# Insurance Insights

**MARK R. GREENE**

Distinguished Professor of Insurance
College of Business Administration
The University of Georgia

**PAUL SWADENER**

Associate Professor of Finance
College of Business Administration
University of Oregon

F35    *Published by*

**SOUTH-WESTERN PUBLISHING CO.**

CINCINNATI   WEST CHICAGO, ILL.   DALLAS   PELHAM MANOR, N.Y.
PALO ALTO. CALIF.   BRIGHTON, ENGLAND

ISBN: 0-538-06350-5
Library of Congress Catalog Card Number: 73-85778

1 2 3 4 D 7 6 5 4

Printed in the United States of America

# PREFACE

The articles presented in *Insurance Insights* were selected, organized, and edited to form a learning tool and a resource for the student who is taking or who has already had a first course in risk and insurance. In this task we had one primary objective in mind: to awake, inspire, and encourage the reader to think about problems in risk and insurance in some depth.

One way to visualize the objectives sought in designing this collection is to draw a parallel. Consider a mound that is of interest to an archeological team. The team has limited resources and time available to glean as much information from the mound as possible. The investigation will consist of neither a random digging of deep narrow shafts nor a more surface scratching of the entire area. Rather the technique will consist of carefully learning the "lay of the land" followed by intensive and deep study into several small areas down through the multitude of layers below the surface. The first course in risk and insurance introduces the student to the lay of the land. This book of selected readings represents the deeper study in specific areas of the subject.

*Insurance Insights* provides specialized study material to the student who does not have an extensive risk and insurance library collection available to him. To the student who is fortunate enough to have access to a strong selection of risk and insurance periodicals, this book serves as a good introduction to that collection. The book introduces the student to many of the more outstanding authors in the area of risk and insurance as well as to the wide range of periodicals and journals available to the person studying the area. It is believed that the user of this book will effect savings in time and money that might otherwise be used in finding and machine-copying the articles contained therein.

The articles chosen are topical, but they are not presented to reflect mainly current events. The articles extend the treatment of topics given in the major beginning text books in risk and insurance, but they were not chosen to follow patterns of development in these works in lockstep fashion. Controversial topics were included to stimulate discussion. Questions follow each article, not as examination questions, but rather as probes and stepping-stones for further development and learning.

The editors wish to thank those authors who have consented to have their work republished in this book.

M.R.G.
P.S.

# CONTENTS

# PART 6. GENERAL LIABILITY INSURANCE

# PART 7. LIFE INSURANCE

# PART 8. PENSIONS AND LIFE ANNUITIES

# PART 9. HEALTH INSURANCE AND SOCIAL INSURANCE

# PART 10. PUBLIC REGULATION OF INSURANCE

# PART 1
# Risk Theory and Concepts

One of the more difficult tasks of a teacher in a course in risk and insurance is that of helping the student develop a concept of risk. As the authors of the first article in this section point out, authors do not agree on the definition of risk. The articles in this part were chosen to supplement and give depth to the development of a common concept of risk.

Professor Crowe and Mr. Horn, in the first article, discuss various definitional treatments of risk that have appeared in the literature. Professor Swadener, in the second article, attempts to clarify a distinction between two concepts that often carry emotional overtones—insurance and gambling. In the third and classic article, Professor Houston presents a thorough and comprehensive treatment of risk and insurance theory. The section concludes with two empirical research contributions in the application of concepts of risk to actual situations.

# 1. THE MEANING OF RISK *

Robert M. Crowe †
and Ronald C. Horn ††

Joe College is an undergraduate in the College of Business Administration at Typical U. He has enrolled recently in an elective course entitled "Principles of Risk and Insurance."

Being that rare conscientious student, Joe decides that, prior to the first class meeting of this course, it would be well for him to do a bit of background reading on the subject. After all, nothing impresses (or surprises) a professor more than a student who has done some exploratory work on the subject before the semester begins.

Joe assumes from the title of the course that the subject of risk will be taken up first. That one should be duck soup. Everyone knows what risk is! It looks like the early part of this course will be a snap!

Just to be sure, however, Joe decides to check a dictionary, where he learns that risk is "the possibility of loss, injury, disadvantage, or destruction." [1] Just what Joe figured! Now to be doubly sure, Joe checks Chapter I of the text to be used in the course. There he discovers that ". . . we shall define risk as *uncertainty of loss*. As such, it is a psychological phenomenon that is meaningful only in terms of human reactions and experiences." [2] Hmm! Doesn't sound quite the same as the dictionary definition. Maybe insurance people use "risk" in a very technical sense to mean something different from the dictionary definition.

Now the real research begins—Joe heads for the library! There he pores through a few textbooks designed for an introductory course in risk and insurance. His research reveals the following:

1. "Risk will be defined in this text as objective doubt concerning the outcome in a given situation. It is the doubt a person would have concerning the future outcome even if he knew all the possible outcomes and their probability or chance of occurrence." [3] (Joe's confidence in his understanding of risk now is a bit shaken. He begins to feel a bit doubtful. Or is it risky?)

---

* From *The Journal of Risk and Insurance* (September, 1967), pp. 459-474. Reprinted by permission.
† Assistant Vice President for Research Administration and Associate Professor of Insurance, University of South Carolina.
†† Assistant to the President of the Indiana Insurance Company.

[1] *Webster's New Third International Dictionary* (Springfield, Mass.: G. & C. Merriam Company, 1964).

[2] Herbert S. Denenberg *et al, Risk and Insurance* (Englewood Cliffs, N.J.: Prentice-Hall, Inc., 1964), p. 4.

[3] C. Arthur Williams, Jr. and Richard M. Heins, *Risk Management and Insurance* (New York: McGraw-Hill Book Company, 1964), p. 5.

2. ". . . *risk* is defined as the *uncertainty* as to the occurrence of an economic loss."[4] Joe notes that there is nothing "objective" about risk in this definition, and his uncertainty (risk?) mounts.

3. "The essential element of risk is unpredictability, a tendency that actual results may differ from predicted results." [5]

4. "A risk may be defined as the *possibility* (emphasis supplied) of an unfortunate occurrence." [6] (Joe is starting to panic now.)

5. "Risk is the *chance* (emphasis supplied) of loss or the occurrence of an unfavorable or undesirable contingency." [7] (Joe wonders if *chance* of loss is the same as *possibility* of loss.)

If Joe College were to look further into the basic texts on risk and insurance, he would find support for several of the foregoing definitions of risk, as well as a few more variations. Instead, he decides to look into some of the more specialized treatises footnoted in the introductory texts and to look up some of the classics on the subject.

1. "Risk . . . is . . . the objectified uncertainty as to the occurrence of an undesired event." [8] (That sounds familiar.)

2. "Risk may be defined as uncertainty in regard to cost, loss or damage." [9] (What happened to objectivity?)

3. "Risk is a combination of hazards . . ." [10] (Hmm! What are hazards?)

4. ". . . risk can only be satisfactorily understood as a 'variance' concept . . . " [11] From the standpoint of the individual, "risk may be defined as the standard deviation of the monetary outcomes of an action . . . To the insurer, risk is a function of the variation in the pure premium distribution and the number of exposure units and may be defined by the standard error of the mean of the pure premium distribution . . ." [12] Sounds plausible, but man! I'm confused.[13]

---

[4] Mark R. Greene, *Risk and Insurance* (Cincinnati: South-Western Publishing Co., 1962), p. 2.

[5] John H. Magee and David L. Bickelhaupt, *General Insurance,* seventh ed. (Homewood, Ill.: Richard D. Irwin, Inc., 1964), p. 3.

[6] Robert Riegel and Jerome S. Miller, *Insurance Principles and Practices,* fifth ed. (Englewood Cliffs, N.J.: Prentice-Hall, Inc., 1966), p. 20.

[7] James L. Athearn, *Risk and Insurance* (New York: Appleton-Century Crofts, 1962), p. 36.

[8] Allan H. Willett, *The Economic Theory of Risk and Insurance* (Philadelphia: University of Pennsylvania Press, 1951), pp. 9-10.

[9] Charles O. Hardy, *Risk and Risk Bearing*, rev. ed. (Chicago: University of Chicago, 1931), p. 1.

[10] Irving Pfeffer, *Insurance and Economic Theory* (Homewood, Ill.: Richard D. Irwin, Inc., 1956), p. 42.

[11] David B. Houston, "Risk, Insurance, and Sampling," *Journal of Risk and Insurance,* Vol. XXXI, No. 4 (December, 1964), p. 517.

[12] *Ibid.,* p. 524.

[13] The authors of this paper will not attempt to discuss all of the definitions and theories of risk that Joe College might have found in the literature. Excellent work of this type has been done by several others. See, for example, David B. Houston, *op. cit.;* Oliver Wood, "Evolution of the Concept of Risk," *Journal of Risk and Insurance,* Vol. XXXI, No. 1 (March, 1964), pp. 83-91; John D. Long, "Risk and Insurance Theory," *Property and Liability Insurance Handbook* (ed. John D. Long and Davis W. Gregg; Homewood, Ill.: Richard D. Irwin, Inc., 1965), pp. 16-24.

Joe's next move is toward the Registrar's office, where he transfers out of Principles of Risk and Insurance and into Principles of Management. "At least in that course I'll be able to find out what *management* is," Joe sighs. Good luck, Joe!

## WHAT IS RISK?

In this paper, risk is defined as *the possibility that a sentient entity will incur loss.* The next several pages are devoted to a discussion of the implications and justifications of the terms in this definition.

## Loss

As the term is used here, loss means an involuntary reduction in the capacity of an entity to satisfy its wants.[14] The satisfaction of some wants requires financial resources, whereas the satisfaction of other wants does not.[15] Further, each entity has its own set of wants based on its own objectives, preferences, and opinions. In other words, the entity's wants are entirely subjective. Because each entity defines its own wants, each entity also defines what constitutes a loss to it.

To clarify, situations can be visualized where (1) objects have little or no market value but are wanted by an entity, and (2) objects have a market value but are not wanted by an entity. The following exemplify objects in the first category: the sentimental attachment of a father to a photo of his young daughter; the fondness of a college professor for a badly worn chair he uses for leisure reading; and the need of an individual for his contact lenses which have been ground according to a special prescription. With respect to the second category, i.e., objects which have market value but are not wanted by an entity, the following are illustrative: the reluctance of an individual to dispose of a pink necktie given him by his mother-in-law, and the indifference of a monk who has taken a vow of poverty to his relinquishment of a right of inheritance.[16]

---

[14] Thus, loss has been defined in terms similar to (but not precisely equal to) the economists' concept of utility. It was felt that use of the word "utility" in the definition, without explanation, might be misleading to some. One who is not familiar with the economists' technical meaning of utility might confuse utility with "practicality," "functionality," or "usefulness." The point to be stressed is that an object may help satisfy a want even if it has no "practicality," "functionality," or "usefulness" as the layman often defines these terms.

[15] "Money may be the husk of many things, but not the kernel. It brings you food but not appetite; medicine, but not health; acquaintances, but not friends; servants, but not faithfulness; days of joy, but not peace or happiness." (Henrik Ibsen). Of course, in the study of risk and insurance, primary concern is with wants which require financial resources for their satisfaction, but in a theory of risk, wants which do not require such resources for their satisfaction should not be disregarded.

[16] It is also conceivable that a wealthy man would be indifferent to the loss of a $10 tie clasp because it results in no reduction in his capacity to satisfy his wants, i.e., it is conceptually possible that, for an individual of great wealth, such an object would have a marginal utility of zero.

It can be seen from these illustrations that there is no necessary proportionate relationship between market value and want-satisfying capacity and, therefore, there is no occurrence which inherently constitutes a loss. Only if an occurrence results in an involuntary reduction in the capacity of the entity in question to satisfy its wants does that occurrence constitute a loss. To reiterate, since wants are entirely subjective, the concept of loss is entirely subjective. It follows, then, that the existence of risk in a particular situation depends on subjective factors. As will be explained later, however, the authors of this paper do not take the position, as do many risk theorists, that risk is a subjective phenomenon. It does not seem contradictory to hold, as is done here, both that loss is determined by subjective factors and that, once the loss being incurred is primarily an objective phenomenon.[17]

## RISK AND UNCERTAINTY

In the authors' view, uncertainty is a state of mind whereby a sentient entity experiences doubt. As such, it is a subjective phenomenon—one of the possible reactions of an entity to its interpretation of reality. Confronted by a given state of reality, two entities may experience uncertainty of different intensity (including the case where one entity experiences no uncertainty) because of different interpretations of that reality and/or differing reactions to it.

Many decision theorists, economists, and other writers define uncertainty in such a way as to make it essentially equivalent to unpredictability or lack of knowledge concerning the facts relevant to a decision. The view of uncertainty presented in this paper is considerably broader than this. As defined here, uncertainty may be present despite perfect predictability, due, for example, to the particular psychic makeup of the entity in question. Conversely, uncertainty may be totally absent despite the inability to predict, for a similar reason. Moreover, this concept of uncertainty may relate to the past, present, or future, whereas unpredictability, by definition, relates primarily to the future. The authors admit that the presence of uncertainty in a great many cases arises from an entity's limited ability to predict or from his lack of knowledge about the present, past, or future. They are unwilling to go a step further, as some writers have done, and suggest that there is any necessary relationship between degrees of unpredictability and degrees of uncertainty.

It should also be clear that, as risk and uncertainty have been defined in this paper, they are entirely separate and distinct concepts. This approach, of course, places the authors in a position directly opposed

---

[17] Note that risk is viewed as primarily, but not exclusively, objective. The extent to which subjective factors, as part of an entity's environment, give some subjective aspects to risk is discussed in another section of this paper.

to those who have defined risk as uncertainty.[18] Since many of these writers seem, at least implicitly, to agree that uncertainty is a subjective phenomenon, they are forced to conclude that risk is entirely a subjective phenomenon.

That risk is uncertainty and therefore completely subjective is a notion we cannot accept for several reasons. First, we cannot believe that a psychiatrist can eliminate risk simply by eliminating an individual's uncertainty. Nor can we believe that a newly-born infant, who has little or no uncertainty about dying, is not exposed to risk in this regard. Or what of a person who has a hallucination that he is about to be trampled by a herd of pink elephants? Is he, because of this hallucination, in fact exposed to risk from this source? The authors think not. Or what of the person who is in a deep coma and near death? He may be uncertain about nothing. Is he not exposed to risk?

To repeat, then, as risk and uncertainty have been defined here, they are entirely separate and distinct concepts.[19] In further support of this contention, it is suggested that the readers consider the following four situations:

First, *in many situations both risk and uncertainty are present.* For example, an individual may be exposed to risk due to disability and therefore may experience uncertainty.

Second, *there are situations in which both risk and uncertainty are absent.* For example, most modern sailors know that the world is not flat; there is no possibility of falling off the edge of the world; therefore, typically they would experience no uncertainty about such a contingency.

Third, *situations may exist in which risk is present and uncertainty is absent.* For example, a businessman may be exposed to the possibility of loss due to interruption of operations by fire. Nevertheless, he may have no uncertainty concerning this risk—perhaps because he fails to recognize the existence of the risk or perhaps although he recognizes its existence, his individual reaction is not one of uncertainty because he is totally preoccupied with other problems. He may also be exposed to risk due to the possibility that his shoelace will break. He may, however, regard the loss as of such little significance that he experiences no uncertainty whatever.[20]

---

[18] Included in this category are those who define risk in terms of objectified uncertainty. This concept of risk seems especially untenable. As the notion of objectified uncertainty is explained by these writers, i.e., the doubt a person would have concerning the future outcome, even if he knew all the possible outcomes and their probability or chance of occurrence, the entire concept seems rather artificial. Moreover, if doubt is a subjective phenomenon, the entire notion of "objectified subjectivity" seems rather self-contradictory.

[19] The authors happily note that some writers recognize the inherent weaknesses of the contrary definition. See, for example, the excellent work of Herbert S. Denenberg and J. Robert Ferrari, "A Review Article—New Perspectives on Risk Management: The Search for Principles," *Journal of Risk and Insurance,* Vol. XXXIII, No. 4 (December, 1966), pp. 653-655.

[20] A different entity, or the same entity confronted with different circumstances, might regard this same event as of great significance and, hence, experience uncertainty (e.g., a track star about to run the one hundred yard dash with a broken shoelace).

Fourth, *situations can be envisioned in which risk is absent but uncertainty is present.* For example, when Columbus sailed there was no possibility that he would fall off the edge of the world. Nevertheless, presumably he was uncertain about this possibility, primarily because of his lack of knowledge of the shape of the world. Also, consider the case of the man who learns that a plane departing from New York crashed an hour ago. The man knows that his wife was scheduled to fly from New York earlier today but does not know whether she was on the particular plane that crashed. Whether or not his wife was on that plane, there is no risk at present, since risk can relate only to future outcomes. Clearly, however, the man now may be experiencing uncertainty, for uncertainty can relate to past and present realities as well as to future outcomes.

Even in the first type of situation, in which both risk and uncertainty are present, they are different concepts. As explained earlier, risk is primarily an objective phenomenon, whereas uncertainty is a subjective phenomenon.

If risk and uncertainty are separate concepts, what relationship exists between the two? [21] There is no necessary relationship. The two frequently are unrelated, as is shown in the third and fourth types of situations (in which one is present and the other is absent) described above.

The first type of situation (both risk and uncertainty present), on the other hand, does suggest some sort of relationship between risk and uncertainty. It is necessary to examine this type of situation more closely in order to identify the nature of this relationship.

Given a sentient entity confronted with a situation in which risk is present, whenever uncertainty results it is tempting to conclude that risk "caused" the uncertainty. Philosophers have wrestled with the matter of cause and effect for centuries, and no attempt will be made to resolve the issues here; however, it seems more rational to assert that the entity's interpretation of its reality is the necessary and sufficient "cause" of uncertainty in situations where uncertainty is the result. Risk itself, on the other hand, is neither the necessary nor the sufficient cause of uncertainty in such cases. The entity is always the intervening link between risk and the result.[22] Accordingly, the entity's interpretation may not—through ignorance, "irrationality," or otherwise—be one of uncertainty, despite the presence of risk.

---

[21] There is no intention to imply that the concept of uncertainty is germane to risk theory only. Uncertainty has been defined broadly in order to recognize that an entity may be uncertain about many matters which are of no significance to him. For example, he may be uncertain as to the exact number of pages in a particular textbook and may be totally indifferent to this lack of knowledge. This type of uncertainty has no relevance to risk theory. Rather, we are concerned only with uncertainty relating to matters which are of at least some significance to the particular entity, i.e., doubt relative to what the entity regards as the possibility that he will incur loss.

[22] As stated earlier, a corporation (or any other group of sentient entities) cannot literally have wants apart from the complex of wants of the individuals comprising the group. Consistent with that view, any interpretations of reality emanating from the group are reflections of the combined interpretations of its members. How these interpretations are combined, of course, will vary significantly from group to group.

In risk and insurance theory, it may be true that situations where risk gives rise to uncertainty are the most important. Here no harm seems to be done if one regards risk as a kind of "proximate cause" of uncertainty, particularly if there is an unbroken chain between risk and the entity's reaction of uncertainty—and particularly if one is mindful of the fact that risk (even if it is recognized by the entity) does not always give rise to uncertainty.

One might also raise a somewhat different question. Can uncertainty cause, or give rise to, risk? More precisely, can the entity's feeling of uncertainty give rise to the possibility of loss where no such possibility existed prior to its state of doubt? A definitive answer to this question would seem to require omniscience unpossessed by mortal men, since the realm and scope of possibility are not clearly definable in a philosophical sense. Nonetheless, the authors intuitively feel that it is plausible to hold that uncertainty can give rise to risk under certain conditions. For example, a man, while sitting in the comfort of his office, suddenly experiences a feeling of uncertainty about whether or not he left a loaded gun in a place readily accessible to his infant son. His uncertainty turns to fear at the thought of potential consequences and this, in turn, prompts him to race home in his automobile to relieve his anxieties. On the way home a tree falls on his car and he is killed. Again the philosophical issues are perplexing. Did his uncertainty give rise to the possibility that a tree would fall on his car, resulting in his death? Surely it did not create the possibility that the tree would fall—or even the possibility of death—but, in the absence of his uncertainty, one could assume that he would still be alive and in his office. Was it uncertainty, fear, the route he chose to drive home, the speed of his car, lightning, or what that gave rise to the risk? One doubts whether uncertainty by itself can literally create risk, as it has been defined here, but it may set up a chain of events that results in loss to the entity. In the above illustration, and a host of others that occurred to the authors, uncertainty triggered responses on the part of the entity that exposed it to risk in regard to matters usually unrelated to the source of uncertainty. In the absence of some stronger reaction, such as fear, anxiety over potential consequences, etc., it is doubtful whether the somewhat "passive" notion of uncertainty in itself gives rise to risk.

## RISK AND PROBABILITY

If a review of the smorgasbord of risk interpretations that has evolved over the years does not leave one somewhat bewildered, a sampling of the various definitions and interpretations attached to the concept of probability surely will—particularly if one engages in the intricate, though enlightening, task of trying to reconcile conflicting notions of risk with conflicting notions of probability. Since the alternative interpretations of probability have been recorded elsewhere in painstaking detail, there is no attempt here to repeat what others have already articulated, nor is there an attempt to enter the arena of debate over which of the various probability explanations is preferable.

At the same time, the philosophical complexity of the probability problem does not justify a decision to ignore it completely, for it is instinctively felt that further development and refinement of risk theory would require, among other things, a careful exploration of the relationships between risk and probability theory, including the interrelated and fundamental question of whether or not risk is a measurable phenomenon. The authors' search for answers to these questions is by no means complete. At this juncture, they merely have taken as given their definition of risk (i.e., the possibility that a sentient entity will incur loss) and attempted to summarize their current thinking on several matters that seem necessary to clarify their concept of risk. In that spirit the following observations are submitted for consideration:

(1) The authors feel that it is imperative, in examining the relationship between risk and probability, to recognize that the term "probability" has no single meaning that can claim universal approval. Writers who have failed to make this explicit have oversimplified and obscured some of the basic issues in risk theory. Others have observed that the lengthy marriage of risk theorists to the insurer's point of view has beclouded their thinking about both risk and probability. For example, writers who define risk in terms of the "chance of loss" at least imply that there is little, if any, difference between risk and probability. However, because there are multiple interpretations of probability, a similar plurality of meaning is imputed to risk, thereby leaving the latter essentially undefined. That these same writers often adopt a single definition of probability simplifies the matter, but it surely does not satisfy those who see merit in applying other probability notions to risk situations.

Writers who define risk in terms of uncertainty, suggest that risk is largely a psychological phenomenon. The uncertainty view is objectionable on many grounds, as stated before, but still other shortcomings of the uncertainty approach are apparent when explored in connection with the probability relationship. For example, most "risk-equals-uncertainty" advocates have created only a rather fuzzy distinction between risk (so defined) and probability interpreted as a subjective degree of belief or a measure of ignorance "having no existence outside of the investigator's mind." Is this particular objection overcome by defining risk as uncertainty and then rejecting the subjective view of probability in favor of another? It does, to be sure, help distinguish between what the author means by risk and what he means by probability, but such admirable consistency does not resolve other equally perplexing issues.

For example, many writers of the risk-equals-uncertainty school adopt the relative frequency interpretation of probability (or some modifications thereof)—sometimes without explanation and often on the grounds that it is the "most widely-held view." However, the relative frequency notion of probability is exceedingly difficult, if not impossible, to apply logically to the unique or virgin event. Do they reject the usefulness, then, of the personalistic probabilities or subjective weights employed by modern decision theorists in treating risk problems? If not, have they in fact fully and clearly distinguished risk from probability? Do they want to make such a distinction? Do they feel that the individual's risk is conceptually different from the insurer's risk? Would they argue that a nonsentient entity can experience uncertainty? Will the answers to such questions be forthcoming as long as risk theorists insist on adopting a single notion of probability? We think not.

(2) The authors suspect, at this state in their thinking, that no widespread agreement on the meaning of risk (or substantial progress in risk theory) can be achieved unless and until risk as a concept is distinguished clearly from all of the probability meanings. Further, they feel that a single and meaningful interpretation of risk can be developed apart from the multiple views of probability, and thus the philosophical problems inherent in the probability controversy need not be completely resolved either to define risk or to make use of the various probability tools in risk situations.

(3) In developing this view of risk, terms that would suggest probability have been deliberately avoided because none of the probability interpretations, however useful for other purposes, captures the essence of risk as a concept. Many writers have done likewise, but some go on to say that probability measures risk. Does application of any of the probability theories measure risk, as it has been defined here? Can a possibility be measured? More precisely, can a possibility that a sentient entity will incur a reduction in its capacity to satisfy wants be measured? The answer, in part, depends upon what one means by measurement. To measure such a possibility, would not one first have to be aware of it, i.e., be able to identify the specific risk under consideration?

Given a state of reality, a given loss to the entity is either possible or it is not. Furthermore, the entity's state of reality can change. Thus, surely not all loss possibilities can be identified, *ex ante,* even crudely. In other words, if risk has meaning only in the context of a future relative, the process of risk identification is essentially an extrapolation into the future. On the basis of past experience, relevant data, or intuition one may conclude that a loss [23] can happen and therefore risk is present— but can one verify that this is the case? Similar difficulties in verification are encountered when one concludes that a loss cannot happen.

Even if it is granted that certain losses are possible and that we can identify these possibilities (e.g., possible losses due to death), are some losses "more possible" than others? Are there degrees of possibility and hence degrees of risk? If one means by possibility, "can happen," the authors think not. True, some losses are "more likely" in a subjective

---

[23] Loss is used here instead of event, since the occurrence of an event does not necessarily result in a loss to the entity. See earlier discussion.

sense—or "more probable" in a relative frequency sense—but how can they be "more possible." [24] Though it is commonly said that some undertakings are "more risky" than others, such a statement can be explained adequately only in terms of relative uncertainty, probability, or likelihood of loss. One can and often does assign a probability of zero to something he believes cannot happen, and a probability of one to something that he believes is certain to happen. This may not be improper in a world where perfect knowledge of what the future will hold is lacking, but assignment of a probability or of a subjective weight to risk is not tantamount to risk measurement per se.

Many would like to see risk defined as a measurable phenomenon, yet an inability to measure risk does not necessarily impede the further development of risk theory, as many have contended. To the contrary, sophisticated measurement and decision theory techniques (including probability, expected value, and utility notions) constitute a reservoir that has not yet been fully tapped by risk theorists. Are these tools less useful as estimates of loss probabilities and guides to rational decision making if risk cannot be measured? Is an over-zealous effort to measure risk in part responsible for the inconsistencies and communicative difficulties one now encounters in the risk literature? The authors do not have answers to these questions, but it should be obvious that they have their suspicions.

## RISK AND HAZARD

In presenting their view of risk in terms of the possibility of loss arising out of aspects of the reality in which an entity exists, the authors have attempted to distinguish clearly their position from the position of those who define risk in terms of uncertainty. This position results in a somewhat uneasy alliance with others who have viewed risk as a state of the world rather than a state of the mind. This alliance is less than a total commitment because of the many questions regarding closely related concepts which, at the time of this writing, are unresolved. Thus, for example, where risk is defined as "a combination of hazards,[25] the authors sense the presence of a kindred spirit, but must wait for agreement on the meaning of "hazard" and some explanation of how hazards, once defined, can be combined to form risk.

Some of the questions or problems which must be resolved before the authors can truly determine the relationship of their concept of risk to other concepts which regard risk as a state of the world are:

(1) Do the aspects of reality, which in the definition presented here give rise to risk, conform to the commonly-used definition of "hazards"

---

[24] The comments of Kenneth L. McIntosh and Thomas O. Carlson on this point are interesting. See *Journal of Insurance*, Vol. XXX, No. 4 (December, 1963), pp. 587 and 590. Both of these actuaries state strongly that a possibility cannot be measured.

[25] See for example, Irving Pfeffer, *op. cit.*, p. 42.

as conditions which increase the probability and/or severity of loss? Every loss results from a chain of events which can be traced retrospectively in endless directions. What aspect of reality, however trivial or ordinary, might not become a link in the chain? Would the mere presence of a child's teddy bear in a house be considered a hazard? If not, would its presence on a stairway in the house be a hazard? Does not the highly coincidental nature of loss situations make most, if not all, aspects of an entity's reality "hazards"? If not, by what criteria does one distinguish those aspects of an entity's reality that are "hazards" and those which are not?

(2) Since there is a lack of agreement as to the precise meaning of probability, then does not the concept of "hazard," when defined in terms of probability, suffer from a derived ambiguity? Even where insurance writers define "probability," their definitions are usually in terms of a relative frequency concept. Does this suggest that "hazard" cannot be interpreted in the case of a unique event or individual exposure unit?

(3) The search for a precise meaning of the term "hazard" was complicated by a tendency of some writers to change their perspective, often without warning, from risk as viewed by an individual entity to risk as seen by an insurer. One example of this chameleon-like tendency can be seen in textbook discussions of "moral hazards." Frequently cited examples include such situations as fraudulent or exaggerated claims and excessive utilization of medical care facilities due to overinsurance. If these factors increase the likelihood of loss, then to whom? To the insured? The insurer? [26] Or perhaps to society? While it might be contended that excessive recourse to insurance may result in loss to an insured, e.g., subsequent inability to obtain desired insurance, is this type of loss in question? In fact, might not an insured actually experience a gain? In some cases, the fact that it is the insurer's point of view being emphasized is implicit, sometimes explicit, where such discussions are found in the context of discourses on underwriting and rate-making functions.[27] In other cases, it is obviously loss to society through wasted resources, which is the point of emphasis.

(4) Yet another aspect of the concept of hazard which continues to be troublesome is the question of whether the phrase "possibility of loss" suggests only frequency or whether it suggests both frequency and severity of loss. Some writers have directed themselves to the question and, either as part of the definition or in exposition, make it clear that severity is part of the concept of "hazard." Other writers have restricted hazard to a frequency concept, and still others have not made their intent clear. Some may argue that this is an area where preference

---

[26] In this discussion the notion of a group entity, e.g., an insurer, suffering a loss is being used as a convenience. See the earlier discussion of losses to group entities for explanation.

[27] The need for clarity in separating the risk of the insurer and that of an insured has been emphasized by others. See, for example, David B. Houston, *op. cit.*

should be permitted to reign unchallenged, but the authors of this paper continue to be plagued by the barriers to progress which such individualism creates.

(5) Considerable attention was devoted to a consideration of the relationship between the concepts of hazard and peril. Unfortunately the net result was another series of partially answered questions and imperfectly articulated conclusions. The difficulty in agreeing upon the meaning of "hazard" acted as a serious impediment in this regard. Despite the admonitions by some writers of the need to distinguish clearly between "peril" and "hazard," their attempted distinctions were found to be less than totally convincing. Most authors define "peril" in terms of cause or source of loss.[28] It appears, however, that some named event which would be classified as a "peril" in some circumstances more closely meets the definition of "hazard" when the focus of attention is shifted. Can a fire in progress be a peril as regards loss through physical destruction of the property aflame, and simultaneously be a hazard as regards its influence on the likelihood of auto collision losses in the vicinity of the fire? Further, since all losses can be traced to a myriad of "causes," which cause is the peril? What is the cause (peril) when a person dies at the hands of a deranged gunman?

It is suggested that the distinction between the terms "peril" and "hazard" is arbitrary, acquiring meaning only in the context of a discussion of some narrowly defined loss. It is also suggested that usage of the terms "peril" and "hazard" is conditioned to a considerable extent by insurance policy terminology. Somewhat facetiously, one wonders what the impact on usage would be if a policy were designed to afford reimbursement for all physical damage arising out of ownership, maintenance, and use of oily rags?

It is not intended that the above listing of questions and problems be considered exhaustive. The list does, however, illustrate some of the areas where further thought and clarification are needed.

## SUMMARY AND CONCLUSIONS

The authors of this paper have been frustrated by the fact that among scholars of risk and insurance there is little agreement on the question of what risk is. Resolution of this basic question is more important now than ever before, since there is a discernible tendency among these scholars to place more and more emphasis on risk, rather than insurance, in their teaching and research. It is questionable as to how much success will result from attempts to develop a sound theory of "risk management" unless first the very foundation of such a theory, the nature of risk, is firmly established.

---

[28] The principle of "proximate cause," while obviously essential for such purposes as the interpretation of a given insurance contract, affords little insight to the philosophical question as to the "cause of loss."

In this paper an attempt has been made to contribute to the development of this needed foundation. The position has been taken that *risk is the possibility that a sentient entity will incur loss*. The concept of loss is a totally subjective phenomenon, reflecting the particular pattern of wants of the sentient entity in question. The concept of risk, on the other hand, is primarily an objective phenomenon. In no sense is it identical to uncertainty, which is a state of mind whereby a sentient entity experiences doubt. Frequently, however, risk and uncertainty are closely associated, since risk often gives rise to uncertainty. Because of the lack of agreement that exists concerning the nature of probability, it seems important to view risk in terms of loss possibilities. Possibility is a concept which captures the essence of the meaning of risk and yet still permits the logical application of any of the several probability notions to risk problems.

## Questions

1. The authors discuss the use of the word "loss." Could a loss have positive value to an entity?
2. The authors state that their concept of risk is not a subjective phenomenon. Rather, "both that loss is determined by subjective factors and that, once the loss is defined, the possibility of a loss being incurred is primarily an objective phenomenon." Relate this conceptualization with the conceptualization of risk as defined in your textbook.
3. Do you agree with the authors that a person who has an hallucination that he is about to be trampled by a herd of elephants is not exposed to risk? Compare this with the example of Columbus being concerned with falling off the edge of the earth, or of the man who is concerned about whether or not he left a loaded gun on his desk at home, even though he had not.
4. Do the authors once and for all solve the problems of definition of risk?

# 2. GAMBLING AND INSURANCE DISTINGUISHED *

Paul Swadener †

The distinction between gambling and insurance is an important concept which is not at all intuitively clear. This distinction has to be couched in terms of definitions—which by their nature are arbitrary. Moreover, the two terms take on emotional overtones. If the treatment is not carefully handled, it may simply turn into an effort to justify insurance as an institution but fail to be useful as a conceptual basis for further analysis. The following presentation of the distinction has proved helpful in cases where the objective is analysis of insurance as a risk handling device.

## ORIENTATION

I have found the approach presented here to be useful in an introductory study of risk, risk management, and insurance, in a course which is meant to convey ideas about the problems of business decision making under conditions of risk. This approach is also particularly applicable in a theoretical study of insurance as an institution. Because of the narrow definitions employed, this approach is of limited value in a course emphasizing insurance contracts and their provisions. The approach is probably most useful in discussions of probability and expected value and in discussions of optimum insurance premium outlay.

## RISK SITUATION

A risk situation is defined as a set of possible outcomes of an event in which each outcome has a probability of occurrence, and in which the sum of the probabilities is equal to one. These probabilities may be subjectively estimated and personal to a decision maker.

Example: A risk situation in which an event of a toss of a die has six possible outcomes with a 1/6 probability for each face.

Example: A risk situation in which an event of a given dwelling exposed over a period of a year to fire has possible outcomes of occurrence or nonoccurrence of a fire with some probability for each outcome.

---

* From *The Journal of Risk and Insurance* (September, 1964), pp. 463-468. Reprinted by permission.
† Associate Professor of Finance, University of Oregon.

Example: A risk situation in which an event of a group of 1,000 lives at age 35 exists over a period of a year has outcome possibilities of 1, 2, ..., 1,000 deaths during the year with some probability for each outcome.

Example: A risk situation in which an event of stepping off the curb and crossing the street has the outcomes of reaching or not reaching the other side safely. Each outcome has some probability which is, at the very least, subjectively and implicitly evaluated by the decision maker who wants to cross the street.

## LOTTERY

A lottery is defined to be a risk situation in which there are payoffs of economic value to the decision maker for each possible outcome. The payoffs can be positive, negative, or zero, and are always considered with respect to the decision maker—a payoff to some individual or group of individuals acting as a decision maker.

Example: A lottery in which payoffs of a given number of dollars are assigned to each possible outcome of the risk situation of a toss of a die.

Example: A lottery in which payoffs of $6 to win and $0 not to win are assigned to the outcomes in the risk situation of a horse running a race.

Example: A lottery in which payoffs of minus $10,000 if a fire occurs and $0 if the fire does not occur are assigned to the outcomes in the risk situation of a given house exposed to fire for a period of a year.

Example: A lottery in which a negative payoff in the form of a loss of income suffered by a family is associated with the outcomes in the risk situation of the occurrence or nonoccurrence of the death in a given year of the wage earner.

Example: A lottery in which payoffs of profit if successful and loss of capital if unsuccessful are associated with the outcomes of a business venture.

## GAMBLE

Given any lottery a decision maker is either a party to the lottery, in the sense that he will experience the actual gain or loss indicated by the outcome of the actual event, or he is not a party to the lottery. Consider the latter possibility. If he is not a party to the contract he may continue in his present state or he may become a party to the contract. A term describing his becoming a party in the lottery is "gamble." A gamble is defined to be the transfer of the decision maker from a state of nonparticipation in a lottery to one of participation in the lottery in the sense that he stands to experience the gain or the loss associated with the outcome of the event.

Example: The gamble in which the decision maker puts his chips on a red eight at a roulette table.

Example: The gamble in which the decision maker puts $2 on a given horse to win a given race.

Example: The gamble in which the decision maker buys a share of stock.

Example: The gamble in which the decision maker steps off the curb and crosses the street.

Example: The gamble in which the decision maker buys a house.

Example: The gamble in which the decision maker accepts the gift of a house.

## RISK TRANSFER

If the decision maker is already a party to the lottery there are again two possibilities. Either he can remain a party to the lottery or he can transfer out of the lottery. The latter possibility is of interest here. This transfer can be called simply a transfer out of the lottery or risk situation or it can be called a risk transfer. The term risk transfer will be employed here. It is the opposite of a gamble. A risk transfer is defined to be a transfer of the decision maker from a state of participation in a lottery to a state of nonparticipation in a lottery, in the sense that he no longer stands to experience the gain or the loss associated with the outcome of the event.

Example: The risk transfer in which the decision maker buys fire insurance protection against the loss of his house by fire.

Example: The risk transfer in which the decision maker gives his house to someone.

Example: The risk transfer in which the decision maker sells his house to someone.

There is the generic classification called risk transfer devices which includes all of the devices usually covered in a course in risk, risk management, and insurance. Insurance is a risk transfer device. What remains to be done in order to complete the distinction between gambling and insurance is to describe the particular niche occupied by insurance in the class of risk transfer devices. In order to do so a further development of the term "lottery" is necessary.

## THE VALUE OF A LOTTERY

Consider a lottery of the classic variety in which a wheel of fortune is to be spun. This wheel is very large and contains 10,000 stopping points for the indicator. It is agreed that the wheel is "fair" in that the chance that any one of the 10,000 numbers will be the winner is the same as for any other. The payoffs are $1,000 to the holder of the winning ticket and nothing to all the others. The expected value of this lottery is .0001 ($1,000) + .9999 ($0) = +$.10.

Recall that a transfer into the lottery is defined to be a gamble. The transfer could be described as a transfer from a state of certainty to one of risk. Recall that a transfer out (disposing of the ticket already held in the lottery) is called a risk transfer. The transfer out could be thought of as a change from a risk state to a state of certainty.

There are two values that are of interest in this lottery. The first value is the expected value of the lottery which is +$.10 in this example. The second is the value to the decision maker of the situation of *being in* the lottery. It can be argued that in a good many lotteries the value to the decision maker of being in the lottery is higher to him than the expected value. As evidence I would cite the success of lotteries which are loaded in favor "of the house" at horse race tracks and at Las Vegas. Many decision makers would find the value to themselves of a $.50 lottery ticket to be in excess of $.50 (thus inducing the purchase of the ticket). If the lottery is loaded in favor of the house, the $.50 price of the ticket is certainly higher than the $.10 expected value. The expected value of +$.10 is less than the value of the risk situation to the ticket holder, a value at least +$.50 and perhaps more.

The conclusion to be reached from the above discussion is that there are many decision makers who would be willing to pay more than the expected value to change from a state of certainty to one of risk. This conclusion is merely an example of a commonly understood limitation of the concept of expected value as a criterion for decision making. However, progressing through a similar exercise shows that not all lotteries are treated the same as the lottery just explained. Where many decision makers are willing to pay *more* than the expected value to get into a risk situation of a lottery, a lottery is easily created for which many will pay *strictly less* than the expected value in order to get into the risk situation.

Consider the same wheel of fortune but change the payoffs to minus $1,000 for winning and $0 for not winning. The interpretation is that if the decision maker is the winner of the lottery he pays the operator of the lottery $1,000. The expected value of the lottery is now −$.10.

If the decision maker were to treat this lottery in the same manner as the first example he would be willing to pay some value in excess of the expected value of −$.10 to buy into the lottery. Now paying a negative value is the same as receiving a positive value. The value −$.09 is more than −$.10. If he were willing to "pay" −$.09 to get into the risk situation, the operator of the lottery need merely pay the decision maker $.09 to enter the decision maker as a party to the lottery in which the decision maker might possibly end up paying the operator $1,000. Many decision makers in this situation would not pay a value greater than the expected value to become a party to the lottery.

But how much would a decision maker "pay"? Would he pay −$1.00? −$10.00? −$100.00? −$200.00? If the decision maker had a nice large bank account to fall back on he might be willing to buy into the lottery for −$100.00 or anything less (−$200.00, −$300.00, . . .), any one of which is less than the expected value of the lottery.

As evidence that many decision makers could be expected to pay strictly less than the expected value to buy into a risk situation in the case of a lottery of this type, I cite the success of insurance companies which of necessity must charge a premium that is loaded against the insured. In this example the decision maker is buying into the lottery. In the insurance situation the decision maker, who is the insured, is transferring out of the lottery. If to *buy into* the lottery he is willing to *pay* strictly less than the expected value, he may be expected to *accept a payment* of less than the expected value in order *to transfer out*. The expected value is −$.10 in this example. The premium he would be required to pay may be, say, $.20 or more if it is heavily loaded for expenses. Paying a premium of $.20 is the same as accepting a payment of −$.20, which is less than −$.10, in the transfer out of the risk situation.

## CLASSIFICATION OF LOTTERIES

Now an important point must be introduced. Let the decision maker who would pay more than the expected value to buy into a lottery be called a risk-taker. Let him who would pay strictly less than the expected value to buy into a lottery be called a risk-averter. Could a decision maker be both a risk-taker and a risk-averter at the same time? He could under any one of three conditions:

1) If he were acting inconsistently,
2) If he judged the probabilities of the possible outcomes of a lottery to be different from those used to compute the expected value, or
3) If some types of lotteries had a value or appeal to the decision maker that was different from other types of lotteries.

Theoretical analysis of actions of human beings ordinarily depends on the assumption of some degree of rationality concerning decision making. Consistency from decision to decision on identical situations is often one of the conditions of rationality. Even though the possibility of inconsistent behavior must be allowed in reality, consistency of decision making will be assumed.

If the probabilities of the possible outcomes of the event as judged by the decision maker are different from those used to compute the expected value of the lottery, the expected value of the lottery need only be recomputed on the basis of the personal probabilities in order to test his decision making for consistency. Thus, the question of whether he can be both a risk-taker and a risk-averter at one and the same time is left unanswered.

Perhaps there may be some psychological effect on the decision maker in the case of some lotteries, which is different from the effect on him of other lotteries. If such is the case, the decision maker could be consistent and also evaluate the probabilities of the outcomes exactly the same as the price setters in insurance companies and at race tracks. He could buy his fire insurance policy the same day that he spends a day at the track and still be consistent in his decision making. The two examples of lotteries explained in detail earlier were chosen so that a clear distinction of types of lotteries could be made. If the decision maker who is willing to buy into the first lottery at a payment of more than the expected value is also willing to pay strictly less than the expected value to get into the second lottery, a pattern of lottery types becomes clear. The following types of lotteries make up the classification system.

Type I —A lottery in which all possible payoffs to the decision maker are zero or greater than zero (as in the first example).

Type II—A lottery in which all possible payoffs to the decision maker are zero or less than zero (as in the second example).

Type III—A lottery in which at least one possible payoff is negative.

The deductive approach used here leads to the conclusion that the decision maker might rationally be expected to treat a Type I lottery differently from one of Type II. Experimentation with several examples of Type III lotteries will lead to the conclusion that the action of the decision maker will not be so predictable as with the other two types. His action will vary depending on the particular payoffs involved.

The approach used in demonstrating the actions of the decision maker in these examples can be more elaborately treated in terms of von Neumann-Morgenstern utility theory. Such a treatment is beyond the scope of this presentation.

## INSURANCE AND GAMBLING

With the specification of the types of lotteries, an explicit statement of the conceptual difference between gambling and insurance can be made. Irving Pfeffer defines insurance as "a device for the reduction of the uncertainty of one party, called the insured, through the transfer of particular risks to another party, called the insurer, who offers the restoration, at least in part, of economic loss suffered by the insured." [1] Dr. Pfeffer's definition clearly classifies insurance as a device employed by the insured to transfer out of a lottery rather than into a lottery, as in the case of a gamble. The restriction to economic *loss* excludes lotteries

---

[1] Pfeffer, Irving, *Insurance and Economic Theory* (Homewood, Ill.: Richard D. Irwin, Inc., 1956), p. 53.

of Type I from consideration since these lotteries have no negative pay-offs. There are other risk transfer devices that can be applied to transfer out of Type I lotteries. In addition to the exclusion of Type I lotteries, the usual insurance transaction involves only lotteries which have zero or negative payoffs and excludes positive payoffs entirely, that is, the usual insurance transaction involves only Type II loteries.

The conclusive distinction between gambling and insurance can now be stated. Gambling is the transfer of the decision maker from a state of certainty to one of participation in a lottery, which is a risk situation by definition. Insurance, on the other hand, is a method of transferring the decision maker from the situation of participation in a lottery to a state of certainty, the lottery involved being one in which there is at least one possible outcome with a negative payoff. Further, the usual interpretation of insurance limits the type of lottery to one in which there are no possible outcomes with positive payoffs to the decision maker.

## SUGGESTIONS FOR FURTHER ANALYSIS

As a tool for further analysis the conceptualization presented here has many possibilities, a few of which are listed below.

1. As a basis for classification of risk transfer devices as to type of lottery involved.
2. As a basis for discussion of the rationality of a person gambling and insuring at the same time.
3. As a basis for discussion of management decisions involving risk situations.
4. As a basis for development of utility theory.
5. As a basis for determining for an individual firm or person the amount of premium that would be an optimum outlay for him in a given situation.

## Questions

1. How can a person logically buy a fire insurance policy on his house the same day he spends a day gambling at a racetrack, a situation that the author says may be "consistent"?
2. What is the difference between insurance and gambling, according to the author? How does this difference compare to other distinctions between insurance and gambling that appear in textbooks on insurance?
3. The author defines three types of lotteries. Examine each of these types with respect to the definitions of risk and of insurance developed in your textbook. Are any of the types excluded?
4. Do lotteries of Type I really exist? Explain.

# 3. RISK, INSURANCE, AND SAMPLING *

David B. Houston †

## SECTION I: RISK AND UNCERTAINTY

The most fundamental notion associated with risk and uncertainty is variability. Thus, when one tries to predict some future event he says that there is risk and uncertainty present because of the variation of possible outcomes. To the extent that variation of possible outcomes is absent, the accuracy of prediction is increased, and uncertainty and risk are reduced. These foregoing assertions are, of course, not to be taken as rigorous definitive statements about risk and uncertainty, but rather merely as guideposts to indicate the general direction of the present analysis.

The separate notions of risk and uncertainty have been widely analyzed and discussed by economists, insurance theorists, decision theorists, philosophers and writers in both the social and physical sciences. Consideration of these phenomena by such diverse disciplines is not surprising when the trite but true observation is recalled that "risk and uncertainty are all-pervasive and omnipresent."

While analysis from several different points of view is generally desirable, there are also certain costs attached to such a development. Risk and uncertainty can mean quite different things in physics, psychology and statistics, for example. Definitions that are reasonably appropriate for one discipline may be worthless or even detrimental for another. The varying subject matter of different disciplines will call for different concepts, and though these concepts may all be given the same name, e.g., risk, they may describe quite different phenomena.

The definitions of risk and uncertainty which one finds in the insurance literature have often been imprecise because the writers have failed to distinguish which aspects of insurance are relevant to the particular definitions they employ. One might reasonably expect that the scope of the concepts, risk and uncertainty, employed in studying insurance would be substantially narrower than in fields like economics and decision theory since the field of insurance is less all-encompassing.

* From *The Journal of Risk and Insurance* (December, 1964), pp. 511-538. Reprinted by permission.
† Associate Professor of Economics, Pennsylvania State University.

This paper will try to develop a concept of risk which is appropriate to the insurance mechanism and at the same time indicate where alternative notions of risk and uncertainty are relevant or irrelevant for the problems at hand. Primarily because of historical linkages, it will be necessary to review briefly the meanings assigned to risk and uncertainty in economics, decision theory, and insurance theory.

## DIVERSE VIEWS

As will be seen, the following writers have certain common elements and certain dissimilarities in their various approaches to these concepts. While one might develop a more extensive list of discussions of risk and uncertainty, the following were selected since they are generally considered to represent the "major" and "best" discussions of the topic.

Willett in his classic doctor's thesis, published in 1901, is one of the first to attempt to distinguish between risk and uncertainty and to offer a definition of each. He writes: [1]

> Risk is the objective correlative of the subjective uncertainty. It is the uncertainty considered as embodied in the course of events in the external world of which the subjective uncertainty is a more or less faithful interpretation.

and further: [2]

> Risk. . . . is . . . the objectified uncertainty as to the occurrence of an undesired event. It varies with uncertainty and not with the degree of probability (of the undesired event).

and finally: [3]

> The greater the probable variation of the actual loss from the average, the greater the degree of uncertainty.

There are two major aspects of Willett's definitions. The first is the objective-subjective distinction, which is generally carried on by all the writers. Thus, risk is an objective phenomenon which can be measured empirically in the real world and is independent of the individual observer. Uncertainty, for Willett, is subjective and is the personal evaluation of the objective risk situation. Uncertainty is an individual characteristic, and hence one risk situation could give rise to as many different levels of uncertainty as there are individuals perceiving it.

The second aspect of Willett's definitions is his assertion that risk is a concept of variation and is not identified with the degree of probability. Thus a high or low degree of probability of the undesired event does not imply a high or low degree of risk. However, Willett is not

---

[1] Willett, Alan H., *The Economic Theory of Risk and Insurance*, University of Pennsylvania Press, Philadelphia, 1951, p. 6.

[2] *Ibid.*, pp. 9-10.

[3] *Ibid.*, p. 8.

entirely consistent in this regard. He says, in the second quotation above, that risk varies with uncertainty, not with the degree of probability. He then considers the case of simple binomial probabilities and asserts that risk is zero when the degree of probability (p) is either 1 or 0 and risk is a maximum when p = ½ as shown in Figure 1.

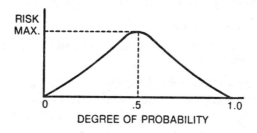

RISK MAX.

DEGREE OF PROBABILITY

0      .5      1.0

FIGURE 1

    Willett, then is saying: (1) risk is not identical to the degree of probability of the undesired event though there may be a functional relationship between them; and, (2) risk refers to variability. However, he never specifies the way in which this variability should be measured. As an aside, one might note that in the third quotation given it would seem more logical to end the sentence with, "... the greater the degree of risk," since he is concerned with objective rather than subjective phenomena.

    Knight, whose important book on this subject [4] first appeared in 1921 was more concerned with the economic aspects of risk and uncertainty, particularly as they were, in his view, the *raison d'etre* for profit.

    Knight attacks the problem by first defining three types of probability: (1) *a priori* which is deductible or obvious from the nature of the situation, e.g., the probability of getting an ace when throwing a six-sided die; (2) statistical which can be arrived at inductively by examining a large number of observations, e.g., the probability that a man age 20 will die within the year; and, (3) estimate or judgment which cannot be determined objectively but can only be believed intuitively, e.g., the probability that a new restaurant opened in your neighborhood will be profitable.

    All three of these types of probability deal with situations of uncertainty, says Knight, but the first two relate to *measurable* uncertainty whereas the third relates to *unmeasurable* uncertainty. Measurable uncertainty is an objective phenomenon which he calls "risk" and un-

---

[4] Knight, Frank H., *Risk, Uncertainty and Profit,* Houghton Mifflin, Boston, 1921.

measurable uncertainty is a subjective idea which he calls "uncertainty." He then elaborates this distinction as follows: [5]

> The practical difference between the two categories, risk and uncertainty, is that in the former the distribution of the outcome in a group of instances is known (either through calculation *a priori* or from statistics of past experience), while in the case of uncertainty, this is not true, the reason being in general that it is impossible to form a group of instances because the situation dealt with is in a high degree unique.

and in dealing with the single case: [6]

> . . . . it is a matter of practical indifference whether the uncertainty is measurable or not.

Knight also notes the objective-subjective distinction. However, it is not clear whether risk and uncertainty are types of probabilities or measures of variability of outcomes. Unfortunately, though he describes risk as measurable uncertainty, he does not indicate how it should be measured e.g., by a probability value or by a measure of variation. The material quoted from Knight implies that measurability depends on the presence of a "group of instances," but the nature of this dependence is never specified.

Hardy, who has contributed two major works on the subject of risk,[7] does not pay particularly careful attention to the problem of definition, and consequently his statements are somewhat vague. He says: [8]

> Risk may be defined as uncertainty in regard to cost, loss or damage. In this definition emphasis is on the word *uncertainty*. Where destruction or loss of capital is certain in connection with a business process, it can be charged up in advance as a cost. It is not a risk.

He does not distinguish between the subjective and objective aspects of the problem, and it is only through a rather tenuous inference that one can argue that Hardy sees risk as a concept involving variability. Thus, Hardy's definition, while it has a superficial clarity, does not really speak to the problem.

The most recent major treatment of risk and uncertainty is Pfeffer's *Insurance and Economic Theory* [9] which, despite its relative youth, one can fairly place in the same class with the works previously cited. Pfeffer discusses the problem as follows: [10]

---

[5] *Ibid.*, p. 233.

[6] *Ibid.*, p. 235.

[7] Hardy, Charles Q., *Readings in Risk and Risk Bearing,* University of Chicago Press, Chicago, 1924.
Hardy, Charles Q., *Risk and Risk Bearing,* Rev. Ed., University of Chicago, Chicago, 1931.

[8] Hardy, *Risk and Risk Bearing,* p. 1.

[9] Pfeffer, Irving, *Insurance and Economic Theory,* Richard D. Irwin, Inc., Homewood, Illinois, 1956.

[10] *Ibid.*, p. 42.

> Risk is a combination of hazards and is measured by probability; uncertainty is measured by a degree of belief. Risk is a state of the world; uncertainty is a state of the mind.

He elaborates further: [11]

> . . . . 'risk' . . . . the combination of hazards to which individuals are exposed. It is an objective relationship between an adverse event and the exposure unit, whose relative frequency of occurrence is measured by a probability value. *Risk and uncertainty are counterparts of one another; the one being measured by objective probability; the other by a subjective degree of belief.*

Thus Pfeffer, whose aim is to develop a concept of insurance suitable for microeconomic analysis, emphasizes most strongly the objective-subjective dichotomy of risk and uncertainty. However, he explicitly states, in contrast to Willett, that risk and uncertainty are each measured by a single probability value (presumably the probability of the adverse event) whether objectively or subjectively determined. Thus, for Pfeffer, risk and uncertainty are not measured by variability but rather by probability.

To summarize, in an effort to determine what ideas contained in the foregoing discussions will be useful in developing consistent definitions of risk and uncertainty, it should be noted first that these concepts must be distinguished as regards their objective and subjective natures, and second that there is no clear cut agreement as to whether these concepts should be expressed in terms of the probability of some unforeseen occurrences or as indications of the variability of possible outcomes in the future. The objective-subjective distinction seems well recognized and in fact must be included in any legitimate explanation of the concepts.

TABLE 1

|  | Probability of unforeseen occurrences | Variability of possible outcomes |
|---|---|---|
| Objective | Empirical Data: Relative Frequencies | Risk |
| Subjective | Degree of Belief: Personal (Subjective) Probabilities | Uncertainty |

However, the second problem, i.e., the question of "probability" vs "variation," is a long-standing one and seems to be responsible for most of the difficulties and confusions of definition which plague the insurance literature both past and present.

To clarify the preceding material, Table 1 is presented, which shows the relationship among the various concepts discussed.

---

[11] *Ibid.*, p. 179. (Italics in the original)

This arrangement provides for a clear distinction between the objective and subjective aspects of the problem and also separates probability and variability. These initially rough divisions will form the basis for further analysis of insurance and risk situations in general. However, before continuing the development of these concepts, certain other statements made about risk, which are usually considered valid and valuable, must be examined.

## RISK DICHOTOMIES

Mowbray [12] provides one of the major distinctions as to the nature of risk. He argues that risk can be separated into what he calls "pure" and "speculative." This distinction rests primarily on the profit and loss structure of the situation. If the individual or firm faces a set of outcomes which include only *status quo* or an economic loss, he is then said to be in a pure risk situation. In contrast, if his outcomes in addition to those already mentioned include the possibility of economic gain, he is in a speculative risk situation.

This distinction can then be used to define insurable and uninsurable risks. Pure risks become insurable since in theory the individual, at best, stands to break even no matter which outcome occurs. Conversely, speculative risks become uninsurable since in certain circumstances the individual would be tempted to use his insurance to make a profit which he would not otherwise earn in the absence of insurance. [13] In addition, it could be considered undesirable to insure speculative risk since, in the view of some economists, it constitutes the *modus operandi* of entrepreneurial profit and provides the incentive for the businessman to allocate optimally the factors of production.

This distinction, while useful for certain types of relatively simple analysis, presents some difficulties which are worth noting. First, it is essentially a dichotomy relating to the kind and direction of losses rather than of risk. In both situations, pure and speculative, there is a plurality of outcomes no one of which is sure to happen. Hence, there is risk present. However, the nature of the risk is unaltered by the fact that the outcomes are not identical. What is in fact being distinguished are loss patterns with different boundaries, i.e., pure losses range from

---

[12] Mowbray, Albert H., *Insurance, Its Theory and Practice in The United States*, 1st ed., McGraw-Hill Book Co., Inc., New York, 1930, pp. 4-5.

[13] The problem of the appropriateness of insuring profit is rather fuzzy. On the one hand, going concerns are permitted to insure against loss of "normal" future profits, e.g., business interruption insurance and rain insurance for outdoor sporting events. The presumption here is that the firm is insuring against the loss of a "sure thing" in that, if the undesired event, fire, rain, etc. did not occur, the profit accruing to the firm would be at least equal to, and most likely greater than, the profit deriving from the insurance policy. On the other hand, industry and public policy discourage or prohibit the use of insurance for speculative gain.

0 to − ∞ while speculative losses range from − ∞ to + ∞. Thus, one might more aptly term the pair as pure and speculative losses.

Additional problems arise from Mowbray's distinction with regard to the insurance institution.[14] It is fair to say that all insurable losses are pure losses if, and only if, all insurance contracts are formulated on a strict indemnity principle. To the extent that some contracts are written on a valued policy basis, i.e., promising to pay a specific sum of money upon the happening of the adverse event, there is a real possibility for speculative gain, and hence the assertion that insurance deals only with pure losses no longer holds.

A second problem, related to the first, arises out of a consideration of moral hazard, i.e., where the insured's behavior increases the probability and/or severity of loss. One of the reasons advanced for not insuring speculative losses is the presence of moral hazard and, further, in a pure loss situation there is, theoretically, no opportunity for gain. Hence, one could reasonably conclude that there is no moral hazard in connection with insurance contracts. This conclusion is so much at variance with reality that it forces one to reexamine the premises of the argument.

It would seem that what is today a pure loss situation may tomorrow be a speculative loss situation; and that the factors causing this are so numerous and complex that it is unlikely that insurers will ever be able to control the situation to their satisfaction. Thus, it appears that insurers do deal with speculative losses, albeit against their wishes.

A final point concerning this distinction should be made. Aside from all previous arguments, this distinction can be misleading if it is unqualifiedly applied to both insured and insurer. It is a valid distinction only when applied to the insured's point of view. He faces pure or speculative loss situations, and the insurance company is desirous of insuring only his pure losses. However, once an insurance company is operating, it, like any other business, is facing a speculative loss situation: it may incur either a profit or a loss.

One may summarize by saying that Mowbray has presented a distinction which is useful in analyzing boundaries of losses from the individual's or firm's point of view. But this distinction must be carefully applied, particularly in those instances where pure and speculative losses are blended into a not easily defined mixture.

A second important risk categorization is Kulp's analysis of fundamental vs. particular risks.[15] This distinction is based on the origin or cause of the risk situation. Kulp writes: [16]

---

[14] The following criticisms are empirical rather than theoretical. It should be noted that failure of Mowbray's concept to correspond one-to-one with the insurance business is not necessarily crucial. It may still provide a useful abstraction as is "perfect competition" in price theory.

[15] Kulp, C. A., *Casualty Insurance*, Ronald Press, N.Y., 1928, pp. 4-7.

[16] *Ibid.*

Fundamental risks are essentially group risks; the conditions which cause them have no relation to any particular individual. Most fundamental risks are economic, political or social; . . .

Particular risks are those due to particular conditions which obtain in particular cases. They affect each individual separately, . . . They are usually personal in cause, almost always personal in their application. Because they are so largely personal in their nature, the individual has a certain degree of control over their causes.

Fundamental risks generally affect an entire society or at least a segment thereof. Individuals have no control over them and hence are not held individually responsible for them. Examples are war, depression, government actions, extraordinary natural disturbances, etc. In contrast, particular risks are controllable by the individual, and so are considered to be his responsibility. Examples are loss of property as a result of negligence, and personal risks such as death and disability.

Kulp notes that this classification rests on social values rather than on any concrete external criteria. Thus, today's particular risk may be tomorrow's fundamental risk. Indeed, one way of describing modern social change is in terms of a shift from particular to fundamental risks, that is, society (government, if one prefers) is placing more and more risks into the fundamental class and thus reducing its notions of individual responsibility.

This dichotomy is not, perhaps, as useful as it appears at first blush. In one sense it is a series of near misses. Thus particular vs. fundamental is *almost* equivalent to: (1) insurable vs. uninsurable; (2) private insurance vs. social insurance; and (3) pure vs. speculative. However, it is, in fact, none of these. It is, rather, simply a way of distinguishing the sources and impacts of losses and must be recognized as a notion which shifts with time and place.[17]

While it would be possible to discuss other risk dichotomies, e.g., Knight's insurable vs. uninsurable, the two here presented are probably the ones most often cited. They indicate the problems with which insurance writers have to cope when trying to understand risk situations, and give the flavor of the solutions generally presented. Basically, these solutions recognize that there are different types of risk and uncertainty to be faced in the world about us.

Distinctions of this type are useful, in fact necessary, but they present at least two problems: first, in that they are not integrated into a larger body of insurance theory, their logic and consistency is never adequately tested, and they remain isolated pairs which are called into use only when they happen to fit; and second, it is possible for classifications of this sort to bias one's thinking in policy decisions, since they implicitly "tell" what is and what is not an insurable risk situation.

---

[17] In examining the three editions of Kulp's book, one sees him modifying the idea to compensate for changes in social values. Also one gets the feeling that the modification represents a continuing and never quite successful effort to classify the notion.

So much for risk dichotomies and other writer's views on risk and uncertainty. The analysis now turns to the author's own development of the concept of risk.


## WHOSE RISK?

A crucial question to any understanding of risk as it is described in the contemporary literature is: risk to whom? The point here is that risk from different points of view may be very different things. While there are innumerable classifications one might choose, the one best suited for this analysis is in terms of the individual and insurer. The following section, then, treats risk, first as seen by the insurer in the context of his operations, and second, as perceived by the individual in general decision making contexts.

This analysis starts with the following premise: risk can only be satisfactorily understood as a "variance" [18] concept, and efforts to conceive of it as a "mean" concept only increase the confusion which surrounds the subject. Unfortunately, many insurance authors, particularly textbook writers, have done just that. The confusion usually springs from some relatively innocuous appearing statement such as: "Risk is the chance of loss."

Since the probability (or chance) of loss is a mean value, equating risk to it is, in effect, defining risk as a mean or average concept and, as will be seen, greatly restricts the analysis. Further, it can be argued that, if risk is equal to the chance of loss, then there is no point in introducing the term "risk" into the discussion, since the term "chance of loss" is already fully defined.

In order to explicate risk in the insurer's context, it is necessary to start by defining the most important mean concepts employed in analyzing risk and insurance situations. First, there is the "frequency" of number of losses suffered by each exposure unit. The mean of this variable is the average frequency where:

$$\text{Average Frequency} = \frac{\# \text{ losses}}{\# \text{ exposure units}}$$

This is a mean concept in the sense that it is the average number of losses for all insureds. In fact, one may conceive of a distribution of number of losses, and the average frequency is the mean of that distribution. Such a distribution might look as follows:

---

[18] The terms "mean" and "variance" are to be taken in their statistical sense. Intuitively, the mean represents an average value, while the variance is a measure of the dispersion of a distribution.

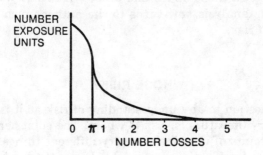

FIGURE 2

The figure indicates that different exposure units or insureds have different numbers of losses and that $\pi$ is the average number of losses for all insureds.

The second notion which must be examined is "severity" or average size loss. This is defined as the ratio of the dollar amount of all losses to the number of losses. Thus:

$$\text{Severity} = \frac{\$ \text{ losses}}{\# \text{ losses}}$$

Here too one may conceive of a distribution of losses at each dollar level as follows:

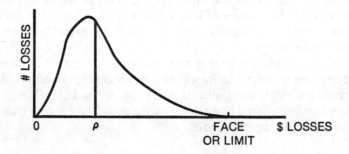

FIGURE 3

When a loss occurs, it may be any positive dollar amount (up to the face of the policy) and this accounts for the severity distribution. The concern here is with, the "severity" for all losses, i.e., the average size loss.

The average frequency tells in some sense how often the event insured against can be expected to occur, and severity indicates, given that loss has occurred, how large it is likely to be. Now, if the average frequency of loss occurrence is multiplied by the average size loss, the insured's loss expectation or pure premium is determined. This is the amount, disregarding expenses, which each insured must pay if all losses are to be met. In a simple formula:

$$\frac{\text{Average Frequency} \; \#\text{ losses}}{\#\text{ exposure units}} \times \frac{\text{Severity} \; \$\text{ losses}}{\#\text{ losses}} = \frac{\text{Pure Premium} \; \$\text{ losses}}{\#\text{ exposure units}}$$

There is also a distribution of pure premiums which results from combining, i.e., multiplying the frequency and severity distributions. Figure 4 illustrates a hypothetical pure premium distribution in which $\mu$ is the mean or average pure premium.

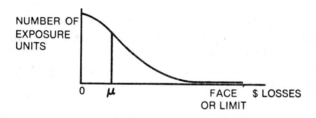

**FIGURE 4**

These concepts are what have here been termed mean concepts. They adequately define the insurance situation in that they produce a logically developed premium. Why then introduce risk at all? By using only the mean values of the distributions referred to, no account has been taken of the dispersion or variation of values around those means. Thus, if the pure premium distribution is widely dispersed, it is quite possible for the actual pure premium to be much greater than the predicted mean pure premium.

What is needed, then, is a notion to indicate (1) the variation within the pure premium distribution, and (2) the expected variation of the actual pure premium.

The first component is the dispersion inherent in the population, i.e., the pure premium distribution. Figure 4 shows that there are many pure premium values ranging from O to F dollars for the population of insureds. A measure of the variability inherent in the population is the standard deviation denoted by:

$$\sigma_{pp} = \sqrt{\frac{\Sigma(pp - \mu)^2}{n}}$$

This is the standard deviation of the pure premium distribution and sufficiently defines the first element of variation. However, variation can arise from another source, sometimes called sampling or random variation. In effect, the insurer does not observe the entire pure premium population, but only a sample therefrom. Thus, when he attempts to estimate, $\mu$, error or variation from the true value of $\mu$ may be present because he has only partial (sample) information. This sampling error or variation is a function of the sample size, usually being inversely related to the square root of the sample size.

These components of variation may now be combined into a single statistic, the standard error of the mean pure premium denoted by,

$$\sigma\mu = \frac{\sigma_{pp}}{\sqrt{n}}$$

where $\sigma_{pp}$ is the standard deviation of the pure premium as defined above and $n$ is the number of exposure units or insureds. This quantity, $\sigma\mu$ represents risk from the insurer's point of view, and the objective of insurance operations is to reduce $\sigma\mu$ by increasing the sample size, i.e., the number of units insured.

To summarize, the variability in the pure premium distribution is the risk which the insurer faces. Several pure premiums (outcomes) are possible, some high, some low, but he may charge only one of those premiums to all of his insureds.[19] The problem then is to choose a pure premium from among the possible ones, which exactly balances the highs and lows or, in other words, is the average of all the pure premiums. The insurer must reduce the variation of the pure premium which he selects, from the true average pure premium, to zero or as close as possible.

Alternatively stated, he must get the best estimate of the true average premium that he possibly can. He accomplishes this reduction in variation or increased accuracy of estimate, by using a large number of exposure units and the laws of large numbers. Since he is concerned with variation in his estimate of the mean pure premium, the standard error of the mean pure premium, $\sigma\mu = \frac{\sigma_{pp}}{\sqrt{n}}$ measures the insurer's risk. It is obvious that $\sigma\mu$ can be reduced by increasing $n$, and thus the insurer controls the risk he faces to the extent that he is able to acquire new business.

One aspect of this development of the notion of an insurer's risk, should be especially noted. All of the concepts used in defining risk are objective. To begin with, the insurer's average frequency of loss is conceived of as objective. Thus, two insurers evaluating the same insurance

---

[19] The reader may assume we are talking about a given class of insureds.

situation will independently produce identical average frequencies of loss.[20]

Further, both severity and pure premium are measured in dollars and are completely objective concepts. Finally, risk itself as herein defined is objective, in that it can be measured empirically independently of the observer. This aspect of insurer's risk contrasts sharply with the subjectivity of the individual's risk [21] which will be considered next.

The individual or firm's point of view is certainly much broader than the insurer's, in that it encompasses a much wider range of behavior. The general problem of individual decision making in the face of risk and uncertainty has received considerable study in the post World War II period. One of the most important contributions in the area is Savage's *Foundations of Statistics*.[22] Savage attempts to formulate a decision theory which has both positive and normative aspects for the individual. First, he contends that a large number of people *do* behave in accordance with his theory, and second, people *should* behave consistently with the theory. Independent of the correctness of these assertions, most writers agree that Savage's formulation is a valuable one, and it has been particularly well received by students of business decisions.[23]

In this section the concept of individual risk, as contained in modern decision theory, is examined. Actually, the contemporary treatment does not measure or deal with risk directly, and so this analysis starts at a more elementary level in which risk can be explicitly defined.

Any decision problem involves three basic components: states of the world, actions, and outcomes. States of the world refer to future or unknown situations which may arise. Since they are unknown they are necessarily hypothetical and hence, are sometimes called hypotheses. The decision maker has no control over these possible states of the world and must simply take them as given. His task in terms of the decision making process is to determine probabilities for these hypotheses. These probabilities, in the Savage formulation, are typically personalistic or subjective. Savage takes the position that: [24]

---

[20] The extreme nature of this statement is recognized. However what we are trying to examine is the "essence" of the insurance situation, and consequently we are looking at an idealized insurer. Of course, to the extent that rates are made in concert by rating boards and bureaus, insurers do "arrive at" identical average frequencies of loss.

[21] The author uses the term "individual's risk" rather than "uncertainty" in order to emphasize the problem basic to both insurer and individual, namely the variability of outcomes. Admittedly this discussion overemphasizes the objectivity of the insurer's measurement and interpretation of risk. Insurers, as all businessmen, continually face critical subjective decisions. But, again, the purpose here is to isolate those aspects of the insurance process which are unique to it.

[22] Savage, Leonard J., *Foundations of Statics*, John Wiley and Sons, Inc., New York, 1954.

[23] For example see Schlaifer, Robert, *Probability and Statistics for Business Decisions*, McGraw-Hill Book Co., Inc., New York, 1959.

[24] Savage, p. 3.

. . . . probability measures the confidence that a particular individual has in the truth of a particular proposition.

Thus, two rational and competent decision makers may assign different probabilities to the states of the world, as a result of differing personal or subjective interpretations of the available evidence. The individual's subjective probability distribution is then defined as follows: if for a given decision problem, there are $n$ states of the world, the individual assigns $n$ probabilities, one to each of the states of the world. These $n$ probabilities sum to one, and measure, for each of the states of the world, the individual's confidence that it will prove to be the true state of the world.

The actions refer to the choices or alternatives available to the individual. He controls these in the sense that he chooses the particular action which optimizes his position according to some specified criterion, i.e., maximizing expected monetary value or utility.

Finally, outcomes are the result of the interaction among states of the world and actions and they are measured in either monetary or utility terms. Each state of the world combines with each action to produce a particular outcome. Thus, if there are $n$ states of the world and $m$ actions, there will be $n \times m$ possible outcomes. This may be represented diagrammatically as follows:

TABLE 2
STATES OF THE WORLD

| Actions | $S_1$ | $S_2$ | . . . | $S_n$ |
|---|---|---|---|---|
| | $P_1$ | $P_2$ | Subjective Probabilities | $P_n$ |
| $A_1$ | $O_{11}$ | $O_{12}$ | . . . | $O_{in}$ |
| $A_2$ | $O_{21}$ | | | |
| . . . | . | | Outcomes | |
| $A_m$ | $O_{m1}$ | $O_{m2}$ | . . . . . | $O_{mn}$ |

Given these ingredients, the rational decision maker, according to modern theory, will choose that action with the highest expected value or utility. The expected value of an action is determined as follows: for each action $A_1$, state of the world $S_j$, probability of $S_j$, $P_j$, and for each outcome $O_{ij}$,

$$E V (A_i) = \sum_{j=i}^{n} P_j \cdot O_{ij}$$

However, this rule of maximizing expected value will hold only if the outcomes are measured by utilities, which are arithmetical statements of the individual's preference relations. If outcomes are measured in dollars, the maximization of expected dollars is unsatisfactory unless further analyzed. A simple example will illustrate this point. Assume that a man with a $10,000 house may insure it against fire for $200 a year, and that his subjective probability estimate of a fire is .01. We may then represent his decision problem as in Table 3.

If he maximized expected value, he will not insure since -$100 is greater than −$200. In fact it is doubtful if any one who maximized expected dollars would ever buy insurance, since the premium would always exceed the expected loss by an amount sufficient to cover expenses.[25]

TABLE 3

STATES OF THE WORLD

| Actions | Fire $P_1 = .01$ | No Fire $P_2 = .99$ | Expected Value of Action | Standard Deviation of Action |
|---|---|---|---|---|
| Insure | −$200 | −$200 | −$200 | $0 |
| Do Not Insure | −$10,000 | $0 | −$100 | $995 |

Therefore, there must be another element present in the situation, in addition to expected value, which encourages him to insure. This element is risk, and it can be defined by the standard deviation or the variance of the action. Thus, just as one can define an expected value for each action, so he can define a risk for each action, and the greater the variability of outcomes, the greater the risk. The last column in Table 3 shows the standard deviation

$$\$\sigma_{Ai} = \sqrt{\sum_{j=i}^{n} (O_{ij} - E V (A_i))^2 \cdot P_j}$$

of each of the two actions. The impact of insuring is very clear. His risk, $\$\sigma_A$, is reduced to zero, and so he considers insuring even though his expected loss will increase from $100 to $200 by so doing.

Intuitively, this definition of risk makes some sense in that if the values of a series of outcomes are all nearly alike, so that $\$\sigma_A$ is small, then the decision maker "knows" that he cannot do badly since the range between the highest and lowest outcomes is small. Thus, any outcome will yield him nearly the same result, so there is little risk involved. On the other hand, if the values of the outcomes vary greatly,

---

[25] This assumes that the individual's subjective probability estimate is close to the insurer's objective probability of loss. If the individual's estimate is much higher, then he would insure even under the rule of maximizing expected dollars.

i.e., $\$\sigma_A$ is large, some outcomes will be very much worse than others, and colloquially, it is a very "risky" situation.

In this framework an individual must examine two parameters, expected values and standard deviations of the actions, in order to make a decision. However, it is not clear how much weight should be given to each factor. The question is: what functional relationship can be established to connect optimal decisions, expected value, and risk?

The modern solution is to move from a dollar scale to a utility scale. Outcomes are measured in "utils" which reflect the individual's preferences. Utility is an indecomposible mixture of the individual's attitudes toward profit, loss, and risk.[26] If outcomes are measured on a utility scale, the rule of choosing the action with the highest expected utility is appropriate since this single measure will reflect all aspects and components of the problem. Hence, in Savage's decision theory, risk is no longer an explicit problem, since it is subsumed under the larger concept of utility.

The relationship between expected dollar value, risk, and expected utility can be indicated by the following analysis: If Figure 5 is an accurate representation of the functional relationship between money (V) and utility (U), that is, shows the decreasing marginal utility of money,

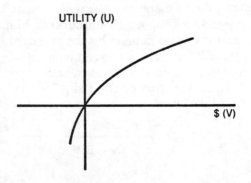

FIGURE 5

then the function is in the second degree of the form: $U = bV - cV^2$. Then, $EU = bEV - cEV^2$ where E means the expected value of the variable. It can then be shown that by algebraic manipulation one gets, $EU = bEV - c(EV)^2 - c\sigma_V^2$. This equation relates expected utility EU, expected value of money EV and risk $\sigma_V$.

---

[26] Schlaifer, *op. cit.*, p. 42.

The constants b and c would vary for each individual. A cautious person or risk averter would have a high c value in which case the curve in Figure 5 would flatten out rather quickly. A risk lover would have a low c value and the curve would not flatten out until he reached the range of high money values. Expected utility is seen to be directly related to the expected value of money but inversely related to risk, i.e., $\sigma_v$.

In summary, individual risk, can be explicated in the context of modern decision theory. It may be defined explicitly as the standard deviation of the outcomes of a particular action, $\$\sigma_A$, if those outcomes are measured in dollars. However, if this is done, it is difficult to know how to combine the expected value and risk of an action and then compare the "mix" with the expected values and risks of other actions. Therefore, the modern solution is to measure outcomes in terms of personal utilities, in which case risk no longer exists as a separate concept but is inextricably bound in with other elements. Risk and all of these other components simultaneously determine the individual's preference ordering.

Individual risk, then, and the entire decision making process is a highly subjective affair as viewed by the modern school. Both the probability estimates and the utilities are subjectivity unique to the individual. These notions of the subjectively of risk are not new. They have been noted in the writings of Willett, Knight and Pfeffer. In each case this subjective risk situation was called "uncertainty" and it was indicated that it was more or less incapable of analysis and quantification. Modern decision theory then represents an important breakthrough or contradiction to the traditional interpretation of uncertainty. However, it is only fair to note that many regard the theory as non-operational in all but the most trivial cases.

Perhaps the most important thing to note about the notion of risk as contained in modern decision theory is its wide applicability. Presumably, every conceivable decision is analyzable in terms of the theory, and hence subjective risk, as defined, enters into all of these situations. Therefore, risk, in this sense, is not the special domain of insurance scholars or theory. Personal decision theory and the notions of risk embodied in that theory are no more nor less applicable to insurance buying than they are to choosing a job or any other decision faced by contemporary man. Whatever aspect of risk is unique to insurance must be determined by looking at the matter from the insurer's point of view.

## INDIVIDUAL AND INSURER RISK COMPARED

How does this subjective risk square with the notion of insurer risk i.e., the standard error of the mean previously developed? The answer is not simple. While there are many parallels there are also structural differences which make it more difficult to apply the standard error of the mean concept to the personal risk situation. Probably the most striking similarity is brought out by comparing frequency with subjective probability, severity with dollar or utility outcomes, and pure premium (expected loss) with expected value or utility. Thus in both formulations we have a probability or frequency, a worth or value, and an expectation. They are mixed together in roughly the same manner to produce in one case a distribution of pure premiums and in the other a set of expected values of actions.

But having established this major parallel, an obvious difference appears. Insurer risk was defined as the standard error of the mean of the pure premium distribution. To be consistent, risk in the subjective context should be defined as the standard error of an action or alternative, i.e., $\frac{\$\sigma_A}{\sqrt{n}}$ where $n$ represents the number of times the alternative was chosen. However, in the individual decision making process, each situation is unique, and there is little chance for repetition, and so $n$ may be taken as equal to one. In that case individual risk becomes $\$\sigma_A$, the standard deviation of an action, which is the definition that was actually developed above.

In the context of the theory of individual decision making, the notion of risk as implying variation in outcomes was preserved. There is, however, not much ground for any reasonable appeal to the laws of large numbers, i.e., increasing the accuracy of one's prediction as a result of increasing the number of cases or exposure units as in insurance.

A second major difference in the two risk notions relates to their empirical natures. Insurer's risk is constructed solely out of objective phenomena, all measurable and independent of the observer. The individual's risk whether explicit in money terms or implicit in utility terms is a personalistic observer dependent phenomenon. From this it follows that the empirical techniques used to study the two risk concepts must necessarily be quite different, the one emphasizing statistical approaches, the other psychological considerations.

The notion of insurer's risk as a standard error is consistent with the idea of risk as a concept of variability, but it also recognizes the importance of sample size. It is a notion which is in the actuarial tradition and is embodied in Risk Theory as formulated by the European actuaries. Willett's treatment of risk, though incomplete, and Dickerson's risk model [27] are respectively implicitly and explicitly in agreement with this analysis. In contrast, Pfeffer (who is emphasizing the individual's point of view), the operations of Lloyds of London,[28] and game theoretic approaches, all tend to support a more subjective individual definition of risk.

---

[27] Dickerson, O. D., "A Conceptual Framework for Insurance Theory," *Review of Insurance Studies,* Vol. II, 1955, p. 26.

[28] It can be argued that certain insurance firms, e.g., Lloyds and marine underwriters, are successful not because of proper application of the principles of insurance and treatment of risk in an insurance context, but rather because they are employing a decision theory similar to Savage's formulation.

One limitation of the foregoing definitions of risk is that they are measured in absolute terms. Thus it is not possible to compare, directly, the risk in one situation with that of another. What is required is a relative measure of risk, e.g., a percentage or a proportion. One possible solution is to divide risk, as defined, by the mean of the distribution. Thus, for the individual,

$$\text{Rel. Risk} = \frac{\$\sigma_A}{\$EV(A)}$$

and for the insurer,

$$\text{Rel. Risk} = \frac{\$\sigma_{pp}}{\sqrt{n.\mu}}$$

For the individual this measure of relative risk is the Coefficient of Variation, a well known measure of the relative variation in a distribution.[29] These definitions, though simple, should be used with caution and only applied to similar risk situations. Thus, a statement comparing the relative risk of a life insurer with that of an automobile insurer is of doubtful value, and even less meaningful is one comparing the relative risk of an individual with that of an insurer.

## SUMMARY

Risk is a concept indicating variability of possible outcomes. It may be studied from either the individual's or insurer's point of view. Risk in an individual context is probably best analyzed in terms of modern decision making theory. Within this theory, risk may be defined as the standard deviation of the monetary outcomes of an action, $\$\sigma_A$. To the insurer, risk is a function of the variation in the pure premium distribution and the number of exposure units and may be defined by the standard error of the mean of the pure premium distribution, $\sigma\mu = \frac{\sigma_{pp}}{\sqrt{n}}$

These distinctions must be recognized in order to distinguish insurance from all other types of decision making in the face of risk and uncertainty.

---

[29] The relationship $\frac{\$\sigma_A}{\$E(A)}$ measures the risk per dollar of expected loss. Both components, $\$\sigma_A$ and $\$E(A)$, are based on the same subjective probability distribution, and this gives the measure a certain internal consistency. However, an alternative definition which is perhaps more satisfactory for consumer analysis, is $\frac{\$\sigma_A}{\$GP}$ where $\$GN$ is the gross premium charged for the insurance. Notice that this measures risk per dollar of premium which may be the most crucial consideration in an insurance buying decision.

An insurance buying decision rule could take the following form: rank all exposures with respect to $\frac{\$\sigma_A}{\$GP}$ and then insure the largest, the next largest, and so on until the insurance budget is exhausted.

## SECTION II. INSURANCE AND SAMPLING ALTERNATIVE
## DEFINITIONS OF INSURANCE

Writers in the field have for some time differed in the definitions of insurance which they put forward. In general, there have been two important definitional schools, i.e., "pooling" and "transfer." The advocates of each of these definitions usually argue that they are irreconcilable and that the definition in opposition to theirs fails to describe the "essence" of insurance. Occasionally textbook writers will attempt to incorporate both points of view but this is usually accomplished through a lack of precision rather than through careful analysis. It is the purpose of the following discussion to show that the definitions of risk offered in the previous section provide a basis for an understanding of both definitions of insurance.

Consider a definition from each of the two schools. Pfeffer offers a precise definition from the transfer point of view: [30]

> Insurance is a device for the reduction of uncertainty of one party, called the insured, through the transfer of particular risks to another party, called the insurer, who offers a restoration, at least in part, of economic losses suffered by the insured.

The most important aspect of the foregoing is the alleged *modus operandi* of insurance, i.e., transfer. In contrast to the definition which follows, no mention is made of grouping or pooling or even of the presence of many insureds. Alfred Manes, an international scholar of insurance, gives the following definition in the pooling tradition: [31]

> ... the essence of insurance lies in the elimination of the uncertain risk of loss for the individual through the combination of a large number of similarly exposed individuals. . .

Thus, Manes, ignoring transfer, sees combination or pooling as the crucial element in describing the insurance device.

In the previous section, risk was defined in two distinct contexts: the individual's and the insurer's. Insurance is a legitimate device for meeting, i.e., reducing or eliminating, risk, and its definition or meaning is a function of whose risk it is dealing with. To an individual dealing with his risk in an individual context, insurance is seen as a transfer mechanism through which he passes on his risk to the insurer. To the insurer, attempting to reduce risk as it appears in the context of his business, insurance is a pooling operation.

An individual confronted with a risk situation has several alternatives, one of which may be insurance. If asked to define insurance or describe it as he sees it, it is unlikely that he would identify himself as one of a large number of individuals facing a similar risk situation who

---

[30] Pfeffer, *op. cit.*, p. 53.
[31] Manes, Alfred, "Insurance, Principles, and History," *Encyclopedia of the Social Sciences,* Vol. 8, MacMillan Co., New York, 1935, p. 95.

combine together in some manner. He will probably say that he gives or transfers his risk to the insurer for a specific price (premium) and that this transfer is based on an individual contract (policy) between him and the insurer. It begins and ends as a personal transaction between him and the insurance company and his only concern is that when he suffers a loss the insurance company will pay him. Thus, in this context, the success of the insurance mechanism is strictly a function of the aggregate financial strength of the insurer. The individual is not directly concerned with the internal workings of the insurance company, only with the payoff.

The foregoing point of view is appropriate for microeconomic analysis. The firm purchases the factor input "insurance service" and transfers its risk of certain losses to the insurer. The effect of this risk transfer is to eliminate extreme variation in the cost curves, from one time period to the next, which would result if catastrophic losses (fire, Acts of God, etc.) were borne by the firm. Thus, some of the irregularities and vissicitudes of the economic life of the firm are smoothed out by insurance. The firm is then freed to concentrate on the entrepreneurial and business risks which are a function of innovation and are essentially uninsurable.

While the phenomenon of insurance itself must be analyzed in a dynamic economic framework,[32] it is interesting to note that the presence of insurance strengthens the realism of static analysis, in that uncertainty as to the future is reduced and the insurance premium is a relatively constant factor price which is substituted for a highly variable loss cost.

To the insurer, insurance is something quite different. His business is to reduce the risk which he faces. This risk has been defined in the preceding section as the standard error of the mean of the pure premium distribution, $\sigma\mu = \frac{\sigma_{pp}}{\sqrt{n}}$. It is possible for the insurer to reduce or eliminate this risk by pooling together a large number of insureds or exposure units. The application of the laws of large numbers enables the insurer to reduce $\sigma\mu$, i.e., his risk. In this context, pooling becomes the central notion, and the insurer's financial success is a function of the successful application of the laws of large numbers.[33] From the insurer's point of view insurance is pooling.

---

[32] Pfeffer, *op. cit.*, Chapter 7.

[33] Pfeffer argues that laws of large numbers are a sufficient but not a necessary condition of insurance and points to the many insurance operations which are not stict examples of pooling, e.g., Lloyds and the nuclear energy exposure. In answer to this we can note that Pfeffer is interested in a definition suitable to microeconomic theory and hence favors a transfer definition. More importantly, it can be argued that these unusual non-pooling insurance arrangements are only possible after an insurer has become established by the successful use of pooling techniques. Thus, the insuring of these "unique" risk situations, which is unlikely with respect to unique risks, is more in the nature of a "guarantee" than an insurance contract, and it is possible for the insurer to give out these "guarantees" simply because of his extensive financial resources. However, from the insured's point of view both a "guarantee" and an insurance contract based on pooling represent a transfer of risk to the insurer.

These alternative definitions of insurance, the individual's and the insurer's, are not identical in scope. The individual would tend to regard as insurance any agreement with an insurance company which enabled him to transfer his risk to that company, whereas to be consistent, the insurer would have to look at this total business as two separate segments: the first, his insurance business based on pooling; and the second, his "unique" business which he hopes he is financially strong enough to cover.[34]

While the discussion to follow develops the technical requirements of insurance, based exclusively on a pooling notion, it must be recognized that these do not define what is insurable except in a very rarefied theoretical sense. In real world terms, economic and social values are critical determinants in assaying what may or may not be insured. Economically, there must be an insurer willing to grant the insurance at a price which the potential insured is willing to pay. Further, the contract must not conflict with contemporary socio-legal values. For example the insurance of uncertain future profits accruing from a business venture is generally considered contrary to public policy in that it would remove the incentive to invest and undertake new business. Attempts at indicating all-inclusive specification of what is insurable necessarily fail since the considerations which determine insurability are more often pragmatic than logical.

## INSURANCE AS A SAMPLING MODEL

If insurance is considered strictly from the insurer's point of view, that is as a pooling arrangement, it is possible to define the criteria of a successful insurance scheme in terms of a random sampling model. Such models have specific requirements which must be met, and these can be shown to be analogous to the factors usually cited as necessary to a sound insurance plan.

Random sampling can be defined as drawing from a population in which each elementary unit has a definite and known probability of being drawn in the sample.[35] Simple random sampling refers to a situation in which the probabilities of drawing all elementary units are equal, and independent. Considering first the simple random sampling model, the necessary criteria of insurance are examined.

(1) *The loss must be objective and accidental.* The requirement that the loss be objective, so that the insurer may be certain that it has occurred, is similar to demanding that the sampler be able to draw elementary units from the population in a definite and unconfused manner.

---

[34] This attitude is partially reflected in insurance companies' attitudes toward their Special Risks Departments which are permitted to "play around" with "oddball risks." The operations in this type of department are viewed as incorporating a substantial element of luck.

[35] R. Clay Sprowls, *Elementary Statistics,* McGraw-Hill Book Co., New York, 1955, p. 11.

If the loss were not accidental, there would be serious moral hazards in that the insured could control its occurrence or nonoccurrence. Similarly, random sampling requires a table of random numbers to determine specifically which elementary units will be included in the sample.

(2) *The exposure units must be homogeneous* with regard to their expected pure premium. This requirement that each insured should have the same loss expectation (the product of his frequency of loss and his severity of loss), is analogous to specifying that each elementary unit have the *same* probability of being drawn into the sample, i.e., the simple random sampling condition.[36]

(3) *Exposure units should be spatially and temporally independent.* Loss occurring to one exposure unit should not alter the loss expectation of any other exposure unit. This requirement renders catastrophe losses extremely unlikely, i.e., spatially independent, and insists that losses are not autocorrelated, that is, what happened in time period "t" has no influence on what happens in time period "t + 1." This is equivalent to the sampling rule that the drawing of an elementary unit does not affect the probability of drawing any other elementary unit.

(4) *There should be a large number of exposure units.* This has the same function in insurance and sampling which is to permit the application of the Central Limit Theorem (discussed below) and thus increase the accuracy of estimation.

(5) *There should be a buffer fund.* This is necessary since it is unlikely that the insurer's predictions will be exactly correct. This buffer fund is not what is normally thought of as the reserve since this latter is for expected losses and is a direct monetary measure of the insurer's risk. It corresponds in sampling theory to the recognition of random or sampling error.

The five foregoing requirements of a sound insurance plan have been treated as analogous to sampling theory. The question now arises as to what extent these requirements are met in actual practice. Is the sampling model a valid representation of insurance practice? Pfeffer has discussed and answered this question in the negative.[37]

> Strictly speaking there is no line of insurance written which is able to meet the complete set of tests implied by any of the Laws of Large Numbers because the universe of insurance experience is constantly changing with the economic and social environment. This means that the results gleaned from the past no longer have the same measure of relevance for the present—much less for the future. For some lines of insurance, it is possible to approximate the requirements of the sampling method; for some, it is possible to meet most of the tests; but, for others, few of the requisites can be established.

---

[36] Under more general random sampling conditions, e.g., stratified, the probabilities need only be known. They are not necessarily equal. The analogous insurance requirement would be that each insured have a definite and known loss expectation.

[37] Pfeffer, *op. cit.*, p. 43, see also p. 66.

However, perhaps the sampling model is not as unrealistic as it first might appear. To begin with, the fact that insurance cannot meet all the requirements of random sampling theory is neither surprising nor unusual. Very few, if any, physical situations correspond exactly to the implicit and explicit requirements of the theorems of mathematical statistics. This is especially the case in the social sciences, and yet sampling is considered one of their most valuable and highly respected tools. Rather than reject sampling theory as too idealized, attempts are made to remove or control as many of the real world discrepancies as possible.

This is exactly what is done in insurance through certain institutional devices. Thus, the conditions most frequently violated are numbers 1, 2, and 3 cited above: accidental and objective losses; homogeneity; and independence. The insurer attempts to guarantee that the loss will be accidental through underwriting, policy provisions, and the court interpretations of the risk situation insured. Losses are made as objective as possible through policy definitions. The problem of homogeneity is usually handled through classifications so that within a given line of insurance insureds are split in classes or groups. The presumption is that all insureds in a given class have identical or very similar loss expectations. This is analogous to moving from a model of simple random sampling to one of stratified random sampling and will be discussed in a later section.

Spatial independence is increased by underwriting rules and retention limits or reinsurance systems. Temporal independence cannot be assumed or increased by manipulation. Autocorrelation of observations made over time is a statistically unpleasant fact in all of the social sciences. Insurers, as do many researchers in economic and related disciplines, simply assume that observations are temporally independent and then make *ad hoc* after the fact adjustments to soften the effect of this erroneous assumption.[38]

On the basis of the preceding arguments it seems reasonable to use the sampling model as representing the insurance process. Certainly the bulk of the transactions which make up the contemporary insurance business are amenable to analysis in terms of this model. A further advantage of adopting sampling theory as a framework is that it permits determination of the extent to which any given insurance transaction deviates from this ideal.

## AN INSURANCE THEORY

There have been developed two important models of the insurance process: "individual risk theory" and "collective risk theory." The

---

[38] More sophisticated treatments of the autocorrelation problem exist, e.g., see, Ezekiel, Mordecai and Fox, Karl A., *Methods of Correlation and Regression Analysis,* 3rd edition, John Wiley & Sons, Inc., New York, 1959, pp. 325-343, but these do not appear to have been applied to any great extent to insurance problems.

formal and technical details of these theories have been described elsewhere,[39] so the purpose of the following treatment is to discuss certain
aspects of these theories verbally, and particularly to examine the form
and implications of individual risk theory.

Collective risk theory is by far the more complicated system. Instead
of considering a single probability of loss (frequency) and a single average
size loss (severity), it analyzes distributions of these two variables. A
whole range of the numbers of losses which can occur is defined, and the
probability of any particular number of losses is specified, e.g., out of
1000 insureds the probability that 75 losses will occur is 0.12, the probability that 100 losses will occur may be 0.02, and the probabilities that
0 or 1000 losses occur are both very small. The sum of all of these probabilities must equal one, and thus define a probability distribution of the
number of losses.

Similarly a loss, when it occurs, may vary, say, from $1 up to $100.
There is a specific probability with which each amount of loss from $1 to
$100 may occur. This is a probability distribution of the amount of loss.
These two distributions are then compounded or multiplied together
to produce a total loss or total pure premium distribution.[40] This is a
third probability distribution, and by examining it over time it is possible
to make statements about the probability of ruin given a certain premium income and risk reserve. This theory, while correct enough, is
mathematically very difficult and hence usefully describes the insurance process to only a very limited audience.

Individual risk theory provides a simpler framework of analysis. It
cons ·rs only the pure premium or total loss distribution and by-passes
the question of the shape or type of any of the three distributions.
This is accomplished by certain sampling assumptions and the use of the
Central Limit Theorem.

First, conceive of a population of all people who are potential consumers of a given line of insurance. The random variable of interest is
the dollars of loss produced by each member of the population (elementary unit). The value of the random variable which occurs most frequently
will be $0, since the vast majority will have no losses. The maximum
value of the random variable might be the face of the policy, i.e., no loss
may exceed this amount.

Figure 6 illustrates a hypothetical population. From this population
(note that nothing has been specified about its shape or form) the
insurer draws a random sample of size $n$, where $n$ is equal to the number
of policyholders. The losses of each policyholder are observed, and these
make up the sample data. The sum of the losses divided by the number
of policyholders, is the sample mean pure premium.

---

[39] Houston, David B., "Risk Theory," *Journal of Insurance*, Vol. 27, No. 1, March 1960,
pp. 77-82.

[40] For a description of this process see Dickerson, O. D., "Loss Distributions in Non-
Life Insurance," *Journal of Insurance*, Vol. 28, No. 3, Sept. 1961, pp. 45-54.

According to the Central Limit Theorem: for a sample $(X_1, X_2, \ldots X_n)$ from a distribution with mean $\mu$ and variance $\sigma^2$, the distribution of the sample mean M approaches the normal distribution with a mean $\mu$ and a variance $\dfrac{\sigma^2}{n}$ as $n \to \infty$. This means that the sample mean just determined

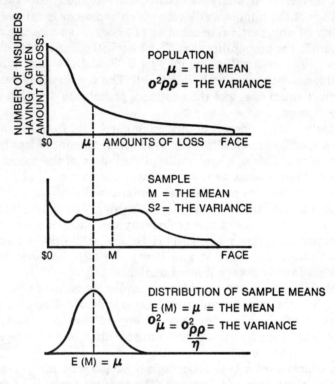

FIGURE 6

may be viewed as an observation from a normal distribution, where the mean of that normal distribution is the same as the mean of the population and the variance of the normal distribution becomes smaller and smaller as the sample size (number of insureds) is increased. This normal distribution is called the distribution of sample means, and is shown in Figure 6.

Thus it can be seen that there are three distinct distributions only one of which, the sample, is ever actually observed. However, since M is distributed normally, and the mean, $\mu$, and variance, $\dfrac{\sigma_{pp}^2}{n}$ of that distribution are known, it is possible to estimate $\mu$ from M and also to make statements, in the form of confidence intervals, about the accuracy of the estimate. Since the variation in the sampling distribution decreases as $n$ increases, the accuracy of these estimates of the true pure premium increases as the number of people insured increases.

Seen within this framework, earlier statements to the effect that the insurer's risk can be indicated by $\sigma\mu = \dfrac{\sigma_{pp}}{\sqrt{n}}$ are perhaps more meaningful.

Thus, a reduction in risk, $\sigma\mu$, implies a compression of the distribution of sample means and improved accuracy in estimating $\mu$. To the extent that estimates of $\mu$ are improved, the size of the buffer fund required to cover chance or random fluctuations is reduced. And it can be seen that the size of the buffer fund decreases as the number of insureds increase. This then, is one of the key economic results of insurance: a reduction of the buffer fund held against unforeseen contingencies.

The individual facing a risk situation must, in order to be safe, set aside the full amount of the potential loss, so that his buffer fund, relatively speaking, is very large. An insurance company never holds funds equal to the total potential losses that might occur. Rather, funds are held equal to average losses expected to occur plus a relatively small buffer fund to cover losses in excess of the average.

Thus, one way of conceiving of the economic worth of insurance is in terms of the added earning power of the assets released as a result of insurance. This may be stated more precisely as follows: suppose an individual faces a loss for which, in order to be safe, he must hold a fund of size $F. He can earn returns on this fund only at the relatively low rate of interest "i" since it must be easily available to cover potential losses. If he buys insurance at a cost of premium $P, he may invest the remainder of his fund at a higher rate of interest "r."

Further, let us assume that half of the premium $P is pure premium or loss dollars and that if he handles the risk himself he can expect an average of $P/2 per year loss. Then, if he does not buy insurance, his financial worth after a year will be $F(1 + i) - \dfrac{P}{2}$ whereas, if he does buy insurance, his worth is $(F - P)(1 + r)$. The difference between these two represents the value of insurance. Thus

$$\text{Ins.} = (F - P)(1+r) - \left[ F(1+i) - \frac{P}{2} \right]$$

This may be rewritten as:

$$\text{Ins.} = F(r-i) - P(\tfrac{1}{2} + r)$$

From this one could conclude that if the loss fund $F$ were very large and/or the interest rate differential $(r - i)$ were substantial, it is likely that the insurance would have a high value to the individual.

Conceiving of insurance in terms of population, sample, and sampling distributions, as above, also enables one to make some precise and fairly useful statements about the distinction between insurance, prevention, and underwriting. Insurance attempts to reduce risk, $\sigma\mu$, that is to compress the sampling distribution and consequently reduce the buffer fund. It does not attempt to alter the mean pure premium or average loss per insured but rather takes this as given.

Prevention aims at altering the population by reducing the pure premium. It may do this by decreasing either the number of losses (frequency) or the average size loss (severity) or both, and prevention activities may be classed according to which variables in the risk situation are being manipulated.

Underwriting is an attempt to redefine, more narrowly, the population from which the sample is being drawn. Often this takes the form of eliminating the upper tail of the population distribution, i.e., those exposure units with a very high average loss potential. The establishment of different underwriting classes is in effect breaking the basic population into several sub-populations and sampling within each. Thus, this theory is useful, not only in describing risk and insurance as such, but also in that it enables one to interpret related phenomena.

## EMPIRICAL EXAMPLES: ESTIMATION AND TESTING

Having examined individual risk theory in rather abstract terms some empirical examples should indicate how the concepts are operationalized. As was implied in the preceding section there are two critical values which the insurer must determine: the mean pure premium, $\mu$, and the buffer fund which is a function of $\sigma\mu$. This idea has been stated particularly well and concisely by a British actuary: [41]

> ... there are two main aspects of general insurance in which a knowledge of the structure of the elements of risk variation is needed—first in the rate fixing process and second in the question of financial stability—and these can be generalized respectively into a knowledge of the mean and variance of the risk involved.

First to be examined is a problem in estimating the pure premium and buffer fund. Suppose an insurer has collected the following data from last year's experience: [42]

TABLE 4

| Dollars of Losses | No. of Insureds |
|---|---|
| $ 0 | 900 |
| $ 75 | 30 |
| $150 | 50 |
| $500 | 20 |

n = 1000

---

[41] Beard, R. E., "Analytic Expressions of the Risks Involved in General Insurance," *Transactions of XVth International Congress of Actuaries,* New York, 1957, Vol. II, p. 232.

[42] Since the universe is treated as unchanging over time, a random sample from last year is theoretically sufficient to estimate this year's pure premium. As discussed above, temporal independence is an assumption, not a reality.

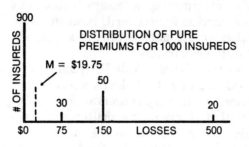

$$\text{FIGURE 7}$$

Figure 7 illustrates the pure premium distribution for 1000 insureds. In relation to Figure 6 it is the sample distribution and has a sample mean M = $19.75 which is the best single estimate of $\mu$, the true population pure premium. In order to determine the size of the buffer fund, it is necessary to have an estimate of $\sigma_{pp}$. The sample variance $S^2$ is a good estimate of the population variance $\sigma_{pp}^2$. So.

$$\text{Est. } \sigma_{pp}^2 = S^2 \; \frac{\Sigma f(X-M)^2}{n-1} = \$5911$$

$$\text{Est. } \sigma_{pp} = \$77$$

$$\text{Est. } \sigma_\mu = \text{Est. } \frac{\sigma_{pp}}{\sqrt{n}} \pm \frac{\$77}{\sqrt{1000}} = \$2.43$$

Knowing that M and $\sigma_\mu$ come from a normal distribution enables the setting up of confidence intervals of the mean pure premium. Suppose that it is desired to operate within the 99 percent confidence interval. This means that, if a random sample of 1000 were taken an infinite number of times, 99 percent of the time the intervals, established by the same procedure which we are using to establish this interval, would contain the true mean $\mu$. The general formula M $\pm$ $Z\sigma_\mu$ becomes

$$\$19.75 \pm (2.58) \, \$2.43 = \$13.48 \text{ to } \$26.02$$

These results imply that for every $19.75 of pure premium which is collected, the company must have a buffer fund, provided through premiums and/or surplus, of $6.27 if it wishes to be 99 percent confident that it will be able to cover all losses. Thus, if the expense loading were 50 percent, the gross premium would be $39.50, so that 1000 insureds would provide premiums written of $39,500 against which a surplus of $6,270 is required.

It should be noted that the preceding is a simple example presented for illustrative purposes only. It is probable that in most practical situations $n$ would be substantially larger thus calling for a relatively much smaller buffer fund. One of the merits of this approach is that it provides a simple method of determining necessary surplus in an insurance company. Most likely, surplus figures for U.S. insurers are high as a result of state regulation of accounting practices and an overconservative bias on the part of the companies.

In this context the Kenney Rule,[43] which asserts that an insurer should have one dollar of policyholder's surplus for every two dollars of premium volume, seems very conservative. If a 50 percent loss ratio is posited, then half of all premiums written are pure or loss premiums. Viewing the policyholder's surplus as the buffer fund, the Kenney Rule may be restated as follows: the buffer fund should be equal to the pure premiums. Intuitively, one would suspect that a much smaller buffer would suffice, since its only purpose is to cover losses in *excess* of those which are expected.

It is also possible to use this sampling approach in a problem of testing hypotheses. Suppose that at the end of the year the company is considering a rate revision. To keep things simple, assume that only two hypotheses (states of the world) are possible: $H_0$: rates are adequate and $H_1$: rates are inadequate. The insurer has two possible actions: let rates alone or increase rates. This can be set up in a 2 x 2 table as illustrated below. In observing the consequences of the mix between states of the world and actions it is noted that two of the possible outcomes are satisfactory whereas two are in error. A Type I error is made when the null hypothesis, $H_0$, is rejected when it is in fact true.

**TABLE 5**

**STATES OF THE WORLD**

| Actions | $H_0$<br>Rate is<br>Adequate | $H_1$<br>Rate is<br>Inadequate |
|---|---|---|
| Let Rate<br>Alone | OK | Type II<br>Error |
| Increase<br>Rate | Type I<br>Error | OK |

In this particular case a Type I error consists in increasing the rate when the present rate is adequate, and the result might be conflict with state regulatory officials and/or loss of business to competitors who do not raise their adequate rates. A Type II error results from rejecting the alternative hypothesis $H_1$ when it is true, e.g., letting the rate alone when the rate is inadequate. The cost of such an action could, in the long

---

[43] Kenney, Roger, *Fundamentals of Fire and Casualty Insurance Strength*, Kenney Insurance Studies, Dedham, 1949.

run, be insolvency. The decision maker must then decide how important, i.e., costly, are the two types of error and then assign probabilities $\alpha$ and $\beta$ to their occurrence. Thus, if a Type I error is very costly its probability, $\alpha$, will be made very small.

Now, suppose the insurer has been charging a pure premium of $40. He wishes to formulate a decision rule to determine if rates are adequate or inadequate and takes a sample of 10,000 insureds. The standard deviation of the population has been estimated from previous data as Est. $\sigma_{pp}$ = $60. He decides that a Type I error (possible conflict with rate regulatory officials) is not too critical and hence sets $\alpha$ = .20. A Type II error (possible insolvency) on the other hand, is critical and its probabilities will be shown by the Operating Characteristic curve which will be developed below. On the basis of the information given, a decision rule can now be formulated.

$H_0$: $\mu$ = $40 (The true $\mu$ in the population is $40.)
$H_1$: $\mu$ > $40 (The true $\mu$ in the population is greater than $40.)
$\alpha$ = .20 (Probability of increasing rate when rate is adequate)
n = 10,000 (Number of insureds—sample size)
Est. $\sigma_{pp}$ = $60 (Estimate of standard deviation of the population).

The problem is to determine a decision point or value such that, if the sampling is from a population in which $\mu$ = $40, i.e., $H_0$ is true, the probability of concluding that the true $\mu$ is greater than $40, is 0.20. Figure 8 illustrates this.

Then

$$\text{Est. } \sigma_\mu = \text{Est.} \frac{\sigma_{pp}}{\sqrt{n}} = \frac{\$60}{\sqrt{10,000}} = \$.60$$

$$M^* = \mu + Z\alpha \text{ Est. } \sigma_\mu$$
$$M^* = 40 + (0.84) \$.60$$
$$M^* = \$40.50$$

Decision Rule: If M (the sample pure premium) is less than $40.50 let the rate alone. If M is greater than or equal to $40.50 increase the rate.

$\beta$, the probability of a Type II error is now specified by the OC curve.

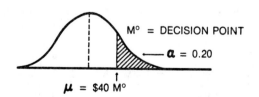

$M^\circ$ = DECISION POINT

$\alpha$ = 0.20

$\mu$ = $40 $M^\circ$

FIGURE 8

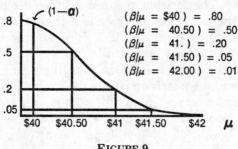

$$(\beta/\mu = \$40\ ) = .80$$
$$(\beta/\mu = 40.50\ ) = .50$$
$$(\beta/\mu = 41.\ ) = .20$$
$$(\beta/\mu = 41.50\ ) = .05$$
$$(\beta/\mu = 42.00\ ) = .01$$

FIGURE 9

Given the decision rule and the oc curve the insurer has an objective framework for analyzing rate changes. This example is not necessarily realistic in terms of quantities, but rather it is the interpretation which is useful in analyzing all cases. The only way that the insurer can decrease $\beta$ while holding $\alpha$ constant is by increasing $n$. Whether or not $\beta$ is "too large" depends upon the buffer fund which is available from past operations. A final point about the example: it would be possible to reformulate the problem with hypotheses reversed. This would enable the insurer to control $\beta$ (risk of insolvency) directly, and might be more satisfactory, if the insurer is greatly concerned about this error.

The two preceding examples, one of estimation and the other of testing illustrate what can be done generally with this kind of sampling approach. They also bring out, indirectly, a very important point in connection with successful insurance operations. All insurance schemes involve two applications of the Laws of Large Numbers. First, the insurer must apply the Central Limit Theorem to estimate the true pure premium. Second, he must insure a large number of exposure units so that the relative variation of his actual results from his expected results will be small (Law of Large Numbers). While it is true that last year's insureds become the basis for this year's estimation, it is still useful to conceive of two distinct applications in describing the insurance process.

## CLASSIFICATION AND STRATIFIED RANDOM SAMPLING

Having described the basic idea of insurance as related to a sampling model and given examples in the areas of estimation and testing,[44]

---

[44] The number and types of examples which can be developed from the sampling model are limited only by one's imagination. One novel approach would be to consider insurance as a random production process. Then, on the basis of some large aggregate of data, upper and lower control limits could be established and relatively small periodic samples could be taken to determine whether or not losses were in control. New rates would be established not periodically, but only when the insurance "process" went out of control and could not be remedied by some other action. This approach is presented as possible, but not necessarily practical, although it may be that some of the implications are both interesting and valid.

attention is now turned to the possibility of modifying the simple random sampling model. Recalling that the three ratemaking criteria established by the states are "reasonable," "adequate" and "equitable," it may be observed that the process so far described meets the first two requirements. Rates are reasonable since an attempt has been made to estimate the true pure premium in the population. They are adequate in that a buffer fund has been established to cover random fluctuations. However, they are equitable only to the extent that the population is homogeneous, i.e., *a priori,* all insureds have identical loss expectations. This is never the case for an entire line (e.g., fire, auto, life, etc.) of insurance, and the very presence of rating factors implies that there are some grounds on which exposure units may be distinguished. These factors are used to establish classifications, and the presumption is that homogeneity exists within a classification and hence equity is achieved.[45]

A straightforward method of conceptualizing the process of classification is as a stratified random sample. Thus, the population is divided into sub-populations which are mutually exclusive and exhaustive. These sub-populations are called *strata,* and a simple random sample is independently drawn from each. The primary advantages are brought out in the following quotation: [46]

> Stratification may bring about a gain in the precision in the estimates of characteristics of the whole population. The basic idea is that it may be possible to divide a heterogeneous population into subpopulations each of which is internally homogeneous. This is suggested by the name *strata,* with its implication of a division into layers. If each stratum is homogeneous, in that the measurements vary little from one unit to another, a precise estimate of any stratum mean can be obtained from a small sample in that stratum . . . these estimates can then be combined into a precise estimate for the whole population.

Two main considerations, then, are first the ability to estimate more precisely in a homogeneous class and second, the ability to get a more precise estimate of the pure premium for the entire line of insurance and hence to reduce the standard error of the mean pure premium for the entire population. Since this reduces the risk $(\sigma\mu)$, and since the buffer fund is a direct function of the risk, stratified random sampling, i.e., classification, will result in a reduction of the aggregate buffer fund necessary for a given line of insurance.

Another way of saying this is that $\sigma\mu$ based on stratified random sampling is less than $\sigma\mu$ based on simple random sampling. Thus, the classification process in insurance not only introduces equity among

---

[45] This idea and the problems which attend it are discussed at greater length in Houston, David B., "The Effectiveness of Rating Classifications," *Journal of Insurance,* Vol. 28, No. 2, June 1961, pp. 83-86.

[46] Cochran, William G., *Sampling Techniques,* John Wiley & Sons, Inc., New York, 1953, pp. 65-66.

insureds but also reduces the insurer's risk and coincidentally the buffer fund.

A stratified random sampling model, then, has certain advantages in describing the insurance process. The mechanics of applying this framework to insurance operations will not be dealt with here. Essentially, the techniques are simply expansions of the techniques described in connection with simple random sampling.

## EQUITY, CREDIBILITY AND BAYES' THEOREM

Equity, as indicated in the foregoing discussion, is a primary consideration in insurance. Rates for individual insureds and for classes should be proportional to loss expectations. If a class or insured (say a business firm) which possesses a large number of exposure units is being considered, this is no particular problem. Such a class or insured may be considered as a population in itself and an appropriate pure premium and buffer fund can be determined.

If, however, the number of exposure units is substantial but not sufficient to provide the level of confidence at which the insurer wishes to operate, the problem arises as to how to treat such experience. On the one hand, the insured or class cannot be treated as a separate self-determining population, and on the other, it seems unfair to ignore the body of experience which it has generated. What is required is a system of weights which determine how much emphasis is to be given to the loss experience of the insured or class as opposed to the experience of the population of which it is a member.

This is known as the credibility problem in insurance. Actuaries have been working with the credibility question for decades and have established formulas, some simple, some complex, which provide methods of weighting the experience of the individual insured and the population. The basic question raised is: how credible or believable is the experience generated by the individual insured? To what extent could it have occurred as a result of chance or random factors? The answer is usually given by the following general type of formula:

$$PP_E = ZPP_i + (1-Z)PP$$

where $PP_E$ is the composite pure premium, i.e., the appropriate pure premium for the individual insured.

$PP_i$ is the pure premium based solely on the insured's experience.

PP is the population or manual pure premium.

Z is the weight or credibility factor where $O \leq Z \leq 1$, and Z is so constructed that as the number of exposure units (n) on which $PP_i$ is based increase $Z \rightarrow 1$.

This formula provides weights, Z and $(1 - Z)$, to be applied to the individual and population pure premiums. The larger the number of exposure units determining $PP_i$ the more weight given to this factor, the limiting case being $PP_E = PP_i$ where $Z = 1$, and the experience of the insured is said to be 100 percent credible, i.e., the insured is self-rating. The other extreme is the case where $Z = O$ and $PP_E = PP$ and the insured is given the manual or average rate for the population.

This credibility procedure may be conceived of in slightly different terms. Thus, PP represents the initial or background or *a priori* information available before the individual experience of the insured was ever examined. $PP_i$ is the new information which has just been observed. $PP_E$ is the result of combining the *a priori* information and the new data and may be viewed as an after the fact or *a posteriori* determination. It is a modification of the *a priori* information on the basis of the new data. Thus, the equation given above verbally could be written as:

*A posteriori* Pure Premium = (New Data)
Z + (*A priori* Pure Premium) (1-Z)

Formulated in this manner, credibility can be seen to be an instance of the general problem of statistical inference to which Bayes' Theorem provides a solution. Simply stated, Bayes' Theorem combines *a priori* or past knowledge and new observations into a new set of knowledge termed *a posteriori*.

The following example indicates one way in which Bayesian inference can be used in credibility problems. Suppose it is desired to determine the average mortality rate among employees of a large firm. Past experience from all insureds indicates that there are three possible rates of mortality (.01, .02, and .05) and that these rates occur with the following respective relative frequencies (.5, .3, and .2). This is the basis of the manual rate or the *a priori* information. If the death rates are identified as Q and their probabilities as K(Q), they can be set up in the following table:

TABLE 6

| Death Rates<br>Q | Probability or Relative Frequency<br>of Death Rates<br>K(Q) |
|:---:|:---:|
| .01 | .5 |
| .02 | .3 |
| .05 | .2 |
| | — |
| | 1.0 |

This indicates that the average manual or *a priori* death rate, $\Sigma Q \cdot K(Q)$ is. 021. Now, suppose that a random sample of 100 employees' records is examined, and it is observed that five have died. This new sample information is the insured's experience and indicates an average death rate of $5/100 = .05$. The question then is: How much weight should be given to the manual rate of .021 and how much to the insured's experience rate of .05? Bayes' Theorem presented in the following form [47] provides an answer:

$$E(Q/S) = \frac{\Sigma \, [Q \cdot K(Q) \cdot P(S/Q)]}{\Sigma \, [K(Q) \cdot P(S/Q)]}$$

The left hand side of the equation can be read as: "the expected or average death rate, Q, given the sample information, S, is equal to . . ." Table 7 shows how the terms on the right hand side of the equation are determined.

TABLE 7

| Death Rate Q (1) | A *Priori* probability of death rate K(Q) (2) | Conditional Probability: Probability of the sample evidence given the death rate P(S/Q) = Pr (r = S/n = 100, P = Q) (3) | Joint Probability of a given Q existing and the sample evidence occurring K(Q) · P(S/Q) (4) | Joint Probability Multiplied by the random variable Q Q · K(Q) · P(S/Q) (5) |
|---|---|---|---|---|
| .01 | .5 | .0029 | .00145 | .0000145 |
| .02 | .3 | .0353 | .01059 | .0002118 |
| .05 | .2 | .1800 | .03600 | .0018000 |
|  | 1.0 |  | .04804 | .0020263 |

Columns (1) and (2) in Table 7 are simply reproduced from Table 6. Column (3) is the binomial conditional probability. Thus, the first entry, .0029, is the probability of observing exactly five deaths out of a sample of 100 drawn from a population in which the death rate is .01. These probabilities show how likely the sample was to have been drawn from each of the three possible universes. As would be expected the sample has the highest probability of occurring (.1800) when drawn from a population in which the death rate is .05.

Column (4) shows the joint probability of a given population existing and the sample being drawn from it. It is the probability of Q and S, i.e., P(Q and S) = K(Q) · P(S/Q). The sum of this column is the denominator of the Bayes' Theorem equation given above. Column (5) is column (4), the joint probability, multiplied by the value of the random variable Q. The sum of column (5) is the numerator of the Bayes' equation.

---

[47] Technically, this is a generalization of Bayes' Theorem which is usually given in a slightly simpler form.

$$E(Q/S) = \frac{\Sigma[Q \cdot K(Q) \cdot P(S/Q)]}{\Sigma[K(Q) \cdot P(S/Q)]} = \frac{.0020263}{.04804} = .042$$

Thus, according to Bayes' Theorem, the average death rate is .042 given the *a priori* knowledge and the sample information. Conceptually, this can be represented as follows:

(*A priori* Q = .021)+(Sample Q = .05)  = (*A posteriori* Q = .042)

This is perfectly analogous to experience rating techniques, and the credibility factor Z is implicit in the above analysis. In this particular example, by solving the following equation

.021 (1 - Z) + .05 (Z) = .042

we find that Z = .72. Here, the credibility is relatively high because of the sample size (100).

Suppose, with the same *a priori* information, a sample of only 20 employees' records is drawn and it shows that one had died. Here, the sample death rate is also the same, 1/20 = .05, but the sample size is much smaller. If the same analysis is applied as that contained in Table 7, the *a posteriori* average death rate will be .026. In this case,

(*A priori* Q = .021) + (Sample Q = .05)  = (*A posteriori* Q = .026)

The impact of the sample evidence is much less here because of its limited size, and the *a posteriori* death rate is little different than the *a priori* death rate. Again it is possible to solve for Z:

.021 (1 - Z) + .05 (Z) = .026

A Z value of .17 indicates that the insured's experience is not very credible. Thus, the Bayesian solution is generally consistent with one's intuitive notions of how credibility factors should operate, e.g., the larger the body of experience the more weight it should be given. In fact, it has been shown that credibility formulae such as the above are employed in casualty insurance and can be derived from Bayes' Theorem and mathematical statistics.[48]

The purpose of the foregoing example is not to define operationally credibility procedures in terms of Bayesian analysis. Rather it is to demonstrate that the latter provides a useful conceptual framework for understanding the former. Thus, the insurer wishes to determine to what extent he should modify his *a priori* view (the manual pure premium of the population or class of which the insured is a member) on the basis of new information (the pure premium developed solely from the individual's insured's experience). This modification results in an *a posteriori* view (the complete pure premium appropriate for the insured).

[48] Bailey, Arthur L., "Credibility Procedures," *Proceedings of the Casualty Actuarial Society*, Vol. 37, Part I, No. 67, 1950, pp. 7-23.

individual insured's experience). This modification results in an *a posteriori* view (the complete pure premium appropriate for the insured).

## CONCLUSIONS

The definitions of risk developed in Section I provide a basis for distinguishing between and accounting for alternative definitions of insurance. To the individual, insurance is a device for transferring his risk to the insurer. The insurer views insurance as a pooling process in which the risk is reduced by increasing the number of exposure units insured. The essentials of a sound insurance plan may be formulated and explained in terms of the requirements of a random sampling model. "Individual Risk Theory" provides a simple and useful conceptual framework for understanding the insurance process. Classification of exposure units can be explained in terms of a stratified random sampling model. Credibility procedures may be viewed as an example of Bayesian inference.

### Questions

1. What condition must be satisfied in order for the product of the frequency of loss distribution and the severity distribution to be the pure premium distribution, as the author sets out?
2. Why does the author stress the dispersion of the distribution of losses?
3. What are the two primary distinctions between insurer and individual risk as set out by the author?
4. How does a collective risk theory differ from an individual risk theory?
5. In the following example what is the value of insurance as formulated by Houston: To protect himself from theft of merchandise, a merchant can purchase theft insurance at a cost of $1,200 per year. If he does not have insurance, he feels he must have a reserve in near liquid form to replace his missing stock on short notice if a loss occurs. He feels that this fund must be $20,000 and he can earn 5% interest on it. If he were to insure, however, he would have this fund available as working capital, on which he earns 10%.
6. Is there any difference between credibility as used by Houston and the term as used in reference to, say, the credibility gap in the White House?

# 4. ATTITUDES TOWARD RISK AND A THEORY OF INSURANCE CONSUMPTION *

Mark R. Greene †

Many scholars have questioned the existence of true "theory" in the so-called applied sciences such as those taught in the typical school of business administration. Thus no large body of literature exists under the caption, the "theory of marketing," the "theory of finance," the "theory of production," the "theory of insurance," etc. This should not be taken to mean that no true theory exists in these areas. It is an indication, however, that the various business administration disciplines have not yet matured sufficiently to allow a well rounded body of "scientific" literature to be developed. In many respects business is still more of an art than a science.

One approach in the development of a science of risk and insurance is to build on truths developed from other disciplines. In particular, scientists from the areas of economics, mathematics, psychology and sociology have been interested in the area of risk and have made contributions toward understanding its basic nature. Few, however, have attempted to relate their findings to any applied area such as insurance, although they of course have made passing references to different possible applications.

It is the purpose of this paper (1) to review what certain recent economic and psychological literature has to say about one aspect of insurance theory, namely, psychological attitudes toward risk, and (2) to report on an experiment by the author to measure attitudes toward risk and to use this measure as a predictor of insurance buying behavior. The reader should be forewarned that this review of behavioral science literature is not complete and is not meant to be, and that the results of the experiment suggest only tentative conclusions. It is hoped, nevertheless, that the paper will stimulate others to pursue investigations of a similar nature, and to extend the review of behavioral science literature and to apply the findings of other social scientists to buttress a more highly developed theory of insurance consumption.[1]

* From *The Journal of Risk and Insurance* (June, 1963), pp. 165-182. Reprinted by permission.

† Professor of Insurance, The University of Georgia.

[1] The author wishes to acknowledge the support given to him for this research under a grant by the Western Management Science Institute in the Summer of 1962.

## LABORATORY STUDIES IN RISK TAKING BEHAVIOR

It is difficult to present a neat classification of studies which have a bearing on attitudes toward risk. Many of the studies reviewed below overlap in their objectives, findings, and even in their basic subject matter. In general, only those studies which appear to have been done under controlled conditions and which might be said to have scientific value in establishing truths relating to attitudes toward risk, are reported. The various factors which appear to have some bearing on risk attitudes are: (1) Age and sex, (2) Subjective interpretation of probability, (3) Personality patterns, (4) Intelligence, (5) Utility for additional increments of money, and (6) Preferred risk levels.

### Influence of Age and Sex

Wallach and Kogan [2] have studied the relationship of age and sex upon willingness to take risk. They constructed a test which they called "Deterrence of Failure." The construction of the items on the test was similar to the items reported in this study (see "The Experiment" section) with the exception that the risk situations described were not confined to economic situations. For example, the subject might be asked what minimum probability he would require for success before he would recommend that a good friend of his undergo a serious surgical operation, etc.

The experimenters found a significant difference in the scores on the deterrence of failure index as between young and old men, and young and old women. The older person generally requires a larger probability of success than a younger person. It was found that attitude change was more abrupt for men than it was for women. Some of the reasons for this may have been that there is a time in the typical man's life in which he ceases to work and this is likely to introduce some type of an emotional change, affecting his attitudes towards risk.

The findings of Wallach and Kogan seem to contradict the often held feeling that young people today are "too conservative." Certainly the findings point to none too surprising conclusion that young people are less conservative than old people. Applied to insurance buying, the study would lead to one to suppose that young people are less apt to buy insurance against a given risk than older people, a finding often confirmed in practice.

### Subjective Interpretation of Odds

Preston and Baratta, [3] in a gambling experiment with play money, found a significant difference between what a person conceives a given

---

[2] Wallach, M. A. and Kogan, N., "Aspects of Judgment and Decision Making: Interrelationships and Changes with Age," *Behavioral Science,* Vol. 6, No. 1, January 1961, pp. 23-36.

[3] Preston, M. D. and Baratta, P., "An Experimental Study of the Auction-Value of an Uncertain Income," *American Journal of Psychology,* Vol. 61, 1948, pp. 183-193.

probability to be and what the true probability actually is. In general, it was found that when the probability of an event is less than 5 percent, the players conceive probability to be higher than it really is, and when the probability exceeds 25 percent, the players conceive of the true probability to be lower than it actually is. Preston and Baratta suggest that an *indifference point* between these two figures lies at about .20. That is, if the true probability is .20, individuals are most likely to interpret this probability more correctly than any other value for probability.

The findings of Preston and Baratta are of considerable interest in explaining insurance buying behavior where typical probabilities are small. An average person conceives of small probabilities to be larger than they actually are. He is therefore more likely to purchase insurance against a loss with only a small probability of occurrence than he would if he conceived the probability to be as small as it actually is.

For example, in the experiments of Preston and Baratta, when the probability was 1 percent and the prize $5, the expected value of winning would be $.05 = ($5.00 × .01). Subjects in the experiment however, were willing to pay 51 cents to play this game. Thus, they were willing to pay 10.2 times the expected monetary value of the prize (.51 ÷ .05). The larger the probability and prize value, the smaller the premium the subjects were willing to pay for the right to play. If the prize were $50, the subjects were willing to pay only 8.88 times the expected monetary value of the prize to play, etc. Similarly, if the probability were 5 percent instead of 1 percent, the subjects were only willing to pay 3.92 times the expected monetary value of the $5 prize to play; 1.06 times the expected monetary value of a $50 prize to play, etc.

Conversely, if the probability of an insurable loss is very high, say above 50 percent, the Preston and Baratta experiment would indicate that people would be likely to underestimate the probability and therefore pay less for avoiding the risk of loss. An interesting side light from the experiment showed that there was little difference in the scores of those who were fairly sophisticated in their knowledge of probability and those who were not so sophisticated. Thus, several of the participants who were professors or mathematics students erred as much in their estimation of true probabilities as did those who were uninitiated in ways of statistics. This seems to suggest that education in the field of probability does not necessarily change one's attitudes toward risk.

Preston and Baratta suggest that the indifferent points are a direct function of the amount of money available to the participants for the play. In other words, the more play money a participant was furnished the greater is his indifference point and vice versa. This finding seems to support the Bernoulli hypothesis [4] that the relative size of a person's wealth affects his willingness to assume risk and to purchase insurance against loss.

---

[4] Bernoulli, D., "Exposition of a New Theory on the Measurement of Risks" (Translated by Louise Sommer), *Econometrica*, Vol. XXII, No. 1 (January, 1954), pp. 23-36.

While Preston and Baratta's experiment is not conclusive, it never-theless suggests some interesting possibilities for further experimentation in this area.

## Effect of Personality on Risk Attitudes

Various investigators have suggested that decision making, particularly in situations of risk and uncertainty, bears a distinct relationship to the various factors of personality. For example, William E. Henry [5] suggests that risk behavior may profitably be studied in the framework and with the methods of personality research.

**Torrance and Ziller studies.** A psychological study of the relationship of personality factors to risk taking behavior has been made by Torrance and Ziller. [6] These investigators developed a scale to measure risk taking tendencies, using a biographical inventory which they called a life experience inventory. This inventory consisted originally of 136 items and was later reduced to 65 items, after item analysis techniques were carried out. The revised scale had an odd-even reliability coefficient of .98 (corrected by the Spearman-Brown formula), and thus was consistent in selecting those subjects who were willing to take high risk.

The scale was given to 370 combat air crewmen and was validated by a further study of 73 Air Force pilots. The criterion used was a combination of scores on a test describing risk situations involving military settings. The military situations forming the criterion simulated actual emergency flying and survival experience of Air Force personnel. For example, the pilot would be asked what he would do if he had been shot down in an airplane over a foreign country and had certain alternatives to escape, a safe alternative and a relatively unsafe alternative. The subject would be asked to indicate what he considered to be the more dangerous alternative and in addition whether or not he would take that alternative and what minimum chance of success he would require before he would take the risky alternative. Torrance and Ziller concluded that their risk scale composed of life inventory experiences was significantly correlated with risk taking behavior as measured by the criterion.

A personality profile of those who are willing to take high risk was given as follows by the authors:

> A look at the childhood behavior of the high riskers reveals that they early learned skills which give one status and advantage among his peers—driving a car, driving a car frequently, dancing, etc. Thus, they are able to face the world with greater self-confidence and less fear. They tend to have been reared on a farm, in a rural nonfarm area, or in a small

---

[5] Henry, W. E., "Personality Factors in Managerial Reaction to Uncertainty," in Bowman, M. J. (Ed.) *Expectation, Uncertainty, and Business Behavior,* pp. 86-93.

[6] Torrance, E. P. and Ziller, R. C., *Risk and Life Experience: Development of a Scale For Measuring Risk-Taking Tendencies.* Lackland Air Force Base, Texas: Air Force Personnel and Training Research Center, February 1957. (Research Report AFPTRC-TN-57-23, ASTIA Document No. 098926.)

town rather than in a city. Thus, they were better able to experiment and take risks without fear, and early gained a feeling of power over their environment. They were afforded other experiences which give one a sense of adequacy, such as taking overnight trips away from home without parents. They were taught to feel secure in their own resources—started bank accounts at an early age, had fun in changing from one school to another, etc.

They early identified with the masculine role and developed the skills and engaged in the behaviors necessary to validate the masculine role. They engaged earlier in such masculine status-giving activities as smoking, driving a car, playing with snakes, hitchhiking, beer drinking, whiskey drinking, and sexual intercourse. High riskers gave expression to their aggressive drives through more frequent fighting, doing cruel things, taking dares, and the like. They were punished more frequently for bad conduct in school, more of them remember crying as boys, and they were less concerned about pleasing adults. They have also given freer expression of their sexual drives. (More of them remember masturbating before age 15). Although they did not start dating any earlier, they did start necking, dancing, and having sexual intercourse earlier. More of them also tend to have been divorced and remarried.

High risk-tendency individuals also present a picture of physical adequacy and enjoyment of physical activity. Although they express more enjoyment and claim more participation in almost every active sport, the difference is particularly marked for rough sports like football, boxing, and wrestling, and for outdoor sports like hunting and fishing. They are characterized by more frequent participation in football, baseball, swimming, diving, boxing, wrestling, skiing, hunting, camping, hiking long distances, mountain climbing, and the like.

High scores on the risk scale are also associated with greater social aggressiveness during the developmental years. In grade and high school, high scorers were usually "right in the middle of things." In school, other students expected them to have ideas about what to do and how to do it. They were the ones who helped new students get acquainted. They were the ones who were selected for the major offices in high school and served as captains of varsity athletic teams, especially football and basketball.

High riskers differ sharply from their more cautious peers in their attitudes toward competition. The high riskers say that they have always enjoyed competition, considered winning important, performed better than usual under stiff competition, and practiced and tried to improve skills when they suffered losses in competition.

Finally, as would be expected, the high riskers more frequently have engaged in such dangerous activities as auto racing, driving very fast around corners, and motorcycling. More of them also participate in games of chance such as poker, black jack, dice, and craps.

While there are several limitations in the biographical inventory technique, it would appear promising to make further investigations along these lines. For example, do subjects who score high on the revised risk questionnaire also score high on their willingness to accept economic risk? Is the masculine, independent, physically adequate, socially agressive male, also most likely to be the type accepting a position which is relatively insecure but has relatively high rewards? Is this individual likely to be one to purchase a risky investment with a promised high return rather than a safe investment with a relatively low or fixed return? Is such an individual likely to be a great purchaser of insurance or not?

One might be tempted to think that the high-riskers will be more likely to reject insurance, except in some minimal amount, than would be true of the conservative person. However, it may well be that a person willing to take risk is also a large purchaser of insurance and this might not be inconsistent with his risk-taking behavior. The reason for this is that our high-risker may wish to confine his risk taking activities to those situations which have a very high chance of reward. He may, very prudently, use some of his resources to avoid certain types of risks that can be transferred through insurance, leaving his resources free for the greater risks of business activity. A number of possible hypotheses can be posed about the connection between personality factors and risk-taking behavior, including that risk-taking behavior which encompasses insurance buying activities. A first step, however, seems to be to determine what, if any, correlation exists between personality factors and observed insurance buying behavior. This first step has been undertaken in the current study and is reported on in "The Experiment" section.

## Effect of Intelligence

Further studies, Scodel, Ratoosh, and Minas,[7] have also examined the effect of personality in risk-taking behavior. These investigators found that in a gambling experiment, intelligence was not significantly related to the degree of risk taking but is inversely related to variability in risk-taking. Apparently, the more intelligent was the subject, the less was the range of risk he was willing to accept in a gambling experiment. A further conclusion of the study was that those subjects seeking low payoffs displayed greater fear of failure than those seeking high payoffs. Another finding was that, corroborating the findings of Preston and Baratta noted above, sophisticated subjects are no more likely to maximize expected value than unsophisticated subjects. In any case, expected value appears to have a negligible effect in determining betting preference. It was also interesting to note that the subjects with military backgrounds in the group of participants, selected more high payoff, low probability, bets than the college group, conforming to the high-risker profile described by Torrance and Ziller.

It can be observed that the findings of Scodel, Ratoosh, and Minas seem to square fairly well with observed insurance buying behavior. The highly educated and presumably more intelligent person is more likely to be an insurance buyer than the less educated person. Insurance has the definite purpose of narrowing the range of uncertainty

    [7] Scodel, A., Ratoosh, P., and Minas, J., "Some Personality Correlants of Decision Making Under Conditions of Risk," *Behavioral Science*, Vol. IV, No. 1, January 1959, pp. 19-28.

within which the purchaser operates, thus confirming the finding that more intelligent persons do not want to play the long shot.

Kipnis and Glickman [8] have studied the effect of risk-taking attitudes and subsequent school grade performance. These investigators found that scores by the radiomen on a risk scale correlated .31 with school grade performance one year after the test was given. School grade performance in turn was measured by over-all school grade scores received in taking code and in evaluations of supervisors. Apparently, there is some relationship between good grades and willingness to take risk. This limited study, of course, is not conclusive, but suggests a new direction for predicting school performance or college performance.

If one assumes that the intelligent person also tends to be the person who gets the best grades in school, there is an apparent conflict here with the findings of Scodel, Ratoosh, and Minas, stated above, that apparently there is no significant correlation between intelligence and willingness to take risk. Certainly further research in this area is indicated.

Motivation for higher achievement appears to be an important determinant of risk taking behavior and gambling choices. Experiments by Atkinson [9] and others, for example, have shown that fear of failure in the individual helps determine his gambling choices and his preferred probability preferences in games with equal expected value. His risk taking behavior is also importantly affected by his general achievement level, with the less capable preferring either very high or very low probabilities rather than intermediate ranges of probabilities.

## Utility and Attitudes Towards Risk

A great deal has been written by economists, psychologists and others on the subject of utility. The utility hypothesis states that individuals behave as if they have a subjective scale of values for determining the real worth to them of different amounts of commodities in the market place. Presumably their assessment of the value of goods is translatable in terms of money. Very early Bernoulli [10] hypothesized that an individual who has a great deal of wealth ascribes less value to an additional dollar of income than a poor man ascribed to the same additional dollar of income. In Bernoulli's mind, the degree of wealth possessed by the individual was the major determining factor in his scale of utility values. He applied his conclusions to insurance buying behavior, holding that the richer a person is the less economical it is for him to buy insurance.

---

[8] Kipnis, David and Glickman, A. S., "The Development of a Non-Cognitude Battery; Prediction of Radiomen Performance," *U.S.N. Bureau of Naval Personnel Technical Bulletin* (June 1959).

[9] Atkinson, J. W., Bastian, J. R., Earl, R. W., and Litwin, G. H., "The Achievement Motive, Goal Setting, and Probability Preferences," *Journal of Abnormal Psychology,* January, 1960, Vol. 60, pp. 27-36.

[10] Bernoulli, *op. cit.*

As noted above, however, apparently several other factors can affect a person's attitude toward risk and, indirectly, his scale of utility values.

What is the connection between utility and attitudes toward risk? The connection is simply this; if an individual has a choice of two alternatives, one risky and one not so risky, in general he will probably reject the risky alternative unless the possible reward for assuming the risky alternative is sufficiently high. It is in the meaning of the words "sufficiently high" that utility enters in. What is sufficiently high to one person may not be sufficiently high to another person. In other words, one person has a different subjective evaluation of a risky alternative than another person—i.e., a different "utility curve." Utility then is a subjective concept, but it can be made into an objective concept to measure a person's attitude toward a risky alternative.

Stimulated by the basic contribution of John von Neumann and Oscar Morgenstern [11] in their book, *Theory of Games and Economic Behavior*, Friedman and Savage [12] attempted to show how traditional utility analysis can be extended to analyze decisions involving risky alternatives. The authors imply that if one develops a utility curve for an individual by a method which they set out in their article, a mathematical picture of a person's attitude toward additional increments of money is possible, when the additional increment of money is the result of a risky alternative. Friedman and Savage left to others the problem of experimenting with empirical investigations of utility curves of individuals. They conceptualized an experiment in which the consumer would be asked to indicate his choice between a certain income of say $600 or an uncertain income of $1000. The uncertain income of $1000 was to be measured by a certain chance $a$ of receiving $500 and a $1-a$ chance of receiving $1000. For example, the consumer might be asked to choose which he would prefer, a certain income of $600, or a game in which he had a 10 percent chance of winning $500 and 90 percent chance of winning $1000. If the consumer chooses the latter alternative, the experimenter is to reduce the probability of winning $1000 and to increase the probability of winning $500 until the consumer is indifferent between the two alternatives. Once the consumer is indifferent between these two alternatives, a numerical value of his utility can be arrived at by a formula. These numerical values can be plotted against increasing amounts of income and a utility curve thus derived.

Presumably this utility curve can then be used to predict a person's economic behavior when confronted with similar alternatives involving risk. For example, the utility curve can predict whether or not a person

[11] Von Neumann, J. and Morgenstern, O., *Theory of Games and Economic Behavior*, Princeton: Princeton University Press, 1944.

[12] Freidman, M. and Savage, L. J., "The Utility Analysis of Choices Involving Risk," *Journal of Political Economy*, Vol. LVI (1948), pp. 279-304 and reprinted in *Readings in Price Theory*, American Economic Association (Richard D. Irwin, Inc., Homewood, Illinois, 1952), pp. 57-96.

will enter into a gambling contract if his income has achieved a certain level. Similarly, a utility curve can predict whether or not that person will be a likely insurance buyer. It is this latter prediction which is of considerable interest to the current investigation.

**Mosteller and Nogee experiments.** Perhaps the first somewhat extensive study in which the experimenters sought to obtain an objective measure of utility attitudes in individuals was done by Mosteller and Nogee [13] reported in "An Experimental Measurement of Utility." This article was part of Nogee's doctoral dissertation at Harvard University in 1953. The Mosteller and Nogee experiments concerned the willingness of their subjects to play various poker hands with differing probabilities of winning. The subjects were undergraduate students at Harvard and National Guardsmen from the Massachusetts National Guard. The subjects were given poker chips worth one dollar at the beginning of each session and were asked to gamble with these chips. A player could keep all the money he won. From the player's choices of various gambling hands utility curves were derived. The authors concluded that it was not unreasonable to conclude that the players maximized their expected utility and that on the basis of empirical curves drawn it was possible to estimate future risk-taking behavior in more complicated playing situations. They also concluded that the subjects are not thoroughly consistent about their preferences and indifferences as between risk situations.

**Other studies.** Other investigators have studied various technical problems in measuring utility. For example, Adams and Fagot [14] tested the transitivity hypothesis in measurement of utility and found that this hypothesis was verified. Briefly, the transitivity hypothesis is that if a subject prefers A to B and B to C he will also prefer A to C. Such a principle is necessary before a concept of utility means a great deal.

Royden, Suppes and Walsh [15] have also set up a model for the measurement of the utility of gambling. They attempted to measure total utility by taking the sum of the expected utility of the expected winnings plus the utility of the pleasure of gambling. In another investigation, Suppes and Walsh [16] found it possible to measure utility and that a person's utility curve could predict later gambling choices with significant accuracy. Coombs and Komorita [17] after reviewing the work of others, concluded that one can measure utility and one can predict with it. They

[13] Mosteller, F. and Nogee, P., "An Experimental Measurement of Utility," *Journal of Political Economy,* Vol. 59, 1951, pp. 371-404.

[14] Adams, E. W. and Fagot, R., "A Model of Riskless Choice," *Behavioral Science,* July 1959, Vol. 4, pp. 1-10.

[15] Royden, H. L., Suppes, P., and Walsh, Karol, "A Model for the Experimental Measurement of Utility of Gambling," *Behavioral Science,* 1959, Vol. 4, pp. 11-18.

[16] Suppes, Patrick, and Walsh, Karol, "A Non-linear Model for the Experimental Measurement of Utility," *Behavioral Science,* July 1959, Vol. 4, pp. 204-211.

[17] Coombs, C. H. and Komorita, S. S., "Measuring Utility of Money Through Decision," *American Journal of Psychology,* Vol. 71 (1958) pp. 383-389.

showed that people have preferences among bets with equal monetary values on a "play once basis."

**W. Edwards study.** Ward Edwards [18] also found in his experiments that certain probabilities were preferred over other probabilities in gambling experiments. Edwards postulated that if this were true the Friedman and Savage method of measuring utility cannot succeed. Edwards' objection to the existence of any simple method of measuring utility appears to be well supported, since other investigators have found that such factors as personality variables, education levels, age, and intelligence enter into the willingness to take risk.

**Conclusions.** A growing body of literature has been developing in the post World War II period which suggests the considerable usefulness of utility analysis in the study of risk-taking behavior. Not only has the theoretical foundation been laid by von Neumann and Morgenstern and by Friedman and Savage, but several experimental studies have been confirmed regarding the potential validity of these theories. However, there is still considerable doubt that it can be said with certainty that the conclusions from the laboratory studies will hold in the real world.

In particular, a great deal more must be proved before a valid test of risk-taking behavior can be developed and before a person's "utility curve" can be ascertained and relied upon to predict this person's decisions in real-life situations. Nothing is known for example, as to how long a person's utility curve might be said to hold constant or in what manner it changes over time and in what situations it is a reliable predictor of a person's true preference or behavior. Nevertheless, continuing studies using the utility hypothesis format should be very productive in the light they can cast upon this important economic problem.

## Preferred Risk Levels

Closely related to the utility analysis and yet differing from it is another approach to the study of behavior in risk-taking situations, known as preferred risk levels. Developed by Nogee [19] in his doctoral dissertation and studied further by Ward Edwards, [20] the preferred risk level approach starts out with a basic assumption that people differ either in their ability to tolerate or in their desire for variability or change in their affairs. This might be aptly summarized by stating that some people like the *status quo* and other people do not, and if one can differentiate between these two groups of people, he will have a valuable

---

[18] Edwards, Ward, "The Theory of Decision Making," *Psychological Bulletin*, Vol. 51, No. 4, July, 1954.

[19] Nogee, Philip, *Experimental Studies of Behavior in Risk-Taking Situations*, 1953. Unpublished Ph.D. Thesis, Harvard University.

[20] Edwards, *op. cit.*

measure of differing attitudes toward risk. For example, a person with a high preferred risk level is likely to adopt a "kill or cure" approach to life, while a person with a low preferred risk level is likely to be one who will take more modest doses of a medicine in the hopes of a more gradual cure. A preferred risk level approach is similar to other concepts developed by psych͜ologists. For example, Else Frenkel-Brunswik [21] reported on "The Intolerance for Ambiguity" and George S. Klein [22] writes of a personality dimension entitled "Tolerance Versus Resistance to the Unstable."

Formally, the preferred risk level is defined as that level giving a person the least variance from his present position in selecting an alternative. Nogee conducted an experiment involving twelve subjects who were given three choices; one risky, one medium, and one safe. Scores on this questionnaire were correlated with the subjects' risk-taking behavior in the card playing experiments referred to earlier. It was concluded that, with certain exceptions, those preferring high risks on the questionnaire also preferred high risks in the selection of card hands.

Other findings in Nogee's study of preferred risk levels were (1) in general a person will take a considerably longer time to make a decision when this decision involves a choice running against his general tendency or general preferred risk level. In other words, if a person is basically conservative, a decision involving risk will take him considerably longer than a decision involving relative safety. This conclusion is none too surprising. (2) There is a positive relationship between impulsiveness, as measured by the reaction time in deciding between two likely alternatives, and preferred risk levels. (3) There is a high relationship between level of aspiration and preferred risk level. Thus, a person with a high preferred risk level is more likely to desire change from his present situation, than is a person with a low preferred risk level.

Applied to a theory of insurance consumption, these findings seem to suggest that people with low preferred risk levels will be the first to purchase insurance and probably will spend a larger portion of their incomes in avoiding risks and in loss prevention activities. These individuals should be among the last to drop an insurance policy even when the need is gone, and are unlikely to be impulsive in their insurance buying decisions. They are probably also a better "underwriting risk."

Successful use of the verbal questionnaire by Nogee, in relating preferred risk levels to gambling behavior, suggests that a similar procedure can also be used to predict real-life economic risk-taking behavior such as insurance consumption behavior. However, an attempt to do this was not successful in the current experiment.

[21] Frenkel-Brunswik, Else, "Intolerance of Ambiguity as an Emotional and Perceptual Personality Variable," *Journal of Personality*, 18, 1949, pp. 108-143.

[22] Klein, George S., "The Personal World Through Perception," in *Perception: An Approach to Personality*, R. R. Blake and G. V. Ramsey, Ed., New York, Ronald Press, 1951.

## Summary

Various researchers have conducted psychological experiments on risk, the results of which help to explain insurance consumption patterns and thus contribute toward a theory of insurance consumption. If one can accept tentatively the assumption that basic attitudes toward risk ought to have a bearing on insurance consumption, then variables such as age, sex, personality, childhood experiences, intelligence, utility for money, and preferred risk levels, all of which are apparently related to risk attitudes, should likewise be of value in explaining insurance buying behavior. The studies reviewed above are far from conclusive and in some cases suggest contradictory results. For example some studies seem to imply that a more intelligent person should be more willing to accept risk than a less intelligent person, but other studies suggest that intelligence is not a factor in risk attitudes. On the other hand there is considerable evidence that attitudes toward risk can be measured and that these measures permit one to make fairly good predictions of future risk taking behavior.

## THE EXPERIMENT

## Purpose

Several investigators, including some of those whose works are reviewed above (Suppes and Walsh, Coombs and Komorita, Mosteller and Nogee) have concluded that behavior in gambling situations is predictive of subsequent behavior in similar, but often more complicated, gambling procedures.

Their experiments usually involved actual gambling games in which the subjects participated. Presumably actual games were carried out because of the findings of several investigators that specific acts or action attitudes often cannot be predicted very accurately from elicited verbal attitudes (Green [23]). However, it would seem that gambling games in which the subject is supplied play money, or is given real money to play with, are about as artificial as a verbal questionnaire. One advantage of a verbal questionnaire is that hypothetical gambling choices over a wide range of monetary values can be elicited, instead of being restricted to small stakes because of limited funds available to the experimenter. Furthermore, while the studies reviewed above are valuable additions to the literature, they have attempted to predict only future gambling behavior, not real-world risk-taking behavior involving other risky economic decisions. It is in this area that more work needs to be done.

The questions posed here are, "Can attitudes toward risk be reliably measured by a verbal questionnaire and can subsequent

[23] Green, B. F., "Attitude Measurement," *Handbook of Social Psychology* (Cambridge: Addison Wesley, 1954) pp. 335-369.

real-life economic behavior involving risk be predicted by scores on such a test?" If so, a valuable tool of behavioral science would be available to apply in practical situations in business administration. Accordingly, as detailed below, the present experiment involved the development of a verbal questionnaire and an attempt to assess its validity against a criterion of real-life economic behavior involving risk, in this case insurance buying behavior of undergraduate students at the University of Oregon.

## Hypotheses

1. *It is possible to construct tests that produce reliable measures of attitudes toward risk by using verbal questionnaires.* An assumption underlying this hypothesis is that within each individual there exists a set of attitudes or preconceptions which tend to make him either willing to accept risky economic situations or to reject them. By "reliability" is meant that the test produces a satisfactory degree of consistency of replies. Ideally, a reliable test is one which produces similar results upon repeated administration.

2. *If a sufficiently reliable test of measurement of attitudes toward risk is developed, scores on this test should be closely related to a measure of actual risk-taking behavior in real-life economic situations, i.e., the test is valid in distinguishing between those willing to take risk and those less willing to do so.* The particular economic behavior in the experiment is the past history of insurance buying behavior. Another hypothesis which should be tested (but is not tested here) is that a person's attitude toward risk is fairly constant and does not change rapidly. If this were true, at least within the age range and education level of the subject group, then past insurance buying behavior could be assumed to be typical of future insurance buying behavior. If both of these hypotheses could be proved true under given conditions, a valuable predictor of insurance consumption would be forthcoming.

3. *There is a tendency for those who say they are willing to participate in gambling games for large stakes to be among those most likely to say they will take the more risky alternatives in other economic situations involving risk, and vice versa.* It will be observed that this hypothesis is stated in terms of what people *say* and not in terms of what they actually *do*. It is well known that there is often a considerable difference between what people say and what they finally do, and that those who are undecided are large enough in number so that it is difficult to predict aggregate behavior of the entire group. Therefore, even if this hypothesis is accepted, it still has limited predictive value in forecasting, but can be used to serve as a basis for further investigation.

4. *Personality characteristics as revealed by biographical inventory methods are associated with risk-taking attitudes and with insurance mindedness as measured by verbal questionnaire.* Specifically, is the

Torrance and Ziller biographical inventory scale correlated with attitudes toward risk or insurance mindedness on the questionnaire developed in the current experiment? In other words, are basic attitudes toward risk closely associated with childhood emotional and physical activities? Apparently, some association does exist as far as military behavior in risky situations is concerned.[24]

These hypotheses were tested by administering three verbal questionnaires to a group of subjects and by analysis of the responses.

## Subjects

Seventy undergraduate students at the University of Oregon served as the subjects. They were taken from different classes offered at the University during the summer and fall of 1962 as follows:

| | |
|---|---|
| Mathematics | 6 |
| History | 7 |
| Accounting | 6 |
| Finance | 5 |
| Business Law | 4 |
| Personnel Management | 15 |
| Insurance | 27 |
| Total | 70 |

All were male, and all owned automobiles for which they were solely responsible. Practically all subjects were between the ages of 18 and 23. They were told that the purpose of the test was to measure their attitudes toward risk. They were not given any instructions or help in completing the questionnaire. Practically all of them had no difficulty in completing the test within one class hour, fifty minutes. Many were through in thirty minutes.

It was recognized that selection of undergraduates as subjects for the experiments was not ideal in some respects, since in many cases these students might be influenced by parents and not completely free to make up their own minds regarding insurance buying. Furthermore, their funds might be limited and their actual insurance consumption affected more by this factor than by basic attitudes toward risk. On the other hand these subjects were young enough so that their insurance buying behavior had not had a chance to become set or routine in nature and hence relatively unresponsive to changing attitudes toward risk. To offset the limitations noted above, a test of "insurance mindedness" described below, selected only those types of insurance in which the subject might reasonably be said to have some discretion in selection, and in which income limitations of the student might not be unduly important. Students from several different departments in the University were

---

[24] Torrance and Ziller, *op. cit.*

selected to help average out any unknown bias in response resulting from different types of academic training.

## Description of Tests

Three separate tests, by means of questionnaire, were given to the subjects at one sitting: (1) a risk attitudes test consisting of 20 items, (2) the biographical inventory test developed by Torrance and Ziller, and (3) an insurance-mindedness questionnarie concerning certain elements of their insurance buying behavior. A high correlation of (1) with (3) would support Hypothesis 2, stated above, indicating that test (1) is a "valid" measure of insurance mindedness. A high correlation of (1) with (2) and (2) with (3) would support Hypothesis 3, stated above.

(1) **Attitudes toward risk test.** Twenty items were developed, each of which was to be scored according to the degree of willingness to take risk. One group of ten items set forth questions to the subjects in the form of how large a prize would be required before they would be willing to enter into a gambling game with stakes varying from small amounts to very large amounts. A second group of questions patterned after Wallach and Kogan's "deterrence of failure" test, presented risky economic situations to the subjects and asked each subject to indicate among a scale of alternative decisions a choice of a solution which would be most appropriate to him. A sample of each type of question follows:

*First Group*

You have just inherited $100 which you didn't expect to receive and for which you have no immediate plans. You are given the opportunity to enter into a game which may be described as follows: There is an urn containing 90 red balls and 10 black balls, mixed at random. Since the urn is painted black you cannot see which ball you might draw before actually drawing it. You can play the game as long as you wish. A prize is to be paid to you if a black ball is drawn. You get nothing if a red ball is drawn. How large would the prize *have to be* (at the minimum) before you would be willing to enter the game, if the cost for each draw is $1.00?

    1. $ 5
    2. $10
    3. $15
    4. $20
    5. $30
    6. $40
    7. I would not enter the game under any circumstances.

Other questions in this group increased the size of the prize to a maximum of $400,000; and the size of the stake to $10,000, but the expected value of the game remained constant.

A thoughtful subject answering the question in the first group should have reasoned that since he had a 10 percent chance to win, and since he could play as long as wished, any prize exceeding $10 would mean a profit to him if the stake were $1. Accordingly he should have checked (3) to the question shown above. If he demanded a higher prize than $10 he could properly be said to demand a premium over the expected value of the game to accept the risk of loss. (Actually, the only risk to him is that he might not be able to play long enough to offset any bad run of continuous losses). The size of this premium, then, is the measure of his willingness to take risk.

*Second Group*

You have a $10,000 savings account which you have been considering withdrawing for purposes of going into business. A real estate broker offers you the opportunity of purchasing a business in which you are interested. Reliable statistics in this line of business show that sales and profits are very closely related to weather in the summer. If weather is unfavorable for your business you will lose half of your investment, whereas if weather is favorable you will double your investment within five years. Please indicate the lowest probability of favorable weather, as revealed by reliable weather bureau records, which you would accept before making the investment:

1. ——The chance of favorable weather must be at least 1 in 10.
2. ——The chance of favorable weather must be at least 3 in 10.
3. ——The chance of favorable weather must be at least 5 in 10.
4. ——The chance of favorable weather must be at least 7 in 10.
5. ——The chance of favorable weather must be at least 9 in 10.
6. ——Check here if you would not make the investment but would prefer to leave your savings account undisturbed.

Other questions in this group were concerned with risky choices involving stocks and bonds, selection of an occupation, purchase of materials from a foreign supplier, selection of a new product by a manufacturer, building construction contracting, staying in college for graduate work, settling of a strike, and insurance.

*Scoring*. If a student checked item one he was given a score of one for that item. If he checked item two he was given a score of two for that item, etc. His test score was the sum of all individual scores on each item. A high total score indicated that the student had a low preferred risk level, i.e., was quite unwilling to take risk. A low score meant a high preferred risk level, a high degree of willingness to take risk.

(2) **Biographical inventory.** Torrance and Ziller's biographical inventory [25] was developed under an Air Force research project and was designed to predict the risk taking behavior of Air Force pilots. The test was refined and was validated against another questionnaire administered to the pilots eliciting their willingness to take risk in various military situations. Torrance and Ziller concluded that certain items on their biographical inventory correlated highly with the willingness

---

[25] Torrance and Ziller, *op. cit*.

of the Air Force pilots to take risk. The items correlating highly with risk taking behavior indicated a pattern of childhood behavior identified with masculine activities. (See full description of the personality profile above). Typical of the 65 items were:

26-33. At what age did you first do the things listed below in items 26-33? (Answer each item separately, using the key below.)
   (1) 12 or younger
   (2) 12 to 14
   (3) 15 to 16
   (4) 17 to 18
   (5) 19 to 20
   (6) 20 or over
   (7) not yet

26. Going out on dates
27. Necking
28. Dancing
29. Having sexual intercourse
30. Smoking
31. Drinking beer
32. Drinking whiskey
33. Hitchhiking

For example, answers of question 28 or 29 as (1) or (2), indicated a high risk pattern, as did answers to questions 31 and 32 of (1), (2) or (3) or answers to question 33 of (1).

The subjects in the current experiment were given the Torrance and Ziller biographical inventory to determine if there was any significant correlation of scores between those having high risk attitudes and those with a biographical pattern found by Torrence and Ziller to be characterized by "the high riskers." Since a high score on the risk scale meant low unwillingness to take risk, one would expect a negative correlation between the risk scale and the biographical scale, which was scored according to how many of the significant items the subject checked.

(3) **Insurance mindedness scale.** Several possibilities existed in solving the problem of measuring a subject's "insurance mindedness." Questions could have been framed according to "what *would* you do if you were faced with a possibility of loss with probability $p$ and were offered insurance at a premium of $y$ percent?" Or, questions might have been in the format, "If you were advising your best friend who is faced with a given probability of loss, and were offered insurance at a certain price how would you advise him?" Instead it was decided to try a very simple direct type of question designed to measure insurance mindedness by actual decisions made in the past by the subjects who have been faced by real-world risks and have either purchased insurance or have not purchased it.

Accordingly, the insurance mindedness scale was developed by asking direct questions of the subjects as to what type of insurance, and in some cases in what amounts, did they actually purchase. Examples of questions asked are:

1. Check below if you pay individually for any of the following types of health insurance.
   - (1)——voluntary student health insurance—accident only.
   - (2)——voluntary student health insurance—accident and sickness.
   - (3)——Blue Cross plan.
   - (4)——other type of health insurance (please identify briefly).
2. Indicate the type of automobile insurance, if any, you carry.
   Physical Damage Insurance
   - ( 1)——$50 deductible collision
   - ( 2)——$100 deductible collision
   - ( 3)——comprehensive
   - ( 4)——other
   - ( 5)——carry physical damage insurance, but unsure of amount or type.

   Liability Insurance
   - ( 6)——$5000/$10,000 bodily injury liability
   - ( 7)——$10,000/$20,000 bodily injury liability
   - ( 8)——higher limits of bodily injury liability than $10,000/$20,000
   - ( 9)——carry bodily injury liability; unsure of amount
   - (10)——medical payments
   - (11)——$5,000 property damage liability
   - (12)——$10,000 property damage liability
   - (13)——higher limits than $10,000 property damage liability
   - (14)——carry property damage liability; unsure of amount
   - (15)——I own a car, but do not carry any insurance on it of any type.

*Scoring.* Scores to the insurance mindedness scale were assigned according to the completeness with which the subject purchased insurance against each exposure to loss. For example, items (1) through (4) of question 1 were scored 1, 2, 2, and 2, respectively. Items (6) through (15) in question 2 above were scored 1, 2, 3, 1, 2, 1, 2, 3, 1, and 0, respectively.

The rationale of the scoring procedure may be illustrated as follows: Each student at the University had the opportunity to purchase student health insurance as he passed through registration lines at the beginning of the academic year. He could purchase an "accident only" plan or a more comprehensive plan, which is similar to Blue Cross coverage. These plans generally do not duplicate any other coverage the student might be expected to have. Parents' health insurance usually does not cover the student at college. Furthermore the student health insurance is integrated with services provided at the student infirmary. The subject was assumed to know these facts. His score was zero if he checked nothing, 1 if he checked accident only coverage, and 2 if he had a more complete plan. Similar reasoning underlay other scores on the insurance mindedness test.

## Results

Table 1 shows the correlation matrix, and Table 2 the mean, standard deviation and coefficient of variation of several scores as follows:

1. Scores of 70 subjects on insurance mindedness scale.
2. Scores of 70 subjects on all 20 items on the attitudes toward risk test.
3. Scores of 70 subjects on the Torrance and Ziller biographical inventory scale.
4. Scores of 70 subjects on odd numbered questions on attitudes toward risk test.
5. Scores of 70 subjects on even numbered questions on attitudes toward risk test.
6. Scores of 70 subjects on first 10 questions on attitudes toward risk test, posing hypothetical gambling choices.
7. Scores of 70 subjects on second 10 questions on attitudes toward risk test, posing required odds for success.

Tests (1), (2), and (3) were total scores on the three basic tests described above. Scores on tests (4) and (5) above were procured in order to determine the reliability, or internal consistency, of test (2) the attitudes toward risk scale, and thus to test Hypothesis 1. Tests (6) and (7) were procured in order to test Hypothesis 3.

**Hypothesis 1.** The evidence supports this hypothesis. The odd-even correlation (test 4 with test 5 Table 2) was .798. Corrected by

TABLE 1

COEFFICIENTS OF CORRELATIONS OF SEVEN SCORES CONCERNING
ATTITUDES TOWARD RISK
(N = 70)

| Test No. | Description | Test 1 | 2 | 3 | 4 | 5 | 6 |
|---|---|---|---|---|---|---|---|
| 1 | Insurance Mindedness | — | | | | | |
| 2 | Attitudes Toward Risk | .150** | — | | | | |
| 3 | Biographical Inventory | .068 | .086 | — | | | |
| 4 | Odd Numbered Questions on Test 3 | .137 | .938* | —.086 | — | | |
| 5 | Even Numbered Questions on Test 3 | .161 | .943* | —.108 | .798* | — | |
| 6 | Gambling Choices | .138 | .928* | —.071 | .891* | .885* | — |
| 7 | Required Odds For Success | .138 | .742* | —.127 | .692* | .724* | .468* |

* Significant at the .005 level, in a single tailed test.
** Would have had to be approximately .2 for significance at the .05 level. Significance levels were determined from tables developed by R. A. Fisher, *Statistical Methods for Research Workers* (Oliver & Boyd, Ltd. Edinburgh.)

TABLE 2

MEAN, STANDARD DEVIATION AND COEFFICIENT OF VARIATION OF
SEVEN TEST SCORES CONCERNING ATTITUDES TOWARD RISK

| Test | Mean | Standard Deviation | Coefficient of Variation |
|------|------|--------------------|--------------------------|
| 1 | 10.01 | 4.25 | .424 |
| 2 | 84.67 | 18.70 | .221 |
| 3 | 23.31 | 7.69 | .330 |
| 4 | 41.02 | 9.72 | .237 |
| 5 | 43.35 | 10.39 | .240 |
| 6 | 46.64 | 14.31 | .307 |
| 7 | 37.68 | 7.57 | .201 |

the Spearman-Brown formula [26] this correlation becomes .89 which is satisfactory as an estimate of reliability.

**Hypothesis 2.** This hypothesis is not supported by the current experiment. Reference to Table 2 shows a correlation between scores on the insurance mindedness test (test 1) and scores on the attitudes toward risk test (test 2) of .15.

While this correlation coefficient of .15 is not statistically significant at the .05 level, it was positive and suggests that certain refinements in the criterion might have been successful in producing a significant correlation. The standard deviation of the insurance mindedness test was very large (See Table 2) being 4.25 compared to a mean of 10.01, producing a coefficient of variation far higher than any other test. This large variation may be due to one or more of the following factors:

1. The criterion measure was heavily weighted in automobile insurance buying behavior, since this type of insurance is semi-compulsory and all subjects had cars, they got substantial scores in this section of the test. For other types of insurance, however, variability was great, probably due to the fact that some subjects had faced an exposure to loss covered by the insurance listed on the questionnaire and others had not. In many cases, for example, it was evident that the student's parents purchased and maintained life or health insurance for them, reducing the degree to which the student purchased this coverage.

---

[26] This widely used formula rests on the assumption that the variances of the error factors in two segments of the test are equal, that the error factor in a set of scores is uncorrelated with the true scores, that the error factor in one set of obtained scores is uncorrelated with that in another set, and that the variable error factor has an expected value of zero. The greater the error variance in a test the more unreliable it is because the numerical value of reliability of a test corresponds proportionately to the variance associated with *individuals* in the quality being evaluated. If error variances in two segments of a test are not equal it is clear that a high correlation of performance in two tests cannot be ascribed to individual performance, but merely due to an unknown error. See Robert L. Thorndike, "Reliability," in Lindquist, E. F. (editor), *Educational Management* (Washington, D.C., American Council on Education, 1951) pp. 566-567, for a full discussion of this point. The Spearman-Brown formula gives an estimate of the reliability of a whole test as determined by the correlation of two halves as

$r_{(1+2)} = \dfrac{2r_{12}}{1+r_{12}}$ where $r_{12}$ is the correlation of part 1 with part 2 of a test, and $r_{(1+2)}$ is the correlation coefficient for the whole test, or its reliability.

2. Due to faulty memory, accurate information on the questionnaire may not have been forthcoming. It was not possible to check on the accuracy of the answers. Students may well have forgotten what limits of liability were carried on their automobiles.

**Hypothesis 3.** This hypothesis is supported by the current experiment. Reference to Table 1 shows a correlation of .468 between scores on the first 10 questions and the second 10 questions of the attitudes toward risk test. This is significantly different from zero at the .005 level. It will be recalled that the first 10 questions of the attitudes toward risk scale posed hypothetical gambling games in which the higher the score, the higher the prize required to make the subject willing to pay a hypothetical stake. In the second 10 questions the high score meant that greater and greater odds for success were required before the subject would be willing to accept a risky alternative in an economic problem. Whether the subject would actually behave in this manner in a real-life situation is a matter for speculation, of course.

**Hypothesis 4.** This hypothesis must be rejected. Reference to Table 1 shows a small negative correlation (-.086) between Test 2 and Test 3, as predicted, but this correlation is not statistically significant. If there is any statistically significant relationship between personality attributes as measured by the biographical inventory technique, and attitudes toward risk, as measured by verbal questionnaire, this experiment did not reveal it. Neither is there any significant relationship between scores of the subjects on Tests 1 and 3 (.068) and thus there is no apparent connection between insurance mindedness and biographical history as measured by the particular test employed.

**Conclusions.** Several findings with interesting implications for a theory of insurance consumption arise out of a review of certain psychological literature bearing on attitudes toward risk and out of an experiment conducted by the author in measuring attitudes toward risk.

The experiment demonstrated that it is feasible to construct a reliable verbal questionnaire to measure attitudes toward risk. Furthermore, answers of subjects to questions relating to gambling preferences were significantly correlated with answers to questions relating to other risk taking behavior in real-life situations. Thus there is evidence that individuals possess a basic set of attitudes toward risk and these attitudes affect importantly their attitudes toward different types of risk economic alternatives.

While the current experiment did not go further than testing attitudes toward hypothetical decisions involving risky alternatives, the next step obviously is to determine if risk attitudes actually affect real life behavior. An attempt to obtain a significant relationship between risk attitudes and past insurance buying behavior did not succeed, but the experiment suggested ways by which this might be accomplished. In future experiments it may be necessary to control for the variables of income and wealth, and certainly a more refined criterion of insurance mindedness is needed.

The author could find no connection between biographical histories and risk taking attitudes involving economic situations, or insurance mindedness, as measured by given tests. Experiments by others have established a connection between biographical histories and military risk taking behavior but apparently this behavior in military situations does not carry over to the economic world.

## Questions

1. The author believes that the findings of Preston and Baratta, reported in this article, suggest that insurance buying behavior may, in part, rest upon errors by people in interpreting true probabilities. Do you agree? Why or why not?
2. What personality characteristics tend to be associated with risk-taking attitudes?
3. Does the experiment conducted by the author support the finding that there is a consistency between risk-taking attitudes and subsequent behavior in decisions involving risk? Discuss.
4. The Torrance and Ziller experimental results were not supported in the present study. What is your conclusion about early life experiences as a reliable indication of basic risk attitudes in later life?

# 5. ATTITUDES TOWARD SPECULATIVE RISKS AS AN INDICATOR OF ATTITUDES TOWARD PURE RISKS *

C. Arthur Williams, Jr. †

The psychological aspects of risk-bearing have attracted increasing attention in recent years. Professor Mark Greene has provided the readers of this *Journal* with an excellent summary of the literature and with some findings based upon original research.[1] The growing importance of this field is perhaps best evidenced by the publication in 1964 of a 278 page book entitled *Risk Taking* which is devoted entirely to a better understanding of risk attitudes.[2]

For the most part, this literature is devoted to determining those factors which affect risk attitudes. For example, Professor Greene has reviewed the influence of age, sex, the odds, personality, and intelligence upon risk attitudes.[3] Professors Kogan and Wallach emphasize the complexity of the decision-making process but they are impressed by the roles of (1) "test anxiety" or the motive to avoid failure and (2) "defensiveness" or excessive concern with maintaining one's image.[4] Researchers have determined the effect of these factors by asking several groups of subjects with varying characteristics (for example, a male group and a female group) to participate in a laboratory experiment or by changing the experimental condition (for example, the odds) for a given group and noting the differences in risk attitudes induced by the change in the feature under study.

As important and as informative as this research may be, the purpose of this article is (1) to inquire into the relevance of this research to the study of pure risk attitudes and insurance buying habits and (2) to suggest some new avenues that might usefully be explored.

---

* From *The Journal of Risk and Insurance* (December, 1966), pp. 577-586. Reprinted by permission.

† Professor of Economics and Insurance, University of Minnesota.

[1] Mark R. Greene, "Attitudes Toward Risk and A Theory of Insurance Consumption," *The Journal of Insurance*, XXX, No. 2 (June, 1963), pp. 165-82.
Mark R. Greene, "Insurance Mindedness—Implications for Insurance Theory," *The Journal of Insurance*, XXXI, No. 1 (March, 1964), pp. 27-38.

[2] Nathan Kogan and Michael A. Wallach, *Risk Taking* (New York: Holt, Rinehart, and Winston, 1964).

[3] Greene, "Attitudes Toward Risk. . . .," *op. cit.*, pp. 166-70.

[4] Kogan and Wallach, *op. cit.*, pp. 13-14.

## PURE RISK vs. SPECULATIVE RISK

Insurance textbooks have distinguished for many years between pure-risk and speculative-risk situations.[5] In both situations there is doubt or uncertainty concerning the outcome, but in the pure-risk situation there is no chance of gain. The person faces only a loss of the status quo. In the speculative-risk situation there is a chance of gain. Although many situations involve both pure and speculative risks, it has proved useful to distinguish between those aspects involving pure risks and those involving speculative risks.

Speculative risks present both favorable and unfavorable consequences. The favorable consequences may indeed be so great that a person deliberately creates a risk (through a wager, for example) where one did not exist previously. Pure risks, on the other hand, are always undesirable. Consequently, one might hypothesize that most people would be more adverse to pure risks than to speculative risks and that, as a result, they might take steps to avoid pure risks while accepting speculative risks. Such behavior has been observed enough to warrant a theoretical explanation by Professors Friedman and Savage who, in a classic article on utility theory, have explained why the same person might buy insurance and still be interested in accepting speculative risks.[6]

The Friedman-Savage article, however, does not explain this behavior in terms of varying attitudes toward pure and speculative risks, but by the shape of the individual's utility function.

One hypothesis, based on an "ignorance" factor, supports a contrary finding. The "gambling" involved in accepting or retaining a pure risk is often obscure. A person who shys away from a speculative risk because of the gambling associated with acceptance or retention of that risk may fail to recognize the gambling associated with the acceptance or retention of a pure risk.

Still another hypothesis, based on an "inertia" factor, suggests that the type of risk involved is not as important as whether the decision-maker must act to assume or transfer the risk and the type of action required. In many, perhaps most, risk situations, individuals tend to prefer their present position unless persuaded to act by some other person or presented with what appears to be a clearly preferable alternative. This may be one reason why it is much easier to convince a person to renew an insurance policy than to purchase the initial contract. This hypothesis suggests that in any experiment designed to determine attitudes toward different types of risk, this factor should be controlled. It also suggests that this factor itself deserves further study.

---

[5] For example, see Albert H. Mowbray and Ralph H. Blanchard, *Insurance*, 5th edition, (New York: McGraw-Hill Book Co., 1961), pp. 7-8).

[6] Milton Friedman and L. J. Savage, "The Utility Analysis of Choices Involving Risk," *Journal of Political Economy*, LVI (August, 1948), pp. 279-304.

Other hypotheses can no doubt be developed but these are sufficient to indicate the need for research in this area. More specific suggestions for additional research are presented in the concluding section of this paper.

## PURE RISK AND EXPERIMENTS ON RISK ATTITUDES

To the author's knowledge, all of the experiments on risk attitudes except those of Professor Greene deal entirely with speculative risks, not pure risks. Three of the five experiments conducted by Professors Kogan and Wallach are typical.[7] First, they computed a deterrence of failure index based on the subject's required probability of success before he would select the risky alternative over a safe alternative in each of twelve situations. Each risky alternative offered a chance of a larger reward than the safe alternative but a less satisfactory outcome was also possible. Second, subjects were asked to choose one of a pair of dice bets. Strategy indexes were then developed according to the number of times the subject selected the alternative keyed for each strategy (e.g., choice of that alternative with the larger potential winnings). All bets involved speculative risks. Third, the subject was asked to place bets on his performance in a game of skill and another strategy index was developed. As in the previous cases, all bets involved speculative risks.

Because all of these experiments were concerned with speculative risks, one should not accept uncritically the findings with respect to the influence of age, sex, and other factors upon attitudes toward pure risks.[8] Although the same relationships may obtain, it would be worthwhile to test this hypothesis with similar experiments using pure-risk situations.

Professor Greene has included one pure risk situation (a question on insurance) in his attitudes-toward-risk test [9] but he did not construct a separate questionnaire on pure risk attitudes. It is interesting to note that in the Greene experiment there was a correlation of .468 between the subject's risk score in gambling situations and his score in other economic situations.[10] Since both scores are, with one exception, based on attitudes toward speculative risks, one would expect the correlation to be even higher.[11] There was no statistically significant correlation, however, between an insurance mindedness scale based on actual insurance purchases and scores on the attitudes-toward-risk test. Although

---

[7] Kogan and Wallach, *op. cit.*, pp. 25-32.

[8] One may also question whether the results of a particular laboratory experiment should be generalized as much as is sometimes the case. For example, if the maximum gain in the experiment is $5 and the maximum loss is −$5 (Practical considerations often dictate the amounts since to "involve" the subjects, they often are allowed to keep their winnings.), the experiment may be misleading for gains and losses outside, this range. Researchers themselves, however, commonly emphasize the limitations of their work.

[9] Greene, *op. cit.*, pp. 175-76.

[10] *Ibid.*, pp. 174, 180.

[11] For one possible explanation why the correlation is not higher, see footnote 13.

several reasonable explanations are suggested for this lack of correlation, one reason not mentioned may be that attitudes toward speculative risks are not related to actions in pure risk situations.[12]

In summary,

1. All of the experiments on risk taking to date deal primarily or exclusively with speculative risks.
2. These experimenters have assumed implicitly that the subject's attitude toward risk is not affected by whether the risk is pure or speculative.
3. Speculative risk aversion scores have not enabled experimenters to predict insurance buying behavior of the subjects.
4. Two hypotheses should be tested. The first asserts that a subject's attitude toward pure risks differs from his attitude toward speculative risks. The second states that a subject's pure risk aversion score will enable the experimenter to predict with confidence the subject's behavior in situations involving pure risk, including his insurance buying habits.

## A PILOT EXPERIMENT

In order to test whether (1) attitudes toward pure risk are not the same as attitudes toward speculative risk and (2) attitudes toward pure risk are more closely related to insurance buying habits than are attitudes toward speculative risks, the author designed three tests to be administered to 51 graduate students in the Evening Master of Business Administration Program of the School of Business Administration at the University of Minnesota. This group of students was selected (1) because it is a fairly homogeneous group with respect to age, sex, intelligence, income level, and property holdings and (2) because most of the students were old enough to have made many insurance decisions. Undergraduates were not used because their insurance purchases are limited.

### Test Construction

Test 1 asked the subject to imagine that he was aged 35, married, and had two young children. He was also asked to imagine that his prospects for the future were bright, that he owned a car and a house, subject to a mortgage, and that he had $15,000 in savings and investments of various sorts. For the subjects in the test group, these assumptions were not unrealistic. The subject was then asked to indicate the LOWEST probability of gain that he would require before he would participate in each of twelve different ventures. If he did not want to participate in

---

[12] *Ibid.*, pp. 177-80. In his more recent article (Greene, *Insurance Mindedness, op. cit.*, pp. 29-30), Professor Greene improved his insurance mindedness scale but the correlation coefficient with a different group of subjects was even smaller. More promising results were obtained by correlating insurance attitudes with insurance behavior. The insurance attitude test asked the subject to record the extent of his agreement with statements about insurance buying behavior. It can be viewed as one version of a test of attitudes toward pure risk.

the venture under any circumstances, he was instructed either to check a special space provided for this purpose or to indicate a probability of 1.0. Each venture was to be treated separately as if the other ventures did not exist. The twelve ventures were as follows:

| Venture | Possible Gain | Possible Loss |
|---------|--------------|---------------|
| 1 | $ 100 | $ 100 |
| 2 | 4,000 | 1,000 |
| 3 | 160 | 40 |
| 4 | 12,500 | 12,500 |
| 5 | 20 | 980 |
| 6 | 4 | 196 |
| 7 | 500 | 24,500 |
| 8 | 800 | 200 |
| 9 | 100 | 4,900 |
| 10 | 2,500 | 2,500 |
| 11 | 20,000 | 5,000 |
| 12 | 500 | 500 |

For ventures 5, 6, 7, and 9, the probability of loss which produces an expected dollar value of 0 is 1/50. For ventures 1, 4, 10, and 12, the corresponding probability of loss is 1/2 and for ventures 2, 3, 8, and 11, 4/5. The ventures were ordered on a random basis in order to avoid any order bias.

Test 2 asked the subject to imagine that he was the same person under the same economic circumstances but in this case he was asked to indicate the LOWEST probability of loss which would have to be present before he would be willing to pay a stated fee to transfer each of twelve potential losses (with no offsetting potential gain) to someone else. The twelve potential losses and the related transfer fees were as follows:

| Loss | Potential Dollar Loss | Fee to Avoid Loss |
|------|----------------------|-------------------|
| 1 | $ 5,000 | $ 100 |
| 2 | 1,000 | 500 |
| 3 | 5,000 | 4,000 |
| 4 | 25,000 | 12,500 |
| 5 | 200 | 4 |
| 6 | 5,000 | 2,500 |
| 7 | 25,000 | 20,000 |
| 8 | 1,000 | 20 |
| 9 | 200 | 100 |
| 10 | 200 | 160 |
| 11 | 25,000 | 500 |
| 12 | 1,000 | 800 |

For losses 1, 5, 8, and 11, the probability of loss for which the expected loss equals the transfer fee is 1/50. For losses 2, 4, 6, and 9, the corresponding probability of loss is 1/2 and for ventures 3, 7, 10, and 12, 4/5.

These losses, like the ventures in Test 1, were arranged randomly in order to avoid any order bias.

A subject who is a speculative risk averter would be expected to require a high probability of success before he would participate in the ventures presented in Test 1. A subject who is a pure risk averter would be willing to pay the Test 2 fee for a small probability of loss. Consequently, high "break-even" probabilities of gain under Test 1 and low "break-even" probabilities of loss under Test 2 indicate risk aversion.

Several comments should be made here about these two tests. First, the manner in which the question is asked can influence the subject's response. In both of these tests the subject was asked to indicate "break-even" probabilities of gain or loss. For each venture or loss, a probability could have been specified and each subject asked to indicate the "break-even" amount that he would pay to participate (and possibly lose) in the venture or to transfer the loss. This approach was not used in this experiment because the absence of a maximum dollar payment and the wide range of possible replies might make it more difficult for some subjects to respond. This alternative approach, however, should be tested at a later date.[13]

There might also be a difference between an open-end question, which was the approach used in this experiment, and a more directed approach which would indicate several probabilities, one of which was to be selected by the subject as his required highest probability of gain under Test 1 or required lowest probability of loss under Test 2. To check on this problem, two forms of each test were administered to the first 20 subjects. Although the analysis was at most suggestive, the responses to the two versions were fairly consistent with one another. The open-end questionnaire was chosen over the multiple-choice version because it was more sensitive to differences in the preferred probabilities. Some distortion may also have been introduced by asking for a probability of gain in one case and a probability of loss in the other.

Second, these two tests require the subject to state what he would do in a given situation. What he would actually do in each situation might be quite different. It is, of course, impossible to run a laboratory experiment in which the subject actually may lose $25,000. On the other hand, an experiment in which he loses at most a quarter is also of limited value. Although the subjects appeared to become sufficiently "involved" during the administration of these tests, this is a facet of the experiment that needs to be improved.

Third, the questionnaires are designed to test reactions to low, moderate, and high probabilities of loss and to four loss sizes ranging from very small to very large amounts. Although the moderate and high

---

[13] Professor Greene has provided a partial test. In his gambling questions, he asked the subject to express his answer in dollar amounts while in the questions on other economic situations, the answers were in terms of probability. Greene, "Risk Attitudes," *op. cit.*, pp. 175-76.

probability findings are interesting, future tests will include only low probability of loss because more pure risk managers are concerned with probabilities of less than .10.

Fourth, for each venture in Test 1, there is a "corresponding" loss in Test 2 which presents a similar decision. For example, venture 9 presents a possible gain of $100 and a possible loss of $4,900. Loss I presents a possible loss of $5,000 which can be avoided for a fee of $100. If the person decides not to pay the fee, he assumes a possible "gain" of $100 and a possible "loss" of $4,900. His starting point, of course, is $100 less. In losses 1, 5, 8, 9, and 10 the differences in the starting point are $200 or less; in the other instances they are $500 or more and the "correspondence" between the two situations is weak.

Fifth, despite the warning noted in the introductory section about controlling the effect of a human tendency to inertia, this control was not introduced in this experiment. Indeed, as often occurs in experimental research, the hypothesis was suggested by the research results.

Test 3 asked the subject to indicate his insurance buying habits with respect to life insurance, health insurance, automobile insurance, and homeowner's insurance. In each section, the subject was asked to indicate the type and amount of insurance he owned. In the life and health insurance sections, he was also asked how much of the protection was provided under a compulsory employee benefit plan and how much individual protection he had purchased since becoming eligible to participate in the employee-benefit plan. An insurance index was computed for each subject on the basis of his answers to these questions.

## Conduct of the Experiment

Each of the tests was administered in a separate week. About twenty minutes were allowed for the completion of the questionnaire and all subjects completed the questionnaire within the required time. Subjects were told in advance that there would be three tests in all (five tests for the initial 20 subjects) but they were not told the nature of the tests and the experiment was described only in general terms. The reasons for administering the test over a period of time were to reduce test fatigue and to reduce the chance that the subjects would notice any correspondence between the ventures in Test 1 and the potential losses in Test 2. No subject mentioned noticing this correspondence in post-experimental discussions.

Fifty-one subjects completed the first two tests. Thirty-nine of these fifty-one subjects also completed the insurance questionnaire.

## Analysis

The test results were analyzed in the following ways:

1. The "break-even" probability of loss for each person for each venture under Test 1 was computed by subtracting the "break-even"

probability of gain from 1. The average "break-even" probability of loss for each venture under Test 1 for all subjects was compared with the average probability of loss for the "corresponding" loss under Test 2. The results are presented in Table 1:

TABLE 1

AVERAGE "BREAK-EVEN" PROBABILITIES FOR<br>EACH VENTURE OR LOSS UNDER TESTS 1 AND 2

| Test 1 | | Test 2 | |
|---|---|---|---|
| Venture | Average Probability | Loss | Average Probability |
| 9 | .01 | 1 | .10 |
| 12 | .30 | 2 | .72 |
| 2 | .41 | 3 | .93 |
| 4 | .08 | 4 | .72 |
| 6 | .02 | 5 | .31 |
| 10 | .21 | 6 | .67 |
| 11 | .29 | 7 | .92 |
| 5 | .02 | 8 | .15 |
| 1 | .35 | 9 | .80 |
| 3 | .58 | 10 | .94 |
| 7 | .01 | 11 | .14 |
| 8 | .48 | 12 | .94 |

In each case, the average probability required before the subject would transfer the potential loss for the stated fee was larger than the probability of loss required before he would refuse to participate in the "corresponding" speculative venture. Loss 1 and venture 9 are particularly interesting on this score. The subjects would, on the average, require a probability of loss of .10 before they would pay $100 to transfer a potential loss of $5,000. On the other hand, they would not participate in a venture offering a possible gain of $100 and a possible loss of $4,900 if the probability of loss were more than .01. Apparently, the subjects perceived these two situations as being quite different despite their many similarities.

Not only did the average break-even probabilities in Test 2 exceed the average "corresponding" probabilities in Test 1, but with only a few exceptions, each individual's Test 2 break-even probabilities exceeded his "corresponding" Test 1 probabilities.

One can argue that the answers to Test 2 are not realistic. For every loss, the average break-even probability of loss exceeds the probability that would equate the stated fee and the expected value of the loss.[14] For example, in loss situation 1, the average break-even probability of .10 would produce an expected loss of .10 ($5,000) = $500 which is

---

[14] With one exception, the average probabilities under Test 1 indicate a willingness to participate in the speculative venture only if the odds favor participation.

five times the stated fee. A probability of .02 would equate the expected loss and the stated fee. Particularly with respect to the low-probability cases, it is doubtful that so many (all but a few in this experiment) would refuse to pay a fee which is less than the expected loss. The insurance buying habits of the group as revealed in Test 3 are clearly not consistent with such behavior. Perhaps, however, the subjects were not aware of the implications of their responses. The consistency of their replies is also impressive.

In summary, this comparison suggests that (1) the subjects did not perceive the similarties in the "corresponding" situations and (2) the subjects were more willing to retain pure risks than assume speculative risks in similar situations.

2. The effect of the potential loss size upon the subjects' behavior was studied by rearranging the average break-even probability data in Table 1 as shown in Table 2. As would be expected from modern utility theory, subjects under both tests displayed a greater aversion to risk-bearing when the potential losses were large. For example, when the potential gain and the potential loss were both $100, the subjects said that they would participate in the speculative venture if the probability of loss were no higher than .35. When the potential gain and the potential loss were both $12,500, the subjects became much more conservative and would participate only if the probability of loss were under .08. Utility theory would explain this behavior in terms of diminishing marginal utility which would cause (1) a dollar lost to mean a greater loss in utility than the increase in utility associated with a dollar gained and (2) the loss in utility to increase faster than the loss in dollars. An additional finding was that, except in the "low-probability" cases, as the size of the potential loss increased, the subjects tended to increase their average break-even probabilities more in the speculative risk situations than in the "corresponding" pure risk situations than in the "corresponding" pure risk situations. In the low-probability cases, the subjects were already so conservative under Test 1 that the change in attitude was more difficult to detect.

Displaying the data as in Table 2 also indicates the degree to which the Test 1 and Test 2 situations "correspond." As noted earlier, the correspondence is strong only in the low probability cases.

3. The subjects' attitudes toward pure risks were correlated with their attitudes toward speculative risks. In order to correlate these attitudes, it was necessary to construct some risk aversion index which would measure each subject's relative attitude toward risk. Several alternative procedures were considered.

The method which appeared to be most satisfactory first subtracts each subject's break-even probability of loss for each venture or loss from the average probability for all subjects for that venture or loss. This difference is then divided by the standard deviation of the subjects' probabilities for that venture of loss. To illustrate, one subject indicated a break-even probability of .15 for loss 1 under Test 2. Subtracting this

TABLE 2

AVERAGE BREAK-EVEN PROBABILITIES OF LOSS FOR EACH
VENTURE OR LOSS UNDER TESTS 1 AND 2 CLASSIFIED BY
SIZE OF POTENTIAL LOSS AND BY PROBABILITY THAT WOULD
PRODUCE AN EXPECTED VALUE OF ZERO UNDER TEST 1 OR
EQUATE THE TRANSFER FEE AND THE EXPECTED VALUE
UNDER TEST 2

### Low Probability Venture or Losses
#### (p = .02)

| Test 1 | | Test 2 | |
|---|---|---|---|
| Potential Loss | Average Probability | Potential Loss | Average Probability |
| $24,500 | .01 | $25,000 | .14 |
| 4,900 | .01 | 5,000 | .10 |
| 980 | .02 | 1,000 | .15 |
| 196 | .02 | 200 | .31 |

### Medium Probability Ventures or Losses
#### (p = .50)

| Test 1 | | Test 2 | |
|---|---|---|---|
| Potential Loss | Average Probability | Potential Loss | Average Probability |
| $12,500 | .08 | $25,000 | .72 |
| 2,500 | .21 | 5,000 | .67 |
| 500 | .30 | 1,000 | .72 |
| 100 | .35 | 200 | .80 |

### High Probability Ventures or Losses
#### (p = .80)

| Test 1 | | Test 2 | |
|---|---|---|---|
| Potential Loss | Average Probability | Potential Loss | Average Probability |
| $ 5,000 | .29 | $25,000 | .92 |
| 1,000 | .41 | 5,000 | .93 |
| 200 | .48 | 1,000 | .94 |
| 40 | .58 | 200 | .94 |

probability from the average probability of .10 yields .05. Dividing
this .05 by the standard deviation of .14 yields +.36 which is the
subject's risk aversion index with respect to this loss. A positive index
indicates a lesser aversion to this risk than the average; a negative
index indicates a greater aversion.

The division by the standard deviation corrects for the difference
in the dispersion of the replies among the different ventures. The standard deviations ranged from .10 to .24 for the twelve ventures under

Test 1 and from .11 to .90 under Test 2.[15] The sum of each subject's standardized differences for the ten ventures under Test 1 is his speculative risk aversion index. The sum of his standardized differences for the ten potential losses under Test 2 is his pure risk aversion index.

The correlation coefficient between the 51 pure risk aversion indices and the 51 speculative risk aversion indices was $-.39$. Although not large, this correlation is significant at the .05 level. The negative sign is particularly interesting because it indicates that as the pure risk aversion index increases, the speculative risk aversion index tends to decrease.[16] This finding supports the hypothesis that attitudes toward pure risks differ from attitudes toward speculative risks.

Because of a risk manager's special interest in the low-probability cases, a separate correlation coefficient was computed for indices based only on the four ventures and the four potential losses associated with low probabilities. The answer was $-.24$. Although not statistically significant at the .05 level, the coefficient is nevertheless suggestive. The failure to achieve a large coefficient for these cases is best explained by the fact that 40 of the 51 subjects had the same pure risk aversion index. Because of the low probability (.02) for which the stated fee would equal the expected loss, the questionnaire failed to discriminate adequately among pure risk attitudes.

4. The subjects' insurance indices as indicated by their insurance purchases were correlated with their speculative risk aversion indices and with their pure risk aversion indices. Constructing the insurance indices was a highly subjective task. Two and a half points were assigned to each of the four types of insurance included in the questionnaire—life insurance, health insurance, automobile insurance, and homeowner's insurance. Scores for each of these four types of insurance depended upon the types and amount of insurance owned. The life and health insurance scores weighted individual insurance more heavily than group insurance because an individual insurance purchase usually represents a more active decision by the employee.

The correlation coefficient between the insurance indices and the speculative risk aversion indices was .0353 which is not significantly different from .0 at the .05 level. The correlation coefficient between the insurance indices and the pure risk aversion indices was $-.139$

---

[15] The magnitude of these standard deviations is disturbing and sheds some doubt on the validity of the aversion indices. The standard deviation was greatly increased in some cases by the presence of one or two extreme responses. For example, except for one .95 break-even probability, the standard deviation for the replies to venture 9 would have been .01 instead of .13. An attempt was made to correct for these extreme cases, but the observations to be excluded would have involved some highly subjective judgments. Elimination of these extreme cases would not change significantly the average probability comparisons in Table 1.

[16] In a pilot study, the author administered the study to a husband and wife. The husband would enter ventures under Test 1 under conditions that the wife would refuse, but the husband was willing to pay the stated fee under Test 2 for lower probabilities of loss than the wife. Can this difference in behavior among the sexes be generalized?

which is surprising because of the negative relationship. However, this coefficient is not significantly different from zero at the .05 level. Both correlation coefficients, therefore, are not significant. The experiment thus failed to support the hypothesis that pure risk attitudes as measured in this way can be used to predict with confidence insurance buying behavior.

Some possible explanations for the discrepancy between those correlation coefficients and the expected results are not difficult to develop.[17] (1) The pure and speculative risk indices are based upon how the subjects stated they would act in hypothetical situations; the insurance index is based upon actual behavior. (2) Although the insurance indices are based upon reported insurance programs, the weighting process introduces so much subjectivity into the indices that they may not correctly measure insurance buying behavior. (3) The pure and speculative risk aversion indices depend upon the subjects' reactions to situations involving low, medium, and high probabilities and potential losses of various sizes. Insurance buying behavior may be related only to the risk aversion indices for low probability cases or for low-probability—high potential cases. (4) Custom and social pressures may be more important than risk attitudes in determining insurance buying behavior, particularly with respect to family insurance. (5) Negative attitudes toward insurance companies may have affected responses to Test 2.

If the correlation coefficients had agreed with the expectations, this agreement could have been challenged on these grounds. These observations emphasize why experimental research must be carefully conceived and conducted and why one must be careful not to over-generalize from the results.

In order to test the third explanation above, pure and speculative risk aversion indices were calculated based upon only the four low probability ventures and their corresponding potential losses. The correlation coefficient between the pure risk aversion indices and the insurance indices is .1084 which is in the expected direction but is not significantly different from zero. Since only four ventures and four potential losses are involved and for all of the potential loss situations over half of the subjects had the same pure risk aversion score, these results are at most suggestive, but they do provide leads for further research.

## IMPLICATIONS FOR FURTHER RESEARCH

Although the results of the pilot experiment reported above have not produced a pure risk aversion index which can be used to predict insurance buying behavior, the results do suggest that people react differently to pure risks and speculative risks, a fact which has been ignored in almost all experimental research to date. Because the readers of this

---

[17] See also footnote 15.

*Journal* are more interested in pure risks than speculative risks, it is important for them to recognize that this difference may exist.

Even if the correlation coefficients had all been significantly different from zero and in the expected direction, generalizations would be dangerous because of the relatively crude nature of the experiment and the importance of slight changes in variables which have been held constant (such as sex) or ignored (such as Wallach and Kogan's test anxiety). Enough success has been achieved, however, to justify devoting more resources to experiments exploring basic attitudes toward pure risks to determine whether they differ from attitudes toward speculative risks.

First, the basic experiment must be improved in the ways already mentioned (low probabilities only, greater involvement on the part of the subjects, alternative scoring devices, alternative ways of asking the subject to respond, and other methods of analysis). In order to make the gambling aspect of the pure risk situation more apparent and to make the "corresponding" pure and speculative risk situations more symmetrical, the pure risk situation could be rephrased to give the subject the chance to recover the transfer fee or to continue his protection. This would also remove the differential effect of action being required in one case to assume a risk and in the other case to transfer a risk. It may also be possible to restate the question in such a way that the person's attitudes toward the insurance business do not cloud his expressed attitudes toward pure risks.

Second, the experiment may be expanded to test the effects of numerous variables upon attitudes toward pure risks. Income, sex, intelligence, education, occupation, acquaintance with pure risk management, whether decisions are made individually or in a group, test anxiety, and defensiveness are perhaps the most promising variables to include in future studies.

This research is of potential value to persons drafting insurance contracts, preparing advertising copy, selling insurance, selecting insureds, or engaged in a variety of other insurance activities. From this research risk managers may obtain better insights into the reasons for their own risk attitudes. The possible pay-off is so great and the problems so numerous that this type of research appears to merit the attention of more students of risk and insurance.

## Questions

1. Administer Test 1 and Test 2 to yourself or a friend. After completing the tests, answer the following questions:
   a. One test asks you to evaluate situations concerning probabilities of gain; the other refers to probabilities of loss. Do you feel that this change between the two tests distorts your answers from what would have happened had the questions been consistent?
   b. Do you feel that the fact that real money was not involved distorted your answers from what they might have been if real money had been used?

    c. Discuss whether or not you are able to distinguish between risk situations in which the probabilities differ by, say, .005 or less.

    d. What do you feel to be the relationship between the two tests?

    e. Do you feel that your answers differed as you "warmed up" to the task of taking the tests?

2. Do you feel that answering questions such as those in Tests 1 and Test 2 in the article is a different exercise for you than for someone who has not or is not studying risk as you are in this course?

3. How do your answers to the questions in Test 1 and Test 2 compare with the result of the survey conducted by the author?

4. One of the interesting findings of Williams' study is that his subjects had less aversion toward pure risks than toward speculative risks. Explain why this was apparently true. Do you believe it is true of people generally? Why or why not?

5. Williams found that pure or speculative risk attitudes are measured in his study were not correlated with insurance buying behavior. How does this finding compare with that of the study made by Greene in "Attitudes Toward Risk and a Theory of Insurance Consumption" (Article 4 in this book)?

6. "There is a difference between what people say they will do and what they will actually do when put to the test." In your opinion, to what extent is this statement relevant to Williams' experiments involving his subjects' decisions about hypothetical losses or gains of money, as compared to what their decisions might have been if real money were used?

# PART 2
## Risk Handling and Management

One of the more significant additions to courses in risk and insurance in the past decade has been material on the topic of risk management. Explicit treatment of this topic gives recognition to the reality that there is something to be studied which falls between theory and its application by institutions, and between definitions, theories, and technicalities and descriptions of institutions and contracts of insurance.

The profession of risk management is a growing one. A specialized branch of the American Management Association and a separate specialized professional association, the American Society of Insurance Management, are two organizations with the purpose of bringing practitioners in this field together to share developments and techniques. There are also specialized risk management publications. Three of the articles in this part are from one of these publications.

The function of the risk manager is treated in the first article by Professor Reavis. The articles by Professors Hofflander and Schkade and by Mr. McRell discuss ideas in the two areas in which the more significant quantitative models have been developed, the size of deductible and self-insurance. The article by Professor Hedges speaks to the illusive concept of the maximum limit of liability insurance decision. Professor Greene's article develops some of the major problems to be solved in the area of risk management.

# 6. THE CURRENT ROLE RISK MANAGERS PLAY *

Marshall W. Reavis III †

. . .

## FORTY-YEAR EFFORT

Although the term risk manager is relatively new, there has been an effort for nearly 40 years to professionally isolate and up-grade the status of that individual who is responsible to protect the firm from a sudden and unexpected financial downturn as a result of loss by a natural disaster or negligence.

Until the 1930s little thought was given to static risk as a specialized problem worthy of high level management concern or programs. Companies bought whatever insurance policies were considered necessary by their peers who happened to be in the sales aspect of the insurance industry. Mowbray says that "those otherwise intensely practical executives abdicated their authority when questions on risk and insurance arose and left decisions to their brokers or agents, keeping some control over amounts expended in premiums." [1] He adds that what records were kept and what planning was done were usually assigned to some minor individual in the office of the treasurer or the controller.

There was little analysis of the risk problems and little planning on any aspect except to transfer the risk to an insurance carrier for a seemingly reasonable premium. How this was done can only be assumed to have been generally haphazard.

## CURRENT STATUS

The risk manager has evolved through four stages: insurance clerk, insurance buyer, insurance manager and risk manager (see box on page 98). It would appear that the current status of the majority of role-incumbents is somewhere beyond insurance manager but not quite at the risk manager level. [2]

It is interesting to note that while few firms would attempt to market a new product or attempt new production techniques without intensive study of the dynamic or speculative risks, they will unfortunately enter

---

* From *Risk Management* (August-September, 1971), pp. 7-11. Reprinted by permission.

† Member of the faculty of the Department of Risk Management and Insurance, University of Georgia.

[1] Mowbray, Albert H. and Ralph H. Blanchard. *Insurance, Its Theory and Practice in the United States.* New York: McGraw-Hill Book Co., Inc., 1955, 4th ed. p. 534.

[2] Only 5 percent of those replying to the survey had the title "risk manager."

into these same projects without the benefit of analysis of the pure or static risks by a qualified risk manager.

In an effort to measure the status of the risk manager in today's organization in the Fall of 1970 a questionnaire was sent to 135 members of the Chicago Chapter of the American Society of Insurance Management. Inquiry was made about such areas as responsibility, reporting senior, size of organization by sales and employees, annual premiums and size of department. Replies totaled 64 or 46 percent.

We analyze in Chart I the individual to whom the risk manager reports. An overwhelming majority, 63 percent, report to an individual within the financial area. Of the remainder, five percent reported to the chairman and three percent to the president. One begins to wonder how the risk manager became so ingrained in the finance area of the organization.

| CHART I | | |
|---|---|---|
| REPORTING SENIOR IN ORGANIZATION FOR RISK MANAGER | | |
|  | Number | % |
| Chairman | 3 | 5 |
| President | 2 | 3 |
| Assistant to the President | 1 | 2 |
| General Council | 5 | 8 |
| Vice President-Administration | 8 | 13 |
| Vice President-Industrial Relations | 2 | 3 |
| Vice President-Insurance | 2 | 3 |
| Vice President-Finance | 5 | 8 |
| Treasurer | 25 | 40 } 63% |
| Assistant Treasurer | 4 | 8 |
| Controller | 4 | 7 |
|  | 62 | 100 |
| Source: Author's Survey | | |

However, if the growth of an individual firm is observed, one finds that the entrepreneur is generally production or sales oriented. The first staff member he adds to his fledgling organization is a bookkeeper. Once he begins to loosen control of some of the managerial chores, he normally will assign his bookkeeper the task of maintaining the records of insurance and paying the premiums.

As the firm prospers, so does the financial staff which then lays claim to the insurance function. However, as the risk management concept developed these duties were expanded beyond the scope of only supervising purchased insurance. At that point many risk managers found their hands tied because a financial officer was interjected between themselves and the chief executive.

Another area of analysis was with respect to the size of the risk management department. Chart 2 indicates the total nonclerical personnel in the department and shows the range of dollars of sales for the firm.

The Evolution of the Risk Manager

There are four steps in the evolution of the risk manager. Any or none of these four levels may be found in individual firms today. They are:

*The Insurance Clerk:* He serves the role of maintaining policies sent to him by the chief executive officer or an insurance salesman. He pays authorized bills, sends in the claims and really neither wants, nor can have, any say in the determination of what is insured, or what is not, or who writes the business or how.

*The Insurance Buyer:* His source of insurance may be an agent or broker writer but the choice of whom probably still remains with top management. He cares little about the insurance market conditions, nor the insurance carriers nor his own claim experience. What is important is that each renewal is bid by three or more companies and the lowest net price gets the business regardless of any other factors.

He also believes that for every premium dollar spent there should be a claim dollar returned and that the insurance carrier is obligated to live on its investment income. He cares little about safety or insurance company inspection recommendations. His is a world of companies and coverages only.

*The Insurance Manager:* A skilled insurance technician, he knows coverages, markets and insurance programs. He designs plans to fit the needs of his organization using what markets are available. Although he may believe in deductibles and some approaches to self-insurance, he tends toward one big package at the lowest possible price, all things considered. His choice of broker or agents is probably dictated from above although he may be able to express a limited opinion in some firms. His approach to safety and property preservation is limited. Instead he develops his savings through tough premium negotiations. He tends to protect his own position through broad all-inclusive policies with high limits (referred to in the trade as "sleep insurance") which will protect the firm and his job from any known and most unknown happenings.

*The Risk Manager.* Responsible for determining potential fortuitous loss to corporate personnel and assets. And, after analysis of the effect on the corporate position, fiscal and otherwise, recommends the proper approach to protecting these personnel and assets from loss. His tools are Contracts (insurance and other); Retenetion (full and partial); Reduction (loss control and parties).

His knowledge of the pulse of the insurance community is fine-honed and he is well-educated in his field. (His background will include a speaking knowledge of insurance, finance, business administration, industrial engineering, human relations, labor relations, loss control, construction engineering, and fire protection.) He must have access to top management planning at an early stage and have full backing of management to cross corporate lines with his recommendations. As his is a staff function, he can only recommend steps to be taken by line personnel, thus he must have corporate stature. His risk management responsibility includes all lines of coverage, on a worldwide basis, over all corporate personnel and assets. His authority toward insurance includes agent or broker choice, coverage and premium negotiations and settlement of claims and power to implement his programs.

He may or may not insure; the choice of Contracts or Retention must be his. Following his analysis

The Evolution of the Risk Manager (Continued)

and identification of risk, he decides whether to assume, control, eliminate or transfer the risk. It is also necessary that he be vitally concerned with the Reduction of risk through Loss Control and Property Preservation and the Recovery of loss through his claims control program.

CHART II

SIZE OF RISK MANAGEMENT DEPARTMENT

| Sales | Department personnel excluding clerical | | | | | | | | |
|---|---|---|---|---|---|---|---|---|---|
| | 1 | 2 | 3 | 4 | 5 | 6 | 7 | 8 | Total |
| Over $1.5 Billion | | | 1 | | | 1 | | | 2 |
| Over $1. Billion | | 1 | 1 | | | | | | 2 |
| Over $750 Million | 1 | 2 | 1 | | | 1 | | | 5 |
| Over $500 Million | | 1 | 1 | 1 | | | | | 3 |
| Over $400 Million | 1 | | 1 | 1 | | | | 1 | 4 |
| Over $300 Million | 4 | | 1 | | | | | | 5 |
| Over $200 Million | 5 | 2 | | | | | | | 7 |
| Over $150 Million | 8 | 2 | | | | | | | 10 |
| Over $100 Million | 6 | | | | | | | | 6 |
| Over $50 Million | 5 | | | | | | | | 5 |
| Over $10 Million | 1 | 1 | | | | | | | 2 |
| Under $10 Million | 2 | | | | | | | | 2 |
| Sales not reported | 3 | | | | | | | | 3 |
| | 36 | 9 | 6 | 2 | 0 | 2 | 0 | 1 | 56 |

Source: Author's Survey
Also excludes 5 banks, 1 university and 2 blank returns.

This stage of the study was disconcerting because it is generally accepted that in most firms the premium dollars spent on voluntary insurance programs total between 1 1/2 to 2 percent of gross sales.[3] In addition there are programs of assumption as well as involuntary insurance programs which can easily raise the total cost that organizations face to as much as 10 percent of gross sales.

## ONE-MAN DEPARTMENTS PREVALENT

What would knowledgeable stockholders think of a chief executive officer and his board of directors who permit the responsibility of millions of dollars to be handled by an understaffed one-man department? Or of the fact that these millions of dollars are often paid from a variety of departments of the firm with little or no centralized control. The difficulty

[3] Reavis, Marshall W. "Corporate Risk Manager's Contribution to Profit," *The Journal of Risk and Insurance,* Vol. 36, No. 4, Sept. 1969.

with the one-man department is that one individual cannot adequately keep track of the basic insurance problems today in the complexity of the organization and the world it operates in, let alone have time to be an analytical risk manager.

Our chart reveals that until the firm passed $400 million in sales, risk management is generally handled by one man. Beyond that point no definite pattern was revealed as departments ranged from one to eight members.

Perhaps then it is the duties of the risk manager that become significant to his role. What is he responsible for? Chart 3 indicates 100 percent of those reporting handled property and casualty insurance while only 60 percent were involved with insured employee benefits. Loss control and property preservation were handled by but one half of the departments.

In most undergraduate business schools curriculums for accounting, finance or personnel management do not require a course in Risk Management and Insurance. Neither does the CPA certification touch this area. Few law schools offer more than one or two insurance courses and they are electives. This would indicate that management is allowing a large number of unexposed individuals to process millions of dollars of voluntary and involuntary premiums.

It is questionable that a prudent chief executive would allow any other single area of organizational expenses to be scattered about the firm so recklessly. But what can be done? How does the risk manager become properly placed in the firm and adequately staffed?

## PROGRAM OF AWARENESS

Without question, top management must become fully aware of the importance of recognizing risk management within their organization. It would appear that only a direct continuing program to educate management can accomplish this. Unfortunately this must be done largely from outside the individual firm. Consideration must be given on a local and national basis to such a program of awareness. Local chapter functions designed to include top management is one recommended method.

Better education and training of current risk managers and their staffs is also a must. In addition to college curriculums in Risk Management and Insurance the industry offers a wealth of educational opportunities. The CPCU and CLU programs as well as the Associate in Risk Management program from the Insurance Institute of America are but a few of the offerings. Many seminars and programs are offered by the industry throughout the year. Successful completion of these programs are to the risk manager's benefit and can lead to personal recognition within the organization.

Our study revealed limited work with employee benefits by the risk managers. Perhaps it is time to invite those in the personnel areas to

CHART III

AREAS OF RESPONSIBILITY FOR RISK MANAGERS

| Responsibility | Number having Responsibility | % of Total Reporting |
|---|---|---|
| Property Insurance | 60 | 100 |
| Casualty Insurance | 60 | 100 |
| Insured Employee Benefits | 36 | 60 |
| Loss Control (safety) | 30 | 50 |
| Property Preservation | 34 | 56 |
| Pension | 17 | 28 |
| Profit Sharing | 5 | 8 |
| Stock Purchase Plans | 1 | 1.6 |

Source: Author's Survey

some insurance functions. This might enlighten some as to your qualifications to work with the benefit programs. Then the risk manager can become more than an "advisor" to the personnel staff.

The image of the risk manager must be transformed from one who only spends money (after all, what is the image of insurance to your chief executive within his own home) to one who has the ability to contribute to profits through new techniques and programs of risk management.

The risk manager must work toward developing the "static" risk management concept through studies and projects relating to this important phase of organization life. For example, examine the situation of the firm's decision to build a new plant. The person responsible for long range planning does studies on the need for production to meet the needs of sales forecasts and selects a size of plant to construct and its location. But what is the role of the risk manager? Management must realize that he is interested in the physical site, the history of natural disasters in the area, labor attitudes toward insured benefits and work injury claim, water supplies, transportation facilities, planned inter-plant interdependence, physical structure, size of work force, inventory storage and size, product line and hundreds of other areas which touch virtually every department of the firm.

It is difficult to perform this role locked beyond the myopic view of a financial department which is mainly concerned with obtaining and controlling the funds to pay for the new plant. And equally difficult for the risk manager to be effective after the fact.

However, until the risk manager can attain a position on the chief executive officer's staff he will have to continue to work around others, tactfully, and assist other departments in their work while continuing to be generally understaffed and awkwardly located on the organization chart.

Teddy Roosevelt once said, "Every man owes some part of his time to the building up of the industry or profession of which he is a part." It behooves all of us in risk management to heed his advice and through our individual, local or national efforts see that our profession succeeds.

## Questions

1. If, as concluded by the author, the academically defined risk manager "fails to exist in practice today except in very few organizations," what is the justification for studying risk management?
2. The author suggests that the management of employee benefits be placed with the risk manager. Discuss.

# 7. A RULE FOR LEAST COST SELECTION OF COLLISION DEDUCTIBLES

Alfred E. Hofflander †
and Lawrence L. Schkade ††

## INTRODUCTION

In the selection of deductible collision insurance a consumer, who has free choice of available deductible amounts, weighs the advantage of a reduction in premium for choosing a larger deductible against the disadvantage of sustaining a larger unindemnified loss in the event of a collision. The total expected cost of coverage for any selected deductible is the sum of the premium plus the expected outlay for unindemnified losses that are less than or equal to the deductible. In monetary terms, the optimal choice of deductible is the one for which total expected cost is a minimum.

A recent article in the *Journal of Risk and Insurance* [1] suggests that, from a purely monetary standpoint, insureds would be better off by purchasing a deductible which is larger than the one typically selected. In terms of deductible amounts, the study indicates that in the vast majority of cases, total expected cost is minimized for deductibles of $100 or more. In more than half of the rating areas analyzed, a deductible of $150 or more is suggested to minimize total cost, whereas a deductible of $50 is indicated only for vehicles in the lowest original price range and located in rating areas with unusually high premium rates.

Over the nation, an overwhelming majority of owners continue to choose $50 or $100 deductible coverage for their automobiles with approximately half of the premium volume arising from the purchase of

* From *The Annals of the Society of Chartered Property and Casualty Underwriters* (March, 1967), pp. 5-17. Reprinted by permission.

† Assistant Professor of Insurance, University of California at Los Angeles.

†† Professor of Business Administration, The University of Texas at Arlington.

[1] Lawrence L. Schkade and George H. Menefee. "A Normative Model for Deductible Collision Insurance Selection," *Journal of Risk and Insurance*, Vol. XXXIII, No. 3 (September, 1966), p. 427.

$50 deductible coverage.[2] The results of the study cited above indicate that the majority of owners do not select deductibles that minimize total expected cost. In effect, individuals who choose deductibles that are smaller than the optimal choice are paying an additional price for coverage.

Several criteria can be suggested to explain why individuals do not select deductible coverage from the point of view of minimizing the expected total dollar outlay for coverage. First, an individual may select a small deductible in order to avoid a more sizeable unplanned outlay in the event of a collision loss, especially if income is heavily committed and personal liquidity is limited. Second, limits may be placed on the range of deductible amounts from which an individual may choose. There is a tendency for the holders of liens on vehicles to restrict an individual's selection of coverage to deductible amounts of $100 or less. Third, a person may choose a deductible by adding the premium and deductible amounts for available choices and selecting the deductible amount for which this sum is a minimum. This well established rule of thumb results in selecting a deductible that is smaller than the one for which total expected cost is a minimum. Finally, the purchase of a small deductible may reflect imperfect knowledge of the range of available choices of collision insurance. For example, while $75 and $150 deductible coverages are available generally, less than one percent of insureds select these amounts.

While the selection of deductible coverage by individuals may be considered rational on the basis of any of several criteria, it would appear that there exists a sizeable group of people who would seek to minimize total expected cost and choose a larger deductible if the optimal deductible were known. Part I of this study presents an easily applied rule for determining the optimal deductible for any selected collision risk in any rating area. This rule provides the basis for improving the service rendered by agents and companies in marketing collision insurance, because now consumers can be provided with more complete economic information with which to select deductibles that are more consistent with their personal financial positions and views toward the assumption or aversion of risk.

Assuming that the application of the rule would suggest a larger deductible than is currently chosen by many consumers, Part II of this paper examines the attitudes of agents and companies toward the selection of larger deductibles. This analysis provides the basis for conclusions concerning the potential benefits that would accrue to customers, agents and underwriters through the selection of deductibles that minimize total expected cost.

[2] For states under the jurisdiction of the National Automobile Underwriters Association, $50 and $100 deductible policies account for about 99 percent of the total private passenger business. In 1958, 66 percent of vehicles were insured with $50 deductible policies; in 1962 the volume dropped to 56 percent. In recent years, the volume of $25 deductible policies has decreased markedly, while the selection of $250 deductibles has increased slightly.

## A SIMPLE RULE FOR OPTIMAL DEDUCTIBLE SELECTION

The purchase of collision insurance reflects the inclination of vehicle owners to avert the risk of loss from collision damage. In most cases, people do not insure collision losses fully, but elect to assume a portion of the loss by selecting a fixed deductible amount in order to reduce the premium payment. In selecting deductible coverage, one pays out the premium amount and assumes the risk of sustaining losses that are less than the deductible plus the risk of incurring a loss of the amount of deductible if collision damage exceeds the deductible. The outlay for coverage, therefore, may be expressed as the total expected cost for coverage for the insured period, which may be written

Total Expected Cost = Premium + Expected Unindemnified Loss.

The expected unindemnified loss varies with the driver of the vehicle, the value of the vehicle, and the experience of the rating area in which the vehicle is driven. This expected loss is always less than the deductible amount as seen in the following example. Suppose a deductible of $50 is selected. The expected loss in the event of a single collision is the average of all possible losses which the insured can sustain. If the collision damage is less than $50, the loss is sustained by the owner, but if collision damage exceeds the deductible, the owner sustains a $50 loss. The average or expected loss is less than $50, for if one averages a set of values, some of which are less than $50 and the remainder are equal to $50, the average will be less than $50.

In selecting deductible coverage, one exchanges the reduction in premium in choosing a larger deductible for the likelihood of incurring a larger loss in the event of a collision. The rate of exchange is reflected in the inverse relationship between premium and deductible amounts. The total expected cost associated with various available deductible amounts can be computed, provided credible experience data are available for the rating area. In most instances, however, loss experience data for local rating areas lack credibility and are not sufficiently complete for computing the loss frequency or the expected unindemnified loss. Fortunately, these values can be derived from the relationship between premium and deductible amounts. The results of this derivation are summarized here, for the complete derivation is too lengthy for purposes of this discussion. The essence of the derivation is summarized as follows:

1. Let q denote the relative frequency of collision loss for the period of a year.
2. The expected unindemnified loss, while less than the deductible (D), is approximated closely by the amount (D) for deductible amounts most commonly selected.
3. The premium amount ($R_D$) varies inversely with the deductible (D), for the larger the deductible, the smaller the premium.
4. The expected outlay in the event of a collision may be written

$$q(D + R_D).$$

In words, the expected outlay is the collision loss frequency times the amounts paid, deductible plus premium, if collision loss is sustained.

5. The expected outlay if no collision occurs may be written

$$(1 - q)R_D.$$

This states that, if no collision occurs, the expected outlay is the likelihood that no collision will occur times the premium.

6. Total expected cost is the sum of the premium plus the expected unindemnified loss and is approximated by

$$TEC = R_D + qD. \tag{1}$$

In words, expression (1) states that total expected cost (TEC) is equal to the premium ($R_D$) for a given deductible (D) plus the expected number (q) of collisions during the period of a year times the selected deductible (D). The average value of the expected number of collisions during the period of a year is estimated to be 0.20.[3] The rule stated by expression (1) may be applied for an average risk as follows:

1. Obtain the premium amounts for all available deductibles for a given risk from the automobile physical damage manual (as determined by vehicle valuation, age and use).
2. Multiply each deductible amount by the collision probability (q) to obtain qD.
3. Add the corresponding values of premium ($R_D$) and expected unindemnified loss (qD) for each available deductible to obtain the total expected cost.
4. Determine the optimal deductible by identifying the smaller value of total expected cost (TEC).

This procedure is illustrated by use of the deductible and premium data for a typical class of risk with an average probability of collision occurrence of 0.20. The selected risk is a private passenger vehicle with driver class 2A, symbol class J-K, age groups 2 and 3, rating area 23, State of Illinois. The available deductible amounts and corresponding premium rates for 1963 for this risk are used to compute the total expected cost. The premium rate for \$25 deductible coverage is \$101.00, as shown in Table 1. The total expected cost for a collision probability of 0.20 is found by computing

$$
\begin{aligned}
TEC &= R + qD \\
&= \$101.00 + (0.20)\,(\$25) \\
&= \$101.00 + \$5.00 \\
&= \$106.00
\end{aligned}
$$

The value of \$106.00, which appears in Table 1, corresponds to a deductible of \$25 and a value of q = 0.20. Similarly, the total expected cost of selecting a deductible of \$250 for the same risk and a probability of 0.20 is computed

---

[3] This value is derived from 1960-62 experience data for states under the jurisdiction of the National Automobile Underwriters Association. The same result was obtained for a cross section of rating areas over the nation. An example of the method for obtaining values of q is shown by Schkade and Menefee, *Op. Cit.*

$$TEC = R + qD$$
$$= \$26.00 + (0.20)(\$250)$$
$$= \$26.00 + \$50.00$$
$$= \$76.00$$

The total expected cost values for all deductible choices for the risk in this example, assuming a collision probability of 0.20, are shown in Table 1, Col. (5). The minimum value, indicated by an asterisk, corresponds to a deductible of $100. Total expected cost data for a range of values of collision probability are also computed and presented in Table 1, Cols. (3)-(7). This is done because the collision probability varies from driver to driver (within a rating area) as well as from one rating area to another for the same driver.

Variation in total expected cost for relatively low valued vehicles (symbol class A-G) and relatively higher valued vehicles (symbol class N-O) for a range of values of q also are shown in Table 1. These data illustrate the effects of vehicle valuation, driver class, and collision probability on least total expected cost. The optimal deductibles range from the extremes of a $50 deductible for the lowest valued vehicle with the highest collision frequency (least total expected cost of $35.50 and $38.00 for vehicle symbol class A-G for values of q of 0.25 and 0.30, respectively) to a deductible of $250 for the highest valued vehicle with the lowest collision frequency selected for this example (least total cost of $79.00 and $91.50 for vehicle symbol class N-O for values of 0.10 and 0.15 respectively).

## TABLE 1

### TOTAL EXPECTED COST OF PREMIUM PLUS DEDUCTIBLE

| Classification of Risk | Deduc- tible | Pre- mium | Probability of Collision Loss | | | | |
| --- | --- | --- | --- | --- | --- | --- | --- |
| | | | 0.10 | 0.15 | 0.20 | 0.25 | 0.30 |
| | (1) | (2) | (3) | (4) | (5) | (6) | (7) |
| Symbol Class A-G | | | | | | | |
| Age Group 4, | $ 25 | $ 36.80 | $ 39.30 | $ 40.25 | $ 41.80 | $ 43.05 | $ 44.30 |
| Driver Class 1 | 50 | 23.00 | 28.00 | 30.50 | 33.00 | 35.50 * | 38.00* |
| | 75 | 17.50 | 25.00 | 28.75 | 32.50 | 36.25 | 40.00 |
| | 100 | 12.00 | 22.00* | 27.00* | 32.00* | 37.00 | 42.00 |
| | 150 | 10.00 | 25.00 | 32.50 | 40.00 | 47.50 | 55.00 |
| | 250 | 8.00 | 33.00 | 45.50 | 58.00 | 70.50 | 83.00 |
| | 500 | 5.40 | 55.40 | 80.40 | 105.40 | 129.40 | 154.40 |
| Symbol Class J-K | 25 | 101.00 | 103.50 | 104.25 | 106.90 | 107.25 | 108.50 |
| Age Groups 2, 3, | 50 | 63.00 | 68.00 | 70.50 | 73.00 | 75.50 | 78.00 |
| Driver Class 2A | 75 | 53.00 | 60.50 | 64.25 | 68.00 | 71.75 | 75.50 |
| | 100 | 43.00 | 53.00 | 58.00 | 63.00* | 68.00* | 73.00* |
| | 150 | 34.00 | 49.00* | 56.50* | 64.00 | 71.50 | 79.00 |
| | 250 | 26.00 | 51.00 | 63.50 | 76.00 | 88.50 | 101.00 |
| | 500 | 19.40 | 69.40 | 94.40 | 119.40 | 144.40 | 169.40 |
| Symbol Class N-O | | 204.00 | 206.50 | 207.75 | 209.00 | 210.25 | 211.50 |
| Age Group 1, | 50 | 128.00 | 133.00 | 135.50 | 138.00 | 140.50 | 143.00 |
| Driver Class 2C | 75 | 108.00 | 115.50 | 119.25 | 123.00 | 126.75 | 130.50 |
| | 100 | 88.00 | 98.00 | 103.00 | 108.00 | 113.00 | 118.00 |
| | 150 | 70.00 | 85.00 | 92.50 | 100.00* | 107.50* | 115.00* |
| | 250 | 54.00 | 79.00* | 91.50* | 104.00 | 116.50 | 129.00 |
| | 500 | 39.60 | 89.60 | 114.60 | 139.60 | 164.60 | 189.60 |

The total expected cost data in Table 1 are obtained by use of the simple rule that yields conservative approximations. In other words, the values of total expected cost are overstated, since it is assumed that the average unindemnified loss is equal to the deductible (*i.e.*, every collision will result in a loss at least as large as the deductible). In reality, the average unindemnified loss is less than the deductible, and the difference becomes more pronounced for larger deductibles. Consequently, the total expected cost values are actually less than the ones shown in Table 1. The optimal deductibles indicated by Table 1, however, suggest the selection of larger deductibles than typically are purchased. These recommendations are conservative, since total expected costs are overstated.

The values of total expected cost that correspond more closely to actual values are shown in Table 2. These values are obtained by use of an appropriate fraction of deductible amounts in the computations.[4] For example, the expected unindemnified loss for a deductible of $100 is 88 percent of the deductible. This amount is substituted into expression (1) to solve for the total expected cost for vehicle symbol class A-G and collision probability of 0.15 to give

$$
\begin{aligned}
\text{TEC} &= R + qD(0.88) \\
&= \$12.00 + (0.15)\,(\$100)\,(0.88) \\
&= \$12.00 + \$13.20 \\
&= \$25.20
\end{aligned}
$$

This value of $25.20 is shown in Table 2 and is comparable to the corresponding total expected cost of $27.00 shown in Table 1. By either method a deductible of $100 is shown to be the optimal choice for the selected risk and collision probability.

The differences in the computed results are more pronounced for the higher valued vehicle and for larger deductibles. For example, the expected unindemnified loss for a deductible of $500 is approximately 48 percent of the deductible. This amount is included in the use of the expression (1) to solve for the total expected cost for vehicle symbol class N-O and a collision probability of 0.20 to give

$$
\begin{aligned}
\text{TEC} &= R + qD(0.48) \\
&= \$39.60 + (0.20)\,(\$500)\,(0.48) \\
&= \$39.60 + \$48.00 \\
&= \$87.60
\end{aligned}
$$

This value of $87.60 is shown in Table 2 and is compared with the corresponding total expected cost value of $139.00, shown in Table 1. The minimum of the more precise values in Table 2 for a value of q of 0.20 corresponds to a deductible of $500, while the optimal deductible suggested by the approximate least total expected cost value in Table 1 for a value of q of 0.20 is $100.00 and corresponds to a deductible of $150.

---

[4] Values of appropriate fractions of deductible amounts can be obtained from loss experience data as illustrated by Schkade and Menefee, *Ibid.*

The use of the approximation method, in which the expected unindemnified loss is assumed to be equal to the deductible, has the advantage of suggesting conservative deductible amounts. The more valuable the vehicle, the more conservative the recommendation. In this manner, the approximate method has an intrinsic hedge against the assumption of inordinately large risks by the insured.

TABLE 2
TOTAL EXPECTED COST OF PREMIUM PLUS PROBABLE LOSS
WITHIN DEDUCTIBLE

| Classification of Risk | Deductible | Premium | Probability of Collision Loss | | | | |
|---|---|---|---|---|---|---|---|
| | | | 0.10 | 0.15 | 0.20 | 0.25 | 0.30 |
| (1) | | (2) | (3) | (4) | (5) | (6) | (7) |
| Symbol Class A-G, | $ 25 | $ 36.80 | $ 39.30 | $ 40.55 | $ 41.80 | $ 43.05 | $ 44.30 |
| Age Group 4, | 50 | 23.00 | 27.90 | 30.35 | 32.80 | 35.25 | 37.70 |
| Driver Class 1 | 75 | 17.50 | 24.48 | 27.96 | 31.44 | 34.92 | 38.40* |
| | 100 | 12.00 | 20.80* | 25.20* | 29.60* | 34.00* | 38.40* |
| | 150 | 10.00 | 22.45 | 28.68 | 34.91 | 41.14 | 47.37 |
| | 250 | 8.00 | 25.50 | 34.25 | 43.00 | 51.75 | 60.50 |
| | 500 | 5.40 | 29.40 | 41.40 | 53.40 | 65.40 | 77.40 |
| Symbol Class J-K | 25 | 101.00 | 103.50 | 104.75 | 106.00 | 107.25 | 108.50 |
| Age Groups 2, 3, | 50 | 63.00 | 67.90 | 70.35 | 72.80 | 75.25 | 77.70 |
| Driver Class 2A | 75 | 53.00 | 59.98 | 63.46 | 66.94 | 70.42 | 73.90 |
| | 100 | 43.00 | 51.80 | 56.20 | 60.60 | 65.00* | 69.40* |
| | 150 | 34.00 | 46.45 | 52.68 | 58.91* | 65.14 | 71.37 |
| | 250 | 26.00 | 43.50 | 52.25* | 61.00 | 69.75 | 78.50 |
| | 500 | 19.40 | 43.40* | 55.40 | 67.40 | 79.40 | 91.40 |
| Symbol Class N-O | 25 | 204.00 | 206.50 | 207.75 | 209.00 | 210.25 | 211.50 |
| Age Group 1, | 50 | 128.00 | 132.90 | 135.35 | 137.80 | 140.25 | 142.70 |
| Driver Class 2C | 75 | 108.00 | 114.98 | 118.46 | 121.94 | 125.42 | 128.90 |
| | 100 | 88.00 | 96.80 | 101.20 | 105.60 | 110.00 | 114.40 |
| | 150 | 70.00 | 82.45 | 88.68 | 94.91 | 101.14 | 107.37 |
| | 250 | 54.00 | 71.50 | 80.25 | 89.00 | 97.75* | 106.50* |
| | 500 | 39.60 | 63.60* | 75.60* | 87.60* | 99.60 | 111.60 |

Since insurance "costs something" in that insureds must pay for the cost of company and agency operation, the *long run* minimum expected cost for an insured who has average or better than average loss probability as compared to his rate class is at the point where no insurance is purchased. Many, if not most, individuals, however, exhibit an aversion to risk and hence purchase some collision insurance. The approximation method, in reality, points out the least total expected cost value over the range of deductibles available from $25 to $500. This minimum value of total expected cost corresponds to the deductible for which there is an equal trade-off between the conditional expected cost in the event of a collision and the conditional expected cost should no collision occur.

In summary, the simple rule for selecting deductibles can be applied readily to data obtained from the physical damage manual, given a range of collision probabilities, to indicate to consumers the deductible for which the expected cost should no collision occur is equal to the expected cost should collision damage be incurred.

## INDUSTRY VIEWS ON DEDUCTIBLE SELECTION

While it can be expected that many consumers would utilize the knowledge of optimal deductibles determined by use of the total expected cost minimizing rule, the potential use of this rationale is contingent upon its acceptance by the insurance industry. The attitudes of agents and insurers toward deductible selection are of considerable interest, for many consumers are likely to be influenced by these views. In an effort to gain insight into these views, a survey of agents and companies was conducted. A series of questions concerning aspects of deductible selection by consumers was asked.

### Agents' Attitudes on Larger Deductibles

A sample of forty-five agents was selected and semi-structured interviews were conducted with each. The responses elicited in the interviews touched on a broad range of considerations. The responses of greatest interest are those related to the selection of deductibles by consumers and the influence of agents in the selection process. These responses to selected questions asked during the interviews are summarized briefly in the following paragraphs.

*If a client has no stated preference, what deductible do you recommend? Why?*

The overwhelming majority of agents recommended a $100 deductible. The major reason stated was the difference in premium cost to the insured *vs.* the difference in coverage. Agents emphasized, however, that they had strong reservations about recommending one deductible over another for fear of hostility on the part of the client when a loss occurs. Most agents were cognizant of the paradox that exists in that the insured who could least afford to bear a large deductible was also the one who could least afford to pay the higher premium associated with the smaller deductible. Many noted that the size of the deductible was also a function of the age and value of the car. Higher deductibles were also recommended on older and less expensive cars.[5] Agents also pointed out that a point is soon reached where the client is best served by having no collision insurance at all.

A small minority of agents felt that the client generally was best off with a $50 deductible. Occasionally a $100 deductible is suggested by these agents, but *never* one over $100. The philosophy here is that the client dislikes having to absorb any of the cost of an accident, and the higher the deductible, the unhappier he becomes with the agent.

---

[5] This advice is *not* consistent with the results of Tables 1 and 2, and probably occurs because insureds and agents tend to look at total premiums (physical damage plus liability) for an automobile. When the total cost begins to appear high, relative to the value of the car, some coverage must be dropped. Since the liability is almost mandatory, the collision insurance is dropped.

*What do you feel would be the effect of clients' choosing the next larger deductible than is currently selected?*

The majority of agents indicated that the company(s) they represent do not seem to prefer one deductible over another. Several companies, however, do not issue policies with deductibles of less than $50. Two companies represented by agents interviewed strongly encourage a deductible of $100. Some agents intimated that companies they represent apparently fear government intervention if only high deductibles were available. This feeling is based on the anticipation that if only large deductibles are available, the public may feel that it is not covered adequately because of insufficient indemnification for losses resulting from being forced to choose too large a deductible.

## Insurance Companies' Attitudes Toward Deductibles

Thirty executives of major insurance companies were sent letters which contained questions concerning the possible effects of a shift to larger deductibles and any preference their company might have for any particular deductibles. The responses to these questions are summarized briefly.

*What effect would a market shift toward the selection of larger deductibles have on the marketing and operational aspects of your company?*

Strikingly similar responses were received from the executives. Nearly all who responded felt that a change to a higher deductible on an industry-wide scale would have little effect on their operations. They felt that premium rates would adjust to reflect the changed experience in both losses and expenses. The total premium dollars would decrease with the change, but new business, which had been self-insuring (sic), would be attracted back to the market. Claim costs would be lowered somewhat by the change, but not to any significant degree since many of the costs of handling a claim are constant, regardless of the deductible. The expected final result is that total premium volume would decrease very little and that chances of profitability to the industry would be enhanced.

A minority of executives expressed the view that the purchase of higher deductibles by the general public would cause less favorable experience, and thus shift the price upward eliminating the price advantage to the buyer. A factor which would tend to propel the rate upward is the temptation to pad collision damages to absorb the deductible. Further, encouraging the purchase of higher deductibles would simply create another problem for the industry as the point was approached where the industry would be failing properly to service the average insurance buyer.

*Does your company have any preference regarding deductible amounts? If so, why?*

Most respondents agreed that from a company standpoint, they did not favor a specific deductible. Nearly all recognized the move to higher deductibles as a trend in consumer preference, with the $100 deductible becoming the most popular. However, nearly all emphasized that consumer preference should be the guiding factor, and that the economic condition of the insured should determine the size of the deductible. Some stated that due to the preference of finance companies, the $50 deductible was "pushed."

Everyone felt that deductibles were necessary to prevent insurance being used for the purpose of maintenance. However, there was a wide range of reasons for choosing one deductible over the other and for the general tendency to move to a higher deductible. Some respondents felt that the savings in premium dollars would not compensate for the increased losses to the insured, especially if he were unfortunate enough to have two losses in one year. Some felt that the lower ($50) deductible gave a sense of security to the insured since he would lose very little financially in the event of a loss. Others expressed the opinion that the driver who chose a higher deductible was more careful because he had the chance of a considerable economic loss in the event of a collision. However, one executive mentioned that the experience so far with the largest deductibles was not adequate to base decisions as to the advantages of the higher deductible to both the insured and the company.

## SUMMARY AND CONCLUSIONS

Recent research in the behavior of consumers in the selection of collision insurance indicates that the majority of insureds purchase deductibles that are smaller than the ones that correspond to least total expected cost. It can be assumed that a sizeable portion of insureds do consider cost in the selection of deductibles and would select deductibles that are more consistent with least total expected cost if this information were available.

A simple rule can be employed to compute the approximate value of the deductible for which total expected cost is a minimum. This rule provides conservative recommendations, for it assumes that every loss is equal to or greater than the deductible with the resulting overstatement of the consequences of choosing too large a deductible. This rule provides the basis for finding a table of total expected cost values that relate to a given risk. The relative magnitude of total expected cost values for alternative deductible choices provides information with which a consumer can evaluate the economic consequences of selecting a particular deductible.

The responses of agents and insurance company executives to a possible increase in the amount of deductible selected by customers indicate that the recommendation of larger deductibles is valid on theoretical and practical grounds. Agents tend to be reluctant to make such recommendations, however, for fear of being held responsible by the consumer for a larger loss in the event of a claim. Insurance companies apparently would benefit from the selection of larger deductibles by insureds, for claim frequency would decline and claim costs and adjustment expense would be reduced. The vast majority of persons interviewed indicated that the consumer should have freedom of choice in the selection of deductibles.

The agent and the company can benefit from providing the consumer with economic information with which to select coverage that is more consistent with his financial position and preference for averting or partially assuming loss. It would seem that a company could adopt a marketing strategy for capturing a larger segment of the higher deductible business by use of the results obtained from the application of total expected cost rule. First, it should emphasize the savings which accrue to the insured through the use of higher deductible (showing tables similar to Tables 1 and 2 in this article). Second, it should overcome concern regarding personal liquidity by agreeing to lend the insured an amount of money equal to the deductible in case of large losses (at a reasonable rate of interest). This also would go a long way towards convincing prospective insureds that companies have their best interests at heart. Finally, it seems that both companies and agents must be more forceful in advising clients regarding their best deductible buy. The agent's commission is partially justified on the basis of increased service. A major part of this service should be accurate advice regarding deductibles. The information provided by the application of the least total expected cost rule can enable agents and companies to advise clients in the selection of deductibles that are more consistent with their financial position and their preference for averting or partially assuming the risk of collision loss.

## Questions

1. What is the basic difference between data presented in Table 1 and Table 2?
2. The total expected cost of premium plus probable loss within the deductible as listed in Tables 1 and 2 for various deductible amounts starts high for small deductible amounts, decreases, and then increases again for very large deductibles. The decision rule stated by the authors is to choose that deductible amount for which this cost is the smallest, i.e., the low point on the total expected cost curve. Why does not the curve keep going down over the entire range, or start low and go up throughout the range?
3. Develop and discuss your decision rule with respect to how old a car must be before collision insurance is dropped.

# 8. "PROPER" LIMITS IN LIABILITY INSURANCE—A PROBLEM IN "DECISION MAKING UNDER UNCERTAINTY" *

Bob A. Hedges †

The problem of proper selection of policy limits in buying liability insurance is both chronic and epidemic; recurrent and widespread. Proposed cures for it are like those for the common cold, most of them have been heard many times, and none of them can be counted upon to work most of the time.

What is here suggested is an *approach*. The theory here employed comes from a recent body of study and thought about business problems, a body called "decision theory." It is a contemporary effort to apply the knowns of logic and mathematics in a systematic and usable way to the unknowns in business situations. The branch of decision theory to be drawn upon uses probability and statistics to aid in making business decisions under conditions of uncertainty. Certainly the problem of selecting proper limits in one's liability insurance is a problem in this category!

## PREREQUISITES

To apply decision theory to this problem, three things are needed:

(1) A measure of the relative ultimate financial effects of different sizes of liability losses.[1]

(2) A probability distribution on these losses.

(3) The cost of insuring against various liability contingencies.

Possessing these three things, it would be possible to use the probability distribution to evaluate the total financial importance of the losses. Then this effect could be measured against the financial importance of the insurance premium, and the lesser evil selected.

Contemporary decision theory will suggest a way to get a measure of the effects of losses. Dr. Rennie has just suggested a basic form or model for the distribution of losses. The cost of insuring is a figure which can be obtained.

* From *The Journal of Risk and Insurance* (June, 1961), pp. 71-76. Reprinted by permission.
† Associate Professor of Finance, University of Illinois.
[1] The term "liability losses," as here used, includes all costs and outlays directly due to a claim that one is liable for damage or injury.

Robert Schlaifer, in the second chapter of his *Probability and Statistics for Business Decisions*,[2] presents a series of "utility scales" for evaluating gains and losses. This analysis is not easy reading, but it demands only "college algebra" as a mathematical background. The method requires, first, that the decision-maker place a dollar figure on the best event that can happen. With respect to liability losses, the best possible result is zero. But what is the worst? To many people, that "worst" figure is exactly the subject of this paper. For these persons, the worst possible liability loss is the amount of liability insurance which should be carried.

This question can be solved by adopting another standard for "worst": the worst possible loss, it is assumed, is the loss of the business. In lieu of the loss of a certain number of dollars, the descriptive phrase, "the business goes into receivership," will be used as the extent of the "worst possible loss."

The next step is to consider the following question: If the decision-maker, were thrust into a situation which confronted him with a 50 percent probability that his business would be bankrupt tomorrow, how much would he be willing to pay to get out of that situation? One thousand dollars? One million dollars? Something in between? Suppose the answer in a given case is $500,000.

Now consider, successively, other probability figures for the same disastrous event. Since these probabilities are small, consider such chances of total loss as one percent, one-half of one percent, one-tenth, one-fiftieth, one-one hundredth, and so on. For each probability figure, decide on a fixed price equivalent.

Among the practical problems involved here is the difficulty of thinking concretely about figures like "one-tenth of one percent" and "one-one hundredth of one percent." How can one get any real feel for abstract quantities like these? This visualization may be tried.

## AN ILLUSTRATION

Imagine 10 urns, each containing 100 marbles, well stirred. One is required to select one of the 10 urns and to draw from it one marble. If the marble is black, the task is over. But if the marble is red, tomorrow his business will be in the hands of the receivers. Suppose he knows that the total number of red marbles in the 10 urns is 100. How much would he pay to get out of the game before drawing? Suppose that he knows the total number of red marbles is 10, how much would he pay to get out? Suppose the number were known to be one? Thus can 1.0, 0.1, and 0.01 percent be presented in a manner which gives some "feel" to them.

Suppose that the decision-maker finally comes up with the set of answers presented in Table 1.

---

[2] New York: McGraw-Hill Book Co., Inc., 1939.

TABLE 1

A SET OF VALUES ON PROBABILITIES OF LOSS OF BUSINESS

| Probability of Loss of Business | Fixed Dollar Equivalent |
|---|---|
| 30.00% | $500,000 |
| 20.00% | 300,000 |
| 10.00% | 125,000 |
| 1.00% | 12,000 |
| 0.50% | 5,000 |
| 0.10% | 1,000 |
| 0.01% | 100 |

Now a reasonable estimate of the present going-concern value of the business is required. For an example, assume this value to be one million dollars.

The next question is, how *small* a sum of liability losses over a year (or other approximate period) could cause this business to be thrown into receivership? The answer depends on all the usual considerations in financial analysis: current ratio, acid-test ratio, cash balance; asset turnover, receivables turnover, inventory turnover, cash flow; operating ratio, equity ratio, number of times fixed charges are earned; credit lines, present and potential; attitude, ability and flexibility of management; and so on. One thing is sure: an unexpected cash loss of considerably less than $1 million can wreck a business worth a million. For this example, suppose the crucial liability loss figure is best estimated as $500,000.

But consider the effect of a loss of $490,000, or even $400,000? Are the real costs, the ultimate financial effects, of losses below the crucial figure to be taken at their face amount, with a sudden jump in their effect when the crucial five-hundred-thousandth dollar is added? Clearly not. It follows that there is need for a whole set of relationships between size of liability loss—defined as total *direct* cost and outlay caused by the claim—and size of ultimate financial effect on the business firm.

## TYPICAL CHARACTERISTICS

All that will be attempted here is to suggest some of the characteristics likely to be found in such a set of relationships:

(1) There will be a range of relatively small losses which have no particularly disturbing effects on the firm's finances beyond their direct costs.

(2) Beyond this comes a range in which the effect can reasonably be estimated by adding to the direct loss a figure which represents the cost of going to the money market for the additional funds needed.

(3) Beyond this, the picture gets complicated. As losses get bigger and bigger they have even more and more serious effects on the ability

to finance the firm's regular operations, for they disarrange cash flows and exhaust credit lines.

An example of such a function can be adopted for the business concern being used for this example. Suppose that over a period of a year it can handle liability losses up to $10,000 without any strain on its resources. In the range, $10,000 to $100,000, it would have to pay for extra money at an average rate of 4 percent, and would need to borrow the money for a length of time proportionate to the amount borrowed. Beyond $100,000, the financial effects of loss increase rapidly, until for a $500,000 direct loss the ultimate damage is $1,000,000—the value of the business.

## A CRUCIAL THEOREM

Now comes the crucial theorem in decision theory. Its explanation appears in an appendix at the end of this paper. Its operation will be illustrated in connection with this example. Suppose the probability distribution on losses for this company shows a probability of 1 percent that losses for a year will come to $10,000.[3] Table 1 shows that $10,000 lies between the $12,000 value placed on a ruin probability of 1 percent and the $5,000 value placed on a ruin probability of 0.5 percent. Various reasonable methods of interpolation are possible; suppose that an appropriate one gives $10,000 as equivalent to 0.85 percent probability of ruin. Now there is produced an abstract figure which represents the "utility" (disutility) to the business of the 1 percent chance of having the year's losses produce $10,000 of damage to the firm's finances. This figure is secured by multiplying the 1 percent chance of a $10,000 direct loss by the 0.85 percent derived from Table 1, and getting 0.85 as this abstract measure, or index.

Suppose that in this business a year's losses totaling $100,000 would have a financial effect of $120,000 because of the cost of borrowing $90,000. Interpolating again in Table 1, $120,000 can be said to be about equivalent to 9 percent chance of ruin. If the chance of the $100,000 direct loss is, say, 0.5 percent, 0.5 is multiplied by 9 and the product, 4.5, is the measure of the relative importance of this particular possibility to this given business. When all the index figures so obtained (one for each possible size of loss) are added, the result is an index of the total undesirability of carrying this risk.[4]

But the question under consideration is not *whether* to insure, but *how much*. Suppose some particular amount of insurance, say $100,000, were carried. Then the premium on the policy would be a "loss" of that amount with a "probability" of 100 percent that it would be lost. By

---

[3] The actual distribution of losses will be continuous, of course, with probability figures applying only over ranges of loss figures, not to particular figures. But in an illustrative example, no damage is done by speaking as though certain individual figures did have probabilities of occurrence.

[4] Since the distribution is continuous the process is integration rather than summation.

going through Table 1 an index figure can be secured to represent the "undesirability" or "disutility" of this outlay. To this must be added an index value for the amounts by which losses may exceed the insurance. The sum of these two figures is the total index for this insurance. This can be compared with the index value previously obtained for the total risk, and the smaller index number will represent the lesser evil. Comparisons for different amounts of insurance then need to be made to search out the lowest over-all figure.

### SUMMARY

The entire procedure is reviewed as follows:

(1) The decision-maker needs to determine what it is worth to him to avoid various probabilities of ruin to his business.

(2) The true financial effects of different dollar amounts of loss in a given business must be discovered, with particular attention to the smallest amount of loss which will bankrupt the business.

(3) A probability distribution on the losses must be obtained.

(4) From Step 1 a table of dollar values and probabilities is developed.

(5) From Step 2 a set of dollar values is secured. Taking these to the table of Step 4, the dollar values are converted to probability figures.

(6) The probability figure obtained from Step 5 is multiplied by the probability figure from Step 3 to get an index of the "importance" or "onerousness" of each loss probability.

(7) The figures obtained in Step 6 are cumulated over the entire range of losses to get the index for noninsurance.

(8) Index figures are developed for different amounts of insurance, using premium-plus-uninsured losses here as losses alone were used to get the index for noninsurance.

(9) The lowest index from Steps 7 to 8 is then selected.

Perhaps a few words are in order about probability distributions on losses. Lacking better evidence (or any evidence at all!), the "log normal" distribution can be adopted as representative. Any normal distribution has two free parameters, its mean and its standard deviation. One must use any possible clue to these. For the mean, in a given case, one could adopt the fire insurance rating philosophy, which holds that direct engineering analysis of the hazards of a given situation provides a basis for arriving at an informed judgment of the extent to which that situation differs from the average for its class. Some statistical help may be available, such as data on the difference in size of dollar claims for similar injuries—for example, a public utility may find itself paying 50 percent more for simple leg fractures than local retail merchants have to pay. Or a chemical manufacturer may find his claims frequency is twice that of a machinery manufacturer. From relationships such as these, individual businesses' loss distributions may be deduced from general averages.

For the standard deviation, it would be expected that the figure for a general class would be close, although it might be better to take the standard deviation as a percentage of the mean rather than as an absolute figure.

If one can assume in advance the nature of the distribution (such as that it is "log normal"), small quantities of data gain considerably in usefulness. And if one is investigating the behavior of a sum of several losses, such as all the losses in a year, rather than the behavior of the values of losses individually, then reasonable guesses become even more possible.

Two related questions still remain. Will such elaborate machinery for decision making actually produce better results than the methods presently in use, whatever they may be? More important, will results from the new methods be sufficiently better to justify the considerably greater cost involved? These are basic questions.

## APPENDIX

The special theorem referred to, depends on the following three assumptions:

I. A smaller probability of losing K dollars is always preferred to a larger probability of losing K dollars (where the differences in probabilities are the only differences between the two situations).

II. Outlay of a smaller sum is always preferred to outlay of a larger sum (where the differences in outlays are the only differences between the two situations).

III. If a man is indifferent between two options A and B and also between options B and C, he will then be indifferent between A and C.

The argument proceeds as follows:

Suppose indifference is established as between the following choices, which together shall be called Pair A:

(1) Pay X dollars.

(2) Draw from an urn containing 100 balls, $k$ of them red, the rest black. The business is lost if a red ball is drawn.

Now consider the choices in Pair B:

(1) A roulette wheel is spun and if one certain specified number comes up, no losses or costs are suffered. If any other number comes up, X dollars are paid.

(2) The same wheel is spun and if one of the same previously specified numbers comes up, no losses or costs are suffered. If any other number comes up, draw from the urn with $k$ red and $100 - k$ black balls, the business being lost if a red ball is drawn.

Each of the choices in Pair B offers the same chance at an identical result (no outlay) and each offers the same chance at results different in form but in the opinion of the decision-maker, not different in worth.

Therefore, it is argued, the decision-maker who is indifferent as between the choices in Pair A is also indifferent as between the choices in Pair B. Furthermore, let the probability of a "bad" number on the roulette wheel (a number which costs X dollars in Choice 1 or causes a draw from the urn in Choice 2) be $q$. Then Pair B is identical to Pair BB described below, and indifference between the choices in B is indifference as between the choices in BB.

Pair BB:
Choice 1: Probability $q$ that X dollars will have to be paid.
Choice 2: Probability $q \times k$ that the business will be lost.

Now suppose the decision-maker furnishes a whole collection of pairs like Pair A, each with a different value of X and the appropriate, matching value for $k$. Such a collection is represented by Table 1 in this paper. Assumptions I and II state that whenever the dollar value of the sure loss is higher, the matching probability of loss of the business will also be higher, and vice versa. These assumptions also make interpolation in the Table (or construction of a continuous, monotonic function on it) a reasonable extension of it.

Now consider the choices in Pair C:
1. Pay X dollars.
2. Pay nothing with probability $r$, pay Y dollars with probability $s$, pay Z dollars with probability $t$, lose the business with probability $u$, where $u = 1 - r - s - t$.

Given values for Y, Z, $r$, $s$, and $t$, the Table can be used to find the value of X which is necessary to establish indifference between the choices in Pair C. First it is necessary to look up Y in the Table (interpolating if necessary), getting a probability $v$ for loss of the business which is equivalent to sure loss of Y; similarly there is found a probability $w$ for loss of the business equivalent to sure loss of Z. Now a choice can be created which is equivalent to the second choice in Pair C: by adding $s \times v$ plus $t \times w$ plus $u$ a sum can be secured which can be called $m$. From the Table find the dollar figure X such that this decision-maker is indifferent between a sure loss of X and a probability $m$ of losing his business.

This gives the choices in Set CC, between which this decision-maker is indifferent:
1. Pay X dollars.
2. Have probability $m$ of losing the business.

Therefore, it is concluded that the following theorem holds:
Given the assumptions made at the beginning of this appendix, and
If the decision-maker can state equivalent fixed-price (sure cost) values for each of a set of different probabilities of suffering maximum loss,
Then for each given distribution of loss possibilities (including losses of all sizes) it is possible to state a fixed dollar amount which is for that decision-maker the sure cost equivalent of that loss distribution. Any sure cost less than that amount is for him more desirable than the loss

exposure, any sure cost greater than that amount is for him less desir-able than the loss exposure.

From this it is concluded that if the necessary data were available, this theorem would show whether or not insurance of a given amount and under given price conditions [6] should be purchased by a given decision-maker.

## Questions

1. An important discussion in this article is the discussion about the relation-ship between amount of loss and the degree of disturbance or effect on the operation of the firm of that loss. The author hypothecates such a func-tional relationship as an example. On the horizontal axis of a graph will be the amount of the liability loss. What is the vertical axis? Draw a graph that shows the general pattern of the relationship set up in the article.
2. Do you feel that the technique outlined in the article is a practical method of making a decision about the proper limits of a liability insurance policy? Discuss.

---

[5] A fixed price for the insurance is not necessary if a probability distribution can be put on the various possible prices which may be paid.

# 9. ADVANTAGES OF A SELF-INSURANCE PROGRAM *

Robert J. McRell †

We know from our basic insurance training that there are four ways to handle exposure: avoid, assume, shift, or reduce. This article will deal with the assuming of exposure from the standpoint of a self-insurance program. A considerable amount of ground work is necessary to investigate the feasibility of installing a self-insurance program. Some companies have saved up to 25 percent by using this approach; on the other hand, implementing a program of self-insurance could possibly prove disastrous to your company.

As a professional risk manager it is your duty to assess and determine the proper approach for your corporation. Hopefully, this article will provide you with the tools to determine how your present operation would stack up against a program of self-insurance.

Two phrases have become common in the insurance field in the past few years—self-insurance and risk retention. Some experts insist that there is no such thing as self-insurance. They point out that this is nothing more than a way of putting dollars away today to pay for the claims of tomorrow. Others feel that self-insurance is a formal method of premium allocation to a fund for the future payment of claims. I believe that the difference between risk retention and self-insurance is the word "fund" which, in fact, refers to funding of monies that are made available due to long term pay-out claims.

How will you know when your company is ready for a program of self-insurance? I believe the answer to this question is when your own insurance department is able to do a better job than the insurance company. This means being able to control the insurance program at a lesser cost and still perform all the functions that an insurance company provides. Your safety program must be better and this can be tested by the amount actually spent on insurance, including the cost of the claim itself and all other expenses involved. The engineering department must be better and this can be tested by ferreting out dangerous conditions. New accident situations appearing on your loss runs indicate that an exposure existed but was not discovered until after the claim occurred. When you are convinced that your department can perform these functions better than an

* From *Risk Management* (October, 1970), pp. 23+. Reprinted by permission.
† Director of Insurance of Eastern Freight Ways, Inc.

insurange company, you have completed the first step towards a program of self-insurance.

## STATISTICAL STUDY

The second step is a statistical study to determine the economic feasibility of instituting a self-insurance program. It will become the prime motivating factor in your decision to enter a program of self-insurance.

At some point you must purchase excess coverage from an insurance company, since obviously no corporation today is in a position to insure from the first dollar up to the maximum potential loss for any situation. Remember, under a program of self-insurance, you are retaining the lower level of claims. You may elect to assume a 10, 15, 25, or $50,000 deductible, and this becomes the self-insured portion of your program. When you have reached this level you are purchasing "excess insurance".

Actually you are doing nothing more than what the insurance companies are doing. They merely retain a certain amount of your risk and then go out into the marketplace seeking additional coverages from their re-insurers. Similarly, under the self-insurance program you bypass your primary insurer, and purchase excess insurance. The statistical study will determine at what level you need the financial assistance of your excess insurer for the payment of claims of a serious nature. You are responsible for the first 10, 15 or whatever amount is on each and every claim that occurs. If you have a thousand claims in a year, then you have a potential 1,000 claims each of which could be worth up to the retention of your program, so that the statistical study will determine at what level you want the excess insurer to assume the liability and protect your corporation's interest up to the policy limits.

A statistical study starts with past loss history. This material is available from your insurance company—both your present insurer and any insurers you have had in the past. The further back you go in developing this loss data, the more accurate the study will be. You must work off what insurance companies call "seasoned" or "up dated" loss runs. If you deal from the original loss runs, you may find claims that were originally reserved at $1,000 and after investigation and reevaluation, the loss was determined a serious one and the reserve increased to $10,000. By operating your study from the original loss run rather than the "seasoned" or "up dated" loss run you can readily see how distortions will occur.

The mechanics of doing this study are relatively simple. Set up charts by year with captions starting at claims paid and reserved under $1,000 and continue up as high as you wish, listing the amount of each claim in the appropriate box. A claim settled at $5,000, for example, will appear in the claims under $1,000, $2,000, $3,000, etc. To encompass your company's growth factor into this loss history, the statistical study will show you the claims cost in relationship to the volume of business at any given period. By applying this formula to anticipated growth, you will have some idea of the additional claims to be handled in the future. This figure will serve as a guide and can only be considered factual if there is no drastic change in the company's operations. For example, if it is primarily a sales firm and management purchases a string of butcher stores, you cannot relate past Workmen's Compensation experience because it just will not work, as they are two different operations and generate different types of claims. For a company that is acquisition oriented the statistical study can tend to be a time consuming but necessary tool, if a self-insurance program is to succeed.

## FORMAL FUNDING METHOD

A formal method of funding dollars for the payment of future claims is a must in a self-insurance program. Assume the study shows you will pay $600,000 in claims the first year. The cost of the excess insurance must also be paid, but since this will be paid monthly, it does not present a funding problem. Future claims do present a funding problem. Some claims will be denied, some contested, many will wind up in court and some will eventually be paid. A liability case can take as long as six years to reach trial and eventual conclusion.

Workmen's Compensation claims are paid over a period of time which means that the corporation will be holding this money in anticipation of future payments. What are you going to do with this money? The answer is simple. Invest it. No matter what the return, it reduces the value of the claim. So you can see that a formal method of investment is a necessity in a self-insured program. Let us take our assumed $600,000 in claims' payments. That is $50,000 a month set aside for the payment of claims. Ten thousand dollars should be available in checks or drafts, and $40,000 should be invested. As the plan progresses, more will be placed in a checking account and less will be free for investment. During the initial months, however, much of the money set aside for claims payment's will not be used, making it available for investment. The reason being that claims occurring in the initial months must be investigated; this takes time and time is where you obtain the use of the money.

Some companies do not invest the monies freed through a program of self-insurance, but rather use the available money as operating capital. The theory being that money retained precludes the necessity of borrowing from the outside. This is a management decision, and when computing the cost of a self-insurance program, you must reduce the cost of the program by the interest rate the money would have earned had a formal investment program been adopted. By following this course you have no formal method of funding dollars and this falls more in line with a program of risk retention rather than a formal program of self-insurance.

Premiums paid to insurance companies are tax deductible and under a program of self-insurance the excess premium paid to an insurance company may be treated as a tax deduction but the self-insurance portion will not receive the same treatment. The Internal Revenue will not permit a tax deduction for funds set aside for the payment of future losses unless certain rules are followed. Reserves set aside for anticipated losses cannot be claimed as this would be expending funds for contingencies which have not yet occurred. In order to qualify for the deduction the accident must have occurred, investigation performed and a reasonable reserve set up. If your reserve picture is such that you have settled claims within a reasonable area of the reserves, then you have backup information to prove the deductions taken should the Internal Revenue request an audit.

## POSSIBILITY OF PENALIZATION

Assuming the Internal Revenue Service audits and disallows the reserves you have taken in the year the accident occurs, you would be charged a six percent penalty plus the back taxes. Since it would probably take two to three years before this audit would be performed under a new self-insurance plan, many of the claims which made up this deduction would be closed. If this money was invested wisely, the return should be greater than the penalty. The majority of companies operating under a self-insured plan treat their allocated loss reserves as expense, and deduct them in the year the reserves are created.

Throughout this article, the word "claims" keeps recurring so let us discuss the handling of these claims. Part of instituting a program of self-insurance is the creation of an organization to handle the claims. You are dealing with your corporation's money from the first dollar up to the maximum of your retention. There being no primary insurance, you do not have the services of an insurance company claims department to fall back on.

The final decision whether to pay a claim, deny the claim, or force it to suit, is yours to make. The system you install and the people you engage to control your claims will be tested on a daily basis. The various claims organizations used by other corporations who are self-insured and their evaluation of these organizations can assist you in the initial setting up of the outside investigating and adjusting agencies required for your operation.

The volume of claims anticipated, as shown on the statistical study, will determine the size of the staff you will need. Self-insurance programs require the services of trained claims people, particularly in the areas of liability and Workmen's Compensation so it may be advantageous to hire experienced personnel and train them in your specific business. In addition to salary each of these people will require a company car and expense account, thus making for a very expensive method of doing claims work. Alternatively you may choose to employ a small staff plus independent adjusting firms and coordinate the investigations through your staff. If frequency of claims is what your business has generated in the past, this method could be quite expensive; most adjusting companies operate at a rate of $7.50 per hour plus expenses. If the problem is severity rather than frequency, then the independent adjusting firms will provide the most economical method of handling claims.

## WORKMEN'S COMPENSATION

In the area of Workmen's Compensation you will be dealing with state regulatory bodies as this line of coverage is controlled by statutory regulations. After you have qualified as a self-insurer, you will be obliged to pay temporary disability, medical bills and attend hearings for the assessment of a permanent disability award (in the states which have permanent awards). The services of medical doctors and hospitals for treatment of your injured employees will be required as well as the services of attorneys to represent you when petitions are filed by your employees.

In the liability area you may elect to adopt the "payment in advance" method of handling absolute liability claims. Fairly new, this method has met with a good measure of success by the insurance companies and the self-insurers who have tried it. The company admits liability in cases where absolute liability exists and commences payment to the claimant for car repairs, ordinary living expenses and medical bills. The theory is that by relieving the claimant of the financial burden the greed angle is removed and the claimant will more readily return to work since no profit can be made by incurring additional medical expenses. At no time during the initial period is the claimant asked to sign a release. Once he has returned to work and all bills have been paid, the settlement negotiations begin. In cases of serious injuries under the "payment in advance" method, you will have control of the medical treatment and if necessary, rehabilitation can begin.

You may elect to handle claims on a settle or defend by liability method which is the usual claims handling procedure. In any event you will need the services of both independent adjusting firms and legal counsel.

Some corporations have approached the group life and hospitalization program from a self-insured basis. If the volume of lives insured is high enough and the face value of the policy low enough, perhaps it is better to self insure. The average rate for group insurance with 500 lives runs about .06 per 1,000 per month. Of course, this is subject to change depending on the actuarial outcome of your group.

Assume each of the 500 lives is insured for $5,000. You are then dealing with $2,500,000 x .60 or $15,000 per month premium dollars. This leaves $18,000 per year for payment of claims or a death reserve expectancy of three and one half lives per year. On a group of 500 people the actuarial odds are in your favor, plus you have the investment income.

In this area of group hospitalization/medical, assume you pay $19 per month per employee and family. By assuming a $1,000 deductible and purchasing excess insurance up to $10,000, thus providing a $10,000 major medical policy to your employees, the rate would drop to about $4.00 per month per employee and the monthly outlay would be greatly reduced. Another advantage of this plan is the fact that a competent staff could expedite the payment of claims, since 95 percent of the claims would be under the $1,000 figure. Claims could be processed and paid the day of presentation. This is good public relations and relieves your employees of immediate financial burdens.

## COST WITH NO PLUS

The foregoing does not take into account the present retention factors you have with the insurance company, but it does, as in all self-insurance programs, give you the use of money. By cutting out the middle-man, expense factors are lower and basically what you are talking about in retention is cost plus. Why not cost with no plus?

Market facilities are tighter now than at any other time in the history of our industry. The rapid growth of business in this country and its insurance demands have drained the available market's capacity to a point where unless your company has a good potential of making a profit for the insurer, your request for insurance will either be denied or the rate quoted will be prohibitive. Many insurance companies are requesting corporations to accept deductions. However, it is a rare case where the insurance company permits a corporation to handle its own claims. I believe this to be the future course of the insurance companies and it appears that the deductible type approach is the insurance of the '70s.

If so, then self-insurance is one of the few courses left open to us. The plans today are usually retrospective rating plans with a loss conversion factor of anywhere from 13 to 15 percent, which means, in effect, that you have built in 13 to 15 percent additional expense relegated to the handling of your claims. What this will do is drive the cost of your insurance program to a point where you may be forced into a program of self-insurance before you are ready. Preparation is one of the keys to a successful self-insurance program, without which the chances of success are greatly diminished. The trend of business today is mergers and acquisitions. The entire insurance program of your corporation could drastically change overnight. With the flexibility of a self-insurance program, you are able to absorb these changes without major revisions in your basic program. As a risk manager, investigation of the possibility of self-insurance for now, or for the future, is your duty to the corporation you represent.

## Questions

1. Is the use of a deductible insurance plan the same as the use of a self-insurance plan for the amount of loss below the deductible?
2. What three important points must be kept in mind when gathering data about losses in the firm in order to decide whether a self-insurance plan is desired?
3. In speaking of the method of funding the self-insurance program, the author identifies the case in which the monies in the fund are not invested outside the firm, but rather are used by the firm as operating capital. He states that "by following this course you have no formal method of funding dollars and this falls more in line with a program of risk retention rather than a formal program of self-insurance." The author also comments about investing the funds where they will result in some return to the firm. How would the risk manager convince the president of the firm that he should invest money outside the firm as a self-insurance fund?
4. What are the implications of the federal income tax regulations with respect to self-insurance programs? A discussion with an instructor or a practitioner in the area of tax accounting may be helpful in obtaining information about current procedures.)

# 10. PITFALLS IN INSURANCE MANAGEMENT *

Mark R. Greene †

Over 60 years ago a student of economics wrote in his dissertation, "To live and labor in uncertainty is the common lot of all men." [1] These words are more true today than they were then. It seems that the degree of uncertainty with which we are surrounded is increasing year by year. This increase in uncertainty is so gradual that many of us do not notice it. Yet silently and almost unobserved, the insurance industry—that business dedicated to the reduction of uncertainty— has grown to become one of America's giant industrial complexes. Insurance has become an important "growth industry," accounting for between 10 and 15 percent of U. S. national income. In spite of the importance of insurance, it is one of the least understood aspects of modern management, one of the most neglected areas for business research, and contains some of the most potentially rich soil for the harvesting of economies in modern business management.

The cost of insurance for a typical business firm is a significant item in the cost of doing business. No reliable data exists which enables us to say with great precision just what this cost is, but we all know it is substantial. The cost of social insurance programs alone— premiums for workmen's compensation, unemployment insurance, social security taxes—will amount to between six and seven percent of payroll for the typical business firm. In a survey of risk management conducted at the University of Oregon in 1959 among 385 retailers, it was reported that the average amount spent by retailers for insurance was slightly over $260 annually.[2] This cost amounted to an average of three percent of total operating expenses or less than one percent of net sales. Thus, insurance premiums can easily run

---

* From AMS Professional Management Bulletins (February, 1970), pp. 1-6. Reprinted by permission.

† Professor of Insurance, The University of Georgia.

[1] A. H. Willet, *The Economic Theory of Risk and Insurance* (New York: Columbia University Press, 1901).

[2] Donald Watson and A. G. Horman. *An Analysis of Risk Management Problems of Small Retailers* (University of Oregon, Bureau of Business Research, January 1961). The amounts spent for insurance range from about $100 to over $2600, but there was a concentration in the $200 to $400 range. This study did not cover life, health, and hospitalization insurance, nor any special insurance; therefore, the estimates are considerably understated if one is estimating total insurance costs.

10 percent of payroll or more for a business. Certainly management has spent large sums researching things that cost less than 10 percent of its payroll. Yet the scientific management of the risk and insurance program is one of the most commonly negelected areas for research or control.

## SUMMARY OF MAJOR ERRORS

There are a number of aspects of insurance management that are often neglected. Some of the major areas where errors occur are discussed below.

1. Underinsurance. Surveys find that management in general runs needless risks which could be economically handled by insurance often without a significant increase in total premium cost. Underinsurance takes the form of inadequate coverage or lack of coverage altogether, leading to unintentional assumption of risk.

2. Organization and policy. A common error here is failure to pinpoint responsibility for handling the insurance program. Usually this takes the form of having more than one insurance agent. It may also take the form of not appointing someone within the organization to deal with several agents used by the firm.

3. Inadequate planning. Among the errors here are failure to set down a clear statement of insurance buying philosophy or policy, failure to centralize insurance buying for most economical handling of coverage, failure to set up procedures so that all new exposures can be recognized and either insured or otherwise disposed of. Inadequate budgeting for self-insured losses or loss prevention activity is a common failing.

4. Failure to initiate, supervise, or maintain loss prevention programs.

5. Failure to review insurance and exposures periodically. The objective here is to increase the likelihood of rate reductions and better coverage. Failing to insure property which has been newly acquired or not eliminating insurance on property which has been disposed of are common errors which can be corrected by formal reviews. Competitive bidding has produced very large savings for many buyers.

6. Errors in insurance coverage. Included in this group are overlapping coverage, nonconcurrencies, inadvertent omission of coinsurance clauses or inclusion of coinsurance clauses, failing to render insurance reports on inventories when required, and inadequate procedures to establish both notice and proof of loss when loss occurs.

7. Failure to insure the serious exposures before the less severe exposures. A good example is the purchase of full coverage collision insurance or any collision insurance on an old automobile and neglect of placing coverage on large limits of liability under bodily injury exposures.

8. Failure to use insurance as a financial device. Use of insurance to reduce the size of cash reserves which would otherwise be necessary for various contingencies is an example of wise use of insurance for financial purposes. For example, life insurance on the president of the company or other key officers or stockholders can prevent losses to the firm which are serious enough to cause bankruptcy in case of death of important persons in the firm. Proper use of group life, or group health, or group pensions as employee incentives can be a significant tool in personnel policy.

9. Failure to keep insurance records. This includes keeping of loss records. Adequate insurance accounting can mean large savings when it comes time to renegotiate rates for coverages and in establishing proofs of loss.

10. Using self-insurance when certain conditions for self-insurance do not apply. Among the conditions which do *not* favor self-insurance are the following:

(a) Desire by management to avoid instability in profits in years of unusual loss. This condition is particularly likely when there are too few exposure units to produce loss stability.

(b) Lack of adequate personnel to keep the necessary records and perform other insurance functions.

(c) Desire by management to avoid unpleasant relations with employees or customers. Employee or customer relations can be damaged when losses are to be paid by the firm rather than an outside party. For example, in workmen's compensation, there are distinct advantages to having a third party deal with the injured employee.

(d) There is need for important insurer services such as engineering inspection, glass replacement, etc.

(e) Management expresses unwillingness or inability to set aside adequate financial reserves to absorb uninsured losses.

In one study among 1100 member firms of the American Society of Insurance Management, it was found that approximately 23 percent practiced self-insurance to the extent of retaining a minimum loss of $10,000 or more per occurrence. It was discovered that for those firms self-insuring fire and liability losses, the loss experience fluctuated more than 50 percent from an average over a previous three-year period. Loss experience was more stable in the case of workmen's compensation insurance. It was concluded that firms, even large firms, do not generally evaluate self-insurance programs to determine whether or not savings are being made or whether other objectives are being reached. Evidently, self-insurance has not yet reached the point of development where it is feasible for any but a small minority of firms.[3]

[3] Robert Goshay, *Corporate Self-Insurance and Risk Retention Plans* (Homewood, Ill.: Richard D. Irwin, 1954).

11. Failure to coordinate risk management with other functions of the business. The risk manager must work closely with the accounting, finance, production, marketing and transportation, and personnel departments. For example, failure to understand clauses used in purchase and sale orders may create liability exposures of which the insurance manager should certainly be aware. If the firm is taking title to goods at the plant of a supplier but the firm's insurance coverage does not apply until products reach its own plant, it is obvious that all perils of loss during the period of transportation are not being insured.

## CASE EXAMPLES OF PITFALLS

In the 1959-60 study of 385 small retail firms referred to previously, there was an attempt to determine how well the insurance management function was being carried out. A further analysis of 116 retailers on attitudes toward insurance was also done. Another study was undertaken in the summer of 1961 with business firms in Roseburg, Oregon to determine how adequate were the insurance programs of Roseburg merchants after the explosion and fire which rocked the city on August 7, 1959.[4]

Examples of insurance errors from these studies are summarized below.

1. *Underinsurance.* Only about half of all firms surveyed had insurance equal to 90 percent or more of the sound value of their buildings. Sixteen percent covered less than 50 percent of the sound value of buildings. Yet, it was discovered that over half of the firms carried coinsurance clauses equal to 90 percent or more. It seems very likely that many of these firms could not collect in full for partial losses even though the limits of coverage exceeded the amount of loss due to the operation of the coinsurance clause. This finding was corroborated in the Roseburg study, where about five percent of the firms in that explosion suffered coinsurance penalties in their loss settlements.

It is interesting to find out that over 3 percent of the building owners in the surveyed firms carried *no* fire insurance on their buildings. About 10 percent carried *no* fire insurance on stock, and about 18 percent carried *no* fire insurance on equipment. It was noted that underinsurance was less prevalent in larger cities than it was in smaller cities.

In the field of liability insurance, 16 percent of the 385 carried no premises liability or operations liability in any form. About 10 percent of the firms carried bodily injury liability limits of less than $20,000 per accident. Only a little over seven percent of all firms carried bodily

---

[4] Mark R. Green, *Risk Management in a Catastrophe* (University of Oregon, Bureau of Business Research, 1962).

injury limits equal to or exceeding $100,000/$300,000. The popular limit was $50,000/$100,000 for bodily injury liability limits. About a quarter of all the firms carried property damage limits of $5,000 or less, and 50 percent carried $10,000 or less for property damage liability.

The survey also revealed that 30 percent of all retailers carried no crime coverage whatever, and only 9 percent carried business interruption insurance.

2. *Coverage errors.* It was found that of 71 firms in the survey not using coinsurance clauses in their fire policies, 27 firms or 38 percent, were eligible for coinsurance but had either rejected the use of the clauses or were unfamiliar with its use. By using a coinsurance clause, savings in the fire insurance premium are possible and range from a low of five percent to a high of 70 percent depending upon the class of fire protection and the type of building construction. Thus it appears that many retail firms are needlessly denying themselves of savings available in the purchase of fire insurance.

There were, in about 6 percent of the cases, one or more instances of non-concurrency in the fire coverage.

3. *Uneconomic allocation of expenditures.* Failing to insure serious exposures before the less severe exposures is a common error. As examples of this error, it was found that 28 percent of the retail firms in the study referred to carried $50 deductible collision insurance on automobiles. At the same time, around a quarter of these firms carried only $5,000 property damage limits of liability in connection with automobiles. Twenty-two percent of the surveyed firms had no automobile bodily injury liability insurance for accidents arising out of the operation of the business. Only six percent of the firms carried replacement cost coverage on property.

4. *Organization errors.* It was found that managers in the retail survey had an average of 1.93 agents for business coverage. Only 34 percent used a single agent; 47 percent had two agents, 17 percent had three agents, and 2 percent had 4 agents handling their coverages. Forty percent of the managers stated that they would not entrust their agents with significant facts of their business and pertinent personal financial circumstances. It seems unsurprising, therefore, that 75 percent of those interviewed indicated they did not feel insurance salesmen are well enough informed about the risks of their businesses to be able to recommend policies.

5. *Loss prevention techniques.* Very often the risk manager fails to take a broad view of loss prevention and concentrates on more mundane affairs such as seeing that each employee wears safety helmets, etc. Consider the case recently illustrated by the risk manager of the Reynolds Tobacco Company in which the design of tobacco storage sheds is integrated closely with the risk management department. To prevent wind damage, the sheds are placed 80 feet apart and built in groups of 16 which are 500 feet apart. Additionally, installa-

tion of an automatic sprinkler system reduced the annual fire insurance premium from $11,000 to $1480. The savings in insurance rates
paid for the cost of the sprinkler system within two years in this
particular case. In the same company, a loss prevention program for
industrial accidents reduced the accident rate from 9.15 to 2.0 losses
per million man-hours. Such a record resulted after a monthly meeting program was installed with 30 employees at each meeting. During
the meetings, a discussion leader showed safety movies, reviewed
certain hazards, and described recent accidents.

6. *Review of insurance.* An example of a large saving here occurred
when a construction company permitted a broker to examine its
policies in connection with Shea Stadium in New York. It was discovered that through a misclassification of payroll under workmen's compensation coverage, the sum of $37,000 was being paid for
a particular class of work which was not being performed on this
particular job.[5]

As another example, a firm required a professional appraiser on a
certain property. As a result, at this plant the insurance coverage
was increased to $2 million from $1 million, its former level. One year
later the plant burned to the ground and was a total loss. In another,
less fourtunate, example in the Roseburg disaster, a firm was found
to have eliminated extended coverage a few months before the
explosion as an economy measure. The resulting loss to this firm
was over $200,000, which was uninsured.

## CONCLUSION

It seems clear that the science of risk management is important
enough to warrant greater study in the future than it has in the past.
Large dollar savings are possible through better planning for risk
and insurance management. Eventually, therefore, the risk manager
will assume a far more important role in the organization structure
than he plays currently.

## Questions

1. Is the risk and insurance management function an important factor in
   producing profits for the firm, or is it simply a "necessary expense" to be
   minimized wherever possible? Explain.
2. Which of the various "pitfalls" do you think are most important to avoid?
   Why?
3. Make a list of "pitfalls" of which you have been guilty as an individual in
   the recent past. What were the results of these errors or omissions?

---

[5] William Guest, "Broker Saves Construction Firm $37,000 on Shea Stadium Job,"
*Business Insurance,* March 11, 1968, p. 15.

# PART 3
## Institutional Aspects of Insurance

By any measure, the institution of insurance is a large and significant part of our economy. Because of the magnitude and the complexity of the institution, and because the early authors in the area of risk and insurance had strong backgrounds in the institutional aspects of insurance, textbook and course material for many years was primarily devoted to a descriptive survey of the institution company structure, insurance salesmanship, contract analysis, and regulatory problems. Study of this structure is necessary for a proper analysis of problems and risk decision making. The articles in this part were selected to illustrate analytical treatment of some institutional aspects of insurance.

In the first article, Mr. Rodda treats insurer insolvency. Professor Greene's article discusses some social obligations of insurers and develops a list of different areas that may be of future importance as research topics in insurance.

# 11. INSOLVENCY FUNDS: A DESIRABLE SECURITY OR A NEEDLESS EXPENSE FOR THE POLICYHOLDER? *

William H. Rodda †

Insurance company insolvencies have caused a clamor for some method under which claimants against insolvent companies would be paid for their losses. The number of insurance companies that have failed in recent years has been small, but it is the number of policyholders affected that causes the clamor rather than the number of insolvencies. Several thousand insureds whose property losses are not paid, or whose liability claims are not met, can raise a furor that is heard in Washington as well as in all of the state capitals.

Several different proposals have been made to pay the claims of those who are unfortunate enough or unwary enough to buy insurance in companies that subsequently failed. These plans range from supposedly simple plans within a single state to an elaborate federal scheme that would encompass the entire insurance business. This discussion is not an attempt to promote or support any plan but is rather an analysis of the various proposals as they may affect the policyholder. The reader can decide whether he feels that there is social or economic justification for him to pay the costs which ultimately will be borne by those who buy insurance.

The acceptance of the Federal Deposit Insurance Corporation and the Federal Savings and Loan Insurance Corporation in the banking and savings and loan fields poses the question whether a similar corporation would be desirable for insurance company failures. The FDIC and the FSLIC have paid depositors of insolvent institutions up to the prescribed limits. FDIC and FSLIC have not eliminated failures. Banks have failed during 1969 at a rate of almost one a month in the United States. It is impossible to say whether supervision by the federal organizations has prevented other failures. Supervision of any kind, and particularly an inquiring supervision, probably brings to light questionable practices by some institutions in time to prevent failures.

---

* From *Business Insurance* (February 2, 1970), pp. 21-22. Reprinted by permission.
† President, Marine Insurance Handbook, Inc.

The payment of $15,000 per account in an insolvent organization by FDIC or FSLIC does not in itself prove that a similar arrangement is feasible in the insurance business. The rules can be fairly simple as to who will be paid in the case of a bank failure. An "account" can be defined and a maximum amount set for payment to each account. It is worthy of note that the amount payable per account is relatively small. The businessman and the corporation whose accounts necessarily are more than $15,000 are expected to choose banks that will not fail. They are smaller in number so that fewer votes would be affected by losses on their part.

Proposals for insurance company insolvency funds vary greatly as to what kinds of insurance should be covered. Automobile insurance has been the primary objective of all the funds so far proposed or enacted. This is the result of two things. First, many people are affected by the insolvency of an automobile insurance company. There is a higher proportion of claims to the number of policies written in automobile insurance than in almost any other field, perhaps with the exception of accident and health insurance. Thus the failure of an automobile insurance company leaves more people without the protection they paid for.

A second reason for greater interest in automobile insurance company insolvencies is that many of the failures have been among these companies. Automobile insurance has been unprofitable. It is impossible to prove whether financial difficulties have resulted directly from inadequate rates, but certainly they have been a factor. The establishing of loss and claim reserves in automobile insurance requires a high degree of competence and honesty. Competence has been lacking in some companies, and lack of honesty has been alleged in other failures. The high initial premiums in automobile insurance makes this an ideal situation for the unscrupulous operator who wants to accumulate a lot of money rapidly so that he can siphon off the assets for himself, and then let the company go broke.

An insurance company insolvency plan is inherently more complicated than a bank insolvency plan. A primary problem is the determining of what kinds of insurance shall be included. Should the plan cover merely automobile insurance which has been the most troublesome, or should it include other property and liability insurance? Should life insurance and accident and health insurance be covered? What limits should be imposed upon the recoveries? There is controversy whether the plans should cover the extremely high verdicts which occasionally are returned by the courts. It may logically be asked why the really high verdict should be eliminated. Such claims are the ones which clobber the insured in a catastrophic way. The limit of $15,000 per account of the FDIC would be wholly inadequate for liability insurance purposes.

There is controversy whether unearned premiums should be covered. An automobile insurance premium with an insolvent insurer may be several hundred dollars. Loss of this unearned premium may be a greater loss to the policyholder than an automobile collision claim. There is also the question whether claims are to be paid in full, such as is the case with FDIC for insolvent banks—or is there to be a deductible of $100 or $200, or some other figure?

Still another question is of great importance to the business insured. Proposals are geared to help the person who has little or no assets. The insured who has a net worth of $1,000,000 is considered as not needing relief. Such policyholders would be excluded from benefits under some plans. Surplus lines coverage in unauthorized insurers would probably be excluded.

Two general proposals are emerging as probable patterns. It is no longer a question of whether there should be an insolvency fund but rather what kind of fund should be enacted. One proposal is for a federal fund similar to the FDIC. Assessments would be collected from insurance companies and held in a fund to pay the claims from insolvent insurers. The other proposal is for state organizations which would collect no funds, or only minor administrative funds, in advance of insolvencies, but which would collect assessments after the fact of insolvency of an insurer.

Two principal objections have been voiced to the federal proposal. One is the cost. It has been charged by opponents of a federal insolvency fund that the administrative costs for such a fund would exceed $36,000,000 per year even before a single insolvent insurer were handled. It is obvious that a substantial cost would result from a federal fund and that this would have to be added to the cost of insurance premiums.

The second principal objection to a federal fund is the allegation that it would supplant state regulation of the insurance business with federal regulation. There is justification for this belief. It is almost certain that such a federal organization would establish requirements for an insurer to participate in the protection of the fund. This has been the pattern in the banking field under FDIC. These federal requirements as to solvency, examination, and underwriting would take the place of state regulation in these areas. It does appear that the establishment of a federal insolvency fund for insurers would lead to a substantial degree of federal regulation of the participating insurers.

The proposals for state administered insolvency funds have the dual purpose of keeping the costs at a minimum and of preserving state regulation of insurance. This second objective of preserving state regulation of insurance is getting a major part of the attention in the current discussions. This tends to obscure some of the more important differences between the federal and the state proposals.

Federal administration of insolvency funds could be better evaluated if the issues were not clouded by arguments over the merits and demerits of federal versus state regulation of the insurance business.

A federal fund would be strong financially. Its administration would be relatively uniform throughout the country. Payments of claims because of insolvency would be expected to be reasonably prompt, if the experience with FDIC can be taken as an indication. Proponents of the plan anticipate that supervision by a federal bureaucracy would bring about more adequate rates than have been achieved in some areas under state regulation. This may be wishful thinking. The same pressures for low cost insurance would be exerted upon the federal bureaucracy that have been evident in the states. Such a collateral benefit to insurers is certainly conjectural ,and by no means certain.

The proposals for state funds appear to have the advantages of lower cost and simplicity of operation. The only money which would be collected in advance of an actual insolvency in a state would be minor administrative funds for a body that would be set up to operate the plan. Assessments would be levied after the fact of an insolvency. Insurers in states that have had few or no insolvencies also feel that they would avoid a sharing of the costs of insolvencies in other states. There are states in which no insolvencies have occurred in recent years. Insurers which operate only in such states are reluctant to share the cost of insolvencies from states which in their opinion have insolvencies because of weakness in the insurance requirements in those states.

Typical of the proposals for state insolvency funds is a so-called "model bill" which has been prepared by a committee of the National Association of Insurance Commisioners. This proposes a post-insolvency assessment arrangement. Insurers operating in a state would be required to join the organization. If an insolvency occurred, all the other companies would be assessed according to their premium volume in order to meet the claims against the insolvent insurer. Insurers in the state would set up an association which would administer the collection and distribution of funds to meet claims against the insolvent insurer. Methods probably would follow those now in force for FAIR plans, assigned risk pools, and similar state operations.

It has been argued that some states might fail to enact the necessary legislation for an insolvency fund. There would inevitably be differences in the operations and in the claims to be paid. It is debatable whether such differences are desirable or undesirable. Advocates of the state plans argue that state differences can take into account the regional differences in social and economic conditions.

Several states have already enacted state insolvency fund plans. These vary greatly as the kinds of insurance that shall be paid as a claim against the fund, whether there shall be a deductible from the amount to be paid, and what limit shall be placed upon the amount of any claim.

The Insurance Commissioners' "model bill" contains limitations and restrictions which appear to represent a consensus of present thinking. There is a "non-duplication of recovery" provision which would force an insured to collect first under the provisions of any insurance which he carried. This is aimed primarily at the uninsured motorist coverage of a claimant against an insured of the insolvent insurer. Many automobile losses in the past have been sustained by persons who had claims against the policyholders of an insolvent company. Uninsured motorist coverage as written by most companies now covers any claim which is uncollectible because the insurer of the defendant is insolvent. The "non-duplication of recovery" provision would prevent a double collection by the injured party.

The commissioners' bill also has a $100 deductible from any claim. This is intended to simplify administration and also to keep down the cost. Unearned premiums would be considered an allowable claim, subject to the $100 deductible.

One of the more important limitations in the Commissioners' "model bill" is an upper limit of $300,000 on a claim. However this is a more lenient provision than the current law of one state which eliminates the claim of any person or corporation having net assets above $1,000,000. Another important limitation is the definition of an "insolvent insurer" to be an insurer authorized to do business in the state when the policy was issued or when the insured event occurred. Insurance in an unauthorized insurer would be excluded.

The insolvency fund is aimed to protect the small claimant, the person who has purchased insurance without a professional knowledge of insurance company solvency and who would be hurt by inability to collect his claim. It is in effect a social type of legislation because its benefits do not extend to all insureds nor for unlimited amounts. Like the bank insolvency funds of FDIC and FSLIC, it is the small policyholder who will benefit most. The cost will be spread over the entire insurance business, including policyholders who will not benefit in proportion to their added costs. The questions to be considered by business policyholders are whether the general benefit to society and to the economy of the country would be sufficient to justify enactment of the proposals, and which would be best.

## Questions

1. Would insolvency funds duplicate the service of reinsurance? Discuss.
2. The article explains the model insolvency fund in which an insurer not authorized to write insurance in a particular jurisdiction would not qualify as an insolvent insurer. Such a provision would seem to eliminate from protection by the fund those who purchase certain mail—order insurance or insurance from companies writing insurance through unlicensed agents in a state. Discuss.

# 12. RESEARCH PROBLEMS FOR MARKETING INSURANCE IN THE 1970s *

Mark R. Greene †

It is possible that the decade of the 1970s will be a decade in which more changes in the economy and in the ways in which business firms must operate will occur than any other previous decade in history. This generalization can apply as easily to many other industrialized nations as it can to the United States. In the minds of many, such a comment immediately would imply technological changes and their impact upon the way in which business must adapt. This paper, however, will focus on: (a) social and economic changes which may occur partly because of the technological changes which are in store; (b) the possible effects of these changes on the insurance industry; and (c) the rationale and nature of research which should be conducted by insurance companies to help them understand the climate in which they will operate in the 1970s, if they are to operate successfully.

## The Problem

It is often believed that social and economic environment is a matter that is of concern only to sociologists or other esoteric social scientists, and is of no direct concern to marketing. It is argued below that the social and economic environment *is* the marketing environment and that problems called "social" are really important problems in insurance marketing.

Many believe that the marketing environment changes only slowly. This in turn leads to the belief that business firms will have plenty of time to adapt to new conditions as they emerge. It is the argument in this paper, however, that social and economic changes in the 1970s are likely to accelerate at a pace never before experienced. With it will come the necessity of relatively rapid adaptation on the part of business firms to new conditions.

In the past, it has been the tendency of business in industrial countries to focus on "the mass market" without examining too closely the specific characteristics or conditions within that market. Often there is the implicit assumption that no change will occur in the market or that customers are perfectly homogeneous. There is a tendency to measure

* From *The Annals of the Society of Chartered Property and Casualty Underwriters* (December, 1971), pp. 293-312. Reprinted by permission.
† Professor of Insurance, The University of Georgia.

market size almost solely in terms of its income. It is argued here that industry will have to begin generally to study market changes more closely than it has in the past and to recognize better the varying and non-homogéneous aspects of the market in order to prosper, or even survive.

In the United States, for example, it has been the tendency of the insurance industry to assume great market stability and high market homogeneity. Its basic products are tailored to a "mass market," which is assumed to demand a fairly uniform coverage. This, the ordinary life insurance policy, a standard automobile policy, a standard fire insurance policy, etc. have been developed and marketed with little regard to changing or varying needs of the consumer. Not only has the basic product tended to remain about the same, but the methods of distributing these products have tended to remain the same for most insurers. However, a few insurers dared to change and have profited. Since 1945, for example, the traditional insurers in the automobile industry in the United States using the American Agency System have lost a major share of their market to a new class of competitors, the exclusive agency companies, who have tailored both the product and the distribution methods to the needs of the postwar consumer.

Similarly, the traditional life insurance industry since 1945 has seen its market share of the consumer savings dollar decline as the demand for equity investments has increased. It is likely that market shifts of this nature could have been predicted, or at least better understood, had there been a better understanding by insurers of social and economic forces producing market demands for protection against inflation and for lower cost, more flexible, automobile insurance.

It is the argument of this paper that in the 1970s the insurance industry will have to take a closer look at the changing nature of the economic and social environment so as to understand the forces which will affect the needs of the consumers of their products. Perhaps one of the main forces affecting these needs will be the ways in which society handles the growing number of social problems which have come to characterize industrialized countries around the world. It would appear that insurance companies should be doing more research on basic social problems rather than on problems which are mainly surface indications of deeper ills. In other words, the attack should be on the causes of the disease rather than on its symptoms.

In the automobile insurance field, a very good illustration exists of some of the points suggested. Dr. William Haddon, President of the Insurance Institute for Highway Safety, reported on the results of some crash tests conducted on late model cars.[1] Results of this research show, for example, that at five miles per hour the damage to one type of "fragile" automobile when crashed into a wall might be double the damage to

---

[1] McDonnell, John, "Fragile Cars Fought by Insurance Firms," *Chicago Tribune,* November 21, 1969.

another car. The clear implication is that the more fragile car should have a higher collision insurance rate. Yet, insurance rates usually do not vary according to susceptibility to damage. One may ask why this type of research was not sponsored by the insurance industry long ago and the findings incorporated into the rate structure. It is an example of the type of "homogeneity reasoning" underlying marketing which the insurance industry has long used.

The type of research illustrated above, as valuable as it is, does not go far enough, however. Not only should insurance companies conduct research which will assist them in developing a sounder rate structure for collision insurance, but they will increasingly be required, for their own survival, to investigate basic reasons for accidents in the first place, and to work harder for loss prevention generally. Thus, it will not be sufficient to develop statistics showing which type of vehicle is most susceptible to loss, or which class of driver is likely to cause accidents, but rather research should be focused on improving the social and economic environment within which automobiles and their drivers operate, in such a way that fewer accidents will occur and insurance rates may reflect this fact.

Another example of this point is in the field of life insurance. For many years, long-run inflation has tended to characterize industrialized nations, causing gradual loss of purchasing power of the dollar. Life insurers generally ignored this situation, which of course tended to undermine the real value of savings invested in life insurance policies. To the writer's knowledge, only a few life insurers conducted basic research on different types of solution. Prominent among those who did were the Teachers Insurance and Annuity Association (T. I. A. A.) and the Prudential Insurance Company. The T. I. A. A. offered the first variable annuity through its companion organization, The College Retirement Equity Fund (C. R. E. F.) in 1950. Most life insurers watched and waited and fought regulatory battles with the Securities and Exchange Commission (S. E. C.). In the meantime, the share of consumer savings collected by life insurers declined steadily. Between 1950 and 1970, for example, private life insurance reserves in the U.S. increased threefold. During the same period the funds invested in investment company shares rose nineteenfold. Savings and loan associations, whose shares are also of a "fixed dollar" type, increased thirteenfold over this period.[2]

Only recently have several life insurers in the U.S. begun to take vigorous action to stem the loss of market share of the consumer savings dollar by entering such areas as variable annuities, mutual funds and expanding their pension business through "separate accounts" invested in equity securities. This action attacks a basic cause of the relative loss

---

[2] Calculated from data reported in *Life Insurance Fact Book, 1971, Federal Reserve Bulletin*, August, 1971 and *The Economic Almanac*, 1964 (New York: National Industrial Conference Board). Over the period 1950-1970, life policy reserves increased from $55 to $168 billion, savings and loan assets from $14 to 176 billion and mutual fund assets from 2.5 to 48 billion.

of business. One may inquire why U.S. life insurance companies took so long to plan for corrective action, when inflation has characterized the U.S. economy almost continuously since 1930, and in other countries for longer periods still.

A considerable area for debate is the extent to which insurance companies can go in paying for research. What are their limits? What kinds of basic research should be conducted? Basic research in these areas is expensive and insurance companies will have to become accustomed to this fact. If insurance companies do not become interested in and support basic research, however, funds that are devoted to this purpose by others (often administered through governmental agencies) may not go toward solving problems of interest to insurance companies, but rather will be directed toward other purposes.

In the decade ahead the following changes in basic economic and social factors have been forecast [3] for the United States, as shown in Table 1.

TABLE 1

PROJECTED ECONOMIC AND SOCIAL CHANGE IN THE U.S.

|  | 1969 | 1980 |
| --- | --- | --- |
| Gross national product * | $932 billion | $1500 billion |
| Disposable consumer income * | $627 billion | $1000 billion |
| Average family income before taxes * | $8600 billion | $20,0000 |
| Residential construction | 1.3 million units | 2.3 million units |
| Auto production | 8.3 million | 15 million |
| Number of new families formed | 925,000 | 1,500,000 |
| Persons with college degrees | 11.5 million | 18 million |
| Total population | 207 million | 243 million |

* In constant dollars.

In foreign countries, markets are growing much faster in some areas than others. For example, the percentage growth at constant prices in private consumption expenditures in selected countries over the period 1961-1966 is estimated as follows: [4] United States, 30 percent; Turkey, 71 percent; Spain, 101 percent; Japan, 52 percent; United Kingdom, 15 percent; Italy, 28 percent; Mexico, 60 percent; and Brazil, 35 percent.

Is the world's insurance industry in the U.S. prepared to cover nearly twice as many cars and houses in 1980 as it now is insuring? Are plans being made to work constructively with 60 percent more new families whose average incomes will be perhaps twice as large in ten short years? Will sales appeals be geared to the college-educated market, which will be over half again as large as it now is?

Are insurance companies writing business throughout the world aware of potentially large increases in demand for coverage in countries

---

[3] Collected and reported by National Securities and Research Corporation, December, 1969.

[4] Business International, *Indication of Market Size for 135 Countries*, 1969.

such as Mexico, Spain and Turkey as compared to more gradual market development in other countries such as Italy, U.S., United Kingdom and Brazil?

The developments in store will create many new problems for insurers which can be solved only by research and planning. Not the least of these problems is how insurers' markets will be affected by ways in which societies react and adjust to a much larger world population with increased congestion on highways, with continuing racial strife and civil unrest, with rising levels of air, water and noise pollution and with rising rates of crime and family breakdown. The ways in which some of these conditions may affect insurance and insurance marketing are explored below.

## Implications of Social Problems and Unrest as They Affect Insurance

The starting point in this inquiry is to examine the role of insurance in society and the implications that social problems and their solutions have on the insurance industry. Three premises may be advanced:

(a) Insurance is a social institution, and its survival and development depend upon the health of the society in which it operates.
(b) Insurance does not tend to develop as a social institution until a certain stage of development in society is reached.
(c) A society does not advance in its industrial development in a "straight line" but rather in stops and starts. It is possible for interruptions in progress to develop into long periods of retrogression. If such periods of retrogression develop with sufficient momentum, serious effects on the development of institutions within the society occur.

### INSURANCE AND SOCIETAL STAGES

Basic development of society has been said to follow three general stages. First, all energies of society are concentrated upon the job of political integration and defense. Governments tend to be absolute powers. Second, after the first task has been completed, there is a struggle for personal freedom and an effort to combine liberty with stability through constructive evolution of municipal and constitutional law. Third, cultural and economic development takes place. Egypt and Babylonia * did not get much beyond the first stage, and Greece and Rome did not complete the second. Western civilization appears to be well into the third phase of development.

It does not appear accidental that insurance institutions do not begin to develop as major social bodies until a society reaches this "third phase" of development of its civilization. Of course, insurance has been practiced

---

* And Viet Nam?—Ed.

to some degree in societies which are only in the first stage of development, but only on a small scale. Insurance appears to wait for its major development until a society is far enough along in its specialization of labor to permit accumulations of wealth to develop a stable monetary system and to allow for leisure time.

Well developed insurance systems do not usually emerge while society is devoting its entire energies to reaching minimum subsistence levels or to establishing its military and political security. However, once trade develops requiring exchange of goods which are manufactured in specialized factories requiring heavy investment, the need for protecting exposed values against loss from various perils also becomes evident. Furthermore, once society has progressed to the point at which human lives become recognized as being valuable, perhaps because of lengthy specialized periods of education or experience, the idea of insurance as a device to protect this investment emerges. Life insurance is not used widely in developing nations such as those in Africa or South America, but it may be expected to make large gains there as industrialization in these nations proceeds.

If conditions necessary for the development of insurance exist in any society, one may expect insurance or insurance-type institutions to appear and to flourish. The basic similarities of insurance institutions in most nations of the world which are industrially developed suggest that each country has responded similarly to needs for solutions to problems towards which insurance is directed. Insurance is a type of social institution that is created by each society as it faces the need for formal ways to handle certain risks in the same manner that societies see the need for developing money, banking systems, governmental procedures, and legal structures. Insurance seems to be a universal technique of society and it can be studied as one of the basic sociological processes.

## INSURANCE AND SOCIETAL FORCES

Giddings, writing in 1900, listed seven internal forces recognized by sociologists as operating within any aggregates of population which tend to give these population groups a common purpose and dignify them as belonging to one "society." These are: (1) A common language or other recognized methods of communication, (2) A recognition of fellow beings as being of one's own kind and unlike all other objects, (3) Imitation, (4) Conflict, (5) Toleration, (6) Mutual pleasure or play and (7) Mutual aid or alliance.

A study of these forces can give some important clues for explaining the existence of social institutions such as insurance. For example, sociological research has tended to establish that war is not a natural state of affairs even though conflict characterizes most population aggregates. Toleration is an important mitigating force to conflict. Mutual aid, although it may start in society on an accidental basis, is consciously perpetuated when its full benefits are appreciated.[5]

Study of the interaction of the forces of conflict, toleration and mutual aid in a society can form an important part of the knowledge of the insurance underwriter who is trying to understand the probability of losses due to crime, disability and illness, which are affected importantly by the ways in which these separate forces interact. Insurance as a technique of mutual aid is made feasible in stable societies where toleration tends to be a more powerful force than conflict. It is important to note that mutual aid seems to be a basic sociological force which, at least in part, is effected through the method of formal insurance in most modern civilizations.

Knowledge of the interaction of different social forces would appear to be valuable information for the underwriter in the international scene. In France, for example, the existence of social classes that are fairly rigid in their dimensions facilitates the underwriting of property insurance without the customary limitations of policy amounts for individual families living in given types of apartment. Reliance on the central government for "family allowances," in many countries tends to limit the market for private life insurance, but helps refine the demand for private annuity policies.

It is worth observing that, just as a basic sociological force of mutual aid is a prerequisite of an institution such as insurance, relative absence of such a force in a country may either prevent insurance from growing or will cause a relative diminution of the importance of insurance which had been previously developed. Insurance is a basic social institution that depends on cooperation, self-sacrifice, mutual trust, and basic honesty of members of a society that has reached the third phase of development of its civilization, that of a relatively high degree of economic and cultural development. If political instability, loss of freedom, or other factors characterizing the development of the first two stages of civilization are allowed to reappear, the insurance institution seems bound to retrogress, just as the incipient Roman insurance institutions declined with the general decline of the Roman empire.

To what extent will the social problems now developing in the 1970s affect the insurance industry and its growth, unless appropriate solutions are found? Some specific suggestions are listed below as possibilities. To the extent that civil unrest and social problems are unsolved, the quality of life in the environment tends to deteriorate and with it the basic social institutions such as insurance. For example, here are some of the ways in which civil unrest in metropolitan areas could affect private insurance adversely:

---

[5] Giddings, Franklin H., "Sociology," *The Universal Cyclopaedia,* (Appletons, 1900). p. 602.

(1) Underwriting losses due to the destruction of property and injury of persons in riots may cause insurance losses to be far larger than those which were anticipated when the rate structure was developed. A vicious circle of public resentment against insurance companies may develop. As losses mount, underwriting standards and rates tend to rise. It becomes more difficult to get insurance. At the same time the demand for coverage increases among the least desirable applicants from an underwriting standpoint. Governmental assistance is sought. Ensuing unrest causes larger damage claims to occur resulting in even higher underwriting standards and rates and the process is repeated. Underwriting losses produce a squeeze on profit which makes it even harder to attract new capital to the insurance industry, heightens the bad public image, and produces even stricter underwriting standards.

(2) During periods of civil unrest, moral and morale hazard are greatly increased. Part of the causes of such an increased moral and morale hazard are the changing attitudes toward the sanctity of private property. For example, investigations by social scientists reveal that looting after natural disasters is quite rare. In looting during the Detroit riots, however, studies revealed that normally-law-abiding individuals from all income brackets within the society strongly support looting as a defiance against the system which created private property in the first place.[6] Furthermore, buying motives of the consumer are affected by civil unrest. Lack of sympathy with "the rich insurance company" may increase the tendency to buy insurance for purposes of collecting on the policy.

(3) Because insurance may have a public relations problem during periods of civil unrest, there may be unwillingness of young people, particularly college-trained persons, to enter the insurance field as a vocation. Although insurance companies have long faced this problem, it is likely to get worse in the decade of the 1970s unless insurers take positive steps to counteract it.

(4) Lack of insurance underwriters' financial capacity resulting from some of the above problems may force a permanent loss of some markets for coverage. These losses are filled by self-insurers, "captive" insurers and foreign insurers.

In 1971 the federal government entered the crime insurance field, an area formerly reserved exclusively to private insurers, with direct insurance in several states being offered to individuals and to firms against burglary and robbery through the Federal Insurance Administration. Under the Urban Property Protection and Reinsurance Act of 1968, the federal government has also offered reinsurance in conjunction with state-sponsored "F.A.I.R." plans (Fair Access to Insurance Requirements) to make property insurance more readily available to

---

[6] Dynes, Russell, and Quarantelli, E. L., "What Looting in Civil Disturbances Really Means," *Trans-Action*, May, 1968, p. 9.

blighted urban areas. Similar reinsurance is offered against flood risks under the National Flood Insurance Act of 1968, with the federal government reserving the right to offer flood coverage directly if private insurers fail to meet the need for insurance.

(5) A likelihood of governmental intervention and participation in the insurance field increases. If private business fails to meet a social need, governmental activity may be demanded. For example, this has occurred recently in the United Kingdom and the U.S. with government-sponsored health insurance.

(6) Tighter underwriting standards and stricter and less liberal policy provisions make it harder to sell new insurance, particularly to new and expanding market segments. The volume of the industry may suffer and costs may increase (such as advertising and sales commissions). This reduces the funds available for basic research aimed at achieving lasting solutions to these problems.

(7) The legal environment for enforcing contracts in their strict sense is jeopardized. Courts continually attempt to circumvent policy provisions and require payments of claims that were not anticipated when the rates were formulated. Due in part to public awareness of insurance, liability insurance losses in the U.S., for example, have been rising spectacularly in recent years.

## Some Evidence on the Extent of Social Problems

Few will doubt that there are many ways in which insurance may be adversely affected by social problems. Some suggestions were offered above as to ways in which this may occur from civil unrest in metropolitan areas. What of other social problems such as divorce, crime, and poverty? There seems to be a tendency to be complacent about such problems in general. Some statistical highlights adding some quantitative dimensions to this problem in the U.S. are given below:

### DIVORCE

As one social scientist stated, "Disorganization of the family is considered by most critics of the contemporary scene as the basic and most crucial problem in American society." [7] Clearly, breakdown of the family structure is of basic importance to insurance companies for it is in the family that the child develops his basic attitude toward society and toward the institutions which bind the society together. Children from divorced families and illegitimate children clearly do not make the ideal customer for insurance companies as a group.

How serious is the rate of family breakdown in American soceity? As shown in Table 2, the percentage of female population who are divorced

---

[7] Goldman, Nathan, "Social Breakdown," *The Annals of The American Acadamy of Political and Social Science,* Vol. 373, (Sept., 1967), p. 158.

TABLE 2

DIVORCE RATES IN THE U.S.

| Year | Percent of Female Population Divorced | Divorces per 1000 Population * |
|------|---------------------------------------|-------------------------------|
| 1940 | 1.8 | 2.0 |
| 1955 | 2.4 | 2.3 |
| 1969 | 3.7 | 3.3 |

* Includes Annulments.
Sources: Department of Health, Education, and Welfare, *Vital Statistics of the United States;* U.S. Department of Commerce, Bureau of Census, *Current Population Reports,* Series P-20.

in the United States has about doubled since 1940, running nearly 4 percent in 1969. In a similar manner, illegitimate births have increased 3.5-fold since 1940. The illegitimate birth ratio for non-white persons in the United States is about six times that for white persons. While only five percent of white births were illegitimate as shown in Table 3.

TABLE 3

ILLEGITIMATE BIRTH RATIO IN THE U.S.

| Year | Ratio Per 1000 Live Births | | |
|------|-------|-----------|-------|
|      | White | Non White | Total |
| 1940 | 19.5 | 168.3 | 37.9 |
| 1950 | 17.5 | 179.6 | 39.8 |
| 1960 | 22.9 | 215.8 | 52.7 |
| 1968 | 53.3 | 312.0 | 96.9 |

Source: *Vital Statistics of the U.S., 1968,* op. cit., Vol. I, p. 1-22.

## CRIME

Crime rates for each 100,000 inhabitants in the United States have increased approximately 120 percent during the period 1960-1969, as shown in Table 4. The brief period was selected because of reasonable consistency in the statistics over this period. The data probably understate the true crime rate in absolute terms but are shown here for comparative purposes. Crime plagues minority races more than the white population. About 26 percent of black households experienced some serious crime in 1965, compared to 19 percent of white households. Low-income groups suffer higher rates of victimization than higher-income groups for all crimes except larcenies and auto theft. A classification of the crime loss according to type is given in Table 5. Total cost of crime in the United States in 1965 was estimated conservatively at $21 billion. Very little of this crime loss, incidentally, is insured, but must be borne directly by the victims.

TABLE 4

CRIME RATES IN THE UNITED STATES, 1960 AND 1969

| Types of Offense | Crimes Per 100,000 Inhabitants | | Percent Increase |
|---|---|---|---|
| | 1960 | 1969 | 1969/1970 |
| Forcible Rape | 9 | 18 | 100 |
| Murder | 5 | 7 | 40 |
| Robbery | 60 | 147 | 146 |
| Assault | 85 | 152 | 79 |
| Burglary | 501 | 966 | 93 |
| Larceny ($50 up) | 282 | 749 | 165 |
| Auto Theft | 182 | 432 | 138 |
| Total | 1123 | 2471 | 120 |

Source: Federal Bureau of Investigation, *Uniform Crime Reports for the U.S.*

TABLE 5

ESTIMATED COST OF CRIME IN THE U.S., 1965
(BILLIONS)

| | |
|---|---|
| Crimes against persons | $ .815 |
| Crimes against property | 3.932 |
| Miscellaneous | 2.036 |
| Illegal goods and services | 8.075 |
| Cost of Police department and courts | 4.212 |
| Prevention | 1.910 |
| Total | $20,980 |

Source: President's Committee on Law Enforcement and Administration of Justice, *The Challenge of Crime in a Free Society,* 1967, p. 145.

In the meantime, the prison population in the United States has been increasing steadily, reaching in 1966 the figure of 194,000 persons, a rate of 99 individuals for each 100,000 of population. In 1967 nearly 78,000 new prisoners were received from the Courts for imprisonment in the various federal and state prisons in the United States.[8]

## POVERTY

Although the United States has been making progress in reducing poverty, there are still 25 million "poor" people representing approximately 13 percent of the people. The definition of what constitutes poverty varies considerably. Although the most common way to define "one who is poor" is the income standard, many social scientists would add other dimensions to the definition, such as the ability to move from one social

---

[8] U.S. Department of Justice, Bureau of Prisons, *National Prisoner Statistics,* Bulletin Nos. 43 and 44.

class to another, to participate in decision making, income stability, education, political position, and status and satisfaction. Using an income standard, the percentage of people who are poor in the United States has dropped from 22.1 percent in 1959 to 12.8 percent in 1968. About 10 percent of all white persons are poor under the definition and 35 percent of all non-white persons are poor.[9]

One of the dimensions of poverty other than income level is that of social mobility. A person who is poor and has little or no chance of ever changing this situation clearly has a worse position than another person who does have such an opportunity. A society with good social and economic mobility clearly will make a better market for products, including insurance, than a society which does not have this situation. In the United States, for example, work in the area of social and economic mobility reveals the following facts: [10] 51 percent of a group of individuals age 55-64 who were in the lower third of families ranked by income in 1928 were still in the lower third by 1960. However, 30 percent had moved to the middle third of the income bracket and 18 percent to the top third. One topic for research would be to determine who it is within these groups who moved, and what the characteristics are of a poor person who is likely to be permanently poor. In formulating marketing plans, for example, for insurance it would appear that this factor ought to be taken into consideration.

## Does Business Have a Social Obligation to Help?

In the three areas of social patterns mentioned above, a picture which should be very disturbing to insurance evidently has been sketched. The sketch portrays the threat of family breakdown, rising crime rates and substantial poverty. Is the insurance industry or business generally concerned about the social environment which will affect marketing plans for the 1970s?

Increasingly, business does appear to be recognizing that it does have a social obligation to make an effort to cooperate with other groups in curing some of the social problems outlined above. For example, in a study sponsored by the National Industrial Conference Board, more than a thousand executives responded to a questionnaire on what problems faced them and the extent to which they would be willing to institute actions to effect solutions. Out of 13 socioeconomic issues, more than 50 percent of the executives were willing to initiate action on ten. Table 6 summarizes their opinions on some of the issues. As one writer stated, "If indeed American business ever did exist in a state of splendid and arrogant isolation from the larger community, those days have long since

---

[9] U.S. Department of Commerce, Bureau of the Census, *Correct Population Reports,* Series p. 60.

[10] Miller, S. M., Rein, M., Roby, P., and Gross, B. M., "Poverty, Inequality and Conflict," *Annals of The American Academy of Political and Social Science,* Vol. 373, p. 24, Sept. 1967.

passed. I take it as axiomatic that businessmen not only have a great need to know about the changing social environment within which they operate, but, in addition, they are required to act upon this knowledge if they are to meet the minimum expectation which the public has of them." [11]

TABLE 6

BUSINESS ATTITUDES TOWARD SOCIAL PROBLEMS

| Problem | Percent of Executives Favoring Initiatory Action by Business |
|---|---|
| Air Pollution | 73.5 |
| Retraining unemployed displaced by automation | 72.6 |
| Improvement work/career opportunities for minorities | 69.2 |
| Improving and purifying water supply | 68.3 |
| Better medical facilities | 62.1 |
| Better law enforcement | 61.4 |
| Better urban transportation | 60.4 |
| Better cultural facilities | 59.1 |
| Better education and recreational facilities | 55.6 |
| Problems of school dropouts | 53.9 |
| Improving local school curriculum | 48.5 |
| Medical care for aged | 35.9 |
| Low-income housing | 31.3 |

Source: Finley, Grace J., "Business Defines Its Social Responsibilities," *The Conference Board Record,* November 1967, p. 10.

In spite of the personal feelings of executives, however, business as a whole is only beginning to act in a tangible way. For example, some business firms in the United States are currently taking an aggressive stance in addressing themselves to some of the current social problems. Some examples of these efforts are listed below:

(1) U.S. life insurance companies have pledged $2 billion to help rebuild inner cities. An ultimate goal of $60 billion investment in central cities exists.

(2) The Citizens Southern National Bank has invested $2.5 million in the slums of Savannah, Georgia, and since has broadened its program to include eleven other cities in Georgia served by the bank. It has promoted a trash cleanup, financed new business firms, purchased 75 new homes and renovated 1000 other homes.

(3) The National Alliance of Businessmen, with 18,500 member companies, has placed more than 200,000 ghetto residents in jobs, and has a goal of placing 614,000 others by June, 1971. General Electric Company

---

[11] Riley, John W., "Broadening Dimensions of Public Affairs," *Public Affairs Conference, Report No. 3,* November 1967.

donated $5 million and a 200,000 square foot building to the local school system and helps a "school factory" to educate and train school drop-outs.[12] In most cases, the contributions made so far by businessmen have, at least in part, a profit motive. For example, one company, The Eastern Gas and Fuel Association, helped rehabilitate 3,000 apartments in the city of Boston and thereby added 3,000 gas-using customers. A social motive also exists. As Henry Ford stated, "Improving the quality of society—investing in better employees and customers for tomorrow—is nothing more than another step in the evolutionary process of taking a more farsighted view of return on investment." [13] Yet in 1966 all manufacturing industries spent only 1.69 percent of their total capital expenditures on air and water pollution control.[14]

Insurance executives gradually appear to be recognizing the need for greater involvement. As Gilbert W. Fitzhugh stated, companies "do have social responsibilities; they did not seek them, but they are inescapable. They are part of the warp and woof of society in which we live." [15]

This statement of Mr. Fitzhugh shows some apparent reluctance to accept increased responsibility for active attempts to solve social problems. Undoubtedly this opinion is typical of much opinion among executives who feel the corporations do have a social responsibility, but who may not be quite ready yet to take action to implement some of the programs which they feel could be of value. However, as Adolph A. Berle warns, "The bankers of 1925 didn't interest themselves in public affairs. The resulting crash caused the power to go to Washington and most of it never came back." [16]

A conclusion would be that at least some corporations gradually are recognizing that a healthy social and economic environment is necessary for good business health. In particular, marketing success is affected vitally by social environment. This applies particularly to insurance since this industry is linked closely to society as one of its basic and indispensible institutions.

## What Types of Research Should Insurance Companies Support?

It is the argument in this paper that insurance companies should support more subsurface (as opposed to surface) research than they have in the past. This does not mean that surface research should be abandoned, or that subsurface research has no application to practical problems, but rather more emphasis should be placed on more fundamental

[12] The above examples are based on a *Business Week* feature article, "The War that Business Must Win," *Business Week,* Nov. 1, 1969, pp. 63-74.

[13] *Ibid.*

[14] Watson, John H., III, "Capital Expenditures for Pollution Abatement," *Conference Board Report,* Sept. 1967, p. 27.

[15] Fitzhugh, Gilbert W., "Company Responsibility—Too Much or Not Enough," *Conference Board Report,* April, 1964, pp. 7-17.

[16] *Conference Board Report, op. cit.,* p. 10.

problems affecting the marketing environment of insurance. Some examples will indicate the nature of the difference between surface research and subsurface research:

### Surface Research Problems

1. Studies to determine the extent to which "fragile" cars cost more to repair than more durable cars with implications for insurance rating.

2. Ways in which design of industrial machinery may be changed to prevent accidents.

3. Adequacy of pensions and other retirement programs in meeting current living costs of retirees.

4. The effectiveness of advertising in producing sales.

5. Adequacy of fire insurance rates in given geographical areas.

### Subsurface Research on Identical Topics

1. Research on emotional attitudes of automobile drivers and ways and means to predict the attitudes and conditions under which emotionally-wrought individuals drive and cause accidents.

2. Studies to determine ways of teaching workers to avoid accidents in the first place through better social adjustments within the work environment.

3. A study of factors producing a good adjustment in retirement including, but not restricted to retirement income.

4. Basic psychological and sociological studies of the consumer as a prerequisite to the design of advertising campaigns.

5. Development of a credible fire insurance rating structure which genuinely reflects actual fire hazards.

Examples of recent subsurface research which are of potential value to insurers in predicting their future marketing environment are given below:

(1) In a certain study, two sociologists examined the social role of a sick person in an industrial situation. They found that there is a measured tendency for being "sickness prone," a concept analogous to "accident proneness." The insurance underwriter might be guided considerably by such a study in helping to predict disability income claims, workmen's compensation costs, and tailoring policy provisions to the specialized needs of insureds for health insurance.[17]

(2) In a survey of 312 Negro men in the Watts area of Los Angeles, California, some social scientists asked a series of questions concerning the willingness of the subjects to use violence in order to obtain Negro rights. In comparing answers to the question "Have you ever done anything social with white people, like visiting each others' homes?", 44 percent of those with low contact also expressed a willingness to use violence in order to get Negro rights, compared to only 17 percent who were willing to use violence and who were high in their rate of having

---

[17] Mechanic, David, and Volkert, Edmund, "Stress, Illness, Behavior, and the Sick Role," *American Sociological Review*, Feb. 1961, Vol. 26, No. 1, pp. 51-58.

contact with white people. Of the group, only 16 had actually participated in the Watts riots.[18] Would this study provide any leads to insurers in offering coverage to persons living in ghetto areas?

(3) In an experimental study 13 orphans less than three years old were removed from a state orphanage and put into a home for retarded women. Two years later their I.Q.'s increased sharply from those which had been measured at the time they left the orphanage. Meanwhile, those remaining at the orphanage had lower I.Q.'s. When the 13 orphans grew up they were normal. Most of the others spent their entire lives in institutions. The study demonstrated the role of the love and attention from the retarded women in bringing about a better adjustment for the 13 children who left the state institution.[19] Could such a finding be used to support advertising or sales themes for life and health insurance designed to keep families from being broken apart due to loss of life or health of the parents?

(4) In a study about unemployment of young people, an author [20] noted that the unemployment rate for youths 16-19 typically is double the national rate. Many of these youths are high school dropouts. For many, the only possible employer is the government. Reasons for their unemployment are not, as commonly believed, the slow growth of teenage-intensive industries, the effect of minimum wages, or unemployed due to a mismatch of skills (structural unemployment). Major reasons were seasonality of industries, employer discrimination, and in general an increased supply of young people. Does this study have relevance to the need for increased manpower in the insurance industry?

One may question from the above three examples what type of relationship, profitable or otherwise, the insurance industry is likely to have with (a) youths 16-19, (b) the orphans who remained in the state institution, and (c) the Negro men in the Watts area who had relatively little contact with white people and were relatively willing to use violence to obtain Negro rights. Are these individuals whose attitudes as potential customers, employees, claimants, or regulators the insurance industry can afford to ignore? The decade of the 1970s is likely to witness conditions under which minority groups such as these may have considerable influence on public opinion. Any industry whose markets are as affected by public opinion as insurance certainly must learn as much as it can about the forces affecting public opinion if it is to operate successfully.

(5) A large American insurance company supported the work of a psychologist who studied basic attitudes toward automobile insurance held by a sample of its customers. It was discovered that at the time of an automobile accident a typical victim tended to look around for somebody to protect him. In a state of emotional insecurity he looked upon

---

[18] *Trans-Action,* Feb. 1969, p. 8.

[19] *Trans-Action,* Sept. 1969, p. 6.

[20] Folk, Hugh, "Oversupply of the Young," *Trans-Action,* Sept. 1969, pp. 27-32.

insurance as a "father figure." Many types of painful image passed through his mind as he wondered what was going to happen to his damaged automobile, how he was to pay for medical losses and whether or not he would have to pay for other people's injuries and property damage. A subsequent advertising campaign capitalizing on this situation was developed and proved to be enormously effective in fostering a protective image of this particular company's attitude toward accident victims. One should contrast this situation with the attitude of other insurance companies when faced with a claim by one of their own insureds. Adjustors may tend to be distant and deal with clients at "arms length." A legalistic approach to negligence may be assumed. Doubt is shown as to whether the insurance is "good" or not or whether or not the client has met all the terms of his contract. Advertising campaigns of some agents even suggest the need of the agent's services to protect the interests of customers against their own insurers. Such an approach is hardly likely to foster customer loyalty.

(6) A study was made of nine poverty neighborhoods in Cleveland.[21] Six of these neighborhoods had predominantly non-white population and three had only a few blacks. Ninety-one percent of the city's Negro population lived in these nine poverty areas which contained 29 percent of the city's population in 1960. Five years later, in 1965, the percentage of Negroes living outside the nine areas rose from nine to 15 percent. The Negro groups who had escaped the nine poverty areas enjoyed a steadily rising income, but those who remained had a worsening position. For example, in one of the poverty areas unemployment rose to more than 20 percent in 1965. Cleveland was characterized by extensive riots in 1965. The predominant reason for these was attributed to the deteriorated nature of the social life in the poverty-stricken area.

Should insurance companies be concerned with the isolating and analysis of a deteriorating situation such as that which occurred in Cleveland? What should insurance companies have done, if anything, (a) to detect the deteriorating condition in the first place, (b) to assume a leadership role in helping correct substandard conditions, and thus (c) to help prevent the tremendous property losses and other upheavals which occurred in this city in 1965? In the decade of the 1970s there will be increasing numbers of insurance executives who will answer such questions positively, with constructive suggestions, if the insurance industry is to extend its understanding of the marketing environment.

(7) Some researchers made a study of 83 four-year Negro colleges in 1965, 21 classed as "good" (six of these were elite), 32 "fair," and 30 "poor." The colleges were evaluated according to their students' standings on nationwide tests and a subjective evaluation by six experts from education foundations. The 30 poor institutions had little hope for any

---

[21] Moynihan, Daniel P., "Urban Conditions: General," *The Annals of the American Academy of Political and Social Science,* Vol. 371, May 1967, pp. 159-177.

change for the better. Most of the teachers for Negro high schools and grade schools come from these colleges. Over half of the students attending these Negro colleges (some 60,000) are "unlikely to be helped by their education" because of poor background, inadequate preparation, and poor teaching.[22]

Will the growing Negro market for insurance be taught by increasingly inadequate teachers? Should the insurance industry do anything to correct this situation as its contribution toward improving their nature as insurance consumers in the 1970s?

A recent report [23] indicated for example that over the decade 1960-1969 more blacks finished college than ever before, but the high school dropout rate in 1970 for black males was still nearly 16 percent, compared to 6.7 percent for whites; unemployment for non-whites was nearly double that of whites, 8 percent $v$. 4.5 percent. It seems doubtful that a healthy and growing market for insurance will exist among persons who are uneducated and unemployed even though they may need insurance badly.

(8) A widely used argument for life insurance is to provide a fund from which the costs of a college education may be met for the children. Implicit in this assumption is that if the funds are available the child, will in all likelihood, go to college. Research shows, however, that education of the father, not family income, is the major factor in predicting whether or not the child will go to college. For example, in the U.S. in 1960, for families with incomes between $7,500 and $10,000, about 86 percent of the children age 16-20 enrolled in college from families in this income bracket if the father attended college compared to about 44 percent in families where the father did not graduate from high school.[24] Two families of the same income obviously have many other differences in insurance-buying habits besides insurance to provide a college education for children. Should insurance marketers conduct studies to learn of these differences?

## Conclusion

This paper has attempted to present some of the reasons why the insurance industry should be concerned with the changing marketing environment in the decade of the 1970s. The argument runs as follows:

1. The decade of the 1970s promises to be one of very rapid change in all basic demographic measures—population, income, production, education and family formulation—factors affecting insurance markets significantly.

2. Insurers will have less time to adjust to changes than formerly.

---

[22] Jaffe, A. J., Adams, Walter, and Meyers, S. G., *College Board Review*, Winter, 1967-1968.

[23] *Time*, August 9, 1971, p. 16.

[24] Miller, S. M., Rein, M., Roby, P., and Gross, B. M., *op. cit.*, p. 38.

3. Evidences of social disorganization are appearing which especially complicate the marketing problems of insurers, which depend on social and economic stability for growth and even for survival. Insurance is a basic social institution in developed societies and its fortunes are vitally affected by the health of these societies.

4. Past history contains many examples of marketing failures among insurers, when basic research and planning would have at least mitigated, if not prevented, these failures.

5. Basic investigation into the nature and causes of social disorganization should be initiated and supported by insurers as a fundamental approach to understanding the new marketing environment in the 1970s. In this way it is possible that insurance effectively, efficiently, and profitably can serve the growing markets of the 1970s without devoting as much energy as it has in the past of treating symptoms, rather than causes, of the underlying economic malfunction.

### Questions

1. The author states that insurers should be doing research on basic social problems rather than on "problems which are mainly surface indications of deeper ills." Give some examples, either from the article or from your own experience, of problems that are "mainly surface indications of deeper ills." Explain.
2. In what sense is the insurance mechanism in society a basic sociological function? Does insurance characterize all societies?
3. Which of the three basic social problems discussed—poverty, crime, and divorce—do you think is most closely related to the growth and survival of insurance? Why?
4. If you were attempting to sell life insurance policies for the purpose of educating a child in college, what sociological phenomenon might influence your decision as to which type of potential customers to approach? Explain.

# PART 4
## Property Insurance

The articles in this part have been selected to expose the reader to some of the legal questions in property insurance and to indicate how these questions are treated in depth in the literature. The areas of insurable interest, actual cash value, strict liability, and other insurance are discussed. Although these legal concepts, at first glance, may seem to be clear-cut, they involve many important and complex concepts that help the student to gain a deeper understanding of the insurance contract.

# 13. THE LAW OF INSURABLE INTEREST IN PROPERTY INSURANCE *

Gary I. Salzman †

Historically, a factor in the public prejudice against insurance was the failure on the part of the insurers and the law to require an insurable interest in the subject of the insurance. Early forms of insurance policies frequently could not be distinguished from gambling or wager contracts.

The development of the concept of insurable interest is not entirely clear. Early policies on people's lives were frequently condemned as immoral wagers on human lives and were prohibited. Although insurable interest in the subject of the insurance was held essential[1] at an early period in the history of English common law, public policy seemed to grow lax and permitted the enforcement of gambling contracts. In the 18th century public policy became more effective.

The English judges opposed contracts that were pure wagers and attempted to discourage their enforcement, but did not declare them invalid. To keep these contracts from becoming legal under common law, there apparently developed the concept that a contract must not be contrary to public policy.[2]

"At common law insurances by way of gaming or wagering were valid, but a policy which did not contain a clause expressly dispensing with proof of interest, or which did not otherwise show that the contract was not intended to be one of indemnity, was deemed to be a contract of indemnity on which the assured could not recover without proof of interest. A policy expressly made "interest or no interest" or 'without further proof of interest than the policy itself or 'without benefit of salvage to the insurer' is commonly called a 'p. p. i. policy' (that is, policy proof of interest) or an 'honour or wager policy.' "[3]

Gambling and wagering were not prohibited by English common law but were void by the common law of Scotland.[4] A mutual intention

* From *The Insurance Law Journal* (July, 1966), pp. 394-405. Reprinted by permission.
† Professor of Business Law, University of Miami.
[1] Vance, *Insurance* 159 (3d ed. 1951).
[2] 18 *Columbia Law Review* 381 (1918).
[3] 22 Halsbury, *Laws of England* 106 (3d ed. 1958).
[4] MacGillivray, *Insurance Law* 427 (4th ed. 1953).

to enter into a wagering transaction was, however, necessary before a policy made without interest could be supported. If the policy purported on the face of it to be a contract of indemnity, and was in fact made by the assured without interest, the assured could not recover and the practice of the court was to assume that all policies which could possibly bear that construction were indemnity policies made on interest. Policies, therefore, which were intended to be mere wagering contracts had to be expressed as to show that the promise to pay was not a contract of indemnity but a promise to pay irrespective of interest. It was for that reason that the clause known as the p. p. i. (policy proof of interest) clause was introduced.

The courts, however, still upheld the validity of wagering contracts but stipulated that the face of the contract had to indicate that it was intended as a wager, and thereby dispensed with the need for an insurable interest.[5] Finally when it became apparent that a gaming use of insurance increased the loss ratio, legislative action prohibited the making of marine insurance contracts if the insured had no insurable interest in the subject of the insurance.[6]

"It seems to have been anciently the doctrine of the common law that mere wager policies, that is, policies in which the insured has no interest whatever in the matter insured, were void as against public policy. This was the law of England prior to the Revolution of 1688. After that period a course of decisions grew up, sustaining wager policies. The legislature finally interposed and prohibited such insurance, first in regard to marine insurance, by the statute 19 Geo. II, c. 37, and later with regard to lives, by the statute 14 Geo, III, c. 48,"[7]

Some cases say the requirement of insurable interest originated with the English statute, others say the statute was merely declaratory of the common law.[8] The uncertainty, however, ends with the passing of the statute of Marine Insurance Act, 1745, 19 Geo, II, c. 37.

The Act of 1745 prohibited policies made, "interest or no interest or without further proof of interest than the policy," and that was construed as requiring the contract to be a contract to pay on interest subsisting at the date of loss, and no other interest was required.[9]

The Act itself says:

"An act to regulate insurance on ships belonging to the subjects of Great Britain, and on merchandizes or effects laden thereon.

---

[5] *Connecticut Mutual Life Insurance Co.* v. *Schaeffer*, 94 U. S. 457, 24 L. Ed. 251 (1876).

[6] Marine Insurance Act, 1745, 19 Geo. II, c. 37.

[7] 16 *The American and English Encyclopedia of Law* 845 (2d ed. 1900).

[8] 16 *Minnesota Law Review* 569, n. 3 (1932).

[9] Work cited at footnote 4, at p. 434.

"Whereas, it hath been found by experience that the making assurances, interest or no interest, or without further proof of interest than the policy, hath been productive of many pernicious practices, whereby great numbers of ships, with their cargoes, have either been fraudulently lost and destroyed, or taken by the enemy in time of war; . . . and by introducing a mischievous kind of gaming or wagering, under the pretence of assuring the risque on shipping, and fair trade, the institution and laudable design of making assurances, hath been perverted; . . . be it enacted . . . That . . . no assurance or assurances shall be made by any person or persons, bodies corporate or politic, on any ship, or ships belonging to his Majesty, or any of his subjects, or on any goods, merchandizes, or effects, laden or to be laden on board any such ship or ships, interest or no interest, or without further proof of interest than the policy, or by way of gaming or wagering, or without benefit of salvage to the assurer, and that every such assurance shall be null and void to all intents and purposes."[10]

It seems that this insurable interest statute of 1745 was not adopted by the American states as part of the English law.[11] Therefore, some of our states require insurable interest by statute.

Although the statute of 14 George III, c. 48 (1774) dealt primarily with insurable interest in lives, it also included some reference to interest on other events. For instance:

". . . That from and after the passing of this act, no insurance shall be made by any person or persons, bodies politick or corporate, on the life or lives of any person or persons, or on any other event or events, whatsoever, wherein the person or persons for whose use, benefit, or on whose account such policy or policies shall be made, shall have no interest or by way of gaming or wagering: and that every assurance made contrary to the true intent and meaning hereof, shall be null and void, to all intents and purposes whatsoever"[12]

Whether these statutes were declaratory of the common law or not, the courts of the American states have generally held that wager policies are against public policy and void.[13]

Subsequently came the Marine Insurance Act 1906, 6 Ed. 7, c. 41 which said in part:

"Every contract of marine insurance by way of gaming or wagering is void."

---

[10] Keeton, *Basic Insurance Law* 76 (1960).

[11] Patterson and Young, *Cases and Materials on The Law of Insurance* 75 (4th ed. 1961).

[12] Work cited at footnote 11, at p. 226.

[13] Work cited at footnote 1, at p. 184.

"The assured must be interested in the subject-matter insured at the time of the loss though he need not be interested when the insurance is effected."

"Where the assured has no interest at the time of the loss, he cannot acquire interest by any act or election after he is aware of the loss."

"A partial interest of any nature is insurable."[14]

This Act states that "contracts of marine insurance made without interest and with no expectation of acquiring interest in the subject matter and all p. p. i. policies are deemed to be gaming or wagering contracts. The Act does not, however, prohibit such contracts and therefore it does not make them illegal as well as void.[15]

Let us look at what the encyclopedias, texts, and court cases say insurable interest is.

## What Is Insurable Interest?

An insurable interest, generally, is that interest (required by law) created by the relation between the insured and the contingent event insured against which would cause a loss to the insured should the event actually occur.[16] It is also such an interest which precludes any wagering intent on the part of the person who will benefit by the event occurring.[17]

In property insurance, this requirement is intended to indemnify the insured against loss.[18] Generally it need not exist when the policy is insured but must exist at the time the event insured against occurs.[19]

Vance[20] and Richards[21] both say that the insurable interest must exist in the insured at the time of loss but need not be present at the time of purchase.

There is authority that claims the interest must also exist when the contract is originally made. "In property insurance an insurable interest generally must exist both at the time of the making of the contract and at the time of the loss. . . . ."[22]

"When the insurance is upon property, not only must the insured have an interest in the subject-matter of the contract at its inception, but also at the time of the loss; for the contact being one of

---

[14] Work cited at footnote 10, at p. 77.
[15] Work cited at footnote 4, at p. 43.
[16] Patterson, *Essentials of Insurance Law* 109 (2d ed. 1957).
[17] Work cited at footnote 1, at p. 157.
[18] Riegel and Miller, *Insurance Principles and Practices* 109 (3rd ed. 1947).
[19] Work cited at footnote 16, at p. 153.
[20] Work cited at footnote 1, at p. 159.
[21] Richards, *Law of Insurance* 327 (5th ed. 1952).
[22] 44 *Corpus Juris Secundum* 871.

indemnity, the recovery by the insured is limited to the loss actually sustained by him. As soon as his interest ceases in the property, the contract is at an end, from the impossibility of any loss happening to him afterward."[23]

"The books, both texts and reports, are full of statements to the effect that the insured must possess an interest at the time insurance is procured on property, as well as at the time the loss occurs, in order to free the contract from the fatal fault of being a wager. But notwithstanding the great volume of authority to this effect, it seems that the existence of an insurable interest at the inception of the contract is not at all necessary to its validity, unless made so by statute."[24]

Numerous attempts at defining or explaining insurable interest have been made.

"At all events, it has become a fixed rule of insurance law that the assured must have an interest of some kind in the subject matter of the insurance, whether property or life. Two reasons may be assigned for this rule. In the first place, it is inexpedient that a contract so necessary for the protection of legitimate business should be prostituted to illegal uses as a mode of speculation; and in the second place, it is opposed to public policy, because demoralizing to the insured, that he should be permitted to enter into any contract under which he would have an interest in the destruction of the subject-matter rather than its preservation."[25]

It is generally recognized that the law requires the existence of insurable interest in property in order to prevent wagering, to minimize the temptation to intentionally destroy the insured property, and to limit the insurer's liability.[26]

Harnett and Thornton suggest there are four broad types of insurable interest in property: property right, contract right, legal liability, and factual expectation of damage.[27] Patterson suggests the addition of a fifth type—representative insurable interests[28] (for the interest of another) which usually also involves one or more of the other types.

Theoretically, there is virtually universal agreement that insurable interest is necessary. There is however, much conflict of opinion as to what constitutes insurable interest and why it is required. Insurable interest has been defined as whatever furnishes a reasonable expectation of pecuniary benefit from the continued existence of the

---

[23] Work cited at footnote 7, at p. 846.
[24] Work cited at footnote 1, at p. 180.
[25] Work cited at footnote 7, at p. 846.
[26] Work cited at footnote 11, at p. 71.
[27] 48 *Columbia Law Review* 1162 (1948).
[28] Work cited at footnote 16, at p. 123.

subject of insurance,[29] or whatever would cause the suffering of a loss from its destruction.[30]

"The requirement of an insurable interest to support a contract of insurance is based upon considerations of public policy, which condemn as wagers all agreements for insurance of any subject in which the contracting parties have no such interest. That is to say, proof of circumstances that negative the existence of a wagering intent establishes the existence of an insurable interest."[31]

Generally, there are three potential harms which may result from issuing an insurance policy to one who does not have insurable interest: (1) the insured may cause the event; (2) a pure and simple wager may have been effected; (3) the insured may be paid more than he has lost. If the insured has no insurable interest he should not be entitled to any recovery since he cannot suffer any loss. The insured must have a right or interest which the law will recognize and protect. This right or interest must be such that the property destruction will have a direct effect upon it, not a remote and consequential one.[32]

Vance attempts to summarize the concept:

"A person has an insurable interest in property when he sustains such relations with respect to it that he has a reasonable expectation, resting upon a basis of legal right, of benefit to be derived from its continued existence, or of loss or liability from its destruction. More specifically, an insurable interest exists in the following cases:

"(a) When the insured possesses a legal title to the property insured, whether vested or contingent, defeasible or indefeasible.

"(b) When he has an equitable title, of whatever character and in whatever manner acquired.

"(c) When he possesses a qualified property or possessory right in the subject of the insurance, such as that of a bailee.

"(d) When he has mere possession or right of possession.

"(e) When he has neither possession of the property, nor any other legal interest in it, but stands in such relation with respect to it that he may suffer, from its destruction, loss of a legal right dependent upon its continued existence."[33]

Richards says it this way:

"By insurable interest in property is generally meant the relationship of a person or persons to the fortuitous event which causes loss or liability from its destruction, or benefit or advantage from its continued existence. A person has an insurable interest in

---

[29] *North British & Mercantile Insurance Co. v. Sciandra,* 7 Fire and Casualty Cases 671, 256 Ala. 409, 54 So. 2d 764, 27 A. L. R. 2d 1047 (1951).

[30] 29 *Am. Jur.* 438.

[31] Work cited at footnote 1, at p. 156.

[32] 18 *Atlantic Reporter Digest* 114 (1941).

[33] Work cited at footnote 1, at p. 161.

property when he has a right on or against the property, or a right derivative from some contract about the property, or a legal liability to make good the loss, or a factual expectation of economic advantage on benefit if the property continues to exist and of economic disadvantage or loss if the property is destroyed."[34]

It is difficult to define exactly what will comprise an insurable interest in all instances. Legal sources are not in agreement with each other. An early writing says that "an insurable interest can only be founded on a legal or equitable title; and a mere claim which the law cannot admit to be either legal or equitable, is not an insurable interest."[35] A more recent case says, "Everywhere there is a tendency to broaden the definition of an insurable interest; neither legal nor equitable title is necessary."[36] There apparently is developing a greater liberality in determining whether interest in property exists. The more complex economic society and relationships become, the stronger the impetus to extend the concept of insurable interest also becomes.

"Any interest in property, legal or equitable, qualified, conditional, contingent, or absolute, or merely the right to use the property, with or without the payment of rent, is sufficient."[37]

One does not need to have an absolute insurable right of property in the thing insured. If one's relationship to the property is such that he could reasonably anticipate a loss if the property were destroyed, there is insurable interest.[38] Neither legal, equitable or property interest in the subject matter is necessary.[39]

"One who is under a duty to insure property, the violation of which by failure to insure renders him liable for damages in the event of a loss of the property, should be deemed to have an insurable interest in the property. Anyone who has made himself responsible for property may insure it against loss."[40]

Our courts do not consistently concur as to when insurable interest exists.

"Although the courts differ somewhat as to the weight to be accorded the various policies underlying the requirement of an insurable interest, there is a general agreement that they must be served to some extent in every property insurance contract. But sharp disagreements arise in regard to the types and extents of interest in property that will constitute an insurable interest.

---

[34] Work cited at footnote 21.

[35] Marshall, *A Treatise on the Law of Insurance* 80 (1805).

[36] *Liverpool & London & Globe Insurance Co., Ltd. v. Bolling*, 2 FIRE AND CASUALTY CASES 534, 176 Va. 182, 10 S. E. 2d 518 (1940).

[37] 3 *Couch, Insurance* 88 (2d ed. 1960).

[38] Joyce, *Law of Insurance*, 1922 (2d ed. 1917).

[39] *Ben-Hur Manufacturing Co. v Firemen's Insurance Co. of New Jersey*, 11 FIRE AND CASUALTY CASES 694, 18 Wis. 2d 259, 118 N. W. 2d 159, 161, 162 (1962).

[40] Work cited at footnote 37, at p. 90.

The cases on point are voluminous and often difficult to reconcile even within a given jurisdiction."[41]

## SPECIFIC AREAS

### Title

It appears to be universally agreed that sole and unconditional ownership of legal title and beneficial interest constitutes an insurable interest in property.[42]

"Any legal title in property of whatever character, constitutes an insurable interest therein. The interest may be contingent and remote, but is yet insurable."[43]

Possession of an equitable title, however obtained, gives an insurable interest in the property. A vendee before conveyance, a mortgagor in some situations, a mortgagee, and the beneficiary under a deed of trust have all been held to have the necessary interest.[44]

### Contracts

"Any binding contract giving rights which will be injuriously affected by the destruction of any designated property will afford an insurable interest in such property."[45]

Where a contract is unenforceable or void, at law or in equity, no insurable interest exists when the only right derives from such contract.[46] Yet the insurable interest of a buyer is not marred where the purchase contract is not enforceable under the statute of frauds.[47]

Generally a person has no insurable interest when his right comes from a contract which is void or unenforceable.[48] Some cases, however, seem to imply that insurable interest may exist despite this.[49]

### Extent of Interest

Neither the courts nor the statutes attempt to measure the amount or degree of insurable interest that one has in the property in question. It appears to be unimportant that the insured's interest is overvalued, providing he has a substantial interest relative to the amount of insurance purchased.[50] The policy, however, will be deemed

---

[41] 44 *Iowa Law Review* 515 (1969).

[42] Work cited at footnote 41, at p. 516.

[43] Work cited at footnote 1, at p. 163.

[44] Work cited at footnote 1, at p. 167.

[45] Work cited at footnote 32, at p. 115.

[46] Work cited at footnote 30, at p. 294.

[47] Work cited at footnote 30, at p. 306.

[48] *Perry v. Mechanics' Mutual Insurance Co.*, (cc) 11 F. 478 (1882).

[49] *Redfield v. Holland P. Insurance co.*, 56 N. Y. 354, 15 Am Rep. 424.

[50] Work cited at footnote 37, at p. 67.

to be a wager where the insured's interest is grossly disproportionate to the amount of insurance.[51]

"A valued policy is not rendered a wagering contract merely because the value placed on the property is greater than the actual value, although recovery will be limited to the extent of the actual interest,"[52]

"Both American and English law, with some statutory limitations, permit the insured and insurer to agree in advance on the value of the insured's interest, and such a valuation, fixed in the policy (hence, a valued policy), will be accepted, in the absence of fraud or a subterfuge for wagering, as the basis for measuring the insured's provable claim."[53]

The general rule appears to be that a limited interest in a property will keep an insured from recovering the full value of the property. In fact, the courts limit recovery to the amount of the actual interest.[54] The courts apparently utilize both the principles of indemnity and subrogation as guideposts in deciding how much of the insured's interests are protected by the insurance contract.

## Expectation

Insurance encyclopedias and texts point out various properties which are characteristic of insurable interest. Vance stresses that an expectation of benefit to be derived from the continued existence of the subject, however likely and morally certain of realization it might be, will not afford a sufficient insurable interest unless that expectation has a basis of legal right.[55]

In Lord Eldon's famous words:

"If moral certainty be a ground of insurable interest, there are hundreds perhaps thousands, who would be entitled to insure. . . Suppose A. to be possessed of a ship limited to B. in case A. dies without issue; that A. has 20 children, the eldest of whom is 20 years of age; and B. 90 years of age; it is a moral certainty that B. will never come into possession, yet this is a clear interest. On the other hand, suppose the case of the heir at law of a man who has an estate worth £20,000 a-year, who is 90 years of age; upon his deathbed intestate, and incapable from incurable lunacy of making a will, there is no man who will deny that such an heir at law has a moral certainty of succeeding to the estate, yet the law will not allow that he has any interest, or any thing more than a mere expectation."[56]

---

[51] Work cited at footnote 37, at p. 68.
[52] Work cited at footnote 37, at p. 67.
[53] Work cited at footnote 16, at p. 109.
[54] Work cited at footnote 11, at p. 107.
[55] Work cited at footnote 1, at p. 157.
[56] Work cited at footnote 10, at p. 87.

# Possession

It is usually held that one having a mere right of possession of property may insure it to its full value and in his own name.[57] Whether one has an insurable interest in property is tested by the question of whether he will be directly and financially affected by loss of the property.[58]

"When a sale of property is made by one who is not the owner and does not have authority to sell the property, it is held that the vendee, not having acquired any title as against the true owner, does not have an insurable interest."

There is authority, however, that when property is delivered into the possession of a third person by the unauthorized act of an agent or purported owner, the possessor may still have an insurable interest although he has no right to possession. The theory here followed is that as he is accountable to the true owner for the restoration of the property he will suffer pecuniary loss if the property is damaged.[59]

"A person having a 'qualified property' in chattels, entitling him to possession and the right of using or dealing with them in accordance with the terms of the bailment has such an interest in the chattels as may be the subject of a valid contract of insurance."[60] This would be equally applicable to all classes of bailees, as innkeepers, warehousemen, commission merchants, factors, receivers, and so forth.

## SPECIFIC INTERESTS

Stockholders of a corporation may usually lawfully insure the corporation's property to the extent of the interest which they possess.[61] There appears to be much inconsistency in the state determinations in this area. Some courts hold that a stockholder has neither legal title to nor insurable interest in a corporation's building.[62]

"So it is generally held that a stockholder may insure the property of the corporation, although he has no legal interest whatsoever in such property. His expectation of benefit to be derived from the continued existence of such property, however, is based upon his legal right as stockholder to demand participation in the profits of the corporation, or in its assets upon dissolution."[63]

---

[57] Work cited at footnote 32, at p. 115.
[58] Work cited at footnote 1, at p. 173.
[59] Work cited at footnote 37, at p. 73.
[60] Work cited at footnote 1, at p. 168.
[61] Work cited at footnote 37, at p. 180.
[62] Work cited at footnote 32, at p. 115.
[63] Work cited at footnote 1, at p. 58.

Remaindermen,[64] curtesy[65] and dower consummate, any other life estate,[66] reversioners,[67] lessors,[68] and lessees[69]—all are deemed to have the requisite interest.

"A debtor who owns property has like any other property owner an insurable interest in the property by virtue of the fact that he will sustain loss by its destruction. A debtor assigning his assets for the benefit of creditors has an insurable interest in the property assigned as he is entitled to a return of any surplus left after the payment of his creditors."[70]

"Even a person in adverse and open possession of a building has an insurable interest, since in course of time he will acquire a good title if the true owner does not oust him."[71]

"On the other hand, a mere squatter, who does not hold adversely to the true owner and hence will not become an owner by lapse of time, has no insurable interest." [72]

"It is generally held that the husband has no insurable interest in the separate property of his wife when statutes deny him the right of possession or the enjoyment of profits, although he may be in actual possession. This is true even where the wife may not sell or incumber the property without the consent of her husband manifested by his signature to the conveyance. Likewise, the husband has no insurable interest although he might under the law of intestate succesion inherit her property."[73]

"It is apparent that the instances in which the husband may insure the property of the other spouse are exceptional rather than general. Perhaps the most generally recognized of these exceptions is the right of the husband to insure the property which is occupied as a homestead even though the title is in his wife [sic, wife's name]. His interest in the homestead is of such a character that its destruction would result in a direct pecuniary loss to him." [74]

"Household goods represent one of the most conspicuous exceptions to the general rule. The husband and the wife each have an insurable interest in all the household furniture used in the home, regardless of how the title was acquired or who may be the separate owner thereof for other purposes."[75]

---

[64] Work cited at footnote 1, at p. 163.
[65] Work cited at footnote 1, at p. 164.
[66] Work cited at footnote 1, at p. 164.
[67] Work cited at footnote 1, at p. 164.
[68] Work cited at footnote 1, at p. 164.
[69] Work cited at footnote 1, at p. 164.
[70] Work cited at footnote 37, at p. 115.
[71] Work cited at footnote 16, at p. 112.
[72] Work cited at footnote 16, at p. 112.
[73] 15 *Iowa Law Review* 482 (June 1930).
[74] Work cited at footnote 73.
[75] Work cited at footnote 73, at p. 484.

There is conflict in the case decisions whether a husband retains insurable interest in real property which he conveys to his wife, although he personally paid the consideration at the time of the original purchase.[76]

The encyclopedias and law books are full of cases individually determining whether specific relationships constitute insurable interest in property. These run the alphabetical gamut from advances (of money) to warehouseman situations. Most follow the general rules indicated throughout this article.

"Any interest in property, legal or equitable, qualified, conditional, contingent, or absolute, or merely the right to use the property with or without the payment of rent, is sufficient."[77]

Sometimes, the general rules do not seem to apply.

"A simple contract creditor, without a lien, either statutory or contractual, without a *jus in re* or *jus ad rem,* owning a mere personal claim against his debtor has no interest in the property of his debtor, and insurance contracts based on an alledged interest therein arising out of such a claim are void as against public policy. Similarly, a simple contract creditor of a corporation does not have any insurable interest in the corporate property."[78]

"The making of contributions does not create an insurable interest in the property purchased with the contributions. A turnpike company which voluntarily contributes to the erection of a bridge, to be used by its customers and the general public, has no insurable interest in the bridge, nor can the county intervene, in case of loss by fire, to claim the insurance effected by the company, nor is either the company or the county entitled to claim compensation, as part of the insurance, for loss of tolls while the bridge is rebuilding."[79]

There is conflict whether a life tenant who insures his interest beyond its value may retain this excess or hold it in trust for the remainderman.[80]

"The only point upon which courts can be said to be in universal agreement is that sole and unconditional ownership of legal title and beneficial interest constitutes an insurable interest in property. Beyond that there is substantial agreement that the holding of legal title without a beneficial interest in the property is adequate and that an equitable interest will suffice."[81]

This is what the encyclopedias, texts, and cases say insurable interest in property is. Now let us look at the various state statutes.

---

[76] Work cited at footnote 37, at p. 137.
[77] *First National Bank v. Burnside National Bank*, 314 Pa. 536, 172 A. 641 (1934).
[78] Work cited at footnote 37, at p. 88.
[79] Work cited at footnote 37, at p. 113.
[80] Work cited at footnote 37, at p. 182.
[81] Work cited at footnote 41, at p. 516.

## STATUTES

Half of the states have no statute. on insurable interest in property insurance.[82] Additionally, four states have statutes restricted to the interest of a railroad and owner of property adjoining the route of the tracks.[83] Pennsylvania[84] has a statute on insurable interest in goods sold, and Wyoming[85] has a statute on insurable interest limited to prohibiting overinsurance. Montana[86] repealed its statute.

California,[87] North Dakota,[88] and South Dakota[89] have statutes which are quite similar in wording. California is illustrative:

"If the insured has no insurable interest, the contract is void."

"Definition. Every interest in property, or in any relation thereto, or liability in respect thereof, of such a nature that a contemplated peril might directly damnify the insured, is an insurable interest."

"In what may consist. An insurable interest in property may consist in:

1. An existing interest;

2. An inchoate interest founded on an existing interest; or,

3. An expectancy, coupled with an existing interest in that out of which the expectancy arises."

"Contingency or expectancy. A mere contingent or expected interest in anything, not founded on an actual right to the thing, nor upon any valid contract for it, is not insurable."

"Measure of interest. Except in the case of a property held by the insured as a carrier or depositary, the measure of an insurable interest in property is the extent to which the insured might be damnified by loss or injury thereof."

"Carrier or depositary. A carrier or depositary of any kind has an insurable interest in a thing held by him as such, to the extent of its value."

"When required to exist. An interest in property insured must exist when the insurance takes effect, and when the loss occurs, but need not exist in the meantime. . . ."

---

[82] Alabama, Alaska, Delaware, Illinois, Indiana, Iowa, Kansas, Maine, Michigan Minnesota, Mississippi, Missouri, Montana, Nevada, New Mexico, North Carolina, Ohio, Oregon, Rhode Island, South Carolina, Tennessee, Texas, Utah, Vermont, and Wisconsin.

[83] Connecticut, Massachusetts, New Hampshire and New Jersey.

[84] Purdon's Penna. Stat. Ann., V. 12A Sec. 2-501 (1954).

[85] Wyo. Stat,. V. 7, 26-77 (1957).

[86] Rev. Codes of Mont., V. 3, Pt 1, 207 (Ch. 40) (1947), repealed by Sec. 673, Ch. 286, Laws 1959.

[87] Deering's Cal. Codes, Secs. 280-286, Ins. Ann. (1963).

[88] N. D. Century Code Ann., V. 4, 26-02-04—26-02-08, 26-02-10 (1960).

[89] S. D. Code, V. 1, 31.2202-31.2205 (1939).

Arizona,[90]Florida,[91]Georgia,[92]Hawaii,[93]Idaho,[94]Oklahoma,[95]andWest Virginia[96] have virtually the identical statute. Arizona is illustrative:

"A. No insurance contract on property or of any interest therein or arising therefrom shall be enforceable as to the insurance except for the benefit of persons having an insurable interest in the things insured.

"B. 'Insurable interest' as used in this section means any actual, lawful, and substantial economic interest in the safety or preservation of the subject of the insurance free from loss, destruction or pecuniary damage or impairment.

"C. The measure of an insurable interest in property is the extent to which the insured might be damnified by loss, injury or impairment thereof."

Arkansas,[97] Kentucky,[98] Louisiana,[99] Virginia,[100] and Washington[101] also use this statute but eliminate Section C.

Hawaii and Louisiana add the following:

"Interest of the Insured: When the name of a person intended to be insured is as specified in the policy, such insurance can be applied only to his own proper interest."

The New York[102] Statute says:

"No contract or policy of insurance on property made or issued in this state, or made or issued upon any property in this state, shall be enforceable except for the benefit of some person having an insurable interest in the property insured.

## Questions

1. From the discussion by the author, deduce a definition of a gamble or wager contract and explain its implications.
2. The author lists five types of insurable interest at one point, but does not develop them. They are (a) property right, (b) contract right, (c) legal liability, (d) factual expectation of damage, and (e) representative insurable interest. Discuss their possible meanings.
3. Is insurable interest a matter of degree or is it an absolute yes or no? Does it or does it not exist? Discuss.

---

[90] Ariz. Rev. Stat., V. 7, Sec. 20-1105 (1956).
[91] Fla. Stat. Ann., V. 18A, 627.0104 (1959).
[92] Code of Ga. Ann., B. 17T, 56-2405 (1960).
[93] Rev. Laws of Hawaii, V. 2, 181-414, 181-415 (1955).
[94] Idaho Code, V. 1A, 41-1806 (1947).
[95] Okla. Stat. Ann., Title 36, Sec. 3605, p. 629 (1958).
[96] W. Va. Codes Ann., V. 2, Sec. 3373, Ch. 33 (1961).
[97] Ark. Stat. 1947, Ann. Spec. Ed., V. 6, Title 66, 1963 Cum. Supp.
[98] Ky. Rev. Stat., V. II, 304.651 (July, 1962).
[99] La. Rev. Stat., V. 15A, 22:614 (1959).
[100] Code of Va., V. 6, 38.1-331 (1950).
[101] Rev. Code of Wash. Ann., 48.18.030, 48.18.040 (1961).
[102] McKinney's Consol. Laws of N. Y. Ann., Book 27, Pt. 1, Art. 7, 148 (1949).

4. Does one have an insurable interest in a piece of stolen property that he has unwittingly acquired?
5. Define each of the following and discuss why each is deemed to have an insurable interest in the subject property: (a) remainderman, (b) curtesy, (c) dower consummate.
6. Discuss the difference between the term "squatter" and the term "person in adverse and open possession of property." How do each of these affect insurable interest?
7. Do both the lender of funds and the creditor have insurable interest in the property used to secure the loan? Is this an instance in which it is possible to double insure some item of property?

# 14. THE MEANING OF "ACTUAL CASH VALUE" *

B. David Hinkle †

The words "actual cash value," which are used in most property insurance policies, have aroused a great deal of litigation. Citing a large number of these cases, Mr. Hinkle concludes that where the nature of the property or some other element makes it impractical to apply a fixed evaluation rule, our courts seem to have no hesitancy in knocking over the rule and allowing whatever evidence will employ the principle of indemnity. Mr. Hinkle presented this paper at the first annual loss seminar of the Baltimore Insurance Adjusters Association in Baltimore, Maryland, on October 10, 1967.

The term "actual cash value" is used in nearly all property insurance policies. Where property is of such nature that its market value can be readily determined, market value has usually been the basis of determining actual cash value at the time of loss under property insurance policies. Where market value is difficult or impossible to determine and where its determination would, for special reasons, not reflect the true loss, other criteria have been used. Thus, there are no universal or standard rules which apply to all jurisdictions.

Although the New England standard fire policy refers to "actual value," the courts seem to have treated it exactly the same as the term "actual cash value" which appears in the New York standard fire policy. We will, therfore, use the New York policy as a reference base:

*This policy states that the insured is protected "to the extent of the actual cash value of the property at the time of loss but not exceeding the amount which it would cost to repair or replace the property with material of like kind and quality within a reasonable time after such loss. . . ."*

The New York standard fire policy is typical of all property policies which are written on the basis of actual cash value, although the wording is not exactly the same in many other types of property contracts. Note that the following limitations are manifestly clear:

(1) Actual cash value is the established maximum.

(2) The value is to be established at the time of loss.

(3) In no case will the amount exceed the cost of repair or replace the property, with these limitations:

---

* From *The Insurance Law Journal* (December, 1967), pp. 711-723. Reprinted by permission.

† Vice-president and assistant director of education for Crawford and Company, insurance adjusters, Atlanta, Georgia.

    (a) The material will be of like kind and quality.

    (b) The repair or replacement will take place within a reasonable time after the loss.

Beginning with line 141 of the 1943 New York standard fire policy the insurance company is given two options in case of loss, in addition to cash payment. The company may repair or replace the property itself; or it may, if the loss is partial, take the property at its agreed or appraised value.

Lines 123 to 140 of the contract specifically provide for an appraisal in case the insured and the insurance company cannot agree as to either of two contingencies: (1) actual cash value of the property or (2) the amount of loss. The methods of the appraisal and the limitations of the appraisers and the umpire are spelled out in that section of the contract.

Since our discussion will be limited to the meaning of the term "actual cash value," then we must presuppose that neither replacement insurance nor valued policy laws are to be a factor in our discussions. However, since both replacement insurance and valued policy laws are frequently used to affect "actual cash value," we will attempt to dispose of each subject with a few brief comments.

Replacement cost insurance, when used at all, changes the effect of the actual cash value provisions in the basic fire contract. This concept is now frequently used in homeowners policies and other similar contracts. It affects the building itself and only in the event of a total loss. Furthermore, no insured may recover the actual replacement cost of his dwelling building until and unless he actually replaces it. Generally speaking, this means replacing the building structure itself with the same or similar materials.

Thus, we can see that the actual cash value concept is not involved in this instance.

A number of states[1] have enacted valued policy laws. Generally, they provide that the face amount of the policy must be paid in case of a total loss to the insured property. There is great variance from state to state as to the precise application, but it is safe to say that these laws usually apply to real property only (buildings) and not to personalty. They usually apply only to total losses. In many states they are limited only to fire insurance.

Here again, if a valued policy law were to apply to a given loss, then there would be no dispute between the insured and the company as to the meaning of "actual cash value."

---

[1] Those states having valued policy laws are: Arkansas, California, Delaware, Florida, Georgia,* Idaho,* Iowa, Kansas, Kentucky, Louisiana, Massachusetts,* Minnesota, Mississippi, Missouri, Montana, Nebraska, New Hampshire, North Carolina, North Dakota, Ohio, Oklahoma,* Oregon, South Carolina, South Dakota, Tennessee, Texas, West Virginia, Wisconsin, and Wyoming.*
\* Extremely limited.

## The Criteria

Through the years there has been a great deal of litigation over the meaning of "actual cash value," and, while the results from state to state have been at variance, the views of the several states and of the federal district courts may be observed in a framework of three criteria categories:

(1) The "market value" criterion.
(2) The reproduction or replacement cost criterion.
(3) The "broad evidence" rule.

## Market Value

The courts have held fairly uniformly that "market value" is determined by viewing the property immediately prior to the loss in a hypothetical situation. If there is both a supply and demand for such property and an established market, then its market value is determined by such established market. However, in those cases where there is no established market, the market value must be estimated at such amount as in all probability would have been arrived at by fair negotiations between the owner willing to sell and a purchaser desiring to buy. The hypothetical sale in the latter situation would, therefore, not be a "forced sale." The insured would not be placed in the position of a seller attempting to "unload" undesirable property on an unwilling buyer.

A large number of states[2] have adopted this criterion, although some of these states do not use it in connection with all classes of property.

---

[2] The following states, in the cases indicated, applied the market value criterion partly or entirely:

United States (in states indicated): *Liverpool, London & Globe Insurance Co. v. McFadden,* 170 F. 179, 27 L. R. A. (N. S.) 1095 (CA-3 Pa. 1909) (cotton in warehouse); *Mechanics' Insurance Co. v. C. A. Hoover Distilling Co.,* 182 F. 590, 31 L. R. A. (N. S.) 873 (CA-8 Iowa 1910) (whiskey); *Prussian National Insurance Co. v. Lawrence,* 221 F. 931, L. R. A. 1915 E. 489 (CA-4 W. Va. 1915) (bar fixtures); *Globe & Rutgers Insurance Co. v. Prairie Oil & Gas Co.,* 248 F. 452 (CA-2 N. Y. 1917) (oil in storage tanks); *Mack & Co. v. Lancashire Insurance Co.,* 2 McCrary 211, 4 F. 59 (Mo. 1880) (stock of clothing).

California: *Hughes v. Potomac Insurance Co.,* 11 Fire and Casualty Cases 81, 199 Cal. App. 2d 239, 18 Cal. Rptr. 650 (1962) (dwelling).

Georgia: *Southern Railway Co. v. Grogan,* 113 Ga. App. 451, 148 S. E. 2d 439 (1966); *Kenner v. Whitehead,* 156 S. E. 2d 136 (1967).

Idaho: *Boise Ass'n of Credit Men v. United States Fire Insurance Co.,* 44 Idaho 249, 256 P. 523 (1927), (stock of merchandise).

Illinois: *Birmingham Fire Insurance Co. v. Pulver,* 126 Ill. 329. 18 N. E. 804 (1888) (stock of dresses and cloaks).

Iowa: *Farmers Mercantile Co. v. Farmers Insurance Co.* 161 Iowa 5, 141 N. W. 447 (1913) (stock of drygoods); *Citizens Insurance Co. v. Foxbilt, Inc.,* 226 F. 2d 641, 53 A. L. R. 2d 1376 (CA-8 1966).

Kansas: *Lambert v. St. Paul Fire & Marine Insurance Co.,* 178 Kan. 533, 289 P. 2d 1057 (1954) (wheat in bins).

Kentucky: *Stokes v. Huddleston,* 227 Ky. 613, 13 S. W. 2d 784 (1929) (flour-mill machinery); *Insurance Co. of North America v. McCraw,* 255 Ky. 839, 75 S. W. 2d 518 (1934) (stock of general merchandise); *State Automobile Mutual Insurance Co. v. Cox,* 31 Automobile Cases 134, 309 Ky. 480, 218 S. W. 2d 46 (1949) (automobile).

(footnote continued)

## Reproduction or Replacement Cost [3]

Replacement or reproduction cost, *less depreciation,* has been favored by a number of courts as the test of the actual cash value

---

Louisiana: *Engolia v. Houston Fire and Casualty Insurance Co.,* 65 So. 2d 814 (La. App. 1953) (automobile); *Darvie v. American Bankers Insurance Co.,* 9 AUTOMOBILE CASES (2d) 454, 80 So. 2d 541 (La. App. 1955) (automobile).

Michigan: *Mitchell v. St. Paul German Fire Insurance Co.,* 92 Mich. 594, 52 N. W. 1017 (1892) (lumber, building materials).

Mississippi: *Motors Insurance Corp. v. Smith,* 2 AUTOMOBILE CASES (2d) 1060, 218 Miss. 268, 67 So. 2d 294 (1953) (automobile).

Missouri: *Leer v. Continental Insurance Co.,* 250 S. W. 631 (Mo. App. 1923) (household furniture, farm products, and livestock); *Hayward v. Employers Liability Assurance Corp.,* 214 Mo. App. 101, 257 S. W. 1083 (1924) (intoxicating liquors); *Cass v Pacific Fire Insurance Co.,* 6 FIRE AND CASUALTY CASES 1140, 224 S. W. 2d 405 (Mo. App. 1949) (personal property and personal effects); *Barton v. Farmers Insurance Exchange,* 33 AUTOMOBILE CASES 1023, 229 S. W. 2d 23 (Mo. App. 1950) (automobile); *Barton v. Farmers Insurance Exchange,* 1 AUTOMOBILE CASES (2d) 727, 255 S. W. 2d 451 (1953 Mo. App.) (automobile).

Nebraska: *Gibson v. Glens Falls Insurance Co.,* 111 Neb. 827, 197 N. W. 950 (1924) (automobile); *Clouse v. St. Paul Fire & Marine Insurance Co.,* 7 FIRE AND CASUALTY CASES 26, 152 Neb. 230, 40 N. W. 2d 820, 15 A. L. R. 2d 1008 (1950) (building and office furniture and equipment); *Borden v. General Insurance Co.,* 8 FIRE AND CASUALTY CASES 20, 157 Neb. 98, 59 N. W. 2d 141 (1953) (stock of groceries and meats, store fixtures and equipment); *Grantham v. Farmers Mutual Insurance Co.,* 11 FIRE AND CASUALTY CASES 823, 174 Neb. 790, 119 N. W. 2d 519 (1963).

New Jersey: (Note that the following are cases in which the New Jersey courts have used the market value rule. However, there is a recent case mentioned under footnote 5 which indicates that New Jersey has adopted the broad evidence rule.) *Bartindale v. Aetna Insurance Co..* 7 N. J. Misc. 399, 145 A. 633 (1929) (household furniture).

North Carolina: *Travelers Indemnity Co. v. Plymouth Box and Panel Co.,* 99 F. 2d 218 (CA-4 1938) (steam turbine); *Fraylon v. Royal Exchange Assurance,* 131 F. Supp. 676 (1955), modified as to the amount of recovery permitted to be insured, 8 FIRE AND CASUALTY CASES 852, 228 F. 2d 351 (CA-4 1955) (building).

North Dakota: *Rohlik v. Farmers Insurance Co.,* 49 N. D. 235, 191 N. W. 347 (1922) (stacked grain);*Butler v. Aetna Insurance Co.,* 64 N. D. 764, 256 N. W. 214 (1934) (building).

Pennsylvania: *Frick v. United Firemen's Insurance Co.,* 218 Pa. 409, 67 A 743 (1907) (whiskey).

Tennessee: *Shipley v. American Central Insurance Co.,* 21 Tenn. App. 259, 109 S. W. 2d 100 (1937) (automobile); *Clift v. Fulton Fire Insurance Co.,* 9 FIRE AND CASUALTY CASES 501, 315 S. W. 2d 9 (Tenn. App. 1958) (household goods).

Texas: *Manchester Fire Insurance Co. v. Simmons,* 12 Tex. Civ. App. 607, 35 S. W. 722 (1896) (stock and medical goods); *Virginia F. & M. Insurance Co. v. Cannon,* 18 Tex. Civ. App. 588, 45 S. W. 945, error ref. (1898) (cotton bagging); *Hartford Fire Insurance Co. v. Cannon,* 19 Tex. Civ. App. 305, 46 S. W. (1898) (cotton bagging); *Detroit Fire & Marine Insurance Co. v. Boren-Stewart Co.,* 203 S. W. 382, error ref. (Tex. Ct. of Civ. App. 1918) (stock of merchandise, furniture, and office equipment); *American Indemnity Co. v. Jamison,* 42 S. W. 2d 801 (Tex. Ct. of Civ. App. 1931) (automobile); *Commercial Standard Insurance Co. v. First State Bank,* 142 S. W. 2d 621 error dism'd (Tex. Ct. of Civ. App. 1940) (automobile); *Smith v. American Fire and Casualty Co.,* 242 S.W. 2d 448 (Tex. Ct. of Civ. App. 1951) (automobile); *Stuyvesant Insurance Co. v. Driskill,* 244 S. W. 2d 291 (Tex. Ct. of Civ. App. 1951) (automobile); *Manhattan Fire & Marine Insurance Co. v. Melton,* 10 FIRE AND CASUALTY CASES 181, 329 S. W. 2d 338 (Tex. Ct. of Civ. App. 1959). (Also refer to *Milwaukee Mechanics' Insurance Co. v. Frosch,* 130 S. W. 600 (Tex. Ct. of Civ. App. 1910) (household and kitchen furniture), along with other cases cited therein.)

Wisconsin: *Engh v. Calvert Fire Insurance Co.,* 266 Wis. 419, 63 N. W. 2d 831 (1954) (automobile); *Cassel v. Newark Insurance Co.,* 274 Wis. 25, 79 N. W. 2d 101 (1956) (stock of merchandise).

[3] Reproduction or replacement cost as the criterion for determining the meaning of "actual cash value" is illustrated by the following cases:

United States (for states indicated): *Western Massachusetts Insurance Co. v. Norwich & New York Transportation Co.,* 12 Wall 201 (1871) (steamboat).

Arkansas: *Good Canning Co. v. London Guarantee & Accident Co.,* 8 FIRE AND CASUALTY CASES 569, 128 F. Supp. 778 (1955) (boiler).

Idaho: *Boise Ass'n of Credit Men v. United States Fire Insurance Co.,* cited at footnote 2 (store and hotel building).                              (footnote continued)

of buildings under policies insuring them to that extent.[4] This criterion has also from time to time been applied to machinery and personal property.

## Broad Evidence Rule[5]

There has been a fairly recent trend on the part of a growing number of courts to reject both of the other criteria as the sole test

---

Illinois: *Smith v. Allemannia Fire Insurance Co.*, 219 Ill. App. 506 (1920) (building); *Knuppel v. American Insurance Co.*, 9 FIRE AND CASUALTY CASES 1094, 269 F. 2d 163 (CA-7 Ill. 1959) (building occupied as restaurant and tavern).

Massachusetts: *Agoos Leather Cos. v. American & Foreign Insurance Co.*, 174 N. E. 2d 652 (1961).

Montana: *Lee v. Providence Washington Insurance Co.*, 82 Mont. 264, 266 P. 640 (1928) (building); *McIntosh v. Hartford Fire Insurance Co.*, 106 Mont. 434, 78 P. 2d 82, 115 A. L. R. 1164 (1938) (building).

Pennsylvania: *Post Printing & Publishing Co. v. Insurance Co. of North America*, 189 Pa. 300, 42 A. 192, 44 L. R. A. 272 (1899) (linotype machines); *Fedas v. Insurance Co. of Pennsylvania*, 300 Pa. 555. 151 A. 285 (1935) (house and household furniture); *Metz v. Travelers Fire Insurance Co.*, 6 FIRE AND CASUALTY CASES 193, 355 Pa. 342, 49 A. 2d 711 (1946) (terminal building); *Farber v Perkiomen Mutual Insurance Co.*, 7 FIRE AND CASUALTY CASES 882, 370 Pa. 480, 88 A. 2d 776 (1952) (building); *Gardull v. Royal Insurance Co.*, 133 Pa. Super. 257, 2 A. 2d 504 (1938) (building).

South Carolina: *South Carolina Electric and Gas Co. v. Aetna Insurance Co.*, 10 FIRE AND CASUALTY CASES 919, 120 S. E. 2d 111 (1961).

Tennessee: *Burkett v. Georgia Home Insurance Co.*, 105 Tenn. 548, 58 S. W. 848 (1900) (building); *Gulf Compress Co. v. Insurance Co. of Pennsylvania*, 129 Tenn. 586, 167 S. W. 859 (1914) (compress machine).

Texas: *Security Insurance Co. v. Kelly*, 196 S. W. 874, error ref. (Tex. Ct. of Civ. App. 1917) (building); *Fire Ass'n of Philadelphia v. Coomer*, 4 FIRE AND CASUALTY CASES 27, 158 S. W. 2d 355 (Tex. Ct. of Civ. App. 1942) (furniture); *Manhattan Fire & Marine Insurance Co. v. Melton*, cited at footnote 2.

[4] The standard clause expressly provides for the consideration of depreciation in computing actual cash value, and a number of courts, in arriving at the measure of the insured's recovery, have considered depreciation in connection with the determination of the actual cash value of the building at the time of loss, particularly in applying the replacement or reproduction cost rule or the broad evidence rule.

Idaho: *Boise Ass'n of Credit Men v. United States Fire Insurance Co.*, cited at footnote 2.

Iowa: *Britven v. Occidental Insurance Co.*, 5 FIRE AND CASUALTY CASES 133, 234 Iowa 682, 13 N. W. 2d 791 (1944).

Louisiana: *Stenzel v. Pennsylvania Fire Insurance Co.*, 110 La. 1019, 35 So. 271 (1903).

New York: *McAnarney v. Newark Fire Insurance Co.*, 247 N. Y. 176, 159 N. E. 902, 56 A. L. R. 1149 (1928).

Oklahoma: *First National Insurance Co. of America v. Norton*, 8 FIRE AND CASUALTY CASES 1125, 238 F. 2d 949 (CA-10 1956).

Tennessee: *Newark Fire Insurance Co. v. Martineau*, 4 FIRE AND CASUALTY CASES 633, 26 Tenn. App. 261, 170 S. W. 2d 927 (1943).

Vermont: *Citizens' Savings Bank & Trust Company v. Fitchburg Mutual Fire Insurance Co.*, 86 Vt. 267, 84 A. 970 (1912).

[5] The broad evidence rule has been recognized in the following cases:

Colorado: *Nebraska Drillers, Inc. v. Westchester Fire Insurance Co.*, 8 FIRE AND CASUALTY CASES 511, 123 F. Supp. 678 (1954) (supplies and equipment).

Florida: *New York Central Mutual Fire Insurance Co. v. Diaks*, 8 FIRE AND CASUALTY CASES 217, 69 So. 2d 786 (1954) (restaurant furniture and equipment); *Worcester Mutual Fire Insurance Co. v. Eisenberg*, 11 FIRE AND CASUALTY CASES 755, 147 So. 2d 575 (Fla. App. 1962).

Iowa: *Britven v. Occidental Insurance Co.*, cited at footnote 4 (building).

Maryland: Refer to *Schreiber v. Pacific Coast Fire Insurance Co.* 7 FIRE AND CASUALTY CASES 221, 195 Md. 639, 75 A. 2d 108, 20 A. L. R. 2d 951 (1950) (dwelling house).

(footnote continued)

of the actual cash value of buildings. In rejecting the reproduction or replacement cost and the market value criteria for determining the actual cash value of buildings, these numerous courts have permitted the trier of the facts to receive and use any evidence logically tending to show actual cash value. This criterion seeks to effectuate complete indemnity for the insured and thus wants the trier of the facts to consider any or all facts or circumstances which would logically tend to influence the outcome. The trier of the facts might consider the original cost of the building, the cost of its reproduction, opinions upon its value given by qualified witnesses, declarations against interest made by the insured and even the gainful uses (rental value, and so forth) to which the building might have been put.

## Pinet v. New Hampshire Fire Insurance Company[6]

We will use this case as an example because it covers a number of interesting points which we can use to illustrate the criteria for determining the meaning of "actual cash value." Here are a few of the factors involved in this particular case:

(1) New Hampshire is a valued policy state as to *realty*.

(2) The property involved in this case was personalty, namely, a herd of pedigreed chinchillas.

---

New Hampshire: *Pinet v. New Hampshire Fire Insurance Co.*, 8 FIRE AND CASUALTY CASES 1096, 100 N. H. 346, 126 A. 2d 262, 61 A. L. R. 2d 706 (1956) (chinchillas).

New Jersey: *Messing v. Reliance Insurance Co.*, 77 N. J. Super, 531, 187 A. 2d 49 (1962).

New York: *McAnarney v. Newark Fire Insurance Co.*, cited at footnote 4 (building); *Gervant v. New England Fire Insurance Co.*, 8 FIRE AND CASUALTY CASES 268, 306 N. Y. 393, 118 N. E. 2d 574 (1954) (building); *Sebring v. Firemen's Insurance Co.*, 227 App. Div. 103, 237 N. Y. S. 120 (1929) (building).

North Carolina: *Garvey v. Old Colony Insurance Co.*, 9 FIRE AND CASUALTY CASES 214, 153 F. Supp. 755 (1957) (tenant house).

Oklahoma: *Rochester American Insurance v. Short*, 7 FIRE AND CASUALTY CASES 1049, 207 Okla. 669, 252 P. 2d 490 (1953) (dwelling house); *National-Ben Franklin Fire Insurance Co. v. Short*, 7 FIRE AND CASUALTY CASES 1052, 207 Okla. 673, 252 P. 2d 495 (1953) (building).

South Dakota: *Lampe Market Co. v. Alliance Insurance Co.*, 6 FIRE AND CASUALTY CASES 81, 71 S. D. 120, 22 N. W. 2d 427 (1946) (market and office building).

Texas: *Home Insurance Co. v. Tydal Co.*, 6 FIRE AND CASUALTY CASES 1, 152 F. 2d 309 (Ca-5 1945) (gasoline refinery plant), motion denied on rehearing, 6 FIRE AND CASUALTY CASES 8, 157, F. 2d 851.

Vermont: *Citizens' Savings Bank & Trust Co. v. Fitchburg Mutual Fire Insurance Co.*, cited at footnote 4 (building); *Eagle Square Mfg. Co. v. Vermont Mutual Fire Insurance Co.*, 12 FIRE AND CASUALTY CASES 645, 125 Vt. 221, 212 A. 2d 636 (1965), reargument denied 125 Vt. 226, 213 A 2d 201 (1965).

Virginia: *Harper v. Penn Mutual Fire Insurance Co.*, 11 FIRE AND CASUALTY CASES 144, 199 F. Supp. 663 (1961).

Washington: *Morgan v. Union Automobile Insurance Co.*, 150 Wash. 443, 273 P. 527 (1929) (automobile).

Wisconsin: *Wisconsin Screw Co. v. Fireman's Fund Insurance Co.*, 11 FIRE AND CASUALTY CASES 3, 297 F. 2d 697 (CA-7 1962); *Wisconsin Screw Co. v. Fireman's Fund Insurance Co.*, 10 FIRE AND CASUALTY CASES 684, 193 F. Supp. 96 (1961).

[6] Case cited at footnote 5.

(3) The loss resulted from fire, and at the time, the insured had contracted to sell and deliver 12 pairs of the chincillas for a total of $15,00.

The coverage was a Scheduled Property Floater Policy containing a valuation clause (Condition 4) stating,

"4. Valuation. Unless otherwise provided in form attached, this company shall not be liable beyond the actual cash value of the property at the time any loss or damage shall be ascertained or estimated according to such actual cash value with proper deduction for depreciation, however caused, and shall in no event exceed what it would then cost to repair or replace the same with material of like kind and quality."

There was also an endorsement attached to the policy which specifically insured the chinchillas with a limit of $750 for "any one animal." The endorsement provided that it was subject to the conditions of the policy.

The plaintiff apparently attempted to recover under the market value criterion. He indicated that the term "actual cash value" should be given to ordinary meaning they (the words) convey to the common mind. . . ." In addition to his attempt to raise an ambiguity over the terminology, he also contended that the company could not apply the limitation clause (". . . and shall in no event exceed what it would then cost to repair or replace the same with *material* of like kind and quality. . .) because registered pedigreed chinchillas were not "material." The plaintiff then contended that the market value should be the test of the meaning of "actual cash value" (and he cited prior New Hampshire cases). He then contended that the contract of sale which existed for the chinchillas at the time of loss should be considered the "greatest probative value" in determining ths loss sustained.

The defendant insurance company sought to apply the reproduction or replacement cost criterion, relying upon the valuation clause in Condition 4. The insurer argued that what it would cost the insured in cash after the loss to purchase property of like kind and quality as that destroyed would be a reasonable and equitable test of the damages sustained, as well as a test of the meaning of actual cash value.

The Supreme Court of New Hampshire, upon a reserved case transferred by the trial court in advance of trial, held that the contract price was admissible though not conclusive with respect to the actual cash value of the property destroyed by the fire, but that the insured's right to recovery was limited by the valuation clause to the *lesser of two figures*: *cash value* or *replacement cost*. In committing New Hampshire to the broad evidence criterion, the court said,

". . . in the last analysis the 'actual cash value' of the plaintiff's loss must be expressed in terms of money which is a matter of opinion. The trier of fact in determining that question may receive evidence whether there is a fair market value or replacement cost and in either case what it may be. Both fair market value and replacement cost are permissible standards for determining fire losses but they are standards and not shackles. . . ."

The court also stated:

". . . we are impressed with what might be denominated a third rule which has received support in New York,[7] Massachusetts and South Dakota. . . . . In these jurisdictions neither market value nor replacement cost is an exclusive test. Evidence of both market value and replacement cost with depreciation may be introduced as evidence of actual cash value. These jurisdictions stress the fact that variations in the types of property and the conditions under which they are destroyed prevent the adoption of any single test for all cases. The objective of these cases is to see that the insured should incur neither economic gain nor loss if he is adequately insured. . . ."

## McAnarney v. Newark Fire Insurance Company[8]

This is a New York case which also illustrates the broad evidence rule. Invariably, as we search legal journals and writings in search of the meaning of "actual cash value" we stumble across this case time after time. It is one of the classics. The case was decided in 1928 by the New York Court of Appeals.

McAnarney owned a brewery, and the National Prohibition Act put him out of business. He had fire insurance on his buildings, and the buildings were still standing. However, by the very nature of the buildings and the equipment therein, they were not usable for any "legal venture" which was available to McAnarney. A fire destroyed the premises.

Prior to the fire McAnarney had put the place up for sale for $12,000. After the fire he filed a proof of loss for $43,000. The insurance company, apparently feeling that $12,000 was enough, made an offer for that amount less the value of the land. The jury in the lower court returned a verdict of $43,000 plus interest.

The higher court rejected both the market value test and the replacement cost less depreciation as sole measures of "actual cash value." The court stated,

". . . Actual cash value must be interpreted as having a broader significance than 'market value.' Moreover, if market value were the rule, property for which there is no market value would possess no insurable value, a proposition which is clearly untenable. The

---

[7] *McAnarney v. Newark Fire Insurance Co.*, cited at footnote 4 (N. Y.); *Kingsley v. Spofford*, 298 Mass. 469, 11 N. E. 2d 487 (1937); *Lampe Market Co. v Alliance Insurance Co.*, cited at footnote 5 (S. D.).

[8] *McAnarney v. Newark Fire Insurance Co.*, cited at footnote 4.

clause was not intended to restrict a recovery for this insurance loss to the market value of the insured buildings. For methods by which actual value may be ascertained, we must look beyond the terms of the policy to *general principles of the law of damages. . . .*"

The court pointed out that no principle of law requires that the recovery in such cases be restricted to the market value of the buildings. On the other hand, the court did not entirely agree with the insured who contended that the sole measure of damage was the cost of reproduction less depreciation. The court commented,

". . . Where insured buildings have been destroyed, the trier of fact may, and should, call to its aid in order to effectuate complete indemnity, every fact and circumstance which would logically tend to the formation of a correct estimate of the loss. It may consider original cost and cost of reproduction; the opinions upon value given by qualified witnesses; declarations against interest which may have been made by the insured; the gainful uses to which the buldings may have been put; as well as any other factor reasonably tending to throw light upon the subject. . . ."

Thus, while the court rejected the market value criterion, (it did not ignore the facts of obsolescence, a deteriorated neighborhood, the inability to use the property in determining the actual cash value), it did hold that these factors justified a recovery of a smaller amount than replacement cost less depreciation.

## Schreiber, et al. v. Pacific Coast Fire Insurance Company, et al.[9]

There had previously been verdicts for the plaintiffs against two insurance companies as a result of a fire to real property in this Maryland case. The plaintiffs appealed due to dissatisfaction with the appraisal. The appraisal clause in the policies provided that if the insured and the insurance company failed to agree as to "actual cash value" or the amount of loss, each should select "a competent and disinterested appraiser," who should then appraise the loss and, if the two appraisers disagreed, they were to submit their differences to an umpire, and so forth.

One of the plaintiffs' objections to the appraisal was that the award had been unlawfully arrived at by adding the figures of the two appraisers and the umpire and dividing by three. While holding that a "quotient verdict" was unlawful, the court found nothing unlawful in this particular procedure, because there was no evidence that the appraisers had agreed *in advance* to be bound by the result of such quotient.

---

[9] Case cited at footnote 5.

The record of this case also reveals that Maryland has adopted the broad evidence rule in determining the meaning of "actual cash value." When the plaintiffs contended that the appraisers did not properly consider all the proper evidence, the court looked far enough into the procedure to determine that the appraisers and umpire did *consider* the evidence submitted by the plaintiffs and defendants, although they chose to ignore at least a part of it.

The court held:

". . . The award on the subject matter, in the absence of fraud or mistake, is binding and conclusive upon the parties. . . . A mistake which will be sufficient to avoid the award must be one that is plain and palpable, such as an erroneous computation or calculation of the amount. . . . Where the award finds or announces concrete propositions of law, unmixed with facts, its mistake, if one was made, could have been corrected in the court below, and can be corrected here. Where a proposition is one of mixed law and fact, in which the error of law, if there be one cannot be distinctly shown, the parties must abide by the award. . . ."

The original judgments were affirmed.

## Insurance Company of North America v. McCraw[10]

Kentucky is one of the states committed to the market value criterion, and we have noted three cases[11] which have used this rule in determining the actual cash value where the property was, respectively, flour-mill machinery, stock of general merchandise, and an automobile.

*Insurance Company of North America* v. *McCraw* is a 1934 case involving stock of general merchandise. It was an action upon a fire insurance policy which limited the insurer's liability to not more than three-fourths of the actual cash value of the property at the time of the loss. The court said that the term "cash value" meant market value, which was the price, considering the original or *wholesale cost price with freight added*, and the quantity, quality, material, finish, style and self-worn condition, if any, of the merchandise at the time of its destruction by fire, which it would bring when offered for sale by one who desired to sell but was not compelled to do so, and bought by one who desired to purchase, but was not compelled to do so.

## Boise Ass'n of Credit Men v. U. S. Fire Insurance Company[12]

This was an action upon fire policies which insured a store and hotel building. The court stated that since the proper test of loss

---

[10] Case cited at footnote 2.

[11] *Stokes v. Huddleston*, cited at footnote 2 (;our-mill machinery); *Insurance Co. of North America v. McCraw*, cited at footnote 2 (stock of general merchandise); *State Auto Mutual Insurance Co. v. Cox*, cited at footnote 2 (automobile).

[12] Case cited at footnote 2.

was the cost of a new building of the same material and dimensions as the one destroyed, less the amount the destroyed building had deteriorated by use, the instruction that actual cash value meant what it would cost the insured in cash to purchase or replace property of a like kind and quality was erroneous. This Idaho case is an example of the replacement or reproduction cost criterion applied to realty. The criterion considers depreciation.

## The Variables

Any effort to draw a chart which would accurately categorize each state neatly into one of the criteria might result in a failure to take into consideration the many variables in the conceptual approach. A given state may lean toward the market value rule when determining the actual cash value of buildings and may use the replacement or reproduction rule with regard to household furniture, general merchandise, and other items of personal property.

For example, in determining the actual cash value of buildings, Pennsylvania[13] may be said to follow the replacement or reproduction cost criterion, and there are cases to support this statement. However, in 1938 in the case of *Gardull v. Royal Insurance Company*,[14] it was held that evidence of the *rental value* of a building destroyed by fire had a bearing on the actual cash value and was therefore admissible. In other Pennsylvania cases the replacement or reproduction cost rule was used in connection with household furnishings,[15] trade fixtures,[16] and so forth. In a 1907 case[17] in Pennsylvania, the market value rule was used to determine the actual cash value of whiskey.

Thus, if one wishes to learn what a particular state does with the term "actual cash value," he will be forced to read a number of cases decided within that state dealing with the varieties of property which are to be the subject of his research.

## Actual Cash Value of Automobiles

We will now see how some of the states have applied the tests or criteria to particular types of property. Cases are not readily available for reading in all states.

With regard to determining the actual cash value of automobiles, it would be an oversimplification to simply say that some

---

[13] *Cummins v. German American Insurance Co.*, 192 Pa. 359, 43 A. 1016 (1899); *Fedas v. Insurance Co. of Pennsylvania*, cited at footnote 3.

[14] Case cited at footnote 3.

[15] *Fedas v. Insurance co. of Pennsylvania*, cited at footnote 3.

[16] *Post Printing & Publishing Co. v. Insurance Co. of North America*, cited at footnote 3.

[17] *Frick v. United Firemen's Insurance Co.*, cited at footnote 2.

states apply the market value test. However, we are unable in this effort to go into great detail as to how "market value" is determined. By briefly citing a few specific cases, we hope to give some idea of the complexities involved.

During wartime, special problems are created because of the shortage of automobile materials and the near impossibility of purchasing new automobiles and their tires, batteries, and other supplies. In the Kentucky case of *State Automobile Mutual Insurance Company v. Cox*,[18] the court noted that for a period of time subsequent to World War II many slightly used automobiles sold for more than the dealers' retail price for new cars. Therefore, in this case the court held that the actual market value of the insured's stolen automobile, as a used car, although inflated, should be considered the actual cash value rather than the dealers' retail price for a new car, which was less.

The use of the "average retail value" in a used car price guide book was the basis for determining "actual cash value" in Louisiana in the case of *Darvie v. American Bankers Insurance Company*.[19] In that case, the appellate court fixed the measure of damages as the "highest value fixed by the insurer's witnesses, which was based upon valuation carried in valuation books used by automobile dealers in determining the value of secondhand automobiles."

Another case in which the market value test was used in determining the "actual cash value" of an automobile was in Tennessee,[20] where the state court refused to deviate from the market value test. The insured's automobile had been stolen, and the court held that in cases such as this where there was a proper determination that the automobile was a total loss, if there was no "fair market value" for the particular automobile in the community, the burden of proof was upon the insured to establish the location of such a market and the cost of transportation thereto.

Texas seems to follow the market value test and does not consider "cost of replacement" the "actual cash value" of an automobile. In *Ohio Casualty Insurance Company v. Stewart*,[21] using the distinction between the insurer's options to "replace" or "pay," it was found that the measure of recovery was the cost of replacement because this was found to be less than the actual cash value of the automobile immediately prior to the fire. Another Texas case, *American Indemnity Company v. Jamison*,[22] more clearly illustrates the Texas concept. It appeared that the cost of repairs

---

[18] Case cited at footnote 2.
[19] Case cited at footnote 2.
[20] *Shipley v. American Central Insurance Co.*, cited at footnote 2.
[21] 76 S. W. 2d 873 (Tex. Ct. of Civ. App. 1934).
[22] 62 S. W. 2d 197 (Tex. Ct. of Civ. App. 1933).

exceeded the difference between the value of the automobile before and after the accident. The court held that the trial court had correctly determined the extent of the insurer's liability to be the difference between the value of the automobile before and after the accident.

In dealing with partial losses, Mississippi has injected the market value test for the protection of an insured whose automobile has been repaired but, following those repairs, has not been restored to its "actual market value" prior to the contingency. In *Motors Insurance Corporation v. Smith*,[23] the court held that if repairs could restore the truck to its market value as of the date of damage, such cost of repairs was the measure of the insurer's liability, but if, despite such repairs, there yet remained a loss in *actual market value* estimated at the time of the collision date, such deficiency was to be added to the cost of repairs. The court stated that it was not the value to the owner which controlled, but the value to those who consitute the market in used cars.

The Mississippi concept in the handling of partial automobile losses is also followed by Georgia[24] and by South Carolina. In the case of *Campbell v. Calvert Fire Insurance Company*,[25] the South Carolina Supreme Court Stated,

". . . Restoration of the car to its former condition 'may or may not be accomplished by repair or damaged parts. It cannot be said that there has been a complete restoration of the property unless it can be said that there has been no diminution of value after repair of the car'. . . ."

This South Carolina case cited additional cases in other states[26] which seem to hold likewise and also referred to a prior South Carolina case[27] similar in concept.

Let us now look at another of the many wartime cases on record. The Oklahoma case of *Motors Insurance Corporation v. Dooms*[28] is a 1945 case in which the insured's tires and wheels were stolen. Neither the insured nor the insurance company could purchase tires due to government wartime restrictions, so the insurance company made a tender of payment to the insured of the ceiling price of labor and materials necessary to repair the car. The court held that this was not sufficient to discharge the liability of the insurance company, in order to discharge its liability, must pay

---

[23] Case cited at footnote 2.

[24] *Southern Railway v. Grogan*, cited at footnote 2; *Kenner v. Whitehead*, cited at footnote 2.

[25] 109 S. E. 2d 572 (1959).

[26] *Rossier v. Union Auto Insurance Co.*, 134 Ore. 211, 291 P. 497, 500 (1930); *American Standard County Mutual Insurance Co. V. Barbee*, 262 S. W. 2d 122, 123 (1953).

[27] *Padgett v. Calvert Fire Insurance Co.*, 23 S. C. 533, 77 S. E. 2d 19 (1953).

[28] 195 Okla. 21, 154 P. 2d 955 (1945).

the *depreciation in market value* of the stolen car after its recovery.

Thus far, in discussing the meaning of "actual cash value" as it applies to automobiles, we have cited market value criterion. A few states follow the broad evidence rule.

Stating that in showing the actual cash value of a truck  at the time it was destroyed by fire, the insured was entitled to show all the circumstances having a bearing upon the question, the court in *Morgan v. Union Automobile Insurance Company,*[29] a Washington case, held that a witness who had sold the truck to the insured and who knew the original cost, the care given the truck, and the use to which it had been subjected, was qualified to give an estimate of the value of the truck *when sold* to the insured.

A Canadian case [30] stated that a policy provision that the insurer could not be liable beyond the actual cash value of the insured automobile at the time of loss was held to mean its *value to the insured,* and not necessarily its market or replacement value. In that case some consideration was obviously given to the fact that the car, a very expensive one, was kept in perfect condition, and the court held it to be worth to the insured at least the amount for which it was insured.

One question which, seemingly, has not been specifically litigated in a large number of states has been answered in Louisiana. In *Guaranty Plan Corporation v. Mechanics,*[31] it was held that under the actual cash value clause of the policy insuring an automobile against theft, the insurer's liability must be determined, not upon the full amount of the debt due by the purchaser, but upon the actual cash value of the automobile at the time of loss.

Kentucky handled a similar problem in *General Exchange Insurance Corporation v. Kinney,*[32] in which the court said that in determining actual cash value, the actual cash selling price rather than the *total price* representing carrying charges, insurance on the car, and the interest, must be considered as the value of the car at the time of the original sale, and that in view of the subsequent use, this value must be reduced, so that the trial court erred in entering judgment in an amount equal to the original selling price.

## Actual Cash Value of Household Furniture and Personal Effects

Only a few states seem to have clung to the market value criterion in this area. One Missouri case used the market value test

---

[29] Case cited at footnote 5.
[30] *Viner v. Union Insurance Society,* 62 C. S. 308 (1924).
[31] 7 La. App. 767 (1927).
[32] 279 Ky. 76, 129 S. W. 2d 1014, 122 A. L. R. 920 (1939).

in a *partial loss*. In *Cass v. Pacific Fire Insurance Company*,[33] the court said that the actual cash value of the damages was the difference between a fair and reasonable market value immediately before the fire and the fair and reasonable market value immediately after the fire.

Perhaps the best illustration of the rule adopted by the majority of states in personal property valuations is illustrated by the Idaho case of *Boise Association of Credit Men v. United States Fire Insurance Company*,[34] in which the court specifically rejected the fair market test, but stated that the difference between the value of such property in its used condition and of similar property entirely new (depreciation) must be recognized. The court in this case also noted that household furniture and personal effects ordinarily have no well-recognized market value except as second-hand articles and that the value of such property to the owner was not ordinarily appraised at what would be paid by a second-hand dealer.

## Conclusion

We live in an era where hard and fast rules of law are being battered and tested. Some fall, and often it is because they should fall.

It may be seen that where certain classes of property may be readily evaluated by a fixed rule, such rule is usually employed; but, where the nature of the property or some other element make it impractical to apply to fixed rule, our courts seem to have no hesitancy in knocking over the rule and allowing whatever evidence will employ the principle of indemnity.

### Questions

1. Refer to the court case *Pinet v. New Hampshire Fire Insurance Company* discussed in the article. What is the relationship between replacement cost and market value in profits insurance, as developed in *Pinet*?
2. If the real issue of the actual cash value problem is the enforcement of the principal of indemnity, why does not the insurance company simply write into the policy that payment of loss shall not exceed indemnification of the insured?
3. Study the appraisal clause in the Standard Fire Insurance Policy. In the case *Schreiber, et al. v. Pacific Coast Fire Insurance Company et. al.* discussed in the article, the two appraisers selected by the insured and the insurer did not agree on the amount of the loss. According to the terms of the contract, they selected an umpire. The umpire made his estimate of the loss, which was apparently different from the other two. He (they?) apparently decided that the solution was the average of the three values. The court upheld this procedure as being within the terms of the contract. From your study of the clause, can you structure an example in which a solution would not be according to the terms of the contract?

---

[33] Case cited at footnote 2.
[34] Case cited at footnote 2.

# 15. WRESTLING WITH STRICT LIABILITY *

Don M. Jackson †

No branch of the law today is as exciting, alive and changing as is the law of products liability. In the space of only a few years, we have gone from a complete lack of liability in the absence of privity, with those few exceptions resulting from *MacPherson v. Buick Motor Company* [1] and the cases involving products for human consumption, through an almost universal elimination of the requirement of privity, to the present ground swell of strict liability which is sweeping the country.

The "assault upon the citadel of privity" so eloquently described by Justice Cardozo in his second landmark case of *Ultramares Corporation v. Touche* [2] has now reached the point of an almost complete victory. The citadel is in ruins! All of this has been occurring with such rapidity that Dean Keeton, of the University of Texas School of Law, an outstanding authority in the field, calls it "the exploding law of products liability."

As the law now stands in the vast majority of the states, a manufacturer may be held liable in an action brought by a consumer or purchaser, an employee or member of the family of the consumer or the purchaser, or even in an action by persons in the vicinity of the use of the product. He may be held liable regardless of how remote in distance from the point of manufacture the accident occurs. In many cases, liability is imposed regardless of the lapse of time between the time of manufacture and the use of the product. His liability may rest in negligence, or it may be based upon strict liability, entirely apart and aside from any negligence on his part. In fact, revised Section 402A of the *Restatement of the Law of Torts* expressly states that one who sells any product in "a defective condition unreasonably dangerous to the user or consumer" is liable for injuries to the ultimate user or consumer caused by that defect; that this is so even though the seller "has exercised all possible care in the preparation and sale of his product."

Likewise, with respect to liability for negligence, the manufacturer has been increasingly required to give more specific and full warnings of the hazards or dangers involved in the formulation or construction of his product, which may expose the user to danger, while using it for the purpose for which it was made and intended. In fact, in some cases, this duty has been extended to the point of requiring the manufacturer to

* From *The Insurance Law Journal* (March, 1966), pp. 133-139. Reprinted by permission.

† Member of the law firm of Jackson, Wade & Barker in Kansas City, Missouri.

[1] Product Liability Cases 827, 217, N.Y. 382, 111 N.E. 1050 (1916).
[2] 225 N.Y. 170, 174 N.E. 441.

warn of the dangers of using it in the manner and for the purposes intended.

Such rapid development in this area of the law has provoked such a storm of controversy with criticism by many of the defense attorneys and plaudits by many plaintiff's attorneys. The former claim that manufacturers are put in a completely untenable and undefensible position by these developments; the latter claim that such developments are creating a plaintiff's paradise. The truth of the matter would appear to lie somewhere about midway between these two extremes. I think the time has come for us to examine this area of the law coolly, critically and dispassionately.

## Historical Basis of Strict Liability

In the first place, I believe it is helpful for us to take a look historically and sociologically at those factors and developments which have brought us to this present state of the law. As late as the turn of the century, most commerce and industry were conducted on a reasonably local basis with small manufacturers supplying the needs of local consumers, with whom they dealt directly. Machinery, when used, was simple and uncomplicated, and the average consumer knew almost as much about the machine as did the manufacturer. Chemicals, where used at all, were of the basic organic type, such as the lye soap grandmother made in the black iron kettle over an outdoor wood fire. If a machine broke or a product was defective, the consumer immediately went to the manufacturer and presented his claim."

Those "good old days" are gone, forgotten and buried in the complexities of modern manufacturing and marketing methods of our modern society. In this age of complicated, high speed machinery, made of strange and exotic alloys of metal or other materials, the true potential for injury is often hidden from all but the scientifically trained user, even though the machinery is designed and intended for use by workmen of limited education or knowledge. In this time of complex chemical products, containing synthetic chemicals designed and intended to do everything from opening a clogged kitchen drain to killing crab grass in the family back yard, even the most highly educated chemists outside the manufacturer's research department have absolutely no knowledge of contents of many of these products. Yet, these are the very products manufactured and placed on the market for use by the unsuspecting housewife, the amateur gardener and the great mass of people who have not even had so much as a basic course in inorganic chemistry.

Can anyone deny, therefore, that it is right, logical, equitable and just to require the manufacturer of machinery, who alone knows what components he has put into the machine, and who, by making the necessary tests and inspections could know what dangers might lurk in the machinery from such things as overspeeding, overloading, or failure to maintain, should be required to give that knowledge to the consumer? It is not equally right, proper, just and equitable to require the manufacturer of a complicated synthetic chemical product to tell the user precisely and specifically what dangers he may encounter in using that product? Should he not be required to give a clear and adequate warning of the true dangers, in language that the least educated user can understand? And if he chooses not to do so because, by doing so, he may be destroying the sales value of his product by frightening the prospective purchasers, should he not pay for taking that risk?

Many of the products on the market today are in fact so highly dangerous that, if the public were given a full and complete warning of their potential hazard, their marketability would be seriously damaged. Yet, these same products are of such great utility in our modern society that, even though the dangers were fully, adequately and completely stated on the container, there would be a public demand for them, even though not as great as would be the case if the warning was not so specific.

These factors are the basic reasons which have led to the evolution of the law of products liability, to the point where it stands today in American jurisprudence. For those interested in a complete delineation of the liability of persons supplying chattels for the use of others, up to the adoption of the rule of strict liability, I refer you to Chapter XIV, Vol. 2, *Restatement of the Law of Torts*, particularly Sections 388, 389, and 395.

## Leading Cases

Having thus progressed to the present state of our society and our industry, let us examine the leading cases dealing with the liability of the manufacturer for negligence. Any discussion of this phase of products liability requires an examination of one of the landmark cases, *Tampa Drug Company v. Wait.*[3] In that case the Florida Supreme Court had before it an action for death caused by inhalation of fumes of carbon tetrachloride. The label of the container in that case warned the user that the product should be used only in a well ventilated area, and further indicated that certain toxic effects might result from failure to do so. There was nothing, however, on the label indicating that prolonged exposure in an ill ventilated area could be fatal. Plaintiff brought the action against the manufacturer for negligence in failing to adequately warn of the dangers, claiming that the failure to warn of possible death from exposure was negligence, that the product was so dangerous that the manufacturer should have given warning of the lethal hazard. In affirming a verdict for the plaintiff on this theory, the Supreme Court of Florida stated:

---

[3] *Negligence Cases* (2d) 262, 103 So. 2d 606 (1958).

"The measure of the duty of the distributor of an inherently dangerous commodity is now well established to be the reasonable foreseeability of injury that might result from use of the commodity. The care exercised in fulfilling this duty is in turn measured by the dangerous potentialities of the commodity, as well as the foreseeable uses to which it might be put. When a distributor of an inherently dangerous commodity places it in the channels of trade, then by the very nature of his business he assumes the duty of conveying to those who might use the product a full and adequate warning of its dangerous potentialities to the end that the user by the exercise of reasonable care on his part shall have full and adequate notice of the possible consequences of use or even misuse."

The court also stated:

"Implicit in the duty to warn with a degree of intensity that would cause a reasonable man to exercise for his own safety the caution commensurate with the potential danger. It is the failure to exercise such degree of caution after proper warning that constitutes contributory negligence in a case such as this. . . ."

A similar result was reached in the equally important case of *Martin v. Bengue, Inc.*[4] where the plaintiff, who had applied a widely used product to his chest to relieve discomforts of a cold, was severely burned when he lighted a cigarette and ignited fumes of this product. The evidence in that case revealed that there was no warning on the container of any such hazard. The defendant contended that the plaintiff was guilty of contributory negligence in undertaking to strike a match and light a cigarette in those circumstances, contending that he should have anticipated and foreseen the possibility of his hazard without any warning on the package. As to this question of contributory negligence, in holding it to be a question for the jury, the court made the most pertinent observation that:

". . . Care is to be taken that the reasonable man be not endowed with attributes which properly belong to a person of exceptional perspicuity and foresight."

The State of Illinois in *Beadles v. Servel, Inc.*[5] expressly approved Section 388 of the *Restatement of the Law of Torts* in holding that a manufacturer who makes an inherently dangerous article is liable for bodily injury caused by such article to those whom he should expect to use the chattel or to be in the vicinity of its probable use. In *Bean v. Ross Manufacturing Company* [6] the Supreme Court of Missouri dealt with an accident which occurred in the State of Illinois in which the plaintiff was blinded by the explosion of a drain solvent. Although the court reversed the case for errors in instructions, it held that Illinois recognizes liability without privity in the case of an inherently dangerous article, and said:

---

[4] 25 N.J. 359, 136 A.2d 626.
[5] *Negligence Cases* 875, 344 Ill. App. 133, 100 N.E. 2d 405 (1951).
[6] *12 Negligence Cases* (2d) 381, 344 S.W. 2d 18 (1961).

"The supplier of a chattel is subject to liability for injury in its use by another when the supplier knows or should know that its use is or is likely to be dangerous and when there is no reason to believe that the user will realize this, if, further, he fails to use reasonable care to warn. . . ."

The facts in the *Bean* case are significant because they indicate the extent to which modern manufacturers have gone in preparing complex chemical products of which the consuming public has no knowledge, or means of knowledge. In that case, the defendant had manufactured a drain solvent, designed and intended for use in unclogging stopped-up plumbing. The product contained as its basic ingredient sodium hydroxide, the label so stating. Sodium hydroxide is nothing more than a commercial form of lye. In order to create a stirring action within the drain, the manufacturer added zinc and aluminum chips, both also identified on the label. What the label did not state was that, when these ingredients were poured into water there was a chemical reaction between them which produced hydrogen gas. Hydrogen is colorless, odorless and tasteless, so that its presence cannot be detected. If this product was contained within a closed chamber while in use, the hydrogen gas thus formed would cause a substantial pressure, sufficient to cause a violent explosion if the container should rupture. The plaintiff, in order to keep down the odor in the drain after pouring the solvent into the water, immediately plugged the hole with a plumber's test plug. Within a very short space of time thereafter, because the drain was completely plugged at the trap, there was a violent explosion and the lye solution was sprayed into his eyes, immediately blinding him. Not only did the label fail to inform a user that hydrogen gas would be created, but there was no warning as such, against plugging a drain. Contained in the instructions and directions, as opposed to any warning, was the very innocuous, unemphasized statement that the drain should not be plugged, carrying with it no hint of any danger if this should be done. The court held that whether there was a sufficient and adequate warning of the danger was, in this case, a question of fact for the jury. To the same effect in a case where a workman was burned by the explosion of hydrogen gas created by the identical product of a competitor, the court made the same ruling in *Kieffer v. Blue Seal Chemical Company.*[7]

In all these cases, and the many other cases holding to the same effect, liability was imposed upon the manufacturer through testing the adequacy of the warning given by him against the dangerous potentiality of the product. The net result has been that, where the product is capable of producing great physical harm such as total blindness or death, the duty of the manufacturer to warn and the adequacy of the warning given by him is far different from the warning which would be considered adequate in those cases where the risk of injury is small. I submit that

[7] *20 Negligence Cases* 614, 196 F. 2d 614 (CA-3 1952).

no one can take issue with this reasoning, particularly where the manufacturer, and he alone, knows the full extent of the dangerous propensities of his product.

## Developments in Strict Liability

Turn now to the developments in the field of strict liability. It is here that we see the wringing of hands and the anguished cries of some defense attorneys. Yet, when we analyze the holdings in these cases, it is my opinion that the rule of strict liability is both fair and equitable to the manufacturer and to the consumer. Beginning with *Henningsen v. Bloomfield Motors, Inc.*,[8] continuing through *Greenman v. Yuba Power Products, Inc.*,[9] and coming down to the very recent decision of the Illinois Supreme Court in *Suvada v. White Motor Company, et al.*[10] the courts have swept away both the requirements of privity and of proof of negligence. As concisely stated by the court in *Suvada,* an opinion which reviews and analyzes all the leading cases on this point:

> "... (I)t seems obvious that public interest in human life and health, the invitations and solicitations to purchase the product and the justice of imposing loss on the one creating the risk and reaping the profit are present and as compelling in cases involving motor vehicles and other products, where the defective condition makes them unreasonably dangerous to the user, as they are in food cases."

## Essential Information is Available to Manufacturers

Many defense attorneys have taken the position that decisions such as *Suvada* have left them completely without defense in a products liability action. Nothing could be further from the fact. Neither *Suvada* nor any of the other cases cited and relied upon by it create any liability on a manufacturer unless the plaintiff establishes (1) that there was a defect in the product as a result of the manufacturing process, (2) that the defect made the product unreasonably dangerous, and (3) that the injury to the plaintiff resulted from that defect. The plaintiff must prove all three of these factors before he is entitled to a submission on the theory of strict liability. In this respect, the difficulties encountered by the plaintiff are far greater than those faced by the defendant. In the first place, the defense has available to it all the records of the manufacturer dealing with the developments, testing and production of the product, as well as all the technical personnel, highly skilled and trained in their respective fields who have developed, tested and produced the product. In the vast majority of cases, these records and these personnel know everything there is to be known about the product and whether or not there is in fact a defect. If proper, adequate and complete inspections

---

[8] *19 Automobile Cases* (2d) 610, 32 N. J. 358, 161 A. 2d (1960).

[9] *16 Negligence Cases* (2d) 35, 59 Cal. 2d 57, 377 P. 2d 897 (1963).

[10] *CCH Products Liability Reports* 5405, 32 Ill. 2d. 612, 210 N.E. 2d. 182 (1965).

and tests have been made during the development and testing of the product, evidence of that fact can strongly influence the jury against a plaintiff.

Additionally, in the modern methods of doing business, most manufacturers of industrial equipment or chemicals belong to one or more trade associations, made up of competitors in the same line. All the expert and technical personnel of those competitors usually will be available to one of the members through the association in supporting his defense of a products liability case. The defendant, therefore, will have the added weight of persons thoroughly familiar with competitive products of like nature, together with their tests and their knowledge and information of the product and its claimed lack of defects. All of these witnesses will be available to the defendant without excessive cost, expense or time.

## Difficulties Encountered by Plaintiff

Contrast this with the position in which the plaintiff finds himself when he claims injury from the use of a product, allegedly resulting from a defect in manufacture. In the first place, as soon as the happening of the accident is known, all avenues of information from the manufacturer, and usually from its competitors, are completely closed off. He frequently must, and usually will, resort to the necessity of engaging the services of independent experts whose knowledge of the product in question may be limited or completely absent. He must proceed solely on the basis of their educational background and basic qualifications, frequently being required to make complete tests or analyses, starting from scratch. In most cases, these are time consuming, extremely expensive, and often inconclusive. The financial burden alone thereby imposed upon the average plaintiff is frequently insurmountable. Thus, for example, I have in mind a fairly recent case in which, in order to determine whether there was a harmful ingredient in a chemical product, the plaintiff was required to hire an expert chemist to work solidly for a period of two weeks in order to find the synthetic ingredients in the product which were a trade secret of the manufacturer and not discoverable.

Even when the plaintiff does succeed in getting expert opinion to substantiate a claim of defeat, he still is met with a united front of the defendant's experts, all armed with formidable knowledge and records concerning the product. Finally, in many cases, after the expenditure of large sums of money and vast amounts of time, the plaintiff reaches the point where a defect cannot be proved. All of which, viewed as a whole, discourages all but the most flagrant cases of actual defect in manufacture. Of course, in those cases, no one can dispute the fact that the manufacturer should be held responsible to a consumer seriously injured as a result thereof. In these respects, therefore, far from being the nemesis of the defense bar, the rule of strict liability still leaves the defense with its complete arsenal of expert knowledge and know-how.

## Conclusion

In conclusion, I think it is safe for us to assume that the trend in products liability cases will be more and more toward the imposition of absolute and strict liability upon any manufacturer who exposes the public to risk of serious injury by putting into his product a defect as to which he either fails to inform himself by adequate and proper tests, so that he can, in turn, either give an adequate warning or correct and remedy the defect.

## Questions

1. Select a child's toy, a household cleanser, a spray can product, or another common product used in the home that could be potentially dangerous. Examine the product with a suspicious and cautious eye and write a sample label giving the user full warning of the characteristics, uses, and misuses of the product. Compare this with the notice actually given with the product. Discuss the differences and their possible reasons.
2. The author cites *Suvada v. White Motor Company, et al.* as the landmark case stressing strict liability of a manufacturer of a product. Do you feel that the issue discussed in that case is the same as that discussed earlier in the article about warning messages? Discuss.

# 16. THE "OTHER INSURANCE" DILEMMA *

Jack L. Watson †

A major area of conflict in the insurance industry today involves the recurrent situation where one party finds himself seemingly entitled to coverage under two policies of insurance, yet both companies disclaim either all or part liability by virtue of the existence of the other policy.[1] The problem arises from the fact that most insurance policies include conditions which provide that in the event of "other valid and collectible insurance" the particular company's coverage either (a) will assume a pro rata share of the damages, (b) will be noneffective or (c) will be excess insurance over the limits of the other policy's coverage. Thus, where a party is covered by two insurance policies and both policies have "other insurance" clauses, a difficult question arises as to what effect to give the respective provisions therein.

The most common situation involving this problem arises where a party incurs liability as the result of an occurrence in which he was driving a nonowned vehicle. The usual situation finds the driver insured by one company, $A$, while the owner of the vehicle is insured by a different company, $B$. The driver's policy generally has a provision covering his use of nonowned vehicles, while the owner's policy, with Company $B$, usually contains a "Definition of Insured" clause which extends coverage to anyone driving the named vehicle with the owner's permission.[2]

Thus, the driver's own policy with Company $A$ offers coverage to him under this fact situation, inasmuch as he was driving a nonowned vehicle, and the owner's policy with Company $B$ also offers coverage to the driver under the terms of its "Definition of Insured," under the so-called "omnibus clause."

## The "Other Insurance" Clauses

Furthermore, both policies usually contain an "other insurance" clause which limits the respective liability of each company either in

---

* From *Illinois Bar Journal* (March, 1966), pp. 151-159. Reprinted by permission.
† Associated with the law firm of J. V. Schaffenegger in Chicago, Illinois.
[1] See Billings, "The 'Other Insurance' Provision of the Automobile Policy," 318 INSURANCE LAW JOURNAL 489 (July 1949), wherein the author enumerates eight types of policies which can involve conflicting "other insurance" clauses as follows: (1) a garage liability policy, (2) a premises policy, (3) a lessor-lessee policy, (4) a nonownership policy, (5) a mortgagor-mortgagee policy, (6) a burial policy, (7) a life policy with special death benefits and (8) other automobile policies; 1 Couch, *Insurance*, Sec. 1.29 (2d ed. Anderson 1959).
[2] See 16 *Insurance Counsel Journal* 190 (1949).

part or *in toto* in the event there is other valid and collectible insurance. The following are illustrations of the various type clauses commonly used:

(a) "If the insured has other insurance against a loss covered by this policy the Company shall not be liable under this policy for a greater proportion of such loss than the applicable limit of liability stated in the declarations bears to the total applicable limit of liability of all valid and collectible insurance against such loss. . . ." [3]

Type (a) is termed a "pro rata" clause by virtue of the fact that it provides for an apportionment between the two insurance policies.

(b) "The insurance contained in this policy is not applicable to any person with respect to any loss against which he has other valid and collectible insurance. . . ." [4]

Type (b) is termed an "escape" or "no liability" clause for the reason that it disclaims (escapes) liability completely in the event of other insurance.

(c) "If there is other insurance against a loss covered under this policy the insurance provided under this policy shall be excess insurance over any other valid and collectible insurance. . . " [5]

Type (c) is termed an "excess" clause for the reason that it provides that its coverage shall be excess coverage only over any other valid and collectible insurance.

As can be imagined, the various type policies have come into conflict in different combinations, that is, prorata v. prorata, prorata v. excess, prorata v. escape, escape v. escape, escape v. excess, and excess v. excess. The effect has been that different combinations have led to different results although the reasoning behind the various decisions has varied considerably.

## IDENTICAL "OTHER INSURANCE" CLAUSES

Where the applicable portions of the two conflicting clauses are identical, that is, pro rata v. pro rata, escape v. escape or excess v. excess, the result nearly always reached is that the two insurers must prorate the liability, [6] and the few decisions supporting a contrary result seem confined to the unusual fact situations involved therein. [7]

---

[3] See *Woodrich Construction Co. v. Indemnity Insurance Co.*, 13 AUTOMOBILE CASES (2d) 1460, 252 Minn. 86, 89 N. W. 2d 412 (1958).

[4] See *Zurich General Accident & Liability Insurance Co. v. Clamor*, 12 AUTOMOBILE CASES 1117, 124 F. 2d 717 (CA-7 1941).

[5] See *Cosmopolitan Mutual Insurance Co. v. Continental Casualty Co.*, 15 AUTOMOBILE CASES (2d) 1345, 28 N. J. 554, 147 A. 2d 529 (1959).

[6] See *Consolidated Shippers, Inc. v. Pacific Employers Insurance Co.*, 11 AUTOMOBILE CASES 864, 45 Cal. App. 2d 288, 114 P. 2d 34 (1941); *Insurance Co. of Texas v. Employers Liability Assurance Corp.*, 15 AUTOMOBILE CASES (2d) 458, 163 F. Supp. 143 (DC Cal. 1958); Appleman, *Automobile Liability Insurance* 134-135, 325 (1938); Annotation, 69 A.L.R. 2d 1122 (1960).

[7] *Hartford Steam Boiler Inspection & Insurance Co. v. Cochran Oil Mill & Ginnery Co.*, 26 Ga. App. 288, 105 S.E. 856 (1921).

It should be noted that the word "applicable" is stressed for the reason that it is common to find two insurers who have identical "other insurance" clauses *in toto,* yet when applied to the facts at hand the pro rata portion of one comes into play as against the excess or escape portion of the other. This situation arises from the fact that many insurers provide that as to other insurance generally they will prorate therewith, but in certain situations, such as when the named assured is driving a temporary substitute vehicle or nonowned vehicle, the coverage either will be "noneffective" or "excess" insurance only. Thus, the particular fact situation may bring the pro rata portion of one policy into play against the excess portion of another policy, despite the fact that the two policies are identical in their entirety.

The reasoning behind the apportionment rule for identical policies is that there is no rational cause to give the language in one policy preference over identical language in the other policy.[8] Furthermore, a completely literal interpretation of the "excess v. excess" or "escape v. escape" situations might well result in a finding that the presence of the other policy relieved both insurers from any liability whatsoever, with the result that the assured would find himself with no coverage where it at first appeared that he had double coverage. Such a result would violate the basic rule that no insured party should be *deprived* of coverage as the result of the presence of two or more insurers and, hence, this possibility is carefully avoided by the courts.[9]

## DISSIMILAR "OTHER INSURANCE" CLAUSES

While the courts have been basically in agreement as to the proposition that *identical* "other insurance" clauses are necessarily indistinguishable and, therefore, to be disregarded, the opinions have varied greatly in attempting to resolve the problem of dissimilar clauses. When the conflicting clauses present a conflict between pro rata and excess, escape and excess, or pro rata and escape, the courts have used several different formulas to reach varying solutions.

### The Prior in Time Theory

A few early decisions looked to the date upon which each policy became effective and placed full liability upon that policy which first came into effect.[10] The reasoning behind this approach was that at the

---

[8] See *Continental Casualty Co. v. Buckeye Union Casualty Co.,* 91, 143 N.E. 2d 169, 180 (C.P. 1957).

[9] See Russ, "The Double Insurance Problem—A Proposal," 13 *Hastings Law Journal* 183, 185 (1961).

[10] *New Amsterdam Casualty Co. v. Hartford Accident & Indemnity Co.,* 5 AUTOMOBILE CASES 1195, 108 F. 2d 653 (CA-6 1940); see *Kearns Coal Corp. v. United States Fidelity & Guaranty Co.,* 10 AUTOMOBILE CASES 435, 118 F. 2d 33, 35 (CA-2), cert. denied, 313 U.S. 579 (1941); *Michigan Alkali Co. v. Bankers Indemnity Insurance Co.,* 3 AUTOMOBILE CASES 345, 103 F. 2d 345, 347 (CA-2 1939); *Air Transport Manufacturing Co. v. Employers' Liability Assurance Co.,* 91 Cal. App. 2d 129, 204 P. 2d 647 (1949).

time the first policy was entered into there was no "other insurance," whereas at the time the subsequent policy was entered into the first policy was, in fact, "other insurance." This view was subsequently criticized as being based on a false premise that the insurers intended their policies to be interpreted as of the time they became effective, whereas, in fact, the accepted rule is that policies are to be examined as of the date of the occurrence for which coverage is being sought.[11]

## The Prime Tortfeasor Theory

Another view adopted by a minority of courts was to place full liability on the insurer of the prime tortfeasor.[12] Thus, in the situation where one party was driving another party's vehicle this theory placed full liability on the insurer of the driver as opposed to the insurer of the owner. The reasoning, of course, was that the fault for the particular occurrence rested on the driver rather than the owner. While this view had a certain equitable appeal, it, too, was subsequently abandoned for the reason that it failed to take into account the fact that the insurers did not intend such a result.[13]

## Primary v. Secondary Coverage

Yet another view attempted to make a distinction between primary and secondary coverage and placed the full liability on the primary insurer.[14] While this distinction has been made in many of the decisions the truth seems to be that the courts have first decided which company should bear the liability and have then labeled it the primary insurer, rather than first applying any accepted tests of primary or secondary. A further difficulty with this approach has been that it offers no solution to those situations in which both insurers appear to fall in the same category and yet still have different "other insurance" clauses.

## The Majority View

While an occasional reference is still made to the aforementioned theories, the situation today is such that two major conflicting theories have emerged as representing the present prevailing approaches to this dilemma.

The result reached by the majority of the courts has been that the different type "other insurance" clauses are distinguishable and

---

[11] See 38 *Minnesota Law Review* 838, 846 (1954).

[12] *American Auto Insurance Co. v. Pennsylvania Mutual Indemnity Co.*, 26 AUTOMOBILE CASES 1114, 161 F. 2d 62 (CA-3 1947); *Maryland Casualty Co. v. Bankers Indemnity Insurance Co.*, 51 Ohio App. 323, 200 N.E. 849 (1935).

[13] See *Maryland Casualty Co. v. Employers Mutual Liability Insurance Co.*, 2 AUTOMOBILE CASES (2d) 932, 112 F. Supp. 272, (DC Conn. 1953).

[14] See 8 Appleman, *Insurance Law and Practice* 333, Sec. 4914 (2d ed. 1962).

represent different limits of liability.[15] Thus, wherever one "other insurance" clause is of the "excess" type, it will be given full effect and held not to come into play where the conflicting clause is of either the "pro rata" or "escape" type.[16] In so holding, the courts have acknowledged the fact that the different language is intended to produce different levels of coverage and the courts have attempted to give full effect to the intent thus manifested.

## The Zurich v. Clamor Decision

The most frequently cited decision in support of this view is the case of *Zurich General Accident & Liability Insurance Company v. Clamor*.[17] This case involved a conflict between an escape clause (in Zurich's policy) and an excess clause (in Car & General Insurance Corporation's policy) and in holding that Car & General's policy did not come into effect until the limits of the Zurich policy were exhausted, the court stated: [18]

> "There is no case, so far as we are aware, where the precise question has been decided. There are cases which have held or indicated, under somewhat similar circumstances, that the specific language is controlling over the general. We think that construction should be applied in the instant situation. Any other construction would ignore the specific language employed by Car & General. The 'excess insurance' provided by the latter is not 'other insurance' required by Zurich. We think the logic of this reasoning is made apparent by assuming that neither of the policies contained an 'other insurance' provision, or that both policies contained an 'other insurance' provision in exactly the same language. It could not be seriously argued, in our opinion, but that under either of such situations the two insurers would be liable in proportion to the amount of insurance provided by their respective policies. *Here, however, as pointed out, the 'other insurance' provision of the two policies is different. In order to give effect to such difference, it is logical to conclude that Zurich is liable to the extent named in its policy, and that Car & General is liable only for any excess over that provided by Zurich."* (Italics supplied.)

This view is generally recognized as representing the established and better rule, and it has enjoyed wide acceptance.[19]

----

[15] *Citizens Mutual Automobile Insurance Co. v. Liberty Mutual Insurance Co.*, 18 AUTOMOBILE CASES (2d) 815, 273 F. 2d 189 (CA-6 1959); *United Services Auto Association v. Russom*, 10 AUTOMOBILE CASES (2d) 647, 241 F. 2d 296 (CA-5 1957); *Schweistal v. Standard Mutual Insurance Co.*, 31 AUTOMOBILE CASES (2d) 795, 48 Ill. App. 2d 226, 198 N.E. 2d 860 (1964); Annotation, 46 A. L. R. 2d 1159 (1956).

[16] *Continental Casualty Co. v. American Fidelity & Casualty Co.*, 19 AUTOMOBILE CASES (2d) 238, 275 F. 2d 381 (CA-7 1960); Annotation, 76 A. L. R. 2d 502 (1961).

[17] Case cited at footnote 4.

[18] Case cited at footnote 17, at 720.

[19] See work cited at footnote 14, at Sec. 4913; 29A *American Jurisprudence* 795 (1960); Annotation, 76 A. L. R. 2d 502 (1951).

This same approach has been used to hold that a conflict between an escape clause and a pro rata clause should be resolved in favor of the former.[20] In this regard, another expression of the *Zurich* decision's reasoning is found in the recent Iowa decision of *Burcham v. Farmers Insurance Exchange*.[21] In holding that a combination excess-escape clause should be given preference over a pro rata clause, the court stated as follows:

> "Though the reasoning may be criticized as circular and arbitrary, we believe the better rule is that where the insurance companies would be liable except for the other, the excess-escape clause policy should be held to be not other similar insurance to the policy containing the pro rata clause, conversely, the policy with only its pro rata clause applicable is regarded as other similar insurance as used in the excess-escape policy. A fair construction of the intention as expressed in the policies is that each company intended to provide and the insureds intended to buy coverage to the extent stated in the excess-escape clause." [22]

## The Minority View—The Oregon Cases

A drastic departure from the majority approach emanated from the Ninth Circuit in 1952 in the case of *Oregon Auto Insurance Company v. United States Fidelity Company*.[23] In this case the court ordered a proration between an excess clause and a pro rata clause and stated as follows:

> *"In our opinion the 'other insurance' provisions of the two policies are indistinguishable in meaning and intent. One cannot rationally choose between them. . . . Here, where both policies carry like 'other insurance' provisions, we think (they) must be held mutually repugnant and hence be disregarded."* [24] (Italics supplied.)

Subsequent to the *Oregon Auto* decision the Supreme Court of Oregon had occasion to follow the lead of the Ninth Circuit in the case of *Lamb-Weston, et al. v. Oregon Auto Insurance Company*.[25] In an extensive opinion, the court reviewed many decisions and acknowledged that the majority rule was contrary to the *Oregon Auto* view. Nonetheless, the court elected to follow the minority approach and, in ruling that an excess policy must apportion damages with a pro rata policy, the court concluded as follows:

> "The 'other insurance' clauses of all policies are but methods used by all insurers to limit their liability, whether using language that relieves them from all liability (usually referred to as an 'escape clause') or that used by St. Paul (usually referred to as an 'excess clause') or that used by

---

[20] *McFarland v. Chicago Express, Inc.*, 1 Automobile Cases (2d) 51, 200 F. 2d 5 (CA-7 1952).

[21] Automobile Cases (2d) 1107, 255 Ia. 69, 121 N.W. 2d 500 (1963).

[22] Case cited at footnote 21, at 503.

[23] 38 Automobile Cases 917, 195 F.2d 958 (CA-9 1952).

[24] Case cited at footnote 23, at 960.

[25] 219 Ore. 110, 341 P. 2d 110, modified 219 Ore. 129, 346 P. 2d 643 (1959).

Oregon (usually referred to as a 'pro rata clause'). In our opinion, whether one policy uses one clause or another, when any come in conflict with the 'other insurance' clause of another insurer, regardless of the nature of the clause, they are in fact repugnant and each should be rejected *in toto*." [26]

The minority view has gained acceptance in several other jurisdictions since its inception [27] and has found favor with various authors.[28] Indeed, it is not difficult to understand the appeal which this approach has to those who seek a simple, convenient solution to the problem.

However, while the *Oregon* approach results in a convenient method by which to dispose of a troublesome situation, it is submitted that it fails to take into account the foremost rule of the law of contracts, which is that the courts will attempt to give full effect to the intent of the parties.[29]

## The Intent of the Parties

While the *Oregon* view is quick to suggest that the different type clauses are indistinguishable in intent and meaning, this approach fails to attach any significance whatsoever to the fact that the policies contain different words with different accepted meanings. A basic rule of contracts is that consideration must be given to *all* the language in a policy to determine its meaning and intent.[30] This rule becomes especially important in resolving the particular problems involved here due to the fact that many policies have more than one clause within their *own* "Other Insurance" provision. To illustrate, a typical "Other Insurance" provision reads as follows:

*"If an assured has other insurance against a loss covered by this policy the company shall not be liable under this policy for a greater proportion of such loss than the applicable limit of liability stated in the declarations bears to the total applicable limit of liability of all valid and collectible insurance against such loss;* provided, however, that the insurance . . . with respect to other automobiles . . . shall be excess insurance over any other valid and collectible insurance available to the assured, either as an insured under a policy applicable with respect to said automobiles or otherwise." [31] (Italics supplied.)

---

[26] Case cited at footnote 25, at 119.

[27] *Continental Casualty Co. v. Weeks*, 5 AUTOMOBILE CASES (2d) 234, 74 So. 2d 367, 46 A. L. R. 2d 1159 (Fla. 1954); *Arditi v. Massachusetts Bonding & Insurance Co.*, 15 AUTOMOBILE CASES (2d) 275, 315 S. W. 2d 736 (Mo. 1958); *Cosmopolitan Mutual Insurance Co. v. Continental Casualty Co.*, cited at footnote 5; *Woodrich Construction Co. v. Indemnity Insurance Co.*, cited at footnote 3; *Beattie v. American Automobile Insurance Co.*, 156 N. E. 2d 49 (Mass. 1959); *New Amsterdam Casualty Co. v. Lloyds' Underwriters*, 33 AUTOMOBILE CASES (2d) 623, 56 Ill. App. 2d 224, 205 N. E. 2d 735 (1965). However, for a contrary Illinois opinion, see *Schweistal v. Standard Mutual Insurance Co.*, cited at footnote 15.

[28] 65 *Columbia Law Review* 319 (1965); 38 *Minnestoa Law Review* 838 (1954).

[29] See *Corbin on Contracts*, Sec. 538 (one volume ed. 1952).

[30] See work cited at footnote 29, Sec. 545-554.

[31] See *Citizens Mutual Auto Insurance Co. v. Liberty Mutual Insurance Co.*, cited at footnote 15.

It is to be noted that the first portion of this provision, in italic, pertaining to other insurance generally, provides that the coverage shall be prorated therewith, whereas the second clause, after the semicolon, provides that in a special situation the coverage shall be "excess" coverage over other insurance.

While the various policies may differ as to the conditions in which they will prorate with other insurance, escape liability or be excess coverage, the fact remains that most policies provide different "other insurance" clauses for different fact situations and a solution to these disputes thus requires a determination as to which part of each company's "other insurance" clause was put into effect under the particular facts involved. The conclusion to be reached from this situation is that since each party has seen fit to distinguish the different type clauses in its own policy, each party necessarily must have intended and understood that the different language used would result in different and distinct levels of liability.[32] And, in our example clause, the most obvious way to distinguish between the two "other insurance" clauses is to hold, as does the majority view, that "excess" means exactly what it says and, accordingly, this coverage is not collectible until all other policies have been exhausted.

As stated in *American Auto Insurance Company v. Republic Indemnity Company of America:*

> "The only construction of the 'other insurance' clause under which both its parts will be meaningful is that the *excess* provision alone controls in every situation which falls within its terms . . . and that the *pro rata* provision alone governs in all other situations, for example, when more than one policy has been issued to the same person." [33]

## An Example of Common Intent

To elaborate on this point, let us assume a conflict between two insurers who both have exactly the same provision *in toto* as the example policy above-cited. Let us now say that Company *A's* assured is involved in an accident while driving a car which is owned by a party insured by Company *B*.

When the matter enters litigation, Company *B* adopts the *Oregon* position that the difference in the language of the two clauses, "prorata" v. "excess," is meaningless and indistinguishable and, therefore, the two policies should prorate. Yet, the fact remains that Company *B* saw fit to make the very same distinction between pro rata and excess in its own policy. If Company *B* truly felt there was no difference in the two type clauses, it surely would not have bothered to distinguish between them in its own policy but, rather, would simply have said that in *all* situations it would prorate with other insurance.

---

[32] See work cited at footnote 2, at 198.
[33] 52 Cal. 2d 513, 341 P. 2d 675, 678 (1959).

In this situation it seems obvious that each company has made exactly the same distinctions, with exactly the same intent, in each policy, that is, as to other insurance generally it will prorate, but as to that one situation where its assured is driving a nonowned vehicle it will be excess only. Neither policy intended to prorate where its assured was driving a nonowned vehicle and both policies spelled out this intent clearly. How, then, can Company *B* now be heard to say that it cannot see any distinction in the language?

If one will accept the premise that it seems improper to force companies in the above situation to prorate in direct contradiction of the expressed and understood intent of both policies, it requires but one short step to accept the fact that wherever a company uses two different type clauses in its own policy, it intends and understands that the different type clauses should produce different results. Such being the case, the fact that the two insurers may not have exactly the same "other insurance" clauses does not alter the fact that both companies understand the fact to be that the different clauses represent different levels of liability. Furthermore, the widespread use of these different clauses suggests that *all* insurers know and understand the different levels involved and should be held to their accepted interpretations.

In this vein it must be noted that the *Oregon Auto* opinion fails to set out the policies in full, and it would be interesting to know whether the complaining companies in that case, had, in fact, distinguished between the different levels in their *own* policies.

## A Recent Development

A relatively recent decision by the Oregon Supreme Court indicates the lengths to which the minority courts will go to force proration. The case referred to is *General Insurance Company and Moore Timber Products, Inc. v. Saskatchewan Government Insurance Office and British Commercial Insurance Company, et al.,*[34] wherein a particular company had contracted with one insurer for basic primary coverage and had then contracted with two other insurers for additional coverage. The terms of the additional coverage policies provided, in effect, they would provide excess coverage over the primary policy. A fact situation arose whereby the company's insurers were asked to contribute to the satisfaction of a judgment by virtue of the fact that the judgment debtor was entitled to coverage under the broad terms of the primary insurer's policy's "Definition of Insured." The judgment debtor's insurer was another insurance company and its policy provided that it, too, would be excess coverage over other valid and collectible insurance. The court required *all* the insurers to prorate the liability in the same proportion which each company's applicable limit of liability bore to the total limit

---

[34] 31 Automobile Cases (2d) 369, 238 Ore. 8, 391 P. 2d 616 (1964).

of liability. Thus, the two additional insurers who had specifically contracted with the assured as additional excess carriers were required to prorate with the primary carrier and the judgment debtor, despite the fact that the limits of the assured's primary policy never were exhausted. This appears to represent a complete disregard of the intent of the additional insurers.

This result bodes ill for those insurers in the business of writing additional "excess" insurance. Not only does the *Oregon* view force the additional insurers to prorate liability without the primary coverage first being exhausted, but, due to the fact that the monetary limits of additional insurance policies are often much greater than the limits of primary policies, the net result of this approach is to place the bulk of liability on the additional insurer, in direct derogation of the intent of the parties. Such a result seems extremely harsh and appears to be an additional argument for a return to the majority rule.

## CONCLUSION

It seems clear from the widespread use of different type "other insurance" clauses, including the use of two different types within one policy, that the insurance industry has long recognized, understood and intended that different type "other insurance" clauses should, and do, represent different levels of coverage. Such being the case, it becomes the duty of the courts to make every effort to give full effect to the manifest intent of the parties and to give expression to the different type clauses. To hold that no distinction can be made is to completely disregard both the language of the policies and the intent of the parties. It is submitted that the reasoning and experience attendant to the majority rule should prevail over mere conveniences.

## Questions

1. Locate the "definition of insured" clause and the "other insurance" clause in your automobile policy. Study them and discuss whether there would be a problem of coverage if the situation arises as set up by the author of this article: You are driving a friend's car. You have your policy on your car and your friend has an identical policy with another company on his car. Follow the principles as described by the author in discussing the situation.
2. It is becoming increasingly common for health insurance policies to have an "other insurance" clause applying, particularly if the other insurance is medical payments insurance in an automobile policy. This type of limitation characteristically appears in student group health and accident insurance policies. Check the terms of the student insurance available at your school. Discuss the relationships between your automobile insurance policy and this student insurance policy.
3. Check your automobile policy with respect to coverage of a trailer towed by the automobile and the "other insurance" provisions.

4. "Umbrella" liability insurance is a very high-limit liability insurance policy that is specifically written as excess coverage over conventional liability insurance coverages. Locate an "umbrella" liability insurance policy. Discuss the "other insurance" clause in the policy and the relationship of the "umbrella" policy to other existing insurance. How would the "Oregon interpretation" as described by the other author apply to the "umbrella" policy?

# PART 5
## Automobile Insurance

Nearly all state legislatures, as well as the Congress, are actively considering alternatives to the negligence reparation system for automobile crash victims. The bulk of the available research results, including the U.S. Department of Transportation twenty-six volume series of studies of 1970-71, attest to the complexity of the issues involved, to the magnitude of the problems, and to the serious inequities that exist in the present system. It is not certain whether acceptable solutions will be found soon or in the future.

The articles in this part were selected to develop ideas in the various facets of the "automobile problem." The first article by Professor Ross discusses societal problems. The economic consequences of the automobile crash are taken up in the article by Professors Rosenbloom and Lee. In the final article of this part, Professor Keeton, who co-authored the book *Basic Protection for the Traffic Victim* to which many attribute the beginnings of serious consideration of no-fault insurance in the United States in 1965, looks beyond the currently offered reform measures to talk to the new issues that may arise later on, after "no-fault" laws are adopted generally.

# 17. SOCIAL PROBLEMS OF THE AUTOMOBILE *

H. Laurence Ross †

## INTRODUCTION

For the foreseeable future, American society is committed to the automobile as a means of transportation. Despite the fulminations of some critics, the people have made it clear, putting money behind their words, that they will take nothing less than the family car as their ordinary means of transportation, whether to work, to shop, or for any other common, everyday activity. This commitment has led to a transformation of society, in which the average man has realized the dream of his home on his own land, and this transformation of homes, stores and factories has sealed solid the commitment to the automobile.

All major social changes, however beneficent in general, bring undesired consequences. If the magnitude of those attending the automobile seems very great, it is necessary to recall the magnitude of the change that the automobile has brought to society since 1900, and the magnitude of the benefits the public enjoys as a consequence. However, the fact that the benefits may exceed the problems does not imply that the problems need be neglected. The purpose of this paper is to review some of the many problematical aspects of the automobile, as they have been stated by critics both friendly and unfriendly, to evaluate the criticisms, and to offer some suggestions as to the direction of possible and desirable changes in the realm of automobile insurance.

## AUTOMOBILES

The extent of society's commitments to the automobile is easily documented with figures. In 1966, there were 78 million passenger cars registered in the United States—more than half of all cars in the world—and four out of five American families own at least one car. One-eighth of United States income was spent on transport, and one-seventh of all persons employed were in the vehicle transportation business. One-quarter of all retail sales were automotive.[1] Perhaps the best testimony

* From *The Annals of the Society of Chartered Property and Casualty Underwriters* (September, 1968), pp. 227-234. Reprinted by permission.
† Professor of Sociology and Law, University of Denver.

[1] Data are from Automobile Manufacturers Association, *Automobile Facts and Figures,* 1967 edition, and Greer, Scott, "Traffic, Transportation and Problems of the Metropolis," in Merton, Robert U. and Nisbet, Robert A., *Contemporary Social Problems,* New York: Harcourt, Brace & World, 1961, pp. 605-650.

to this commitment is the everyday experience with congested streets, which very much reduce the effectiveness of the automobile. Rush hour traffic in some cities averages about 16 miles per hour, but this has not resulted in many abandoning use of the automobile.

The most dramatic consequence of the automobile has been the impact on cities. The city of 1900, densely built at its throbbing core, and strung out like a starfish along lines of public transportation at the periphery, has been transformed into a sprawling structure with relatively much less centralization and much lower density. The single-family detached residence has triumphed over the row house, the tenement, and the middle-class apartment house. The preference for single-family houses has its roots in the longing of English forefathers for a castle in a park; its realization depended on the automobile. Today, the majority of Americans live in metropolitan areas, and more than half of these live in the suburbs. Not only has housing become decentralized because of the automobile, commerce quickly followed, based on the same means of transportation, drawn by clientele to the Elysian Fields. It has been joined increasingly by industry, chasing the workers and liberated from the rail lines by the car's cousin, the motor truck.

These developments have rendered their cause, the automobile, a true necessity. With home, job and shopping all suburbanized, the new metropolitan man cannot exist without his automobile. The driver's license, which could be considered a privilege when driving was a mere convenience, is coming to be considered a right as driving becomes a necessity. Deprivation of a license may well be a sentence to economic death. It is a rarely imposed sanction, and on those occasions when it is imposed large numbers of people continue to drive in violation of the law.[2]

The transformation of the city into the suburbanized metropolis has involved some sacrifices. The street life of the old central cities may have become less lively, and some of the valued institutions there complain of loss of patronage. The threatened institutions have responded in different ways. Some successfully have followed their clients to the suburbs. Others have provided the impetus behind urban renewal, with rather mixed results. Central city interest groups have spurred construction of new and better highways and parking facilities to attract the suburbanites back into town, a project that can probably never be completely successful because the scale of the transformation has been so great.

The effect of the automobile in transforming the city has frequently been cited as a major social problem. From the vantage point of those with economic or sentimental interests in the central cities, this view

---

[2] See Ross, H. Laurence and Campbell, Donald T., "The Connecticut Speed Crackdown: A Study of the Effects of Legal Change," in Ross, H. Laurence, (ed.), *Perspectives on the Social Order*, (2nd ed.), New York: McGraw-Hill Book Company, 1968, pp. 30-38.

When Connecticut in 1955 started to suspend driver's licenses in large numbers for conviction of speeding, convictions for driving without a license rose astronomically.

may be reasonable. However, the studies that have been made by social scientists have shown rather conclusively that the suburbs are a success as judged by the feelings of those who live there.[3] The horrors of commuting described by the critics do not seem to disturb the suburbanites, who may have received a slow but comfortable journey by car in exchange for a shorter but much less comfortable trip by mass transportation. The specialty shops and little theaters may not be missed at all, or may be compensated for by television, shopping centers, and the pleasures of an active community life. The most important satisfactions of suburbia, according to the best studies, are those centering around the family and the private house, which the city of the pre-automobile age was much less capable of offering to its resident masses.

The current technology of the automobile lends support to a related criticism, the validity of which is again documented by everyday experience. This is air pollution. If congestion can be said to have its positive aspects, testifying as it does to the use that people make of their cars, the same cannot be said for pollution. Even relatively thinly settled metropolitan areas like Denver are unable to cope with the intensive use of the automobile that occurs today. Fortunately, current and prospective technical devices for reducing polluting emissions promise to be effective, although they will raise the price of the automobile and will not be purchased on a large scale unless required by law. The problem is soluble, although temporarily discomforting, probably without the need to develop a new source of power by which to run the automobile.[4]

## ACCIDENTS

If the previously mentioned problems associated with the automobile seem on reflection to be overestimated or inherently soluble, the death, injury and economic loss associated with automobile accidents present a much less hopeful picture. According to the National Safety Council, the 13.6 million accidents experienced in 1966 caused 53,000 deaths and nearly two million disabling injuries, and the cost in terms of lost wages, medical expenses, and maintenance of the insurance system equalled 6.7 billion dollars.[5] Much progress has been made in the past in reducing the automobile death rate. This progress can be accounted for largely by the construction of safer highways and improvements in medical skills applied to traumatic injuries. However, the mileage death rate has fluctuated between 5 and 6 per hundred million vehicle miles for

---

[3] See Gass, Herbert J., *The Levittowners*, New York: Pantheon Books, 1967.

[4] This is the conclusion of a report to the Commerce Department and others by a private Panel on Electrically Powered Vehicles. See *U. S. News and World Report*, October 30, 1967, and *Science News*, November 4, 1967. According to the latter, the report stated: "Pollution controls, although expensive, are economically feasible with known devices and those in sight. Any alternate low pollution propulsion, such as electric cars, steam engines, and turbines, are too far down the road to get into production fast enough to help."

[5] Data are from National Safety Council, *Accident Facts*, 1967 edition.

the last decade, suggesting that the source of major improvement in this matter may have dried up. Barring a major break-through, it would appear that additional safety measures will produce smaller increments of benefit than those of the past. The traffic system is probably one in which a certain minimal level of accidents will have to be tolerated, and as the use of the automobile continues to increase, the absolute number of fatalities, and of injuries and economic loss, may be expected to increase.

## COMPENSATION

No one can give back the life lost in a traffic accident, nor in any fundamental way can the sufferer of an injury be made completely "whole." What can be done, however, is to repay the economic consequences of an accident to the point where the sufferer is not out of pocket, or above and beyond this point so that the sufferer may be less unhappy with his lot in general. This payment is the function of insurance in society, and it is made through two different forms of insurance, which correspond to two different philosophies of the automobile accident.

The first of these philosophies is that of fault, and of the liability insurance policy. According to this view, if recompense is to be made, it is because the damage was caused by the imprudent and unreasonable conduct of someone, who did not fulfill a legal duty to the injured party. The loss should rightly be that of the party who caused the injury rather than of the party who suffered it innocently. Although, as Fleming James and many others have pointed out, the existence and near universal use of liability insurance means that the guilty party pays no part of the damages * (but rather transfers his burden to the insured owners of automobiles generally), the underlying conceptualization is of individual responsibility. In this light, the requirements on the sufferer to prove the fault of the other, and to do so with his own hands being "clean," are eminently reasonable.

In contrast, medical payments and similar policies put the idea of fault aside. The concept on which this compensation depends is that of an accident. Although fault may be involved in the cause of the accident, it is not held to be relevant in deciding upon payment. The accident is here regarded as a possible but unpredictable event, and its consequences can be insured against because its occurrence in the mass can be calculated statistically, and its cost divided proportionately.

Although the majority of people working in the automobile insurance field seem to find the fault model more persuasive than the payments model, this author believes that current scientific studies of accidents show the latter to be more persuasive. In the Case Studies of Traffic

---

* Provided his liability limits are adequate. Adequate currently is defined as $5,000,-000 excess over $500,000/$1,000,000 underlying—Ed.

Accidents project at Northwestern University, it became clear that the principal causes of the accidents observed were the failure to observe an approaching hazard, or a miscalculation of its course.[6] Seldom did the failure or miscalculation appear abnormal. Rather, it appeared that the requirements of safe driving exceed the capacities of ordinary men, given the streets and vehicles with which they must operate, and assuming a reasonable rate of speed for traffic. Accidents appeared to the investigators on that projects as inevitable results of ordinary gaps in attention and understanding on the part of reasonable and prudent drivers. Although it could be surmised that a given accident might have been avoided if the driver's gaze had been turned in another direction, in that case, a different hazard might have been overlooked. One could not say that a driver's general performance of his task was faulty, in the majority of the accidents studied. Given this perspective, the fault philosophy appears unrealistic and artificial.

It stands to reason from the viewpoint of one adopting the accident philosophy that a compensation system based upon the fault philosophy is unfair and capricious. The Keeton and O'Connell study *Basic Protection for the Accident Victim,* summarizes the flaws in the tort system as follows:

> First . . . some injured persons receive no compensation. Others receive far less than their economic losses . . .
> Second, the present system is cumbersome and slow. . .
> Third, the present system is loaded with unfairness. Some get too much . . . and most often it is the neediest (those most seriously injured) who get the lowest percentage of compensation for their losses. . .
> Fourth, the present system is marred by temptations to dishonesty that lure into their snares a stunning percentage of drivers and victims. . .[7]

With the exception of the fifth point, perhaps, these criticisms make sense as stated only if one rejects the fault principle. If the principle is not rejected, the remaining points may be quite invalid, depending on the facts underlying these generalizations. For instance, if some people receive nothing in compensation, these may be the very people whose negligence caused their accidents, and who do not deserve compensation according to the fault criterion. Of course, it is possible that lack of assets or financial failure of the defendant's insurance company may underlie some cases of non-payment, and these are defects even granting the fault principle.

Likewise, it can be argued that a slow, cumbersome and expensive system is necessary, in order to be sure that fault is properly diagnosed, and fair payment made accordingly. Much of the effort involved in adjusting automobile insurance claims goes into recreating the accident

---

[6] Ross, H. Laurence, "Awareness of Collision Course in Traffic Accidents," *Traffic Safety Research Reviews,* Vol. 5, No. 1 (March, 1961), pp. 12-16.

[7] Keeton, Robert E. and O'Connell, Jeffrey, *Basic Protection for the Traffic Victim,* Boston: Little, Brown, 1965, pp. 1-3.

and determining who was at fault, and this process is expensive and time-consuming.[8] If the fault principle is an element of justice in the accident situation, the procedures in use may be warranted.

Even the apparent unfairness cited in Keeton and O'Connell's third point becomes more comprehensible, if fault is meaningful. Much of the apparent overpayment of small claims reflects a realistic generosity of insurance companies in small claims, where fault of the insured may be contestable, but the price of contesting it makes the contest prohibitive. In the large claims, where the game is worth the candle, this type of minor blackmail can be eliminated and payment can be related more closely to fault.

In support of these arguments the author wishes to cite a study he currently is making of 2,200 automobile injury claims randomly selected from the files of a large insurance company that writes automobile policies throughout the United States. Among these cases were 285 rear-end collisions in which the claimant was in the rear car. It may be presumed that virtually all these cases were strictly speaking instances of no liability. However, some payment was made in 108 of them, and the mean payment was $145.00. There were 70 claims in which the claimant car but not the insured car was cited by the police, again strongly suggesting no liability; in 34 of these cases some payment was made, the mean payment being $376.00. In 232 cases, the adjuster stated in the file his opinion that the case was one of no liability; some payment was none the less made in 78 of these, the mean payment being $130.00.

These findings suggest that the company studied is making payments in a significant proportion of claims in which liability may be very questionable. The company is by no means eleemosynary,* nor is it atypical of insurance companies generally. Management's policy is to make payment only where payment is due. That this is not in fact what happens is largely due to the strong pressures upon adjusters to economize company resources by closing files.

In brief, the administration of the law of negligence by insurance companies seems to be distorted in the direction of payment without fault, which is exactly the direction for which the critics of the present system are pleading. If inequities remain, from the viewpoint of the critic who rejects the fault principle, it is because the principle, though bent in its administration, is far from being completely discarded as the *sine qua non* for recompense through liability insurance. Moreover, the tort route is still depended on for approximately half of all recoveries for losses in traffic accidents. The retention of the liability question in

---

[8] In the study of insurance claims referred to below, the average time to close a claim was 411 days when the adjuster was of the opinion that the insured was liable; 457 days when the adjuster was of the opinion that the insured was not liable; and 621 days when the adjuster believed that liability was questionable.

* Some companies, however, seem to be non-profit.—Ed.

the handling of claims requires a costly and time-consuming recon-
struction of the accident, and results in a distribution of funds which,
from the critics' viewpoint, can be regarded only as capricious. However,
it is important to emphasize that if the road to be followed is that sketched
by the critics, one must be prepared to follow them first in renouncing
the philosophical commitment to fault in interpreting traffic accidents.
This is a renunciation that the author is prepared to make, based on
his own studies, the studies of others, and his own experiences as a
driver.

It is interesting to note the direction in which it seems the insurance
industry ought to be going in protecting the accident victim, assuming
that the fault principle is rejected as a basis for allocating payments.
These thoughts are not very original, and the author acknowledges a
debt to Keeton and O'Connell, as well as to other pioneers in reassess-
ing automobile insurance.[9]

1. Economic loss suffered in an automobile accident should be repaid,
regardless of fault. If fault is as fictional as it appears to be, it has no
business drastically affecting human lives. This can best be accomplished
on the basis of the first-party insurance contract, where the auto policy
can be excess over more general types of insurance, such as Blue Cross-
Blue Shield, major medical insurance, disability income insurance, and
similar coverages. The first party relationship seems to be the most
satisfactory one between an individual and an insurance company, and
the author has too much respect for the accomplishments of the insurance industry to be swayed by the argument that rating problems would
be insuperable.

2. Coverage should be universal, as the benefits of the automobile
are universal, but the machinery should be private. Compulsory private
automobile insurance has now been shown to be sound and workable.
A system whereby insurance must be shown to obtain an automobile
license is tried and true, as are the capacities of private insurance companies efficiently to handle claims. Although dishonesty and ineptitude
may from time to time create gaps in the planned system, a variety of
supplementary techniques is available for handling these, for instance
uninsured motorist coverage and state guarantee funds for insolvencies.

3. Deterrence and punishment should have no place in the injury
reparation system, but should be allocated to the agencies of the criminal
law. Some accidents do seem to be caused by culpable and blameworthy
behavior. The author does not wish to dismiss such matters as drunken
and reckless driving, but to allocate them to their proper place in the
system of legal control.

The findings of the recent studies of the plight of automobile accident
victims can support no other conclusion than that change is needed.

---

[9] See Keeton and O'Connell, *op. cit.*, Chapter 4, pp. 124-240, for a complete review
of proposals for change.

However, the needed changes are not largely a matter of improving the operation of insurance companies. Saddled with law based on antiquated and unrealistic assumptions, the reputable companies are doing more than is legally required in cases of plaintiffs' contributory negligence and absence of fault on the part of the defendants. It is the underlying legal system, as applied to the automobile, which most requires change.

## Questions

1. Compare current automobile crash data as listed in *Accident Facts* with the figures listed in this article. Do you see any changes or trends? What is the difference between data reported in the form "x number of accidents" compared to the form "x accidents per million miles traveled?"
2. What research findings cause the author to favor the "no-fault" principle?

# 18. ECONOMIC CONSEQUENCES OF AUTOMOBILE ACCIDENT INJURIES: AN ANALYSIS *

Jerry S. Rosenbloom †
and J. Finley Lee ††

## INTRODUCTION

*The Economic Consequences of Automobile Accident Injuries* is a two-volume work in the Department of Transportation's series concerning the motor vehicle insurance and compensation.[1] The study is reputed to be "without question the most comprehensive and carefully conducted study of the plight of people injured by motor vehicles ever produced." The title of the report is indicative of the basic thrust of the research effort in which the current economic system of automobile injuries and the impact of losses and of reparations are analyzed and discussed.

### Objectives of the Study

The objectives of the study are stated in its introduction. Specifically, the researchers, the Westat Research Corporation with assistance from the Bureau of the Census, set out to identify and measure quantitatively "the various contributions to economic loss both to individuals and to family units."[2] Moreover, an attempt was made to identify and measure "the sources of reparations for such economic loss."[3]

### The Method

The researchers utilized mail questionnaires and personal interview techniques. Data were obtained from injured persons and survivors of persons fatally injured in automobile accidents. The Bureau of the Census prepared a stratified sample; counties or other areas were drawn with known probability to represent each stratum. The result was the

* From *The Annals of the Society of Chartered Property and Casualty Underwriters* (June, 1971), pp. 129-142. Reprinted by permission.

† Associate Professor of Insurance and Risk, Temple University.

†† Associate Professor of Business Administration, University of North Carolina.

[1] U.S. Department of Transportation, *Economic Consequences of Automobile Accident Injuries* by U.S. Bureau of the Census and Westat Research, Inc. Washington, D.C.: U.S. Government Printing Office, 1970, p. iii.

[2] For example, the National Safety Council estimated that approximately 52,900 persons were fatality victims of automobile accidents during the year studied (1967) and that between two and four million persons incurred injuries as a result of automobile accidents.

[3] The definition of economic loss generally included: (1) medical expenses, (2) property damage, (3) wage losses, (4) other actual expenses including transportation, funeral costs, household help, and miscellaneous expenses and (5) expected future losses.

development of a simple contiguous area termed a "primary sample unit."

The sample data consisted solely of reported accidents. Generally, state highway department data were used, but other supplementary sources also were utilized to obtain more complete data. The final data included only those reported accidents in which there was a reported severe personal injury.[4]

## SUMMARY OF MAJOR FINDINGS

The report was devoted mainly to an analysis of economic loss to seriously injured persons. Specifically, to be included in the sample, the person had to have a serious injury that resulted in:

Medical costs (excluding hospital) of $500 or more, or two weeks or more of hospitalization, *or,* if working, three weeks or more of missed work, *or,* if not working, six weeks or more of missed normal activity.[5]

## Economic Loss

The technique used for the measurement of economic loss included five main categories of loss.[6] Additionally, these loss categories were further divided into (1) losses to date and (2) future losses.

"Losses to date" consisted of "actual expenses or losses incurred during or attributable to the period of time between the date of the accident and the date of the interview." Such losses included: actual hospital costs, other medical costs, property damage, and accumulated wage losses during the period. The second part of total economic loss, *i.e.,* that relating to future losses included: (1) the *respondent's* estimate of anticipated future medical and other expenses and (2) a *derived estimate* of the respondent's future earnings loss[7] [emphasis added].

Future earnings losses were measured or estimated in two ways. First, "societal" losses were estimated. "Societal" losses include the present value of the losses of incomes associated with fatalities and serious injuries in automobile accidents. The second estimate was personal and family losses. "Societal" losses represented the loss to society as a whole, while

---

[4]The primary net screened sample included 8,021 cases. The final number of cases tabulated was 1,376 which was inclusive of the subcomponent of the screened sample termed "total seriously injured and fatalities."

[5] The report admits that this criterion is arbitrary, at best. Moreover, it notes that errors were encountered in the screening process. Apparently, the researchers believed that underreporting of injuries was a serious bias as they objectively retained data from persons known to be suffering injuries. This judgment is highly suspect and introduces a serious question of data bias.

[6] *Supra,* Note 3.

[7] The researcher noted the problems associated with the nature of expectations. Data were provided with and without the estimation of future losses. The method of estimating the present value of future earnings was cited in the paper. The method was taken from Miller, Hermon P. and Dornseth, Richard, "Present value of estimated lifetime earnings," Technical Paper 16, U.S. Department of Commerce, Bureau of the Census (undated).

personal and family losses were adjudged to be those losses directly affecting the micro-family unit.

## Economic Losses by Category of Losses

The analysis of the economic losses by category of losses was apparently developed to bring out, through segregation of data, the most important loss findings of the research effort. Each is discussed in turn.

**Individual Economic Losses.** From data produced through the mail questionnaires, the researchers ascertained that approximately 513,000 persons were seriously injured or killed during 1967. In the seriously injured group, the average losses were found to be slightly in excess of $4,200. This average loss was comprised primarily of medical costs ($1,604) and wage losses ($1,951). The $4,200 figure represented *only* losses to the date of the interview. Thus, future losses expected to approximate an additional $4,100 were not included.[8]

In the serious injury category, the amounts of economic losses were also broken into sub-classifications. The types of loss then were converted to percentages and measured against the total amount of the economic loss. Excerpts from the data are presented in Exhibit 1.

EXHIBIT 1

PERCENTAGE DISTRIBUTION OF ECONOMIC LOSSES

| Amount of Economic Losses | Medical Expenses Percentage to Total Loss | Wage Loss Percentage to Total Loss |
|---|---|---|
| $1-$499 | 67.47% | 16.19% |
| $500-$999 | 54.21 | 23.99 |
| $1,000-$1,499 | 50.45 | 20.77 |
| $1,500-$2,499 | 42.92 | 24.93 |
| $2,500-$4,999 | 45.41 | 29.83 |
| $5,000-$9,999 | 43.07 | 42.41 |
| $10,000-$24,999 | 36.75 | 55.50 |
| $25,000+above | 20.88 | 76.40 |
| Total | 38.16 | 46.44 |

Source: *Economic Consequences of Automobile Accident Injuries*, p. 67.

As can be seen from Exhibit 1, the ratio of medical losses to the economic loss decreases as the economic loss increases. Conversely, as economic losses increase, the proportion of the loss attributable to lost wages increases. This indicates that economic loss is concentrated in lost wages where economic loss is large.

In fatality cases, economic losses were estimated to be $2,300, primarily composed of funeral costs. If, however, discounted future lost

[8] The additional $4,100 was represented primarily by losses of future earnings.

earnings of such fatalities are considered, the average "societal" loss per fatality is $87,000. In 80 percent of the fatality cases, some wage loss is suffered. The principal exceptions are persons over 65 years of age and others not in the labor force.[9]

**Components of Economic Losses.** The highlights of the components of loss suffered by seriously injured and fatality victims who sustained the various types of loss are shown in Exhibit 2.[10]

EXHIBIT 2

COMPONENTS OF ECONOMIC LOSSES PER SERIOUSLY
INJURED PERSON AND FATALITY CASES

| Kind of Loss | Average Loss for Those Sustaining Loss (Seriously Injured) | Average Loss for Those Sustaining Loss * (Fatalities) |
|---|---|---|
| Losses to date of interview or death | | |
| Medical | $ 2,011 | $     848 |
| Hospital | 1,213 | |
| Other medical | 798 | |
| Property damage | 873 | $  1,065 |
| Wage Loss | 2,838 | |
| Other losses | 306 | |
| Total | 6,028 | $  1,913 |
| Expected future losses | | |
| Future Earnings | $40,006 | |
| Medical and other | 1,098 | |
| Total future losses | 41,104 | $109,621 |
| Total Losses | $47,132 | $111,534 |

* Certain components not computed.
  Source: Adapted from Tables 3.1 and 3.2 pages 26 and 27.

Exhibit 2 illustrates that, for seriously injured persons who sustained losses, medical expenses and wage loss were the major loss items to the date of the interview. The largest predicted future loss for this category was discounted future earnings. For the fatalities, medical expenses at date of death were, on the average, $848 with property damage being $1,065; however, future losses were estimated to be $109,621. Exhibit 2

---

[9] In this study, homemakers were considered to be in the labor force and were assumed to have an equivalent "loss value" of $4,000 per year, from which a maintenance cost of $2,000 per year was subtracted for fatality cases.

[10] Data were presented in two ways (1) on an average total loss per person, and (2) on an average loss for those sustaining loss. It was felt that it would be much more meaningful to present the data in Table 2 on an "Average Loss for those Sustaining Loss," basis, otherwise the losses of these victims would be spread out among those who did not suffer a loss.

clearly indicates that predicted future losses can be catastrophic in nature and should be closely analyzed in attempting realistically to assess the current automobile reparations system.

Attempting to estimate future losses was an area where this study could have made significant contributions, but such contributions turned out to be lacking. The questionnaire was deficit in this key area. Only four questions were asked in this critical area. Obviously in attempting to assess any reparations system, future losses are a key element that should have received more careful treatment.

Though the introduction to the study clearly indicates that "pain and suffering" would not be considered, this might be a major flaw in the research design. Without question, pain and suffering is, under the present system, a major component of loss. Additionally, the issue of pain and suffering has been the stumbling block in many previous studies and proposals for reform of the current reparations system. To raise this question in a nationwide research effort and perhaps discuss its role in the reparations system might have increased the study's utility.

**Family Losses.** The research questionnaire included information about the family unit in an attempt to determine the impact of automobile accidents on the family as a group. A series of questions was designed to ascertain which members of a family were injured and to provide information about medical costs, wage losses and sources of reparations for injured members of the household. In 93.3 percent of the families, only a single person was seriously injured or killed in the same accident. Two members seriously injured or killed in the same family in a common accident was found to be 6.5 percent. The remaining .2 percent involved three or more family members being involved in a single accident. Thus, the study concluded that, "the incidence of multiple serious injuries or fatalities within the same family in an automobile accident is relatively rare." [11] The patterns and components of economic loss discussed previously for the individual hold true in every case for the family as well. Therefore, the remainder of this article will deal only with the losses and recoveries of individuals.

## REPARATIONS FOR ECONOMIC LOSS

The sources of reparations for economic loss arising out of automobile accidents formed a major part of the study. The sources of reparations that were considered are shown in Exhibit 3.

Of all the various sources of recovery enumerated in Exhibit 3, tort recovery is the only one based on the fault concept. All other programs pay upon demonstration of loss.

Nine out of ten seriously injured persons responding to the survey reportedly received some form of compensation for economic loss. About 50 percent received payments from medical insurance and 38 percent

---

[11] *Economic Consequences, supra,* p. 32.

EXHIBIT 3

POTENTIAL SOURCES OF LOSS RECOVERIES

---

Recovery of Current Losses

Insurance policies on family members
Medical insurance (including hospital)
Life insurance (for fatality cases only)
Automobile medical payments
Collision insurance
Other insurance programs

Other Sources:

Tort recovery
Sick leave
Workmen's Compensation
Disability under Social Security *
Miscellaneous Sources (Included here are payments made through
Medicare, union and employer medical programs, the Veterans
Administration, Medicaid, and public and private welfare agencies.)

Recovery of Future Losses

Social Security *
Other Sources (Included here are benefits from workmen's compensation,
Veterans Administration, union funds, and other public and private
survivor and disability programs.)

---

\* The term Social Security is used throughout the study, yet the term Social Security is
much broader than its use only for disability income payments in this report. Social
Security includes unemployment compensation, old age and survivors benefits, health
insurance, public assistance, etc. However, to avoid confusion the authors will use the
term Social Security in this article to mean disability income payments under the Old-
Age, Survivors and Disability Insurance (O.A.S.D.I.) system.

acquired benefits under automobile medical payments coverage. There is,
of course, some overlap of these coverages. About 30 percent received
some recovery for property damage from collision insurance, while 20
percent received sick leave benefits. Workmen's compensation benefits
were received by 7.5 percent, and 2 percent received Social Security
disability income benefits.

Under tort recovery, approximately 47 percent of those interviewed
received some reparations. The study cautions that, "In interpreting
this number (47 percent) it should be kept in mind that recovery is
presumably dependent on the injured person not having contributed to
the accident in the fault sense." [12] More will be said about this later
in the article when a review of reactions to the fault concept is evaluated.

In 62 percent of the fatality cases, the beneficiaries of the victim
recovered under life insurance, while only 21 percent received some
benefits from medical insurance. However, it was noted that the substantial number of almost instant deaths contributed to the reduction

---

[12] *Economic Consequences, op. cit.,* p. 38.

in the medical insurance recovery figure as well as from automobile medical payments coverage.

The average reparations and percentage of aggregate loss recovered by seriously injured persons is presented in Exhibit 4. Exhibit 4 reveals

EXHIBIT 4

AVERAGE REPARATIONS AND RATIOS OF REPARATIONS
TO LOSSES BY AMOUNT OF TOTAL ECONOMIC LOSS
FOR SERIOUS INJURY CASES

| Amount of Economic Loss | Average Total Loss per Person | Reparations per Person Receiving Reparations | | Ratio of Aggregate Reparations to Aggregate Losses |
|---|---|---|---|---|
| | | Average | % Receiving | |
| $1-$499 | $    330 | $    829 | 70 | 1.8 |
| $500-$999 | 764 | 1,270 | 77 | 1.3 |
| $1,000-$1,499 | 1,254 | 1,747 | 86 | 1.2 |
| $1,500-$2,499 | 1,947 | 2,234 | 88 | 1.0 |
| $2,500-$4,999 | 3,496 | 3,502 | 90 | 0.9 |
| $5,000-$9,999 | 6,632 | 5,521 | 95 | 0.8 |
| $10,000-$24,999 | 16,482 | 9,681 | 91 | 0.5 |
| $25,000-and over | 71,371 | 12,718 | 94 | 0.2 |
| All Losses Classes | 8,290 | 4,055 | 88 | 0.4 |

Source: *Economic Consequences of Automobile Accidents,* p. 38.

many of the most important findings of the study. For example, this table demonstrates that, on the average, 40 percent of aggregate economic losses of seriously injured persons were recovered. However, while the percentage of those recovering some part of their loss increases from 70 percent for the lowest economic loss class to 94 percent for the highest economic loss class, the ratio of reparations to loss drops from 1.8 to 0.2. That is, those with small economic losses recover, on the average, nearly twice their loss, while those with high economic losses recover only one-fifth of their economic losses. These results are consistent with and supported by several previous studies on the automobile accident reparations system.[13] The previous studies have been focused mainly on local or statewide areas. This research broadens the base of the findings to show that similar results are achieved on a nationwide basis.

---

[13] See, for example: Columbia University Council for Research in the Social Sciences, *Report by the Committee to study Compensation for Automobile Accidents* (Philadelphia: International Printing Co., 1939); State of New York, *Report of the Joint Legislative Committee to Investigate Automobile Insurance* (Albany: J. B. Lyon Co., 1938); Adams, John F., "A Survey of the Economic-Financial Consequences of Personal Injuries Resulting from Automobile Accidents in the City of Philadelphia, 1953," *Economic and Business Bulletin*, Temple University, Vol. III, No. 3 (March, 1955); Morris, Clarence, and Paul, James C. N., "The Financial Impact of Automobile Accidents," 110 *U. of Pa. Law Review* (1962), pp. 913-33; Conard, Alfred F., Morgan, James N., Pratt, Robert W., Jr., Voltz, Charles E., Bombaugh, Robert L., *Automobile Accident Costs and Payments* (Ann Arbor: U. of Michigan Press, 1964); Keeton, Robert E. and O'Connell, Jeffrey, *Basic Protection for the Traffic Victim* (Boston: Little, Brown and Co., 1965); Rosenbloom, Jerry S., *Automobile Liability Claims*, (Homewood, Ill.: Richard D. Irwin, Inc., 1968).

One interesting aspect of this study is that no reference or footnotes are made to the many previous landmark studies devoted to the same problems of the reparations of automobile accident victims. Perhaps this was the intent to ignore or place little dependence on what has previously been written, or perhaps it was felt that the earlier studies were either too out of date or wouldn't be useful for a nationwide sample study.

Similar results were achieved in the fatality and family sample. Some of the overpayment of the smaller claims may be accounted for by the "nuisance value" of such claims. That is, some insurers will pay a relatively small amount of payment on a claim hoping that this will close the case, avoiding a lawsuit. Also, in some cases, it would cost an insurer more to investigate a claim than to make a small payment on a claim.

Exhibit 5 shows how the proportion of reparations received from each principal source varies as the amount of economic loss changes. As the study points out, "the patterns of change are irregular and are somewhat distorted by the inclusions of life insurance, as a source of reparation." [14]

Nevertheless, Exhibit 5 does show (1) that recovery under the tort system is relatively less for large losses than for small losses and (2) that recovery from medical payments insurance increases relatively with the size of the loss except for very large losses. Wage replacement sources are relatively more important for losses over $25,000, and most of that recovery is represented by Social Security disability income benefits.

Exhibit 5 is confusing, for inspection of the $1,500-$2,499 category under "Total Economic Losses" reveals that the various components of

EXHIBIT 5

PERCENT OF REPARATIONS RECEIVED FROM PRINCIPAL SOURCES
AS COMPENSATION FOR SERIOUS INJURY OR FATALITY,
BY AMOUNT OF ECONOMIC LOSS

| Total Economic Loss | Total | Medical Insurance | Life Insurance | Auto Medical Payments | Collision Insurance | Net Tort | Wage Replacement * |
|---|---|---|---|---|---|---|---|
| $1-499 | 100 | 4.1 | 11.8 | 3.6 | — | 74.4 | 4.3 |
| $500-999 | 100 | 9.7 | 7.0 | 5.6 | 3.6 | 59.6 | 13.2 |
| $1,000-1,499 | 100 | 10.9 | 6.1 | 10.3 | 5.6 | 56.6 | 5.9 |
| $1,500-2,499 | 100 | 10.4 | 23.3 | 6.1 | 9.5 | 38.4 | 13.0 |
| $2,500-4,999 | 100 | 15.2 | 5.9 | 6.2 | 11.4 | 40.0 | 11.7 |
| $5,000-9,999 | 100 | 17.7 | .8 | 9.5 | 10.6 | 39.1 | 16.6 |
| $10,000-24,999 | 100 | 19.9 | 6.2 | 3.4 | 3.8 | 42.5 | 19.9 |
| $25,000 and over | 100 | 5.5 | 23.7 | 0.9 | 1.2 | 17.3 | 49.2 |
| Total | 100 | 11.1 | 14.1 | 4.3 | 5.5 | 32.1 | 27.4 |

* Sick leave, workmen's compensation, social security, and similar sources.
Source: *Economic Consequences* (Table 3.15), p. 45.

[14] *Economic Consequences, supra,* p. 44.

reparations sources total 100.7 percent, while the other rows vary from totals of 90.4 percent to 98.7 percent. The table indicates that the total of the separate percentages should be 100. Rounding fails to account for the differences between the real and the supposed totals.*

## Recovery under the Tort System

In view of all the discussion concerning changing the present automobile system for compensating automobile accident victims, this section is perhaps the most vital part of the voluminous study. It is this section that will interest most readers.

Exhibit 6 illustrates that about 43 percent of those persons recovering some reparations for serious injury or fatalities received some compensation under the tort system. This exhibit also illustrates that those receiving tort reparations obtain about 60 percent of their total recovery from the tort system. Columns (4) and (5) of the table indicate that persons receiving part of their compensation from tort, receive, on an average basis, a substantially greater recovery than do persons with no tort reparations.

EXHIBIT 6

COMPARISON OF REPARATIONS RECEIVED FOR SERIOUS
INJURY OR FATALITY BY PERSONS
WITH AND WITHOUT TORT RECOVERY

| Total Economic Loss (1) | Estimated persons with some recovery (2) | Percent with tort recovery (3) | Ratio of net recovery to loss | | Percent tort of total recovery for those with tort (6) |
|---|---|---|---|---|---|
| | | | with tort (4) | without tort (5) | |
| $1-499 | 19,500 | 54.3 | 4.5 | 0.8 | 92 |
| $500-999 | 42,700 | 62.6 | 2.6 | 0.5 | 72 |
| $1,000-1,499 | 54,000 | 49.3 | 2.4 | 0.7 | 79 |
| $1,500-2,499 | 93,600 | 46.9 | 2.0 | 1.0 | 63 |
| $2,500-4,999 | 109,300 | 43.6 | 1.6 | 0.6 | 64 |
| $5,000-9,999 | 57,000 | 44.2 | 1.1 | 0.6 | 63 |
| $10,000-24,999 | 28,200 | 52.3 | 0.7 | 0.4 | 72 |
| $25,000-over | 42,600 | 41.8 | 0.3 | 0.3 | 42 |
| Total | 448,900 | 47.7 | 0.6 | 0.4 | 60 |

Source: *Economic Consequences* (Table 3.17), p. 47.

Another controversial issue considered in the research report was that of legal fees and expenses involved in the settlement of automobile claims under the current tort system. The legal costs, on the average, amounted to 25 percent of total recovery. (The median figure was 32.5 percent, with a range of 22.5 to 52.5 percent.)

---

* It is also confusing to combine death and disability claims in one table.—Ed.

This research again supports previous works in concluding that approximately 65 percent of those who make claims for tort reparations retained counsel, and 74 percent of this group actually filed lawsuits. Both of these percentages tend to increase as the amount of economic loss increases.[15] Also about 8 percent of lawsuits filed reached a court verdict.

EXHIBIT 7

NET TORT RECOVERY FOR SERIOUS INJURY AND FATALITY BY RETENTION
OF COUNSEL BY FILING OF SUIT, AND BY TOTAL ECONOMIC LOSS

| Total Economic Loss | Ratio of Recovery to Economic Loss | | | |
|---|---|---|---|---|
| | For Those Retaining Counsel | For Those Without Counsel | For Those Filing Suit | For Those Not Filing Suit |
| $1-499 | 3.05 | 2.79 | 2.94 | 1.88 |
| $500-999 | 1.77 | 1.65 | 1.28 | 1.52 |
| $1,000-1,499 | 1.48 | 2.27 | 1.19 | 1.34 |
| $1,500-2,499 | 1.18 | 1.26 | 0.92 | 0.87 |
| $2,500-4,999 | 1.06 | 0.68 | 0.82 | 0.82 |
| $$5,000-9,999 | 0.73 | 0.43 | 0.59 | 0.42 |
| $10,000-24,999 | 0.45 | 0.37 | 0.43 | 0.21 |
| $25,000 and over | 0.11 | 0.01 | 0.09 | 0.04 |
| Total | 0.32 | 0.36 | 0.25 | 0.21 |

Source: *Economic Consequences* (Table 3.21), p. 51.

Exhibit 7 contrasts the ratio of recovery of economic loss for those retaining counsel and those without counsel, and compares those who filed suit with those who did not file suit. As can be seen from this exhibit, those who retained counsel generally recovered a larger portion of their economic loss. The exceptions were those with losses in the $1,000 to $2,499 range, in which those who did not retain counsel received a larger portion of their economic loss.

The last statement illustrates one major limitation of this study. Much of the information is presented in strictly quantitative form without much of an attempt to ask why certain results were achieved. Perhaps trying to find causal relationships is beyond the scope of the report; yet if it is the most comprehensive and carefully conducted study of automobile accident victims, shouldn't some attempt be made at seeking explanations to questions raised? This is especially so if it is to serve as a basis for fundamental changes in the current system.

Those filing suit generally received slightly more in terms of recovery than those who did not file suit. As elsewhere in the study, the conclusion is drawn that persons with small economic loss tend to recover a higher ratio of recovery to loss than do persons with high economic loss.

---

[15] These findings also have been found by the studies mentioned in footnote number 13.

Another key issue explored is the lapse in time between injury and recovery. The study demonstrates that an average of 16 months elapses between the date of the accident and the date of the final settlement. The report concludes that, "the lapse in time is positively correlated with the total amount of economic loss." [16] That is, the larger the prospective economic loss, the longer the delay.

## Demographic Influence

Some of the more important demographic highlights of the research showed that there is a tendency for persons with higher education attainments to retain counsel, as well as showing that such individuals tend to recover a higher proportion of their losses. Similarly, there seems to be a clear indication that families with larger incomes are more inclined to retain counsel, and to recover a larger proportion of their economic losses.

## Attitudes of Who Was at Fault

Still another controversial dimension of the current automobile reparations system is discussed, that is, can it really be ascertained who is at fault in an automobile accident. This was the only attempt in this work to measure attitudes and opinions.

While approximately 82 percent of the total in the survey responded that it is relatively easy to determine who is at fault, about 65 percent of those admitting fault made claims against another party. Seventy-six percent of those placing fault on the driver of the other vehicle made claims. Additionally, 42 percent of those indicating that both drivers were at fault made claims, while 17 percent of those indicating "nobody's fault" made claims. It appears that the question of who is at fault in an automobile accident is still as unanswered as ever!

### CONCLUSION

This is without question the most comprehensive study of the plight of people injured by motor vehicles ever produced. The hundreds of statistical tables contained in the report bear out this connection.

There is a little new contained in the study. This is not meant as a criticism, because it has researched the automobile problem on a national basis whereas most previous studies have done so on a local, state or regional basis. Moreover, by supporting what has been garnered from earlier studies, perhaps the nation or individual states now have enough data to decide that the kinds of problems pointed out in the study not only pertain to a particular geographic area but are nationwide in scope.

Perhaps the greatest contribution this study has made is that the major findings are presented in unambiguous language with hundreds

---

[16] *Economic Consequences, supra,* p. 51.

of supporting tables, computer runs, and other data. This will enable the report to accomplish two key objectives: (1) wide distribution of the major findings, because they are so uncomplicated and direct, and (2) use of the supporting data for further clarifications of the major findings and as an invaluable source for future studies on the automobile reparations system.

The major limitation of this report is unquestionably its lack of evaluation, conclusions, or recommendations. More searching attempts at analysis of the data and of possible courses of action would have contributed immensely to the value of the research.

Whether intentional or inadvertent, the failure to build on or highlight differences and similarities with earlier automobile accident studies detracts from the impact of this work. If this research had indicated that the findings on approaches of previous works, the meaningfulness of these results would have given direction. If, however, it was expressed that the nationwide results differed from previous localized studies (as many have suggested), then new approaches would be indicated.

One lingering question still remains. Where does the United States collectively, or individually as separate states, go from here? At some point, major actions will have to be instituted to improve the automobile reparations system. The debate will inevitably stop, and actions, probably in the form of compromises, will be taken. *The Economic Consequences of Automobile Accidents* may have narrowed the gap between debate and action.

## Questions

1. The article discusses the discounted expected "societal" loss of future earnings attributable to the victim of a traffic accident. How is this discounted expected future income derived? Discuss this loss (a) as a loss to the family of the victim and (b) as a loss to society.
2. An argument for a change in the reparation system for automobile crash victims that seems to be common to most studies is that the present system overcompensates the small losses and undercompensates the large losses. Identify and discuss the data in this DOT study that supports or disputes this charge.
3. Is it true that there is a tendency for our "fault" system to reward the rich and penalize the poor?

# 19. BEYOND CURRENT REFORMS IN AUTOMOBILE REPARATIONS *

Robert E. Keeton †

Proponents of reform of human institutions tend almost inevitably, it seems, to engage in microscopic examination of current and recent ways of doing things. From this perspective, they soon discover that human institutions are remarkably resistant to change. The point was expressed dramatically by the President of the American Insurance Association, T. Lawrence Jones, on June 15, 1972.[1] He observed that between October, 1968, when the American Insurance Association first announced its support of "complete no-fault reform,"[2] and June, 1972, only four states (Massachusetts, Florida, Connecticut and New Jersey) enacted what could be called genuine no-fault statutes. Meanwhile, American astronauts made five landings on the moon.

Yet we know that from a perspective of longer range, the only constant is change. In relation more particularly to the subject of this symposium, even one of those quick glances into the past that is tolerable to the least history-minded among us is enough to discover that in the long perspective of political, social and economic development, the duration of any reparations system without change is short.

In looking beyond current reforms, then, perhaps we can focus attention most usefully on principles. That is, we can gain a better understanding of the direction of change and where it may lead us by trying to identify and understand, first, the principles underlying current developments and, second, the principles competing for dominance in the future. Though issues of implementation are of tremendous practical significance as well as great interest, this paper concerns only the broader questions bearing upon the central nature of the reparation systems under discussion.

---

* From *The Journal of Risk and Insurance* (March, 1970), pp. 31-37. Reprinted by permission.

† Professor in the Law School of Harvard University.

[1] T. Lawrence Jones, Remarks, Insurance Information Institute Seminar, Marriott Hotel, Philadelphia, June 15, 1972.

[2] American Insurance Association, Report of Special Committee to Study and Evaluate the Keeton-O'Connell Basic Protection Plan and Automobile Accident Reparations (October, 1968).

## EMERGING REFORMS

### Combined Public and Private-Enterprise Insurance

The first no-fault automobile reparations system involving some degree of tort exemption, as distinguished from merely a crediting of no-fault benefits against tort liability (as under the Saskatchewan Plan),[3] was enacted in Puerto Rico and became effective on January 1, 1970.[4] Its no-fault benefits are provided from a social-security type of public fund, financed by fees paid for annual vehicular licenses. At the present date, two states have operating no-fault systems with partial tort exemptions (Massachusetts[5] since January 1, 1971, and Florida[6] since January 1, 1972) and two more (Connecticut and New Jersey) have enacted systems of this type to become operative in 1973.[7] The no-fault benefits under all these state plans are provided by private-enterprise insurance.

No-fault statutes enacted in the United States within the decade of the 1970's probably will rely upon private-enterprise insurance as the principal source of no-fault benefits. However, it is also probable that benefits from other compensation systems that are to some extent publicly funded (such as social security, workmen's compensation, and nationally sponsored health care benefits) will increasingly be treated as "primary" and automobile insurance benefits as "secondary" or "excess."

In the present context, private-enterprise automobile insurance benefits are referred to as "primary" if the law imposes liability on the automobile insurer for payment of the benefits, regardless of the extent to which benefits may also be due from other sources because of the same loss. In contrast, the automobile insurance benefits are "secondary" or "excess" if either, first, the automobile insurer may, after paying the benefits, recoup its loss by proceeding on its own account or in the name of its payee to recover against a third person (usually a tortfeasor or his liability insurer) or, second, the automobile insurer may

---

[3] The Automobile Accident Insurance Act, 1946, 10 Geo. 6, ch. 11 (Saskatchewan). For a description and analysis of the Saskatchewan Plan, see Keeton & O'Connell, *Basic Protection for the Traffic Victim,* (Boston: Little, Brown & Co., 1965), pp. 140-148.

[4] See Juan B. Aponte & Herbert S. Denenberg, "The Automobile Problem in Puerto Rico: Dimensions and Proposed Solution," *The Journal of Risk and Insurance,* Vol. XXXV, No. 2 (June, 1968), p. 227; "The Automobile Problem in Puerto Rico: An Addendum," *The Journal of Risk and Insurance,* Vol. XXXV, No. 4 (December, 1968), p. 637.

[5] Mass. Laws ch. 670 (1970), as amended by Mass. Laws ch. 744 (1970).

[6] Fla. Laws 71-252 (1971).

[7] The Connecticut and New Jersey laws are Conn. Laws 1972, P. A. No. 273, and N. J. Laws 1972, ch. 70. More recently Michigan has enacted a no-fault law with a declared effective date of October 1, 1973. Mich. P. A. 294 (1972).

escape liability for benefits otherwise due to showing that the claimant is entitled to recover compensation from some other source. From the perspective of a focus on the automobile reparations system, the benefits from some other source are commonly referred to as "collateral source" benefits.

The interplay between choices of principle and choices concerning issues of implementation is well illustrated by current controversy over the relationship between automobile insurance benefits and "collateral source" benefits. The major policy interests bearing on the extent to which private-enterprise automobile insurance benefits shall be made primary, or instead secondary or excess, are concerned with resource allocation, efficiency, and freedom of choice for the consumer. Among the host of additional issues that become involved in the formulation of any specific reparations plan are competitive interests among different segments of the insurance industry as well as competitive interests between governmental benefit-paying institutions on the one hand and private-enterprise insurers on the other. In the immediate future, these issues of intra-industry competition may substantially affect the shape of emerging reforms. From a longer range perspective, however, they probably will have less impact than public and legislative reaction and response to the three major policy issues.

On the first of these major issues, in general, spokesmen for automobile insurers have joined with a number of academicians in urging that motoring should pay its way in our society. Of course there are difficulties in translating this general goal into concrete prescriptions, but in general the point is that making automobile insurance benefits primary will advance the objective of causing motoring to pay its way and that making automobile insurance benefits secondary or excess will tend, in contrast, to elsewhere—for example, on the social security system, or the workmen's compensation system, or the healthcare system, including accident and health insurance.

In contrast, arguments based on data concerning the relative efficiency of different benefit sources[8] tend to favor public sources such as social security over private sources such as insurance and, among private sources, tend to favor health and accident insurance over automobile insurance. Thus, although the inference that the same or similar disparities in efficiency will continue in a reformed

---

[8] See, e. g., Alfred F. Conard, James N. Morgan, Robert W. Pratt, Jr., Charles E. Voltz & Robert L. Bombaugh, *Automobile Accident Costs and Payments: Studies in the Economics of Injury Reparation,* (Ann Arbor: The University of Michigan Press, 1964), pp. 53-66; State of New York Insurance Department, *Automobile Insurance. . . . For Whose Benefit?* (1970), pp. 34-37.

system are subject to challenge and debate, in general the higher value one places on the goal of efficiency the more likely he is to set this off against the goal of resource allocation expressed in a general way in the assertion that motoring should pay its way.

Another way in which the goal of efficiency may affect choices in the controversy over whether automobile insurance benefits are to be primary is that additional administrative costs are generated by any arrangement involving a second round of loss shifting, such as occurs when a "secondary" source pays a benefit and then seeks reimbursement from a "primary" source. One may conclude, of course, that other values that are realized more than compensate for the cost of this second round of loss shifting; in doing so he is finding that in the particular instance the goal of efficiency is out-weighed by other goals.

Concern with the goal of freedom of choice for the consumer, in relation to the question whether automobile insurance is to be primary or excess, grows out of the fact that a significant portion of the bodily injury liability insurance premium dollar has been used to pay benefits that duplicate benefits from collateral sources.[9] This leads to the conclusion that, as a practical matter, the consumer has been compelled to pay for this duplication even though he might have preferred a system of dove-tailed benefits under which he could either pocket the premium savings or else apply the savings to purchase additional nonduplicating coverage.

Even such a brief sketch as this of the policies of resource allocation, efficiency, and freedom of choice for the consumer discloses that they are in some respects competing and contradictory. Any plan of reparations that emerges for any given time and place is likely to be a compromise, or an accommodation, in which each of these three goals is to some extent sacrificed in order to give effect, to some extent, to the other two. If there is a discernible trend at this time, however, it is surely in the direction of less emphasis on making motoring pay its way and more emphasis on efficiency, with perhaps a modest increase as well in the extent to which the consumer is given some freedom of choice.

## Combined Federal and State Sponsorship

No-fault automobile reparation systems currently in operation are state sponsored. But the support for prompt enactment of more inclusive and more incisive reforms in outrunning the pace of action in state legislatures. Two developments occurring in early August, 1972, provide clues concerning the kinds of legislation that might be enacted both in Congress and in the states during the decade of the 1970's.

---

[9] *Id.*

On August 10, 1972, the National Conference of Commissioners on Uniform States Laws voted to approve and to recommend state-by-state adoption of the Uniform Motor Vehicle Accident Reparations Act (UMVARA) developed by a Special Committee of the Conference during a period of intensive study of the automobile reparations system commencing June of the preceding year.[10] The Conference study was supported by a grant from the United States Department of Transportation. Under standing procedures of the Conference, the recommended Uniform Act has been placed before the House of Delegates of the American Bar Association for its consideration.

Earlier in the same week, the United States Senate, by a margin of three out of 95 Senators voting, effectively terminated any prospect of federal legislation on this subject in 1972 by referring to the Judiciary Committee the National No-Fault Bill previously recommended by the Senate Commerce Committee.[11]

Both UMVARA and the Senate Bill contain provisions for a tort exemption very much more extensive than those in the acts of the four states thus far enacting some kind of tort exemption (Massachusetts, Florida, Connecticut and New Jersey). The National Conference, in adopting UMVARA, proposed state-by-state adoption of a tort exemption that would preclude negligence claims against motorists except for (1) general damages in cases of what might appropriately be termed very severe injury and (2) economic losses in a very limited group of cases involving losses exceeding the weekly limit of $200.

The recommendation of UMVARA by the National Conference of Commissioners on Uniform State Laws substantially improves the prospects for effective action in state legislatures and to some extent diminishes the prospects for Congressional action. The type of Congressional action for which there is greatest support is a bill establishing minimum standards, including a tort exemption, that would be effective only in states that had not enacted laws consistent with the minimum standards.

Unless state legislatures respond promptly with legislation of the UMVARA type, including both extensive no-fault benefits and a strong tort exemption, it seems likely that Congress will act in this matter before the end of the calendar year 1973. In turn, this will mean that the system emerging by the mid-1970's will

---

[10] Proceedings of the National Conference of Commissioners on Uniform State Laws, Meeting in its Eighty-First Year, Session of Thursday Afternoon, August 10, 1972, to be published in *Handbook of the National Conference of Commissioners on Uniform State Laws* (1972).

[11] 118 Congressional Record S 13069-S 13093, August 8, 1972.

[12] See, e. g., Donald McDonald, editor, "Medical Malpractice—A discussion of alternative compensation and quality control systems" (Santa Barbara: Center for the Study of Democratic Institutions, 1971).

be one that is still administered and regulated to a substantial extent by the states but is subject to very significant federally imposed standards, with a partial shift of regulation to Washington.

## Combined No-Fault and Tort Liability Insurance

All five no-fault automobile accident reparation systems referred to thus far (Puerto Rico, Massachusetts, Florida, Connecticut and New Jersey) preserve the tort liability to some extent. So does the draft statute developed by a special committee of the National Conference of Commissioners on Uniform State Laws. Tort liability is preserved to even greater extent in other states that are sometimes referred to as "no-fault" (for example, Delaware and Oregon). At least through the 1970's our automobile reparations systems will combine no-fault with tort-liability insurance, though substantially reducing the role of tort-liability insurance.

The extent of no-fault benefits and the extent of the tort exemption are closely related as a practical matter. In a sense a trade-off is involved. Comparisons of costs between an existing system and a proposed system are necessarily estimates that are subject to dispute. Varied estimates submitted to the Special Committee on UMVARA from three major industry sources ranged from modest savings to modest increases in comparison with costs of the existing system on average. For a particular policyholder in a particular community, variances in either direction might be greater. For the purpose of illustrating a key question one might ask himself, assume that you are a citizen for whom the costs of the existing and the proposed system would be approximately the same. The proposed system would give you guaranteed life-time coverage for economic losses sustained in automobile accidents, regardless of negligence, but no chance of recovering general damages for noneconomic detriment unless you sustain a very severe injury. The existing system gives you a right to recover for both economic losses and general damages if you have a valid claim based on negligence, but no right to recover either kind of damages if you have a valid claim based on negligence, but no right to recover either kind of damages in other cases and no assurance of the financial responsibility of the negligent party above $25,000. The key question is this: if these two were offered to you at about the same price, which would you choose?

As comparative cost data accumulate and more precise comparisons of costs for various levels of no-fault benefits and tort exemptions become available, it seems likely that the trend of public choice during the current decade will be toward greater assurance of compensation for economic losses with a corresponding reduction in the role of tort law and tort liability insurance.

## LONG-RANGE PROBABILITIES

The first part of this paper has been focused on principles underlying emerging reforms of the automobile reparations system—principles that are likely to shape developments within the decade of the 1970's. What are the longer-range prospects for reparation systems both in relation to harms sustained in automobile accidents and in relation to other harms? Here, even more plainly than in speculations about the short-range future, an attempt to identify the major principles that will shape change seems more appropriate than an attempt to envision details of a plan of implementation.

## Competing Principles

The key ideas underlying reparation systems thus far developed may be classified as expressions of various combinations of six principles: (1) tort liability based on fault; (2) third-party liability insurance; (3) loss insurance applying to defined areas of loss (or no-fault insurance, as it has come to be called in recent years); (4) private-enterprise funding and management of insurance; (5) broad protection securing a minimal level of economic welfare; and (6) public funding and management of the security system (either as an insurance system or as a tax system).

As a matter of empirical observation, these principles have commonly been used in one of the following three combinations, though these do not exhaust the range of theoretical possibilities: (a) a combination of (1), (2), and (4)—that is, fault-based tort liability with liability insurance funded and managed by private enterprise; (b) a combination of (3) and (4)—that is, loss (or no-fault) insurance applying to defined areas of loss, funded and managed by private enterprise; and (c) a combination of (5) and (6)—that is, social welfare protection publicly funded. These are the three major sets of principles that appear destined to compete for dominance in the future. What are the probabilities regarding their respective degrees of influence?

*Tort-Liability and Third-Party, Private Enterprise Insurance.* This set of principles has been predominant since the automobile was invented. Proposals for a no-fault automobile insurance system have been founded on the view that this predominant set of principles has not worked well in relation to harms sustained in automobile accidents. Projections in this paper of increased acceptance of no-fault plans are, conversely, projections of declining influence of the present set of principles. However, those projections referred to the automobile reparations system only.

Moreover, even in that context it was noted that the emerging reforms will preserve some tort actions. In the longer range, as well as for the immediate future, it seems unlikely that negligence claims and liability insurance will be completely abandoned.

*No-Fault, Private-Enterprise Insurance.* Systems founded on this pair of principles, as indicated earlier in this paper, are currently moving into dominance in reparations for injuries caused by automobile accidents. In addition to this development through legislation, a dramatic turn has occurred through court decisions of the last decade in another area—that is, in relation to compensation for harms resulting from defective products. In that context the newly established theory is referred to as strict liability rather than no-fault insurance. The two new theories are alike in dispensing with fault as the basis for compensation. They differ in that strict liability recoveries for harms resulting from defective products include general damages for such matters as pain and suffering. That is, they are not subject to limitations of the type incorporated in no-fault statutes as part of the trade-off, under which prospects for general damages are sacrificed in return for assurance of compensation for economic loss.

In light of this judicially established strict liability for harms resulting from defective products it seems unlikely that no-fault statutes will be extended to that area. What are the prospects of extension to other areas? Already there is wide discussion of possible extension of no-fault, private-enterprise insurance to injuries resulting from accidents in the course of medical treatment.[12] But formulating a viable no-fault law for medical accidents poses substantially greater difficulties than those that had to be dealt with in developing a no-fault automobile accident reparations systems.

Two examples will underscore the above point. First, the trade-off referred to previously makes it possible to provide life-time protection for economic losses through no-fault insurance at costs in the same general range as those for no more than $25,000 tort liability insurance. In contrast, similar no-fault benefits to all persons sustaining injury from a physician's mistake or some other accident in the course of medical treatment probably would cost far more than is now paid in malpractice liability insurance premiums. Since there is already a great hue and cry about the high costs of medical malpractice insurance, obviously there would be tremendous resistance to still greater increases in insurance costs.

Second, the shift from fault to no-fault would not be as effective in reducing administrative costs in medical accident cases as in automobile accident cases because the causation problem looms larger in the medical context. For example, it would often be disputed whether the patient's disability after medical treatment was due to some accident or mistake in treatment or instead was simply the unavoidable consequence of the ailment for which he sought the treatment.

The foregoing illustration makes the point that a quick, general shift from a tort-and-liability-insurance system to a no-fault system for all types of injuries and harms is not a realistic possibility. The viability of this set of principles will have to be examined area by area. Moreover, the choice will not be merely one between a tort-and-liability insurance system and a no-fault system. Rather, current and proposed increases in the scope of social security suggest that an accurate projection of the full range of choice must take account of this possibility too.

*Social Welfare Protection, Publicly Funded.* Systems founded on this set of principles have gained ground in the last decade. Moreover, in light of the present state of the controversy over national intrusion into the health care system, it appears that this set of principles will gain substantially more ground in the future. This is not to say, however, that the trend in this direction should be expected to continue to the point that a social security system becomes the principal reparations system in our society. That seems improbable in the near future and only one of the major possibilities for the longer range.

## SUMMARY

Our society has adopted not one but many reparation systems, founded on differing sets of principles that are to some extent in competition for dominance both in general and as well in relation to particular problem areas. In relation to automobile accident reparations, emerging reforms are establishing a system that combines no-fault reparations for economic losses with limited opportunities for recovering general damages through the tort system. Currently the major controversy centers on this shift from a fault system to a blended system in which no-fault insurance is predominant.

However, the trend toward diminishing influence of fault and liability insurance seems well established. In the long range, then, the key question that remains in doubt is whether no-fault, private-enterprise insurance will be dominant or instead publicly funded systems of the social security type will gain greater ascendancy. It is in relation to this key question that there is the greatest chance that wise decisions of today's political leaders, executives, and perhaps even academicians may have substantial impact on the shape of the future.

### Questions

1. Should "motoring pay its way," or should the burden be spread over the wider population? What are the implications of this question for auto insurance?

2. Should auto insurance be "excess" over other coverage? What is the relationship of this question to that of the market share of insurance held by auto insurers?

3. "Preservation of negligence liability after a basic level of no-fault benefits are paid will benefit the rich because they will be the class of persons able to afford to press a negligence liability case, while the poor will be forced to accept only the no-fault benefits." Do you agree? Why?

4. What is your answer to the question presented by Professor Keeton as a consumer choice between the two systems—no-fault and tort liability? Discuss.

5. What combination of the six principles listed by Professor Keeton are currently in effect in your state?

6. Do you see any similarities between the developments in automobile liability and products liability? Discuss.

# PART 6
## General Liability Insurance

The liability of the operator of a car involved in a crash and the popularity of automobile liability insurance as a means of protecting the operator have given new dimensions to the area of negligence liability. The observation at the scene of a crash of one party asking the other "Do you have insurance to cover me?" is an indication that liability insurance is perceived to be coverage for the injured party as much as protection for the driver. This dimension to liability insurance was not a part of its original design.

Another new dimension is the quantity of lawsuits and the public awareness of recourse available to an injured person against the person causing the injury. This awareness influences the size of judgment asked as well as the number of suits. The awareness also influences the filing of suits for injuries other than those resulting from an automobile crash. With this awareness, there has been significant growth in several areas of liability insurance other than automobile insurance.

The articles in this part were chosen to introduce the student to basic concepts of legal liability in specific areas typically covered by insurance. Malpractice insurance for medical practitioners has its counterpart as professional liability insurance to protect corporate directors and officers, lawyers, accountants, and other professionals. The first article in this part discusses developments in this area. Two other areas, pollution and products liability, are developed in the articles by Mr. Bromwich and Mr. Thompson. Finally, a well developed treatment of the effect of inflation on risk and insurance is presented by Mr. Kelley.

# 20. SOME OBSERVATIONS ON THE PERSONAL LIABILITY OF PROFESSIONALS, INSURANCE AGENTS, AND CORPORATE DIRECTORS AND OFFICERS FOR MISCONDUCT AND MALPRACTICE *

William E. Knepper †

Our subject-matter involves consideration of some trends in professional malpractice litigation, the errors and omissions of insurance agents, and the  legal liability of corporate officers and directors arising out of their official activities. No attempt will be made to discuss medical malpractice, although some of the matters to be dealt with trace their origins to decisions in the field of medical malpractice. Neither will any effort be made to cover these subjects in any substantial depth. Our purpose is merely to note trends and to try to take cognizance of developing areas of exposure to liability.

## ARCHITECTS AND ENGINEERS

In past years the courts erected a protective legal structure around architects and engineers, which was sufficient to shelter them from any extensive liability for their misconduct. However, in recent years there have been substantial changes in that situation, and the pendulum is swinging away from such holdings. Under today's decisions architects are held liable for defects attributable to plans and specifications, for injury to or the death of a third party from defective plans or specifications, and for the results of an improper certificate by an architect who gave such certificate in the acceptance of the work performed by the contractor. In other miscellaneous instances liability has also been imposed.

Because of the unique problems involved in an action to impose liability upon an architect for injury to a third party on account of a defective design, reference should be made to the New York case of

---

* From *Insurance Counsel Journal* (January, 1971), pp. 39-48. Reprinted by permission.

† Member of the firm of Knepper, White, Richards & Miller in Columbus, Ohio.

*Inman v. Binghamton Housing Authority.*[1] This case involved some aspects of privity, but was primarily concerned with an open and obvious defect. Six years after an apartment house had been completed and turned over to the owner, this action was brought against the architects who designed the structure, the builder who constructed it, and the owner, to recover for injuries suffered by a child of a tenant when he fell off a stoop or porch.

In the first instance, the court held that the "principle inherent" in *MacPherson v. Buick Motor Co.,*[2] applies to determine the liability of architects or builders for their handiwork. However, in this case the complaint did not allege that "the structure possessed a latent defect or an unknown danger" or "any recital that the absence of a railing or other device was unknown or undiscoverable." Such omissions were held fatal and the action was dismissed.[3]

While the action also involved an attempt by the housing authority to hold the architects and builder liable as indemnitors, the court refused to extend their contractual obligations to apply to such liabilities after a lapse of six years following completion of the construction. This is in line with the trend which excludes the passage of an extended period of time as an element of successful defense.[4]

The earlier cases of this type invoked the doctrine of privity of contract,[5] but more recent decisions have followed the general trend and have repudiated that doctrine.[6] For example, in a 1966 Illinois decision, the court said:

(T)o prohibit recovery from injury caused by his negligently drawn plans, upon the ground that no contractual relationship existed between the injured member of the public and the negligent furnisher of the plans, is to enforce outmoded concepts of liability dependent upon contract-law doctrines that no longer belong in the law of tort liability. Negligence which proximately causes injury will require the negligent actor to respond in damages for the harm suffered, where the injury is foreseeable, regardless of the prior relationship of the parties.[7]

The "latent-patent defect" principle underlying the *Inman* decision has been criticized severely [8] and has come close to repudiation in a New Jersey decision which verges on strict liability. In this case,[9] Levitt &

---

[1] 3 NY2d 137, 143 NE2d 895, 59 ALR2d 1072 (1957).
[2] 217 NY 382, 111 NE2d 1050, LRA 1916F, 696.
[3] See also Gouldin, "Liability of Architects and Contractors to Third Persons: Inman v. Binghamton Housing Authority Revisited," 33 Ins Counsel J 36 (1966); Thornton and McNiece, "Torts and Workmen's Compensation," 32 NYULRev 1465 (1957).
[4] See Hale v. DePaoli, 33 Cal2d 288, 201 P2d 1 (1948).
[5] E.g., Geare v. Sturgis, 14 F2d 256 (1926).
[6] See Annotation, 13 ALR2d 191, supplemented in 58 ALR2d 865.
[7] Laukkanen v. Jewel Tea Co., 222 NE2d 584 (Ill App 1966).
[8] See, e.g., Messina v. Clark Equipment Co., 263 F2d 291 (2 Cir 1959); Tracy v. Finn Equipment Co., 310 F2d 436 (6 Cir 1962).
[9] Schipper v. Levitt & Sons, Inc., 207 A2d 314 (1965).

Sons, a mass developer of residential subdivisions, was held liable to the infant son of the lessee of a home constructed to the developer's specifications. The child was scalded by hot water coming from a bathroom sink. The mixing valve was known to be dangerous to both the owner and the lessee but, of course, the child had no such knowledge. The New Jersey court stated that it found a need to impose "an implied obligation of reasonable workmanship and habitability" which would carry over to the ultimate user of the property.

The expansion of the liability of contractual engineers has been said to result from a decision of the Supreme Court of Alabama in 1963.[10] In that case the engineering firm was to design and specify a drainage system for a subdivision. The plans and specifications did not provide what amounted to adequate drainage, and the plaintiff filed suit based on the implied warranties of the contract for professional services. In its opinion, the court distinguished the professional services in this case from those of physicians, attorneys, and architects, stating that in such professions there are so many elements of judgment to be dealt with that any expectation of implied warranty is negated. The Alabama court believed that the elements involved in the drainage survey were ascertainable to the point that it was reasonable and just for a person to expect a specific result. The court said, in part:

> Certainly a contracting party has a right to expect the survey to be done with reasonable accuracy, changeable to the profession, and should not be dependent in his efforts to recover damages on an allegation of negligence or unskillful and imprudent work.

Another somewhat recent development in the liability of engineers and architects has to do with that of responsible supervision of the methods used by construction contractors. Illinois joined the ranks of states applying the *MacPherson* rule to architects in an action where a contract between an owner and architects provided that the architects' duties included general administration of the construction contract and general supervision and direction of the work. The architects had authority to stop the work to insure proper execution of the contract. It was held that the architects were not required to specify the method the contractor should use in performing the work, but did have the right to interfere and stop the work, if the contractor performed in an unsafe and hazardous manner.[11] In that case, the complaint charged common law negligence and the court held that the jury could find from the evidence that the architects were guilty of negligence in failing to inspect and watch over a shoring operation which resulted in the collapse of a roof on which the plaintiff was working.[12]

---

[10] Broyles v. Brown Engineering Co., Inc., 275 Ala 35, 151 So2d 767 (1963).

[11] Miller v. DeWitt, 37 Ill2d 273, 226 NE2d 630 (1967).

[12] See also Arness, "Architects and Engineers: A Consideration of Basic Liability Principles and Legal Trends in Foundation Engineering," 34 INS COUNSEL J 334 (1967).

Thus it appears that the architect may be held liable not only for a breach of duty owed to the owner, but also for a breach of duty owed to workmen on the project.   In measuring his duty to inspect and supervise, he must bear in mind the potential dangers to others from a defective condition, even though it may have been created by a contractor performing work on the job-site.[13]

The duty of an engineer is substantially the same as that of other experts or professionals. In a leading case decided in Minnesota in 1915,[14] the courts said that an engineer, in performing the work which he undertook, had the "duty to exercise such care, skill and diligence as men engaged in that profession ordinarily exercise under like circumstances." Noting that the engineer was not an insurer that the contractor would perform his work properly in all respects, the court held that it was the duty of the engineer to exercise reasonable care to see that the contractor did so.

In connection with construction costs, an architect or engineer may be liable for the negligent approval of progress payments to a building contractor as well as for their fraudulent approval,[15] and can be held liable for negligently estimating the initial cost of structures or projects.[16] In a California case decided half a century ago, an architect was held liable for intentional misrepresentation of the final estimate of the cost of construction, although the court pointed out that it would be inequitable to allow the owner to retain the more valuable building and still recover the difference between the estimate and the actual cost.[17]

There is a duty upon the architect to ascertain whether labor and material bills have been paid,[18] and to obtain lien releases or require the contractor to submit evidence that such obligations have been satisfied.[19] The Eighth Circuit has stated:

> (I)f the architect knew or should have known that the contractor was not paying his bills for material and labor on work already performed and on which he had been reimbursed, then the architect probably would have a duty to make inquiry and take steps to correct that situation before making any further certification on work performed.[20]

It is also the responsibility of the architect to see to it that the cost of construction is at least reasonably close to his cost estimate.[21] But if the

---

[13] See, e.g., Erhart v. Hummonds, 334 SW2d 869 (Ark 1960); Alexander v. Hammarberg, 230 P2d 399 (Cal App 1951).

[14] Cowles v. City of Minneapolis, 128 Minn 452, 151 NW 184 (1915). See also Pittman Const. Co. v. New Orleans, 178 So2d 312 (La App 1965).

[15] Corey v. Eastman, 166 Mass 279, 44 NE 217 (1896).

[16] Beachman v. Greenville County, 218 SC 181, 62 SE2d 92 (1950).

[17] Edward Baron Estate Company v. Woodruff Company, 163 Cal 561, 126 P 351 (1912); see also Capitol Hotel Company v. Rittenberry, 41 SW2d 691 (1931). And cf., Kellogg v. Pizza Oven, Inc., 402 P2d 633 (Colo 1965).

[18] Palmer v. Brown, 273 P2d 306 (Cal App 1954).

[19] State v. Malvaney, 72 So2d 424 (Miss 1955).

[20] See Aetna Insurance Co. v. Hellmuth, Obata and Kassabaum, Inc., 392 F2d (8 Cir 1968).

[21] See Goodrich v. Lash, 146 A2d 169 (Vt 1958).

owner changes the plans and thereby increases the cost of construction, the architect will not be held liable, as a general rule.[22]

The United States Court of Appeals for the Sixth Circuit handed down an interesting decision on the liability of engineers, in a 1964 Tennessee action. An engineering firm, which prepared boring log drawings showing the results of test borings at a tunnel site, inadvertently failed to include, in its summary, information about core recoveries contained in the reports of a testing firm. The tunnel contractor sued the engineers for damages because the job, as performed, was different than it had appeared in the plans. However, the court held that, without proof of wilful, intentional or fraudulent misrepresentation by the engineers, they were not liable for mere failure of disclosure.[23] The report of the other firm was available for inspection in the owner's office.

The contract under which an architect or engineer operates in performing his duties for the owner by whom he is employed is of substantial significance in determining the extent of his professional liability.[24] Such a contract is usually negotiable, and the professional has only himself to blame if he accepts contractual obligations greater than should be imposed upon him.

Also the construction contract, under which the contractor builds the project, may have a definite bearing on the professional liability of the architect or engineer. In the case of an architect, in particular, he ordinarily prepares the construction contract and writes its specifications, and, again, has only himself to blame if he permits it to impose unreasonable legal or contractual requirements upon him.

In far too many instances an architect or engineer will be tempted to sign whatever is placed before him, or will employ some so-called standardized forms of specifications to fix the obligations of the parties. When this occurs, there may be little that a lawyer can contribute after a loss has resulted.

## INSURANCE AGENTS OR BROKERS

The insurance agent or broker is vulnerable to legal attack on several grounds, and may incur liability on a variety of theories ranging from breach of implied warranty to fraudulent misrepresentation. For example, in a 1970 decision, the Supreme Court of California [25] imposed liability upon a corporate general agent for recommending a poor insurance risk and negligently fixing its premium rate. The insurance company principal was awarded the difference between the net premium received by it and the money it was legally obligated to pay out in losses and expenses.

---

[22] E.g., Martin v. McMahan, 271 P 1114 (Cal App 1928).

[23] Texas Tunneling Co. v. City of Chattanooga, 329 F2d 402 (1964).

[24] E.g., Miller v. DeWitt, Note 11, supra.

[25] United States Liability Ins. Co. v. Haidinger-Hayes, Inc., 83 Cal Rptr 418, 462 P2d 770 (1970).

However, the president of the corporate agency was absolved from individual responsibility to the insurance company. The court followed the rule that directors or officers of a corporation do not incur personal liability for the torts of the corporation merely by reason of their official position, unless they participate in the wrong or authorize or direct that it be done.

In actions involving insurance agents and brokers, it is generally considered that the duty to use reasonable care carries with it the implied warranty that the agent possesses the skill which is ordinarily possessed by agents in this field. For example, one text states: [26]

> (I)f an agent accepts an order to insure, he . . . must exercise such reasonable skill and ordinary diligence as may fairly be expected from a person in his profession or situation . . . and in all this he is obligated to exercise the strictest . . . good faith toward both his employer and the insured.

A failure to procure insurance caused by a lack of such skill may make the defendant agent liable in contract or tort, depending on the jurisdiction in which the failure occurs, and whether concurrent remedies in contract and tort exist.

The contract theory holds that when an agent promises to procure coverage, the promise must be performed with reasonable care or the agent will be liable in damages for a breach of the contract. The tort theory holds that when the duty emanating from the contract is not performed with reasonable care, the resulting damage creates a tort. As a practical proposition, under the liberalized procedure and simplified pleading which exists today in most states, this is a distinction without a difference. In fact, there is authority that the owner of property has a choice of bringing his action against his agent under either the tort theory or the contract theory.[27]

As is indicated by the California decision mentioned above, aside from his liability to an owner it is likely that an agent may be held responsible to an insurer on the theory of respondeat superior after liability has been imposed upon the insurer. For example, in an Iowa case [28] the decedent had sought life insurance, and the prospective insurer's agent negligently procrastinated in obtaining the insurance. The decedent died before the policy was issued. The estate of the decedent recovered from the insurer on the ground that is was liable for the tort of its agent in his procrastination. While that case did not actually involve an action over by the insurance company against the agent, it would appear that under the rule of the California case previously mentioned, such an action could have been maintained.

---

[26] 2 Couch, Insurance Law, Section 462 (1929).
[27] See Ursini v. Goldman, 118 Conn 554, 173 A 789 (1934).
[28] Duffy v. Bankers' Life Association, 160 Iowa 19, 139 NW 1087 (1913).

Generally, an agent or broker who contracts to obtain adequate insurance on specific property will be held liable if he fails to procure an effective and adequate policy.[29]

An agent will be held liable to his principal for failure to obey its instructions. This rule will apply, for example, when the insurance company directs its agents to cancel an insurance policy. While the agent may believe that he has superior information and should be entitled to exercise his own judgment, he may be held liable to the insurance company if he fails to carry out its directions.[30]

## ATTORNEYS AT LAW

Back in 1895, the California court applied a strict rule of privity and refused to impose liability upon an attorney for a mistake in drafting a will, where the result deprived one not his client of benefits under the will.[31] That case was expressly overruled in *Lucas v. Hamm*,[32] decided in 1961. The court followed its own earlier decision in which a notary public prepared a will and was held liable in tort to an intended beneficiary who was damaged because of the invalidity of the instrument.

In *Lucas v. Hamm,* the plaintiffs were held entitled to maintain their action as third-party beneficiaries of the employment contract between the lawyer and the testator. The court found the situation comparable to those in which (1) a bank was held liable to beneficiaries of a life insurance policy which lapsed because the bank failed to pay the premiums,[33] and (2) persons who agreed to procure liability insurance but failed to do so were held liable to injured persons who would have been covered by the insurance.[34]

However, the California court concluded that Attorney Hamm could not be held negligent on account of his mistakes in the drafting of the will. The errors involved the rules relating to perpetuities and restraints on alienation. These areas of the California law were termed "fraught with confusion" and "concealed traps for the unwary draftsman." Accordingly, no lack of proper diligence, skill or prudence was found in failing to avoid such traps.

Mr. Hamm was held liable, however, because he neglected to obtain releases which would have precluded subsequent claims against the estate, and his neglect thereby reduced the amount distributable to the beneficiaries.

---

[29] Hampton Road Carriers v. Boston Insurance Company, 150 FSupp 338 (1957); Case v. Ewbanks, Ewbanks & Company, 194 NC 775, 140 SE 709 (1927). See also Annotation, 129 ALR2d 171 (1953).

[30] See Mitton v. Granite State Fire Insurance Company, 196 F2d 988 (10 Cir. 1952).

[31] Buckley v. Gray, 110 Cal 339, 42 P 900, 31 LRA 862 (1895).

[32] 15 Cal Rptr 821, 364 P2d 685.

[33] Biakanja v. Irving, 49 Cal2d 647, 320 P2d 16, 65 ALR2d 1358 (1958); Walker Bank & Trust Co. v. First Security Corp., 9 Utah2d 215, 341 P2d 944 (1959); Johnson v. Holmes Tuttle Lincoln-Mercury, Inc., 160 CalApp2d 290, 325 P2d 193 (1958).

[34] James Stewart & Co. v. Law, 149 Tex 392, 283 SW2d 558, 22 ALR2d 639 (1950).

A sequel to *Lucas v. Hamm* was the 1969 California decision in *Heyer v. Flaig*.[35] It presented the question: When does the statute of limitations commence to run against an intended beneficiary of a will who acquires a right of action against an attorney for malpractice in failing to fulfill the testamentary directions of his client?

The court fixed that time at the date of the death of the testatrix and ruled that "the defendant's negligence was continuing and incomplete until that time." The testatrix could have changed her intention or her will until she died. Accordingly, the intended beneficiaries acquired no legal rights under the will until the testator's death occurred.

In an excellent discussion of this case in 37 INSURANCE COUNSEL JOURNAL 258 (April 1970), Mitchell Lee Lathrop, of Los Angeles, expresses the view that the decision will "open the door to an enormously expanded class of plaintiffs who will in the future be permitted to maintain actions against attorneys with virtually no time problems to contend with, insofar as limiting statutes may be involved." He bases that statement upon his view that, under this decision, "as long as any errors committed by the attorney could be corrected, the statute of limitations would be tolled."

According to ALR, "the rule that finds support among most of the cases is that the statute of limitations begins to run, against an action for damages arising out of the negligent act or omission of an attorney, from the time of the occurrence of the neglect or omission complained of." [36]

In New York state, since a 1968 decision of the Supreme Court, Appellate Division, Second Department, in *Siegal v. Kranis*,[37] it has been established that the statute of limitations will not begin to run until the attorney ceases to represent the client in the particular matter in which the malpractice occurred. This is similar to the "continuous treatment" doctrine that obtains in medical malpractice actions.[38] Since the attorney-client relationship is marked by a trust comparable to that existing in the physician-patient relationship, the New York courts generally apply the same rules to both. There are some contrary decisions.[39]

There is a rule in some states that the statute begins to run at the time damages are sustained.[40] That rule seems to be in line with the California decisions previously mentioned. Ohio has refused to hold that the statute begins to run when the attorney-client relationship terminates, although it applies that rule in physician-patient cases.[41]

---

[35] 74 Cal Rptr 225, 449 P2d 161 (1969).

[36] Annotation, "When Statutes of Limitations Begin to Run Upon Action Against Attorney for Malpractice," 18 ALR3d 978, 986 (1968).

[37] 20 AD2d 477, 288 NYS2d 831 (1968).

[38] See Borgia v. City of New York, 12 NY2d 151, 187 NE2d 777 (1962).

[39] Cf., Troll v. Glantz, 57 Misc2d 572, 293 NYS2d 345 (1968).

[40] Ft. Myers Seafood Packers, Inc. v. Steptoe & Johnson (AppDC 1967), 381 F2d 261, 18 ALR3d 974, and cases cited in Annotation, 994-996.

[41] Galloway v. Hood, 69 Ohio App 278, 43 NE2d 631 (1941).

In any professional malpractice case, the subject of the statute of limitations is significant and usually troublesome. A Maryland case, decided in 1969, is an excellent example.[42] Its facts disclose that in 1954 a partner in the defendant law firm examined a real estate title and advised his client to accept a deed to certain real estate. She did so. In 1965, when she sought to sell the property, it developed that her grantors had no lawful interest in the property and her title was worthless. After her deed was declared null and void, she sued the only surviving partner of the defendant law firm and the firm to recover damages for the loss of the property. The trial court granted summary judgment for the defendants on the ground that the relationship between lawyer and client was contractual and the statute of limitations began to run in 1954 when the title opinion was rendered.

In the appellate court, the summary judgment was reversed. The court followed its earlier decisions dealing with the liability of physicians,[43] and surveyors,[44] and declared that the action sounded in negligence even though the relationship between the parties was contractual. Consequently, it was held that the statute of limitations did not begin to run until the wrong was discovered. Therefore, the action was commenced in time, even though some twelve years after the title opinion was rendered.

More than any case in recent years, the decision of the California District Court of Appeals, First District, on January 23, 1968,[45] has caused casualty insurance companies and their counsel to reappraise the consequences that may result from their actions in conflict-of-interest situations. That case in analyzed in several articles, including Snow, "Excess Liability—Crisci and Lysick," 36 INSURANCE COUNSEL JOURNAL 51 (1969) and Knepper, "Conflicts of Interest in Defending Insurance Cases," 19 Defense Law Journal 515, 529-532 (1970). It merits careful study on the question of the potential liability for malpractice of a lawyer retained by an insurer to defend its insured, who finds himself ensnared by the conflicting interests of his client and his employer.[46]

## CORPORATE OFFICERS AND DIRECTORS

Liabilities of corporate officers and directors generally fall within three categories:

(1) Negligence in their official actions;
(2) Failure to comply with their fiduciary responsibilities to the corporation and its stockholders; and

[42] Mumford v. Staton, Whaley & Price (CA, Md 1969), 255 A2d 359.
[43] Benson v. Mays, 245 Md 632, 227 A2d 220 (1967).
[44] Mattingly v. Hopkins, Md., 254 A2d 904 (1969).
[45] Lysick v. Walcom (1968), 258 CalApp2d 136, 65 Cal Rptr 406, 28 ALR3d 368.
[46] See also, Knepper, "Insurer's Duty to Defend: Recent Developments," 17 Defense L J 391 (1968).

(3) Violation of the duties imposed upon them by virtue of the Securities and Exchange laws.

While an exhaustive analysis of these various liabilities is not practical on this occasion, an attempt will be made to discuss each of the three categories to some degree.

Reference has already been made to the 1970 California decision in which the president of a corporate insurance agency was absolved from personal responsibility to a third party with which his employer had contractual relationships. The court in that case followed the rule that directors or officers of a corporation do not incur liability for the torts of the corporation merely by reason of their official position, unless they participate in the wrong or authorize or direct that it be done.[47]

The standard of care imposed upon corporate officers and directors is "due care" or "reasonable care." In Delaware that has been defined as the degree of care which reasonably prudent persons exercise in the conduct of their own affairs of like kind.[48]

The rule defining the degree of care required of corporate officers and directors as that expected of "ordinarily prudent and diligent men under similar circumstances" was first declared in *Briggs v. Spaulding,* in 1891.[49] That same rule has been followed in the Sixth Circuit,[50] and in many other states. In Pennsylvania, the adoption of the Business Corporation law of 1933, enacted the "personal affairs rule" into law. It imposed the duty upon a director to discharge his responsibilities "with that diligence, care and skill which ordinarily prudent men would exercise under similar circumstances in their personal business affairs.[51]

In a 1966 decision of the Supreme Court of Pennsylvania, construing that statute, it was held that, even in the absence of fraud, self-dealing, or proof of personal profit or wanton acts of omission or commission, directors of a business corporation, "who have been imprudent, wasteful, careless and negligent, will be personally liable if their actions result in corporate losses on account of the insolvency of the corporation."[52] Of course, a director is not an insurer and he does not guarantee the fidelity of the officers and agents to whom the board of directors may delegate the responsibility of conducting the corporation's affairs.

It is true that a corporation officer, like any other agent, may impose liability upon his principal for torts committed by him in the course of his employment and within the scope of his authority. In any such case

---

[47] United States Liability Insurance Company v. Haidinger-Hayes, Inc., 83 Cal Rptr 418, 462 P2d 770 (1970), citing Knepper, "Liability of Corporate Officers and Directors," Chapter 6.

[48] Graham v. Allis-Chalmers Manufacturing Company, 40 Del Ch 335, 182 A2d 338 1962).

[49] 141 U.S. 132, 152 (1891).

[50] Atherson v. Anderson, 99 F2d 883 (6 Cir 1938).

[51] Purdon's Pennsylvania Statutes Ann., Title 15, Section 140B.

[52] Selheimer v. Manganese Corp. of America, 423 Penn 563, 224 A2d 634 (1966).

he would also be personally liable to the injured party for his own wrong-doing. When a corporation is held vicariously liable for an officer's tortious acts under the rule of respondeat superior, it probably will have a right of indemnification to recover over from that officer what it was compelled to pay by reason of such vicarious liability.[53]

Generally speaking, a director is not liable for the misdeeds of his co-directors, where he has not participated in the acts resulting in the damage,[54] but he may be held liable to creditors for his negligence in not preventing a misappropriation of funds by a co-director. For example, in a Colorado case [55] decided before the turn of the century, the court reasoned that while Nix, a director, had not himself committed a fraudulent act, his complete inattention to corporate activity constituted "gross negligence" and made him accountable to a creditor, just as if he had personally performed the acts causing the damage.

Corporate directors are treated as fiduciaries with respect to the corporation and its stockholders. While they are not "trustees" in a technical sense,[56] their relationship to the corporation and its stockholders involves responsibility and accountability similar to that of trustees.[57] They may not use the trust property or their relation to it for their own personal gain, and it is their duty to administer the corporate affairs for the benefit of all the stockholders, and exercise their best care, skill and judgment in the management of the corporation business solely in the interests of the corporation.[58]

In 1932, the Harvard Law Review published a famous debate between Professor Adolf A. Berle and the late Professor E. Merrick Dodd on the subject of the fiduciary responsibilities of corporate directors.[59] Since then the subject has had much attention by numerous writers. And Professor Berle recently looked back at that debate with some interesting observations.[60] He indicated that, pragmatically, "Professor Dodd won the debate." He continued, "I was not convinced as a matter of doctrine that social responsibility should not be left to government—but there was no doubt that the event conformed rather to his prediction than to mine." [61]

---

[53] See, e.g., Maryland Casualty Company v. Frederick Company, 142 Ohio St 605, 52 NE2d 795 (1944); Klatt v. Commonwealth Edison Company, 55 IllApp2d 120, 204 NE2d 319 (1964).

[54] See, e.g., Holland v. American Founders Life Insurance Company, 376 P2d 162, 166 Colo 1962).

[55] Nix v. Miller, 26 Colo 203, 57 Pac 1084 (1899).

[56] Bosworth v. Allen, 168 NY 157, 61 NE 163, 55 LRA 751 (1901).

[57] See Cohen v. Beneficial Industrial Loan Corporation, 337 U.S. 541, 93 LEd 1528, 69 Sup Ct 1221 (1949).

[58] See Western States Life Insurance Company v. Lockwood, 166 Cal 185, 190, 135 Pac 496, 498 (1913).

[59] See Berle, "For Whom Corporate Managers are Trustees," 45 HarvLR 1365 (1932); Dodd, "For Whom are Corporate Managers Trustees?", 45 HarvLR 1145 (1932).

[60] Address before the Association of the Bar of the City of New York at its program on "The Future Direction of the Modern Corporation," presented April 23, 1968.

[61] See Practising Law Institute Handbook No. B4-2526, "Protecting the Corporate Officer and Director from Liability" (1969), at p. 102.

This subject matter has a direct bearing on the potential liabilities of corporate directors today. Air and water pollution, the safety of products manufactured and sold, servicing of such products after their acquisition by the retail customer, "built-in obsolescence," unattractive billboard advertising and the like, are all matters of social significance as well as of economic consequence. The decisions of corporate directors as to such matters may be of some importance with respect to corporate earnings. The failure of corporate directors to recognize the social significance of such problems may result in corporate losses which, in turn, may bring down the wrath of the shareholders upon them.

Professor Berle sums up the present situation thus:

> Corporation decisions that yesterday did not materially affect other people today powerfully impinge on their lives. . . . My hope is that corporations will themselves be aware of the areas of reaction, and in that awareness will reconsider some of their policies before government intervenes.[62]

The cases and text writers generally agree that "directors owe three duties to the corporation they serve:" obedience, diligence, and loyalty.[63] The duty of *obedience* contemplates that ultra vires corporate activities are to be avoided. Directors may be held to absolute liability if they cause their corporation to engage in business activities beyond the scope of its charter or prohibited by law.

The duty of *diligence* contemplates that a director will exercise the degree of care previously mentioned, namely, that which ordinarily prudent men would exercise under the same or similar circumstances in the conduct of their own affairs. In New York, for example, the statute,[64] requires directors to discharge the duties of their positions with that degree of diligence, care and skill which ordinarily prudent men would exercise under similar circumstances in like positions.

The third duty is *loyalty*. It contemplates that a director must refrain from engaging in his own personal activities in such a manner as to injure or take advantage of his corporation. In this connection, it is generally held that directors may not make secret or private profits out of their official positions, and must give to the corporation the benefit of any advantages they may obtain in their official positions.

In one New York case, the Supreme Court said: [65]

> In the last analysis, whether or not a director has discharged his duty, whether or not he has been negligent, depends upon the facts and circumstances of a particular case, the kind of corporation involved, its size and financial resources, the magnitude of the transaction, and the immediacy of the problem presented.

---

[62] Ibid, at p. 109, reprinted from 24 BusLaw 149 (1968).

[63] See 6 Cavitch, Business Organizations, 1092, Sec. 127.01 (1968).

[64] McKinney's Consolidated Laws of New York, Business Corporation Law, Section 717.

[65] Litwin v. Allen, 25 NYS2d 667, 678 (1940).

A director who seeks to be insulated from potential liability ought to direct his efforts toward doing a conscientious job in behalf of his corporation. Regardless of the likelihood of misbehaviour by fellow directors or officers, a director should always give attention to his particular obligation and duties, and keep himself adequately informed of the company's activities. The failure of a director to make sufficient inquiry is probably the most common cause of liability upon him. Where he is a so-called "outside" director, or even an "accommodation" director, the potential hazards of his position are even greater.

The responsibilities of a director may be expected to include:

1. Making sure that all technical requirements of law have been met before the corporation commences to do business.

2. Keeping informed of the provisions of the articles of incorporation, code of regulations, and by-laws, which relate to his powers and duties as a director.

3. Keeping informed of the general activities of the corporation, and the general business area in which it functions.

4. Having a competent knowledge of the duties of his office.

5. Obeying all statutes which prescribe specific duties to be performed by directors.

6. Avoiding self-dealing in any matters relating to the corporation's business.

7. Avoiding any contract to serve his own interests, or to assume any position to bring his interests into conflict or competition with the interests of the company.

8. Attending director's meetings regularly; if meetings must be missed, being sure the records show a valid reason for his absence.

9. Registering dissent when in disagreement with board action, and being sure such dissent is made a matter of record in the minutes of the meeting, and that he (the director) has verified the accuracy of the minutes.

10. Exercising the utmost good faith in all dealings with and for his corporation, and being prepared to prove that he has done so.

11. Assuring complete and accurate disclosure of all the details of all transactions involving the sales of securities.[66]

It has been well said that "the life blood of business depends upon the quality of guidance which officers and directors can give to the corporations they serve." Consequently, and in order to be able to obtain high quality guidance from such officers and directors, there has been a strong movement toward adequate indemnification of corporate officers, directors and employees, and the provision of liability insurance to supplement the indemnification and protect both the officers and directors from potential losses.

Despite some earlier criticism of the Delaware indemnification statute, it and Section 4A of the Model Business Corporation Act from which it is taken, have served as the pattern for similar enactments in 38 other jurisdictions.

The New York law contains a unique provision in Section 726(c) of the Business Corporation Law. If indemnification is paid other than

---

[66] Knepper, "Liability of Corporate Officers and Directors," 16018, Sec. 1.08.

pursuant to a court order or action by the shareholders, the corporation must mail to its shareholders of record a statement specifying the persons paid, the amounts paid, and the nature and status at the time of such payment of the litigation or threatened litigation. The time limits for such mailing are prescribed in the statute.

The Delaware and New York statutes are examples of the methods by which legislatures have been attempting to avoid misuse of indemnification and, at the same time, endeavor to provide reasonable protection for corporate officers and directors. While this is not a new problem, the fear of liability and the resulting difficulty in attracting high-quality persons as corporate directors continues and increases largely because of new and greater hazards under federal laws relating to securities and antitrust matters.

Faced with such problems, corporate counsel have turned to the drafting of byla·s and charter provisions intended to afford the broadest possible indem...ification and insurance permissible under applicable legislative enactments. However, until the statutes themselves have been amended to deal adequately with such problems, it is difficult to solve them by corporate by-laws and charter provisions. Professor James H. Cheek, III, in his discussion of the Delaware and New York statutes,[67] has taken a significant step in this direction.

Liabilities of corporate officers and directors in securities transactions have increased to a great extent over the last decade. In particular, Section 10(b) of the Securities Exchange Act of 1934 and Rule 10b-5, promulgated thereunder by the Securities and Exchange Commission, have been the focal point for a spectacular growth in the law arising out of transactions in securities. Judge Irvin R. Kaufman, in a decision rendered in 1968, said that Rule 10b-5 generates almost as much litigation as all the other anti-fraud provisions combined.[68]

Because so many of the significant decisions in this area have been handed down by the United States District Courts in New York, and by the United States Court of Appeals for the Second Circuit, it is to be expected that lawyers practicing in these courts will have a substantial exposure to this kind of litigation.

Also, the New York state courts have rendered some important decisions in this field. For example, *Diamond v. Oreamuno*,[69] decided by the New York Court of Appeals in 1969, is of major significance, although the question presented was one of first impression in that court. This question was whether officers and directors might be held accountable to their corporation, in a stockholder's derivative action, for gains realized by them for transactions in the company's stock as a result of their use of material inside information.

---

[67] See Cheek, "Control of Corporate Indemnification: A Proposed Statute," 22 Vanderbilt LR 255 (1969).

[68] Green v. Wolf Corporation, 406 F2d 291 (CA2, NY 1968).

[69] 24 NY2d 494, 248 NE2d 910 (1969).

In the *Diamond* case, the complaint alleged that the corporation's board chairman and president knew that the corporation would suffer a 75 percent decrease in its net earnings, but did not make this information public for several months. Meanwhile, these two officers sold off 56,500 shares of the corporation stock, which they owned, and realized $800,000 more than if the inside information had not been available to them. The action sought an accounting to the corporation for those profits.

The opinion was written by Chief Judge Stanley H. Fuld. He expressed the view that there were practical difficulties inherent in an action under Federal law for such relief (especially since Sec. 16(b) of the Securities Exchange Act of 1934 was not applicable because the corporate officials had held their stock for more than six months). Accordingly, the Chief Judge considered that there was manifest desirability of creating an effective common-law remedy. He found "nothing in the Federal law which indicates it was intended to limit the power of the States to fashion additional remedies to effectuate similar purposes."

In the opinion it was noted that:

> When officers and directors abuse their position in order to gain personal profits, the effect may be to cast a cloud on the corporation's name, inure stockholder relations and undermine public regard for the corporation's securities.

Also, in considering whether such a claim might be asserted in a derivative action, the Chief Judge pointed out that "a corporation fiduciary, who is entrusted with potentially valuable information, may not appropriate that asset for his own use even though, in so doing, he causes no injury to the corporation." He continued:

> The primary concern, in a case such as this, is not to determine whether the corporation has been damaged but to decide, as between the corporation and the defendants, who has a higher claim to the proceeds derived from exploitation of the information.

It was the court's unanimous conclusion that there could be no justification for permitting officers and directors to retain for themselves profits derived from exploiting information obtained by virtue of their inside position as corporate officials.

Professor Ernest L. Folk, III, of the law school of the University of Virginia, has described *Escott v. BarChris Construction Corporation*,[70] as arguably the most important decision yet rendered under the Securities Act of 1933, principally because of the remarkable and sometimes emotional public response to that case in various quarters. As Professor Folk points out,[71] *BarChris* is unprecedented because of the number

---

[70] 283 FSupp 643 (SDNY 1968).
[71] 65 Va LR 1, 5 (1969).

and variety of defendants held liable. When that case is considered along with *Texas Gulf Sulphur*,[72] it is apparent that all those having any connection with corporate securities transactions are presently confronted with far greater potential liabilities than heretofore were ever anticipated.[73]

## CONCLUSION

The misconduct and malpractice of those who undertake to serve their fellow men for compensation, whether they be professionals or laymen-with-expertise in particular fields, is an ever-expanding source of claims and litigation. Today's trial lawyer cannot afford ignorance or incompetence in such matters, else he may find himself in the defendant's chair charged with his own professional liability. These areas of the law are not complicated but they do require the day-by-day updating of a lawyer's knowledge.

## Questions

1. Research the statute of limitations in your state. Discuss the statute with respect to malpractice of one of the classes of professionals in this article.
2. If a small businessman turns over his insurance program to his agent with the instruction, "Cover me for anything that is really important," what should the agent do, in your opinion, to fulfill his professional liability to the businessman? Why?

---

[72] Securities and Exchange Commission v. Texas Gulf Sulphur Company, 401 F2d 833 (CA2, NY 1968).

[73] See, e.g., J. I. Case Company v. Borak, 377 U.S. 426, 12 LEd2d 423, 84 Sup Ct 1555 (1964).

# 21. POLLUTION AND INSURANCE *

G. R. E. Bromwich †

The pollution liability insurance situation is both simple and complex. Limitations on coverage can be understood quickly; unfortunately, if not amended or eliminated they often leave the risk manager with a serious uninsured exposure. The background is more complicated, but must be understood if one is to make the best out of a bad business. Most of the examples given here refer to Canada and Canadian law but they are applicable in the United States because the questions involved are fundamental.

## Insurers Concerned

I do not think there is any doubt that the insurance market, both direct and reinsurers, is perturbed about the possibility of large pollution liability claims. Their immediate reaction has been to introduce endorsements which attempt to define the limited extent of coverage they wish to give for most risks and to exclude virtually all liability for pollution in the case of risks associated with the petroleum industry. I believe Lloyd's was first to introduce what it called Seepage, Pollution and Contamination clauses which went beyond previous similarly named clauses. This was in the early part of last year and INA was not far behind with its clause termed, Environmental Pollution Exclusion. Other versions put out by insurers have such titles as Environmental Exclusion.

Insurers rarely react immediately to any situation and the origins of the present concern over pollution go back for some years.

For example, any fisherman will confirm that for years people writing about fishing have been bemoaning the extent to which rivers and lakes have become polluted. Attempts have been made to counteract this but conservation, as far as I am aware, never made a great deal of headway.

## Torrey Canyon Aroused Interest

It was not until the tanker *Torrey Canyon* went aground off the south coast of England and the oil spill fouled the coasts of England and France that general interest in pollution was aroused. The British Navy attempted unsuccessfully to salvage the wreck; the R.A.F. tried to set the oil on fire by bombing it, also without success. Subsequently, a sister

* From *Risk Management* (April, 1971), pp. 14-19. Reprinted by permission.
† Manager of the Research Department at Reed Shaw Osler Limited in Toronto.

ship was "arrested" in Singapore harbor and eventually the British and French governments recovered about $7.8 million from the charterers, Union Oil Company of California, who apparently owned the vessel through a subsidiary.

Then came the enormous spill from a drilling rig operated by Union Oil in the Pacific Ocean near Santa Barbara, California. Representatives of the parties damaged, which included fishing and boating industries, beach front property owners and the beach-using public, have filed suit for $1.3 *billion* (not million) damages against the four companies involved (although Union Oil was operating the rig, it was in partnership with Mobil Oil, Gulf Oil and Texaco). There have been other smaller spills in Canada and elsewhere. One of these "smaller" spills involves suits for $100 million against Chevron Oil Company for damage done to shrimp and oyster fishing in the Gulf of Mexico.

## Voluntary Action

As a result of various oil spills from tankers, an arrangement was reached between the majority of the world's tanker owners to provide compensation to governments who incur expense in clean-up. This arrangement is known as TOVALOP (Tanker Owners Voluntary Agreement concerning Liability for Oil Pollution). There is a corresponding scheme for owners of cargo—CRISTAL (Contract Regarding Interim Supplement to Tanker Liability for Oil Pollution).

A special Canadian act, The Arctic Waters Pollution Prevention Act, has been passed in recognition of the fact that oil pollution in arctic areas would take far longer to disperse than in a warmer climate. Although passed by Parliament the Act will not come into force until proclamation and it is mainly "skeleton" legislation to be fleshed out by regulations. Provision is made, among other matters, for evidence of financial responsibility by way of insurance to be required of developers, ship owners, etc. The Arctic Waters Act is complementary to the proposed changes in the Canada Shipping Act.

## Other Causes, Effects

There are, of course, other types of water pollution. For instance, there has been a good deal in the news recently about mercury, which discharged as a result of the industrial process, is poisoning fish in the Great Lakes. Subsequently, warnings have ensued about eating fish from these waters. As a result the livelihood of commercial fisherman has been affected and the tourist fishing industry has suffered a blow. The discharge of great quantities of domestic detergents, which contain phosphates, is also a problem.

Near the city of Elliot Lake, Ontario, radioactivity has been discovered in certain waters to an undue extent as the result of uranium mining. Various industries have unfortunately allowed their effluents to flow into waters of lakes or rivers in quantities that foul the waters and prevent safe swimming. Insufficiently treated sewage has caused the rivers and lakes near some of our big cities to become polluted. Regulations have been introduced recently forbidding pleasure boats over a certain size to dump their sewage in the waters they use.

In conjunction with the proposed changes in the Canada Shipping Act to control water pollution (Bill C-2), an attempt is being made to obtain U.S. agreement so as to lead to some international standards regarding sewage disposal from commercial vessels. Incidentally, this same bill will likely impose heavy fines for the discharge of oil or other pollutants and set up a fund to compensate anyone whose property is affected by such discharges, the money being obtained from a levy on oil imported into Canada.

Liability under the Act, as amended by the bill, would be absolute. No proof of negligence would be necessary, but there would be a limit of $140 per ton of the ship's tonnage with a total limit of $14 million. Of course it is not yet known what will be the final terms of the bill when passed. In the U.S. the Water Quality Control Act has been passed to handle similar matters though the Canadian bill appears broader in scope.

## Air Pollution

Another area of concern is over air pollution. In Toronto and many other large cities a special watch is kept on the extent of air pollution and when it reaches a certain level, industry is warned to reduce its activities. Recently a number of large concerns were cited as being warned about the extent of the emissions they were permitting and the press report stated that relatively speaking the emissions by smaller concerns were probably just as bad, but it was impossible to identify them individually.

Airlines can be seen every day trailing black smoke from their engines and this undoubtedly adds to the air pollution. Attempts are being made to reduce the extent of the fouling of the air from this cause. Then there is pollution from automobile exhausts. Los Angeles, for example, has had particular problems with smog and has taken steps against the pollution caused by automobile exhausts. Various devices have been developed by auto manufacturers to reduce the exhaust emissions and the intention is to make the installation of these compulsory in new model cars. Lead free gas, which has been the subject of advertising campaigns by certain oil companies and counter-campaigns by others, is another attempt to reduce the emissions from car exhausts.

Not only is water and air being polluted, but the ground and even the animals we use for food can be affected. Governments have become satisfied that DDT, although of great use in killing insects, is dangerous in large quantities and steps have been taken to ban its use.

The above gives some idea of the scope of the problem and the fact that it crops up in so many different situations.

## Public Interest Awakened

Some of the pollution which is now being so widely publicized is inevitable. It is the price of living in urban areas which supply the types of service and comforts to which we have become accustomed. Also, pollution has crept up over a period of generations and it will take a long time and a great deal of money to reverse the trend and improve matters to an acceptable level.

We have to face the fact that pollution is one of the social concerns of the day and a happy hunting ground for politicians. It's like motherhood; one cannot be against motherhood. Who can be against purer environment?

Just recently the Canadian Government announced the formation of a new department, to be controlled by the present Minister of Fisheries, that will be called the Department of the Environmental and Renewable Resources. This development appears to be in line with the increased interest in what is loosely called consumer protection. Industry of all kinds, I feel, is going to be under increasing pressure to reduce pollution and will be subject to considerable penalties where it seems to have fallen short.

Another trend which is appearing over the horizon in Canada is the "class action," a legal action by one or a few persons on behalf of a number of others having the same interest. The enormous suit arising out of the oil drilling spills off the California coast and that in the Gulf of Mexico are class actions.

Thus we have on the one hand a recent awakening of the public to the extent of pollution and the continued dramatization of this in the media coupled with legislative pressure on industry to reduce it by all possible means, and perhaps increasing opportunities for actions for damages where pollution does occur. It is this combination of circumstances which provides the background to the action taken by the insurers in restricting their policies.

## Position of General Liability Policies

I believe that we are going to see endorsements placed on most General Liability policies restricting the coverage provided in respect of pollution. This may become as routine as exclusions relating to nuclear risks.

Some policies will no doubt continue in force without any special restriction and it is well to consider how far pollution liability may be covered by these policies. Of course, we can only deal in general terms, but even this has some value.

First of all, inevitable damage is not covered under any type of wording. The relevant legal cases have usually been concerned with policies providing coverage on an accident basis. But even in policies extended to include occurrence basis property damage, there is normally some provision which requires that the damage must be unexpected.

Accordingly, a couple of Ontario decisions are relevant. The first one was Crisp v. Great American (CILR 1-046 1961) in which the insured contractor undertook to grind terazzo tiles at a customer's house. The contractor took virtually no precautions with the result that dust permeated throughout the house causing considerable damage to the furnishings. Although there was no doubt that the contractor was liable to the homeowner, he failed to recover under his Liability policy on the grounds that what he had done inevitably led to the damage. In the case of McCollum v. Economical Mutual (CILR 1-084 1962), the insured was cleaning the outside of a building by sandblasting. Some of the windows of the building were damaged in the very center, which indicated that the workmen had made no use at all of wooden shields which were provided to protect the windows. Again the decision was that no recovery was allowable since damage was virtually certain.

## Must Be Accidental

It, therefore, seems that coverage will not apply if an insured has made pollution damage virtually inevitable by his act or omission. Further, while unexpected damage will be covered, unless the insured takes prompt steps as soon as he realizes that damage has arisen, subsequent damage will not be covered.

With property damage coverage on an accident basis, some insurers maintain that an accident must take place at a specific point in time and if unintentional pollution occurred over a period of time without being discovered, the policy would not apply. While most insurance companies would use this contention, it is doubtful whether it is correct in law and I do notice that most of the endorsements relating to pollution, where they permit limited coverage, require what happens to be *sudden* as well as accidental, indicating that the word accident or accidental does not necessarily imply suddenness.

In summary and in general terms, if you have liability coverage without any special endorsement—and how long this state of affairs will be enjoyed is questionable—you almost certainly do not have coverage if the actions of your company inevitably lead to pollution and no reasonable steps have been taken to avoid it. If you have accident rather than occurrence basis property damage insurance you will be faced probably with a further contention that only a sudden happening is covered.

## Endorsements Limiting Coverage

A number of different endorsements are now being used by various insurers to limit or exclude their liability for pollution risks. They seem to have taken separate legal advice on what to say. Lloyd's produced one set of clauses, INA produced another, and still other versions have been set forth by Great American and other insurers. Perhaps eventually we shall have some type of standardization. In the meantime here is a general review of common features although it is most important to examine thoroughly the wording actually employed in a particular instance.

These endorsements generally exclude completely any liability in connection with the oil business and sometimes the gas business—often closely connected with oil.

As regards other types of risks, they tend to provide coverage for a happening which is accidental and sudden, although the exact wordings vary. Some spell out what is meant by pollution in detail (references to smoke, gases, alkalis, acids etc.) and some deal with it in general terms only, so that in examining a clause at least three questions should be borne in mind.

(1) Does it eliminate all coverage for pollution caused by oil and gas? If so, how is this phrased?

(2) Are pollution, contamination or other similar words defined and if so, in what terms? If not defined, how far would the general terms extend in the circumstances involved?

(3) Is coverage limited to sudden and accidental happenings?

## Short Term Phenomenon

Taking first the trades which are fortunate enough to have been left with some form of coverage, it seems clear that if damage is inevitable, owing to the actions of the insured, there is no coverage. As explained previously, this almost certainly exists even if there is no special endorsement, but the situation is now spelled out. It is usually stated that the damage must be *sudden* and this certainly is new to the majority of insureds who have property damage coverages on an occurrence basis. What seems to be the intent is to provide for some very short term phenomenon, for example, a breakdown in some filtering apparatus which permits the discharge of a pollutant into a river or a lake. How far the use of such a word as "sudden" limits the time during which damage must occur is uncertain, but it does seem that the insured must take prompt steps to remedy whatever led to the pollution. Perhaps some form of device which would give warning of pollution over the minimum acceptable limit is implied by the wording.

The imposition of these endorsements has been so recent that no cases on the subject have yet come to court which makes it virtually impossible, even for lawyers to say what their exact effect will be.

## What Can Be Done About Pollution

We are in the early stages of dealing with pollution as an insurance problem. There appears to be no change of an overall solution which would apply to all insureds. Rather, I believe that whenever the question of restricting or eliminating pollution liability coverage is raised by an insurer, and it is likely to be raised in virtually every instance where there is any chance of the risk arising, that each case must be dealt with on its own merits. We, if I may speak for a moment for our competitors in the agency and brokerage field as well as my own firm, will have to be very energetic on your behalf in making representations to the insurers and I am confident that we shall be.

You as risk managers should, I suggest, provide us with some additional ammunition. We shall have a much better chance negotiating if we can say that A.B.C. Company is very much alive to the pollution problem, although it is perhaps never had a claim made against it on these grounds. We should like to be able to say, for instance, something to the effect that a senior company official has been given the task of preventing pollution and that under his direction a special survey of the company's operations has been carried out to pin-point types of pollution which might occur and to eliminate any weak spots where it could take place. If definite amounts of money have been spent for special machinery such as filters of some sort, this would certainly be a help. We should also like to think that there is, if the circumstances are appropriate, some special monitoring device from which a warning is immediately given if an acceptable level is exceeded. If special investigation has been made by the company's research staff, or by some outside firm at its request, or perhaps by a trade association, with a view to changing methods so that pollution is made less likely, this too will be helpful.

If we can jointly put together a case which shows considerable activity by your particular group, then we can go to the insurer with a good hope of success. You may think that this sounds as though the insurer will only give cover when there is very little likelihood of a claim, but no amount of precaution will eliminate all chance of something going wrong and I suggest that the procedure I have outlined is in accordance with one of the basic risk management philosophies: to eliminate risks as far as possible and only insure what cannot be eliminated.

Probably insurers will gradually come to realize that the risk in some industries is far less than in others and we may be able to secure better terms for some of our clients accordingly. It may be that the use of considerable deductibles will eventually provide partial answers where insurers still oppose wide forms of coverage.

Out of our efforts to obtain improvements, we can hope there will gradually evolve a more logical and less restrictive approach to the problem of pollution as an insurable risk.

## Questions

1. The author indicates that exclusion of pollution-caused losses may be universal in the future. He raises the issue of doing this on a select industry-by-industry basis as compared to a universal exclusion under all policies. Why does he favor the former course?

2. If an industrial company conducts activities that inevitably lead to pollution and take no reasonable steps to avoid it, would any resulting liability be covered under the general liability policy, even if it is written on the occurrence basis? (Refer to the *Crisp v. Great American* case). Why?

# 22. PRODUCTS LIABILITY: LOSS CONTROL KEY TO CONTINUED COVERAGE *

A. Edward Thompson †

As risk managers you know about the rise and fall of "privity of contract," the implications and variations in court interpretation of "express" and "implied" warranties, the revision in the slogan "let the buyer beware" to "let the seller beware" the increasing number of plaintiffs' verdicts based on "failure to warn" decisions, down to our present position of practically "strict" liability in most instances and for most products. It is this idea of "strict" liability that creates many of our problems.

The direction which future laws will take will probably be influenced by the National Commission on Product Safety which was established by Congress in November 1967 to, among other things, "conduct a comprehensive study and investigation of the scope and adequacy of measures now employed to protect consumers against unreasonable risk of injuries which may be caused by hazardous household products. . . ."

The Commission was to explore:

1. "The extent to which insurance companies are seeking to stimulate the development of safety in the manufacture of household products, as against the possibility that insurers are giving less than full attention to this area and are willing to pass on to policyholders the resultant higher premiums.
2. "The adequacy of compensation of those insured; timeliness of civil remedy; statute of limitations problems; statutory ceilings on recovery, and related legal questions.
3. "Uniformity of common law remedies in different states; scope of manufacturers' distributors' and retailers' liability; effect of emerging doctrines of strict liability on manufacturers, distributors, retailers, and on consumers, and related questions in this area of legal issues.
4. "Efforts of individual companies to cure defects in design or manufacturing and prevent injury and avoid liability, including recall from the market and from home; effect of proof of compliance by the manufacturer with mandatory or voluntary standards; influence of criminal statutes on manufacturers' conduct; ramifications of imposing punitive standards.
5. "Effect of product warranties on liability and product safety."

* From *Risk Management* (February, 1971), pp. 13-19. Reprinted by permission.
† Assistant Vice President of Aetna Life & Casualty Insurance Company.

This Commission is presently in the process of drafting a "Uniform Consumer Products Liability Act" for presentation to and consideration by the states. Obviously many changes will be made before it is in final form and even then the individual states will go on to work on it. However some of the proposed wording makes me shudder—in fact, I contend that if it really becomes law in a majority of our states in essentially its present form—we will not be able to continue to provide Products Liability insurance as it is known today.

Several sections of this Act presently under review are quoted below:

*Section 102: Definitions*

(a) The term "product" or "consumer product" shall mean all products customarily sold at retail intended or used for personal, family, household, transportation, farming or recreational purposes.

(b) The terms "defect" or "defective condition" shall mean any aspect, feature or characteristic of a product or its design which causes physical or emotional injury or property damage.

(c) The term "seller" shall include the manufacturer of a product or of any of its components, the distributor, assembler, retailer, lessor, importer, and all other persons who contribute to the creation or dissemination of a consumer product.

(d) The terms "consumer" or "user" shall include one who uses, consumes, or is affected in any way by a consumer product and shall include bystanders who are injured thereby.

(e) The term "certifier" shall mean any party that places or allows to be placed on a product or in the advertisements or written sales materials concerning the product or in any other manner uses or allows to be used in connection with the product its seal, symbol, certification, guarantee or other endorsement pertaining to the safety of the product, or which may reasonably be understood to pertain to the safety of the product.

*Section 103: Strict Liability of Seller*

(a) A seller of any consumer product in a defective condition unreasonably dangerous to the user or consumer or to his property shall be liable for physical or emotional injury or property damage thereby caused if:

(1) the seller is engaged in the business of manufacturing, selling, assembling, distributing, retailing, leasing, importing, or otherwise contributing towards the creation or dissemination of a consumer product; and

(2) the product is intended to and does reach the user or consumer without substantial change in the condition in which it is sold.

(b) The rule stated in Part (a) applies even though:

(1) the seller has exercised all possible care in the preparation and sale of the product;

(2) the user or consumer has not bought the product from or entered into any contractual relation with the seller;

(3) the user or consumer has used the product in a manner other than that which was intended by the seller, so long as the actual use made of the product should reasonably have been anticipated by the seller and no adequate instructions for proper use or warnings against such reasonably foreseeable misuse were given to the consumer. In the case of toys

or other products intended primarily for use by or around children, no warning against reasonably foreseeable misuse shall be considered adequate;

(4) the product has been manufactured and assembled as designed and intended but the design of the product creates a defective condition unreasonably dangerous to the user or consumer. In the case of such a defective design, no warning by the seller will alter the liability under this Act;

(5) the user or consumer has failed to (i) inspect the product, (ii) discover the defect, (iii) guard against the possibility of the existence of a defect in the product or (iv) has otherwise contributed to the injury, other than assuming the risk or misusing the product as defined in Section 105.

*Section 104: Presumption*

(a) In the absence of proof of substantial change in the condition of a consumer product under Section 103 (a)(2) (for which the burden shall rest with the seller), proof by the consumer of a defect in the product at the time of the injury shall be deemed presumptive evidence that the defect existed when it left the seller's possession.

*Section 106: Defenses*

(a) Assumption of the risk shall be a defense to an action brought under this Act, if the user or consumer

(1) knew or reasonably should have known of the defect or defective condition; and

(2) knew or reasonably should have known the magnitude of the risk and the potential for harm presented by the defect or defective condition; and

(3) could reasonably have avoided exposure to said defect or defective condition.

(b) Misuse of the product shall be a defense to an action brought under this Act, only if

(1) the misuse was of a type which could not reasonably have been anticipated; or

(2) adequate warnings against the type of misuse causing the injury were supplied, provided that no warning shall alter the liability under this Act for defective design.

(c) Compliance with any Federal, state, local or voluntary safety code, standard or regulation applicable to the consumer product is not a defense to an action brought under this Act.

(d) Failure to comply with any Federal, state or local safety standard or regulation applicable to the consumer product shall constitute a defect or defective condition per se.

A further section to be known as "Class Actions" is still to be drafted. I shudder to think what this will do!!

Where are we headed? Against what has happened so far we see these statistics:

|  | 1960 | 1969 |
| --- | --- | --- |
| No. of claims | 35,000 | over 300,000 |
| Value of claims | $25,000,000 | over $100,000,000 |

Look also at the size of some recent awards:

- $25,000 for a fractured wrist when a backhoe tilted.[1]
- $90,000 for burns caused by a fertilizer.[2]
- $117,000 for amputation of a leg when a rotary lawnmower backed over it.[3]
- $220,000 for burns caused by a highly inflammable article of wearing apparel.[4]
- $322,000 against the seller and manufacturer for lacerations caused when a sight glass exploded.[5]
- $500,000 against the manufacturer for eye injuries from the use of a drug product.[6]

Try to relate the single $250,000 verdict resulting from a defect in one of your products to the profit per unit regardless of unit cost! Consider also the insurance rate per $1000 of sales which would be necessary to cover that one loss!

Our underwriting programs with respect to Products Liability are undergoing constant scrutiny and updating. We are requiring a much more thorough evaluation of the exposures of each account we insure, or expect to insure. A comprehensive survey, including the completion of a questionnaire, is required from our Engineering Department. In addition to an evaluation of the types of products involved, this survey deals in depth with the account's attitude toward loss prevention, quality controls, record keeping, warning labels used, etc.

In establishing future prices we are placing much less emphasis on past experience and concentrating more on what can be reasonably expected in the future. This has resulted in higher premiums and continued upward movement must be expected especially for excess limits and higher aggregates.

We have always contended that the larger commercial account could not expect to "sell" its "normal" losses to an insurance carrier at a profit. With the increasing value of Products Liability losses and the increasing frequency of such losses, it becomes evident that the self-retained limits (whether retrospective or otherwise) in insurance plans must go up. Some of our Products programs now require our insureds to self-insure (through retrospective plans) a minimum of $100,000 each claim and aggregates as high as $1,000,000 to $1,500,000 annually! Insurance must be used for the unexpected or catastrophe loss, and if the insured will not self-retain its normal losses there simply will not be capacity at realistic premiums for limits up to and even beyond $5,000,000.

---

[1] Sylestor vs. Warner & Swassey Co., CA-2 NY 1968.
[2] Land O'Lakes vs. Hungerholt, CA-8 Minn. 1963.
[3] South Austin vs. Thomison, 421 SW 2d 933.
[4] LaGorga vs. Kroger Co., 275 F Supp 373.
[5] Penn vs. Inferno Manufacturing Co. et al., 199 So 2d 210.
[6] Toole vs. Richardson-Merrell Inc., 60 Cal. Rptr. 398.

The last, but not least important item, in our Products underwriting program concerns loss control. The term "loss control" as here used encompasses both safety engineering, products loss prevention activities and a sound products claim defense program.

We all accept the importance of safety engineering and the part loss control programs have played in reducing both the frequency and severity of Workmen's Compensation accidents. I'm sure that few commercial insureds attempt to operate their businesses without giving some consideration to the safety of their employees while on the job. In fact, their Workmen's Compensation insurance carrier assists in the efforts as part of the service function of the insurance program. There is no question that it has proven sound financially, effecting savings not only in insurance costs but in operating expenses as well.

The concepts of applying these programs to the Products Liability field are not new, but they have been developed to only a very limited extent. Much more effort by both the insurance industry and the insured public must be expended in applying loss control principles to the production and distribution of products if Products Liability insurance is to continue to be available in any form. As is the case with other loss control efforts, we cannot expect to prevent or eliminate *all* accidents or losses which may result from the "products" exposure. Our objective will be realized if we in the insurance industry can, in cooperation with our insureds, reduce these loss producing potentials to an absolute minimum by use of control procedures.

## Loss Control Program

The model Loss Control Program involving close cooperation of the Underwriting Department, Engineering Department and Claim Department of the insurance carrier, with the insured, consists of nine basic elements:

**1. An efficient organization with full top management backing.** Management alone recognizes exactly how much is at stake in their total investment in plant and equipment, and a part of this investment must be their public image and good will. They control the advertising budgets which often run into the millions and are designed to promote the company's image and produce increased sales. Management must accept the responsibility to adopt and vigorously support a policy of producing the safest product possible, and establishing the necessary programs to be certain their policy is actually put into effective practice. It must be clear at all levels that the safety program and policy enunciated will *never* be sacrificed for any competitive reasons. The statements of management policy on this important subject must be explicit, positive and realistic; and they must be effectively communicated to the entire organization. If the organization is one of multiple operating divisions, each such operating division should establish its own divisional controls within the framework of the overall corporate program.

The best means of coordinating a Plant-wide Engineering Product Control Program is through a Product Loss Control Committee. Representation should include those areas or departments responsible for legal advice, design, engineering, production, quality control, advertising, and purchasing. The Product Loss Control Committee provides a channel for interdepartmental communication, and prevents accident reports, test results, complaints, and other information concerning the product's quality or safety from being filed away before corrections or improvements are made. A loss control coordinator is used sometimes in lieu of a committee. In such cases the coordinator must work directly with the various area or department representatives.

Once the "organization" has been developed it is vital that written statements of "policy" be disseminated to the entire organization. This must follow for each part of the program.

**2. Research and design controls, so that products are developed with the safety of the consumer in mind.** Product loss control begins with research and design. The manufacturer must keep abreast of the latest developments in engineering technology, so that he can build the utmost safety into his products. He must have qualified research and design personnel, who are kept up to date in their fields through constant training.

The manufacturer must try to foresee and eliminate all possible dangers that could arise from either normal or unusual use of his product. If a potential hazard cannot be engineered out of an item, or a back-up system provided, serious consideration should be given to the discontinuance of production and possible withdrawal of the product from the market. It is important that those responsible for developing manuals, sales literature, and advertising material be aware of potential hazards so they can take them into consideration when describing the product and its uses.

The insurance carrier's Engineering Department should be able to give assistance in evaluating the safety of a product. Most have research laboratories available for testing purposes. Bear in mind this must be a joint effort and in some instances an insurance engineer can pinpoint a source of danger which has been overlooked by plant technicians.

**3. Quality Control Procedures must be clearly delineated in writing with standard recorded reports required.** The manufacturer must establish procedures for controlling quality from raw materials to finished product. He should test raw materials and purchased components even though they have been certified as meeting the specifications outlined in the purchase orders. Many concerns conduct these tests in special quality control laboratories, or in sections of the research laboratories that have been set aside for the purpose.

The manufacturer should test a product in various stages of production, especially if critical sub-assemblies are involved. Final tests are necessary on each individual product or on representative samplings of the plant's output.

Testing procedures should be in writing, in accordance with accepted standards and thoroughly understood by all research and testing personnel. Permanent records should be maintained on all test results, as such procedures and test results may be important in the defense of any losses which ultimately occur.

**4. Manuals of use and installation must be carefully prepared with assistance from a competent legal staff.** Great care should go into developing maintenance, installation, assembly, operational and parts manuals.

This literature should describe procedures for minimizing wear and tear on the product, and show how often parts should be inspected or replaced. It should cite the product's limitations, warn of hazards that could not be engineered out, and stress the danger of not following printed manual procedures. The consequences of misuse should be emphasized.

To guard against misstatements regarding function, use, etc., the manufacturer should have his manuals reviewed by his legal staff before they are published. It should be reemphasized again that at no point in these efforts should "competitive" pressures be used as reasons for deviating from the basic purpose—the control of losses and product safety.

**5. Advertising and sales material must present a true picture of the product and have the approval of the legal staff.** Advertising and sales personnel must present a true picture of the product. This is important because a manufactuer can be held responsible for any promises that that he makes—through either an expressed or an implied warranty when he puts a product on the market. An expressed warranty is a promise or representation made at the time of the sale to induce a person to buy. Implied warranties arise from the sale itself as an assurance that the product is merchantable and fit for the purpose for which it is being sold.

The manufacturer should keep advertising and sales personnel up to date on the product, and should have advertising and sales material reviewed by his engineering and legal departments to avoid the danger of exaggeration.

The manufacturer should avoid using all-inclusive terms, such as "moisture proof", "tamper proof", and "completely non-toxic." "Resistant to moisture," "tamper resistant," and "non-toxic" are terms that can be defended more easily.

The Legal Department should be involved in a review of all advertising and sales material as it is produced. In many instances part of a plaintiff's claim will be based on statements contained in the advertising material used.

**6. Warning and instruction labels must be clear and unambiguous.** One of the most important functions of the Product Loss Control Committee or Coordinator involves the review of all warning and instruction labels to be used in connection with their products.

The program must be so designed that it will:

(a) Warn the public of any dangerous properties in the product which would not be apparent and understood in the absence of such disclosure. These warnings must apply to both use and disposal of the product or any part of it.

(b) Give the using public clear and unambiguous instructions and directions for use of the product for its intended purpose. Warnings of the dangers of misuse should be made clear also.

(c) Comply with all Federal and state statutes, national and local codes and trade association standards. Some of the federal acts involved are:
   (1) The Federal Food, Drug and Cosmetic Act.
   (2) The Federal Hazardous Substances Labeling Act.
   (3) The Federal Insecticide, Fungicide and Rodenticide Act.
   (4) The Child Safety Act.

It is important to have all labels and instructions reviewed by the Law Department and/or outside attorney familiar with products claims and labeling statutes.

**7. Packaging and shipping problems must be given proper consideration in relation to the product's peculiarities.** If the product is to reach the purchaser complete and in good condition, the manufacturer must package and ship it properly. He should use cartons designed to prevent damage, and adequately label them to guarantee safe handling. The manufacturer should compare the shipping invoice with the purchase order to be sure he ships all parts and material as ordered. He should also check to see that instruction and maintenance manuals are included.

Important in this section must be consideration to the protection of any shippers if the product has dangerous propensities which might be activated as a result of improper handling during shipping.

**8. All complaints and alleged accidents resulting in injury or damage must be promptly and adequately investigated and reports committed to writing.** The manufacturer should investigate each complaint that he or his representatives receive. He should report discovered flaws in the product to the engineering and production departments so that immediate steps can be taken to eliminate them. The manufacturer should keep a permanent record of each complaint, showing what corrective actions were taken and why.

If investigation reveals that a product is creating a hazard, it should— depending on the degree of danger—be withdrawn from the market, modified, or labeled with a warning to the user.

The Products Loss Control Committee or Coordinator must establish procedures and control devices to be certain that all complaints and reports of accidents are investigated fully and completely. All complaints should be reviewed by personnel who can distinguish a potential liability claim from a complaint. A complete analysis of complaints in many instances will reveal where the product needs improvement, defects in the quality control program, or labeling deficiencies. However, the investigation of complaints should be carried on so that they are not magnified into claims; but if it is indicated a potential claim exists it should be investigated promptly and completely.

Direct and immediate cooperation and communication with the Claim Department of the insurance carrier is essential. The adjuster and/or attorney will need full and complete technical data concerning the claim. Copies of quality control records will be important defense documents. Be assured that insurance company claim people are alert to the significance of products claims. They should be given all information immediately so that they may know when and how to pay a claim, if indicated, without damaging the good will of their insured.

In making the investigation for either a complaint or as the result of an alleged accident causing injury or damage, it is essential to develop sufficient details concerning any possible defect in the product and when such defect might have developed. Was it in existence when the product left the plant? Did some middleman create the defect? To what extent is there an indication of negligence on the part of the manufacturer? These are all questions which must be answered by the survey.

We must admit that all accidents will not be prevented—but the damages resulting from them can be controlled by proper, timely cooperation with the insurance carrier during the defense procedure.

9. **Appropriate written records must be maintained throughout the entire manufacturing process and any investigation procedures.** It is important to keep written records on each phase of production, from procuring raw materials to marketing the finished product. Test records should include dates conducted, reasons for rejection, action taken to correct any deficiencies, and identifying data. Records should also be kept to identify units or batches that have passed all tests successfully.

Records will assist the manufacturer in adjusting complaints, and will aid the insurance carrier in defending against unjust claims. Service records will also be helpful in future litigation, especially if the serviceman has noted and recorded negligence by the purchaser on other parts of the equipment. The manufacturer should permanently maintain all records of design information, raw materials and components, production, and final testing. He should also keep all purchasing and shipping papers.

The claim portion of the program must be involved at almost each step to be certain that whatever is done as a "loss preventive" measure will react favorably when the unforeseen accident occurs and a claims defense must be entered.

We cannot offer this as a panacea but I assure you that unless our industry accepts the responsibility to enforce some such program it may well find itself without any Product's insurance available.

You are aware of the great strides made by industry and their insurance carriers in reducing the incidence of work-connected injuries to employees which came about as a result of the development of statutory Workmen's Compensation laws. The same opportunity exists here, it seems to me, and you as risk managers have the obligation to see that your companies take the lead. In the long run the company that can effectively control its Products losses will have a distinct advantage over its competitor.

## Questions

1. Under the definition of "strict liability of the seller" the author believes that the insurance industry will not be able to provide products liability insurance as it is known today. Suggest reasons for this.
2. What types of loss control are recommended in the model program? How will this relate to the availability of products liability insurance?

# 23. INSURANCE AND INFLATION *

Ambrose B. Kelly †

Insurers deal with money. They collect premiums from their policy-holders, from which they pay present expenses and future losses. In many types of insurance such as life insurance, it may be many years after the insurance contract is issued before a claim must be paid. At any moment in time insurers are required to maintain capital, surplus and mandatory reserves proportionate to the business they are doing. Any change in the value of money, therefore, vitally affects their business.

I am certain that all of you understand what is meant by "inflation"—an economic condition in which prices are steadily rising for a period of time for a representative group of commodities or services. Inflation, long continued and of substantial aggregate effect, may so decrease the value of any currency in terms of other currencies or of gold that the government decides to recognize the change which has taken place by a currency devaluation. Such a devaluation may also be necessary in order to preserve or strengthen the economic condition of a country, particularly one which is heavily involved in world trade. This results in a change in the official rate at which the currency of any country may be exchanged for the currency of other countries or for gold, but it seldom makes a dramatic change in the purchasing power of the currency in question. International examples were the devaluation of the British pound in 1967 and that of the French franc in 1969—both moderate in extent. The economic history of the world, particularly in the past 60 years, would seem to indicate that some degree of inflation is to be expected each year. As the result of war or political or economic conditions, the value of a country's currency may be sharply reduced and currency devaluation may be necessary. Even though all economists are in agreement that inflation must be kept to about 2 percent or 3 percent a year to be manageable, it is a hard and unpleasant fact of existence that it is often much larger in extent.

A study has been made of currency development in 83 countries during the 10-year period from December 1956 to December 1966.[1] A sharp rise in the amount of money in circulation is, as a general rule, connected with an increased loss of the purchasing power of the currency. In the 10-year period under study, the money in circulation in

* From *Risk Management* (January, 1970), pp. 32-40. Reprinted by permission.
† General counsel for the Factory Mutual Companies.
[1] *Experiodica*, Vol. 3, No. 11.

Indonesia increased by 185,788 percent, the purchasing power in the same period fell to approximately 1 percent; in El Salvador the money in circulation increased only by approximately 6 percent, whereas the loss of purchasing power was nil. In the United States there was a 37 percent increase of monetary circulation, which was coupled with an 18 percent decrease in purchasing power. There are wide fluctuations, as already noted, in the extent of inflation, and the countries of the Americas illustrate both extremes. During the 10-year period which ended with 1966, there was a loss of purchasing power of 99 percent in Brazil and of 95 percent in Argentina and Uruguay. In the same period, Guatemala and El Salvador had no loss in the purchasing power of their currency, and in Nicaragua the change was less than 10 percent. Approximately one-half of all countries with a loss of purchasing power of more than 50 percent were in South America.

## EXHIBIT "A"

### AVERAGE ANNUAL INFLATION RATES 1960-1966

#### AMERICA

| | | | | | |
|---|---|---|---|---|---|
| El Salvador | 0 % | Canada | 2.0% | Greenland | 5.0%[6] |
| Venezuela | 0 % | Mexico | 2.2% | Bolivia | 5.1%[1] |
| Guatemala | 0.4% | Dominican Republic | 2.3% | Paraguay | 5.3%[1] |
| Panama | 9.4% | Puerto Rico | 2.4% | Peru | 9.3% |
| Netherlands Antilles | 0.8% | Trinidad | 2.4% | Columbia | 13.6% |
| British Honduras | 1.3% | Honduras | 2.5% | Argentina | 24.5% |
| USA | 1.6% | Surinam | 2.7% | Chile | 26 % |
| Costa Rica | 2.0% | Jamaica | 2.8% | Uruguay | 36 % |
| Guyana | 2.0% | Ecuador | 4.1% | Brazil | 60 % |
| Nicaragua | 2.0% | Haiti | 4.5% | | |

(1) 1960-1965
(6) 1960-1964

(Source: EXPERIODICA, Vol. 3, No. 11, Published by Swiss Reinsurance Company)

During the 6-year period from 1960 to 1966, the inflationary tides continued to sweep the world. Population growth led to demand for food and all kinds of raw materials, failure of supply to match the demand increased prices, and the rising price level had to be matched by wage increases to give the inflationary spiral new impetus. The development of price changes occurs unequally in a geographic sense, but the same fundamental factors affect all countries. The U.S., which had maintained a relatively stable economy after the Korean War, found inflationary trends constantly stronger after 1964. At the moment, the highest priority has been given by the Nixon Administration to efforts to control the present inflationary forces; tax increases, coupled with high interest rates, are being used to cool the boom and restrain business activity.

Despite these efforts, the increase in price levels continued unabated in the first half of 1969. The degree to which this problem is present throughout North and South America is shown very clearly by Exhibit A, giving the average annual inflation rates during the period from 1960 to 1966. We normally think of inflation as being some vague formless evil which increases prices, results in hardship to those living on a fixed income and works for the benefit of creditors and against debtors. The economists who study the problem are much more likely to feel that inflation is a fact of life which has been present many times in history and which is not going to go away. There are those who argue that some inflation is necessary to give emphasis to the economy and prevent unemployment.

In *The New Inflation,* by Willard Thorp and Richard Quandt, the statement is made, "Moderate inflation is not necessarily all bad, because it may encourage full employment and maintain economic growth. Monetary and fiscal policies are probably not adequate for dealing with inflation from other causes, because they are likely to arrest inflation at the cost of unemployment." [2]

Since inflation has been until recently a relatively minor factor in the United States economy, other countries have been much more concerned with the problems resulting from inflation, and their insurers have had to take steps to protect themselves at an earlier point in time. It has only been within the last few years that those analyzing the poor underwriting experience suffered by insurers in the U.S. have given sufficient attention to the effect of the inflationary spiral. It has had wider recognition in other countries.

In a very widely reprinted talk given by J.A.S. Neave on September 11, 1968, at the Monte Carlo Rendevous, of reinsurers he said: "There is a third major contributory factor to which reference is also made later, and this is the capricious and widespread influence of inflation, which affects the industry as a whole and reinsurers on the long end of the business more than most. In this situation we are the involuntary and somewhat passive victims of an influence on underwriting which in our long-term business is impossible to prevent and very hard indeed adequately to control."

He was dealing with the disastrous recent experience of reinsurers, which has been responsible for the shrinkage in capacity so evident today, but his remarks are also applicable to the direct insurers themselves. In any study of the effect of inflation on the insurance business, it must be realized that it does not fall with equal impact on the three major divisions of property insurance, life insurance and liability insurance. It must also be realized that reinsurers writing coverage on an excess basis are more vulnerable than insurers writing direct full coverage policies. The usefulness of the loss retention as a cushion between the reinsurance and the economic loss due to the occurrences diminished with every drop in the purchasing power of the currency.

---

[2] *The New Inflation,* Thorp and Quandt, Published by McGraw-Hill, 1959.

A property insurer assumes an obligation to indemnify a person with an interest in property in the event the property is damaged or destroyed over a future period of time by a described peril. In determining the amount of insurance to be purchased on the property, the person with an interest in it is normally dependent upon estimates of value made in the past. Quite commonly a current appraisal is not available and the amount of insurance purchased may be based on the cost of the property at an earlier period, without proper adjustment for increases in construction costs or the rise in the market value of the property. This is particularly true when dealing with residential property, but it may also occur with industrial, commercial or institutional risks.

Policies are written for an extended period in the future. In the United States the most common term for property insurance policies is three years and some policies are written for a period of five years. Quite obviously, if the property was insured for 100 percent of its value at the beginning of a 5-year term and there was an average annual inflation of 4 percent, by the end of the 5-year period the amount of insurance would represent less than 80 percent of the value of the property. Since most losses under property insurance policies are partial, the policyholder would collect his loss in full if it occurred in the fifth year, even though the premium paid would only have provided insurance to 80 percent of the value at the time of the loss.

As attorneys interested in insurance regulations and in the drafting of insurance contracts so that they will provide proper coverage under changing circumstances, we are naturally interested in those acts which can and should be taken to protect the policyholder and the insurer from inflationary forces. A survey of insurance statutes and regulations in the United States, however, disclosed that the thrust of insurance regulation is to protect the members of the public during a period of depression or devaluation.

When dealing with property insurance contracts, for example, the state legislatures, in statutes enacted 50 to 70 years ago, attempted to protect the unsophisticated purchaser from the agent or company wishing to over-insure the property in order to collect an excessive premium, with every intention of settling a loss which had occurred on the basis of actual value of the property at the time of loss. It was for this reason that several states adopted statutes whose effect was to require that in the event of a total loss of the property the insurer could not question the value or deny that the property was worth the amount for which it was insured.[3]

---

[3] The states of Arkansas, California, Florida, Iowa, Kansas, Kentucky, Louisiana, Minnesota, Mississippi, Missouri, Montana, New Hampshire, North Dakota, Ohio, South Carolina, South Dakota, Tennessee, Texas, West Virginia and Wisconsin have adopted statutes which provide that the insurer must pay the face amount of the policy in the event of a total loss of the property of the insured. The Wisconsin statute (§ 203.21, Wis. Ins. Code) is representative: "Whenever any policy insures real property and the property is wholly destroyed, without criminal fault on the part of the insured or his assigns, the amount of the policy shall be taken conclusively to be the value of the property when

In the same way, several states in the United States impose restrictions and regulations on the ability of an insurer to add a co-insurance clause to its policies. Under such a clause, the amount which will be paid by the insurer after a loss is the same proportion of the loss as the amount of the insurance placed on the property bears to the stated percentage of its actual cash value required under the provisions of the co-insurance clause. Thus, if an 80 percent co-insurance clause is used, it would be necessary for the property to be insured up to 80 percent of its value. If it were found after loss that the property was insured to only 50 percent of its value, the policyholder could recover only 5/8ths of the amount of the loss. Thirteen states have provisions which generally limit the writing of co-insurance in connection with Fire Insurance.[4]

The danger to the public, in the eyes of the insurance departments and state legislatures, was over-insurance. Such over-insurance might be the result of the aggressive sales approach of an agent, with the result that an honest insured would pay premium for insurance in excess of the value of his property. It might be the result of conscious planning by a dishonest insured, who expected to arrange for the destruction of his property by fire to his own profit. Consider the following sections of the Nebraska Insurance Law:

(§ 44-601) "It shall be unlawful for any insurance company or any agent to knowingly issue any fire insurance policy upon property within this state for an amount which, with any existing insurance, exceeds the fair value of the property or of the interest of the insured therein, or for a longer time than for five years, except as provided in § 44-812."

(§ 44-602) "It shall be unlawful for any party having an insurable interest in property located in this state to knowingly procure any fire insurance policy upon his interest in such property for an amount in excess of the fair value of his interest in the property, or for an amount which, with any existing insurance thereon, exceeds the fair value of his interest in the property."

---

insured and the amount of loss when destroyed." Some of the statutes provide that the property must be examined by an agent or other representative of the company within 90 days and the value agreed upon with the insured. If this is not done, the face amount of the policy is conclusively presumed to be reasonable and settlement made on that basis.

[4] Florida, Iowa, Kentucky, Louisiana, Michigan, Minnesota, Mississippi, Missouri, North Carolina, South Carolina, Texas, Vermont & Wisconsin. The Wisconsin statute (§ 203.22) is typical of those normally used and reads as follows: "Except as otherwise provided by law, no fire insurance company shall issue any policy in this state containing any provision limiting the amount to be paid in case of loss below the actual cash value of the property, if within the amount for which the premium is paid, unless, at the option of the insured, a reduced rate shall be given for the use of a coinsurance clause made a part of the policy. Any company may, by so providing in the policy, distribute the total insurance in the manner and upon as many items as specified therein, or limit the amount recoverable upon any single item, article or animal to an amount not exceeding the cost thereof, or to an amount specified in the policy. Any company, officer or agent violating any provision of this section shall upon conviction thereof, be punished by a fine of not less than $100 nor more than $500 and the license of such agent and company may be suspended for a period not exceeding one year." The suspicion with which such clauses are regarded is indicated by statutes requiring that the policy give notice on its face, sometimes in red ink, that the policy contains a Co-Insurance Clause.

There is no corresponding concern over under-insurance, even though it might result in the payment of substantially less than the value of the insured property in the event of a total loss. The states have also disregarded the average rate inadequacy which would result from consistent under-insurance. It has been the feeling of insurance department personnel reviewing rate filings that responsibility for the preparation of rate modifications that would be calculated using trend factors based on inflation was squarely on the insurers and their rating bureaus. If such factors were used in the development of rates, they would be carefully considered but, if they were omitted, the rating supervisors would not be concerned.

The problem of adjusting the amount of insurance for changes in the purchasing power of the currency was recognized in Europe long before it was in the U.S. The policies used in many countries provide for an automatic adjustment of sums insured proportionate to the movement of an agreed index, which may be geared to changes in prices or wages, the cost of construction or any other yardstick acceptable to insurers and policyholders.

## Indexation Clause

In 1960 a comprehensive survey of the use of such a clause in Europe was made by Mr. Robert Beinex.[5] He found that an indexation clause, similar to that used in France, was also used in Germany, Spain, Norway and Sweden, but it was not generally used in Austria, Belgium, Denmark, Greece, Italy, Luxembourg, Switzerland or Turkey. Since that time, there has undoubtedly been a wider use of such clauses in other countries as the problem has been more generally recognized.[6] It will be most interesting to the members of the United States delegation to learn from our colleagues in the other countries of the Americas what steps have been taken by them to provide adequate coverage and adequate premium during periods of inflation and currency devaluation.

---

[5] *L'Assurance Indexee en Europe*, M. Robert Beinex, May 1960.

[6] In France an Indexation Clause is used which gears the sum insured to a cost of construction index. The policies provide for an automatic adjustment of the sums insured proportional to the movement of the index. Furthermore, the insurance of simple risks in France is available in a form where no sum insured is determined at all, the premiums being expressed as a function of other factors, such as the number of rooms, the size of the apartment, the surface cover of the building, etc. These premiums are also adjusted automatically to the movement of the cost of construction index. The problem has been considered in most other European countries which have used similar clauses. Switzerland has recently adopted the use of an automatic adjustment clause which can be roughly translated as follows: "This insurance has been contracted when the cost of construction index as published by the statistical bureau of—was at—points. The sum insured is automatically increased proportionately to the increase of the said index, subject, however, to a maximum of 30%. This arrangement to be in force for a period not exceeding five years, after which the sum insured and the cover for further cost of construction increases shall anew be agreed upon."

The United States insurance companies have been very slow to provide such an indexation clause. Its first use has been in the field of homeowners coverage, and several companies in 1968 and 1969 announced that their homeowners policies would be endorsed to provide an automatic increase in the amount of insurance of 1 percent every three months, or an automatic increase of 4 percent a year. This is the first tardy recognition through contractual change by United States property insurers of the economic facts of life.[7]

In the rating of property insurance, it is obvious that inadequate coverage results in inadequate premium, which in turn results in an underwriting loss to the companies. The rating bureaus have realized that inflationary trends must be taken into account in determining future rates. They have attempted to compensate for the inflationary factors by including in their rate calculations a trend factor based on the expected rate of inflation. Some of the regulatory authorities who have a responsibility for reviewing and approving rates have been willing to approve the use of such trend factors when they can be justified. In some cases the trend factors have been disapproved and in others the use of such factors has been permitted for the current year only.[8] It is obvious, however, that rates made on past experience, when average rates of inflation were less than one-half of those currently existing, are almost certainly inadequate when the inflationary spiral accelerates. In commenting on the unfavorable underwriting result in property-liability insurance, an Industry Advisory Committee to the National Association of Insurance Commissioners said, "It is attributable in varying degrees to inflation, a series of seven catastrophes, defects in the premium rating process, high and rising damage judgments and changing patterns of social and personal responsibility." [9]

## Impact on Multi-National Operations

Up to this point we have been concerned with the problems faced by an insurance company, most of whose business is transacted in its own country. In such case of course, the economy moves as a unit and the insurer, being a part of the national economy, is carried along on the business stream, with compensating advantages and disadvantages whenever the value of currency changes. Some attention should be given to the situation in which an insurer finds itself when it is doing business in several countries which have varying degrees of inflation or currency devaluation. Some of its reinsurance contracts may be

---

[7] This is very similar to the practice of providing an automatic increase of insurance on household contents followed in some European countries. A Swiss clause reads: "At inception of each new policy year the sum insured is increased by 5% of the basic amount originally declared in this policy. In the same way the original premium is also increased by 5% per year."

[8] In Pennsylvania the trend factors extend only to January 1, 1970.

[9] "Report of the Industry Advisory Comm. to the (D1) Sub-comm. the NAIC on Holding Company Legislation." Dec. 2, 1968.

expressed in local currency, some in soft currency and some in hard currency. If it is operating in South America it may be writing some important business in United States dollars or other hard currency, especially for North American interests. At the moment of governmental devaluation, it may have funds abroad in foreign currency, have some hard currency assets, and owe reinsurers balances on account. Claims will be in process of settlement on either direct or reinsurance contracts.

In discussing these problems in the *International Insurance Monitor*, Charles E. Howe made the following comments:

"The insurance written in national currency on properties, for fixed sums and for fixed periods, will continue unchanged in amounts, save where a devaluation clause has been incorporated into the contract; in this last-mentioned case, the sum insured will automatically readjust to the new exchange level in accordance with the terms of the clause, up to any maximum limit imposed. Such readjustments, however, are few and far between. If, as is probable, property insurance incorporates a 100% co-insurance clause, insured will be under-insured, especially in respect of all imported goods and machinery or raw materials which require imported parts or portions. This situation may be put right as soon as business reopens, and the premium will be pro rata for the period of additional cover.

"Where the insurance is written without a co-insurance clause, which is usually the case in covering automobiles, some fire business, some theft business, fidelity and similar classes of property insurance, the effect of devaluation will be to increase claim payments without additional premium compensation.

"For a number of property policies issued on a monthly reporting basis, changes in values of goods will raise the sums to be declared and produce higher claims against earned premiums. As the insured find themselves confronting the upward trend of declarations, they may find it necessary to call for additional amounts of insurance in good time to avoid co-insuring. Reinsurances will then be ceded for higher amounts.

"In most of the cases covered by devaluation, retentions for company accounts will remain unchanged in national currency, and the amounts ceded to reinsurers will increase. And although new claims will increase in national amounts, there will be a lag in the payment of fixed back claims." [10]

There are some conclusions which can be drawn from the material presented.

• Inflation, or currency devaluation, is a substantial factor in determining the operating results of property insurers. Unless its effect is anticipated and compensated for in both rating procedures and policy contracts, it will have an adverse effect on their results.

• Insurers in the United States, because of the relative price stability in earlier years, have been slow in recognizing the effect of inflation on their business.

---

[10] C. E. Howe, *International Insurance Monitor*, Vol. XXII, No. 11, Nov. 1968.

● The insurance statutes and regulations of the United States have been concerned with the prevention of over-insurance and have not given equal attention to the problems which result during a period of chronic under-insurance.

● Other countries have adopted contractual provisions for the automatic adjustment of insurance contracts in a period of inflation which are just beginning to be used in the United States and which will become increasingly important if inflation continues.

● An insurer operating in a number of countries must be constantly aware of the economic trends so that necessary steps may be taken through adjustment of insurance, reinsurance or investments to protect itself during a period of inflation.

## Life Insurance

The very nature of life insurance requires the accumulation of reserves over a long period of time so that the insurer may meet its obligations when they mature under outstanding policies. Reserves are much greater in proportion to premium than is the case with property or liability insurance. If the funds of the life insurance company are invested in securities or other assets whose value reflects changes in the price level, the life insurance company may improve its financial position during inflation, since its obligation is normally expressed in terms of a fixed amount to be paid the named beneficiaries on the death of the policyholder. The whole problem of currency devaluation in life insurance was considered by the Society of Actuaries in April 1968. At that time Dr. Irving Pfeffer, leading the discussion of the subject said:

"Logically, the position of the life insurance industry ought to be that of a rational creditor; a rational creditor, in a period of the type we are describing, should be shifting out of fixed-interest obligations which are pegged into obligations having a greater variable factor. The proportion of total assets of life insurance companies invested in United States government bonds is one indicator of this kind of shift. In 1945 the life insurance industry had 45.9% of its total admitted assets in United States government bonds, 21.0% in 1950, 9.5% in 1955 and 5.4% in 1960. In 1965 the percentage was 3.4%. The move was clearly out of the fixed-interest, hard-bound type of security into other things, primarily mortgages. Mortgages had some equity characteristics because of prepayment penalties and the relatively short turnover period of what looked like long-term mortgage instruments." [11]

## Holding Companies

Dr. Pfeffer also called attention to the impetus which steady inflation had given to the drive to create holding companies in an attempt to escape from the investment restraints that had been imposed on life

---

[11] "Transactions of the Society of Actuaries." Vol. XX, April, 1968.

insurance companies as a result of the Great Depression (1929 to 1933). A study made of the effect on life insurance portfolios of the decline in value of equity investments gave rise to stringent restrictions on such investments for life and other insurance companies. As Dr. Pfeffer said, "Breaking the shackles of this kind of outmoded legislation has proved too great a burden to bear for the insurance industry; consequently, holding companies have been the logical response."

In the discussion which followed, attention was paid to the effect on life insurance companies when the home office was located in a country which had experienced a currency devaluation. Speaking of the experience of the Canadian branch of a British life insurance company, it was pointed out that the effect of the devaluation may be offset in whole or in part by the appreciation of the company's assets which were held in equity-type investments.

Mr. Donald J. Leapman, discussing this point, said, "The proportion of life insurance funds invested in such assets in the United Kingdom has been much greater than is usual in North America. This is due perhaps to the considerable inflation which has continued in the United Kingdom since the end of World War II but also to the insurance legislation which permits each company to determine the constitution of its own investment portfolio without restriction. Also lacking are very discriminatory asset-valuation procedures, which may create an artificial preference for certain investments by reason of such procedures rather than per se."

Mr. Leapman also commented that, "The ability to invest to a high degree in equity-type assets is of prime importance in offsetting inflation from devaluation. While it is uncertain how quickly common stock values will respond to such inflation (since for a time profit margins may be reduced), investments in 'bricks and mortar' should respond more rapidly."

It would seem, from these comments, that inflation or currency devaluation will only be a major problem for a life company if restrictions on its investments have made it impossible for it to arrange its investment portfolio to avoid fixed-amount obligations which would be reduced in real value by devaluation. At the same meeting, Gerald M. Brown of the Manufacturers Life Insurance Company, in discussing the effect of sterling devaluation, said:

> "The immediate effects of devaluation on life insurance are rather small. The morning after devaluation the currency locally is unaltered, and it is only in export-import matters that an immediate change is felt. Since devaluation is part of a long process, the idea that the local currency is not necessarily a strong currency may accelerate a gradual change already in process. The factors leading up to devaluation—gradual depreciation, cost-of living increases, and so forth—tend to promote larger sums assured, swings to lower premium plans, and, where possible, equity investments. These trends are furthered by devaluation and the cost-of-living increase which inevitably follows.

"The effects on insurance of the sterling devaluation last November (1967) follow the theory. There has been in the United Kingdom for some time a trend toward larger policies and lower premiums, as well as a rapid development in a variety of equity products. These trends have continued in the five months since devaluation with possibly even more emphasis on the equity items. However, the change in Britain's insurance markets and possibly even its devaluation are closely tied into the dramatic shift in incomes in the last ten years. The rapid increase of the middle-income group in Britain has opened up a large insurance market and has increased average policies.

"The above comments apply to a country where devaluation is a somewhat unique and startling event. An example of another form of devaluation would be Israel, where money has depreciated at more than 5% per annum over the last tcn years. Here depreciation must be looked upon as continuous devaluation and its effects met in other ways. Many Israeli companies sell indexed insurances, where the premiums, values, death benefits, and so forth, are tied in with the local government index. The premium income for these policies is invested in Israeli-indexed government bonds. The Manufacturers Life has attempted to avoid the problems in that approach by issuing a basic fixed-amount policy with a rider permitting purchase of evidence-free additional insurance, whenever Israeli currency has depreciated 20% in terms of United States dollars. The policy has been quite successful, and a number of policyholders have taken advantage of the rider."

In conclusion, it would seem that there is no apparent need for any change in contractual provision or government regulation to protect life insurers or their policyholders from inflation or currency devaluation. However, as the trend towards variable equities and mutual funds has indicated, the public, conscious of the degree to which the value of fixed-amount life insurance is lessened in a period of inflation, may very well switch to other types of investment for protection against financial hardship in the future.

## Liability Insurance

The problems of liability insurers differ from those of property and life insurance, primarily because of the long time lag between the occurrence which gives rise to a claim and the actual determination of the amount which must be paid. The rates charged for liability insurance are an actuarial attempt to determine the monetary value, including cost of defense, of handling claims in the future based on the experience of the past. In a period of inflation, the average value of all outstanding casualty claims increases with any change in the general price or wage levels. Attention has also been called by many students of the problem to what is termed "super-imposed inflation."

This is the tendency of large claims, already affected by price inflation, to become still larger through the effect of less-obvious inflationary forces arising out of a wide variety of new influences associated with the changing society in which we live, such as the advances in medical science which make it possible for long-term disability cases to have a much longer life expectancy than would have been true a few years ago. Not only may the annual costs be expected to increase in proportion to the increase in the cost of medical services generally, but they will continue for much longer periods of time.

A further complicating factor is a tendency of the courts to allow larger and larger sums of money in serious cases. There has been a steady broadening of the legal principles which determine liability for negligence and a liberal construction of policy provisions. In consequence, liability insurance, in a period of inflation like that of the last several years, suffers not only from the impact of normal changes in the price level but must also cope with those changes resulting from medical progress and changes in court attitude. In considering liability insurance it must always be kept in mind that the reinsurer, particularly where reinsurance is written on an excess basis, will suffer even more than the primary insurer.

The first loss retention of the insurer was intended to shield the excess of loss reinsurer from ordinary losses, with the reinsurer only called on for payment in the exceptionally heavy claim. As the cost of claims increases, there will be many more losses above the pre-agreed deductible and the reinsurer will find itself paying an increasing share of the total loss. Realizing the cumulative effect of a small average inflation, reinsurers are more and more requiring an indexation clause which will ensure that the values prevailing at treaty inception will be maintained until the final settlement of all excess losses occurring during the treaty period.

## Wage Vs. Cost of Living Index

As was pointed out by W. Mantel of the Swiss Reinsurance Company, the effectiveness of an indexation clause naturally depends largely upon the index chosen.[12] The predominant yardstick for the application of the indexation clause in Europe has been the official cost-of-living index. In many cases the loss emanates from serious bodily injuries for which the amount of the claim is dependent upon the index development. Studies have been made of the variation between an index based on wages as compared with cost-of-living. The study made by Mr. Mantel included the development of the cost-of-living index and a wages index in seventeen countries.

Using 1958 as "100," he found that in the five-year period from 1956 to 1966 there not only had been a substantial increase in both indexes, but that in almost every case the increase in the wage index was substantially higher than that in the cost-of-living index. It was also notable

---

[12] "Influences of Inflation," Will Mantel, *International Insurance Monitor,* Vol. XXII, No. 1, January 1968.

that for most countries the pace of inflation has increased in the past five years and the average growth rate per year was much higher in the period from 1961 to 1966 than it was in the period from 1956 to 1961.

Granting that the elements which make up the problem are known, it is much more difficult to suggest steps which might be taken by insurers to protect themselves. A study made by the American Mutual Insurance Alliance indicates that between 1962 and 1967 automobile repair costs jumped 44 percent country-wide. During the same period, hospital room charges increased 54 percent, doctors' fees were up 22 percent and median family income rose 35 percent.[13] Despite these inflationary pressures, automobile bodily injury rates increased only 19 percent. Is it any wonder that underwriting losses continue to be a chronic drain upon the assets of liability insurance companies?

There is one area in which inflation falls with equal effect upon all types of insurers. As was pointed out, insurance codes have always shown a preference for investments in fixed-interest obligations and have looked with suspicion upon investments in equity securities. It has been almost axiomatic that a fixed amount obligation issued by a government or a solvent private corporation was to be preferred to a security which merely indicated a participation by the holder in the ownership of a corporation. Detailed investment codes, like those found in the insurance laws of New York, often limit the percentage of the company's assets which may be invested in equities.[14] Such an investment philosophy, based on economic conditions no longer existing, puts the entire insurance business in the United States in a difficult position when it is trying to arrange its investment portfolio to handle the problems which result from inflation.

In a report, the Industry Advisory Committee to the National Association of Insurance Commissioners found, in the desire to secure freedom from such investment restrictions, a principal reason for the trend toward the creation of holding companies. The committee said, "Three major trends have impelled insurers to diversify their activities. The first is a long-term secular trend of inflation which has accelerated in the past two decades and has become acute since 1963. Continuing deterioration in the purchasing power of the dollar has quickened public interest in and the market for equity-based investments as a hoped-for hedge against inflation." [15]

The need for review of investment laws so that obsolete restrictions can be removed is being recognized. Yet change will almost certainly be slow. Unwilling to wait for such developments, the insurance business in the U.S. is increasingly using the holding company device as a means

---

[13] "What's Really Causing the Boost in Your Automobile Insurance Bill," published by American Mutual Insurance Alliance, 1969.

[14] Article V, Chap. 28 of Consolidated Laws of New York.

[15] "Report of Industry Advisory Comm. to (D1) Sub-committee of the NAIC on Holding Companies," Dec. 2/68, NAIC Proceedings, 1969, Vol. 1, Page 176.

of securing the investment freedom it feels is required in an inflationary period.

This paper has been concerned with the manner in which the insurance business has been affected by inflationary forces. There can be no doubt that insurance can fulfill its function in society in a period of inflation and that alert management, with the cooperation of regulatory authorities, can compensate adequately for changes in the price level or the effect of currency devaluation. To do so, however, requires willingness to recognize the existence of inflationary forces and their continuance over a period of time. The problems suffered by insurers in modifying rates and contracts show that insurance executives, accustomed to a period of price stability, may find it difficult to adjust their thinking to today's conditions. Unhappy with the world as it is, they continue to feel optimistically that price stability can be reestablished so that other action on their part will not be necessary. In the light of the experience of the past five years in the Americas, there would seem to be no ground for such continued wishful thinking.

## Questions

1. Why may inflation reduce the profits of an insurer of buildings against physical loss by fire?
2. How have some countries handled the inflation problem as it affects owners of buildings?
3. How is the effect of inflation alleviated for insurers issuing policies with co-insurance clauses? Is this an acceptable solution for the insured?

# PART 7
## Life Insurance

Life insurance is the largest single element of the private insurance industry in the United States. It channels billions of savings dollars into the capital markets each year, providing investment growth of our economy. This segment of the industry is also perhaps the most visible segment to the college-age student, being typically the first overt insurance buying decision this person is invited to make. Likewise, it is a decision involving a planning horizon many years greater than this person is typically concerned with to this point in life. These features combine to make the life insurance section of any risk and insurance textbook or course a section that justifiably consumes a substantial portion of the student's effort and time.

This part presents a selection of papers focusing on several important areas of life insurance. Professor Mehr projects the industry to the year 2000 in the first article, based on many years as a teacher and student of the topic. Professors Olson and Winklevoss, in the second article, describe proposals to design life insurance to protect against the risk of inflation. The part concludes with an article by Professor Belth, who considers the point of view of the consumer.

# 24. LIFE AND HEALTH INSURANCE— THE YEAR 2000 *

Robert I. Mehr †

and Seev Neumann ††

This paper summarizes some aspects of a broader research effort dealing with long range effects of inflation, advancing technology and growth of the institution of private insurance in the United States.[1] Of concern here are only those aspects relating to the forecasted shape of the life and health insurance industry in the year 2000.

## THE METHODOLOGY

The forecasts reported here represent the median of the distribution of the individual forecasts of a panel of experts, arrived at via the Delphi Technique. The Delphi Technique involves interrogating panel members several times. First, a questionnaire is sent to each panel member and their responses are tabulated and classified. Next each panel member is sent a summary of initial responses and asked to reconsider his answers and revise them if he wishes. For responses to questions on the second time around that deviate significantly from the norm of the initial responses by falling outside the interquartile range, the panel members are asked to explain why their judgment is atypical. Then each panel member is sent the second-round results with a summary of the reasons given in support of deviating opinions. Panel members are asked to reconsider their second-round responses in the light of these responses and respondents are asked why they were unimpressed with the arguments supporting extreme positions at the opposite end of the spectrum. These reactions are summarized and sent to panel members for a final opportunity to change their responses. The median of the fourth-round responses is taken as the consensus of the panel.

These four rounds of interrogation took place in 1968-1969 and involved 58 panel members. The panelists were drawn from scholarly

---

* From *The CLU Journal* (October, 1971), pp. 11-18. Reprinted, with permission, from the JOURNAL of the American Society of Chartered Life Underwriters, Volume XXV, No. 4 (October, 1971). Copyright 1971 by the American Society of Chartered Life Underwriters, 270 Bryn Mawr Avenue, Bryn Mawr, Pa. 19010.

† Professor of Finance, University of Illinois, Urbana-Champaign.

†† Member of the faculty at the Graduate School of Business, University of Tel Aviv, Israel.

[1] Robert I. Mehr and Seev Neumann, *Inflation, Technology and Growth: Possible Implications for Insurance* (Bloomington, Indiana: Bureau of Business Research, Graduate School of Business, Indiana University, 1971).

institutions, government bodies, corporate insurance buyers, journalists, and top executives of both property-liability and life-health insurers. The panelists were provided with background material on the American economy, on possible technological developments and historical facts about the insurance business for the period 1950-1966. Panelists were encouraged to draw on whatever means they could employ in arriving at their forecasts. In fact, forecasts submitted by a number of panelists were based on deliberations and analyses involving staff members of their organizations.

## THE INSURANCE INDUSTRY IN GENERAL

1. It is expected that by the year 2000 the insurance industry still will be segmented into the traditional branches of life-health insurance and property-liability insurance; that life-health insurers will hold 80 percent of total admitted assets of insurance companies and will collect 55 percent of insurance industry premiums; and that property-liability insurers will hold 20 percent of total admitted assets of insurance companies, and will collect 45 percent of insurance industry premiums. These are the percentage distributions of 1966.

Of special significance, however, is that a quarter of the panelists anticipate that all-lines insurers will collect 5 percent or more of the total premium volume and will hold 4 percent or more of total admitted assets of insurance companies. About 20 percent of the panelists anticipate that all-lines insurers will collect 29 percent or more of the total premium volume and will hold 25 percent or more of total admitted assets of insurance companies. These panel members believe that competitive pressures will force insurers to abandon the traditional demarcation between life and property insurers. They anticipate that those life insurers with highly developed group merchandising and underwriting facilities will extend their group activities into property-liability insurance, as expected changes in the regulatory climate make this step possible. While the anticipation generally is that the legal distinction between life-health and property-liability insurers will continue, it is expected that there will be increased activity among all-lines groups. While in 1965 the percentage of total premiums written for all lines of insurance by the 40 leading all-lines groups was 39 percent, the consensus of the panel was that all-lines groups will dominate the insurance business in the year 2000, with 55 percent of total insurance industry premiums collected by the leading 40 all-lines groups.

Taking into account the smaller all-lines groups and the continued development of the "total financial services" concept, it is reasonable to anticipate that a percentage much higher than 55 percent of total insurance industry premiums will be paid to insurers who will be members of all-lines groups.

2. The percentage of total insurance premiums written by the leading companies in life-health insurance business may indicate the degree of

concentration within this industry. The percentages of total insurance premiums written in 1966 by the 20 leading companies in life-health insurance (ranked by total admitted assets), was 59.6 percent. The forecast is that the premium writings will be more heavily concentrated among the 20 leading companies in the industry. In the year 2000, the 20 leading life-health insurers will control 63 percent of the total life-health insurance premiums.

3. Social insurance expenditures in the United States in 1966 amounted to about 3.8 percent of Gross National Product. These are comprised of total expenditures for old-age, survivors, disability, health insurance, and health insurance for the aged. Premiums paid to life-health insurers amounted to about 4.7 percent of Gross National Product. These figures may indicate the relative importance of private and social insurance. It is anticipated that by the year 2000 social insurance will be the predominant form of insurance, with expenditures for social insurance more than doubling as a percentage of GNP, rising to 7.75 percent. The increase in social insurance expenditures will not be at the expense of private insurance expenditures; private insurance expenditures will more than keep pace with the real growth of the economy, being 7.7 percent of GNP in the year 2000 as compared to 7.6 percent in 1966. Life-health insurance premiums will equal 4.5 percent of GNP and property-liability insurance premiums will equal 3.2 percent of GNP in the year 2000. At that year, the public sector of insurance is, thus, expected to be larger than the private sector.

4. The relative importance of group coverage can be measured by the percentage of the total amount of life insurance in force written on a group basis, the percentage of total private health insurance premiums written on a group basis, and the percentage of the total annuity income in force written on a group basis. Table 1 shows these percentages for the year 1966 and those anticipated for the year 2000.

TABLE 1

GROUP INSURANCE AS A PERCENTAGE OF TOTAL INSURANCE

| Covers | 1966 | 2000 |
|---|---|---|
| Life Insurance in Force | 35% | 50% |
| Health Insurance Premiums | 65% | 76% |
| Annuity Income in Force | 80% | 85% |

The forecast is that group coverage will represent a larger share of insurance covers, indicating a growing importance of the group mechanism for the merchandising of private insurance.

## LIFE INSURANCE

1. A higher percentage of disposable personal income will be used for life insurance premiums and annuity considerations in the year 2000

than in 1966: 4.0 percent compared with 2.87 percent. Based on this percentage, the total amount of life insurance premiums and annuity consideration in the year 2000 expressed in 1965 dollars will be between $62.4 billion (low projection) and $103.9 billion (high projection).[2] The following would be the low projections and the high projections expressed in current dollars for the year 2000 assuming various average annual rates of inflation:

| Average Annual Rate of Inflation | Low Projection (In Billion $) | High Projection (In Billion $) |
|---|---|---|
| 2% | 191.5 | 319.0 |
| 3% | 268.9 | 448.1 |
| 4% | 377.1 | 628.4 |

These projections for the year 2000 compare with $19.6 billion for 1966 and $24.3 billion for 1969.

2. The total premiums collected by life insurers includes life insurance premiums, annuity consideration, and premiums collected by the health insurance departments of life insurance companies. The breakdown of total premiums in the year 2000 is anticipated to be significantly different from that for 1966, as illustrated in Table 2.

TABLE 2

PREMIUM INCOME OF U.S. LIFE INSURANCE COMPANIES

| 1966 | Total | Life Insurance Premiums | Annuity Consideration | Health Insurance Premiums |
|---|---|---|---|---|
| $ billion | 126.5 | 17.2 | 2.4 | 6.9 |
| Percent | 100.0% | 64.9% | 9.1% | 26.0% |
| 2000 Low | | | | |
| $ billion (1965 dollars) | 95.9 | 48.0 | 14.4 | 33.5 |
| High | | | | |
| $ billion (1965 dollars) | 159.8 | 79.9 | 24.0 | 55.9 |
| Percent | 100.0% | 50.0% | 15.0% | 35.0% |

---

[2] In 1965 U.S. dollars, the low projection for GNP for the year 2000 is $2,177 billion and the high projection is $3,628 billion. These projections are based on 131 million people working 1600 hours a year producing a total of 210 billion man hours of work for the year 2000. In 1965, one man-hour of work yielded $4.73 in GNP. The high projection assumes that the yield per man-hour worked will increase at an average annual rate of 4 percent reaching about $17.1 in the year 2000. The low projection assumes an average annual increase of 2.5 percent reaching about $10.6 in the year 2000. See H. Kahn and A. Wiener, *The Year 2000, a Framework for Speculation on the Next Thirty-Three Years* (New York: MacMillan Company, 1967).

The expectation is that annuities will grow in relative importance among life insurance products. Annuity considerations and health insurance premiums will generate one half of the premium income of life insurance companies in the year 2000. The increased proportion of health insurance premiums to total premium income of life insurance companies results from the forecasts of an intensification of the trend of the concentration of health insurance writings in life insurance companies and a further reduction in the proportion of health insurance premiums written by property-liability and monoline companies. Also it reflects the forecast that insurers, in comparison with the Blue Cross and Blue Shield type plans, will write an increasing proportion of the medical care coverage.

3. The expectations are that variable annuities will contribute to an increasing proportion of annuity considerations relative to life and health insurance premiums collected by insurers. The much greater growth of the variable annuity in relation to the fixed dollar annuity is indicated by the forecast that 40 percent of annuity considerations in the year 2000 will be for variable annuities, as compared with an insignificant percentage in 1966.

4. Families will own 50 percent more life insurance relative to disposable personal income than they owned in 1966: 3:1 in the year 2000 compared with 2:1 in the year 1966. Life insurance in force in legal reserve life insurance companies in the year 2000 is projected, assuming 1965 dollars, to be between $4,677 billion (low) and $9,794 billion (high). The following would be the low projections and the high projections expressed in current dollars for the year 2000 assuming various average annual rates of inflation:

| Average Annual Rate of Inflation | Low Projection (In Billion $) | High Projection (In Billion $) |
|---|---|---|
| 2% | 10,280 | 17,131 |
| 3% | 14,443 | 24,068 |
| 4% | 20,252 | 33,748 |

The projections for the year 2000 compare with $985 billion in 1966 and $1,285 billion in 1969.

In addition, life insurance in force underwritten by the government, fraternals, savings banks and assessment societies is projected in 1965 dollars to vary between $187 billion (low) and $341 billion (high) compared with $50.8 billion in 1966. In relative terms this means an increase in the share of legal reserve companies in the total life insurance in force in the U.S. from about 94 percent in 1966 to 96 percent in 2000.

5. Another change in the composition of the volume of life insurance in force will be an increased share underwritten by stock life insurers

and a reduced share underwritten by mutual life insurers, as indicated in Table 3.

TABLE 3

DISTRIBUTION OF TOTAL LIFE INSURANCE IN
FORCE AMONG TYPES OF INSURERS

|  | 1966 | 2000 |
|---|---|---|
| Mutual | 51.8% | 47.0% |
| Stock | 42.4% | 49.0% |
| Others | 5.8% | 4.0% |
| Total | 100.0% | 100.0% |

6. About 6.4 percent of total life insurance in force in 1966 was credit life insurance. The projection is that sales of credit life insurance will increase at a faster rate than will the sales of total life insurance, so that its share in total life insurance in force in the year 2000 will amount to 9 percent. This means that the amount of credit life insurance in force in 2000 expressed in 1965 dollars will vary between $421 billion (low) and $881 billion (high), compared with $62.7 billion in 1966.

7. The composition of life insurance purchases and premiums as to the components of ordinary, group, and industrial life insurance is forecasted (Table 4) to be materially different.

TABLE 4

LIFE INSURANCE PURCHASES * AND PREMIUMS **

|  | 1966 | | 2000 | |
|---|---|---|---|---|
|  | Purchases | Premiums | Purchases | Premiums |
| Ordinary | 73.2% | 73.1% | 69.0% | 72.5% |
| Group | 21.2% | 18.7% | 30.0% | 25.0% |
| Industrial | 5.6% | 8.2% | 1.0% | 2.5% |
| Total | 100.0% | 100.0% | 100.0% | 100.0% |

* Excluding credit life insurance and annuities
** Excluding annuity considerations

Both group insurance purchases and group insurance premiums will increase in relative importance. Industrial life insurance will play an insignificant role in the life insurance picture. The share of ordinary life insurance purchases will decline slightly, while ordinary life insurance premiums will remain relatively stable. Part of the phenomenon of a stable share of premiums with the declining share of purchases of ordinary insurance may be attributed to new products. The forecast is that 30 percent of all ordinary life insurance purchased in the year 2000 will be written under types of policies not issued until sometime after 1968.

8. Ordinary life insurance purchased for business purposes (key-man insurance, insurance to fund stock purchases and partnership buy-and-sell agreements) is forecasted to grow faster than other types of ordinary life insurance.

The projection is that 3.5 percent of all ordinary policies and 17.75 percent of all amounts of ordinary life insurance will be purchased for business purposes in the year 2000. The high ratio of the amount of life insurance purchases to the number of policies purchased, indicates that the exposures to be anticipated for business purposes are far greater than those to be anticipated in the purchase of ordinary life insurance for individuals.

9. In 1962, 3.7 percent and 0.9 percent of ordinary life insurance purchases were extra-risk due to physical impairments and hazardous occupations, respectively. The forecast is that 3.9 percent of the total ordinary life insurance purchased in 2000 will be substandard; 3.2 percent will be substandard because of physical impairment and 0.7 percent because of hazardous occupations. The changes may be attributed to improved rating techniques and improvements in medical technology and safety technology. There is also the possibility that new occupations will be more hazardous, thus, offsetting in part improved safety standards.

10. The forecast of the distribution of annual purchases of ordinary life insurance among plans with "heavy savings" features (retirement income and endowment policies), those with "moderate savings" features (straight life, limited payment, modified life) and plans with "no savings" features (term life) indicate a change in the future importance of life insurance as a savings medium. The forecast is that there will be a significant change in the product mix in the year 2000. The percentage of the total purchases of ordinary insurance with "heavy" and "moderate savings" features will decline to 45 percent and 4 percent, respectively from 54 and 6 percent in 1966). The percentage share of ordinary insurance with "no savings" features will increase from 40 percent in 1966 to 50 percent in the year 2000. In spite of this trend, the amount of annual savings generated through life insurance industry will maintain the industry as one of the important savings media in the American economy. While the last two decades have witnessed a decline in the percentage of life insurance savings in total annual household savings, the forecast is for no further continuation of this trend. Life insurance is expected to generate 23 percent of the total annual household savings in the year 2000, compared with 21.6 percent in 1966.

11. In 1966, about 27 percent of all persons covered in private pension plans and 31 percent of all assets backing pension plans were in insured plans. The forecast is for life insurers to play a relatively more important role in the funding of private pension plans in the year 2000. It is expected that 35 percent of all persons covered under private pension plans in the year 2000 will be covered under insured plans, and that 40 percent of all assets behind private pension plans will be held by life insurance companies. This forecast is consistent with an expectation regarding the growth of segregated accounts as a funding instrument for private pension plans in the economy of the year 2000. The forecast is that 25 percent of the total funds backing insured pension plans will be deposited

in segregated accounts by the year 2000, compared with 2 percent in 1966 and 9.2 percent in 1969.

12. Growth in the number of new active life insurance companies has been rapid since the end of World War II. This growth has increased the share of the younger companies (both of the total assets held by life insurance companies and of the total life insurance in force). However, it is expected that new insurers will be less of a factor in the market over the 31 years ending in the year 2000 than they were in the 20 years ending in 1965. The forecast is that in the year 2000, insurers formed after 1968 will own 5 percent of the industry's assets and will have 8.9 percent of all life insurance in force. These figures compare with 1965 figures of 5.6 percent for assets owned by and 10.5 percent of life insurance in force issued by new insurers formed between 1945 and 1965.

13. The average premium rate per $1,000 of life insurance in force has generally been declining over the years. Two policies were selected to serve as a basis for projection—a $10,000 straight life policy and a $10,000 5-year renewable and convertible term policy, both issued to a male aged 35. The forecast is for a continued downward trend in the premium rates charged for life insurance, with the straight life non-participating premium rate decreasing 14.9 percent (from $18.80 per $1,000 in 1966 to $16 in 2000), and the convertible term insurance premium rate decreasing 15.8 percent (from $5.94 to $5). The decline is attributed to improved mortality experience, relative reduction in expenses and stabilization of investment earnings at an interest rate higher than in the past.

A further question about the behavior of future premium rates relates to their relative uniformity among insurers. The dispersion of premium rates among companies can be measured by the coefficient of variation (the lower the coefficient, the greater is the uniformity of premium rates among companies). For the same straight life and convertible term life policies discussed above, the forecast is for a 21 percent reduction in the coefficient of variation in the distribution of premium rates for the straight life policies in the year 2000, and for a 33 percent reduction in the coefficient for the 5-year term policy. The anticipation is, thus, for a greater degree of uniformity in premium rates charged by life insurers in the year 2000.

14. Contributing to the above mentioned projected decline in premium rates is the improved efficiency anticipated in the operation of life insurance companies. Assuming that an efficiency index measuring the cost of issuing and servicing a homogeneous block of ordinary life insurance policies was assigned a value of 100 in 1966, the index is expected to have a value of 87.5 in the year 2000, an improvement of 12.5 percent.

15. Higher interest rates in the future will also contribute to reduced premium rates. The over-all rate of investment earnings on life insurance funds has been rising steadily from 3.13 percent in 1950 to 4.73 percent in 1966 (net investment income before federal income taxes to mean invested

assets). The projected rate of interest for the year 2000 is 5.5 percent. This projected rate is higher than for any year reported or for this century.

16. The contribution of an increased rate of return on assets employed by life insurance companies will go together with a slightly faster growth of total assets relative to the growth of real GNP. The forecast is that the percentage of life insurance assets to GNP will be 25 percent in the year 2000, compared with 23 percent in 1966. These two factors (assets and rate of return) will affect the composition of the total receipts of life insurers in the year 2000. Of each composite dollar of income received by U.S. life companies during 1967, 77.9 cents represented premium payments for life and health insurance policies and annuities. The remaining 22.1 cents consisted chiefly of earnings on the life insurance companies' investments. The composite dollar of income in the year 2000 will reflect a higher contribution of investment earnings, as computed from Table 5.

TABLE 5

ASSETS AND INCOME OF LIFE INSURERS IN THE YEAR 2000
(BILLION 1965 DOLLARS)

|  | Low Projection | High Projection |
| --- | --- | --- |
| Total Assets | 544.0 | 907.0 |
| Total Investment Income | 29.9 | 49.9 |
| Total Premium Receipts | 95.9 | 159.8 |
| Total Income * | 125.8 | 209.7 |

* Not included in total income are policy proceeds left with the companies under supplementary contracts.

Of each composite dollar of income forecasted to be received by life insurance companies in the year 2000, 76.2 cents will represent premium payments, while the remaining 23.8 cents will consist chiefly of investment earnings.

17. Of the total assets held by life insurance companies in the year 2000, 70 percent are forecasted to be held by life insurers with mutual fund affiliates. This compares with a figure of 12.1 percent in 1967, when about 2.7 percent of the life insurers had mutual fund affiliates or had joint sales activities with mutual funds. These figures may reflect, in part, the trend toward the total financial services concept.

18. The percentage distribution of admitted assets of life insurance companies is forecasted to be materially different from the 1966 distribution, as shown in Table 6.

The change in the relative importance and size of various classes of investments held by life insurance companies is patent. Mortgage loans and corporate debt are expected to continue to be the principal assets held by life insurers, 75.4 percent of total admitted assets in 1966 and 68.5

percent of total admitted assets in 2000. Government debt is expected to decline. A major increase is expected in the holdings of corporate stocks, rising from 5.2 percent in 1966 to 13.5 percent in 2000. A major increase also is expected in the holdings of real estate.

TABLE 6

PERCENTAGE DISTRIBUTION OF ADMITTED ASSETS OF
LIFE INSURANCE COMPANIES

|  | 1966 | 2000 |
|---|---|---|
| Domestic Government Debt | 6.0 | 4.0 |
| Stocks | 5.2 | 13.5 |
| Real Estate | 2.9 | 5.0 |
| Mortgages | 38.7 | 35.5 |
| Corporate Debt | 36.7 | 33.0 |
| Other | 10.5 | 9.0 |
| Total | 100.0 | 100.0 |

The role of the life insurance industry in the capital market will be affected by the distribution of its assets and by the competition of individuals and other financial institutions. The forecast is that life insurers will continue to play an important role in the capital market, but that their role will be relatively less important at the turn of the century than it was in 1966.

The anticipation is that only in the purchases of equities will life insurers play a more important role, holding 5 percent of all corporate stocks outstanding in the year 2000, compared to 1.8 percent in 1966. But life insurers are expected to hold only 20 percent of all corporate debt compared to 26 percent in 1966, 2 percent of all government debt compared to 2.6 percent in 1966 and 17 percent of all real estate mortgages compared to 18.8 percent in 1966.

## HEALTH INSURANCE

1. The percentage of total health insurance premiums written by insurance companies (i.e., excluding payments into Blue Cross, Blue Shield, and prepayment plans) of total disposable personal income is expected to increase from 1.53 percent in 1966 to 2.5 percent in the year 2000. This increase is a continuation of the trend of the last two decades. Based on this figure, total health insurance premiums written by insurance companies in the year 2000 will vary between $39 billion (low projection) and $65 billion (high projection) expressed in 1965 dollars. The following would be of low projections and the high projections expressed in current dollars for the year 2000 assuming various annual rates of inflation.

| Average Annual Rates of Inflation | Low Projection (Billion Dollars) | High Projection (Billion Dollars) |
|:---:|:---:|:---:|
| 2% | 86 | 143 |
| 3% | 121 | 201 |
| 4% | 169 | 281 |

These projections compare with $7.8 billion in 1966.

2. Life insurance companies are expected to follow the trend of the recent past and increase their share of the health insurance market. Health insurance premiums written by life insurers in the year 2000 will vary between $33.5 billion and $55.9 billion expressed in 1965 dollars. This amounts to 86 percent of total health insurance premiums written by insurance companies, (relative to 78.7 percent in 1966), while non-life insurance companies will receive the rest. A further evidence of this trend concerns the distribution of insuring organizations writing health insurance.

Health insurance written by insurance companies currently is sold by life insurance companies, property-liability insurance companies and mono-line companies. In 1966, 68 percent of the insurance companies writing health insurance were life insurers, 28 percent were property-liability insurers and 4 percent were mono-line insurers. It is forecasted that 79 percent of the health insurance companies in the year 2000 will be life insurers, 18 percent will be property-liability insurers and two percent will be mono-line insurers, indicating a continued upward trend in the dominance of the health insurance market by life insurance companies.

3. Total health insurance premiums written by insurance companies can be classified into loss of income protection and hospital-medical (including surgical and major medical) protection, and then subclassified into group and individual (and family) premiums. Table 7 shows the distribution of health insurance premiums written by insurance companies in the year 2000, according to these categories. The premiums are expressed in terms of 1965 dollars, and represent real growth only. To translate these figures into current dollars for the year 2000, the appropriate inflation percentage must be applied.

It can be observed from Table 7 that the division of premiums into loss of income and hospital-medical protection in the year 2000 will be changed only slightly. Group hospital-medical insurance premiums will increase materially relative to their 1966 percentage, while individual policy premiums for loss of income and for hospital-medical protection will decrease significantly.

4. In 1966, insurance companies' share of total health insurance premiums written (excluding loss of income protection) was 53.8 percent. Based on a projected figure of 60 percent for the insurance companies'

TABLE 7

DISTRIBUTION OF HEALTH INSURANCE PREMIUMS OF
INSURANCE COMPANIES

| | Loss of Income | | | Hospital-Medical | | | |
| | Group | Indi-vidual | Total * | Group | Indi-vidual | Total * | Grand Total |
|---|---|---|---|---|---|---|---|
| 1966 ($ billion) | $ 1.2 | $ 0.9 | $ 2.1 | $ 3.9 | $ 1.8 | $ 5.7 | $ 7.8 |
| Pct. | 15.2% | 11.4% | 26.6% | 49.7% | 23.8% | 73.5% | 100.0% |
| 2000 Low Projection ($ billion) | $ 5.9 | $ 2.8 | $ 9.6 | $22.8 | $ 7.0 | $29.4 | $ 39.0 |
| High Projection ($ billion) | $ 9.8 | $ 4.7 | $15.9 | $38.0 | $11.7 | $49.1 | $ 65.0 |
| Pct. | 15.0% | 7.3% | 24.5% | 58.5% | 18.0% | 73.3% | 100.0% |

Note: * Figures for year 2000 do not add up to the totals given because of the use of median forecasts.

share of total health insurance premiums written (excluding loss of income protection) for the year 2000, the distribution of *total* health insurance premiums (including loss of income) between insurance companies and Blue Cross, Blue Shield and other plans will be as follows; expressed in terms of 1965 dollars.

| | Insurance Companies | Blue Shield Blue Cross, Others | Total |
|---|---|---|---|
| 1966 ($ billion) | $ 7.8 | $ 4.9 | $ 12.7 |
| Percent | 61.4% | 38.6% | 100.0% |
| 2000 Low Projection ($ billion) | 39.0 | 19.6 | 58.6 |
| High Projection ($ billion) | 65.0 | 32.7 | 97.7 |
| Percent | 66.5% | 33.5% | 100.0% |

Insurance companies will, thus, increase their share of the health insurance premium volume in the year 2000, gaining particularly in the area of providing hospital-medical protection.

5. Only an insignificant percentage of long-term disability income insurance is written at present on an escalating basis (i.e., income increased by a given percentage annually). A significant share of health insurance premiums written by insurance companies for this type of coverage is forecasted for the year 2000. The premium volume anticipated for the coverage expressed in 1965 dollars will vary between $2

billion and $3.3 billion, amounting to 5 percent of total health insurance premiums written by insurance companies in the year 2000.

6. An intriguing question relates to the development of new health insurance coverages. It is anticipated that 25 percent of total benefit payments by insurance companies in the year 2000 will be provided by new types of coverages developed after 1966.

7. In the year 2000, 90 percent of the civilian population will be protected by one or more forms of private health insurance (including Blue Cross, Blue Shield and other plans). This compares to 80.2 percent in 1966. The most prevalent coverage will be hospital expense plans, protecting 90 percent of the population. Surgical expense coverage will protect 85 percent (73.4 percent in 1966); regular medical expense plans will cover 80 percent (59.1 percent in 1966); major medical expense plans will cover 65 percent (28.8 percent in 1966); and loss of income protection will cover 40 percent of the civilian population in the year 2000 (27.6 percent in 1966). The number of persons with private health insurance has shown a steady growth over the years and these projections reflect a continuation of the trend. The percentage of the population with loss of income protection is limited, of course, by the percent of the population in the civilian labor force. About 37 percent of the population was in the civilian labor force in 1965 and the percentage projected for the civilian labor force in the year 2000 is about 41 percent of the total population.

8. The percentage of expenditures (both public and private) for health and medical care (excluding medical facilities construction) to GNP is expected to increase from 5.4 percent in 1965 to 8 percent in the year 2000, reflecting the steady upward trend of recent years. Based on this figure, public and private expenditures for health and medical care expressed in 1965 dollars will vary between $174 billion and $290 billion in the year 2000, compared with $36.4 billion in 1965. The percentage of private expenditures to total public and private expenditures (excluding medical facilities construction) for health and medical care is expected to decline from the 75 percent level of 1965 to 55 percent at the turn of the century. The result is an anticipated increase in private expenditures of from $27.1 billion in 1965 to between $96.0 billion and $160 billion in the year 2000 expressed in terms of 1965 dollars. The decline is mainly due to the belief that in the year 2000 social insurance will be a predominant form of insurance. The composition of total private health and medical care expenditures is expected to change materially. In 1966, 64.2 percent of this total were direct payments, 31.4 percent were insurance benefits, and 4.4 percent were prepayment expenses. The percentage distribution projected for the year 2000 is 40 percent, 50 percent and 7 percent, respectively. The relative increased amount of financing of private health and medical care expenditures by insurance companies in the year 2000 is attributable to the more extensive protection in terms of persons covered and in terms of new coverages that will be offered by private insurers.

## CONCLUSION

The paper attempted to enumerate the implications of inflation, technological advances and growth for the future of the life-health insurance industry.[3] The purpose was to identify those present characteristics that were likely to prevail until at least the end of the century, and any new characteristics that were likely to have emerged by that time. The forecasts reported here were not made on a normative basis, i.e., what ought to be done to accomplish certain goals. The task of drawing normative conclusions is left to the people in the insurance industry. The projections do not describe the year 2000 as a single year but are descriptive of a time period around that year. It is hence believed that these long-term projections should serve as a benchmark, a frame of reference, for short and intermediate term projections.

### Questions

1. What do the authors conclude about the relative growth of all-lines insurers, the top 20 life-health insurers, group coverages, and social insurance in the U.S. economy by the year 2000?
2. What appears to be the projections for the growth of the life insurance premium income by the year 2000, relative to health insurance and annuities?
3. What is expected to happen to life insurance premium rates by the year 2000? Why?
4. In view of the possibilities for national health insurance in the U.S., do you believe the projections in this article for health insurance are realistic? Discuss.

---

[3] A much more extensive treatment of the subject can be found in Robert I. Mehr, Seev Neumann: *Inflation, Technology and Growth: Possible Implications for Insurance,* op. cit.

# 25. EQUITY BASED VARIABLE LIFE INSURANCE *

Douglas G. Olson †
and Howard E. Winklevoss †

The life insurance industry has been frequently characterized as a conservative set of firms selling products that have remained virtually unchanged for decades. Product "innovation" has consisted of little more than slight variations of the same theme. Under almost all types of policies, the insurance company simply assumes the risk of unexpectedly high mortality and overhead expenses, and provides a *minimum* investment return guarantee. The majority of policies furnish an annual dividend to the policyholder which presumably results in all of the above three determinants of the premium.

Life insurance products are differentiated by the maximum length of time for which benefits are payable, by the period over which premiums are to be paid, and by the emphasis placed on the "pure" insurance, versus the investment element of the contract. It is important to note that under most circumstances, the actual obligation of the company is fixed in advance.

State insurance departments have closely regulated the investment practices of life insurance companies in order to safeguard policyholder benefits. As a result of these regulations, companies are limited in the proportion of their total assets that may be invested in common stock. In fact, a review of life insurance company investment portfolios indicates that, in the aggregate, 5 percent of the total assets are invested in common stock, compared with 36.5 percent in mortgages and 41.5 percent in bonds.[1]

In distinct contrast with traditional practice, life insurers have begun to pursue the possibility of offering a contract where the death proceeds are contingent upon the actual investment performance of the company. As opposed to the normal portfolio consisting of bonds and mortgages, the assets representing these products would be predominantly invested in common stock. The most recent proposal for equity-based products is called variable life insurance. For purposes of this article, variable life insurance shall be defined as life insurance wherein

* From *The Warton Quarterly* (Summer, 1971), pp. 26-40. Copyright 1971 by The Trustees of the University of Pennsylvania. Reprinted by permission.
† Members of the faculty of the Insurance Department, Wharton School, University of Pennsylvania.
[1] Institute of Life Insurance, *1970 Life Insurance Fact Book* (New York: 1971), pp. 70-75.

the obligations of the insurer are directly related to the investment performance of a specifically designated portfolio—composed of common stocks.[2]

The following discussion is designed to expand upon the concept of variable life insurance by analyzing the stimuli for the product, describing the major types of variable life insurance, evaluating how policyholder benefits would have been affected by using these products, and describing probable differences in contractual features between variable life policies and traditional fixed-benefit designs.

## STIMULI FOR EQUITY-BASED PRODUCTS

The proposals for variable life insurance appear to have been stimulated primarily by two conditions. First, inflationary pressures have eroded the real value of fixed-benefit policies, thereby leaving the beneficiary with lower real benefits than anticipated by the policyholder.[3] Second, many insurance company executives believe that there has been a shift in consumer preference away from the type of investment typified by cash value life insurance in favor of more speculative investments. While the effect of inflationary pressures is easily demonstrated, analyses of the second condition are complex.

### Inflation

Using the Consumer Price Index as an indicator of inflationary pressure, Table 1 illustrates the death benefits (in constant dollars) of a $10,000 life insurance policy issued at the beginning of each of the last three decades. Death benefits are evaluated at quinquennial intervals. The table suggests that, for the time period under investigation, the real value of the benefits would have been significantly reduced even when death occurred within a relatively short period of time (five years) after the purchase of insurance. Stated differently, a $10,000 policy purchased in 1940 would have had to increase in face value to $27,700 by 1970 in order to maintain its purchasing power. The policy issued in 1950 would have had to increase to $16,100 by 1970, and the policy issued in 1960 would have had to increase to $13,000 in ten years.

---

[2] This definition excludes a new type of life insurance which some authors may refer to as variable life insurance. This insurance links the face of the policy (death benefits) to the consumer price index (or some other index reflecting purchasing power). These index-linked policies differ from the above definition in two important respects: (i) the assets behind the index-linked policies are not necessarily invested in media which are different than those normally permitted by state insurance regulations, (ii) the company is obligated to change the face value according to the specific index—regardless of investment performance. Under variable life insurance, the face value is determined by the company's investment experience which may or may not be positively correlated with inflationary pressures.

[3] Professor Whittlesey has provided an interesting discussion of the effects of inflation on life insurance and the viability of life insurance companies in a previous article in the *Wharton Quarterly*. Charles R. Whittlesey, "Inflation and Life Insurance," *Wharton Quarterly*, IV (Fall, 1969), pp. 28-32.

DEATH BENEFITS IN CONSTANT DOLLARS
(Face Amount = $10,000)

|  | C.P.I.[a]<br>(1957-59 = 100) | Policy<br>Issued<br>in 1940 | Policy<br>Issued<br>in 1950 | Policy<br>Issued<br>in 1960 |
|---|---|---|---|---|
| 1940 | 48.8 | $10,000 | | |
| 1945 | 62.7 | 7,783 | | |
| 1950 | 83.8 | 5,823 | $10,000 | |
| 1955 | 93.3 | 5,230 | 8,982 | |
| 1960 | 103.1 | 4,733 | 8,128 | $10,000 |
| 1965 | 109.9 | 4,440 | 7,625 | 9,381 |
| 1970 | 135.3 | 3,607 | 6,194 | 7,620 |

[a] Consumer Price Index

Given the persistent nature of inflation, one might reasonably be led to question why the life insurance industry has just recently considered products which would provide the necessary adjustment in benefits. The answer appears to be that most (if not all) insurers previously regarded inflation to be a less significant issue than implied by the above analysis— since there existed various methods by which the policyholder could mitigate the problem. If, for example, real wages tended to remain constant or increase in spite of inflation, the policyholder could simply purchase more insurance, as time went on, without increasing the proportion of real wages devoted to insurance. In fact, companies issue supplementary contracts which guarantee policyholders the right to purchase additional insurance in the future even though, because of poor health or changes in other conditions, they are unable to satisfy normal insurability standards.

Unfortunately, policyholders may encounter some difficulty if they rely on the purchase of additional insurance coupled with a guarantee of insurability. First, the price of insurance necessarily increases with age so that the additional insurance may require a greater portion of total income than originally anticipated. Second, the insurability guarantees are limited in scope. Generally the policyholder is able to utilize the guarantee only once every three years, at certain specified dates, and the amount of insurance which can be purchased on these dates is limited.[4]

A second alternative for alleviating the effects of inflation involves the use of life insurance dividends, which are available only under participating life insurance policies. Policyholders may either leave dividends on deposit with the company or use the dividends to purchase additional insurance. Under either alternative, the proceeds at the time of death

---

[4] These restrictions are needed so that the insurance company will avoid problems of unhealthy policyholders purchasing large amounts of insurance.

will be greater than the face of the original policy, and the premium will have remained level throughout the period.

## Competitive Posture

The increasing importance of life insurance among other financial intermediaries during the first half of the twentieth century has been well-documented. Goldsmith [5] has indicated that, between 1900 and 1952, the assets of private life insurance companies increased from approximately $1.7 billion to $73.4 billion. In comparison with the other nine major financial intermediates that operated throughout the period,[6] the rate of growth of life insurers was exceeded by only savings and loan associations, fraternal insurance organizations, and casualty and miscellaneous insurers.

In spite of the overall favorable performance of the private life insurance sector, studies have suggested that since the beginning of the 1940's life insurers have failed to increase their share of either the flow of saving or of the total assets held by households. We shall examine the flow of saving issue first.

For purposes of this discussion, annual saving in the form of life insurance products is the annual change in adjusted reserves for life insurance and insured pension plans. The measure of total personal saving is the national income account item for personal saving, i.e., the difference between personal income (after taxes) and expenditures. Using these indicators, the suggested comparison is presented in Table 2.

It is worth noting that the percentage of personal saving attributable to life insurance in each of the years since 1965 has been less than the percentage in any year since 1945. During the interim 20-year period, life insurance accounted for an average of 24 percent of personal saving, while in the last four years, the average fell to 17 percent. While the evidence cannot be regarded as conclusive, the data suggest that life insurance is not maintaining its position.

A comparison which may be more meaningful is the trend in the position of life insurers versus other financial intermediaries in the total financial assets held by individuals. The inclusion of tangible assets in personal saving data may serve to cloud the picture if the focus is the competitive position of life insurers in the financial markets. By confining the analysis to financial assets, this problem may be avoided.

Prior analyses by Goldsmith and Friend [7] imply that although life insurers successfully increased their relative importance as suppliers of financial assets to households prior to the 1940's, they have stabilized since that time. The analyses indicate that during the 1940's and 1950's

---

[5] Raymond W. Goldsmith, *Financial Intermediaries in the American Economy Since 1900* (Princeton: Princeton University Press, 1958).

[6] Goldsmith, *Financial Intermediaries in the American Economy Since 1900*, p. 69.

[7] Irwin Friend, Hyman P. Minsky, and Victor L. Andrews, *Private Capital Markets* (Englewood Cliffs: Prentice-Hall, Inc., 1964).

TABLE 2

LIFE INSURANCE AND TOTAL PERSONAL SAVING

| Year | (1) Personal Saving Attributable to Life Insurance[a] (Billions) | (2) Total Personal Saving (Billions) | (3) Percentage of Saving Accounted for by Life Insurance (1 ÷ 2) 100% |
|------|------|------|------|
| 1940 | 1.7 | $ 3.8 | 44.7% |
| 1945 | 3.3 | 29.6 | 11.2 |
| 1950 | 3.4 | 13.1 | 26.0 |
| 1955 | 4.4 | 15.8 | 27.8 |
| 1960 | 4.1 | 17.0 | 24.1 |
| 1965 | 6.5 | 28.4 | 22.9 |
| 1966 | 5.6 | 32.5 | 17.2 |
| 1967 | 6.7 | 40.4 | 16.6 |
| 1968 | 6.7 | 38.4 | 17.4 |
| 1969 | 5.7 | 37.6 | 15.2 |

[a] Annual change in: total life insurance reserves (including insured pension plans) plus dividend deposits, less health insurance reserves, policy loans and premium notes.

Source: Life insurance data supplied by Institute of Life Insurance. Personal saving data for 1940-1968: U.S. Department of Commerce, *Business Statistics, 1969*. Personal saving data for 1969: U.S. Department of Commerce, *Survey of Current Business, April, 1970*.

life insurance company reserves (including those for insured pension plans) accounted for approximately 21 percent of the total assets supplied by financial intermediaries—having increased from 15 percent in 1900. More recent estimates may be obtained by comparing the increase in insurance company reserves with the increase in financial assets of individuals as shown in Table 3.

Again, the data suggest that life insurers have failed to improve their relative position, and the trend is probably toward less prominence.

The apparent change in demand for life insurance might be interpreted as a signal that, as inflation has become more prominent in the last five years, potential policyholders are questioning the value of the security provided by a long term contract with constant benefits. This suggests that life insurance companies might improve their product line by offering contracts where the obligation of the company is a function of the investment performance of an equities portfolio. If the market value of such securities tends to keep pace with inflation (at least in the long run), benefit payments will maintain their purchasing power.

In addition, life insurance companies may also be interpreting the apparent success of investment companies in the past decade as an indicator of individual preference for a managed equities portfolio. An equity-based life insurance product may enable the insurance industry to attract a portion of this market. As will soon become apparent, short term variable life insurance with a high savings element would be closely akin to a share in an investment company.

TABLE 3

THE POSITION OF LIFE INSURANCE AMONG
TOTAL FINANCIAL ASSETS OF INDIVIDUALS

|  | Increase in Life Insurance Reserves [a] (Billions) | Increase in Financial Assets of Individuals (Billions) | Increase in Life Insurance as % of Increase in Financial Assets of Individuals |
|---|---|---|---|
| 1950 | $3.4 | $13.7 | 24.8% |
| 1955 | 4.3 | 27.9 | 15.4 |
| 1960 | 4.4 | 27.7 | 15.9 |
| 1961 | 4.7 | 34.9 | 13.5 |
| 1962 | 5.0 | 39.3 | 12.7 |
| 1963 | 5.7 | 44.9 | 12.7 |
| 1964 | 6.2 | 51.3 | 12.1 |
| 1965 | 6.8 | 56.0 | 12.1 |
| 1966 | 6.6 | 54.4 | 12.1 |
| 1967 | 7.3 | 66.5 | 11.0 |
| 1968 | 7.5 | 63.7 | 11.8 |
| 1969 | 7.7 | 57.1 | 13.5 |

[a] Includes increase in the reserves of insured pension plans.
Source: Increase in life insurance reserves and increase in financial assets for 1950 through 1968 found in: U.S. Securities and Exchange Commission, *Statistical Bulletin,* January, 1970. Data for 1969 available from April, 1970 issue of same publication.

## VARIABLE LIFE PROPOSALS

Given the above considerations, it is interesting to look at some of the methods by which the face value of a life insurance policy can be changed to reflect the investment yield on a portfolio consisting principally of equities. Before doing this, it is necessary to briefly discuss the nature of a life insurance reserve.

The reserve for a life insurance policy can be thought of as a sum of money which results from the policyholder *prepaying* some of the mortality costs that evolve under the policy. The actual mortality cost for any given year is determined by multiplying the probability that death will occur in that year by the value of the death benefit provided in the policy. Since mortality rates increase with age, this cost continues to rise over time.

If the premium for the policy is to remain constant throughout the period, or if the premium-paying period is shorter than the length of the policy, it should be evident that some degree of prepayment must take place in the early years in order to offset the higher cost of mortality in later years. These prepayments, along with their accumulated investment returns, constitute the reserve under most life insurance policies.

In the computation of the premium, insurance companies assume that a specific investment return will be earned on the assets behind the reserves of a fixed-benefit policy, hereinafter referred to as the assumed investment return (AIR). If the company fails to accomplish this investment objective, it will be actuarially unable to meet its obligations. On the other hand, if the investment return is greater than the AIR, these excess earnings will contribute to the dividend—as previously indicated. Under the variable policy, the difference between the actual yield and the AIR is used to bring about changes in the face value.

With regard to traditional fixed-benefit policies, the reserve takes on especial significance under an endowment policy. Endowment contracts pay the face of the policy to the beneficiary if the insured dies during the protection period, and pays the policyholder the same amount if he survives the period. The policy thus includes a built-in savings program, and the reserve must be sufficient to pay the policyholders who survive. Clearly, the shorter the period of the endowment policy the greater the emphasis on the savings element.

Term insurance is at the opposite end of the spectrum from endowment policies. Such policies are typically issued at relatively young ages and are in effect for relatively short time periods. Unless the policyholder dies during the contract period, there is no benefit payment by the company. Under these conditions the reserve will be relatively low.

Diagram I portrays the reserve under an endowment which matures in 20 years, a term insurance policy which is issued for 20 years, and a whole life policy, each issued to a male age 35. The relative size of these reserves is important in understanding the types of contracts which are likely to be offered on a variable basis. As can be seen, the reserve under a term policy is quite small, and adjustments in the face value to reflect actual investment performance would be practically meaningless. On the other hand, although the endowment policy has an extremely high reserve, it turns out that it is also unlikely to be offered on a variable basis.

The reason for the endowment exclusion is that this policy places much more emphasis on investment than on insurance. Consequently, there is little question that this policy would be considered an investment contract and thereby fall under the jurisdiction of the Securities and Exchange Commission (SEC). This, in turn, would subject the contract to regulation by both the SEC and the state insurance departments. SEC regulation would include: disclosure requirements, a review of sales literature and techniques, and a limitation on the sales commission—which would be substantially lower than commissions currently paid on life insurance contracts.

If the product is subject to SEC regulation, many insurance executives feel that the difference in sales commissions would preclude successful marketing of variable life insurance alongside traditional life insurance products. The insurance industry is now in the process of seeking an SEC exemption for all variable life insurance contracts (except the endowment policy).

The reserve under a whole life policy appears to be large enough to be meaningfully adapted to the variable life design, but not of sufficient size to be considered an investment contract. Thus, variable life insurance will most likely be offered on a whole life basis, and we will concentrate our analysis on this design.

## Variable Policy Designs

It should be made clear at the outset that there are many ways that the face of an insurance contract can be systematically adjusted in recognition of the performance of the equities portfolio. The adjustment methods discussed here have a well-defined rationale and seem to meet best the more technical problems that the insurance industry must solve before the product is made available.

Perhaps the most straightforward adjustment method is one developed by a group of actuaries from the New York Life Insurance Company.[8] Under this approach, the face value of the variable policy rises or falls so that the ratio of the face to the assets in the investment account behind that policy is identical to the ratio of the face of a fixed-benefit policy to its reserve. It should be clear that there will be no change in the face value if the actual yield on the investments behind the reserve during the entire policy period is equal to the assumed investment return (AIR). On the other hand, if the yield is greater or less than the AIR, then the face will be raised or lowered accordingly in order to maintain the proper face-to-reserve ratio.

For example, let us assume that at the beginning of the accounting period the reserve for a $1,000 fixed-benefit policy and the assets behind a corresponding variable-benefit policy, are each $90. We may further assume that, at the end of the period, the accumulated reserve for the fixed-benefit policy is $100. However, because of favorable investment experience, the assets behind the variable policy have accumulated to $125. At this point, the face value of the variable-benefit policy will be increased to $1,250 in order to maintain the face-to-reserve ratio indicated by fixed benefit design (10 to 1).

Although not indicated in the above discussion, the $25 unanticipated investment return will not be sufficient to support a permanent $250 increase in death benefits. Thus, in absence of continued favorable investment returns, the extra death benefit will become less over time. This process is analogous to using the favorable investment experience in one period for the purchase of a paid-up whole life policy which has a decreasing face value. Of course, if the actual investment experience in any period is less than the AIR, the face value of the variable life policy will be reduced accordingly.

This adjustment method, sometimes referred to as the New York Life design after its originators, will be designated the *constant ratio*

[8] John C. Fraser, Walter N. Miller, and Charles M. Sternhell, "Analysis of Basic Actuarial Theory for Fixed Premium Variable Benefit Life Insurance," *Transactions of the Society of Actuaries, 1969,* XXI, pp. 343-378.

*design,* since this name is somewhat descriptive of the underlying concept used in determining face value.

A second design was developed in response to possible objections to the decreasing nature of the additions (or deductions) under the above method. Under this design, the excess investment return in any year is used to purchase a paid-up whole life policy which has a *constant face value* over time. Initially, smaller amounts of insurance will be added (or deducted) under the constant face design than under the constant ratio method. However, since these additions (or subtractions) do not decrease over time, this method provides in the long run a greater benefit than the constant ratio method.

Both of these methods have a logical basis upon which a systematic adjustment of the face is made. However, it should now be apparent that virtually any type of paid-up (single premium) insurance could be added or deducted in response to a favorable or unfavorable investment return on the account. It is unlikely, though, that many significant variations from these two designs will be placed on the market.

It is important to note that both the constant face designs are accomplished with a *level* yearly premium regardless of the increase or decrease in the face value of the policy. A third design, the *unit variable method,* has variable premiums as well as a variable face. The name unit variable comes from the fact that premiums and benefits are expressed in terms of units rather than dollars. At the inception of the contract each unit has a specified monetary value. As time progresses, this value will either increase or decrease depending on the investment performance of the policy account. For instance, one might pay 50 units a year for a policy with a face value of 1000 units. If the value of the underlying unit increases by 50 percent then the dollar face value *and* the dollar yearly premium likewise increase by 50 percent.

Diagram II shows the relative change in the face value under each of the three methods. For purposes of illustration, we shall assume that the investment experience up to age 49 is precisely equal to the AIR. During that year the investment earnings are sufficient to increase the account to a sum which is twice the reserve computed on the AIR basis for age 50. After age 50 the investment experience returns to the AIR.

It can be seen from the diagram that the face value of the unit variable design doubles along with the reserve and is maintained at this level throughout the policy period. As previously indicated, the premium also doubles after age 49. The death benefit for the constant face design is increased by approximately 50 percent, and likewise remains constant throughout the policy period. The face value of the constant ratio design, however, initially doubles, but subsequently decreases and by age 95 is only 20 percent greater than the original face amount.

## Simulated Results

Table 4 shows the experience under each of the variable life insurance designs for a $10,000 whole life policy issued in 1940 to a male

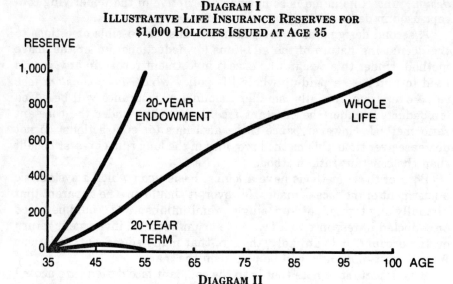

DIAGRAM I
ILLUSTRATIVE LIFE INSURANCE RESERVES FOR
$1,000 POLICIES ISSUED AT AGE 35

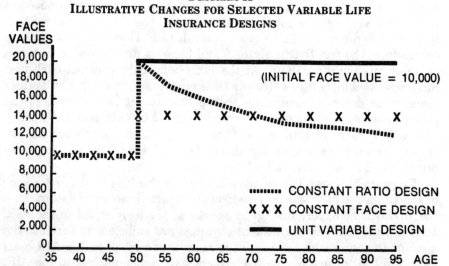

DIAGRAM II
ILLUSTRATIVE CHANGES FOR SELECTED VARIABLE LIFE
INSURANCE DESIGNS

age 35. It is assumed that the assets behind the policy experienced the
yields reflected in Standard and Poor's Composite Index for 500 common
stocks with all dividends reinvested. The AIR adopted for this analysis
was 3 percent. Since inflation was previously cited as a factor that influenced the development of variable life insurance, the results are
shown in both actual and constant dollars (based on the Consumer
Price Index).

The constant ratio design is more responsive to the investment yield
in the early years of the policy than the constant face design. However,
by the end of the 30-year period, their values are nearly equal, amounting to approximately $47,500. If the simulation were continued beyond

age 65, the face value of the constant face design would eventually exceed that of the constant ratio design. In terms of constant dollars, both policies generally fell short of maintaining a $10,000 real face value during the first 15 years, while in the last 15 years they exceed this objective. In fact, by age 65 they are both approximately 50 percent greater than they need to be in order to provide a constant purchasing power of $10,000.

Clearly, the unit variable design is more sensitive to investment performance than either of the other designs. In relation to inflation, the ten-fold increase over the 30-year period reduces to a four-fold increase in death benefits when valued at constant dollars. Premiums, of course, also increase in these same proportions.

One will note that the face value of the variable policies, in actual dollar amounts, rarely falls below the original face value of $10,000. If the policy were issued in some year other than 1940, the number of times the face would fall below $10,000 could either be non-existent or much more frequent. It is believed, however, that all variable policies will guarantee that the face value will never drop below the original amount and that the premium charge for this guarantee will be very small. (Of course, there will be no guarantee with respect to the cash values.) Otherwise, the premium for a variable policy should be nearly identical to that for a fixed-benefit policy.

It should be noted that these results are unique to: the year in which this policy was issued (1940), the age of the policyholder (35), and the yield rate of the Standard and Poor's Index. Changes in any of these variables may have a significant effect on the changes which take place in the death benefits. These results are presented here only to indicate the relative variability of each of the three designs and to provide some indication of the growth that one might expect over a particular 30-year period.

## CONTRACTUAL FEATURES

The fact that the obligations of the company are subject to both positive and negative variations of unspecified magnitude will dictate that some of the current features of life insurance contracts will be modified under the variable design. The analysis below treats the most important of these features: cash surrender values, nonforfeiture options, policy loans and reinstatement privileges.

### Cash and Nonforfeiture Values

As previously indicated, the use of a level premium for a long term life insurance contract clearly implies that policyholders will accumulate an investment account with the company. For purposes of this discussion, we will assume that this investment account is analogous to the reserve. In an effort to protect policyholders, states have enacted statutes

TABLE 4

ILLUSTRATIVE FACE AMOUNTS FOR $10,000 VARIABLE WHOLE LIFE
POLICIES ISSUED TO A MALE AGE 35 WITH ASSETS INVESTED IN
STANDARD AND POOR'S COMPOSITE 500 AND AIR EQUAL TO 3%

| Year | Age | Constant Ratio Design | | Constant Face Design | | Unit Variable Design | |
|------|-----|-----------|------------|-----------|------------|-----------|------------|
| | | Actual $ | Constant $ | Actual $ | Constant $ | Actual $ | Constant $ |
| 1940 | 35 | 10,000 | 10,000 | 10,000 | 10,000 | 10,000 | 10,000 |
| | | 8,807 | 8,879 | 9,946 | 9,461 | 8,807 | 8,378 |
| | | 8,252 | 7,089 | 9,848 | 8,461 | 7,697 | 6,613 |
| | | 9,995 | 8,089 | 9,979 | 8,076 | 8,662 | 7,010 |
| | | 12,182 | 9,698 | 10,315 | 8,211 | 10,555 | 8,403 |
| 1945 | 40 | 13,527 | 10,528 | 10,659 | 8,296 | 12,192 | 9,489 |
| | | 17,085 | 12,261 | 11,600 | 8,324 | 16,153 | 11,592 |
| | | 14,164 | 8,884 | 11,121 | 6,976 | 14,295 | 8,967 |
| | | 13,780 | 8,024 | 11,170 | 6,505 | 14,471 | 8,427 |
| | | 13,804 | 8,116 | 11,322 | 6,657 | 14,978 | 8,806 |
| 1950 | 45 | 15,030 | 8,753 | 11,904 | 6,932 | 16,792 | 9,779 |
| | | 17,803 | 9,600 | 13,167 | 7,100 | 20,538 | 11,075 |
| | | 20,735 | 10,939 | 14,682 | 7,746 | 24,858 | 13,114 |
| | | 22,600 | 11,834 | 15,906 | 8,329 | 28,245 | 14,789 |
| | | 21,297 | 11,103 | 15,719 | 8,195 | 27,738 | 14,462 |
| 1955 | 50 | 29,067 | 15,203 | 20,091 | 10,509 | 39,261 | 20,535 |
| | | 36,211 | 18,660 | 24,621 | 12,687 | 51,009 | 26,285 |
| | | 35,885 | 17,844 | 25,287 | 12,592 | 52,717 | 26,251 |
| | | 30,467 | 14,765 | 22,904 | 11,100 | 46,674 | 22,618 |
| | | 38,998 | 18,750 | 28,977 | 13,932 | 61,900 | 29,761 |
| 1960 | 55 | 41,459 | 19,624 | 31,550 | 14,933 | 68,296 | 32,326 |
| | | 38,220 | 17,900 | 30,321 | 14,200 | 65,262 | 30,564 |
| | | 46,991 | 21,757 | 37,535 | 17,379 | 82,942 | 38,402 |
| | | 40,003 | 18,296 | 33,467 | 15,306 | 73,026 | 33,399 |
| | | 45,796 | 20,674 | 38,902 | 17,562 | 86,196 | 38,912 |
| 1965 | 60 | 50,118 | 22,255 | 43,485 | 19,309 | 97,251 | 43,183 |
| | | 53,012 | 22,873 | 47,123 | 20,332 | 105,988 | 45,732 |
| | | 46,023 | 19,312 | 42,421 | 17,800 | 94,733 | 39,751 |
| | | 52,356 | 21,081 | 49,123 | 19,779 | 110,716 | 44,579 |
| | | 56,818 | 21,713 | 54,469 | 20,815 | 123,424 | 47,166 |
| 1970 | 65 | 47,702 | 16,807 | 47,287 | 16,661 | 106,395 | 37,488 |

(termed nonforfeiture legislation) which establish the minimum size
of the investment account and also guarantee that a policyholder may
receive the cash value of his account if he terminates his policy.

Switching to a variable life insurance policy will alter the nature of
these cash values. Since reserves will reflect the actual investment
performance of an equities fund, cash values cannot be determined in

advance and therefore will not be guaranteed. In this sense, the investment element of variable life insurance will resemble a share in an investment company. While the insurance company will probably guarantee a
minimum death benefit, it will not guarantee a minimum cash value.

Nonforfeiture legislation also specifies that the policyholder who
terminates his contract may elect to use the value of his investment
account to purchase some form of insurance. These same options will
probably be available under variable life insurance.

## Policy Loans

State statutes additionally guarantee that the policyholder will be
able to borrow the funds in his account at a specified rate of interest. In
the event of death, the value of the loan, plus the interest thereon, is
simply deducted from the proceeds paid to the beneficiary. Under these
conditions, policy loans will not disrupt the function of the insurance
mechanism.

Under variable life insurance, loan privileges similar to those under
fixed benefit policies would appear to invite speculation by the policyholder. If the policyholder believes that the equities in the investment
portfolio are currently overvalued and that the value of his account will
soon deteriorate, he may be tempted to speculate by borrowing the funds.
If his predictions are correct and he is allowed to repay the full dollar
value of the loan, he would be credited with more insurance than currently held by those who had left their total funds with the company since
his new account will be of greater value.

Regulatory authorities currently believe that such speculation is not
in the best interest of either policyholders or beneficiaries. Companies fear
that such speculation will subject them to "runs" on their investment
account with subsequent high transactions costs. As a result, it is likely
that state statutes will be amended to remove the *requirement* that
companies offer policy loans in the case of variable life insurance.

Although it appears that companies will devise alternative, acceptable methods by which policyholders can "borrow" against their policies,
these privileges will most probably be similar to simply canceling portions of the policy and taking the cash value of these portions. Thus the
death benefit will be reduced significantly more than it would be under
traditional loan provisions where the death benefit is reduced only by
the amount of the loan. While the company would also permit the policyholder to repay the loan, he will not be able to repay more than a sum
sufficient to restore his insured position to the amount he would have had
if he had not withdrawn the funds.

It should be noted that the modified loan provision described above
will not be sufficient to discourage speculation. For example, assume that
$100 is borrowed and at the time of repayment only $50 is needed to fully
restore the policy due to a deterioration in the investment portfolio.

According to the modified loan provision, the policyholder can repay $50 of the $100 loan and thereby retain only as many benefits as if he had not borrowed the funds. However, he will have $50 more than the policyholder who did not negotiate a loan.

One characteristic of the proposed modified loan provision will adversely affect policyholders. Since the repayment of a loan will increase the insurance protection by a sum which is greater than the loan itself, companies will have to protect themselves by requiring that insureds furnish proof of insurability at the time of repayment. This will preclude from utilizing the loan provision some policyholders who are in ill health. Although actuarially necessary, this loan provision is more restrictive than current loan provisions.

## Reinstatement

Under traditional life insurance contracts, termination of the policy and election of a nonforfeiture benefit does not necessarily preclude the policyholder from reinstating his original insurance agreement at a subsequent time. However, the privilege to reinstate is limited to policyholders who elect one of the nonforfeiture options other than cash.

By statute, the policyholder is guaranteed the right to reinstate his original contract if, within three years of cancellation, he repays all overdue premiums plus any indebtedness on the contract, both accumulated at a specified rate of interest. Of course, the insurer will also require evidence of insurability.

In the case of variable life insurance, the ability to reinstate by simply paying the accumulated overdue premiums may tempt the policyholder to speculate against the company. Since the policy that is granted upon reinstatement is to provide the same protection that would be available if the policyholder had not lapsed, the payment of back premiums alone would discriminate against existing policyholders when investment returns have been greater than the AIR. The benefits that would be granted upon reinstatement would be those which would have been justified by both timely premium payments *and* favorable investment gains. Thus, simply paying the overdue premiums plus the interest rate specified in the contract will not be sufficient to support these benefits.

For the above reason, plus additional considerations, variable life insurance reinstatement will require the greater of: overdue premiums and indebtedness accumulated at a specified rate of interest, or the increase in the cash surrender value resulting from the reinstatement. Such a requirement would appear to discriminate against policyholders who lapse when the policy is high, and then desire to reinstate at a time when the policy value is low. Under such a circumstance, the policyholder would be required to repay overdue premiums plus interest—even though, actuarially, the funds necessary to restore his benefits are much lower.

In review, it appears that moving to a variable benefit contract will offer the possibility for a larger return than the investment element of a traditional policy, and that this return will always be available to the policyholder in case he chooses to terminate his policy. However, the possibility for wide variations in the investment element will also serve to limit supplementary contractual rights which have been considered valuable by owners of traditional forms of life insurance.

## CONCLUSION

Variable life insurance signifies a definite philosophical shift in the life insurance industry. To this time, the industry has evolved under the assumption that the insurance product was to provide guaranteed benefits, with the company assuming the mortality, expense and investment risk for the policyholder. Proposals for variable life insurance essentially shift the investment risk back to the policyholder, leaving the company with only the risk of unanticipated expenses and mortality costs. If the insurer guarantees that the death benefit under the variable life policy will be at least equal to the original face, this characterization must be somewhat modified. However, insurers can minimize their overall investment risk by providing no guarantees with regard to the cash value of the policy and by utilizing an ultra conservative investment return assumption in calculating premiums.

The results of simulating a variable life insurance policy over a period from 1940 to 1970 suggest that this product might offer a partial solution to the problem of inflation. Even though the face value in constant dollars deteriorated somewhat in the early years, the policyholder would appear to have been far better off with this type of coverage than with a traditional fixed-benefit policy.

The choice between a participating fixed-benefit policy and a variable-benefit policy (with a guaranteed minimum face benefit) involves several considerations. Preference for the variable benefit design presumes that the yield on the equity portfolio will result in greater benefits than those available from combining the fixed-benefit policy with its dividends. Additionally, the variable policy will not provide guaranteed loan and nonforfeiture values traditionally found in the fixed-benefit design.

In any event, the availability of both fixed and variable life insurance will provide the insurance consumer with a broader choice of investment and protection combinations.

## Questions

1. The authors define variable life insurance as "life insurance wherein the obligations of the insurer are directly related to the investment performance of a specifically designated portfolio—composed of common stocks." What other type of variable life insurance plans are there? Discuss.
2. For the purchasing power of the proceeds to be maintained at its original level, by what approximate amount must the face of a $10,000 life insurance policy purchased in 1950 be increased by 1970? How might the consumer arrange such an increase? Discuss.

3. (a) In the variable life insurance policy of a constant ratio design, how would the face amount of protection be adjusted during the life of the policy. Explain. (b) How would the insured receive protection against reductions in the purchasing power of the face amount of the policy?
4. How does the constant face design differ from the constant ratio design? From the unit variable design? Explain.
5. Judging from the "constant dollar" column in Table 4, which variable life design is likely to be most responsive to changes in the cost of living in the United States? Can the buyer count on this occurring in the future? Discuss.
6. How will the policy loan provision of the variable life policy probably be changed from ordinary life insurance contracts? Why?

# 26. INSURANCE MARKETS IN A DECADE OF "NADERISM" *

Joseph M. Belth †

For many years I have been interested in the area of deceptive sales and advertising practices in the life insurance business. Early this year, however, following a series of incredible experiences, I became intensely interested in the subject. So I am delighted to have the opportunity to discuss with you several examples of marketing practices that in my opinion are going to come increasingly under fire in a decade of "Naderism."

My purpose in presenting these examples is a constructive one. I hope you will think carefully about them, and if you agree that they are open to serious criticism, I hope you will do everything you can to eradicate such practices. On the other hand, if you feel that such practices are not as serious as I think they are, I hope you will share your reasoning with us during the discussion period.

## I. Why You Shouldn't Buy Term Insurance

In the April 15, 1967, issue of the life edition of *The National Underwriter,* an advertisement covering three full pages was run by *Better Homes and Gardens* magazine. Two of the pages were a reproduction of an article that had appeared earlier in BH&G. The article dealt with various misunderstandings about life insurance, and one section contained a comparison between a $10,000 nonparticipating five-year renewable term policy and a $10,000 nonparticipating straight life policy. The comparison was at issue age 25. I do not know what company's figures were used in the BH&G article, which referred to the company as a typical one, but in this discussion I am using data for policies issued currently by the Connecticut General Life Insurance Company. The figures are similar to those in the article.

The article pointed out that the premiums from age 25 to age 65 for the term policy add up to $5,049. Then it was pointed out that the premiums over the same period for a straight life policy in the same company would be $5,308, but that there would then be a cash value of $5,730. The article concluded that the policyholder's "net gain" in the case of the straight life policy was $422, which might be referred to as a negative cost. The article implied that the straight life policy enjoyed a cost superiority of $5,471 over the term policy.

* From *Best's Review* (November, 1970), pp. 30+. (A paper presented September 17, 1970, at a conference in Chicago sponsored by the Reinsurance Division of the Continental Assurance Company.) Reprinted by permission.
† Professor of Insurance, Graduate School of Business, Indiana University.

322    **PART 7    LIFE INSURANCE**

The analysis I have just described fails to take interest into account (or, stated another way, an interest rate of 0 percent is assumed implicitly). Now let's take 4 percent interest into account. The present value of the term premiums is $1,973. The present value of the straight life premiums is $2,732. The present value of the cash value at 65 is $1,192. The cost of the straight life policy is now $1,540.

In short, when 4 percent interest is taken into account, the apparent cost superiority of the straight life policy is only $433, as compared with $5,471 when the BH&G procedure is used.

If such other relevant factors as mortality rates and lapse rates were taken into account in calculating the present values, the cost superiority of the straight life policy would shrink even further, and the pendulum might even swing the other way. (Please note that I am not arguing for or against term insurance or any other policy form. I am merely discussing questionable sales and advertising practices.)

The byline for the BH&G article carried the name of one of its editors, but I assume that someone in the life insurance industry furnished some input. When the subject under discussion involves long-term financial instruments—in this case life insurance contracts spanning a 40-year period—interest is "the name of the game." I believe that omission of the interest factor, as in the ad discussed here, will come increasingly under fire in a decade of "Naderism."

## II. The Case of the Low-Priced Policy

In the February 1970 issue of *Underwriters Review* magazine, there was a short article entitled "Returns on Life Insurance." The article was attributed to the company magazine of the Massachusetts Mutual Life Insurance Company. I should mention that the company's officials were very upset when I brought this item to their attention, and they have taken strong action to prevent a recurrence.

The article suggested the following technique for handling the question of investment return when it arises in the sales interview:

> Ask the prospect what kind of return he would expect to get if he invested $1,000 a year. Assume he answers 8 percent. Then ask him what kind of return he would expect to get if he invested the $1,000 a year in a life insurance contract. Assume he answers 4 percent.
> What would it cost the prospect to buy the life insurance? Wouldn't it be the difference between what he would have earned on the 8 percent investment and what he would earn on the life insurance investment? This difference amounts to $40 a year.
> If the prospect invests $1,000 a year in a straight life contract at his age of 30, his family would get $50,000 when he dies. "Mr. Prospect, that's $50,000 of death protection for $40 a year. Can you really afford to invest in anything else?"

There are a number of minor flaws in this presentation. But I am going to point out only what I consider to be the major flaw. I am going to point it out not because I think you can't see it, but because I want to make absolutely sure that you see it.

If we accept all of the figures in the article, the life insurance buyer would forego $40 of interest each year for each $1,000 invested in the life insurance policy. In the first year the amount foregone would be $40. In the second year, however, even disregarding compound interest, the amount foregone would be $80, because he would be foregoing the extra interest on the first year's $1,000 as well as the second year's $1,000. By the same token, and again disregarding compound interest, he would forego $120 in the third year. In other words, while the technique suggested in the article refers to $50,000 of death protection for $40 a year, the actual figures should be $40 in the first year, $80 in the second year, $120 in the third year, $400 in the tenth year, $800 in the twentieth year, and so forth. If compound interest were considered, the figures would be $40 in the first year, $82 in the second year, $125 in the third year, $480 in the tenth year, $1,191 in the twentieth year, and so forth.

I feel that the technique described in the article is not only false but also very tricky. I believe that such sales practices will come increasingly under fire in a decade of "Naderism."

## III. The Case of the Low-Priced Rider

In the August 1970 issue of *Life Insurance Selling* magazine, the Wisconsin National Life Insurance Company ran a half-page advertisement concerning a new family income rider "at industry's lowest rates." The ad cited several examples, including an annual premium of $127.60 for a 20-year, $400 per month family income rider for a person aged 25.

This is indeed a low premium. A similar rider in the Connecticut General, for example, requires a premium of $172.80.

The reason for the low premium is the fact that the Wisconsin National now uses 8 percent interest in calculating commuted values for its family income riders. Although the ad makes reference to the "maximum income" of $96,000 payable under the rider, the ad contains no reference to commuted values or to the 8 percent commutation rate.

The initial commuted value of the rider at 8 percent interest is $49,160. The initial commuted value of the Connecticut General rider, in which 3 percent interest is used, is $72,560. These widely differing initial amounts of decreasing term explain the premium differential. Indeed, when the premiums mentioned above are divided by the respective amounts of decreasing term (expressed in thousands of dollars), one finds that the Wisconsin National rate is $2.60 per $1,000 of initial coverage, while the Connecticut General rate is $2.38.

The Wisconsin National does have something to offer here. After all, the beneficiary who is in a position to take the $400 per month enjoys what amounts to a settlement option that guarantees 8 percent interest.

But the ad, while perhaps accurate as far as it goes, omits factors of crucial importance. I believe that this kind of omission will come increasingly under fire in a decade of "Naderism."

## IV. The Case of the 10 Percent Dividend

A few years ago, the Wabash Life Insurance Company offered a specialty policy called the Jet 9-C, for which the annual premium was $500 per unit. The contract was participating and contained a conventional dividend clause. According to the company's dividend scale at the time, the dividends for policy years 2 through 8 were $50, $60, $70, $80, $95, $100, and $110 respectively.

In the sales brochure describing the policy, there was the usual indication that the "illustrated dividends are neither projections nor guarantees," and then the scale was shown as follows:

10% upon the payment of the second annual deposit in full.
12% upon the payment of the third annual deposit in full.
14% upon the payment of the fourth annual deposit in full.
16% upon the payment of the fifth annual deposit in full.
19% upon the payment of the sixth annual deposit in full.
20% upon the payment of the seventh annual deposit in full.
22% upon the payment of the eighth annual deposit in full.

There was no specific indication that the second year's dividend, for example, was $50. Nor was there a specific indication that the second year's dividend was 10 percent *of that one year's annual premium.*

Although it may have been obvious to some people that the dividend was 10 percent of that one year's premium, it was not obvious to everyone. In a hearing before the Oregon insurance commissioner, several of the company's policyholders testified that they bought the policy by withdrawing funds from other savings because they thought they would achieve a higher rate of return by buying the policy.

It is unfortunate that the word "dividend" has become so ingrained in life insurance terminology. In my opinion, it would be a major improvement to substitute the word "refund." Until such an unlikely change comes about, however, it is important to avoid presentations that make the life insurance dividend look like something other than what it is. I believe that presentations of the type described here will come increasingly under fire in a decade of "Naderism."

## V. The Case of the 11 Percent Annuity

In the April 17, 1970, issue of *Life* magazine, The Equitable Life Assurance Society of the United States ran a full-page advertisement on immediate life annuities. The ad provided a brief description of the way in which a life annuity works, including a statement that the income is "derived from both principal and interest," and including a statement that "a portion of the annuity payments you receive is not includible in income for Federal income tax purposes, since a part of each annuity payment is considered a return of principal."

Then the ad stated that "a man 70 years old can get a guaranteed yearly income for life of about 11% of the purchase price of the annuity." The ad also showed a figure of about 13 percent for a man aged 75.

In my opinion, it would be much better to illustrate the operation of an annuity with dollar figures rather than percentages. Most readers of the ad probably do not fully understand the nature of an annuity, and would still not understand it after reading the brief explanation in the ad. Percentage figures might mislead such readers into believing that an investment in an annuity would produce an 11 percent or 13 percent rate of return. I believe that advertising practices of this type will come increasingly under fire in a decade of "Naderism."

## VI. The Case of the Missing Sentence

In March 1970 I submitted a formal statement to a Senate subcommittee concerning what I consider to be deceptive sales and advertising practices in the life insurance business. The statement was in connection with hearings on a consumer protection bill.

In the statement I was critical of the practice of contrasting a given year's premium with the increase in cash value in the same year. One of the illustrations I cited was a "Back Page" advertisement run in 1967 by the American General Life Insurance Company. Benjamin N. Woodson, president of American General and author of the ad copy, referred to a premium payment of $60 in the thirty-seventh year of a policy and a cash-value increase of $86 in that same year. He then indicated that the $86 cash-value increase "grew out of" the $60 premium payment in that year. I believe that the correct explanation is that the $86 cash-value increase arose from two sources—the premium payment for the year and interest on the accumulation of the previous thirty-six years.

Mr. Woodson responded to my criticism in another "Back Page" advertisement that appeared in several places including the July 25, 1970, issue of the life edition of *The National Underwriter.* In the recent ad, he indicated that he was wrong when he attributed the increase in cash value solely to the current premium payment.

In his recent ad, Mr. Woodson also alluded to another aspect of the problem. Let's summarize the situation by considering the following three statements and their truth or falsity:

(1) "The premium payment in the thirty-seventh year is $60." True.
(2) "The cash-value increase in the thirty-seventh year is $86." True.
(3) "The $86 cash-value increase grew out of the $60 premium payment." False.

Now, suppose one substitutes for the third item the statement that "the $86 cash-value increase grew in part out of the $60 premium payment and in part out of interest on the accumulation of the previous thirty-six years." All three statements are now true, and the use of deception has been avoided, in my opinion.

But suppose one makes only the first two true statements and omits the third statement entirely. In my opinion, deception is now involved, because unless the listener is extremely familiar with life insurance and adept at handling financial reasoning, he is apt to infer that the $86 cash-value increase grew out of the $60 premium payment. In other words, if one makes the statement about the cash-value increase, I feel he must go one step further and make the correct statement about the sources of the increase.

I believe that omissions of this kind—failure to make the third statement after having made the first two statements in the above illustration—will come increasingly under fire in a decade of "Naderism."

## VII. Conclusion

Each of the cases I have described constitutes, in my opinion, a deceptive sales or advertising practice. I feel that each of them is serious, although admittedly some are more serious than others. Please note that none of the cases involves mere adjectives and adverbs that tend to exaggerate a bit. Rather, each of them involves *numbers*—in some cases correct numbers arranged in such a way that a false impression may be gained, in other cases false numbers are difficult to detect, and in still other cases numbers that have been omitted.

Incidentally, I use the word "deceptive" to describe the effect of the practice upon the prospective buyer or reader of the advertisement. When I use the word, I do not mean to suggest that the deception is necessarily deliberate on the part of the doer.

I believe that life insurance—including cash-value life insurance—is salable on its merits. I will go one step further. I am convinced that if buyers thoroughly understood cash-value life insurance, they would buy it in much greater quantities than they now do. For these reasons, I find it appalling to observe deceptive sales and advertising practices in the life insurance business. In my view, life insurance neither needs nor deserves such practices.

I would like to propose that each of you give some serious thought to the kinds of sales and advertising practices in which you engage, and do whatever you can to eradicate questionable practices. If at least some of you adopt my proposal, I will feel that my visit with you has been worthwhile.

I would like to conclude with a quotation. Back in 1963, the following statement was made by Robert E. Dineen, then vice president of The Northwestern Mutual Life Insurance Company and now consultant to the National Association of Insurance Commissioners. He was discussing a proposal that was then under consideration in the NAIC, and I think his comments might also apply to the proposal I just made:

. . . . Our performance as a business and our regulation by the states is now being periodically reviewed by Congress and its committees. Our efforts are being judged by men who have created such structures as the Department of Justice, the Federal Trade Commission, and other judicial bodies and regulatory agencies. As a company, we do not relish the idea of explaining to sophisticated people like these—as some day we may be asked to do—the reasons why our business is opposed to this proposal. In our opinion, the better procedure is to support the proposal, adopt any changes necessary to make it workable, and get on with our business.

## Questions

1. In example (1), which compares "term to 65" with "whole life," the author points out that the "apparent cost superiority of the straight life policy" is $433.00, not $5,471.00. Do you agree that the author's cost comparison is legitimate? If so, why? If not, why not?
2. In example (2), what criticisms could be leveled at the investment return comparison other than the one cited by the author? Explain.
3. Advertising can be misleading not only by what it says, but also by what it does not say. By reference to the examples cited in this article, illustrate the above statement.
4. Select an ad for life insurance from a current newspaper or magazine and demonstrate how it either is or is not misleading to the typical insurance buyer.

# PART 8
## Pensions and Life Annuities

Since World War II a strong movement has occurred expanding group insurance, employee benefits, and private pensions in the United States. This movement has been in response to pressures such as growing population, inflation, union organization, and tax incentives. Abuses and weaknesses characterized the movement, however, and corrective federal legislation has been proposed. The article from *Business Week* identifies the major issues involved.

In the second article selected for this section, Wood and Lee examine the performance of mutual funds and variable annuity funds, both of which have been important as hedges against the risk of inflation.

# 27. THE PUSH FOR PENSION REFORM *

For 65-year-old Walter Plawinski and his wife, Jane, the good life began in 1970, when he retired from his job as an expediter at U.S. Steel's South Chicago works. In the past few years, the couple has taken several trips—to Florida and Hot Springs, Ark.—and Plawinski has again found time to indulge his love for music, a field he abandoned when the Depression wiped out his job as an orchestra leader.

"Now, I'm just taking it easy," he says. "We eat well and manage to travel a little. And I still play violin on the side."

The Plawinskis' relaxed life style and sense of financial security are due in part to a Social Security check for $212 a month, and partly to savings. But a big factor is the pension that Plawinski receives as a result of his labor for 43 years with U.S. Steel. That $323 monthly check ensures the Plawinskis relative comfort in the years ahead.

Not everyone is so fortunate. In 1960, Moriz Dreyfus was sales vice-president of Pioneer Industries, a Philadelphia clothing manufacturer. With 32 years of service, he looked forward to a pension of $700 a month. Twelve years and three mergers later, Dreyfus, who retired in 1970 at age 69, was receiving a pension check of just $160 a month.

To Richard Boch, a 45-year-old Pennsylvanian, the thought of retirement is not a happy one. Boch was employed by Acme Supermarkets for 28 years. Starting as a part-time clerk while still in high school, he worked his way up to store manager and into the supervisory ranks. Then last year Acme let him go—and told him that he was ineligible for a future pension because its plan stipulates that an employee must be 50 before his pension rights become permanent. "It doesn't seem just," says Boch, "that a man puts in over half his working life and gets nothing for it."

Gail Patrick Irish, a 56-year-old former jewelry repairman and laborer, agrees—even though he spent most of his productive life working for companies that lack pension plans. Disabled by cancer after more than 25 years in the labor force, Irish scrapes by in a one-room apartment in Los Angeles on a $200 monthly Social Security disability check and "odd jobs on the side." And when he reaches 65, no private pension check will ease his circumstances.

These stories typify the bright—and also dismal—pension prospects of Americans today. Like Walter Plawinski, millions of employees ranging from blue-collar workers to corporate executives will be able to

---

* From *Business Week* (March 17, 1973), pp. 46-50, 52, 56, 68. Reprinted by permission.

supplement their Social Security benefits with substantial private pensions when they retire. Others, such as Moriz Dreyfus and Richard Boch, who have also been enrolled in private plans for extended periods, will receive little or no pension support, either because they were laid off or changed jobs before they acquired permanent rights, or because their pension plans were terminated before adequate funds were accumulated. And millions of other workers (half the private work force), spend most of their lives like Gail Irish, in jobs that offer no pension coverage whatsoever.

This chaotic picture, which reflects the uneven development of a young and still-evolving private pension system, has given rise to a heated national debate. Spurred by employees who insist that pensions should be made an irrevocable part of their compensation, Senator Jacob Javits (R-N.Y.) is one of scores of legislators who are pressing for reform of what he terms "an institution built on human disappointment." Branding private pensions a "comprehensive consumer fraud," Ralph Nader advocates scrapping the present setup and substituting one with far greater employee and government controls. And Merton C. Bernstein, an Ohio State University law professor and long-term gadfly of the pension system, is so upset with its slow pace of reform that he says it may be "beyond effective repair."

## THE CHANGES THAT ARE COMING

Such changes, backed by thousands of letters from disillusioned workers, have stirred Congress and the Administration to act. Observers on Capitol Hill give pension reform legislation an excellent chance of passage by 1974.

For their part, many business groups argue that the pension system's critics ignore its considerable achievements. While conceding that legislation would eliminate some weaknesses, they fear the constraining hand of over-regulation. Even as the debate rages, however, it is clear that major changes are in the works:

■ Companies will have to tell employees and government a lot more about how their pension plans work and are administered.
■ Government-mandated standards will seek to insure that employees receive permanent pension rights after reasonable periods of service and that these rights are backed by adequate funds.
■ Pension fund administrators will find their investment activities closely watched by plan participants, corporate shareholders, and government agencies.
■ The multibillion dollar impact of pension funds on the securities markets and the economy will be scrutinized.

In short, the private pension system, which like Topsy has "just growed," is headed toward a stage of guided development in which it will be increasingly shaped by the imperatives of national social policy.

Realistic businessmen are already accepting the idea that reform is inevitable. Though some worry about the cost, the consensus of pension experts is that the extra outlay by U.S. companies should not be onerous. The critical question, however, is whether the reforms can be accomplished without damaging the system's remarkable vitality.

That vitality is illustrated by the dynamic growth of private pension plans in the last three decades. The number of people enrolled in such plans has soared from 4.1-million in 1940 to more than 30-million in 1971. In the same period, the number of retirees receiving private pensions rose from 160,000 to 5.25-million, and the assets of pension funds multiplied sixtyfold to $153-billion.

It may come as a surprise to thousands of workers who ante up a chunk of their salaries every month, but most private plans are not contributory. Indeed, with employers putting more than $14-billion a year in the kitty, the employee share currently is only $1.5-billion and has been declining in percentage terms. But even with management picking up most of the tab—aided, to be sure, by returns on the invested assets—private pension fund reserves are expected to hit $250-billion by 1980.

Individual pensions are growing apace. The system pays out more than $8-billion in benefits each year, and the average annual pension, which was $822 back in 1950, came to about $1,600 in 1971. Moreover, this average figure includes pensions paid to workers who retired 10 and 15 years ago. Newly retired workers are getting a lot more. More than half of covered workers who retired in 1968 received private pensions in excess of $1,800 a year. The pensions earned by today's crop of retirees are undoubtedly higher.

## CARROTS AND STICKS

What makes this growth especially impressive is that the private pension system in the U.S. is purely voluntary. No law forces a company to set up a pension plan. Furthermore, the system is a relative newcomer on the American industrial scene. To be sure, several railroads and American Express Co. set up pension plans in the late 19th Century, followed by a number of unions and corporations in the early 1900s. But it took the Depression and World War II to transform such developments into a national movement.

The Depression brought into painful focus a number of long-term trends affecting the aged: their deteriorating position in the labor force as the U.S. became industrialized, their loss of support from children as large rural families split up into smaller urban families, and their inability to save for their declining years (lengthened by medical advances) in an economy subject to cyclical fluctuations and swift technological change. The Social Security Act of 1935 recognized the need for systematic ways to provide for superannuated workers, and created a basic "floor of protection" on which private efforts could build.

With the imposition of wage controls and excess profits taxes during World War II, these efforts intensified. Unable to use wage hikes to compete for scarce workers, corporations offered the lure of future pensions instead and funded them with profits that would otherwise have been taxed away. The landmark Inland Steel Co. decision by the National Labor Relations Board in 1948 confirmed the right of unions to bargain about pensions—a right they have doggedly exercised ever since.

Clearly, as Thomas Paine, partner in the actuarial firm of Hewitt Associates, points out, a major reason for the pension system's beanstalk-like growth has been "the absence of constraining regulatory controls." To bolster the system, the government offered some tax inducements: It exempted from taxes both employer contributions to pension funds and the investment earnings of such funds, and it deferred employee taxes on these sums until retirees actually receive benefits (a time when individual incomes and tax liabilities are usually low). It also set certain basic ground rules, one being that benefit schedules cannot discriminate in favor of higher-paid personnel, and another that corporate contributions to pension funds must be enough to cover retirement benefits currently being stored up by workers.

But the government has been far more permissive in other key areas. It has left the matter of fiduciary responsibility—the rules governing the behavior of pension fund administrators—mainly to state trust laws and the common law. And it has allowed companies to make their own decisions about "vesting"—the point at which an employee acquires a permanent right to a future pension.

Moreover, an employer is not required to fund the past service liabilities that are usually created when a plan is set up. The government merely insists that, at a minimum, it must pay interest on them to the fund. Yet past service liabilities are not only generally hefty to begin with, but tend to rise dramatically when benefit formulas are raised retroactively. After American Can Co. negotiated a pension hike with its unions in 1971, for example, its unfunded vested liabilities jumped by $90-million.

## A GUARANTEED RIGHT

Given the lack of regulation, the private pension system has performed remarkably well. Prodded by union demands, competitive pressures, and their own growing sense of social responsibility, most companies have steadily improved vesting, funding, and benefit standards. A recent Bureau of Labor Statistics study indicates that 90% of all employees covered by private plans today are entitled to vested rights or early retirement benefits by age 55 if they have worked 15 years under a plan. Liberal features such as early retirement provisions, death and disability benefits, and final-pay pension formulas have become common. Yet without the freedom to adopt their own funding and vesting practices and thus minimize initial costs, many companies that now boast outstanding pension programs might never have taken the pension path at all.

Whether this degree of freedom is still desirable is another question. In recent years, real and potential weaknesses in the pension system have drawn attention.

For one thing, there has been growing interest in the economic impact of what Senator Harrison A. Williams, Jr. (D-N.J.), calls "the largest single pool of virtually unregulated assets in the nation." Pension funds have become not only a critical source of the investment capital needed to fuel a growing economy, but also a major influence on the behavior of the stock markets.

At the same time, American society has undergone profound changes affecting public expectations regarding job tenure and the permanence of corporate entities. Under the pressure of rapid technological progress and unprecedented economic growth, American workers and companies have become increasingly mobile. And corporate identities have been altered or swept away in a continuing wave of mergers and acquisitions that has left a trail of terminated pension plans and unfulfilled pension promises.

Perhaps most important, public attitudes toward pensions have changed. As companies and unions have boasted about pension advances, and as more and more retirees have actually received benefits, the traditional notion that a pension is a gratuitous reward for long and loyal service has gradually been replaced by the belief that it is—or should be—a guaranteed right, once an employee has completed a reasonable period of employment.

These developments lie behind the pressure for reform that has been building in Congress. At present three legislative plans are given the best chances of adoption:

> ■ A wide-ranging bill introduced by Williams and Javits and 49 other co-sponsors in the Senate. It would set new rules regarding fiduciary responsibility, disclosure, vesting, and funding, and would establish an insurance plan to guarantee pension rights and a government clearinghouse to ease portability of pension credits among employers.
> ■ A similar plan pushed by Representative John H. Dent (D-Pa.) in the form of two bills before the House.
> ■ A more conservative Administration-backed program that was embodied in two House bills in the last Congress and is expected to be reintroduced, with some modification. Besides setting standards for fiduciary responsibility, disclosure, and vesting, President Nixon's plan would allow employees who lack pension coverage to set up their own tax-deductible retirement programs.

All three reform plans recognize that new rules regarding the behavior of pension fund administrators and disclosure of information are necessary —not because misconduct is rife, but because it is hard to expose and to prosecute.

For one thing, the stiffest present federal law, the Welfare & Pension Plans Disclosure Act, requires pension plans to file annual reports that are so general that they are of little use in spotting misbehavior. It took many months, for example, to develop evidence in the classic United Mine Workers case, in which pension money was deposited in a non-interest-bearing account in a union-run bank and also used to invest in electric utilities which were then pressured to use union-mined coal.

Moreover, not only do state trust laws covering fiduciary responsibility often conflict (a knotty problem for plans operating interstate), but they tend to be permissive with respect to questionable practices. "There are a lot of funny things you can do if a plan's trust agreement says they're o.k.," notes Michael Gordon, minority counsel of the Senate labor subcommittee, which drafted the Williams-Javits bill. Gordon points to the cases of Sharon Steel Corp., which used pension fund money to engineer corporate takeovers, and of Genesco, which used its fund to buy and mortgage the stores of S. H. Kress, which it later acquired.

## THE SCOPE OF PROPOSED REFORMS

The new reform measures would ban these and a whole list of other "conflict-of-interest" practices, such as investing more than 10% of a pension fund's assets in a company's own stock. And they would make plan administrators liable to civil and criminal actions in the federal courts, including suits by pension plan participants.

Companies will also have to disclose a lot more about their fund operations, including securities transactions and actuarial assumptions, and such information will be available to plan participants, too. Says Joseph Leary, executive director of the Assn. of Private Pension & Welfare Plans: "Much of the disappointment about pensions has been due to ignorance about the way plans operate." Employers will have to furnish participants with simple, easily understandable descriptions of their rights and obligations, and of the ways in which they can lose out on benefits.

Corporations will also be required to make pension rights permanent after a reasonable period of service. Until last year, the business community had argued heatedly that the pension system's progress makes such legislation unnecessary. It cited a study of 864 plans by the actuarial firm of A. S. Hansen, which indicates that two-thirds of covered employees will wind up with pension rights before leaving their jobs. The reformers replied by pointing to a comprehensive Senate labor subcommittee survey that suggests that only 10% of those enrolled in a private plan stay around long enough to acquire a pension right.

Both studies are open to criticism, but government statistics tend to support the pension system's defenders. A recent study indicates that 43% of recently retired male workers (and 17% of female workers) receiving Social Security benefits also get private pensions from their longest-held job. Since only half of the private work force has pension coverage, most covered workers (or at least male workers) apparently manage to vest benefits by the time they retire.

Nonetheless, a significant number of workers do lose benefit rights after long service because their pension plans have poor vesting provisions. And their ranks multiply whenever an economic slowdown results in massive layoffs. "It's bad enough to lose a job at 50 or 60," says one observer, "but it's devastating to lose your pension, too."

Recognizing the inequity of this situation, the Nixon Administration last year added its voice to those calling for compulsory early vesting. And a number of business groups, such as the National Assn. of Manufacturers, the American Bankers Assn., and the U.S. Chamber of Commerce, reversed their former stands and backed the idea. "When you see the handwriting on the wall," says one man "you give in gracefully."

The NAM has testified in favor of the Dent bill's proposal for 100% vesting after 10 years of covered service, but other business groups favor the Administration's "rule of 50" proposal, which would vest an employee with 50% of his pension when his age and service total 50 and add 10% more annually over the next five years. "This gives security to older workers who need it most," says one man. But backers of the Dent plan and the Williams-Javits bill (30% vesting after eight years, with 10% more each year for the next seven) argue that the rule of 50 could encourage companies to avoid pension costs by hiring younger workers. "Anyone over 45 has enough trouble finding a job," says Vance Anderson, counsel to the pension task force of the House general labor subcommittee.

## PROTECTING VESTED RIGHTS

Whichever vesting proposal wins out, the outlook is dim for "portability" proposals that would set up a clearinghouse to facilitate the voluntary transfer of vested credits from one employer to another. The Administration is dead set against the idea, and reformers are not pushing it very hard. "If you have vested rights," says one, "you don't need to drag your pension around behind you."

Reformers insist, however, on the need for stiffer funding rules and the creation of a federally administered insurance plan to protect employees' vested rights if a plan terminates. And though the Administration is still studying these ideas, it is not entirely unreceptive. In a message to Congress last year, Nixon observed: "When a pension plan is terminated, an employee participating in it can lose all or part of the benefits which he has been relying on, even if his plan is fully vested."

One reason for such losses is obviously the present funding standard. Under Internal Revenue Service rules, a pension plan must fund its currently accruing liabilities, but it can get by with interest payments on its past service liabilities. Plans that stay close to this level often tend to be underfunded. And if such a plan is terminated (when a facility is closed or the company folds or is involved in a merger), the fund may lack assets to cover all vested liabilities. Since retirees almost always have first claim on the assets, many workers with vested rights wind up empty-handed.

This is apparently what happened in some of the cases investigated by the Senate labor subcommittee last year. Hearings were held on the recent termination of such plans as those of White Motor's Minneapolis-Moline Div., New Jersey's P. Ballantine & Sons, and Sargent Industries' Gar Wood division in Cleveland. Although the employers were in compliance with IRS funding regulations, hundreds of vested employees faced benefit losses.

A regulation mandating the funding of past service liabilities would undoubtedly lessen this problem, although most plans are already funding such obligations at a reasonable pace. Indeed, to avoid the loss of tax revenues, the IRS has felt it necessary to forbid companies to fund faster than over a 10-year period. The most frequent schedule for amortizing past service costs, in fact, is 30 years, which is the precise funding period contained in the Williams-Javits bill. (The Dent proposal is for 25-year funding of vested liabilities.)

A 30-year funding rule, however, would not completely erase the risk of losing vested rights—not only because 30 years is a long time, but because most companies periodically improve pensions to keep pace with inflation and workers' demands. And when this happens, even plans that follow good funding practices tend to become seriously underfunded for a while. Before the United Auto Workers negotiated pension hikes with Ford Motor Co. in 1970, for example, the pension plan was 86% funded. After the hikes, the funded level dropped to 70% (it is higher now), and some employees with vested rights would have wound up with only 16¢ on the dollar had the plan suddenly terminated.

A company such as Ford, of course, is not likely to fold up tomorrow, so its temporary underfunded status was not really a problem. But companies do fall by the wayside over the years, leaving unfunded vested liabilities in their wake. "Even if plans follow good funding practices, plan termination insurance is needed," says Michael Gordon.

## INSURANCE FOR THE PENSION

Compulsory insurance to protect the pension rights of employees is not a new idea. Both Sweden and Finland, for example, require employers to guarantee pension promises either by securing credit insurance or by purchasing insurance policies. And many experts such as Dan McGill, chairman of the Wharton School's Pension Research Council, believe that an insurance plan is feasible for U.S. employers, as well. But some business groups are skeptical. For one thing, many companies resent having to pay for something they feel they do not need. Mark Twinney, manager of Ford's pension department, figures that its initial annual premium for such insurance might come to $2-million. "People like us would pay for the financially weak," he complains. Others fear that the availability of insurance would cause costs to spiral. "An employer who knows he's going out of business isn't likely to exercise restraint," declares Andrew Melgard of the U.S. Chamber of Commerce.

Pension reformers are quick to reply. "Large corporations have an exaggerated idea of their permanence," says one. "Who can say that every single one of the big auto and steel companies will be around in 20 years?"

Michael Gordon insists that the insurance provisions in the Williams-Javits bill have "strong safeguards to prevent abuses." Only vested pension rights up to $500 a month would be insured, and no payout would be made for pension increases granted in the three-year period preceding termination. The Secretary of Labor would have power to make sure that the termination is a bona fide action. And if a merger was taking place, the surviving company would have to reimburse the insurance fund for some of its costs.

Just how much would reforms cost pension plan sponsors? Obviously the new fiduciary and disclosure standards entail minimal costs. As for vesting, a computer simulation study made for the House labor subcommittee by Howard Winklevoss, assistant professor of insurance at the Wharton School, indicates that the major reform proposals do not differ significantly in their potential costs. While a few plans might get hit as much as 50%, the vast majority would face modest increases ranging from zero to 7%. On the other hand, the cost of plans with no early vesting at all would rise on average about 10% to 15%. Since pension costs normally range between 3% to 10% of payroll, the average hike in the worst cases would come to 1½% of payroll.

The modest impact of a vesting rule is confirmed by a survey of 491 companies made by McGraw-Hill Publications Co. last year for Standard & Poor's Intercapital, Inc. On average, the companies surveyed indicated that passage of a 10-year vesting rule would force them to raise their pension contributions by a scant 2%.

The costs of insurance coverage will also be modest, at least to begin with. The initial premiums in the legislation range up to half of 1% of unfunded vested liabilities. Further, these liabilities may be smaller than they appear on a company's books. For accounting purposes, most companies value their pension fund assets at less than market value—recognizing that market fluctuations make it prudent to spread unrealized appreciation (or depreciation) over several years. In 1971, for example, the total market value of such assets was $18.6-billion more than their reported value (a difference of 17%). And for insurance purposes, companies would be able to use the market value of assets to calculate the degree to which vested liabilities are funded.

Several years ago, two pension experts, Charles Trowbridge and Frank L. Griffin, Jr., used a similar market-value yardstick to access the funding status of more than 1,000 plans covering 4.5-million workers. They found that 77% of the plans had enough reserves to cover all vested liabilities, and another 10% had assets covering at least 80% of such obligations. This suggests that many companies would find their unfunded vested liabilities—and insurance premiums—far smaller than they have imagined.

## BUSINESS HAS WORRIES

Ultimately, the cost of insurance will depend on experience. And here again, a preliminary study of pension plan terminations just released by the Treasury and Labor departments suggests that it will not be great. The study, which is in line with earlier research, indicates that some 10,000 individuals are losing $20-million to $30-million in vested benefits each year from plan terminations. "From an insurance standpoint, this is peanuts," says one official.

Business spokesmen, however, continue to worry about the possibility that insurance would inspire unwarranted hikes in benefits. "This is a very tricky thing," says one man. "You would be insuring assets that do not yet exist."

The cost of a minimum funding rule appears far less threatening. "It wouldn't be that much of a problem for most companies," says Robert Maggy, manager of Standard Oil of California's benefits division. Indeed, most of the complaining about cost is done by unions, not business.

The sticking point is multi-employer plans, in which a number of employers in an industry contribute to a common fund administered jointly by labor and management. While the AFL-CIO strongly backs the Williams-Javits bill, it argues that multi-employer plans should be exempt from the funding and vesting standards. Because such plans have a portability feature, labor claims that employees are protected against loss of pension rights when an employer lays them off. They merely go to work for someone else in the industry and carry their pension credits with them. Moreover, the argument goes, it makes no sense for multi-employer plans to fund past service liabilities since the bankruptcy of a single employer does not ordinarily affect the solvency of the fund.

Louis Rolnick, who oversees the International Ladies Garment Workers Union's multi-employer plan, estimates that the new proposals could easily double its cost. "We would either have to get employers to kick in a lot more or reduce our benefits, which now run only $75 or $85 a month for retirees with 20 years of service," he says.

Pension reformers concede that multi-employer plans may be safer than single employer plans in many instances. But Vance Anderson points to the anthracite coal and New England shoe industries as examples of multi-employer plans with financial problems. Given the political pressures, however, a compromise on the multi-employer issue seems likely. The Williams-Javits bill, in fact, permits delays in compliance where new vesting and funding rules impose hardships on employers or beneficiaries, and it authorizes the Labor Secretary to set separate filing standards for multi-employer plans.

Meanwhile, what worries some business groups most about funding is the specter of increasing government control. Says Thomas Paine of Hewitt Associates: "Many people fear the government will dictate guidelines on such things as actuarial assumptions and accounting practices."

Paine believes this could damage the private pension system's flexibility. "Each company," he argues, "is a special case, with its unique work force, economic situation, and pension objectives. It must be able to make its own assumptions about labor turnover, investment performance, and other matters, and to act independently. Most companies, for example, make heavy contributions to their funds in good years and cut back sharply in bad years."

Paine also notes that the American Institute of Certified Public Accountants has ruled that companies with unfunded vested liabilities should charge pension costs against earnings, cutting these liabilities by 5% a year or amortizing all past service costs over 40 years. "There's no need for a further government standard," claims Paine.

## THE ROLE OF SOCIAL SECURITY

The ultimate fear of the business community, of course, is that new regulations would be simply the first steps in a process leading to the absorption of private pension schemes into the Social Security system. The recent major increases in Social Security taxes are already preempting some revenues that businesses might have pumped into pension programs. Reform and its costs, the Cassandras argue, will stifle the private system still further.

The reformers reply that their efforts are directed at strengthening private programs and resisting the inroads of Social Security. "I am an ardent advocate of the private pension system," says Javits. "I think workers themselves prefer a private pension to total dependence on Social Security. But it has to be a pension where they have a real chance to get retirement security."

Somewhat surprisingly, the reformers have not yet seriously tackled the most obvious shortcoming of private pensions: the fact that they cover only half of all workers in the private sector. Many small and middle-sized companies simply cannot afford to set up private pension plans. Robert Paul, president of Martin E. Segal Co., consultants and actuaries, believes that this "deplorable situation" is responsible for Social Security's accelerating growth. "Because many workers who retire without a private pension can't get by on Social Security alone," he says, "the political pressure to raise Social Security benefits is unremitting."

## SPREADING THE BENEFITS

The Administration has taken a small step toward filling this gap by proposing that employees who are not covered by pension plans be allowed to contribute up to $1,500 a year or 20% of their income (whichever is smaller) to individual retirement programs, and to deduct these contributions from their taxable income. Participants in existing plans would also be able to sweeten the pot if employer contributions on their behalf are below this level.

This proposal would extend to the working public the same kind of tax incentives already available to the self-employed (under the Keogh Act), but it would still bypass millions of low-wage workers who can ill afford to put money aside for retirement. The AFL-CIO has attacked the proposal as a "new tax loophole for the wealthy." Many pension experts believe the ultimate answer may be a compulsory private pension plan.

In any case, the pension system is in for some major changes in the next few years. Says economist Robert Taggart, executive director of the National Manpower Policy Task Force and author of a recent study of the system: "Pension legislation is inevitable in light of the nation's social goals." Taggart points out that many plans now pay pensions that provide two-thirds or more of preretirement income when combined with Social Security. "For the private pension system," he says, "the next decade may well be a period of consolidation, with the stress on equity, security of benefits, and bringing laggard plans up to par."

Many of the reforms that observers like Taggart are talking about have already become reality overseas: mandatory vesting in the Netherlands, Belgium, and Denmark; systematic advanced funding in several of the Scandinavian countries; portability in France and Britain; insurance in Scandinavia; and compulsory private coverage in Finland. Canada, whose pension system most resembles that of the U.S., has had mandatory funding and vesting standards for years. Private pension experts in these nations do not feel that regulation has hampered growth.

With the pressure for similar reforms mounting in the U.S., some elements of the business community are climbing on the bandwagon. Both the American Bankers Assn. and the Life Insurance Assn. of America have come out in favor of reasonable minimum vesting and funding rules. Says William T. Gibb III, associate general counsel of the insurance group: "The only way to preserve the private pension system is to establish some mandatory standards." Robert Eddy, personnel manager at San Francisco's Levi Strauss & Co., says that his company is "highly in favor" of the Williams-Javits bill even though its pension plan does not yet meet the standards outlined in the proposal.

John F. Manning, treasurer of Philadelphia's ITE-Imperial Corp., comments: "There's a lot of sound and fury now, but if you ask most businessmen 10 years from now what they think of pension legislation, most of them will probably say it was worthwhile."

## Questions

1. The article states that the United States pension system is "purely voluntary." Assuming that this is so, list and discuss reasons why a small, family-held firm might start a pension program and contribute funds to it.
2. Discuss the general effect that each of the following changes in a pension fund has on the cost of the program. What happens in each case if the provision is changed and the firm does not change the contribution it makes?

a. Changing the vesting period from 20 years to 15 years.
b. Decreasing the interest rate that is assumed to be earned by the fund from 4% to 3%.
c. Agreeing with another firm that employees who change jobs from one of the firms to the other firm has the privilege of transferring all of his pension rights and funds to that firm's pension program.
d. Reducing the retirement age from 65 to 62.
e. Increasing the benefit check for those who are already retired and receiving benefits by $50 per month.
3. What consideration should you have and what questions should you ask about the pension plan of a firm with whom you are interviewing for a job?
4. In 1971 it was estimated that about 65% of private nonfarm employees (about 30 million) were enrolled in private pension plans. Yet only about 5 million persons were receiving private pensions in 1971. What accounts for this discrepancy? What major reform would help correct it? Discuss.

# 28. MUTUAL FUNDS AND VARIABLE ANNUITIES: CONSUMER PURCHASE DECISIONS *

Glenn L. Wood †
and J. Finley Lee ††

The prodigious growth of mutual funds in recent years is well known, even to those who are unsophisticated in financial matters. The *1968 Mutual Fund Fact Book* published by the Investment Company Institute reported that the assets of mutual funds increased about 90-fold between 1940 and 1967.[1] This phenomenal rate of growth can be easily explained. An increasing population, greater affluence, increasing acceptance of equity investments, and the rapid appreciation of security prices are among the important explanations of why mutual funds have had such success.[2] Another reason, which is frequently overlooked, is that retirement income planning is becoming much more important, and a high proportion of mutual fund shareowners plan to use their mutual fund shares for retirement purposes. A recent study revealed that about three-fourths of mutual fund owners intend to use mutual funds for retirement purposes.[3]

During the period 1952-1967, when the total net assets of mutual funds increased about 11-fold,[4] the assets behind variable annuities increased insignificantly in comparison. In 1966, the total reserves for variable annuity plans in force with life insurance companies in the United States were approximately $70 million, of which only $10 million represented individual variable annuity plans.[5] In the same year the

* From *CLU Journal* (January, 1969), pp. 8-15. Reprinted, with permission, from the JOURNAL of the American Society of Chartered Life Underwriters, Volume XXIII, No. 1 (January 1969). Copyright 1969 by the American Society of Chartered Life Underwriters, 270 Bryn Mawr Avenue, Bryn Mawr, Pa. 19010.

† Associate Professor of Finance, University of Missouri.

†† Associate Professor of Risk and Insurance, Florida State University.

[1] This figure applies only to the assets of mutual fund members of The Investment Company Institute.

[2] For an analysis of mutual fund growth, see "Factors That Affect Mutual Fund Growth." F. B. Allerdice and D. E. Farrar, *Journal of Financial and Quantitative Analysis,* Vol. II, No. 4 (December, 1967), p. 365.

[3] United States Senate, *Mutual Fund Legislation of 1967,* Hearings Before the Committee on Banking and Currency, (Washington, D. C.: U.S. Government Printing Office), p. 467.

[4] Investment Company Institute, *1968 Mutual Fund Fact Book,* (New York: Investment Company Institute, 1968), p. 16.

[5] Institute of Life Insurance—Division of Statistics and Research, "The Tally of Life Insurance Statistics," (January, 1968), p. 2.

total net assets of mutual funds were approximately $35 billion[6]—about 3500 times greater than individual variable annuity reserves. Uninsured variable annuity plans have also been unpopular. A study in 1967 indicated that only 4 percent of existing trusteed pension plans included a variable annuity option during the liquidation period.[7]

The reasons for the slow acceptance of variable annuities are not difficult to determine. Variable annuities, from their inception in 1952, have been plagued by regulatory problems. For more than a decade the Securities and Exchange Commission fought for regulatory jurisdiction.[8] Many, but certainly not all, of the major regulatory questions have now been resolved, and a large number of life insurance companies are entering the variable annuity market. One study prepared in the summer of 1967 showed that at least forty-four life insurance companies were in the variable annuity market in some form, and that a number of other companies were planning to enter the market.[9]

As greater numbers of life insurance companies enter the equity investment market, comparisons between mutual funds and variable annuities will be made. Such comparisons are already starting to appear. According to one observer, ". . . the variable annuity and the mutual fund are not very different."[10] And, he continues, ". . . I believe the variable annuity is the best *kind* of mutual fund for most men in most circumstances most of the time."[11] (emphasis added)

Comparisons of mutual funds and variable annuities will multiply because of competition among financial institutions for the consumers' savings dollar. These comparisons will be particularly important to life insurance agents and other salesmen who can offer both products to their clients.

The analogies between mutual funds and variable annuities are most interesting. If it is true that variable annuities are virtually the same as mutual funds, one might expect the growth of variable annuities to accelerate rapidly in the future. Moreover, if variable annuities are a superior investment media for "most men in most circumstances most of the time," then it would seem logical to expect that growth in variable annuities would exceed the growth of mutual funds. The possibility of rapid growth for variable annuities is based on the assumptions that consumers have an important role in purchase decisions and that the marketing of

---

[6] Investment Company Institute, *op. cit.*, p. 7.

[7] Edwin T. Johnson, "Variable Annuities," *Pension and Welfare News*, Vol. 4, No. 10, (July, 1968), p. 30.

[8] Many articles have discussed the regulatory problems associated with variable annuities. See, for example, Wiliam A. Kern, "Variable Annuities," *Insurance Law Journal*, No. 543, (April, 1968), p. 277.

[9] "Insurance Companies in the United States Selling Variable Dollar Products," *Pension and Welfare News*, Vol. 4, No. 4, (January, 1968). pp. 26-27.

[10] Benjamin N. Woodson, "The Life Underwriter's Future Role in the Personal Investing Function," *1967 C.L.U. Forum Report*, (Bryn Mawr, Pa.: The American Society of Chartered Life Underwriters, 1968), p. 50.

[11] *Ibid.*, p. 51.

variable annuities will become substantially more effective than it has been in the past. There are important signs that the variable annuity will be marketed much more effectively in the future. The major obstacle (regulatory problems) has been largely removed and large numbers of life insurance companies, as well as competing financial institutions, are attempting to enter the variable annuity market. With roughly comparable marketing effectiveness, the two products—mutual funds and variable annuities—should stand on their merits before the consumer. If these assumptions have some validity, the possibility of expansive growth in variable annuities rests upon the assertion that variable annuities are essentially the same as, or have significant overall advantages over, mutual funds.

The purpose of this paper, therefore, is to analyze the factors a rational consumer should consider in making decisions with regard to mutual funds and variable annuities.[12] It is hoped that the analysis will have some important implications for the probable future growth of each type of investment media.

## ESSENTIAL SIMILARITIES BETWEEN MUTUAL FUNDS AND VARIABLE ANNUITIES

There is a great deal of variation among individuals in the degree to which they plan their financial affairs. Some people have rather detailed, elaborate plans, and others have virtually no plans. At a minimum, practically everyone has some vague ideas concerning his financial needs and how he might attempt to satisfy them. Even the most rudimentary financial plans must involve at least two elements: (1) financial needs must be identified, and (2) financial vehicles must be selected. For example, an individual might decide that he has a need for a retirement fund and that he will use a savings account in a commercial bank to reach this objective.

Mutual funds and variable annuities are two financial vehicles that might be used to meet certain financial objectives. To the extent that consumers view them as substitutes, they may both be used to meet the same financial needs. The degree of substitution between mutual funds and variable annuities depends upon the similarities that consumers perceive between the two products. Consumers might very well view the products as being essentially the same because they share a number of important characteristics. These characteristics are:

(1) The types of investments made by most mutual funds and variable annuity plans are comparable. Although mutual funds and variable annuity companies make investments in bonds and preferred stocks,

---

[12] Only individual variable annuities are treated in this paper. Also excluded from consideration because of their unique characteristics are no-load and contractual mutual funds. In addition, the desirability of whether or not any type of financial institution should enter the variable annuity market is outside the scope of this treatment.

the assets of most mutual funds and variable annuities are invested primarily in common stocks. Because of differences in objectives, the portfolio composition of individual mutual funds and variable annuity plans may vary.

(2) Another similarity between mutual funds and variable annuities is that the success or failure of each is dependent upon investment performance. The value of a "share" in a mutual fund rises and falls according to investment experience. The value of a variable annuity "unit" is also determined by interest, dividend income, and capital gains and losses. While there are differences in terminology, investment performance essentially determines the value of the consumer's investment.

(3) Mutual funds offer an investor a partial solution to the problem of portfolio management. The management company performs the research function, selects and purchases securities, supervises the portfolio, sells securities, and provides an accounting to the mutual fund shareholder. The owner of a variable annuity obtains the same services. In fact, a single professional management company could service a mutual fund and a variable annuity company simultaneously.

(4) Most investors who purchase individual securities cannot obtain a high degree of diversification. However, both mutual funds and variable annuities provide a consumer with a highly diversified investment portfolio. A mutual fund is diversified by the number and types of investments. Each shareowner, in effect, owns a portfolio; diversification by industries and geographical region are also characteristic of most mutual fund portfolios. Diversifications over time can be achieved by a mutual fund shareowner by making periodic purchases. Exactly the same types of diversification are available to variable annuity owners since the same principles of diversification are used in purchasing securities.

## DIFFERENCES BETWEEN MUTUAL FUNDS AND VARIABLE ANNUITIES

Although mutual funds and variable annuities share a number of fundamental characteristics, there are some important differences. If these differences are substantial, they might lead consumers to choose one over the other or use mutual funds to meet one objective and variable annuities to meet another.[13] The major differences—or potential differences—between mutual funds and variable annuities that might persuade consumers to choose one over the other are the annuity principle, the investment return, expense charges, and tax effects.[14]

---

[13] Technical differences in methods of operating or regulating the plans should have no impact on consumers if they do not perceive them as significant for their own personal situations. For a discussion of the differences between mutual funds and variable annuities that seems largely irrelevant to consumers, see, John F. Guion, "Just Like a Mutual Fund," *Personal Insurance,* (February, 1968), p. 81.

[14] A recent study showed that investors are apparently more sensitive to investment performance, sales charges, and expense ratios than commonly believed. Allerdice and Farrar, *op. cit.,* p. 377.

## The Annuity Principle

Technically, an annuity is simply a periodic payment, and a life annuity is a series of payments that are made throughout a designated person's lifetime. The annuity principle is a concept that is utilized by variable annuities but not by mutual funds.

At retirement, many individuals have the problem of converting a principal sum into a series of income payments. There are only three methods by which this conversion can be accomplished. First, a person could elect to receive periodic interest, dividends, or both from the principal sum he has invested, without liquidating the principal. This approach preserves the principal sum, even after death, but it is not an efficient use of funds unless there is a need or desire to leave an inheritance. Moreover, it requires a large sum to provide a sizeable income. For example, at 6 percent interest (or a 6 percent dividend rate) a capital sum of $100,000 is needed to provide $500 a month. Few people have been able to accumulate the principal amounts required for substantial retirement income.[15]

A second approach that can be used in an attempt to obtain a larger retirement income is to liquidate the principal over time. Most mutual funds will allow shareowners to periodically withdraw any amount they choose (subject to minimum amount restrictions). This approach permits considerable flexibility and is popular with many investors. A serious drawback, however, is that a person never knows how long he will live and, therefore, what portion of the principal can safely be withdrawn each year. Thus, there is a distinct possibility that an individual could outlive his income and lose his financial security.

A life annuity represents the third approach to converting a principal sum into a series of income payments. Although an individual cannot know how long he will live, it is possible to predict, rather accurately, average life expectancy. This means that a large group of retired individuals can pool their investments and, using mortality data, liquidate the invested fund over their lifetimes. Funds would be released by those who die soon after retirement to provide continued income for those who live longer than expected. A life insurance company does precisely this when it issues life annuities. Benefit payments from life annuities, as a consequence, are composed of principal and interest. This scientific liquidation of principal is known as the annuity principle and is one reason that the percentage return on a life annuity is considered to be attractive. A male aged 65, for example, can obtain an income through a life annuity (composed of interest earning and liquidated principal) of about 8 percent per annum.[16]

---

[15] In 1963, the median value of financial assets owned by the aged was only $1,340. Only about 15 percent of the aged married couples had financial assets of over $15,000. For a good description of the financial condition of the aged, see John Turnbull, C. Arthur Williams, Jr., Earl Cheit, *Economic and Social Security*, (New York: Ronald Press Co., 1968), p. 70.

[16] Based on current annuity rates of several representative life insurance companies.

A life annuity has several advantages over a mutual fund in providing retirement income. The income is guaranteed for life, and is probably greater than it would be if only interest or dividend income were received. In the past, the major disadvantage of life annuities was a susceptibility to loss of purchasing power through inflation. Since the variable annuity benefit payment is predicated on the investment performance of a securities portfolio, it provides as much protection against the purchasing power risk as a mutual fund that invests its assets in similar securities.

## Investment Performance

A consumer may prefer a mutual fund or variable annuity if he expects the investment performance of one to be better than the other. Advocates of mutual funds may claim that the investment performance of mutual funds will be superior to that of variable annuities, and those who favor variable annuities may believe that the investment performance of variable annuities will be at least as good as, or better than, that of mutual funds. Undoubtedly this debate will develop and intensify in the future.

An examination of past performance records may not be meaningful since the experience of variable annuities is limited; moreover, adequate data are unavailable. The data that do exist are not comparable. The taxes applicable to mutual funds and variable annuities are quite different in effect, and data that are published generally do not adjust for the differences. In addition, the investment performance of individual mutual funds and variable annuities has varied widely; this variation tends to limit the significance of aggregate data. Subject to these major limitations, it is interesting to compare the data that are available.

During the period 1960-1965, the median rate of growth in the unit value of fourteen variable annuity plans was 7.5 percent.[17] A widely accepted index of mutual fund performance showed the following:[18]

| Type of Fund | Rate of Growth* | Representative Dividend Yield |
|---|---|---|
| growth-income | 7.9% | 2.3% |
| growth | 7.7 | 1.3 |
| income | 6.1 | 4.4 |
| balanced | 5.8 | 2.7 |

\* This is the yearly average compound rate of growth. It assumes reinvestment of capital gains.

---

[17] This figure was computed from "Forum: Actuarial and Financial Experience under Variable Annuities." *Proceedings-Conference of Actuaries in Public Practice,* 1965-1966, pp. 156, 160, and 166, and the Annual Reports of several large companies that were selling variable annuities during 1960-1965. The mortality experience is included in the unit value of some companies, but most of the plans were fairly large and mortality deviations would not affect the unit value greatly.

[18] Arthur Weisenberger and Company, *Investment Companies,* (New York: Arthur Weisenberger and Company, 1966), p. 129.

Over the same period (1960-1965) the Dow-Jones Industrial Average grew at an average rate of 5.6 percent. Thus the median variable annuity performance was better than the rate of growth in the Dow-Jones Industrial Average, but was not equal to that of the mutual funds.

The legitimate concern of consumers should be investment performance in the future, not the past. Do variable annuity plans or mutual funds have characteristics that would appear to give one an investment advantage over the other in the future? Proponents of mutual funds state that they have had more investment experience with common stocks. Life insurance companies, they argue, have historically been severely limited by regulatory restrictions in the amount of common stocks they may own. As a result, the argument continues, the investment officers of life insurance companies are relatively inexperienced with common stock investments. Even with the investment regulations that have been liberalized to permit life insurance companies to offer variable annuities, some states still have restrictions that might hamper investment performance. Also, mutual fund advocates assert that life insurance companies have traditionally been conservative in their investment policies and this may inhibit their investment performance. Finally, a number of mutual fund management companies have recently been purchased by organizations that control life insurance companies. According to mutual fund proponents, this may be an admission that life insurance company executives place greater faith in the ability and experience of mutual fund managers with equity investments than they place with their own investment staffs.

Defenders of variable annuities have several rebuttals to these arguments. First, they point out that although life insurance companies have been limited in the percentage of common stocks they could own, the absolute amounts have not been small. Life insurance companies owned about $7 billion of common stock in 1967.[19] One life insurance company alone has over $1.1 billion invested in common stocks.[20] Thus, large life insurers often have sizeable investment staffs and many employees who specialize in common stock investments. Life insurance organizations that have acquired investment personnel from mutual fund companies do not necessarily admit that they have inferior investment talent. They claim there are other reasons for obtaining mutual fund personnel.[21]

According to variable annuity proponents, regulatory restrictions on variable annuity investments will not hamper investment performance. Even though some states continue to have restrictions on the

---

[19] A. M. Best Company, *Best's Insurance Reports*, (Morristown, New Jersey, 1968), p. viii.

[20] *Ibid.*, p. 1230.

[21] Among the reasons given for purchasing existing mutual fund management companies are: ease of entry into variable dollar product markets, administration, possible reduction of regulatory problems, and simplicity.

investments life insurance companies can make with respect to the variable annuity business, these restrictions are minor, and may be fully eliminated in the near future.

Life insurance investment officers have also indicated that they have purchased securities directly from companies over a long period of time, and as a consequence, have learned a great deal about the financial history of their debtors. In addition, the bond indentures frequently require the companies issuing bonds to make periodic reports to the bondholders (life insurance companies). Mutual fund proponents argue that this is not an advantage to life insurance companies because those who manage mutual funds make periodic field visits to companies and obtain similar information.

Investment officers in life insurance companies argue that mutual fund shares are redeemed more often than variable annuities are surrendered. The cash flow through a variable annuity plan, therefore, should be more constant and predictable than the cash flow through a mutual fund. According to variable annuity advocates, this should make it easier for life insurance companies to invest more effectively.

## Expenses

Although some mutual fund shareowners and variable annuity owners are apt to regard the total deposits they have paid into a plan as the amount that has been invested on their behalf, this is obviously not the case. Charges for insurance benefits (if any), distribution expenses, and management fees must be deducted to determine how much is actually available for investment. Expenses, therefore, have a direct impact on overall results and differences in expenses between mutual funds and variable annuities are factors that should be considered in the consumer decision process.

**Charges for Insurance Benefits.** It is quite common for variable annuity plans to provide a death benefit during the accumulation period.[22] Many deferred variable annuity contracts stipulate that if the annuitant dies during the accumulation period, the death benefit payable will be the current market value of the accumulation units credited to the annuitant or the total premiums paid into the plan, whichever is larger. This provision, in essence, is a guarantee that the beneficiary will not recieve less than the annuitant has paid into the plan.[23] This type of benefit is not available with mutual funds, although some mutual funds (primarily contractual plans—which are not treated here) have

---

[22] During the liquidation period, a death benefit is inherent in the type of annuity option selected.

[23] The "insurance" element in this benefit comes into operation only if the accumulation units credited to an annuitant have a value that is less than the total premiums paid. This is a distinct possibility, however, because the value of the accumulation units may decline after they have been purchased, and in any event, deductions for expenses and management fees must be made from the total premiums paid by the purchaser.

completion insurance that pays a lump sum benefit equal to the future purchase payments that would have been paid by the purchaser had he lived. Thus the insurance benefits in mutual funds and variable annuities usually are not comparable. Charges for these benefits, therefore, should be considered separately when a purchaser attempts to compare expenses of the two plans.

**Distribution Expenses.** The cost of distribution in a mutual fund purchase is generally termed the "sales load." The sales load is the largest and most important charge paid by an investor who purchases shares of a mutual fund. The charge is typically 8.5 percent of the purchase price, but it varies among companies. Rarely is the sales load less than 7.0 percent.

The sales charge generally is reduced for large purchases. Many mutual funds lower the sales charge for purchases exceeding $12,500.[24] The reduced sales charge is applied toward the total single purchase.

There are two basic approaches for assessing the sales charge in variable annuity plans. The first approach is to make a level deduction from each purchase payment. The amount of this charge ranges between 8 and 10 percent for the individual contracts of most companies. The sales charge is usually reduced for large purchases, as it is in a mutual fund. The second approach is similar to the traditional life insurance treatment, with a deduction of 30-50 percent in the first year, 8-12 percent for the next 9-12 years, and possibly a small percentage thereafter. (This approach is also similar to that used by contractual mutual funds.[25]) The sales charge for single premium variable annuities is lower, often grading downward from 7 percent depending on the amount of the payment.

**Management Fees.** The contract between a mutual fund and a management company provides for the payment of an advisory fee. This fee compensates the management company for its services, and may cover expenses for salaries and other compensation, office rental, accounting services, office supplies, legal and directors' fees, reports, and custodian fees. While there is some variation in the approaches to the advisory fee, most contracts call for payment on the basis of total assets held by the fund on a specific date. In a report of the Securities and Exchange Commission, the annual expense ratios for large mutual funds were reported to range from approximately 0.45 percent to 0.65 percent of total assets.[26] The fee is scaled down above the stipulated level of assets. A few funds relate the advisory fee to the level of performance.

---

[24] Securities and Exchange Commission, *Public Policy Implications of Investment Company Growth*, (Washington: U.S. Government Printing Office, 1966), p. 52.

[25] A good comparison of endowment life insurance and contractual mutual funds is contained in Herbert Denenberg and Robert Ferrari, *Life Insurance and/or Mutual Funds*, (New York: Pageant Press, Inc., 1967.)

[26] *Report of the Securities and Exchange Commission on the Public Policy Implications of Investment Company Growth*, (Committee on Interstate and Foreign Commerce), December 2, 1966.

Variable annuity companies also make annual deductions for investment expenses. The expenses of most variable annuity plans currently range from 1 percent to 1.5 percent of the assets in the variable annuity account. It is unfair, however, to compare this expense charge with the expense loading in mutual fund plans because the variable annuity loading includes a charge for mortality and expense guarantees. The portion of the charge that is allocated to investment expenses ranges from .3-.5 percent, which is comparable to the charge in mutual funds. The balance of .8-1.0 percent is a charge to guarantee policyholders that deductions from deposits for expenses and mortality cannot exceed the allowance in the contract. This is a valuable benefit because inflation may very well make the expense allowance inadequate and greatly increased longevity may result from medical advances.

Mutual fund plans do not provide mortality and expense guarantees. In comparing expenses, therefore, it is reasonable to exclude this charge from variable annuity expenses. If this is done, the total first year expense rate for a typical mutual fund would be about 9 percent and about 10 percent for (level deduction) variable annuities. This is, of course, a generalization that is subject to many qualifications. Nevertheless, it appears that many mutual funds have a slight advantage over variable annuities when a consumer is comparing total expenses of the plans.[27]

Finally, there is another basic difference between mutual fund and variable annuity expenses for buyers who take their funds from the plans within a short period after buying. Very few mutual funds extract a redemption charge upon the surrender of mutual fund shares. On the other hand, a surrender of a variable annuity contract in the early contract years may incur a surrender charge. This charge may be approximately 1 or 2 percent of the accumulated values in the fund. Most variable annuity companies, however, do not assess a surrender charge after a few years.

## Taxation

Another factor in the consumer decision between mutual funds and variable annuities is the tax treatment of the two vehicles. In some circumstances, a variable annuity owner gains several important advantages; in other cases, mutual funds may have tax advantages over variable annuities.

**Prior to Retirement.** A variable annuity owner is not required to pay federal income taxes on interest, dividends, and capital gains during the accumulation period. Mutual fund shareowners, on the other hand, pay federal income taxes on interest and dividends (subject to the $100 annual dividend exclusion) at ordinary income tax rates, and they typically pay capital gains taxes on distributions of capital gains.

---

[27] It should be noted that there are currently regulatory and competitive pressures to reduce the expense charges in both mutual funds and variable annuities.

This is a significant tax advantage for variable annuities—the magnitude of which depends upon an individual's marginal tax bracket during his productive years.

A major disadvantage may be associated with variable annuities if an annuitant takes the proceeds of his annuity in cash before benefit payments begin. The holder of mutual fund shares is taxed each year on both dividends and capital gains, and when he sells his mutual fund shares, he pays a capital gains tax based on the gain in net asset value per share. If there is a loss in per-share net asset values, he may declare a capital loss that may be applied against capital gains or against limited amounts of ordinary income if there are no offsetting capital gains. An annuitant who surrenders his annuity is in a less advantageous position with respect to a capital gain. When the contract is surrendered, any increase in value in excess of the annuitant's cost is taxed as ordinary income in the year received. Some relief may be obtained, however, from the rather complicated income averaging rules.[28] The taxation of the gain as ordinary income results in a higher tax payment than would be the case if the gain were taxed at capital gain rates.

While a variable annuitant is not required to report any of the insurer's earnings that might be attributable to him, there is a tax liability that arises should the annuitant die during the accumulation period. Specifically the annuitant's estate incurs an income tax liability on the previously untaxed income at the time of the annuitant's death. The estate is then taxed as if the annuitant had surrendered his contract. In contrast, when a mutual fund shareowner dies, the shares are valued in the estate at their fair market value. When the shares are sold, the cost basis is the fair market value in the estate and not the original cost to the deceased shareholder.

**After Retirement.** Variable annuity benefits are taxed in precisely the same manner as benefits under conventional annuities. The "investment in the contract" is divided by the "expected return" (based upon life expectancy) to determine the "exclusion ratio." The "exclusion ratio" is the percentage of each annuity payment that represents a return of principal, and is not subject to taxation. The excess of each benefit payment over the excluded amount, however, represents the accumulation of investment earnings and is taxed. The same principle of taxation applies to amounts received from mutual funds, i.e., returns of principal are not taxed. However, there is a significant difference in the tax impact of amounts withdrawn during retirement from mutual funds and variable annuities. Regardless of how long a variable annuitant lives after retirement, he can continue to deduct that portion of his annual annuity benefit that is considered to be a return of principal. An annuitant who lives beyond his life expectancy obtains a significant income tax advantage because he continues to receive a portion of his annuity benefit without incurring a tax liability. The "exclusion ratio" is applicable for

---

[28] The rule that permitted the gain received in a lump sum under an annuity to be spread over the year of receipt and the two preceding years is no longer available.

the life of the annuitant, even if he outlives his life expectancy. On the other hand, if the annuitant dies after starting to receive benefit payments (but before the end of his life expectancy at the time he retired) his beneficiary does not have the opportunity of liquidating the principal without a tax liability.[29] If the annuity is "pure," i.e., contains no refund feature, there would be no benefits after the annuitant dies and thus no chance of receiving the principal; if the annuity contains some type of refund feature, all benefits received (after the period certain) are taxed to the beneficiary.

It is extremely difficult, if not impossible, for a consumer to evaluate the different tax treatments of variable annuities and mutual funds. A meaningful comparison would necessarily involve a number of assumptions needed to compare the tax treatment of mutual funds and variable annuities would be: (1) the tax bracket of the individual at different points in time, (2) the tax rates that will exist in the future, and (3) the magnitude of interest, dividends, and capital gains. Furthermore, even with assumptions that may not prove realistic, the tax effects could be changed considerably by death or by withdrawing funds from the plans. With all these problems, it is only possible to make generalized statements. Variable annuities certainly have an income tax advantage over mutual funds during the accumulation period and probably a disadvantage if funds are withdrawn from the plan prior to retirement.

## Conclusions

Consumers should evaluate the relative merits of mutual funds and variable annuities in view of their personal financial objectives. For objectives other than retirement, variable annuities appear to have distinct disadvantages. If a person accumulates funds through a variable annuity and surrenders the contract for cash prior to retirement, he may pay a heavy charge for expenses, and the company may assess a charge when the contract is surrendered. Furthermore, the annuitant may have to pay substantial federal income taxes at ordinary income tax rates in the year the contract is terminated. To compare the disadvantages of mutual funds with those of variable annuities, an investor in mutual fund shares would have to analyze acquisition and administrative expenses and the income tax effect. Although each individual case would have to be analyzed on its own merits, mutual funds apparently would normally have overall advantages compared with variable annuities for short range financial objectives.

For the objective of financing retirement, variable annuities have several major advantages over mutual funds. First, the annuity principal guarantees that an individual cannot outlive his income. Second, the expenses involved in variable annuities do not appear substantially different from those incurred in the purchase of mutual fund shares. Third, there seems to be no reason why the investment experience

---

[29] Moreover, the executor cannot claim an income tax deduction for the loss.

should differ greatly. Fourth, the tax treatment of variable annuities used for retirement compares favorably to that of mutual funds. Finally, a variable annuity buyer has other guarantees that are not available with mutual funds. If the annuitant dies during the accumulation period, the beneficiary is assured of receiving the total payments made into the plan; increased longevity cannot adversely affect the annuity benefit payments because mortality is guaranteed; and expense guarantees provide assurance that charges for expenses cannot be increased.

An excellent case can be built in favor of planning retirement income through variable annuities. In order to obtain greater flexibility (particularly considering tax effects) it may be sensible to plan retirement income with both mutual funds and variable annuities. In any event, in the future variable annuities should have a place in the retirement plans of many individuals.

## Questions

1. Which do you believe are the most important *differences* between variable annuities and mutual funds? From whose viewpoint? Discuss.
2. Note that there is apparently little difference in investment performance between variable annuities and some mutual funds. What type of investment objective should a variable annuity plan have? Why?
3. Why does it make a difference whether mutual funds and variable annuities are analyzed in the short run or the long run? Discuss.

# PART 9
## Health Insurance and Social Insurance

Health insurance has been included with the topic of social insurance in this part in recognition of the likelihood that in the next decade more health insurance will be offered as a type of social insurance than as private insurance. Problems of health care in the United States are of great concern to many at the current time. At the time of publication of this book, although many important changes have been proposed, agreement in Congress on the subject of reforms in health insurance and the health care delivery system does not seem to exist.

The two articles by Ms. Kittner and Mr. Parker develop discussions on problems in the decision on health care insurance. Mr. Pettengill, in the article that follows, relates health insurance to the general topic of health care delivery systems.

The remaining articles in this part develop concepts in several aspects of the areas of unemployment insurance and workmen's compensation insurance, both of which have lain dormant to major advances in the past 15 to 20 years, but which are rapidly gaining attention today.

# 29. CHANGES IN HEALTH AND INSURANCE PLANS FOR SALARIED EMPLOYEES *

Dorothy R. Kittner †

Major companies substantially improved the health and insurance protection of their salaried employees during the past 6 years. Although improvements in both the levels and types of benefits provided salaried workers were almost always unilaterally made by the employer, they often reflected gains achieved by production workers through collective bargaining. Some of the changes, however, reflected the employer's awareness of the necessity of broader and greater coverage to meet changing standards of health care protection and rising living costs, particularly medical costs.

Health and insurance plans for salaried workers generally provided greater income protection and more comprehensive coverage than plans for production workers. In particular, plans for salaried workers included optional life insurance, long-term disability benefits, and major medical benefits more frequently than those for production workers. Also, salaried employees, unlike most production workers, often continued to receive their regular pay while temporarily absent from work because of illness.[1]

Some recent improvements in salaried employee benefit plans represent interesting innovations and special benefits supplementing or liberalizing existing private plan benefits, while others involve new ways of supplementing government-provided benefits, such as Medicare and disability pensions. In the income area, a special survivors' benefit, which provided certain survivors a percentage of the deceased employee's salary for at least 12 months, was increasingly superimposed on basic and optional life insurance benefits.[2] In the health area, liberal benefits for convalescent and nursing home care, psychiatric care, and dental care

---

* From *Monthly Labor Review* (February, 1970), pp. 32-39.
† Economist in the Division of General Compensation Structures, Bureau of Labor Statistics.

[1] In 1967-68 for example, about 4 out of 5 of the office workers in metropolitan areas as compared with 1 out of 2 of the plant workers had a major medical benefit, and 7 out of 10 of the former group and 3 out of 10 of the latter group had a paid sick leave plan. Separate data on the incidence of optional life insurance and long-term disability benefits for the various groupings of employees are not available. However, all indications are that these benefits are much more prevalent for salaried employees than for production workers. *Wages and Related Benefits, Part II: Metropolitan Areas, United States and Regional Summaries, 1967-68* (BLS Bulletin 1575-87).

[2] This benefit which provides certain survivors a percentage of the deceased employee's salary for at least 12 months, is also payable in addition to the survivors benefits of a pension plan.

are now added to health care packages. Service benefits, covering surgical-medical care for all employees regardless of their incomes, became more frequent as more plans paid all reasonable and customary charges of physicians and surgeons instead of a fixed allowance.[3]

Although benefits paid for solely by the employer (noncontributory) became more common, many workers still had to pay part of the cost of their health and insurance plans. In 1968, as in the previous 5 years, more than 40 percent of all employees surveyed by the Health Insurance Institute participated in noncontributory programs, and more than half were in contributory ones.[4] Of course, as implied by the term "optional," all employees with optional life insurance coverage paid at least part of its premium, and those with long-term disability and major medical benefits coverage usually helped finance it. As in the past, the proportion of office workers with noncontributory benefits lagged behind the proportion of plant workers whose benefits were similarly financed. The only major exception to this generalization is in the area of major medical coverage, as shown in the following tabulation, showing the proportion of workers in metropolitan areas during 1967-68 covered by noncontributory benefit plans:

| Benefit | Plant workers | Office workers | | |
|---|---|---|---|---|
| | 1967-68 period | 1967-68 period | 1963-64 period | Percent increase since 1963-64 |
| Life insurance ............... | 66 | 58 | 54 | 7 |
| Accidental death ............. | 42 | 33 | 28 | 18 |
| Weekly accident and sickness . | 47 | 26 | 21 | 24 |
| Hospital ..................... | 65 | 50 | 46 | 9 |
| Surgical ..................... | 64 | 49 | 44 | 11 |
| Basic medical ................ | 55 | 44 | 36 | 22 |
| Major medical ............... | 30 | 39 | 28 | 39 |

Nevertheless, since 1963, there has been a noticeable increase in the proportion of office workers covered by plans paid for entirely by their employers.[5]

In 1963 and again in 1969, the Bureau of Labor Statistics compiled a digest of health and insurance plans covering salaried employees of major

---

[3] See Donald M. Landay, "Trends in Negotiated Health Plans: Broader Coverage, Higher Quality Care," *Monthly Labor Review*, May 1969, pp. 3-10, and J. F. Follman, Jr., "Health Insurance Plan Design Trends—Coverage and Benefits," *Pension and Welfare News*, February 1969, pp. 13-22.

[4] *New Group Health Insurance: I. Policies Issued in 1968; II. The Five-Year Trend, 1963-1968*, Health Insurance Institute, New York, N.Y. This survey is based on an analysis of the group health insurance policies, providing health care and income replacement benefits, written by insurance companies between January 1 and March 31, 1968, and an analysis of benefits provided employee groups of 25-499, which the Health Insurance Institute stated represents group health insurance trends.

[5] See BLS Bulletins 1575-87 and 1385-82.

companies.[6] These plans, selected to illustrate only those of large manufacturing and nonmanufacturing firms, are not necessarily typical plans,
nor are they a representative selection. Improvements in the plans contained in the BLS digest frequently occur earlier than in other plans,
and innovations are often made in them which, with appropriate modifications, are later adopted by others, and thus are pattern-setting. The
following discussion, limited to these plans, examines changes made
between 1963 and 1969.

## Prevalence of Benefits

While all plans provided for basic life insurance in 1963 and 1969,
almost twice as many provided optional life insurance as in 1963 and
almost 3 times as many paid special benefits to relatives of deceased
employees. Long-term disability benefits were provided by almost half
the companies studied—a fivefold increase since 1963 when only approximately 1 in 10 provided such benefits.[7]

Since 1963, there has been a slight decline in the proportion of plans
that offer basic hospital and surgical-medical benefits to their active
employees and their dependents, but in 1969, as in 1963, those not offering basic benefits offered comprehensive major medical plans, which
usually provided broader protection than most basic benefit plans. Between 1963 and 1969, three of the plans substituted comprehensive
major medical benefits for basic hospital-surgical-medical benefits. Major
medical benefits now are offered by nine-tenths of the plans studied. In
1963, slightly more than four-fifths of them had this benefit.

Psychiatric care and treatment in facilities other than hospitals are
now specifically offered in three plans. Previously, no plan had a benefit
solely for this type of care. However, the basic hospital benefits of most
plans provided coverage for hospital confinement for short periods due
to mental and nervous disorders, and the major medical benefit, when
available, covered a limited amount of out-of-hospital psychiatric treatment both in 1963 and 1969.

In both years, 4 out of 5 of the companies continued life insurance
coverage for their employees after retirement and 2 out of 3 continued
health benefit coverage. Upon retirement at age 65, optional life insurance is usually discontinued, basic life insurance is reduced, and health
benefits are modified so as to supplement rather than duplicate Medicare.
Since 1963, only three companies, which previously required the retirees
to pay the full cost of their health benefits, discontinued health benefits

---

[6] *Digest of 50 Selected Health and Insurance Plans for Salaried Employees, Spring
1963* (BLS Bulletin 1377), and *Digest of 50 Health and Insurance Plans for Salaried Employees, Early 1969* (BLS Bulletin 1629). All, except one plan, were included in both digests.
Thirty-six of these plans are in manufacturing industries and 13 in nonmanufacturing
industries.

[7] This protection was rarely available in 1963. However, since the exact incidence of
this protection in 1963 is unknown the change in prevalence since then is also unknown.

for retirees. Of course, salaried employees of these companies who retire at age 65 are eligible for Medicare protection, as are most employees age 65 and over in private industry.[8]

## Plans Covering Active Employees

**Financing.** In early 1969 about 1 out of 6 of the companies paid the full cost of all benefits, except optional (added) life insurance. Basic life insurance was provided without charge to employees of more than 2 out of 5 of the companies studied; in 1963, more than half the plans required employee contributions. Optional life insurance was generally offered on a contributory basis but only two of the plans required employees to pay the full cost of their added insurance.

Long-term disability benefits, generally not provided in 1963, were fully paid for by about 30 percent of the firms that offered them. About 30 percent of the other companies with this benefit required employees to pay the full cost of it. In the remaining cases, company and employees shared the cost.

Roughly half of the companies studied paid the full cost of all health benefits covering their salaried employees. Five of these, however, required their employees to contribute toward or pay the full cost of their dependents' coverage. In addition, seven companies paid the basic health program's full cost but required their employees to contribute toward major medical coverage. Six years earlier, more than two-thirds of the plans required employees to contribute toward their own basic benefits.

The striking change in the financing of health and insurance benefits for salaried workers during the past 6 years became apparent only when the same package of benefits available in 1963 was compared with those available in 1969. By early 1969 one-third of the companies paid the full cost of benefits available to salaried employees and their dependents, compared with one-seventh in 1963.

**Life Insurance.** Since 1963 almost half of the companies made one major change or more in the life insurance benefit offered salaried employees. The most typical change being a revision of the benefit schedule or formula to provide almost everyone with greater protection. In a few cases, however, only those workers at the lower or higher salary levels profited by the revisions. Different levels of coverage were eliminated between 1963 and 1969 in those few cases where greater life insurance coverage had been provided men than women. At least for insurance purposes, all of the companies treated men and women employees alike.

The level of life insurance protection for salaried employees is generally geared to salary levels. In early 1969, basic and optional coverage

---

[8] Medicare, the Federal health plan for individuals age 65 and over, became effective July 1, 1966. Hospital benefits are available without charge to those qualifying for Social Security old age benefits and the medical benefits are available to those paying the monthly premiums.

provided by most companies ranged from an amount approximately equal to annual salary to 4 times salary. Six years earlier, maximum coverage provided by several companies was much less than annual salary and only one company had insurance limits which exceeded 3 times salary. A few plans adopted changes between 1963 and 1969 that adversely affected some future participants—generally those to be hired into entry-level jobs—while improving the plan for all others. This type of revision does not adversely affect the benefits of current plan participants, but does occasionally result in lower benefits being offered to future participants at certain entrance-level salaries than prevailed under the superseded plan. One of the ways that this can occur is illustrated by changes in the Douglas Aircraft Co., Inc. plan. In 1969, the Douglas plan provided basic coverage equal to annual salary plus optional coverage in the same amount; 6 years earlier, the plan had offered $9,000 basic coverage to all employees plus optional coverage based on an earnings schedule. As a result basic coverage for employees currently hired at $5,000 and $10,000 is $5,000 a year less than it was in 1963. Those workers previously employed at these salary levels continued to receive the insurance protection they had previously enjoyed. However, because basic coverage under this plan is now based on annual salary, new employees earning over $9,000 yearly get more noncontributory insurance coverage than they would have received in 1963.

Some modifications made by companies in the life insurance benefit increased the basic coverage amount provided by the company on a noncontributory basis without affecting total coverage. This was accomplished in one of the plans by eliminating the contributory optional insurance provided in 1963 and increasing the free basic insurance by a corresponding amount.

**Income Protection Benefits.** Income protection was usually provided during temporary disability periods either by an insured weekly accident and sickness benefit, the company's self-insured paid sick leave plan, or both. The "building block" approach used when both these benefits are provided guarantees employees, with few exceptions, full pay for a specified period and part pay for an additional period.[9] A significant number of companies also provided nonmanagerial employees income protection benefits during long-term disabilities.

**Accident and Sickness Benefits.** For most employees the accident and sickness benefits offered by the companies were considerably higher than those available 6 years ago. Nevertheless, higher-paid employees frequently were eligible for a smaller fraction of their salary than lower-paid employees. For example, with few exceptions, the size of the benefit in early 1969 for the $5,000-a-year man ranged between 50 percent of weekly salary and 75 percent, the median plan paying between 60 and

---

[9] Formal paid sick leave plans which are now provided by about 3 out of 5 of the 50 Digest companies are now discussed in this article. They are summarized in BLS Bulletin 1629.

65 percent. By contrast, the size of the benefit for the $10,000-a-year man ranged from 25 percent to 75 percent with the median plan paying between 40 and 45 percent of weekly salary. The amount of the benefit and the ratio of benefit to average salary rose substantially between 1963 and 1969. For example, the $5,000-a-year employee's benefit in 1969 averaged $59 (62 percent of his weekly salary) as compared with $55 (57 percent of salary) in 1963.

Between 1963 and 1969, only a few plans extended the duration of accident and sickness benefit periods. Three plans made changes with two of them doubling the period to 52 weeks (none had a longer period) from 26 weeks and the other, to 26 weeks from 13 weeks. One out of 5 companies with accident and sickness benefits provided them for 52 weeks in 1969 and 7 out of 10 to 26 weeks. In 1963 about one-eighth of the plans with accident and sickness benefits made payments for 52 weeks and two-thirds for 26 weeks.

**Long-term Disability.** These benefits are usually designed to assure totally disabled employees an income until age 65 when normal retirement benefits under private pensions typically become available.[10] Because age and long service are rarely considered in determining the employee's eligibility, these plans are of special importance to young and new employees, who could not qualify for regular disability retirement benefits under their company's retirement plan, and to employees with short service who are entitled only to small inadequate disability retirement benefits. Following the qualification standards developed under Social Security, the plans required employees to be totally disabled for 6 months to become eligible for benefits. While waiting, they usually collect some weekly accident and sickness benefits, sick leave pay, or both.[11]

Under long-term disability plans, all eligible employees typically are guaranteed a specified monthly income. The benefit paid never equaled full pay, but together with other benefits generally provided at least half pay. The actual amount paid by the plan, however, usually depended on the employee's Workmen's Compensation, Social Security, and private retirement plan benefits. Most of the companies explicitly reduced monthly benefit payments by these other payments. One, however, deducted only half of the employee's Social Security benefit. Of course the few companies paying benefits without a Social Security reduction probably considered Social Security payments in establishing the benefit formula. This type of consideration seemed particularly likely in the case of one plan that established a monthly payment equal to 25 percent

---

[10] Long-term disability benefits are income protection benefits for employees totally disabled for over 6 months. The monthly payments, usually a high percentage of the employee's salary when combined with Social Security and workmen's compensation benefits, generally continue until age 65 (unless he recovers earlier) when he ordinarily becomes eligible for full regular benefits under his company's private pension plan.

[11] Both paid sick leave and weekly accident and sickness benefits have brief waiting period requirements or none at all. Weekly accident and sickness benefits were payable for at least 6 months in all but three of the plans.

of monthly salary plus 35 percent of salary in excess of $550 monthly (in 1966 and 1967, earnings above this amount were not subject to Social Security taxes).

Most plans provided payment until the employee's disability ended or until he reached age 65, whichever occurs first. However, under one plan, the employee's length of service determined the duration of benefit payments. Those with less than 5 years of service received payments for 5 years; those with 5 but less than 15 years received benefits for a period equal to their length of service, and those with at least 15 years of service, received them until normal retirement.

The monthly payment under long-term disability plans (as shown in table 1) was calculated with four exceptions, by using a "percentage of salary" formula, frequently with an upper limit on the monthly benefit. The expected plans either graded the percentage used in the computation according to salary and service, paid a larger proportion of an employee's salary during the first part of his disability than later on, used a combination flat amount and percentage-of-salary formula, or paid a flat amount based on an earnings schedule.

TABLE 1. DISTRIBUTION OF PLANS BY LONG-TERM DISABILITY
BENEFIT FORMULA

| Benefit formula for monthly disability payment | Number of plans |
|---|---|
| All digest plans with long-term disability benefit .......... | 23 |
| Including Social Security and other statutory benefits, and private disability retirement benefits: | |
|     50 percent of salary ................................. | 14 |
|       No maximum payment ............................... | [1] 9 |
|       Maximum payment ($1,000-$3,125 monthly) ........... | [2] 5 |
|     60 percent of salary ................................. | 3 |
|       No maximum payment ............................... | 2 |
|       Maximum payment ($2,000 monthly) .................. | 1 |
|     66⅔ percent of salary (maximum, $2,000 monthly) ..... | 1 |
|     80 percent of after-tax salary (maximum, $3,000 monthly) | 1 |
|     25 percent of salary under $550 monthly; 35 percent of salary over $550 ......................................... | 1 |
|     Graduated amount based on salary .................... | 1 |
|     Graduated percent of salary based on salary and service[3] ..... | 1 |
|     $100 plus 50 percent of salary over $400 monthly[4] .... | 1 |

[1] Under one plan only employees earning $6,600 annually or more, are eligible for benefit. One plan provided a minimum benefit of $265 monthly, another paid two-thirds of salary during first 24 months, and another paid employees with at least 15 years of service, an additional 1 percent of salary for each year of service over 15.

[2] Under one plan only employees with earnings of $400 monthly or more are eligible for benefit, and under another, only employees earning $15,000 annually or more.

[3] Only employees with annual earnings of $7,000 or more were eligible for benefit.

[4] Applicable to employees with less than 15 years of service; employees with at least 15 years of service received $100 plus 30 percent of salary over $400 monthly.

**Hospital Benefits.** Basic hospital benefits are not quite as common in the plans in 1969 as they were in 1963. Two plans that dropped this benefit, as well as one that never had it, helped defray hospital expenses by providing comprehensive major medical benefits. Many of the remaining plans provide hospital benefits that differ in one respect or more from those in effect in 1963. The principal changes involved lengthening the duration of benefit payments, switching from cash benefits to service benefits, and increasing cash allowances for room, board, and ancillary services.

Service hospital benefits, such as those provided by most Blue Cross plans, have a built-in cost adjustment feature. Because they cover the full cost of hospital confinements for specified periods, the monetary value of service benefits increases as hospital charges for room, board, and ancillary services increase and as more services—often requiring expensive new machinery and personnel—are provided owning to technological advances in hospital care and treatment. The value of and protection provided by the plans with service benefits increased significantly during the past 6 years.[12] In particular, the protection provided by the six plans that switched from cash to service benefits since 1963 was superior to that provided previously.

Most of the Digest plans provided service-type benefits with only about 1 out of 5 paying cash allowances. These plans have substantially higher room and board allowances than in 1963, the amounts ranging from $14 to $40 a day compared with $12 to $18 in 1963, and averaged $28 instead of about $15. Only one plan paid under $20 a day but 5 paid at least $30. As a result, since 1963 the 87-percent increase in the average room and board allowance of the plans with cash hospital benefits surpassed the 66 percent increase in semiprivate room and board charges reported in the Bureau's Consumer Price Index.

Not only have the major companies covered a larger proportion of the hospital charge because of a switch to service benefits for room and board or payment of higher room and board allowances, but about half the companies also increased the maximum number of days for which full benefits were payable. By early 1969, over three-fifths of the plans provided full benefits for 120 days or more of hospital confinement compared with one-half in 1963 and the number of plans providing full coverage for at least 365 days of hospitalization increased from 8 to 11.

Additional improvements were made by plans that shifted from cash to service benefits for room and board. They changed their ancillary service benefit from a cash allowance to the full cost of specified services. In addition, plans that increased the duration of room and board benefits also made identical increases in the period during which the ancillary services were payable. The maximum allowances of plans which paid the

---

[12] According to the Bureau of Labor Statistics Consumer Price Index, hospital semiprivate room charges increased 66 percent in the 5-year period, and operating room charges and certain diagnostic services rose over 41 and 16 percent, respectively.

full cost of such services up to a specified amount, ranged from $300 to $450 with two exceptions. One of the excepted plans paid $150 and the other, $800. In 1963 only two plans with cash benefits had an ancillary allowance of $300 or more.

**Surgical Benefits.** Over half of the companies revised their plans' surgical benefits by raising the maximum payable for surgical procedures. In addition, six companies improved their surgical benefit by switching from fee-for-service benefits to full payment of reasonable and customary charges. Under the scheduled benefit plans, allowances for all procedures were not affected to the same extent, the greatest increase generally occurring in those for the most expensive operations.

**Basic Medical Benefits.** Over half of the companies with basic medical benefits (benefits for nonsurgical treatment by a physician) revised these benefits during the past 6 years. In addition to paying the entire surgeon's fee, four plans also paid a reasonable and customary fee to physicians for in-hospital nonsurgical treatment instead of providing a cash allowance as in 1963. These plans, like most of those with basic medical benefits, did not cover medical treatment in the home or doctor's office. The remaining ones slightly raised the allowance for in-hospital (and if covered, out-of-hospital) visits. As a result, 11 plans (up from 4 in 1963) paid at least $5 for an in-hospital treatment.[13]

**Major Medical Benefits.** In early 1969, three-fourths of the 44 plans that had a major medical benefit, specified a uniform amount of medical expenses (the deductible) that employees, regardless of their earnings, had to pay before the major medical benefit became operative. In 1963, two-thirds specified a uniform deductible. This difference from 1969 levels reflected a decrease in the proportion of plans with a deductible graded by employee's annual earnings. However, because all plans dropping a deductible tied to earnings retained a minimum deductible of $100, the change to the uniform amount did not aid lower paid employees. In fact, only two companies reduced the deductible for everyone—one reducing the amount from $100 to $75, and the other, from 4 to 3 percent of earnings. Most plans allowed employees to meet the deductible by accumulating all medical expenses for an entire calendar year. This and other types of deductible accumulation periods are summarized in table 2.

Plans modified the coinsurance provision by raising the proportion of charges the plan paid from 75 percent to 80 percent thereby lowering the proportion the employee had to pay from 25 to 20 percent of costs. These modifications and the addition of three plans that did not have a major medical benefit in 1963 raised the proportion of plans with an 80/20 percent coinsurance provision to three-fourths from three-fifths.

---

[13] For plans that paid a higher allowance for treatment during the first 2 days of hospitalization or a lower allowance after several days of hospitalization, the allowance referred to is the one payable for treatment on the third day.

TABLE 2.  MAJOR MEDICAL BENEFITS:
DEDUCTIBLE ACCUMULATION PERIOD, EARLY 1969

| Accumulation period | Number of plans |
|---|---|
| All Digest plans with major medical benefits  ...... | 44 |
| Per disability  .................................... | 11 |
| 2 months  ......................................... | 1 |
| 3 months  ......................................... | 3 |
| 4 months  ......................................... | 1 |
| 6 months  ......................................... | 4 |
| 12 months  ......................................... | 2 |
| All disabilities  .................................... | 33 |
| 6 months  ......................................... | 3 |
| 12 months  ......................................... | 6 |
| 1 calendar year[1]  ................................ | 23 |
| 2 years[2]  ......................................... | 1 |

[1] With "carry-back" to last 3 months of preceding year.
[2] Applicable to other than hospital and surgical expenses.

The most frequent and often the most significant change in major medical benefits made since 1963 involved the maximum benefit payment. Several plans removed the restriction on plan payments for a single disability, thus providing greater protection for a catastrophic illness. However, they placed a limit ranging from $20,000 to $100,000 on total plan payments to any employee during the employee's lifetime. These lifetime limits were always higher than the maximums "per disability" previously specified. Those plans that retained the limitation on payments for each disability at least doubled the amount the plan paid before coverage ceased.

In 1969 as well as in 1963 the other plans with revised maximum payments had no limit other than a lifetime one. The limit in early 1969 was usually $20,000—double the $10,000 maximum in 1963. Maximum payments specified in the 44 plans with major medical benefits in early 1969 and the period to which they apply are shown in table 3.

## Plans Covering Retirees

About two-thirds of all the companies continued to provide health benefits for retirees, three-quarters provided life insurance coverage, and about one-half of them continued to provide both life insurance and health benefits to retirees. In addition, retirees of some companies carried paid-up life insurance policies (fully paid for during their active working years) into retirement and almost all age 65 and over were eligible for Medicare.

All retiree benefits were paid for by about half of the companies providing these benefits. Almost three-fifths of those with health benefits for retirees paid the full cost, and three-fourths of those extending life insurance paid for it. Of the 14 companies that provided both life insurance and health benefits and required retirees to pay some of the cost,

TABLE 3. MAJOR MEDICAL BENEFITS:
MAXIMUM PAYMENTS AND BASIS OF PAYMENTS, EARLY 1969

| Basis of payment and maximum amount | Number of plans | | |
|---|---|---|---|
| | Total | With disability limit | With benefit period limit |
| All digest plans with major medical benefits .................. | 44 | ............. ...................... |
| Plans with limits applying only to each disability or benefit period, total ............... | 13 | 10 | 3 |
| $5,000 ..................... | 1 | 1 | ..................... |
| 10,000 ..................... | 7 | 5 | 2 |
| 15,000 ..................... | 1 | 1 | ..................... |
| 20,000 ..................... | 2 | 2 | ..................... |
| 25,000 ..................... | 1 | ............ | 1 |
| 100,000 ................... | 1 | 1 | ..................... |

| | Total | Limit for each disability (one-half lifetime maximum) | Limit for each benefit period (one-half lifetime maximum) | No other limit |
|---|---|---|---|---|
| Plans with lifetime limits, total | 31 | 1 | 8 | 22 |
| $5,000 ..................... | 1 | ............. | ............. | 1 |
| 10,000 ..................... | 9 | ............ | 5 | 4 |
| 15,000 ..................... | 4 | 1 | [1] 1 | 2 |
| 20,000 ..................... | 11 | ............ | 2 | 9 |
| 25,000 ..................... | 1 | ............ | ............. | 1 |
| 30,000 ..................... | 1 | ............ | ............. | 1 |
| 40,000 ..................... | 1 | ............ | ............. | 1 |
| 50,000 ..................... | 1 | ............ | ............. | 1 |
| 100,000 ................... | 1 | ............ | ............. | 1 |
| Other ..................... | 1 | ............ | ............. | 1 |

[1] Limit each benefit period is two-third lifetime maximum.

only three required them to contribute toward the cost of both benefits; the remaining companies divided almost evenly between those that required them to contribute only for their life insurance and those that required them to contribute only for their health benefits.

Changes in the financing of health and insurance benefits for retirees during the past 6 years, like those for active employees, were most striking when compared with the package of benefits available in 1963. In 1969, 60 percent of the companies paid the full cost of benefits provided compared with only 35 percent in 1963. This large increase was probably due in part to Medicare's making it possible for five companies with retiree health benefits in 1963 to either assume the full cost of these benefits or to discontinue retiree-financed health benefits.[14]

**Life Insurance.** The amount of life insurance coverage extended to retirees has increased over the years, primarily because a retiree's life insurance coverage is related to his coverage prior to retirement, and, as pointed out previously, life insurance coverage for active workers has increased since 1963. However, the amount extended was still usually much less than that available prior to retirement. The practice of many companies was, as in the past, to gradually reduce employees' retirement coverage over a period of about 5 years to from 25 to 50 percent of that available before the initial reduction. As in the past, a few companies reduced preretirement coverage to a nominal amount, such as $1,000, immediately after retirement.

Employees of some companies that did not continue life insurance coverage after retirement had a combination of group-term and paid-up insurance coverage for active employees. Under this arrangement, the employee's contributions bought units of paid-up insurance, which accumulated over the years, and the employers contributions bought term insurance equal to the difference between the amount of paid-up insurance purchased by the employee and the total amount of insurance specified in the plan. Because the paid-up portion of the employee's total insurance coverage was available to him when his employment terminated, long-service employees of these companies, when they retire, had most or all of the coverage possessed immediately prior to retirement.

**Health Benefits.** Like other employees in private industry who are over 65 years old, salaried employees who retired at that age were generally eligible for the hospital and medical benefits of Medicare.[15] Customarily, companies let their employees, who are eligible for Medicare's Part B (medical) insurance be responsible for paying the premium for their coverage and that of their dependents.[16] However, nine companies paid some of the cost and three of them paid the full premium for the retiree and his spouse.

Two companies purchased Part B coverage for both their eligible active and retired employees and their eligible dependents by paying the entire monthly premium of $4 for each individual. One company paid the original premium of $3 for all eligible groups except dependents of active employees (the employee paid the balance of his premium and

---

[14] Medicare provides more comprehensive hospital, medical, and other health care benefits than virtually any private health plan formerly provided for people age 65 and over.

[15] To be eligible for Medicare hospital benefits employees have to be entitled to primary Social Security benefits. For details on the benefits provided under Medicare, see *Your Medicare Handbook: Health Insurance Under Social Security* (U.S. Social Security Administration, 1968). For a discussion of Medicare's effect on private insurance plans and how private plans have adapted to it see Dorothy R. Kittner, "Negotiated Health Benefits and Medicare," *Monthly Labor Review*, September 1968, pp. 29-34.

[16] Part A (hospital insurance) of Medicare is paid for under the Social Security program by active employees under 65 and their employers.

all of the premium for his dependents).[17] Another company paid the full premium only for retirees; the latter had to pay it for their dependents. The following tabulation shows the number of companies paying the Medicare premium in full or in part for each of the eligible groups:

| Eligible group (65 years and over) | Full Medicare premium | Part of Medicare premium |
|---|---|---|
| Active employees | 6 | 1 |
| Dependents of active employees | 6 | ............... |
| Retired employees | 4 | 2 |
| Dependents of retired employees | 3 | 2 |

All companies providing benefits for retirees in 1963, (except the three that discontinued coverage since then and those adding this coverage, modified their benefits during the past few years to avoid duplication of Medicare benefits. They did this by using one of the following three methods developed by the insurance industry: Under one method, the "benefit carveout," Medicare benefits are deducted from the same or similar benefits provided workers under age 65; under another, the "building block" method, payment is made for specific services or expenses not covered by Medicare; and under the third, the "major medical" method, partial payment (commonly 80 percent) is made for practically all medical expenses not covered by Medicare in excess of a certain amount.

Over two-fifths of the 43 companies with retiree health benefits used the "benefit carveout" approach. However, the benefits extended frequently differed from those available prior to retirement. For example, basic hospital and medical benefits might be available for a shorter period, the major medical deductible might be larger, or the maximum payment under the major medical benefit might be smaller.

Roughly equal proportions of the remaining companies utilized the "major medical" and "building block" methods. Companies using the former method extended to retired employees the major medical benefits available to active employees under age 65 or a cut-down version of it (a higher deductible, lower maximum payment, or both). Those using the last method either paid some or all of the Medicare deductibles and certain charges that the retiree otherwise had to pay, provided benefits for certain major expenses (private duty nursing care and out-of-hospital drugs) that are not covered by Medicare, or both.[18]

---

[17] Prior to January 1, 1969, the premium for Part B of Medicare was $3.

[18] The hospital deductibles are the first $44 during the first 60 days of confinement, $11 daily during the 61st to 90th days, and $20 daily during the 91st to 150th days; the convalescent home deductible is $5 daily for 80 days; and the medical and other health care deductible is the 1st $50 of charges (Medicare pays 80 percent of charges in excess of $50).

## Questions

1. Among the various types of life and health insurance available to salaried employees, which appears to be growing the most rapidly?
2. What has been the major change in the financing of health and insurance benefits for salaried workers since 1963?
3. In the typical long-term disability income plan, what is the definition of "long-term disability"?
4. What have been the major changes in hospital insurance coverage since 1963?
5. What is the typical maximum limit of payment under major medical plans for salaried employees?
6. Is it necessary to have private insurance as a supplement to the basic Medicare coverage, in your opinion? What methods are used to supplement Medicare when the employer decides to offer this service?

# 30. HEALTH CARE INSURANCE— WHERE AND WHEN *

Gerald S. Parker †

## WHERE ARE WE NOW

Here we are in the middle of 1971. In the United States, about 170,000,000 people under 65 years of age have hospital insurance, and another 11,000,000 or so over 65 have some private insurance supplement to Medicare. Of those under 65 over 93% also have surgical expense insurance, and about 43% have Major Medical. For this coverage they paid something over seven billion dollars to insurance companies in 1970, plus over six billion dollars to service-type plans. The total, therefore, was in the area of thirteen to fourteen billion dollars. A study of group insurance claims in 1967 done by the Health Insurance Association of America indicated that the group plans surveyed reimbursed about 86% of covered hospital expenses, 77% of surgical expenses, 84% of anesthetist expenses, 76% of diagnostic X-ray and laboratory expenses, 70% of in-hospital doctor visits, and nearly 60% of home and office doctor visits.[1]

A few years ago almost everyone would have considered this a phenomenal performance. Can we say that today? No. Anything but. It is generally accepted today in governmental circles, legislative circles, academic circles, and even insurance circles that we are in the midst of a health care crisis and a crisis in health care financing. The assertions, generally, run about as follows:

1. The care now being delivered to the people is wasteful and inefficient.
2. Adequate health care is inaccessible to the poor and many low income people.
3. The distribution of health care professionals is unsatisfactory. They are crowded in the affluent, middle-class and upper-class areas. They are avoiding the rural areas and inner-city areas.
4. The costs of health care are increasing so rapidly that soon even the relatively affluent will be unable to afford them.
5. The cost of health care insurance has been following the cost of the care itself, and there is danger that it will be priced out of the market.

---

* From *The CLU Journal* (October, 1971), pp. 22-27. Reprinted, with permission, from the JOURNAL of the American Society of Chartered Life Underwriters, Volume XXV, No. 4 (October, 1971). Copyright 1971 by the American Society of Chartered Life Underwriters, 270 Bryn Mawr Avenue, Bryn Mawr, Pa. 19010.

† Vice President, Health Insurance of The Guardian Life Insurance Company of America.

[1] Sourcebook of Health Insurance Data, 1970 projected.

6. The benefits of most health care insurance, even though it is fairly widely distributed, are often inadequate. (Stronger words are often used.)

There are other charges, but the listed ones paint the picture. As a result of these charges and the intense discussion of them over the past few years, the concept of health care as a right has been generally accepted. Since the acceptance of the concept has not automatically produced the delivery of the care, the present political climate has developed.

## THE POLITICAL CLIMATE

The acceptance of the concept of health care as a right, regardless of income, has led to the present political climate under which many legislatures and the Congress of the United States have been deluged with legislative proposals for dealing with the "health care crisis." The proposals, the assertions, the charges and counter-charges, and all the discussion of them are far too extensive to cover in a short article. Suffice it to say that we are now unquestionably on the verge of political action. Rep. Wilbur C. Mills, Chairman of the House Ways and Means Committee, has stated that hearings on the bills submitted will be held after Labor Day. Because of the limited time available, it is unlikely that the House of Representatives or the Senate will pass some kind of a national health care bill this year. If a bill can be hammered out which can pass both Houses of the Congress and reach the President in 1972, we shall be concerned with its implementation in 1973. In any case, the delivery of health care and its financing will be one of the two or three most important political issues in the 1972 campaigns. This issue is not going to go away. It is going to be resolved, and is going to be resolved in the next two to four years.

## THE INDUSTRY POSITION

The position of the health insurance is not of course, monolithic; but the Health Insurance Association of America, the major trade association of insurance companies providing health insurance, has agreed to five basic principles. They are these:

1. Every American should have access to quality health care regardless of income.
2. The nation needs a new health care system which combines the strengths of our present system with new programs, reforms and additions, where the present system, for one reason or another, does not meet the nation's needs.
3. Such a new system should make maximum use of the private sector and judicious use of government funds.
4. The nation should make comprehensive health insurance coverage available to all of its people at the earliest date consistent with the availability of health care services.

5. Action should be taken simultaneously to improve the organization and delivery of health care and to improve the financing of health care.

The industry has a program, described below, and you will see that it is designed to meet and satisfy the five principles. It is the only program so far which does so. It is very important to understand principle #5. Unless the organization and delivery of health care is improved, improvements in the financing can prove a snare and a delusion, resulting only in increasing the cost of care, and not in its successful distribution to the people who need it.

## THE PROPOSALS

There are numerous proposals now before the Congress. Most of them are of relatively minor importance, but about five are relatively comprehensive in nature and may contain elements which seem likely to be considered by the Congress in developing the bill which finally emerges from the compromises which must be considered inevitable.

The first of these is the "Health Security Act" developed by the Committee for National Health Insurance which was organized by the late Walter Reuther, and by the AFL and CIO. Sponsored by Senator Edward Kennedy, Democrat of Massachusetts, and others, this Act would substitute a monolithic federal insurance plan for all private health insurance. It would be financed 50% by general revenues and 50% by payroll taxes on employers and employees. A complex bureaucracy of federal, regional and local boards would tell institutions what services they could provide and negotiate budgets with institutions and prepaid group practice plans. Any funds left over after the payment of institutions and group practice plans could be used to reimburse those physicians who remained in solo practice on a fee-for-service basis.

This would be a tightly controlled federal scheme. It is apparently designed to completely eliminate private insurance (but might not successfully do so if the Government were unable to deliver on its promises), and its cost has been variously estimated at anywhere from fifty billion dollars to seventy-seven billion dollars per year. Obviously, this proposal fails to meet the second and third of HIAA's principles, and it violates the fifth in offering the care and financing before it is available for delivery.

The proposed National Health Insurance and Health Services Improvement Program developed by Senator Jacob K. Javits, Republican of New York, would provide comprehensive medical service, including hospital, extended care facilities, surgery, diagnostic workups, annual physical exams, maternity, some prescription drugs, dental care for young children, psychiatric care, and medical appliances. The patient would pay the first $52 per hospital stay and some co-payments for long term hospitalization and convalescent care. For other services, the patient would pay the first $50 plus 20% of the bill. Covered prescription drugs would be available at a charge of $1 per prescription to the patient.

This plan would be financed in part from the general revenues and in part from new Social Security taxes. The plan provides for optional contracting out on a private basis with the employer paying 75% and the employees 25%. Whether this part of the plan is workable seems dubious in the light of experience in California and New Jersey with the temporary disability benefits laws in those states. The plan would be administered by the Department of HEW and would use private carriers as intermediaries much as Medicare does. It proposes to phase poor, disabled and unemployed persons into the system first, then extend it to the rest of the population gradually. This plan would seem to fail to meet HIAA principle #3, and it may fail to meet principle #5 if the financing is available before the services are obtainable.

A plan called Medicredit, developed by the American Medical Association, would set up federal standards for benefits and give each family a tax credit equal to a percentage of the premiums paid for the minimum standard benefit plan. This percentage would be 100% for the poor and grade down to 10% for those in upper middle and the top income brackets. Those who do not pay an income tax would receive the credit in the form of a certificate which they could use for the equivalent amount of money in order to purchase the insurance. The plan lays the emphasis on the services of physicians and provides only modest amounts for other services. It is not truly comprehensive, and it is not phased in in accordance with the availability of manpower and the facilities. Furthermore, it has no provision for improving manpower or facilities and does nothing to suggest reorganization of the delivery system in any other way. Since it would use private insurance, it would meet the first four of the HIAA principles, but not the fifth one.

The National Health Insurance Standards Program and Family Health Insurance Plan developed by the Nixon Administration has been introduced in the Senate by Senator Wallace F. Bennett, Republican of Utah, and a number of other Republican senators. In the House, it has been introduced by Representative John W. Byrnes, Republican of Wisconsin, the ranking Republican on the House Ways and Means Committee, Minority leader Gerald R. Ford, Republican of Michigan, and several other Republican congressman.

The Administration Health Insurance Standards Program would require all employers to make a group health care plan available to employees and their dependents. The plan would have to meet minimum quality standards and provide very substantial hospital, surgical, and extended care coverage, diagnostic workups, general and special physicians' services, maternity and well baby care, health maintenance services, low income family counseling, vision care for children, and acute hospital psychiatric services. It would be subject to calendar year deductibles and co-insurance which could leave quite a substantial area available for possible supplementation by group or individual plans of insurance. Premium costs would be divided between employers and employees on a 75%-25% basis, and under the House version there is provision for subsidization of small employers. Insurance companies would write the group insurance policies, and such companies would be required to develop "group" policies with the same benefits for use by small employers and for self-employed individuals and others not eligible for group insurance or Medicare.

The Family Health Insurance Plan would add a new title to the Social Security Act to provide health care benefits for the poor and the near poor. It, too, would provide inpatient hospital care, extended care, home health services, physician services, well child care, maternity care, and family planning services. Psychiatric care is excluded.

These benefits, however, differ very substantially from those provided to employed persons and those who can afford to buy their own insurance. Deductibles and co-insurance vary in accordance with income class of the patient. Premiums are based on the family's income class taking into account the family size, and the lowest income families would pay no premiums. In this plan, too, provision is made for families to have dual choice between a health maintenace organization and coverage by the more conventional means of health care delivery.

The program would encourage the development of health maintenance organizations (prepaid group practice plans) with grants and loans and would permit so-called "dual choice." It would increase the output of health manpower with a per capita grant program to mental and dental training centers, encourage proper distribution of health personnel under incentive legislation now on the books. It would continue Medicare for the aged.

Portions of the Administration plan are distasteful to the industry for several reasons. In particular, it would provide a different kind of coverage for the poor than it would provide for others. It is compulsory rather than voluntary. It would require federal regulation of insurance policy forms and rates. It is weak in the areas of encouraging and requiring better health planning and improving the means of delivery of care. On the other hand, it contains many features of which the industry tends to approve.

The program which has been developed by the Health Insurance Association of America is known as Healthcare. It has been introduced in the Congress by Congressman Omar Burleson, Democrat of Texas, a member of the House, Ways and Means Committee, and by Senator Robert McIntyre, Democrat of New Hampshire. It was designed by a task force of HIAA member company officials, headed by J. Henry Smith, President of the Equitable Life Assurance Society of the United States. Obviously, it meets the five requirements. Its features are briefly described below. Note that the bill contains six major aspects, and only the sixth of them has anything to do with insurance. This bill recognizes the proportions of the problem and comes to grips with the entire problem, not just the financing part.

## THE HEALTHCARE BILL

1. It would provide Federal Scholarship and Loan programs for health manpower training, with partial forgiveness of loan for each year a graduate spends practicing in an area of special need such as inner city and rural areas. It would provide for grants to presently licensed health care personnel who will practice in such areas until the larger graduating classes under the loan program begin to be available. It would provide Federal grants to schools to spur the training of additional health care personnel, particularly those prepared to offer family ambulatory care and administer ambulatory care centers.

2. It would develop ambulatory health care services to promote health maintenance and reduce the amount of costly hospital care needed.

3. It would improve health planning so that current and future health resources can be distributed more equitably and effectively. This would include planning agencies to set priorities on community needs and certify all applications for federal aid as to need.

4. It would more directly contain escalation of health care costs while assuring quality of health care. Payment for health care under federally supported programs would be based on customary and prevailing fees and on peer review of professional services falling outside of professionally established guidelines. Payment to hospitals and other health care institutions under federal programs would be based on a system of prospectively approved charges. This system would require the hospitals, for instance, to establish their charges on a prospective basis, say a year in advance, rather than raising them at any time that it occurred to them that their expenses were increasing, or they decided to buy some new, expensive equipment.

5. The program would establish national goals and priorities to improve health care. It proposes that the President deliver to Congress an annual report on the state of the nation's health, and that the Congress create a Council of Health Policy Advisors to the President to advise him on broad policy and health matters.

6. It would improve the financing of health care for everyone. This is the aspect of the Healthcare program which has the greatest immediate interest to life underwriters and those directly concerned with the health insurance business. The program is too complex to review in detail here, but generally speaking, it would propose a broad, comprehensive package of health care insurance standards to be set by the Federal Government. These standards would provide for ambulatory and preventive care benefits, hospital benefits, and medical care benefits. The minimum benefits would include diagnostic and laboratory work, ambulatory care, institutional care, well baby care, skilled nursing home care, and approved home health care programs. The breadth of the programs would be increased by phases. Given the enactment of this bill in 1971, it would initially be effective in 1973. The benefits would be broadened in 1976,

and again in 1979 as the facilities for the delivery of more care became available.

The same basic benefits would be available to all persons, at least as a minimum. There would be no top limit on what insurance companies could offer in the way of benefits over and above the required minimums. The standard minimum coverage would not be compulsory, but strong tax incentives would be offered to purchase it. The full premiums for a qualifying health care plan would be tax deductible, but only half the premiums for a non-qualified plan.

The poor and the near-poor would be covered under State pools of insurers set up to provide the minimum standard coverage. Because of the limited resources of such persons, the level of benefits in the State pools would be at the level planned for the second phase, right from the beginning. But these persons would have insurance coverage issued by insurance companies, exactly the same as everyone else. The premiums for the poor would be entirely paid by the Government. The near-poor would be subsidized and would pay a portion of their own premiums.

This pool would also be available to provide coverage for the uninsurable, defined as those who were unable to purchase the coverage at double the normal premium or less.

## THE PROSPECTS FOR ACTION

What is likely to come of all these proposals? One thing is certain, and that is that none of them is likely to be enacted in its entirety without amendment. The Congress is a body skilled in compromise. The Senate and the House have different viewpoints on many issues. It seems likely that whatever bill is enacted will contain elements from two or more of the proposals. It seems vital that persons in the insurance business keep the five principles of HIAA strongly in mind and advise their legislative representatives of how they feel about the matter. If this is done, the bill ultimately enacted should be one we can live with.

## THE KEY POINTS AT ISSUE

Perhaps it is optimistic, but I like to think that the HIAA proposal, being by far the most practical and having a reasonable price tag (approximately 3.2 billion dollars of new federal money in the initial year), will contribute most to the ultimate plan. Obviously, the Administration proposal has many points in common with the HIAA Plan. Since it does not appear likely that the Congress will be willing to enact the necessary tax measures to support the more radical plans, such as Senator Kennedy's offering, some plan similar to those of the HIAA and the Administration seems the most likely outcome. Therefore, it may be of value to explore some of the key differences in the insurance end of these plans.

Perhaps the most important difference is that the Administration plan would provide a compulsory arrangement, while the HIAA plan is voluntary and depends upon tax incentives to achieve universal coverage. The second point seems closely related to the first. The Administration would require federal control of forms and rates, while the HIAA plan envisages the federal government setting minimum standards as to benefits, but control of actual forms and rates remaining, as it is presently, within the province of the states. A third important difference is in the way the poor and the near-poor are handled. The Administration plan proposes a completely governmental and "different" plan for the poor; the HIAA approach would give the poor the same coverage as everyone else. Finally, the differences in incentives for the improvement and augmentation of the means of delivery of health care are most important.

The industry will make every effort to retain state regulation of the actual plans and to encourage the stronger planning and delivery augmentation provisions contained in its own Healthcare proposals.

## THE FUTURE OF THE BUSINESS

Where does that leave the agent and the health insurance business? Unless I am very much mistaken, it's fairly obvious that the future of group insurance is assured. Probably, the premium volume will grow enormously. Virtually every employer will have to participate on one basis or another, and for one reason or another, and the quality of the plans will be so much improved that premiums cannot help but increase substantially. It also seems fairly obvious that the business as a whole is going to have to pay very close attention to the costs of its operation. A plan of such universal application will result in demands for high operating efficiency and low retentions.

What of the individual side of the business? One of the disturbing things about the Administration plan is in its provisions for the insuring of certain individuals "at group rates." It appears rather clear that many persons unacquainted with the realities of the insurance business assume that merely labeling something as "group insurance" assures a lower premium rate and lower costs of doing business.

Those of us actually engaged in the business know only too well that this is not so. The lower costs of group insurance emerge in no small part from the fact that the personnel departments of the employers are doing much of the contact work, advice, and actual selling ordinarily done by agents in the handling of individual health care insurance. In the absence of such personnel, if agents are still going to do this kind of work, they are going to have to be paid for it in one way or another.

Individuals who pay their premiums individually to insurance companies are going to have to be billed individually. In the absence of payroll deduction, they are going to have the same disposition to lapse their policies. Just where this leaves insurance companies attempting to show low expense costs in handling inherently expensive business, no one yet knows. However, one thing is certain. It will be necessary to show lower expense ratios under a plan which is either semi-compulsory via the tax-arm-twisting route, or compulsory as under the Administration route, than has been permissible in the past.

What will this do to the rates of compensation now enjoyed by agents? It seems likely that front-end sales commission rates will have to be reduced, because they are and should be based largely on the difficulty of making the sale. On the other hand, if the sale of health care insurance becomes almost a walk-in proposition with most of the agents' work being concerned with service, it might well make much more sense to pay a flat annual service commission or fee, rather than a large sales commission followed by small renewal commissions. But all in all, it seems likely that there will remain a substantial market for individual health care insurance. And, of course, the individual premiums will be much larger, so that the earnings of agents should remain substantial.

One problem which will face the insurance companies will be the problem of making ends meet. As most of these bills are written, any insurance offered on the individual basis would have to be guaranteed renewable. Depending upon the extent to which the rates may be subject to control, companies writing individual insurance might be caught in a very serious trap if they had to offer coverages under guaranteed renewable policies which they could not alter, even to fit changes in the benefit pattern later enacted by Congress, and were, at the same time, at the mercy of political rate regulation. One doubts that health insurance carriers would like to be in a position similar to that of the automobile insurance carriers in recent years! Yet that does not seem an impossible prospect. And the automobile insurance carriers could at least get completely out of the business if they wished to. With guaranteed renewable coverage, even that door may not be open.

Obviously, the shape of the final legislation is far from clear, and many of these problems may be solved before it is. I remain optimistic that there will continue to be a marketplace in which the competent insurance practitioner will find an opportunity for honorable and profitable service. However, whether this market survives will depend in no small part on the contributions that all of us in home office and field alike are willing to make toward educating our representatives in the Congress on the necessity for enacting a bill which meets the five principles. Let us accept our responsibilities to that end, and in so doing, let us keep in mind that National interest as well as our own.

## Questions

1. What weaknesses exist in the labor-sponsored Health Security Act, Medicredit, and the Family Health Insurance Plan judging from the HIAA principles or from your own analysis?
2. Evaluate the Healthcare proposal.
3. If the Healthcare proposal is adopted, would individual health insurance still be sold as extensively as at present?

# 31. WRITING THE PRESCRIPTION FOR HEALTH CARE *

Daniel W. Pettengill †

For over five years, the nation's employers have faced annual increases of 10% to 15% in the costs of their group health care plans, and more increases are coming.

While some of the increase has been caused by improvements in benefits and by union demands for greater employer contributions, most of it is due to the skyrocketing cost of health care. As early as 1960, health care costs were climbing twice as fast as the cost of living—and taking insurance costs with them.

Something must be done; the question is what. With little rhetorical license, it can be said that everyone has a solution to offer. Business has a large stake in the shape health care reform takes, because the current state of the world predetermines one fact—business will pick up a larger share of the bill.

In the early 1960's, all things seemed possible in this country; in the early 1970's, we know that obtaining something new adamantly demands giving up something else. As a recent Brookings Institution budget study points out, the cost of *any* new federal program must be met either by cutting back existing programs or by enacting new taxes.[1]

The same study shows that the lion's share of federal expenditure has not been made in areas that would rebound with the winding down of the war; rather, government has spent most of its money in attempts to assist its citizens. Hence nothing can be pared without pain, and new taxes seem unavoidable. One way or another, business has a vital interest.

## PROBLEMS BEFORE CONGRESS

To prepare itself to judge the various bills proposed by the Administration and by individual legislators, Congress has set 1972 as its target date for reviewing the way the United States provides and pays for health care. To understand the options Congress will be weighing, one must understand the problems facing the nation's health care system.

* From *Harvard Business Review* (November-December, 1971), pp. 37-43; 1971 by the President and Fellows of Harvard College; all rights reserved. Reprinted by permission.

† Vice-President, Group Division, Aetna Life & Casualty.

1 Charles L. Schultze, Edward R. Fried, Alice M. Rivlin, Nancy H. Teeters, *Setting National Priorities: The 1972 Budget* (Washington, The Brookings Institution, 1971) pp. 331-333.

## Manpower Shortage

First, the public demands greater health care services than there is manpower to deliver. Sought after and overworked, doctors are charging higher and higher fees.

The problem is more complex than the obvious solution, "Produce more doctors," would imply. Medical schools in this country can graduate only 40,000 students a year, and this means that through 1975 the number of doctors will rise only slightly faster than the general population. Shortening their schooling, making their courses more "relevant" (an increasingly frequent cry of dissatisfied medical students), encouraging the training of paramedical personnel, and then persuading both physicians and patients to rely on them—these are some of the tough advances we must make.

## Technical Advance and Obsolescence

Burgeoning medical technology has created a host of costly tools for the treatment of acute illness. Because an increased number of specially trained teams of doctors and technicians are required to operate new equipment, the costs of maintaining personnel are higher than ever before. The maintenance of a specialized team, in fact, can become a heavy financial burden.

Perhaps the most familiar instance is the intensive care unit developed for cardiac and pulmonary problems. None of us would be quick to dispense with this increased capacity to save lives or with the knowledge it represents, but we have been slow to face the fact that we must pay for it. And, of course, we must pay for it again and again, thanks to the rapid appearance and the rapid obsolescence of increasingly sophisticated improvements.

## Needless and Wasteful Competition

Technology can induce totally unwarranted cost in a context of unnecessary competition.[2]

The classic and dramatic case is the attempt, made by nearly every major hospital, to offer open heart surgery. Too often the equipment goes largely unused, and the surgical team does not operate frequently enough even to maintain its skills at peak efficiency.

I should like to note that one practical answer to this problem would be to give the voluntary health planning agencies, which have already been established under Public Law 89-749, the authority to require an institution to demonstrate a high-priority community need before it can add major equipment and services.

---

[2] See G. C. Forsyth and D. Glyn Thomas, "Models for Financially Healthy Hospitals," HBR July-August 1971, p. 106.

## Extra Burdens on Hospitals

According to expert testimony, cutting the length of the average hospital stay by a single day could save some $1.7 billion a year in hospital billings. Yet the charge continues to be made that hospitals are overused. Why, then, has the average stay not been reduced?

One reason is that the hospital is the ideal workshop for the doctor. Another is that the public has been conditioned to believe that hospital care is the best care.

But by far the most important reason is the almost exclusive reliance that insurance buyers place on hospital coverage. They are reluctant to seek other care, or to agree to it even if it is prescribed. To relieve hospitals of their "draining" occupancy, first the public must be persuaded to change from in-patient to walk-in/walk-out care. However, such a change will also require a reeducation of the medical profession, building and staffing high-quality ambulatory care centers, and adequate health insurance to finance ambulatory care.

From the physician's vantage, there is a forbidding specter that demands the overuse of hospitals and other health care services: the malpractice suit. An increase in such suits raises the fees he must charge, naturally; but there is another professional reaction that must be considered as well. Fear of suit encourages the physician to order every conceivable diagnostic test to prevent a patient, and a court, from charging him with irresponsibility. He also tends to increase the length of the hospital stay, when less costly care might suffice.

But the most far-reaching consequence of the rise in malpractice suits is the understandable reluctance of the physician to delegate tasks to paraprofessionals. The risks of such care, which lie upon the doctor, are cramping the development of an enormous manpower resource that would permit more care more economically.

## Plague Spots

The whole somber picture is further darkened by the uneven demographic distribution of medical personnel and, to a lesser extent, of health care facilities.

The problem is not so much to produce more personnel as to persuade the personnel we have to locate where they are needed. Even if there were a comfortable surplus of health care personnel, the disadvantages of locating in a sparsely populated region, where professional isolation and exhaustion are real hazards, or in an urban ghetto, where the possibility of violence is disturbingly present, strongly discourage doctors from seeking homes in these areas.

To encourage location in the medically needy parts of the country, government must ensure that financial incentives and rotational relief are available on an adequate scale.

## Vicious Circle: Health and Poverty

Poverty is part of the health care problem, as it is of most of the other major problems facing our nation. Poor health breeds poverty, and poverty exacerbates poor health. No overall solution to our health care problem can overlook the fact that the poor and the near-poor need assistance in financing adequate health care. A system that fragments them from the rest of the population must be suspect on the grounds that it may consign them to second-rate care.

### SOLUTIONS BEFORE CONGRESS

As I mentioned at the outset, everyone has a solution for one or more of these elements of the health care crisis. Although the proposals differ greatly, they can be grouped loosely into three categories:

1. A new system to be run by the federal government.
2. A system of mandatory benefits for catastrophes.
3. An improved version of our present system that allows more effective partnership between the government and private industry.

## A Single Government Program

The perennial suggestion that this country adopt the British system— that is, have the federal government take over both the delivery and financing of health care—falls into the first category. Inasmuch as neither the British nor any other foreign system has been successful in controlling costs, this suggestion has less support today than it did, say, 40 years ago when private health care insurance first started.

In this first category is the Health Security Act proposed by Senator Edward Kennedy (D.-Mass.). Under this bill, a single, compulsory federal health care insurance plan would replace essentially all voluntary private coverage. The program would be paid for half by general revenues and half by payroll taxes.

The employer's share would be 3.5% of his total payroll; the employee's, 1% of his wages and unearned income up to $15,000 a year. Depending on agreements reached through collective bargaining, employers might pay all or part of the employees' portion. It is not surprising that the Health Security bill is supported by organized labor.

The program would be administered by a national Health Security Board, operating in regional units that dictate the services to be provided by health care institutions and negotiate annual budgets with them. Each institution would then be expected to provide the authorized services within its fixed income to an unlimited number of patients. Doctors' traditional fee-for-service bills would be severely discouraged by giving budgetary priority to doctors agreeing to serve a given segment of the population for a specified per capita payment. Certainly prepaid group practice plans have an important role to play in improving our system of delivering health care. However, I do not believe that they are an adequate answer in themselves; and they cannot be established overnight.

And establishing such a plan as the bill proposes might have evil consequences. The end result of this bill would be "nine to five" practice of medicine on an inflexible budget. Congress is naturally concerned about what this might do to the quality of medical care and to the future of medical science in this country.

But this concern of Congress is running second to its concern over the cost factors the Kennedy bill would set in operation. Its rejection is likely to stem from the fact that it would require a shift of more than $55 billion a year from the private sector to the government at a time when the nation is faced with other needs—to appropriate substantial funds and devise administrative solutions for such problem areas as employment, housing, pollution and transportation, to say nothing of defense and foreign aid.

The other entry in this first category is Senator Jacob Javits' (R.N.Y.) proposal to extend Medicare to everyone. His bill allows employers the option of electing a private plan; but to be acceptable, a private plan must provide more liberal benefits than Medicare; and the employer must assume responsibility for at least 75% of its costs.

Does Javits' proposal represent an effective partnership between the federal government and private enterprise? Apparently, *yes;* actually, *no.* The government could not long permit a significant number of employers to opt out of the federal program, because the better risks would generally do so, and this would increase the cost to those who choose Medicare. Thus the conditions for private plans would be likely to become progressively more stringent in order to cut down on the number of plans that would qualify as acceptable. Javits' plan, then, must be classified along with Senator Kennedy's as a federal-monopoly approach.

## Programs for Catastrophes

In the second category are the proposals of those who apparently believe that the federal government is already doing all it should in the health care field, except that it is not providing adequate assistance to families hit by a catastrophic illness.

The key bill here is that of Senator Russell Long (D.-La.), Chairman, Senate Finance Committee. This proposal would increase the Social Security payroll tax so the federal government could pay for various expenses incurred in catastrophic illness after a deductible equal to 60 days of hospital care and $2,000 worth of physicians' and certain other services.

Such a proposal would add to demand without increasing supply and would intensify rather than resolve all of the nation's health care problems. If enacted, I believe it would result in endless pressure on Congress for successive reductions in the amount of the deductible until the initial federal catastrophe benefit finally became a comprehensive federal health care plan.

Ironically, perhaps the greatest catastrophe—that people continue to live long after they have ceased to be able to take care of their daily physical needs—is an *income maintenance* problem, like unemployment, rather than a *medical* problem.

Financing the room, board, and personal hygiene aspects of long-term custodial care is, without a shadow of a doubt, a major problem that cries for a solution. But the many subjective factors at work in this area make the cost virtually impossible to predict or control. Therefore, while provision for the occasional medical needs of the permanently incapacitated should form part of a health insurance plan, financing their ordinary living expenses should be considered a problem in itself.

## Federal/Private Partnerships

Proposals in the third category hold that if adequate health care is to come within the reach of all without requiring the huge additional tax revenues necessary for the government to do the job alone, the federal government must set standards and provide incentives for the private sector to improve the present system. This is, of course, the approach taken by the Nixon Administration.

**Administration Plan:** The National Health Insurance Partnership bill (hopefully to be debated in Congress before the end of the year) would compel every employer to offer his employees and their dependents a minimum basic insurance program plus major medical coverage. The employer would pay 65% of the cost initially and 75% ultimately. He would retain the right to choose the insurance company that would underwrite the plan.

Group health insurance for small employers is more expensive to administer and is subject to greater fluctuations in claim cost than insurance for large employers. To spread this extra cost, small employers and the self-employed persons who elected to purchase coverage would be charged either the same premium rate or some rate not in excess of a prescribed maximum. Losses on the class of business would presumably have to be recovered by charging higher than customary rates to all larger employers.

To supplement his Partnership act, the President also proposes a new federal insurance plan for poor families with dependent children. (The childless poor would remain eligible for the state Medicaid program.) In adopting this dual approach, the Administration appears to have been motivated solely by reasons of budget.

But even if the childless poor were to be made eligible for the new federal plan, the President's proposal would still have the unfortunate and unwarranted effect of filtering out the poor from the mainstream of health care. I agree with those critics who believe this separation will result in health care of inferior quality for the poor.

The President's program does not provide additional federal funds or increased authority for voluntary health planning agencies. It does make funds available for training medical personnel and for planning and developing Health Maintenance Organizations (HMOs). Medical staffs at the HMOs would provide fairly comprehensive health care for those who volunteer for it; this HMO membership would pay for its care in advance, on a per capita basis.

The HMO, then, stands as a variation of a prepaid group practice plan, and it might share the latter's success in shifting the emphasis from expensive in-patient hospital care to less expensive ambulatory care. It is obvious that the President hopes to encourage this all-important redirection.

But since membership would be voluntary, a massive development of HMOs can succeed only if both physicians and the public want it. So far, both seem somewhat reluctant.

**AMA Plan:** The American Medical Association has taken a very different approach to the federal/private partnership. It has designed a financing scheme that would give everyone, including the poor, access to a federally specified plan of private health care insurance.

Under its Medicredit, so-called, each person would receive an income tax credit for the amount he paid to buy health care insurance that meets minimum benefit standards. The percent of credit would decrease as the amount of his income tax increases, with the poor receiving full financing and no one receiving less than 10%. For the portion of the premium that paid for catastrophe coverage, the credit would be total regardless of income.

However, the AMA plan does not provide truly comprehensive coverage, nor does it provide for the phasing in of benefits coordinated with the availablility of manpower and facilities. And one must wonder whether obtaining a certificate from the Internal Revenue Service and then redeeming it with an insurance company would be a convenient and economical way for the poor to secure private coverage. The bookkeeping required to keep 50 million accounts of this kind in order would be a considerable administrative task, to say the least.

**Burleson-McIntyre Proposal:** Also in this third category is the National Healthcare bill introduced in Congress by Representative Omar Burleson (D.-Tex.) and Senator Thomas J. McIntyre (D.-N.H.). In the opinion of members of the insurance industry, this is the most comprehensive, yet pragmatic, proposal thus far advanced. Consider its advantages:

■ In answer to the manpower shortage, it would provide more funds for training and also offer incentives to those serving in areas where scarcities are acute. For example, under the terms of a proposed five-year experimental program, the Secretary of HEW would be enpowered to guarantee a medical worker a higher wage than he might get elsewhere—say, 110%—to work in an area where he is badly needed. In addition, part or all of the expenses of any medical/paramedical education could be waived, according to an incentive schedule.

Funds would also be made available for the construction and initial operation of ambulatory health care centers.

■ Areawide community agencies for health planning, staffed by professionals and consumers, would be given both money and authority to determine health care problems and their priorities. Each agency would survey the health care needs in its area and then recommend or prohibit federal funding for individuals or organizations with plans to meet these needs.

I might note that the prohibiting power is an important one. Currently, groups denied a recommendation for funding through such an agency can go round the back way, through another agency, and get another kind of grant.

■ Cost controls would be strengthened without subtracting quality by encouraging physicians, dentists, and other health professionals to set up "utilization" or "practice" guidelines on county or state bases for insurers to use in screening claims. Claims that fell outside these guidelines would be subject to peer review, and benefits would be paid only if the care was found to be "necessary and proper."

■ Health care institutions would be required to establish budgets and schedules of rates, to be filed and approved in advance by a state Healthcare Institution Cost Commission. Payments for services to all patients would be made according to these rates.

Either inefficiencies would be removed, or the institution would lose money. Presumably the community would be called on to make up the difference; but while contributions may be made fairly cheerfully to hospital funds today, people probably would *not* be willing to cough up money for a hospital which had lost its approved federal funding through its own shortcomings.

■ To guide the President, the Congress, and the nation in developing a sound health care policy, a council of advisors would be established at Cabinet level to ensure that health care would get continued attention amidst the crush of priorities.

In terms of dealing with the problems that plague the nation's health care system, the Burleson-McIntyre bill gains by comparison with the others I have reviewed.

In addition to making the provisions I have just outlined, it also confronts the necessity of making health insurance available to everyone. Its approach is threefold:

1. The federal government would establish minimum standards for coverage, modest at first, but more ambitious in the future as the resources grow.
2. Employers would not be compelled to offer these minimum benefits. They would be encouraged to do so through income tax deductions—100% for acceptable plans, 50% for inferior ones. To help ensure

employee participation in the group plan and to help the self-employed buy individual policies, the personal income tax law would be amended to provide 100% and 50% deduction for individuals, just as for employers.

3. Each state would purchase a single group policy to provide the federal standard of benefits for the poor, the near-poor, and those self-supporting persons who are currently uninsurable for health reasons. The poor would not be required to contribute toward the premium, but the near-poor would make a modest contribution based on income and family status. Self-supporting uninsurables would pay the full premium. The policy would be reinsured by all carriers in proportion to the volume of their health care policies in the state.

Furthermore, the states would be reimbursed for much of their cost by the federal government. Percentages would vary from 70% to 90%, depending on the state's per capita income. By offering such support, the plan guarantees that members of all income levels will receive the same quality care, with the freedom to choose who provides it. Medicaid, but not Medicare, would be phased out.

One of the advantages of the Burleson-McIntyre bill is the modest amount of additional tax revenue it requires: this is estimated at $4.8 billion in fiscal 1974. Because the plan leaves health insurance for those under age 65 in the private sector—and fully 90% of these people are privately covered—it does not require the huge expense of dismantling one part of private industry and building its replacement into the government. Nor does it divert tax dollars to buy coverage for those who can afford to pay for it themselves.

It also allows the employer to retain a degree of freedom in designing the benefits, in setting the level of employee contribution to his company's group health care plans, and in choosing the insurer who can provide him with efficient administration at reasonable cost.

## EITHER/OR

In the last analysis, there are two possibilities: business can champion a proposal that nationalizes health care or one that preserves, but improves, the existing private, pluralistic system.

Under the first, we can expect higher taxes, less take-home pay, and demands for higher wages—the familiar tune of an ever-accelerating merry-go-round.

A plan constructed on the existing framework, however, offers business health care insurance that controls costs and quality, not by fiat, but by response. And because it would offer to all a plan that does not require enormous new taxes, it would not siphon off funds needed to solve other urgent social problems, many of which—the environment, housing, malnutrition, to name a few—can radically affect the *nation's* health.

## Questions

1. Which of the major problems in health care cited by the author do you feel can be solved *only* by some form of federal legislation? Which can be solved within the existing system of health care? Discuss.
2. Under a single government health care system, how might workmen's compensation, OASDHI, and other types of social insurance programs now providing health insurance benefits be affected? How would you propose to prevent duplication of services and benefits? Discuss.
3. Do you favor the Burleson-McIntyre proposal over other alternatives? Why or why not?

# 32. WHAT'S WRONG WITH UNEMPLOYMENT INSURANCE? *

William Papier †

What's wrong with unemployment insurance? Mindful of the hazards of criticism, one recalls the warning of a noted scholar who once wryly observed: "If you grab the bull by the tail, you must face the issue directly!"

The critic of unemployment insurance, no matter how pure his motives, makes himself a target for more than a single bull. He can easily find faults—in the philosophy, in the benefit structure, in the tax provisions, in the administration. And when he does, he risks the joint animus of friends of the program, of organized labor, of organized management, of state and federal colleagues.

Despite its oft-exaggerated flaws, it is suggested that the concept of unemployment insurance is basically sound. "What's right with unemployment insurance" by far outweighs "What's wrong." It provides a system whereby workers laid off through no fault of their own can claim and receive weekly compensation for wage loss, enabling them to maintain their dignity and self-respect, because benefits are paid as a legal right.

If, however, the public image of unemployment insurance leaves much to be desired, the fault lies in part with its friends. To some extent they have searched out, publicized and tried to correct its flaws. To a considerable extent, they have not.

## PERSPECTIVE

What, precisely, is wrong with unemployment insurance? Part of what's wrong is in our own vacillating temperature, which blows hot and cold with the business cycle. During the last recession, in 1961, more than seven million persons received one or more unemployment checks under state programs. Six out of every one hundred covered workers, on the average, were jobless. Many solid citizens were unemployed, including family heads with years of prior employment. Public support of the program was reflected in liberalization of state laws. The Congress extended payments for those still out of work after exhausting state benefits.

* From *The Journal of Risk and Insurance* (March, 1970), pp. 63-74. Reprinted by permission.

† Director of Research and Statistics, Ohio Bureau of Employment Services.

390

More than nine years have elapsed since the last recession. The recovery has been truly remarkable for its duration. The labor market in 1968 was the tightest in 15 years, with thousands of jobs begging for qualified candidates. Fewer than one-half as many weeks of unemployment were compensated last year, under state unemployment insurance laws, as in 1961. The rate of insured unemployment fell to 2.2 percent, the lowest level since World War II.

The composition and quality of the unemployed are far different in boom years than in recession years. Although the available facts are limited, there's little doubt that the proportion of family heads among claimants goes down in boom years, while the proportion of secondary workers with limited attachment to the labor market goes up. Those with least economic pressure and motivation to find new jobs represent a sizeable proportion of all claimants in boom years. Public enthusiasm for unemployment insurance tends to cool.

This note on perspective, in other words, is basic: No matter how perfect the statutes and their administration, public reactions are prone to be most critical in good times and least critical in bad times. Perhaps this is just as well! It should lead to periodic improvements when economic conditions are best, in advance of later recessions.

## PRIMARY GOALS

What improvements should now be considered? Number 1 is the development of a general consensus on primary goals. Twenty years ago the Administrator of the Ohio Bureau, speaking in New York to his assembled counterparts from every state in the Union, asked this pointed question:

Where do we want to go? If we don't know where we're going, it doesn't matter which road we take. But if we all take different roads, and head in different directions, and shift our objectives from one point to another, can we expect anything but public confusion, lack of respect for our program, and eventual disintegration?

We'll all rise or fall together. The sins of one state reach the public mind as the sins of all. The virtues of another state help us all. But sins make more interesting headlines than virtues. In the public mind, we're all good or we're all bad. Right now, our stock isn't very high. Every state must improve.

Maybe it's an insurance program we're operating. Maybe it's the so-called 'dole.' Maybe our primary objective is to develop and stabilize employment. Maybe our program is a combination of all these. Or maybe it's something else altogether. Whatever it is, whatever it's designed to accomplish or try to accomplish, the public has a right to know.

Despite the lapse of two decades since these remarks were first made, and more than three decades since benefits were first paid, this unpleasant fact remains: We still have no generally-accepted philosophy concerning the proper place and purpose of unemployment insurance in our economic system. This is a paramount need—to provide sound policy guides—for statutory implementation and administration.

## Economic Stabilizer

Back in the early days, at the time of the Great Depression, there were many who thought that unemployment insurance would serve as an economic stabilizer. Benefits, they believed, should be highest in bad times, when employer taxes should be lowest—and vice versa. Aggregate benefits, of course, have been considerably higher in recession years than in boom years. But wage losses due to unemployment have also been considerably higher in recession years. Dean Richard A. Lester of Princeton University, in his 1962 book, *The Economics of Unemployment Compensation,* found that benefits in the preceding 13 years replaced only 15 cents on the dollar of wage loss due to unemployment. The tax structure, he also found, had a "tendency to aggravate the business cycle." Several years earlier the University of Illinois published a study on *Experience Rating in Unemployment Compensation,* by Dr. Clinton Spivey. He observed "little evidence that the existing experience rating systems are capable of producing counter-cyclical tax effects." In other words, unemployment insurance as an economic stabilizer apparently leaves much to be desired.

## Broader Coverage

The stabilizing impact of unemployment benefits could be greater, of course, if coverage were broader. This poses the question "Who should be covered?" Presumably, everyone employed by others and subject to layoff should be protected. The U.S. Department of Labor estimates that one out of every four who should be covered—over 16 million—are excluded. Noncovered employees of state and local governments, and of other nonprofit organizations, number over 10 million. Federal employees are covered by federal law. The military services are similarly covered. Why should large noncovered groups continue to be excluded by the states? Reasons vary from different categories of exemptions—constitutional, administrative, financial. All are surmountable. Noncovered workers, through the prices they pay for goods and services, help defray the costs of unemployment insurance for others. Is there any reason why the large, noncovered group should be enthusiastic about the program?

## Eligibility

For those who are covered, however, let's consider the issue of basic eligibility. The program was originally intended for workers firmly attached to the labor market, for those who needed and wanted year-round jobs, for heads of households. The early laws established prior earnings and occasionally employment requirements, which fairly well screened out workers with limited attachment to the labor market. In those days—thirty-some years ago—there were relatively few jobs for such persons. But since then truly remarkable changes have occurred. Tens of thousands of jobs opened up for secondary workers such as housewives and students—full-time jobs, part-time jobs, night-time jobs, "pin-money" jobs—for carryouts at supermarkets, for car-hops at drive-ins, for salesclerks at shopping centers, and so on. There were  some changes, over the years, in basic eligibility requirements. But the screens were not narrowed sufficiently to keep out these new secondary workers with limited labor market attachment. When laid off, they were assured of food, clothing, and shelter whether or not they found new jobs. When they received unemployment benefits—and sometimes showed little interest in new jobs—criticism mounted. Our public image suffered.

Just as the screen of basic eligibility requirements tended to widen with the passing years, for those who cleared the first hurdle, new and finer screens were introduced in the form of disqualification provisions. Some were apparently intended to disqualify the kinds of workers who should never have cleared the initial eligibility test. The laws normally provide that claimants must be able to work, available for work, and jobless because of lack of work. Claimants are disqualified if they quit voluntarily without good cause, or are discharged for misconduct con-nected with their work. Over the years, a wide variety of additional disqualifying clauses were introduced. In some cases they were con-sidered punitive. Needless to note, perhaps, severe disqualification provisions, which denied benefits under specified conditions to claim-ants who had previously established basic benefit rights, disenchanted not only those who were negatively affected but also friends of the pro-gram. Our image was further tarnished.

## Benefit Amounts

For claimants who clear the qualification and disqualification hur-dles, the obvious question is this: How much should they get and for how long? Again we go back to early principles. Employment should always be more attractive, financially, than unemployment. Benefits, it was generally agreed, should always be related to prior earnings. And, except for a relatively small proportion of highest-paid workers, weekly benefits should represent at least one-half prior weekly earnings.

What has been happening with respect to benefits? Most claimants, when unemployed, probably get less than one-half their prior average earnings. In 1968, the average unemployment insurance check for all states amounted to $43 per week—less than three-eighths the aver-age earnings of all covered workers.

The Ohio proportion was similar. Ohio figures also provide earnings data for individual claimants, as distinguished from averages for covered workers generally. Under Ohio Law, three out of every five 1968 claimants were eligible for benefits amounting to less than one-half their prior weekly earnings. For men with dependents the proportion was better than three out of four. This key group of family heads averaged $58 per week in benefits when totally unemployed. When they were employed, however, they averaged $152 per week. Their average benefit, in other words, represented only 38 percent of their average earnings.

Are these family heads likely to be pleased? Probably not—especially not when they learn that women without dependents are treated far more generously. Whereas only one out of every four men with dependents was eligible for benefits equalling at least one-half his prior earnings, better than three out of every four women without dependents were similarly eligible. These women, averaged $77 per week employed, and received benefits averaging $36 per week when unemployed. Their weekly benefit, on the average, replaced 46 percent of their prior weekly earnings. How can anyone defend a system which treats unemployed women without dependents much better than unemployed men who head families? It isn't easy!

Certainly this pattern was not the intent of early proponents of unemployment insurance. It developed, on the one hand because claimants with dependents generally earned considerably more per week than claimants without dependents. They earned more primarily because they had greater tenure, they were more skilled and they worked longer hours in higher-paying industries, such as construction, utilities, and heavy manufacturing. It developed, on the other hand, because weekly benefit ceilings hit higher wage-earners much harder than they did lower wage-earners. Last year, for example, seven out of every eight men claimants in Ohio would have had higher basic benefits (disregarding dependents allowances) at one-half their prior weekly earnings, were it not for statutory ceilings. Only one out of four women, however, was similarly held down by the same ceilings. In practice, therefore, there were two benefit-rate philosophies—one for lower wage-earners, who are predominantly women and secondary workers, and one of higher wage-earners, who are predominantly men with dependents. The lower wage-earners received benefits related to prior earnings. The higher wage-earners were essentially on a flat-rate system, because they were heavily concentrated at the ceilings. The current double standard is indefensible. Those who protest for "equal rights," insofar as unemployment insurance is concerned, should be men!

What should be said about minimum weekly benefits? Are they also vulnerable to criticism? Yes, although relatively few claimants are affected. Many states, including Ohio, pay $10 per week or less to eligible claimants who are totally unemployed. Yet 96 out of every 100 claimants in Ohio average $50 or more per week when employed. Thus, they justify and receive benefits when totally unemployed of $25 per week or more. The federal minimum wage law now requires basic pay rates of at least

$1.45 per hour. This goes up to $1.60 in February, 1971. It seems point-less to write a negligible number of small benefit checks, knowing that recipients were limited in labor market attachment and probably should have been screened out initially.

## Duration of Benefits

What should be said about potential duration of benefits? Here again there are mixed philosophies among the states. A handful or so provide that everyone who establishes basic eligibility can draw bene-fits for as many as 26 weeks in 52. Most states have systems of vari-able potential duration, geared to presumed measures of labor mar-ket attachment. Virtually all states provide potentials of 26 weeks or longer for some claimants. And a few provide for extended duration of benefits when unemployment appears relatively high/ These mixed philosophies stem from the basic and still unresolved issue of who the program should protect. If it is designed to protect those who normally work full-time and want year-round employment, then there is no good reason why such workers should not all be potentially eligible for 26 weeks or more of benefits when unemployed through no fault of their own. If, on the other hand, it is intended also to cover secondary workers with limited attachment to the labor market, shorter potential durations for such workers may be warranted.

Experience shows that the average duration of benefits is con-sistently longer for women than for men. Claimants without dependents draw benefits over a longer period of time than do the claimants with dependents. Does this pattern reflect greater re-employment opportuni-ties for men, especially men with dependents? Or does it reflect greater economic pressure on these men to get back to work as soon as possible? Or both? The women, remember, are preponderantly secondary workers whose benefits, related to prior earnings, are considerably more at-tractive than those paid men who are predominately primary workers.

No one really knows the extent to which employer preferences in filling jobs and economic pressures on different claimants explain vari-ations in the duration of benefits. The fact that the statutes make benefits more attractive to one group than to another, however, can-not be overlooked. Nor can the reluctance of employers to hire unen-thusiastic claimants be ignored. Insofar as these patterns do exist, perhaps more extensively in some areas than in others, cynicism develops. The program suffers from lack of public support.

## Taxation

The discussion shifts now to the unpopular subject of taxes. Bene-fit costs are financed entirely by what the laws euphemistically call "con-tributions." These compulsory "contributions," based on payrolls, are geared to the individual experience of each employer. Rates change every calendar year. Employers experiencing higher unemployment and benefit charges pay higher tax rates. The lowest rates, which go down to zero in some states including Ohio, are enjoyed by employers experiencing lower unemployment and lower benefit charges.

The philosophy that benefits should be financed by a payroll tax is widely accepted, at least in practice. Whether or not all or part of the covered payroll should be taxed, however, is a far different matter. Originally, total and taxable payroll were one and the same. But beginning with 1940 the Federal Unemployment Tax Act, which finances administrative costs of state programs, reduced the federal tax base to the first $3,000 per year of each covered worker's earnings. Many states, Ohio among them, similarly reduced their tax bases. At that time, however, very few workers earned over $3,000 per year. In Ohio, for example, 92 percent of the covered payroll was then taxable.

With nearly three decades of inflation, marked by rising salaries and wages, the pattern changed markedly. Most covered workers today earn much more than $3,000 per year. Nevertheless, the tax base for the Federal Unemployment Tax Act and the tax bases in most states remained at $3,000. The taxable payroll in Ohio last year represented only 45 percent of the total payroll.

A score or so of states, other than Ohio, have raised their tax bases, with ceilings currently ranging from $3,300 to $7,200 per year. None has gone back to taxing total annual payroll. Clearly, the federal government and the states have widely divergent views concerning the best and fairest method of financing unemployment insurance. In terms of results, lower tax rates on a higher tax base could yield the same return as higher tax rates on a lower tax base. The rate structure is the same for all employers in a given state, whether they offer high wages or low wages. The tax base, however, may affect high-wage industries differently than low-wage industries. Retailers in Ohio, for example, now have a taxable payroll which represents about three-fifths of their total payroll. The pattern for Ohio manufacturers, on the other hand, is reversed. Their non-taxable payroll is around three-fifths of their total payroll.

There is no pattern of consistent logic, either in the federal tax base of $3,000 or in the wide variety of tax bases and rates now in effect in the various states. It might be argued that different rates and bases would be immaterial if each industry fully paid its own benefit costs. Yet subsidy is inherent, and sound, in every insurance system, including social insurance. Nevertheless, when a high-wage industry, such as construction, is heavily subsidized by a relatively low-wage industry, such as retailing—as experience in Ohio and doubtless other states indicate—then issues of equity may arise. The problem is compounded by the question "Who ultimately pays the tax? The employer in the form of lower profits? The worker in the form of lower wages? Or the consumer in the form of higher prices?" At any rate, unhappiness among some employers, some workers, and some consumers may well be expected, insofar as unemployment insurance taxes are concerned.

## ADMINISTRATION

Having highlighted some of the factors that seem wrong with substantive aspects of unemployment insurance—in confused philosophy, in inequitable benefits, in questionable financing—there remains the controversial issue of administration. Has the program been well-administered? Top executives, both in Washington and in the states have generally been men of superior ability. Superior executives and good administration, however, are not necessarily synonymous. Trouble is bound to ensue when federal executives control purse strings while state executives are responsible for effective administration. More heat than light is often generated where program philosophies differ markedly, not only by level of government, but also over time.

Ten years ago, speaking at the Annual Conference on Social Security at the University of Michigan, I maintained that the federal-state "partnership" in unemployment insurance, created in 1935 by the Social Security Act, was essentially a "shotgun wedding." In the early days, however

> Despite the initial frigidity of the states, responsibility and authority for administering unemployment compensation had to be theirs. The statutes were then comparatively clear-cut. The federal government had the job of collecting the federal unemployment tax; of reviewing the certifying state laws for conformity; of serving as repository for trust funds; of securing and allocating administrative funds for the states. There was no federal responsibility for administering, assisting in, or controlling the administration of state laws. The states, on the other hand, wrote their own laws—within the broad limits of conformity requirements—set up their own administrative organizations and procedures, and made their own decisions.
> With the passage of time, however, the pattern markedly changed. World War II, federalization of state employment services, the Korean War, periodic shuffling and reshuffling of responsibilities among different federal agencies, demands for complete and permanent federalization, a host of new federal statutes—these all created an atmosphere hardly indicative of "marital bliss" in the federal-state partnership.
> Although responsibility continued to rest primarily with the states, they lost their initial dominance as federal controls were greatly extended and as overlapping and confusing statutes were enacted by the Congress.

In the decade that elapsed since these observations were made, have there been any notable changes? Yes, there have. But in the wrong direction! A new federal "Manpower Administration" has replaced the old Bureau of Employment Security. New programs created by new legislation—in the field of redevelopment, training, readjustment allowances, and so on were "subcontracted" to the states.

New national policies, dealing with "human resource development," and the so called "disadvantaged," reversed the emphasis of state employment services. Whereas, historically they had been concerned with attracting and placing the best-qualified candidates (including claimants), they were diverted in recent years toward attracting, developing, and finding jobs for the least-qualified. Added funds were by no means commensurate with added responsibilities. Services mandated under state statutes suffered. Local offices took on more of the aspects of welfare agencies than public employment offices. The average quality of job-seekers, in all likelihood, deteriorated. The quality of job openings filed by employers with public employment offices probably dropped also. Private employment agencies mushroomed, both in numbers and in payrolls.

Employers, workers, and consumers pay taxes, directly or indirectly, to support public employment offices. These offices were intended to serve everyone who seeks help in filling or finding jobs. If, however, substantial numbers of employers and workers fail to avail themselves of such services, then this conclusion seems inescapable: There must be considerable dissatisfaction with the services rendered.

## CONSTRUCTIVE SUGGESTIONS

### An Objective Appraisal

Finding faults, of course, is much easier than finding remedies. Any jackass, it has been said, can kick down a barn door; but it takes a skilled craftsman to rebuild it. Preferring the role of craftsman, let me offer some constructive suggestions. Needless to note, perhaps, the views expressed heretofore and hereafter are altogether personal, and in no sense official. With this prelude, let me repeat a recommendation first published in the *Industrial and Labor Relations Review* for January 1955:

> The time has come for an objective appraisal of the entire system (perhaps "lack of system" is more accurate) of employment security. Twenty years have elapsed since the Committee on Economic Security developed a comprehensive plan for a system to provide greater economic security. It was based upon a great many detailed and objective studies. Since then, however, the program has doubtless suffered over the years, not only from the labor-management tug of war but also from federal and federal-state differences concerning their respective responsibilities in this field of legislation. A new and comprehensive study, conducted by disinterested persons without administrative, management, or labor ties to the current system, should endeavor to appraise existing and proposed programs, recommend the lines they should follow, and endeavor to fit one into another on some logical and socially desirable basis.

Fourteen years have elapsed and nothing has come of this recommendation. Nevertheless, it still bears repetition. If no more than the delineation of sound primary goals should come of the proposed study, this alone would be a significant achievement.

## Needed Remedies

The "wrongs" already cited are indicative in themselves of some of the remedies. Apart from potential merits of unemployment insurance as an economic stabilizer, if we concede that noncovered workers indirectly help defray the costs of unemployment insurance, then as a matter of equity, as many as possible should also be protected against layoffs. Employees of smaller firms currently excluded should be covered. The large group of non-elective state and local government employees, and employees of nonprofit agencies should also be included.

If we believe that unemployment insurance should be designed to protect those who normally work full-time on a year-around basis, and that secondary workers with limited labor market attachment should be screened out, then stronger basic eligibility requirements are necessary. Prior covered employment in 26 weeks or more of the year preceding separation, plus minimum earnings in such weeks sufficient to justify a meaningful minimum benefit, would tighten the initial screen.

Tighter basic eligibility requirements could and probably should exclude many of those who do not normally support themselves, those who have doubtless engendered much of the more virulent criticism of the past. Once such changes were enacted, it should be easier to win broader public support for more generous benefits and longer potential durations for those who are firmly attached to the labor market. Disqualification provisions which had been aimed chiefly at the first group might well be repealed. Punitive disqualification provisions could be reduced or dropped.

If economic stabilization is considered a major objective of unemployment insurance, eliminating benefits for marginally-attached workers must be offset by far more substantial payments to strongly-attached workers. This poses many problems of the sort which heretofore have been resolved chiefly by a variety of fixed, dollar-amount, statutory criteria. The historic pattern of wage and price inflation, however, has demonstrated clearly that such criteria have been inadequate. They either become antiquated and unrealistic, as usually happened, or they required frequent amendment. The solution, therefore, appears to be enactment of statutory standards in fixed proportions rather than dollar amounts, with dollar amounts established annually by administrative regulation, on the basis of annually-updated experience.

## Proportionate Standards

In developing such proportions, the minimum weekly earnings figure necessary for basic eligibility should be related to the minimum weekly benefit for total unemployment. This minimum benefit, in turn, should be related to the maximum weekly benefit. And the maximum should be related to the level and distribution of prior weekly earnings of claimants.

Suppose we start with the maximum and work backward. President Nixon recently urged, for example, that the maximum be set at a level that would concentrate fewer than one-fifth of all insured workers at the ceiling. He also urged that at least 80 percent of these workers be eligible, when unemployed, for weekly benefits equalling at least one-half their prior weekly earnings.

With four out of five getting 50 percent or more, what would the Ohio ceiling have to be? With statutory authorization, earnings data for claimants filing in 1968 could set our maximum benefit for 1970 at $84. If the minimum benefit were set at one-third the maximum, it would become $28. To justify such a minimum weekly benefit at one-half prior earnings, claimants would be required to have earned at least $56 per week. This seems not unreasonable, since the smallest full week's earnings under the federal minimum wage law in 1970 will be $64.

Most secondary workers with limited attachment to the labor market could be screened out by a basic requirement that they must have been employed in 26 or more weeks of the year preceding separation, and that they must have earned at least two-thirds the maximum weekly benefit amount in each such week. If this were done, and the proposed system of proportions adopted, would the statutes then be as generous to men as to women, in terms of benefits paid as percentages of prior weekly earnings? By no means!

Women who claimed benefits in Ohio last year previously earned $77 per week, on the average. Men claimants, however, averaged $145 per week—88 percent more. To equalize the impact of benefits on men and women it would be necessary to apply the same proportional standards to their respective prior earnings. Thus the maximum weekly benefit for women could be set at a level which held down no more than 20 percent of the women, while that for men would similarly limit no more than one-fifth of the men. This would create lower minimum and maximum benefit amounts for women than for men, and correspondingly different qualifying earnings.

Although no state has adopted—or seriously considered—separate floors and ceilings for men and women, the idea is not as revolutionary as it may seem. Eleven states now provide various forms of dependents allowances. Despite comparable prior earnings, claimants with dependents receive more when unemployed than claimants without dependents. Claimants with dependents, however, are very predominantly men—over 96 percent in Ohio. To the extent, therefore, that men have and claim dependents, while women do not, these states already provide different ceilings for men, in effect, than for women.

Since claimants with dependents earn considerably more than claimants without dependents, dependents allowances as such might well be eliminated, at least for those below the maxima. Thus four out of every five women and four out of every five men could receive weekly benefits at a fixed proportion—one-half, for example—of their individual prior weekly earnings. For the one out of five at the top of each group, supplemental dependents allowances might be added, as percentages of their respective group maxima. This would be of greatest help to men with dependents, enabling the highest paid also to receive benefits approaching one-half their individual prior earnings. It would similarly help the relatively few highest paid women who claim dependents but whose benefit checks would otherwise be held down by their ceiling.

## Benefit Duration

Should the potential duration of benefits go beyond 26 weeks in 52? By limiting the program to workers firmly attached to the labor market, a strong case can be made for lengthening potential duration with length of prior employment. Thus everyone who cleared initial eligibility requirements, with 26 weeks or more of employment in the preceding year and earnings enough to justify a meaningful minimum, would be potentially eligible for at least 26 weeks of benefits. Why not extend their potential duration, on a week-for-week basis, up to 39 weeks? The stronger the prior attachment, in other words, the longer the potential duration.

Certainly this makes far more sense than the federal programs of extended benefits which were in effect during the recessions of 1958 and 1961. In boom years there are localized recessions, and in general recessions there are localized booms. This pattern has occurred within Ohio and doubtless within many other states. The record clearly demonstrates that conditions of the economy greatly affected the duration of benefits. In Ohio, for example, during the recession of 1961, claimants averaged 14 weeks of benefits out of a uniform 26-week potential. During the boom of 1968, however, they averaged less than eight weeks of benefits out of a 25-week average potential.

If secondary workers with limited labor market attachment had been screened out both in 1961 and 1968, and if potential duration had risen to 39 weeks with corresponding weeks of prior employment, the average duration of benefits would probably have been only slightly higher. Claimants most firmly attached to the labor market, in general, are probably the ones most rapidly reemployed. Few, surely, would begrudge more adequate and longer potential benefits for steady year-round workers hit by localized recessions, regardless of the general state of the economy.

## Financing

The entire system of financing unemployment insurance should be carefully reexamined. If a major objective of the program is economic stabilization, then the tax structure should be designed to reinforce the benefit structure. Collections should be highest in boom years—

to check inflation, to build up reserves, to "stockpile" effective purchasing power. Collections should be lowest in recession years—when taxes are hardest to pay, when wage losses due to unemployment are greatest, when the economy needs bolstering through benefits which replace a substantial share of lost wages.

The total payroll, of course, goes up and down with the business cycle. It thus has considerable merit as a stabilizing tax base, provided the average tax rate moves in the same direction. Unless, however, the Congress decides once again to tax total payroll under the Federal Unemployment Tax Act, the states are very unlikely to do so.

Only three states currently require employee as well as employer contributions. Nevertheless, there is much to be said for a flat-rate employee tax. It would help finance more adequate benefits and a longer potential duration. It would give workers a tangible stake in the system with an incentive to help police it. It would help establish unemployment insurance as a "rights" program, unrelated to need or welfare. And flat employee rates could easily be designed to go up and down with the business cycle.

It would not be a simple task, however, to develop an employer experience rating system which would help stabilize the economy. Yet it seems a worthy and most important goal to integrate the tax structure with the benefit structure, to assure that their economic effects were not offsetting. They have been, at least insofar as average rates are concerned. Taxes as a percent of total payrolls in all states averaged 1.2 percent for the recession year 1961. In 1968, the greatest boom year since 1953, the average tax rate was about one-third lower.

## Administration

What should be said about administration? The greatest need, after goals, is to establish clear-cut lines of authority and responsibility. This can be achieved only if unemployment insurance is financed and administered completely by the states or completely by the federal government. Neither alternative, however, seems likely to receive serious consideration. The "shotgun wedding" has already lasted more than three decades, and neither "partner" really wants a divorce. "Family quarrels" were inevitable, of course, as the states were increasingly submerged toward the status of junior partners. They were nevertheless publicly blamed for many faults of a system which could not easily be changed without Congressional action. The "marriage contract" was delineated in detail, by the Social Security Act of 1935. Subsequent federal legislation tightened the tie that "binds."

### FUTURE GOALS

What, then, needs to be done? Unless and until primary goals are established, no one can chart a sound course. Some believe that the employment security system should assume broad-range responsibilities, covering the entire panorama of manpower problems—from entrance to the labor market and first job, to exit toward retirement and the "Pearly Gates." They would embrace far greater functions in the fields of vocational guidance and training, health and income maintenance, geographic relocation, and general welfare. This is the philosophy inherent in most of the new federal programs whose administration has been "subcontracted" to the state employment security agencies.

There are others—this writer among them—who believe that we should concentrate on trying to achieve what we started out to achieve. These early goals include development of a first-rate, nationwide system of free public employment offices, serving jobseekers with every level of skill and ability, serving employers of every size and industry, promoting employment by compiling and releasing authentic and objective labor market information, and paying benefits promptly, in the absence of suitable jobs, to everyone firmly attached to the labor market and otherwise eligible.

Surely these are no mean goals. Yet they fall far short of the goals envisioned by those who see potentialities in the federal-state employment security structure for ultimate solutions to major manpower, poverty, and ghetto problems of the nation.

The original set of goals relates predominantly to 85 percent or more of the civilian labor force, who offer no serious labor market problems. Such goals seem reasonable in relation to administrative funds available in the past, and likely to be made available in the future. When substantial progress toward achievement of such goals is widely evident, the public image of the program may well shift from negative to positive.

The broader set of goals, however, relates largely to the 15 percent or fewer persons in the labor force who do have serious labor market problems. They cannot possibly be achieved within the limits of funds made available thus far or likely to be made available in the future. The scope of the goals, the difficulty of the problems, and the inadequacy of financing assure one prospective result if nothing else—a continued negative image.

The contradiction in philosophy inherent in the two sets of goals makes it difficult to suggest an effective, cooperative, administrative structure. Once primary goals are established and agreed upon, however, there remains only to answer these questions: first, How can the federal government best contribute to their achievement? Second, How can the states best contribute to their achievement? Third, How much will it cost? Fourth, How can the costs and responsibilities be fairly and clearly allocated between the federal government and the states? And fifth, How can they best continue their "partnership" on the basis of full equality, mutual respect, and wholehearted cooperation?

## Questions

1. What is "secondary" employment? Discuss whether you feel that a person in the secondary employment market should be eligible for unemployment insurance benefits on the same basis as a person in the "primary" market.
2. Should there be a "needs" test for receiving unemployment insurance benefits? Discuss your opinion with respect to (a) financing the system and (b) the effect of a "needs" test on solving some of the basic problems defined in this article.
3. Obtain the eligibility requirements for receiving unemployment insurance benefits in your state. Plan out exactly what you would need to do to receive the minimum unemployment insurance benefit. Also plan out what would be necessary to receive the maximum benefit. Then discuss these plans with respect to what you consider to be a *desirable* unemployment insurance benefit from the viewpoint of the employee.
4. What does the author find to be mainly wrong with unemployment insurance?
5. Which of the reforms suggested would you consider the most important? Why?

# 33. A TIME FOR REFORM *

## A. OVERALL EVALUATION OF
## WORKMEN'S COMPENSATION

The Workmen's Compensation Commission was directed to "undertake a comprehensive study and evaluation of State workmen's compensation laws in order to determine if such laws provide an adequate, prompt, and equitable system of compensation." This summary of the Commission's evaluation is based on the five objectives of a modern workmen's compensation program: coverage, income maintenance, medical care and rehabilitation, safety, and an effective delivery system.

## 1 Workmen's Compensation Should Provide Broad Coverage of Employees and Work-Related Injuries and Diseases

Although on an upward trend, workmen's compensation coverage is inadequate. Only about 85 percent of all employees are presently covered. The wide variations among the States in the proportions of the labor force covered are inequitable. Moreover, those not covered usually are those most in need of protection: the non-union, low-wage workers, such as farm help, domestics, and employees of small firms.

In the past, some work-related injuries were not compensable because certain legal tests could not be satisfied, such as the requirement that an injury be the result of an "accident." Because these legal tests have been liberalized, most work-related injuries now are compensable. The status of work-related diseases is less satisfactory. Despite considerable improvement, some 10 States still do not provide full coverage for work-related diseases, and the statute of limitations is so short in some States that many diseases are not compensable because symptoms appear long after exposure.

## 2 Workmen's Compensation Should Provide Substantial Protection Against Interruption of Income

In general, workmen's compensation programs do not provide adequate income maintenance. Disabled workers in the majority of cases receive less than two-thirds of their lost wages. In most States, maximum weekly benefits for a non-farm family of four are below the poverty level of income. Many States also have limits on the duration or

* From *Report of the National Commission on State Workmen's Compensation Laws* (Washington, D.C.: USGPO, 1972), pp. 117-130.

total amount of benefits or both. The inadequacies of benefits mean that too high a proportion of the burden of work-related disability is borne by workers and the taxpayer rather than by employers.

Workmen's compensation income benefits are not equitable. One obvious inequity is the substantial difference among the States in the adequacy of benefits. There are also intra-State inequities in those jurisdictions with low maximum weekly benefits because a higher proportion of wage loss is replaced for low-wage workers than for high-wage workers. Another source of apparent inequity in some States is the substantial amount of benefits paid for minor injuries relative to the benefits paid for serious injuries.

We do not have sufficient data to evaluate definitively promptness of payment. The better private carriers, State funds, and self insurers are doing excellent jobs of beginning payments in uncontested cases. Such promptness appears to be one of the strengths of workmen's compensation. In contested cases, the record is less satisfactory.

## 3 Workmen's Compensation Should Provide Sufficient Medical Care and Rehabilitation Services

The provision of medical care, including physical rehabilitation, is generally adequate, equitable, and prompt. Serious exceptions are found in those few States which limit the duration or dollar amount of medical care.

The vocational rehabilitation record is uneven: some programs are excellent but too many are not. Poor performance is due partially to inadequate supervision by some State workmen's compensation agencies, to insufficient attention to the plight of the industrially disabled by departments of vocational rehabilitation, and to the lack of coordination between the two programs.

The potential of workmen's compensation to return rehabilitated workers to jobs is limited by the unfortunate reluctance of many firms to employ the handicapped. Working within this limitation, workmen's compensation has a reasonably good record. One device for supporting rehabilitation is the second-injury fund, which protects employers from extraordinary workmen's compensation costs associated with employment of the physically impaired.

## 4 Workmen's Compensation Should Encourage Safety

While there is only limited evidence of the actual influence of workmen's compensation on safety, the use of merit rating means the potential influence is significant. As income benefits and medical care and rehabilitation are provided, the assessment against the employers for the benefits should provide automatic incentives to safety. Substantially stronger safety incentives would result from the benefits recommended by this Commission. The safe way will become the economical way.

## 5  Workmen's Compensation Should Have an Effective Delivery System

The four basic objectives—coverage, income maintenance, medical care and rehabilitation, and safety—can be achieved only if employers, insurance carriers, State agencies, and all others involved in the workmen's compensation program are organized into an effective delivery system. With more than 5,000,000 cases a year, administration of benefits is a huge task. Many States now have reasonably effective delivery systems. Some are excellent.

The two main deficiencies in the delivery systems are rooted in attitudes that are passive rather than active. Some States do not initiate programs to protect workers, usually for lack of adequate funding and staffing of the workmen's compensation agencies.

The second deficiency, excessive litigation, results in unnecessary delay, expense, and interference with rehabilitation. Compounding the influence of passive administration, agency rules and procedures often stimulate litigious attitudes. Also, because payments of claims lead to higher costs, employers have greater incentives to resist claims than if benefits were financed by a flat rate tax or assessment.

### Conclusion

The inescapable conclusion is that State workmen's compensation laws in general are inadequate and inequitable. While several States have good programs, and while medical care and some other aspects of workmen's compensation are commendable in most States, the strong points are too often matched by weak.

Consider the record of the States in meeting the recommended standards published by the Department of Labor. (Table 1) These recommendations, have been well publicized. Several are conservative compared to the recommendations of this Commission. If all 50 States were in compliance with the 16 recommended standards, the total compliance "score" would be 800. As of 1972, the actual "score" is 402. The inequities of workmen's compensation are underlined by the wide variation among the States in their record of compliance. Although 9 States meet 13 or more of the recommendations, 10 States meet 4 or fewer.

In recent years, legislatures have adopted many improvements in State workmen's compensation laws. In 1971, more than 300 changes were enacted, about 50 percent more than customary in odd-year sessions. Significant improvements in several States in 1972 include reductions in numerical exemptions to coverage and removal of limits on medical care. This recent burst of activity is encouraging, but some have suggested it was caused by the creation of this Commission and may not be sustained after our activities cease.

Moreover some improvements may slip away. For example, benefit maximums in most States must be amended from time to time to keep

TABLE 1

NUMBER OF JURISDICTIONS MEETING 16 RECOMMENDED STANDARDS,
1 JAN. 72

| Standards Met | States (50) | Other "States" (6) | Federal (2) |
|---|---|---|---|
| 13-16 | 9 | 1 | 1 |
| 9-12 | 13 | 4 | 1 |
| 5-8 | 18 | 0 | 0 |
| 0-4 | 10 | 1 | 0 |

benefits in proper relationship to State average weekly wages. Yet wage increases due to inflation and higher productivity have not been reflected in proportionate increases in maximum weekly benefits.

No member of this Commission wishes to convey an unduly bleak assessment of workmen's compensation. The program has many virtues and the recent life signs are encouraging. Nonetheless, all of us feel that the present program has serious deficiencies. The proper remedy for these deficiencies is the concern of the balance of the report.

## B. IS THERE A CONTINUING RATIONALE FOR WORKMEN'S COMPENSATION?

Does our evaluation suggest that workmen's compensation is permanently and totally disabled, or is there a continuing rationale for the program?

Only an ivory tower iconoclast would answer this question in the abstract. Properly, it must be answered by considering the realistic alternatives to workmen's compensation. While workmen's compensation has weaknesses, it also has strengths. It should be abandoned only if an alternative has a better mix of strengths and weaknesses.

### Damage Suits

One possible alternative is to rely on negligence suits. From the worker's standpoint, this option may be somewhat more attractive than it was 50 years ago, when workmen's compensation was first widely adopted, because the plaintiff's burden subsequently has been eased in negligence suits. Other reasons, however, have convinced us that, for workers and others, workmen's compensation is preferable to negligence actions. For example, the issue of negligence is particularly elusive in the work setting. Most studies of work-related impairments stress the intermingling of employee and employer responsibility in a substantial proportion of accidents. The determination of negligence tends to be expensive and the outcome uncertain. Payments tend to be delayed when negligence suits are prosecuted, and over-crowded court dockets would compound the delays. Some workers eventually would receive damage awards in excess of workmen's compensation benefits, but others would receive no protection. Moreover, even when the worker succeeded in winning monetary damages, the litigation could be a substantial deterrent to successful rehabilitation.

**We conclude that damage suits are a distinctly inferior alternative to workmen's compensation.**

## Disassemble Workmen's Compensation and Assign the Components to Other Programs

Another alternative is to disassemble workmen's compensation and assign the components to other programs. One scheme would assign permanent total disability cases to the Disability Insurance (DI) program of Social Security and temporary total disability cases to State temporary total disability insurance (TDI) programs. The medical component of workmen's compensation could be assigned to an expanded Medicare or national health insurance program, and rehabilitation could be absorbed by the State Departments of Vocational Rehabilitation (DVR). Finally, the safety aspect could be assumed by the enforcement agencies of the Occupational Safety and Health Act of 1970.

**This systematic disassembling of workmen's compensation may become feasible in some other era, but we are convinced the problems associated with this approach are too serious to justify the strategy now.**

Each program to which the components of workmen's compensation would be assigned has at least one serious deficiency compared to workmen's compensation. A few examples of the deficiencies are the following:

The Disability Insurance program under Social Security has eligibility requirements much more stringent than those in workmen's compensation. In workmen's compensation, the worker is eligible from the first day he is hired, whereas workers are only eligible for DI benefits after several quarters of covered employment. Insofar as short term disability is concerned, only five States plus Puerto Rico have temporary disability insurance programs. It is one thing to think about transferring short-term work-related disability cases to well established TDI programs; quite another to think about phasing workmen's compensation into largely nonexistent programs.

Even if permanent total disability cases were absorbed by DI and temporary total disability cases by TDI programs, the most important aspect of cash benefits in workmen's compensation would remain unassimilated. No generally available program other than workmen's compensation pays benefits because of permanent partial impairments. (We exclude veteran's programs from consideration because veterans comprise only about one third of the labor force.) The determination of the extent of permanent impairment is complicated and requires scarce administrative expertise as well as considerable expenditures. There would be significant startup costs if another program were assigned the permanent partial aspect of workmen's compensation.

Moreover, any scheme that would assign permanent total and temporary total cases to other programs but leave permanent partial cases to workmen's compensation would be an administrative nightmare. The typical workmen's compensation case paying permanent partial benefits also involves payments of temporary total benefits, and often eligibility for permanent partial and permanent total benefits is determined at the same time. Unless this component of workmen's compensation were abandoned, an option which we strenuously oppose, there is no choice but to continue workmen's compensation as a source of permanent partial benefits.

We do not believe there is likely to be available in the near future a satisfactory alternative to workmen's compensation as a source of medical care. If national health care were to be extended to cover all work-related impairments, employees would in general be affected adversely. Most proposals for national health insurance contain "deductibles" and other limitations on benefits not found in most workmen's compensation statutes.

We would be reluctant also to see the rehabilitation component of workmen's compensation assigned to another program. One of the difficult tasks of workmen's compensation is the coordination of the medical care and physical and vocational rehabilitation services. The difficulties of coordination would be accentuated if rehabilitation were completely removed from the workmen's compensation system.

The assignment of the safety aspect of workmen's compensation to another program also has disadvantages. The Federal government now has a substantial safety program established by the Occupational Safety and Health Act of 1970. We believe this role will be constructive but the OSHA approach will require extensive appropriations through the decades to assure its effectiveness. Workmen's compensation has the virtue that the linkage of benefits paid to insurance costs should automatically provide a strong incentive for safety.

Finally, no other delivery system is generally superior to workmen's compensation. Most alterntives to workmen's compensation involve an expanded role for the Federal government. This Commission has seen no evidence to suggest that Federal programs are better administered than State workmen's compensation programs. It is true that the administrative costs of workmen's compensation are higher than in some other social insurance programs. These comparisons, however, can be misleading because other programs do not face the same complexities of administration. In particular, because cash benefits for permanent partial disability are the most expensive component of workmen's compensation, and because the determination of permanent impairment requires substantial administrative expense, we caution against any assumption that administrative costs could be significantly reduced by absorbing the services now provided by workmen's compensation into another program.

## Conclusion

We have written this report neither to praise nor to bury workmen's compensation. We would liken our attitude to Winston Churchill's views on democracy.

> Many forms of government have been tried and will be tried in this world of sin and woe. No one pretends that democracy is perfect or all-wise. Indeed it has been said that democracy is the worst form of government except all those other forms that have been tried from time to time.

Perhaps in another decade or two, an attractive alternative to workmen's compensation will emerge. We are unable to predict the social insurance programs that will appear in our social evolution.

**For the present and the foreseeable future, we are convinced that, if our recommendations for a modern workmen's compensation program are adopted, the program should be retained.**

## C. PREVIOUS EFFORTS TO IMPROVE WORKMEN'S COMPENSATION

The work of this Commission is not the first effort to improve State workmen's compensation programs. This section briefly recounts some earlier efforts and attempts to isolate the factors which explain the successes and failures.

## Individual State Reforms

In several States, improvements in the law were preceded by concentrated efforts at reform. In New York, the amendments which restructured the administration of the program followed a series of studies by Moreland Act Commissioners. The most recent study was presented to Governor Rockefeller in 1962 by a Governor's Workmen's Compensation Review Committee.

A California commission, composed of representatives from management, labor, the insurance industry, the medical and legal professions, and the public, issued a report in April 1965 which led to improvements directed toward reducing litigation and separating the administrative and adjudicative functions.

In Oregon, the Act was entirely restructured in 1965 as a result of an intensive negotiating process among management, labor, and other interest groups.

A Governor's Study Commission in Maryland, in continuous existence since 1956, develops its own recommendations and presents them to the legislature and the Governor. Its recommendations are considered a major factor in recent improvements in the Maryland Act.

Idaho revised its workmen's compensation law extensively in 1971 following a two-year study by a commission appointed by the Governor. Improvements included a basic maximum weekly benefit on a sliding scale following 60 to 90 percent of the average weekly wage in the State, full coverage of occupational diseases, and a second-injury fund with broad coverage of impairments.

In Pennsylvania, substantial reforms achieved early in 1972 included the requirement that all hearing examiners be full-time employees. These reforms were not preceded by a formal study but represented a consensus arrived at by the current State administration and the many groups interested in workmen's compensation. Late in 1971, the Pennsylvania AFL-CIO and the Pennsylvania State Chamber of Commerce supported the pending legislative changes with an unprecedented joint press release.

No one model describes the route of these achievements. Only a few elements appear consistently in many States. Reforms can be achieved by a relatively small number of advocates, but their characteristics and following differ from State to State. In general, reforms have resulted from investigations supported or initiated by State officials, although in Oregon the workmen's compensation officials did not participate until the reform effort was underway. Usually two or more years elapse from the initiation of reform to legislative enactment.

Aside from these few generalizations, perhaps the most important conclusion to be drawn about workmen's compensation reforms in individual States is that they are all too rare. There is no guarantee that a State which needs a thorough review of its workmen's compensation law will spontaneously generate such an investigation.

## Standards Recommended by National Organizations

Another approach to improving workmen's compensation has been the promulgation of recommended standards by national organizations. The 16 recommended standards published by the Department of Labor are based on the standards recommended by other organizations such as the American College of Surgeons, the National Rehabilitation Association, and the Council of State Governments. The Department of Labor recommendations were first published in 1959 and, with some modifications, have since appeared in four bulletins together with a record of State compliance.

The International Association of Industrial Accident Boards and Commissions (IAIABC), the professional organization of State workmen's compensation administrators, also has recommended standards. The IAIABC has encouraged States to meet its 22 recommended standards by techniques such as sending a certificate to each Governor indicating the number of standards met by his State. The extent of compliance with these standards was evaluated in 1972 by the IAIABC.

The 50 States plus the District of Columbia and Puerto Rico were reported on average to comply in full with 14 of the 22 standards.

States might be expected to comply with IAIABC standards more readily than those published by the Department of Labor since the IAIABC members administer the State programs and presumably have an intimate and realistic understanding of State needs. However, it is sometimes awkward for an administrator to pursue his own views agressively when he faces a recalcitrant Governor or State legislature. This ambivalence was reflected in our hearings when a representative of the IAIABC said that while the organization strongly supported its own recommended standards, it "specifically rejects the proposition that a State act which does not meet all standards is an inadequate or undesirable act or that such act is not substantially meeting the needs of the worker."

The Atomic Energy Commission since 1965 also has recommended standards for State workmen's compensation laws. The AEC interest in Workmen's compensation stems from the issue of compensability for workers whose exposure to ionizing radiation show no clinical effects until long after the time allowed in some States for claiming workmen's compensation benefits. Several States have modified provisions of their laws relating to radiation hazards, especially with respect to the time allowed for filing claims. The IAIABC mentions effects of radiation in its recommended standards. The Atomic Energy Commission has had reasonable success in promoting its standards, perhaps because it is well financed and has concentrated on a narrow range of issues which encompass a compelling need.

In general, past efforts to improve workmen's compensation merely by recommending the adoption of standards have a sparse record of success. Moreover, the standards recommended tend to be limited in number and detail.

## Lobbying or Other Promotional Efforts

Some interest groups have attempted to improve workmen's compensation by lobbying or other promotional activities. For example, trade unions, by use of their political influence, were a key factor in changes in California and Michigan laws. As their strength varies considerably among the States, unions have not been successful in all their efforts to improve workmen's compensation. Moreover, in States where labor is weak, reform of workmen's compensation has generally received lower priority than goals such as repeal of "open shop" or "right to work" laws.

The insurance industry also has attempted to promote changes in workmen's compensation laws. The industry is in a difficult position, however, because its clients are employers and it is tempted to avoid any stand which could possibly antagonize them. Historically, the insurance industry attempted to be at best "neutral" on any issue about workmen's compensation. Much of its lobbying energy was devoted to opening up exclusive-fund States to the private insurance industry. During the last decade, there has been a heartening change of attitude by the private carriers, which are taking a more active part in promoting needed improvements.

It seems clear that, in efforts to improve workmen's compensation by lobbying or other promotional efforts, one interest group seldom can succeed by itself. In general, reform has been successful only where several interest groups have acted in concert.

## The Model Act Approach

During the 1960s, a coordinated effort among the interest groups in workmen's compensation to improve the program nationally resulted in the proposed "Workmen's Compensation and Rehabilitation Law." This Model Act was drafted by a committee of the Council of State Governments chaired by Arthur Larson, former Under Secretary of Labor. The committee included representatives from industry, labor, State agencies, insurance carriers, the medical profession, the academic community, and Federal agencies interested in workmen's compensation. The law, drafted over a four year period, was published in 1963 and 1965 by the Council of State Governments in *Suggested State Legislation*.

Despite the impressive credentials of the drafting committee and the prestige of the sponsoring organization, no State has adopted the act either in its entirety or in substantial part. In contrast, another model act, the Uniform Commercial Code, has been adopted with only minor modifications in 49 States. Since the U.C.C. is perhaps even more controversial than the model workmen's compensation act, the lack of success in workmen's compensation can best be explained by other factors.

## Evaluation of Previous Effects

Past efforts to improve workmen's compensation have had some success, but it is evident from our evaluation of the workmen's compensation program, that these efforts have been insufficient. The crucial question is why? There appear to be several reasons.

**Lack of interest or understanding**. Workmen's compensation is relatively complex. During our hearings a bewildering array of provisions were described. The terms used have different meanings according to context. We can appreciate that State legislators and other officials have difficulty in understanding workmen's compensation and that lack of understanding too often has led to lack of attention.

Moreover, workmen's compensation is seldom the most compelling topic of the day. The program generally receives far less notice than pollution, or minimum wage laws, or auto insurance. This low visibility persists even though there are millions of workmen's compensation cases a year. The average employee is indifferent perhaps because thinking about industrial accidents is unpleasant; it is only human to assume "It won't happen to me."

For the average employer, workmen's compensation costs represent only about one percent of payroll, a relatively unimportant charge compared to the wages or to other fringe benefits which add about 25 percent to straight-time wages. For trade unions, items such as wages or retirement benefits receive prior attention because these items affect more employees and represent more money and because they are handled by direct negotiations with the employer. Collective bargaining usually is a much more productive use of union time than lobbying to improve workmen's compensation benefits.

Legislators and other State officials for their part are faced with competing demands from many sources on issues which generally command more public attention than workmen's compensation. Too rarely do State workmen's compensation administrators take the initiative to educate the electorate or to espouse legislation to improve the program. They usually respond to requests for assistance from others promoting changes, but in few States do administrators assume responsibility for initiating reform.

In short, deficiencies in workmen's compensation in many States result from lack of leadership, understanding, and interest.

**Veto power of the interest groups.** In many States, substantial reform is difficult because there is more than one interest group with power to veto proposed changes in the law, and it is difficult to find a package of amendments acceptable to all parties. Under these circumstances, a State may be locked into a program despite serious abuses.

This veto power takes strength from the general lack of understanding about workmen's compensation. In some States, the legislatures have reacted to complexities by in effect delegating authority for workmen's compensation to important interest groups. Under the "agreed bill" procedure, legislatures adopt amendments mutually acceptable to labor and management. Unfortunately, these parties often deadlock: employers block action because they object to cost increases associated with general improvements in the law; trade unions because they will not surrender certain cherished practices, such as the right to a de novo trial, which labor in some States considers an important element of protection. Also, some labor officials are unwilling to give up the disproportionate awards in minor permanent partial cases in exchange for increased benefits for serious permanent impairments.

The difficulties confronting labor and management in reaching agreement are sometimes compounded by their use of agents. Employers often rely on trade associations, whose staff people sometimes prove their worth by fighting benefit increases and claiming savings. Attorneys representing the various interest groups abound, and their clients are not always well served. For example, trade unions often are represented by plaintiffs' attorneys who too often view litigation as an end in itself to be protected at the expense of other reforms.

**Competition among States.** The economic system of the United States encourages the forces of efficiency and mobility. These forces tend to drive employers to locate where the environment offers the best prospect for profit. At the same time, many of the programs which governments use to regulate industrialization are designed and applied by States rather than the Federal government. Any State which seeks to regulate the by-products of industrialization, such as work accidents, invariably must tax or charge employers to cover the expenses of such regulation. This combination of mobility and regulation poses a dilemma for policymakers in State governments. Each State is forced to consider carefully how it will regulate its domestic enterprises because relatively restrictive or costly regulation may precipitate the departure of the employers to be regulated or deter the entry of new enterprises.

Can a State have a modern workmen's compensation program without driving employers away? Our analysis of the cost of workmen's compensation has convinced us that no State should hesitate to adopt a modern workmen's compensation program. Interstate differences in workmen's compensation costs for the average employer rarely exceed one percent of payroll. Surely no rational employer will move his business to avoid costs of this magnitude. For most employers, the costs are relatively insignificant compared to other differences among States, such as wage differentials or access to markets or materials. There are, to be sure, a small minority of employers for whom workmen's compensation costs are significant because of their adverse loss experience, but it seems folly for a State to contrive a cheap workmen's compensation program in order to keep these employers from moving elsewhere. In any event, the incentive to relocate is dampened because the Federal corporate profits tax would substantially reduce the benefit an employer would gain by moving to a State with low workmen's compensation costs.

While the facts dictate that no State should hesitate to improve its workmen's compensation program for fear of losing employers, unfortunately this appears to be an area where emotion too often triumphs over fact. Given the degree of uncertainty about the factual costs of workmen's compensation, State legislators cannot be expected to become experts on interstate differences in such costs to employers. Furthermore, whenever a State legislature contemplates an improvement in workmen's compensation which will increase insurance costs, the legislators likely will hear claims from some employers that the increase in costs will force a business exodus. It will be virtually impossible for the legislators to know how genuine are these claims. To add to the confusion, certain States have abetted the illusion of the runaway employer by advertising the low costs of workmen's compensation in their jurisdiction.

When the sum of these inhibiting factors is considered, it seems likely that many States have been dissuaded from reform of their workmen's compensation statute because of the specter of the vanishing employer, even if that apparition is a product of fancy not fact. A few States have achieved genuine reform, but most suffer with inadequate laws because of the drag of laws of competing States.

## D. NEW STRATEGIES FOR IMPROVING WORKMEN'S COMPENSATION

The main body of this report has been devoted to evaluation of the present workmen's compensation program and to our recommendations for a modern workmen's compensation program. We are required by the Act to discuss the "methods of implementing the recommendations of the Commission." At least five methods to improve workmen's compensation were suggested at our hearings.

First, the States could be left to improve their laws without Federal guidance or assistance. This position was supported by witnesses who believed that the present State programs are acceptable, particularly in light of the rate of recent improvements and current reform movements.

Second, additional guidance could be presented to the States, and State action encouraged. This guidance in the form of recommendations by this Commission, especially if endorsed by Congress, could be expected to stimulate State improvements by drawing national attention to the critical needs of injured employees. Reforms might then proceed on a State by State basis, or multistate action might occur through techniques such as an interstate action might occur through techniques such as an interstate compact.

Third, State action could be mandated by the Federal government. For example, Congress could enact basic minimum standards for State workmen's compensation laws and provide an enforcement procedure. Support for this position was urged by some witnesses because of the lack of extensive compliance with previous recommendations by eminent national organizations.

Fourth, State action could be encouraged by Federal assistance, such as grants to develop additional data on the operation of State programs.

Finally, workmen's compensation could be taken over entirely by the Federal government, which would control the substantive terms and administer the program.

These five methods, though not exhaustive, cover the range of possible methods for improving workmen's compensation most commonly suggested to the Commission at its hearings. The second, third, and fourth methods are not mutually exclusive; indeed, most proposals to this Commission have consisted of a mixture of the three.

The members of this Commission have devoted much time and effort to considering the possible methods of implementing our recommendations. No topic received more attention at our hearings. Because we all believe so fervently that the present program must be strengthened, we have thoroughly debated the issues. The result of our debates is that we are in substantial or complete agreement on most aspects of implementations.

**We reject the suggestion that Federal administration be substituted for State programs at this time.**

The States have the distinct advantage of having personnel and procedures in place: a Federal takeover would substantially disrupt established administrative arrangements. Moreover, most Commissioners believe there is no evidence that Federal administrative procedures are superior to those of the States. Several Commissioners believe that a Federal takeover of workmen's compensation may be appropriate in a few years if present deficiencies in the State program are not repaired promptly, but they also believe these deficiencies can be overcome by the States.

**We believe that our recommendations should be adopted by the States as soon as possible.**

In preceding chapters, we have presented the five major objectives of a modern workmen's compensation program and our specific recommendations for achieving these objectives. Although not every aspect of a workmen's compensation program is included in our prescriptions, we believe we have presented sufficient guidance to enable each State to modernize its workmen's compensation program thoroughly.

Adoption of our recommendations will increase the costs of workmen's compensation in all States and for most employers, but we believe that employers and States have the resources to meet these costs.

**Reform of the workmen's compensation programs largely can and should take place at the State level. Nonetheless, we believe that the virtues of a decentralized, State-administered workmen's compensation program can be enhanced by creative Federal assistance.**

This assistance should take two forms: (1) appointment by the President of a new commission and (2) a 1975 review of the States' record of compliance with the most essential of our recommendations. This review should culminate in Federal mandates if necessary to guarantee compliance.

## A New Commission: An Immediate Opportunity for Federal Assistance

**We urge the President immediately to appoint a Federal workmen's compensation commission to provide encouragement and technical assistance to the States.**

One critical role for the commission will be to provide encouragement to the States to modernize their workmen's compensation programs.

Another role will be to help the States learn from one another. We have been impressed by the evidence in our hearings that a superior method in one State is not adopted swiftly by other States. This lag is partially explained by the complexity of workmen's compensation.

The specific activities of the new commission should include:

1. Providing assistance to the States to help them establish committees both to reexamine the State laws in light of our report and to develop support for needed reforms. Some of our recommendations will be modified by each State to reflect variations in size, population, and economic activity. The assistance of the new Federal commission to the State committees should include technical services and, if available, commission funds.

2. Reporting annually to the President and to the Congress on the progress of the States in meeting the recommendations in our report.

3. Analyzing certain critical areas of workmen's compensation, as described below, which could not be adequately examined by this Commission during its limited term.

4. Advising the States on whether their laws are in compliance with the mandates discussed below. The advice could be given to individual States or employers who are uncertain about their compliance status.

5. Assisting in the development of uniform or comparable data, and analyzing data and the operation of State workmen's compensation programs.

## Federal Guarantee of Essential Reform

All of our recommendations are important.

**Nonetheless, certain of our recommendations are essential and particularly suitable for Federal support to guarantee their adoption.**

Each State act should incorporate the following essential recommendations:

1. **Compulsory coverage.** (Recommendation 2.1.)

2. **Coverage with no occupational or numerical exemptions: Coverage should include farm workers, household workers, and State and local employees.** (Recommendations 2.2, 2.4, 2.5, 2.6, and 2.7.)

3. **Full coverage of work-related diseases.** (Recommendation 2.13)

4. **Full medical care and physical rehabilitation services without limitation as to time or dollar amount.** (Recommendations 4.2 and 4.4.)

5. **Employees may file claim in the State where injured, or where hired, or where employment is principally localized.** (Recommendation 2.11)

6. **Temporary total benefits.** A worker's benefit should be no less than 66 2/3 percent of his average weekly wage (Recommendation 3.7), subject to a maximum weekly benefit of at least 66 2/3 percent of the State's average weekly wage by July 1, 1973, and at least 100 percent of the State's average weekly wage by July 1, 1975. (Recommendation

3.8) There shall be no limit on duration or total dollar amount during the period of disability (Recommendation 3.17).

7. **Death benefits.** Surviving dependents should receive no less than 66 2/3 percent of the worker's average weekly wage (Recommendation 3.21), subject to same maximums as temporary total (Recommendation 3.23), with no limit on duration or total dollar amount of benefits during the period of statutory dependency (Recommendation 3.25).

8. **Permanent total benefits.** A worker's benefit should be no less than 66 2/3 percent of his average weekly wage (Recommendation 3.12), subject to same maximums as temporary total (Recommendation 3.15) with no duration or total dollar limits on benefits. (Recommendation 3.17.) The Commission's recommendation for the definition of permanent total disability should be used. (Recommendation 3.11.)

We urge the States to incorporate these essential recommendations into their workmen's compensation programs as soon as feasible. We realize that time is required for this achievement. Some State legislatures meet only biennially. Most states will need time to review these statutes carefully on the basis of all our recommendations. Nonetheless, we believe these essential recommendations are so feasible and essential that every jurisdiction can be expected reasonably to adopt them within three years.

**We believe that compliance of the States with these essential recommendations should be evaluated on July 1, 1975, and, if necessary, Congress with no further delay in the effective date should guarantee compliance.**

We believe the most desirable method to insure that each State program contains our essential recommendations would be to include these recommendations as mandates in Federal legislation, applicable to all employers specified by our essential recommendations.

Compliance with the mandates could be insured by two complementary methods. Any employer within the scope of the Federal legislation not already covered by a State workmen's compensation act would be required to elect coverage under the act in an appropriate State. Also all employers affected by the Federal law would be required to insure or otherwise secure the mandated recommendations. Employer compliance with the election and security requirements of the Federal legislation would be assured by a penalty enforceable through law suits filed by the U.S. Attorney's office in the appropriate Federal District Court.

Most employers can be expected to comply voluntarily with the Federal mandates. For the remaining recalcitrant employers, the most common enforcement mechanism probably will involve suits by the U.S. Attorney's office. There is a second enforcement mechanism that would rely on individual employee action. A workman would file his claim with his State workmen's compensation agency, which would be authorized by Federal law to make awards consistent with the Federal mandates.

The workman and his employer would have the right to appeal issues concerning the mandates to the State courts, with an eventual right of appeal to the Federal courts on the compliance issue. Should the State workmen's compensation agency refuse to assist in the implementation of the Federal mandates, the employee would be entitled to sue his employer for payment in State or Federal courts. If he requests, he should have the assistance of the U.S. Attorney.

The enforcement methods we have recommended lack the attribute of instant intelligiblity. Nonetheless, we believe they represent a workable solution to our desire to preserve workmen's compensation as essentially a State program while providing Federal assurance that injured workmen, no matter where they live, receive prompt, adequate, and equitable protection. For the vast majority of workers, the mandate approach we have recommended would affect only the substance, not the procedure, of their claims compared to the present program.

## The Costs of Adopting Our Essential Recommendations

The estimated costs of adopting our essential recommendations in the 50 States and the District of Columbia are summarized in Tables 2 and 3.

The National Council on Compensation Insurance, the actuarial organization for the workmen's compensation insurance industry, has estimated for 51 jurisdictions the impact of incorporating certain of our essential recommendations into the actual State law in effect on January 1, 1972. These recommendations are: full coverage of work-related diseases; full medical care and physical rehabilitation services; and the designated improvements in temporary total, permanent total, and death benefits. Our benefit recommendations have 1973 and 1975 stages for maximum weekly benefits but even the more expensive stage could be met in 46 jurisdictions by a less than 50 percent increase in workmen's compensation costs. (Table 2)

Data on workmen's compensation premiums as a percentage of payroll for a sample of insurance classifications are available for 41 States and the District of Columbia. (Table 3) These estimates by the Commission staff indicate that the average employer in 37 jurisdictions now expends one percent or less on workmen's compensation premiums. If our 1975 essential recommendations were adopted, the average employer in 37 jurisdictions would spend 1.25 percent or less on workmen's compensation premiums. Workmen's compensation costs would be somewhat more expensive in a small minority of States. Those employers whose workmen's compensation premiums now are above the average for their State would, unless their loss experience improves, continue to pay premiums above the State averages shown for 1973 and 1975. Despite these qualifications, we believe our essential recommendations are realistic as to their cost significance.

TABLE 2

DISTRIBUTION OF 50 STATES AND THE DISTRICT OF COLUMBIA ACCORDING TO
ESTIMATED INCREASE IN WORKMEN'S COMPENSATION COSTS RESULTING
FROM INCORPORATING OUR ESSENTIAL RECOMMENDATIONS INTO EACH
JURISDICTION'S PRESENT LAWS

| Percentage increase in costs over costs of present State program | Cost of adopting our essential recommendations | |
|---|---|---|
| | With 1973 maximum weekly benefits | With 1975 maximum weekly benefits |
| | Number of States | Number of States |
| Less than 10% | 12 | 5 |
| 10/29.9% | 25 | 20 |
| 30/49.9% | 14 | 21 |
| 50/69.9% | 0 | 5 |
| 70.0% or more | 0 | 0 |

TABLE 3

DISTRIBUTION OF 41 STATES AND THE DISTRICT OF COLUMBIA
ACCORDING TO ESTIMATED PERCENTAGE OF PAYROLL DEVOTED
TO WORKMEN'S COMPENSATION PREMIUMS BY EMPLOYERS IN A
REPRESENTATIVE SAMPLE OF INSURANCE CLASSIFICATIONS

| Workmen's compensation premiums as a percentage of payroll | Number of States in which premiums are the indicated percentage of payroll | | |
|---|---|---|---|
| | Actual in 1972 | If our essential recommendations were adopted | |
| | | With 1973 maximum weekly benefits | With 1975 maximum weekly benefits |
| Less than 0.50/% | 7 | 4 | 0 |
| 0.50/0.749% | 17 | 14 | 15 |
| 0.75/0.999% | 13 | 13 | 12 |
| 1.00/1.249% | 3 | 6 | 10 |
| 1.25/1.499% | 2 | 4 | 3 |
| 1.50/1.749% | 0 | 1 | 2 |
| 1.750% or more | 0 | 0 | 0 |

## Other Critical Areas of Workmen's Compensation

Certain subjects of vital importance in a modern workmen's compensation program are not appropriate for the mandates approach at the present time. These areas are more elusive; necessary data are unavailable; and the means of insuring compliance unclear. Still these issues are so important that the vitality of the State system will be tested by the ability of States to resolve them satisfactorily. A primary responsibility of the new Federal commission we have recommended is consideration of the following subjects.

**Permanent partial benefits.** States vary widely in their approach to these benefits. More data are needed to answer questions such as how well do schedules predict actual wage loss and why is an apparently disproportionate amount of resources devoted to these benefits in some States?

**Administration.** Although there is broad consensus on the general requisites of good administration, such as adequate financing, a permanent staff with tenure, an active informal procedures unit, and supervision of medical and rehabilitation services, the methods of insuring compliance with these criteria warrant further examination. Other aspects of administration, such as the appropriate place for compromise and release agreements and the effective use of second-injury funds, presently are matters of controversy and require additional intensive examination.

## Rationale for Commission's View on Methods of Implementing our Recommendations

Having now indicated our recommended implementation procedures, it is necessary to indicate our primary reasons for choosing this course.

We are unanimous in concluding that Congressional intervention may be necessary to bring about the reforms essential to survival of a State workmen's compensation system. The major difference among us concerns the time for urging Congressional action. A majority of the Commission believes there are two major reasons why Congress should not be asked to mandate any State action until after the States are given an opportunity for self-reform.

First, many recommended reforms of a fundamental nature are not susceptible to immediate Federal mandates, and some probably can never be mandated. If only the recommendations which can be Federally mandated are adopted by a State, many needed reforms will be neglected. If our list of mandates is adopted and made immediately applicable to the States, some States are likely to forego the thorough review of their workmen's compensation program which we believe is essential.

Second, an immediate push for Congressional legislation mandating some of our recommendations could precipitate a confrontation at the Federal level which could delay positive action at the State level pending the outcome and would divert energies and resources from reform efforts at the State level.

## Conclusion

The members of the National Commission on State Workmen's Compensation Laws were asked by the Occupational Safety and Health Act of 1970 to provide an effective study and objective evaluation of State workmen's compensation laws. We have done our best to fulfill that assignment. But in the process, we have produced a report which undoubtedly has some limitations imposed by the complexities of the subject and the pressures of time—pressures we felt were justified by the urgency of our task. As a result of these limitations, we know that our report can be misused. We know we cannot entirely stop the possible misuses, but in order to eliminate one possible misapplication, we wish to stress one central point which may be submerged in the details of our recommendations:

**We are without exception supporters of the basic principles of workmen's compensation.**

We have criticized the present State workmen's compensation programs, but not because we believe the basic principles are inherently wrong. Indeed they are right. We voice our criticism because present practice falls so far short of the basic principles, and because there is no possible justification for this short-fall.

Our report must then be understood as a repudiation of the old saw that even your best friends won't tell you. We believe we are workmen's compensation's best friends and, as friends, we are telling those who control the fate of the program that it should and can and must improve. Our disagreements within the commission as to the exact nature of the program's present impairment and as to precisely how the improvements must occur are far overshadowed by our agreement that the time has now come to reform workmen's compensation substantially in order to bring the reality of the program closer to its promise.

## Questions

1. The Commission states that wide variations among the states in the proportions of labor force covered are inequitable. Do you believe it is inequitable for a worker to be covered in one state but excluded in another? Why or why not?
2. What are the alternatives to the existing system of workmen's compensation? Do you favor any of these? Why?
3. The Commission is pessimistic about past attempts to reform workmen's compensation. Which of the five suggestions for a new approach do you think has the greatest chance for success? Why?
4. What reforms in workmen's compensation does the Commission apparently feel are most urgent? Do you agree with its judgment?

# PART 10
## Public Regulation of Insurance

The regulation of insurance, traditionally dominated by states, has recently been carried on by federal agencies as well. Action in the U.S. Congress in the areas of catastrophe insurance, automobile insurance, national health insurance, pensions, and social security have highlighted a seeming neglect by state regulators to cooperate with one another to control this vast industry. Serious questions are presenting themselves now as to which, if either, regulate this industry.

The articles selected for this part deal with important regulatory problems that are within the jurisdiction of the individual states. In the first article Professor Leverett addresses himself to the problem of insurer insolvency. Professor Goodman, in the second article, presents a credible, documented attack on a little-recognized clause in the life insurance contract. The last two articles on ratemaking in liability insurance and on profitability in the property and liability insurance industry develop other concepts of concern to insurance regulators.

# 34. PAID-IN SURPLUS AND CAPITAL REQUIREMENTS OF A NEW LIFE INSURANCE COMPANY *

E. J. Leverett, Jr. †

There is much concern about the financial requirements for a new life
insurance company, but little work has been done to determine an optimum amount of initial paid-in surplus and capital. The purpose of this
study is to determine the amount of funds that a new life insurance company would need in order to stay solvent under current regulatory conditions. Various operating assumptions are made and the amount of initial
paid-in surplus and capital necessary to finance the formative years of
the company are determined.

During the 19 years between 1950 and the middle of 1968, 2,084 life
insurance companies were organized in the United States, and 934 companies were merged, reinsured, or otherwise retired from business.[1]
Many reasons can be cited for the retirement of these companies. Some
start with a lack of managerial experience or unbalanced experience.
Others lack experience in the field and still others start with inadequate
capital.

The dominant reason for the retirement of these companies is unknown, but low capital and surplus requirements during this period
made it relatively easy to organize a stock life insurance company. This
ease of entry attracted people who were more interested in making a
quick profit on a stock promotion than in building a life insurance company.[2] The ease of entry also attracted people who were unable to cope
with the complexities of managing a life insurance company, and companies with this type of management have low probabilities of survival.
It could be argued that the reasons for failure are all a part of poor
management and inadequate capital and surplus simply a function of
poor management.

---

* From *The Journal of Risk and Insurance* (March, 1971), pp. 15-28. Reprinted by
permission.
† Head of the Department of Risk Management and Insurance, University of Georgia.
[1] *Life Insurance Fact Book,* (New York: Institute of Life Insurance, 1969), p. 102.
[2] Address by Leland J. Kalmbach, 58th Annual Meeting of the Life Insurance Association of America, Dec. 9, 1964, p. 4.

## INITIAL REQUIREMENTS

As indicated by Table 1, the initial capital and surplus requirements for the licensing of a life insurance company vary from $70,000 to $3,000,-000.[3] It would appear that most jurisdictions have established these capital and surplus requirements without any evidence of the amount of initial funds needed in order for the companies to survive without repeated infusions of funds. In recent years, the New York Department has attempted to deal with this problem by requiring a company to submit a detailed plan of operation that is supported by actuarial projections meeting department criteria.[4] This type of planning requires a company to examine the relationship between its proposed initial financing and its future financial requirements.

One life insurance executive indicated, in a private conversation with the author, that his newly formed company would need a capital and surplus structure of $5 million to sustain the company's operations until it become profitable. An actuary indicated that an exceptionally well run company would need a minimum of $1.5 million capital and surplus and an average new company would need $3 million to finance operations until it become profitable.[5]

Another prominent insurance executive indicated that the financial requirements of the various states were inadequate and changes needed to be made. He said:

> The minimum requirements of many states are totally inadequate for our type of business, and there is no doubt that many companies which have considered it desirable to merge or reinsure in recent years have had insufficient funds to finance their development programs adequately.[6]

## PURPOSE OF THE STUDY

It is evident that there is much concern about the financial requirements of the various states, but little has been done to arrive at an optimum amount of paid-in surplus and capital. The purpose of this study is to determine the amount of funds that a new life insurance company would need in order to remain solvent, under current regulatory conditions and under various operation assumptions, and be reasonably certain that it would not have to seek additional funds during its formative years. Good management of the company is assumed. The operating variables considered in this hypothetical life insurance company are expenses, mortality, lapsation, price structure, reserves, sales, interest, and paid-in surplus and capital.

---

[3] Arizona required $37,500 initial capital and surplus during most of the period under consideration but raised its requirement to $70,000 in 1966.

[4] 106th Annual Report of the Superintendent of Insurance to the New York Legislature Covering 1964, p. 28.

[5] Melvin L. Gold, "An Actuary Examines the Rash of New Companies," *Insurance (Goldbook)*, Sept. 11, 1965, p. 130.

[6] Kalmbach, *op. cit.*, p. 6.

TABLE 1

MINIMUM CAPITAL AND SURPLUS REQUIREMENTS OF EACH STATE
FOR DOMESTIC LIFE INSURANCE COMPANIES, 1970

| State | Requirement | | Statute |
|-------|-------------|-----------|---------|
|       | $ Capital | $ Surplus |         |
| Alabama | 200,000 | 300,000 | Ala. Stat. Title 28 $1 (1967) |
| Alaska | 200,000 | 100,000 | Alaska Stat. 21.09.070 (1966) |
| Arizona | 20,000 | 50,000 | Ariz. Rev. Stat. 20-210 & 20-211 (1966) |
| Arkansas | 100,000 | 100,000 | Ark. Stat. $$66-2207, 66-2208 (1967) |
| California | 450,000 | 550,000 | Calif. Ins. Code 700.05 & 10510 (1965) |
| Colorado | 200,000 | 100,000 | Colo. Rev. Stat. $72-1-36 (1963) |
| Connecticut | Created by Legislature | | |
| Delaware | 300,000 | 150,000 | 18 Del. Code $511 (1968) |
| D.C. | 200,000 | 100,000 | D.C. Code $$35-508, 35-601 (1964) |
| Florida | 500,000 | 750,000 | Fla. Stat. $$624.0206, 624, 0207 (1968) |
| Georgia | 200,000 | 200,000 | Ga. Code $$56-306,-307 (1963) |
| Hawaii | 200,000 | 100,000 | Hawaii Ins. Law 431-88,-89 (1963) |
| Idaho | 400,000 | 400,000 | Idaho Ins. Code $41-313 (1969) |
| Illinois | 400,000 | 200,000 | Ill. Stat. $73:625 (1965) |
| Indiana | 400,000 | 600,000 | Ind. Stat. Ann. $39-3614 (1967) |
| Iowa | 350,000 | 400,000 | Ia. Code $508.5 (1965) |
| Kansas | 200,000 | 100,000 | Kan. Gen. Stat. $40-401 (1965) |
| Kentucky | 500,000 | 750,000 | Ky. Rev. Stat. $304.072 (1966) |
| Louisiana | 100,000 | 200,000 | La. Ins. Code $22:71 (1966) |
| Maine | 500,000 | 1,000,000 | Maine Ins. Code 24-A $410 (1970) |
| Maryland | 500,000 | 750,000 | Md. Stat. Code Art. 48A $48, 49 (1965) |
| Massachusetts | 400,000 | 800,000 | Mass. Gen. Laws c. 175 $48, 51 (1968) |
| Michigan | 1,000,000 | 500,000 | Mich. Stat. Code 500.410 (1965) |
| Minnesota | 200,000 | | Minn. Stat. $60.29 (1963) |
| Mississippi | 200,000 | 300,000 | Miss. Code $5660 (1962) |
| Missouri | 200,000 | 200,000 | Mo. Stat. Ann. $376.280 (1964) |
| Montana | 100,000 | 100,000 | Mont. Rev. Code $$40-2808 (1965) |
| Nebraska | 500,000 | 500,000 | Neb. Stat. 44-214 (1967) |
| Nevada | 200.000 | 100,000 | Nev. Rev. Stat. $682.160 (1963) |
| New Hampshire | 600,000 | | N. H. Stat. $411:1 (1969) |
| New Jersey | 800,000 | 1,700,000 | N. J. Stat. $17:17-6 (1968) |
| New Mexico | 100,000 | 200,000 | N. M. Stat. Ann. $58-18-24 (1965) |
| New York | 1,000,000 | 2,000,000 | N. Y. Ins. Law $191 (1967) |
| North Carolina | 300,000 | 300,000 | N. C. Ins. Laws $58-777 (1963) |
| North Dakota | 150,000 | 75,000 | N. D. Rev. Code $26.08-04 (1963) |
| Ohio | 400,000 | 600,000 | Ohio Rev. Code 3907.05 (1965) |
| Oklahoma | 250,000 | 125,000 | Okla. Ins. Code 36 $610, 611 (1967) |
| Oregon | 500,000 | | Ore. Rev. Stat. $731:554 (1967) |
| Pennsylvania | 300,000 | 150,000 | 40 Penn. Stat. Ann. $383 (1967) |
| Rhode Island | Created by Legislature | | R. I. Gen. Laws $7-1-5 (1956) |
| South Carolina | 100,000 | 100,000 | S. C. Code $37-181 (1963) |
| South Dakota | 200,000 | 200,000 | S. D. Code $31.1510 (1959) |
| Tennessee | 150,000 | 150,000 | Tenn. Code Ann. $56-303, 305, (1961) |
| Texas | 100,000 | 100,000 | Texas Insurance Code Art. 3.02 (1963) |
| Utah | 200,000 | 500,000 | Utah. Ins. Laws $31-11-1 (1967) |
| Vermont | 250,000 | 150,000 | 8 Vt. Stat. Ann. $3304 (1968) |
| Virginia | 500,000 | 300,000 | Va. Ins. Laws $38. 1-88 (1966) |
| Washington | 400,000 | 400,000 | Wash. Rev. Code $48.05.340 (1967) |
| West Virginia | 750,000 | 375,000 | West. Va. Code 33-3-5 (1968) |
| Wisconsin | 400,000 | 100,000 | Wisc. Ins. Code 201.04 (1966) |
| Wyoming | 200,000 | 100,000 | Wyo. Ins. Laws 26.1-57 (1965) |

## THE MODEL

The model used in this study is a combination of two actuarial techniques known as (1) the asset share, and (2) the model office. This model[7] is designed to generate the data necessary to construct the balance sheet and income statement, as well as a statutory test of solvency of a hypothetical life insurance company.

The first part of the model is based on an asset share formula of the retrospective type. The purpose of this portion of the model is to determine the asset share per $1,000 of business in force at the end of any particular year of analysis. The asset share calculation is based upon ten variables: (1) expenses that vary with the premium, (2) death claim expense, (3) expense per policy, (4) rates of mortality, (5) rates of lapsation, (6) interest rate, (7) cash value, (8) dividend schedule, (9) face amount of insurance, and (10) gross annual premium.

The second part of the model deals with the model office technique. This technique is generally used to illustrate the effect on an entire company of some change in its method of operation. In general, a model office involves the selection of a few plans of insurance and a few ages of issue, and an assumption that all business is issued on these plans and these ages. In order to generate the surplus of a company under various operating assumptions, the asset share for the business written by the company is calculated and applied to the business in force as developed in the model office. The combination of the asset share and the model office technique introduces four additional variables: minimum start-up expenses, the reserve liability, the sales pattern, and the business in force.

## Minimum Start-Up Expenses

Most of the variables used in this study are widely used in the actuarial literature but little has been written about what it costs to start a life insurance company. It is generally conceded that new life insurance companies have high initial expenses. Expenses that vary with the premium and expenses that are a function of the number of policies that the company has in force are expressed in the model as the expenses that are achieved by the company once it is in operation. It is also necessary to forecast the excess expenses prior to the time the company is in actual operation.

Certain expenses cannot be avoided whether or not the company writes any business, and these are in excess of those expense factors contemplated in the premium calculation. These may be referred to as "fixed" or "overhead" expenses and consist of executive and clerical

---

[7] Edgar J. Leverett, Jr., "A Simulation of the Financial Operations of a Life Insurance Company under Various Operating Assumptions with Special Emphasis on Solvency and Paid-In Surplus and Capital," unpublished dissertation, Graduate School of Business, Indiana University, 1967.

salaries, agency expenses in addition to commission, rental expenditures, furniture, printing, actuarial, legal and accounting fees, advertising, postage and other expenses. Although these costs are normally charged against the value of sales during the company's first year of operations, it would be more realistic to amortize such expenses over a number of years. Statutory accounting requirements, however, do not permit this practice.

The determination of an exact division of expenses between the organizational and/or start-up and operating expenses is difficult, but a look at three recently formed companies gives a pattern to follow. The general expenses and insurance in force of the three companies were as follows:

| Company | General Expenses | Insurance In Force At Year End |
|---------|------------------|-------------------------------|
| X | $397,321 | $6,660,655 |
| Y | 434,566 | 2,506,687 |
| Z | 410,951 | 2,017,037 |

It is assumed in this study that all general expenses through the first partial calendar year of operations are organizational and start-up expenses, and $400,000 is used as start-up expenses in the calculation.

## TEST OF SOLVENCY

Solvency is a primary objective for any business firm and a life insurance company is no exception. Business firms can be judged technically insolvent or actually insolvent. If a firm cannot meet its maturing obligations it is considered to be technically insolvent. A business firm with liabilities in excess of its assets in considered to be insolvent in a bankruptcy sense or actually insolvent. Generally, a business corporation would be permitted to continue operations as long as it meets its obligations as they mature.

The critical issue for a life insurance company would be actual insolvency rather than technical insolvency.[8] The regulatory officials of most states would declare a life insurance company insolvent if its admitted assets are less than the total values of its present liabilities and capital required for the company to do business. The statutes of most states give broad powers to the official charged with the regulation of insurance companies. Many states prohibit any impairment of capital and consider a company insolvent when any such impairment occurs. All of the regulatory officials of the states whose statutes permit impairment of capital for a limited period of time indicated they would not permit the impairment even for a limited period of time.

---

[8] Joseph M. Belth, "Observations on Solvency in the Context of Life Insurance Regulation," *The Journal of Risk and Insurance*, Vol. XXXIV (December, 1967), p. 541.

A solvency test for any business firm is arbitrary because of the valuation of assets and liabilities. This is particularly true for a life insurance company as the generally accepted policy of both management and regulatory officials is to "value the assets low and the liabilities high.[9] This conservatism does not appear to be considered since the regulatory officials have clearly indicated they would abide by the no impairment rule or actual insolvency. For purposes of this study, the minimum amount of capital required by the particular state is considered to be the amount of net assets below which the company would not be permitted to fall.

A test of solvency is used to determine whether or not the initial paid-in surplus and capital were adequate to finance the investment in new business and to satisfy the regulatory officials during the assumed period of operation. If the reserve liabilities plus the minimum required capital are greater than the assets generated by the business written plus the paid-in surplus and capital account with compound interest then the company is considered to be insolvent. Assume, for example, a company with $1,000,000 paid-in surplus and capital, of which $400,000 is considered to be the minimum amount of capital. The business it has written has generated $1,000,000 in assets and $850,000 in liabilities. The following test of solvency indicates that the company is solvent by a margin of $750,000.

| Paid-in Surplus and Capital | Generated Assets | Reserve Liabilities | Minimum Capital | Margin of Solvency |
|---|---|---|---|---|
| ($1,000,000 | + $1,000,00) − | ($850,000 | + $400,000) = | $750,000 |

## SUMMARY OF ASSUMPTIONS

A summary of the assumptions that are used in this study is given in Table 2. The breakdown of sales by age and plan of insurance is given in Table 3. The lapse assumptions by plan of insurance age are given in Table 4, and Table 5 gives the gross annual premium for each age and plan of insurance. The figures used for mortality, lapsation, cash values, and policy reserves can be found in most standard life insurance texts.

## COMPANY A

It is assumed that Company A is operating in states that require paid-in surplus and capital totaling $1,400,000 of which $400,000 is the minimum amount of capital. If Company A impairs the $400,000 capital, it is considered to be insolvent, therefore, in the test of solvency, the amount of the minimum capital is treated as a liability.

---

[9] B. Franklin Blair, "Company Annual Statement," *Life and Health Insurance Hand-Book*, ed. Davis W. Gregg (2nd ed., Homewood, Ill., Richard D. Irwin, Inc., 1964), p. 1026.

TABLE 2

SUMMARY OF BASIC ASSUMPTIONS USED FOR HYPOTHETICAL COMPANY

1. The period of analysis is 20 years.

2. Policies are issued to standard males aged—ten, thirty, and fifty.

3. The plans of insurance are ten-year level term, whole life, and endowment at age 65. These plans are written on a non-participating basis. In addition, a preferred whole life is written on a participating basis.

4. The expenses incurred with each death claim are $20 per policy, plus $1 per thousand.

5. The face amount of insurance for each plan is $12,000.

6. The paid-in surplus and capital will be started at $1,400,000, of which $400,000 is considered to be the minimum capital permitted by regulatory officials. The paid-in surplus and capital will be varied to achieve an optimum amount.

7. The assumed sales in the first year are 500 policies of $12,000 each. The number of policies sold in subsequent years is assumed to increase by 40 percent of the number sold in the previous year for the first five years, 12 percent for the next five years, and ten percent for the remaining years.

8. Sale are divided among the ages and plans of insurance according to Table 3.

9. The expense pattern will consist of expenses that vary with the premium and expenses per policy. It is assumed that 103 percent of the first year's premium plus $87 per policy are used for expenses in the first policy year. In addition a higher expense pattern is used to illustrate the impact of expenses. The higher pattern calls for 150 percent of the first year's premium to be used for expenses. The remaining years are the same as the basic expense pattern.

10. The mortality rates are those found in the $X_{18}$ mortality table with Buck's select data for the first five years at ages ten, thirty, and fifty except in the case of term insurance where the mortality rates are increased by 50 percent.

11. The lapse rates vary by age and plan of insurance. Table 4 gives the lapse patterns used for each category.

12. The cash values are determined on the basis of the 1958 CSO Table of Mortality and three and one-half percent interest.

13. Policy reserves are calculated using the Commissioners' Reserve Valuation Method and based upon the 1958 CSO Table of Mortality and three and one-half percent interest.

14. The net annual interest rate is 5.0 percent.

15. All premiums are assumed to be paid annually, and the gross annual premiums are given in Table 5.

16. The start-up or organizational expense are $400,000 which is expended in the first year of operation.

TABLE 3

PERCENTAGE OF SALES BY AGE AND PLAN OF INSURANCE
FOR A HYPOTHETICAL COMPANY

| Age | Ten-Year Term | Whole Life-Par | Whole Life Non Par | Endowment at 65 | Total |
|-----|-----|-----|-----|-----|-----|
| 10 | 0 | 10 | 5 | 15 | 30 |
| 30 | 15 | 5 | 15 | 5 | 40 |
| 50 | 10 | 5 | 10 | 5 | 30 |
| TOTAL | 25 | 20 | 30 | 25 | 100 |

TABLE 4

LAPSE RATES BY AGE AND PLAN OF INSURANCE FOR A HYPOTHETICAL
COMPANY, BASED ON LINTON'S TABLES OF LAPSATION

| Age | Ten-Year Term | Whole Life-Par | Whole Life Non Par | Endowment at 65 |
|-----|-----|-----|-----|-----|
| 10 | — | B | B | A |
| 30 | B+50% | B | B | B |
| 50 | B+50% | A | A | A |

TABLE 5

PREMIUMS BY AGE AND PLAN OF INSURANCE FOR HYPOTHETICAL COMPANY

| Age | Ten-Year Term | Whole Life-Par | Whole Life Non Par | Endowment at 65 |
|-----|-----|-----|-----|-----|
| 10 | — | $ 9.81 | $ 7.91 | $ 9.95 |
| 30 | 5.75 | 18.48 | 14.70 | 20.85 |
| 50 | 17.00 | 38.86 | 32.44 | 65.01 |

## Basic Assumptions

Using the basic assumptions, given in Table 2, in conjunction with the paid-in surplus and capital assumption, the results of the test of solvency is selected years are as follows:

| Year | Total Assets | Total Liabilities | Difference |
|-----|-----|-----|-----|
| 6 | $1,909,632 | $1,709,051 | $ 200,581 |
| 7 | 2,511,333 | 2,416,080 | 95,253 |
| 8 | 3,308,037 | 3,315,745 | −7,708 |
| 9 | 4,214,960 | 4,424,085 | −209,125 |

The above figures indicate that the total assets of Company A are greater than its total liabilities in the first seven years of operations, but the margin of solvency is diminishing rapidly. These figures indicate that Company A's initial capital and surplus are insufficient to cover the statutory minimum requirements and investments in new insurance sales. As indicated in Chart 1, the difference between the total assets and the total liabilities is increasing sharply throughout the period of analysis. The negative difference in the eighth year indicates that the company is insolvent and the margin of insolvency is greater in each subsequent year. This widening difference indicates that insolvency is not a temporary situation, and if Company A is to continue to operate, some significant changes must be made in its operation.

CHART 1

MARGIN OF SOLVENCY OF COMPANY A UNDER BASIC ASSUMPTIONS
AND $1.4 MILLION PAID-IN SURPLUS AND CAPITAL

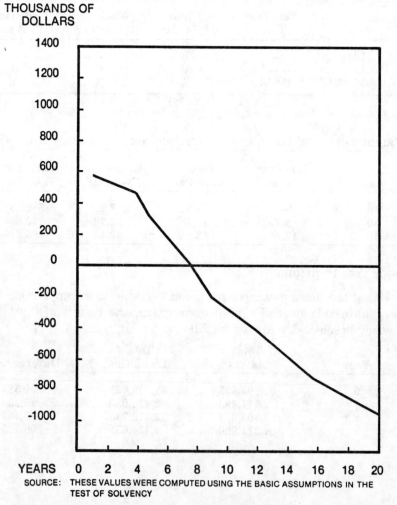

THOUSANDS OF DOLLARS

YEARS

SOURCE:   THESE VALUES WERE COMPUTED USING THE BASIC ASSUMPTIONS IN THE
TEST OF SOLVENCY

temporary situation, and if Company A is to continue to operate, some significant changes must be made in its operation.

## Higher Expense Pattern

Some authorities[10] feel that a new life insurance company will have a higher acquisition cost than that reflected in the basic expense assumption used in this study. In recognition of this possibility, a higher expense pattern is adopted. In this pattern, the expenses that vary with the premium are 150 percent of the first year's premium. This is in contrast to 103 percent of the first year's premium going to expenses in the basic expense pattern.

A shift to the higher expense pattern emphasizes the inadequacy of the initial funds of Company A. The following figures indicate that Company A would be insolvent in the fifth year of operation when the expense assumption is shifted from the basic pattern to the higher pattern.

| Year | Total Assets | Total Liabilities | Difference |
|------|-------------|-------------------|------------|
| 3 | $861,355 | $ 598,862 | $ 262,493 |
| 4 | 843,885 | 782,792 | 61,093 |
| 5 | 841,239 | 1,181,838 | −349,599 |

One of Company A's alternatives is to increase the paid-in surplus and capital sufficiently to enable the company to remain solvent throughout the period of analysis. An increase in the assets of the company could be achieved through the sale of additional stock or through a coinsurance arrangement with another company. These methods could be used individually or in combination, whichever was the more advantageous to the stockholders of Company A.

The most realistic course for Company A would have been to start business with adequate paid-in surplus and capital. This would allow the company to operate without being subjected to the disadvantages associated with frequent infusions of new funds.

### COMPANY B

Assume that Company B is operating under the same conditions as Company A with the exception of paid-in surplus and capital. It is assumed that Company B will start its operations with $1.65 million of paid-in surplus and capital.

## Basic Assumptions

The total assets of Company B exceed its total liabilities and capital stock for the first 12 years of operations. The following selected values

---

[10] Irving Pfeffer, "Measuring the Profit Potential of a New Life Insurance Company," *Journal of Risk and Insurance*, Vol. XXXII, No. 3 (Sept., 1965) p. 419, and Roy H. Owsley, "Cost Study," *Best's Insurance News* (Life Ed.), May 1964, p. 18.

point out the plight of Company B and its need to make adjustments in its operations or return to the market place for additional "risk" funds.

| Year | Total Assets | Total Liabilities | Difference |
|------|-------------|-------------------|------------|
| 10 | $ 5,946,010 | $ 5,759,275 | $ 186,735 |
| 11 | 7,460,759 | 7,341,809 | 118,950 |
| 12 | 9,212,028 | 9,176,650 | 35,378 |
| 13 | 11,257,436 | 11,297,439 | −40,003 |
| 14 | 13,619,646 | 13,725,349 | −105,703 |

Chart 2 indicates Company B's margin of solvency over the entire period of analysis. The inadequacy of initial paid-in surplus and capital is clearly pointed out by the rapidly decreasing margin of solvency after the fourth year of operations. It should be noted, however, that Company B's margin of insolvency is leveling off after the 16th year of operation. This is in contrast to Company A which continues to show a rapid decrease in the margin of solvency throughout the period of analysis. The increased investment income that Company B receives from the additional paid-in surplus and capital explains the difference in the margin of solvency of Company A and Company B.

## Higher Expense Pattern

Continuing the assumption of $1.65 million paid-in surplus and capital, the test of insolvency is applied to the financial structure of Company B when the basic expense assumption is increased from 103 percent of the first year's premium for expenses to 150 percent. The following figures indicate Company B is insolvent in the fifth year of analysis when the expense pattern is changed from the basic to the higher pattern.

| Year | Total Assets | Total Liabilities | Difference |
|------|-------------|-------------------|------------|
| 4 | $1,148,122 | $ 782,792 | $ 365,330 |
| 5 | 1,160,309 | 1,181,838 | −21,529 |
| 6 | 1,306,134 | 1,709,051 | −402,917 |

The net gain from operations is negative for a substantial portion of the period of analysis, when the higher expense pattern is used in Company B's operation. The initial funds of Company B are not sufficient to withstand the drain on surplus beyond the fourth year and the company would be declared insolvent thereafter.

CHART 2

MARGIN OF SOLVENCY OF COMPANY B UNDER BASIC ASSUMPTIONS
AND $1.65 MILLION PAID-IN SURPLUS AND CAPITAL

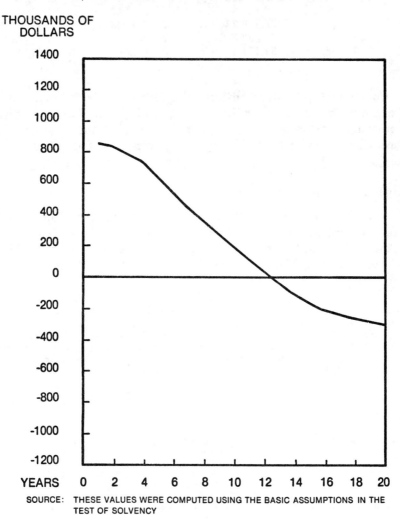

THOUSANDS OF
DOLLARS

YEARS

SOURCE:  THESE VALUES WERE COMPUTED USING THE BASIC ASSUMPTIONS IN THE
TEST OF SOLVENCY

## COMPANY C

## Basic Assumptions

Company C is assumed to begin operations with $1,900,000 paid-in
surplus and capital, of which $400,000 is the amount of capital it must
maintain. It is operating under the same conditions as Companies A
and B with the exception of the amount of paid-in surplus and capital.
The results of the statutory test of solvency for selected years are as
follows:

| Year | Total Assets | Total Liabilities | Difference |
|------|-------------|-------------------|------------|
| 16 | $19,603,530 | $19,262,575 | $340,955 |
| 17 | 22,821,328 | 22,481,255 | 340,073 |
| 18 | 26,350,736 | 25,996,849 | 353,887 |
| 19 | 30,183,389 | 29,801,953 | 381,436 |
| 20 | 34,414,315 | 34,031,589 | 382,726 |

Company C is solvent during the entire period of analysis. The above figures indicate that the earnings and assets of the company are increasing faster after the 17th year than its investment in new insurance. Chart 3 indicates the margin of solvency for the entire period of analysis.

## Higher Expense Pattern

A shift to the higher expense pattern would put Company C in financial difficulties in the 6th year of operation. As indicated by the following figures, Company C would be declared insolvent in the sixth year of operations if it experienced the higher expense pattern:

| Year | Total Assets | Total Liabilities | Difference |
|------|-------------|-------------------|------------|
| 4 | $1,147,762 | $ 782,792 | $ 364,970 |
| 5 | 1,279,379 | 1,181,838 | 97,541 |
| 6 | 1,641,157 | 1,709,051 | −67,894 |
| 7 | 1,935,782 | 2,416,080 | −480,298 |

### COMPANY D

Company D is operating under the same conditions as the previous companies with the exception of the $2.4 million paid-in surplus and capital, of which $400,000 is considered to be capital.

## Basic Assumptions

Chart 4 indicates the margin of solvency during the period of analysis. The turning point for Company D is the 16th year of analysis. In the previous years, the liabilities of the company were increasing faster than the assets. After the 16th year, the assets are increasing at a faster rate than the liabilities because the earnings on the business-in-force is increasing faster than the investment in new insurance written. The following figures indicate the financial position of Company D in selected years of operation:

| Year | Total Assets | Total Liabilities | Difference |
|------|------|------|------|
| 14 | $14,312,620 | $13,725,349 | $587,271 |
| 15 | 16,911,023 | 16,345,700 | 565,323 |
| 16 | 19,821,814 | 19,262,575 | 559,239 |
| 17 | 23,050,527 | 22,481,255 | 569,272 |
| 18 | 26,591,394 | 25,596,849 | 594,545 |

CHART 3

MARGIN OF SOLVENCY OF COMPANY C UNDER BASIC ASSUMPTIONS
AND $1.9 MILLION PAID-IN SURPLUS AND CAPITAL

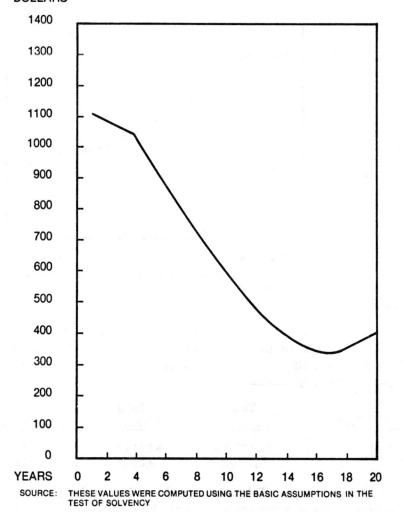

THOUSANDS OF
DOLLARS

YEARS

SOURCE:   THESE VALUES WERE COMPUTED USING THE BASIC ASSUMPTIONS IN THE
TEST OF SOLVENCY

CHART 4

MARGIN OF SOLVENCY OF COMPANY D UNDER BASIC ASSUMPTIONS
AND $2.4 MILLION PAID-IN SURPLUS AND CAPITAL

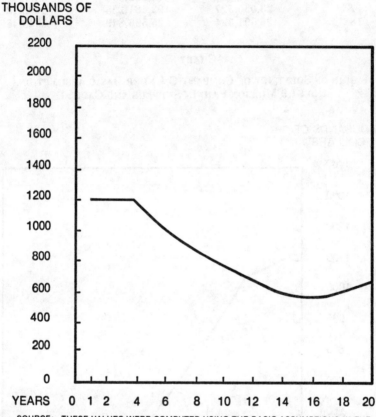

THOUSANDS OF DOLLARS

SOURCE:  THESE VALUES WERE COMPUTED USING THE BASIC ASSUMPTIONS IN THE
TEST OF SOLVENCY

## Higher Expense Pattern

A shift to the higher expense pattern by Company D would put it in financial difficulties in the eighth year of operation. The following figures indicate the financial position of Company D in the seventh and eighth years of operation:

| Year | Total Assets | Total Liabilities | Difference |
|------|------|------|------|
| 7 | $2,639,332 | $2,416,080 | $  223,252 |
| 8 | 2,703,386 | 3,315,745 | −612,359 |

Although Company D is solvent in the entire period of analysis using the basic expense assumption, it would be declared insolvent early in its life if it experienced the higher expense pattern. These figures indicate the need for a substantial increase in initial funds to offset the investment in new insurance being written.

## COMPANY E

Company E is assumed to be operating under the higher expense pattern, in conjunction with the other basic assumptions. It is further assumed that its initial paid-in surplus and capital is $7 million, of which $400,000 is the amount of the capital it must maintain. The following figures of selected years of Company E's operation indicate that the company is solvent during the entire period of analysis.

| Year | Total Assets | Total Liabilities | Difference |
|------|-------------|-------------------|------------|
| 5 | $ 7,988,537 | $ 1,181,838 | $6,806,699 |
| 10 | 11,907,254 | 5,759,275 | 6,210,979 |
| 15 | 20,748,740 | 16,345,700 | 4,403,040 |
| 20 | 34,799,159 | 34,031,589 | 767,570 |

It should be noted, however, that although Company E is technically solvent throughout the period of analysis, the margin of solvency is decreasing rapidly. This would indicate that the investment in the company's new insurance is increasing faster than the earnings generated by the paid-in surplus and capital and the business in force. If company E is to reach the point that its earnings are increasing faster than its investment in new business, it will be necessary to increase its paid-in surplus and capital substantially, decrease its expense factors or decrease its sales performance. A decrease in the expense pattern would be highly desirable, but this may not be a completely controllable item. The other alternative is to increase the paid-in surplus and capital to a point that earnings would increase to a higher level.

Another way to improve Company E's surplus position would be to decrease its sales, but this could have a disheartening effect on the sales force and a long term deterioration of the company's profit picture. It could be argued that part of the regulatory job would be to control the sales pattern of a company.

New York has established limitations on the amount of new business which a company can write in a given year. If a company has more than $750 million of insurance in force, it is not permitted to write in excess of the larger of $200,000,000 or 115 percent of the volume of business during the best of the three preceding years. The Superintendent of Insurance, however, is permitted to suspend the limit for any company if its agency operations are conducted efficiently. This ruling was an outgrowth of the Armstrong investigation and is aimed at discouraging excessive competition and not particularly aimed at new companies.

Small, recently established companies are expected to grow at a faster rate than older, larger companies and it is unlikely the rule would be applied by the Superintendent although it is within his power to do so.

## SUMMARY AND CONCLUSIONS

### Initial Capital and Surplus

The initial capital and surplus requirements for the licensing of a life insurance company vary from $70,000 to $3,000,000. This wide variance might indicate that most jurisdictions have established these limits without any or very little evidence of the amount of initial funds needed in order for the companies to survive without repeated infusions of new funds.

A large ratio of new business to business-in-force depletes the company's assets and creates a drain on its surplus. This drain is an expected occurrence with a new company and if a company is to survive, it must have adequate paid-in surplus and capital to invest in new business.

The purpose of this study was to determine the amount of paid-in surplus and capital that a new life insurance company would need in order to remain solvent, under current regulatory conditions and under various operating assumptions, and be reasonably certain that it would not have to seek additional funds during its formative years.

### Solvency

In the current regulatory environment, a company is generally considered insolvent when the sum of its liabilities and required capital exceed its total admitted assets. For the purpose of this study, the total assets consist of the assets generated by the business plus assets equal to the initial paid-in surplus and capital compounded at the assumed rate of interest. The total liabilities consist of the required reserve liabilities plus the capital required by the state insurance commissioner. Regulatory officials of most states have indicated that they would not permit a company to impair its capital even for the limited period of time permitted in some statutes. Consequently, for all practical purposes, a company may be considered insolvent the moment it impairs its capital, even though the statutory definition of insolvency may be somewhat more lenient.

For the purpose of this study, it is assumed that the minimum amount of capital permitted by the regulatory officials is held constant in this study at $400,000. The time necessary for the company to "turn the corner" would be increased if the amount of minimum capital were increased.

Table 6 indicates the results of the test of solvency on the operating results of five hypothetical life insurance companies. It was determined that Company C with $1.9 million paid-in surplus and capital would

TABLE 6

SUMMARY OF THE TEST OF SOLVENCY APPLIED TO VARIOUS
NEW LIFE INSURANCE COMPANIES USING DIFFERENT EXPENSE
ASSUMPTIONS AND PAID-IN SURPLUS AND CAPITAL

| Company | Paid-In Surplus and Capital | Year of Insolvency | |
|---|---|---|---|
| | | Basic[1] | Higher[2] |
| A .................... | $1,400,000 | 8 | 5 |
| B .................... | 1,650,000 | 13 | 5 |
| C .................... | 1,900,000 | S* | 6 |
| D .................... | 2,400,000 | S* | 8 |
| E .................... | 7,400,000 | S* | S* |

* S = Solvent throughout the period of analysis.

[1] The basic expense pattern calls for 103 percent of the first year's premium plus $87 per policy to be used for expenses.

[2] The higher expense pattern calls for 150 percent of the first year's premium plus $87 per policy to be used for expenses.

be solvent throughout the 20-year period of analysis when operating under the basic assumptions.

When the expense assumption is shifted to a higher pattern, as suggested by some authorities, it would be necessary for a company to start business with $7.4 million paid-in surplus and capital to remain solvent throughout the period of analysis. This points out the tremendous impact of expenses on the financial condition of a life insurance company.

It would appear on the basis of these findings, that the regulatory authorities have been unduly optimistic in the financial requirements of a new life insurance company. The assumptions used in arriving at these findings have been carefully chosen to reflect as realistic a situation as possible. If the assumptions used in this study are realistic, then the minimum financial requirements are indeed too low in 48 of the 50 states. The next question arises as to what assumptions were actually being made when these low requirements were formulated. In Arizona, for example, some heroic assumptions must be made to justify only $70,000 of paid-in surplus and capital. Perhaps, it was contemplated that there would be no start-up expenses, that insurers would earn 30 percent on their investments, or that the rate of acquisition of new business would be very low or some other unrealistic assumption.

This analysis has shown the crucial importance of the rate of new business growth and the expense assumptions in predicting the solvency pattern of new life insurance companies. The effect of other elements of the model on the solvency of the company were not investigated. These could have significant effect on the final conclusions but the study of these variables was beyond the scope of this paper.

The findings of this study suggest two steps that could be taken by regulatory officials in reducing the risk of a new company becoming insolvent. The first recommendation is the requirement of an actuarial projection concerning the use of initial paid-in surplus and capital. This requirement should increase the probability of a new company's survival because management would be forced to give careful thought to its goals, and how they would be reached. A model similar to the one used in this study could be used to make the necessary projections. Other types of long run planning models could be used so long as they required management to think through the various assumptions associated with the model.

The second recommendation would be an increase in the initial financial requirements. A comparison of the financial requirements shown in Table 1 and the results of the test of solvency shown in Table 6 indicates that only two states, New Jersey and New York, have financial requirements that are high enough to maintain solvency under the basic assumptions. If the expenses are increased to the higher level, none of the states has adequate financial requirements.

The requirement of adequate initial financing plus a projection of the operations would do much to increase a new company's probability of survival. It is apparent that inadequate study has been given to the establishment of initial financial requirements. This paper points out the need for careful study on the part of regulatory officials prior to the establishment of paid-in surplus and capital requirments. This increased study and the resulting changes would reduce the large number of companies merged, reinsured or otherwise retired and the industry image of financial soundness would be greatly enhanced.

## Questions

1. What is the difference between actual and technical insolvency for a life insurance company? Which criterion should be used for insurance regulation purposes? Why?
2. Is the question of life insurer insolvency unimportant in today's economy? What is the record of "turnover" among life insurers? Does the existing turnover mean losses to policyholders? Discuss.
3. The author shows that under the basic assumptions stated in Table 2, a company (Company C) must have $1,900,000 of initial capital and surplus in order to avoid the necessity of an infusion of new capital within a short period. Under higher expenses assumptions a company must have $7,400,000 of initial capital and surplus in order to avoid insolvency, as defined.
   (a) How do state laws on minimum capital and surplus measure up to the author's standards?
   (b) In view of the fact that apparently not all new life insurance companies go insolvent within a short time, nor do they all have the minimum capital suggested as being necessary by the author to avoid insolvency, some of the assumptions in Table 2 are apparently not being met in practice. What differences in the assumptions in practice could account for the results noted? Discuss.

# 35. A STATEMENT BEFORE THE NAIC ON PROTECTION OF THE PUBLIC INTEREST AND THE MISSTATEMENT OF AGE CLAUSE IN LIFE INSURANCE CONTRACTS *

Oscar R. Goodman †

I would like to thank The Honorable J. Richard Barnes, C.L.U., Commissioner of Insurance for the State of Colorado, and the other members of the Subcommittee on Life Insurance of the National Association of Insurance Commissioners for extending to me the privilege of presenting this statement on protection of the public interest in the matter of age statements in life insurance applications. My statement will point out that practically all current insurance contracts include three major misrepresentations by omitting essential information. It will also show that, as insurance commissioners, you have been derelict in your duty to protect the public from the activities of insurers in current settlement practices with regard to age statements. I shall review the problem and call upon the state insurance commissioners, individually in their own states, to issue immediately regulations and install procedures in keeping with their responsibilities in this area.

The practice of using death certificates as prima facie evidence of birth date and age in the settlement of life insurance policies has no justification in equity, is a cruel exception to the legal principle that contract ambiguities in insurance contracts are to be interpreted in favor of beneficiaries, and should cease forthwith. The party who contracted with the insurance company for the insurance is usually dead at the time of settlement and is unable to speak from the grave to answer accusations by the insurance company that he misrepresented his age. He did not sign the age statements in the death certificate. The death certificate is evidence of only one fact: death.

State insurance commissioners should place the burden of proving errors in age statements on the insurer. The practice of shifting the burden to the beneficiary on the basis of the death certificate should be stopped immediately. Insurance commissioners who are interested in the welfare of the public should welcome the opportunity to establish this

* From *The Journal of Risk and Insurance* (March, 1971), pp. 147-152. Reprinted by permission.
† Professor of Finance, Roosevelt University.

rule, if necessary, in the courts of their state. State insurance departments should require individual reports of each individual instance of contract reformation on the basis of the age clauses. This should include full facts and proof of the correct age supplied by the insurer beyond a reasonable doubt without use of the death certificate as proof of death.

It is over 100 years since Elizur Wright became the first state insurance commissioner in the United States after he fought to protect widows and orphans who were being victimized by life insurance companies in Massachusetts. The insurance companies used their superior financial strength and the advantage of the death of the insured, who was thus unable to protect himself, to twist the words in the contracts to escape payment of the policy face to beneficiaries at death. I will not rehash in this statement the documentation of these insurer abuses, since this is contained in a recent paper.[1]

It is a plain truth that insureds and beneficiaries are not aware of the fact that beneficiaries will have to prove the correct age and birth date of insureds after the death of the insureds and that life insurance companies are well aware of it. It is also obvious that the correct age and birth date are best proven by the insured, and that the insurance company can ascertain the accuracy of this information at the time of contracting. Yet the policy is silent and misrepresents the actual burden of proof in the payment clause, which purports only to require proof of death to have the insurer meet its contractual obligation. The incontestable clause is conspicuously silent on the exception of age statements from its protection, and the insurer is well aware of the fact that it intends to take advantage of the exception.

The age clause states that reformation will take place if the "correct age" of the insured is proved to be different from the application age. Yet in most contested cases, the "correct" age is never established. The insurer seizes upon the death certificate when it is to his advantage and then refuses to pay face value unless the beneficiary proves the "correct" age. In many cases such proof is impossible to obtain. Thus, the insurance company forces the beneficiary to take the smaller amount. It must be obvious to all here that this results in a substantial profit to stock life insurance companies and an undeserved bonus to the payrolls of mutual life insurance companies.

These omissions are deliberate in spite of the superior knowledge of the insurer of the legal distinction between "contest" and "dispute," and of settlement and litigation practices after receipt of proof of death. Life insurance contracts cannot be held to be contracts of good faith when such omissions and exceptions are part of the policy and of common insurer practices.

---

[1] Oscar R. Goodman, "Public Policy and the Age and Incontestable Clauses in Life Insurance Contracts," *Journal of Risk and Insurance,* Vol. XXXV, No. 4 (December, 1968), pp. 515-35.

It was precisely for situations such as this that insurance companies were forced by the state legislatures to insert the incontestable clause in life contracts to forestall attempts by insurers to take advantage of beneficiaries after the death of the insureds, on all statements as to health and history. These statements are open to question only during a reasonable time period, such as one or two years and age statements should be given the same protection.

The late Dr. Solomon S. Huebner commented on the incontestable clause that:

> . . . it was undesirable to have widows, children, and other dependents protected by a contract under which forfeiture might remain unknown until after the death of the insured, thus negating the essential purpose of life insurance.[2]

Would you gentlemen herein assembled, who are sworn to protect the public interest, suggest that forfeiture is any less repugnant when it only involves part and not all of the policy proceeds?

Insurance companies would have you believe that, where the age in the death certificate differs from the application age and the differential is in their favor, the insured was a liar. Yet many errors are made in home office operations and through deliberate twisting by the agents of the insurance companies. Other errors are made by those who fill out death certificates, unaware of the dangers lurking in the shadows in the form of potential actions of those who have so piously proclaimed that they protect the beneficiaries of their insureds.

Beneficiaries are economically unable to protect themselves in an age contest. As many of you know, two-thirds of all policies are for less than $2,500 in face value. Once an age contest is proclaimed, insurance companies refuse to pay unless the beneficiary agrees to accept the smaller amount and the full burden of proof of correct age to the exacting specifications of the insurer. Such proof is very often either impossible to obtain or so time and expense consuming as to be self defeating.

When proof is sought, the widow is deprived of the policy proceeds, and no interest is paid on the proceeds which remain in the hands of the insurance company and earn at least 7.5 percent interest in today's market. The pious insurance company earns $75 per year on each $1,000 it can keep while forcing a beneficiary to seek proof. In most states, there is no requirement and no voluntary assumption of the necessity to pay interest on proceeds withheld after receipt of proof of death.

If the beneficiary seeks legal help, the cost of such assistance is beyond economic justification, considering the amount at issue. No recovery of legal fees, interest, or expense is allowed in most states even though the insurer may subsequently pay the policy face after the contest.

---

[2] Solomon S. Huebner, *Life Insurance* (New York: Appleton-Century-Crofts, 1935), p. 579.

Surely an administrative regulation could impose very strict rules on clipping the policy face based upon assertions of age misstatements on policies under $5,000 as a bare minimum protection to widows and orphans. State insurance commissioners could, by directive, order every life insurer under their jurisdictions to:

(1) pay immediately the undisputed amount, without requirement of any waiver and without requirement to relinquish control over the policy or over any rights;

(2) put the disputed amount in a trust account at interest under the supervision of the state insurance department;

(3) present to the commissioner of insurance proof beyond a reasonable doubt of the correct age of the insured within thirty days, without use of the death certificate or of proofs of death, or to pay out the disputed portion at the end of thirty days;

(4) provide that the beneficiary is to have no obligation to do anything and should be specifically exempt from appearing at the hearing unless she chooses voluntarily to do so, without jeopardy of any subsequent legal remedies, and that the beneficiary should have no obligation to aid in the investigation and no administrative inferences should be drawn from any lack of cooperation;

(5) use in this hearing information secured from the insured during his lifetime or gathered during the lifetime of the insured, or information gathered without recourse to the beneficiary; and

(6) await an administrative finding by the state insurance commissioner of the "correct" age of the insured before a policy can be reformed by an insurance company, thus placing the burden of proof on the insurer rather than on the beneficiary.

Insurance commissioners should include in their annual reports a statement, by company, of the number of life policies settled at less than face values, with the amounts involved, and with special detail on all policies of less than $5,000 face value.

This is only the top of the iceberg. Beneficiaries become aware of the terms of the policy only at death. They have no way of knowing whether any additional amounts of insurance were purchased by way of dividend additions or by other policy privileges. My paper cited in footnote 1 shows that insurance companies have taken advantage of beneficiaries until ordered by courts of last resort to pay amounts as small as $250.[3]

It is very probable that abuses exist in the area of insurance purchased by dividends also. Insurance companies should be required to report annually to each policy owner the exact amount of extra insurance he has purchased under his option privileges, in the same manner that banks, saving and loan associations, and corporations report annually on interest and dividends paid.

Insurance companies should be required to furnish an affidavit to the beneficiary at time of settlement, specifically warranting that a search has been made of all such possible extra insurance and that they have paid all amounts due the beneficiary. At the present time,

---

[3] Oscar R. Goodman, *op. cit.,* p. 530.

signing sworn statements of accord and satisfaction is a one-way street that is forced upon beneficiaries as a condition precedent to receiving funds, with no commensurate obligation upon the insurer.

I have previously advocated that state legislatures eliminate the age clause from life insurance contracts so that age statements will be protected by the incontestable clause and be immune from attack after the passage of a reasonable time period.[4] Life insurance companies can make whatever examination is necessary before closing the contract and can, within a reasonable time thereafter, discover misstatements by the insured. Presently they have neither incentive nor desire to do so and can in fact profit by refraining from raising the question until after the insured is dead.

I am here today to call upon you as state insurance commissioners to do what the people of your state expect of you—protect the public, and protect the beneficiaries. Cease being neutral in age disputes, thus in fact protecting the insurers. Cease aiding and condoning the reprehensible practice of attacking the statements of a man after he is dead, although during his lifetime representations were made to him that the contract would be construed strongly in favor of insureds and beneficiaries and the protection of the incontestable clause was used as a strong selling point. (The reason most often given by insurers to justify their duplicity in using death certificates as proof of "correct" age is that they are afraid of losing some business if they had to give age statements the protection of the incontestable clause!)

Some say that it is easy to offer correct proof of age. But it is extremely difficult, particularly when the error is based upon a misstatement in a death certificate. Richard L. Wright, an experienced attorney and a former Acting Assistant Attorney General in charge of the Antitrust Division of the United States Department of Justice, has been unable to change the middle name on a birth certificate although he is alive, well, professionally trained, and extremely capable. The newspaper account reports that the county  clerk refused to accept Wright's sworn statement that the doctor's handwriting on the birth certificate had been misread and asked for a baptismal certificate or a school entry record.[5] Wright did not have a baptismal record, and the school records had been destroyed by fire in 1909.

Mr. Wright then sent in an affidavit signed by his brother attesting to his correct middle name. The County Clerk said there was insufficient proof and that he would have to file suit in Circuit Court to force the County Clerk to acknowledge that his correct name is Richard Llewellyn Wright and not Richard Lincoln Wright. The battle continues in Cook County in Illinois, with the last word being that of the clerk's office which says "you are whoever your birth certificate says you are."

---

[4] Ibid., p. 534.
[5] Chicago Tribune, March 24, 1969.

Insurance companies add to their profit by blatantly telling the beneficiary, when it is to their advantage, that the insured was as old as his death certificate says he was! Consider how a widow or orphan would fare trying to safeguard the reputation of the deceased and with $50 to $100 at stake on a $2,000 policy. The insurance company would end up with the money and the widow would take whatever they want to give her. And that is the evil that I am asking you to use your present responsibility to correct.

The amount involved and the number of policies involved are substantial. It should be obvious that the uniform resistance of the life insurance industry to the loss of their self assumed role as defendant, judge, jury, and prosecutor in age contests is grounded upon a realization that there is a golden trickle from this leak in the barriers erected against harassment of beneficiaries and debasement of policy face values. The information gathered from some life insurance companies indicates that around 1 percent of all maturing policies are subject to age contests. About 6/10 of 1 percent of all policies have approximately 5 percent reduced from the face value by the insurance company on the basis of an assertion of age misstatement.

In 1966, $5.2 billion was paid in life insurance death benefits. Approximately $2 million was withheld from the face value on the basis of age contests and was lost to beneficiaries. A clipping of $50 to $100 per policy on a $1,000 or $2,000 policy held by a widow or orphan adds up to a very substantial bonus to life insurance companies. This is particularly true when there is no economic justification to resist the claim, since all the expense, loss of interest, loss of proceeds, and loss of time must be borne by the beneficiaries and deducted from the face value if they elect to resist the insurance company. The state insurance commissioner, sworn to protect the public, is a neutral party in these disputes. Over the past twenty years, it is estimated that 180,000 policies have been so affected and $35 million was withheld from beneficiaries by insurance companies.

State insurance commissioners have the power and the duty to require all life insurance companies to file immediately full and complete information currently and for all years since 1950 so that the information can be made available to the public, by company, classified by stock and by mutual life insurers. The sums involved are substantial since age reformations affect annuities and settlement options as well as face values. At the end of 1967, there was over $1 trillion of life insurance in force in the United States. If all of this coverage were to be settled on the basis of current age clause experience, we estimate that the public would lose over $300 million.

If life insurance companies were held to their contractual responsibility to prove correct age before debasing the policy face, the shoe would pinch and the companies instead of the beneficiaries would have the trama and the substantial expense. The beneficiary under a small insurance policy cannot successfully oppose a multibillion dollar insurance company.

Life insurers candidly admit that some companies settle age contest policies on the basis of the lowest cash outlay to the insurance company but always claim it is the other guy who does it. The life insurers' position is that the correct age can be demonstrated factually, without emotion or trauma and in a relaxed fashion. Life insurance companies state that it would not be in the public interest to make age statements incontestable after a reasonable passage of time. This is a comfortable, profitable, and self serving position, since the company relies on a death certificate, is put to no expense or trouble to prove correct age, and has as an adversary a widow or orphan who needs the sum in question at a critical period and has neither resources nor time to accept the difficult burden of disproving the age statement in a death certificate.

The issue is quite clear. Unless the state insurance commissioners take immediate positive action, the clipping operation will continue. Whom are you going to protect? The beneficiaries, or the insurers? Whom will you require to pay the expense of proving "correct" age? Whom will you require not to use death certificates and proofs of death?

State insurance commissioners have put the burden on the public long enough. It is time for the insurers to accept the expense and responsibility. Each state insurance commissioner should immediately require a full report on each instance where a policy is reformed on the basis of the age statement and should require the insurer to prove correct age beyond a reasonable doubt without use of a death certificate or proof of death which, on its face, is proof only of death and is not and never was intended to be a birth certificate.

## Questions

1. Why does the author claim that most insureds are treated unfairly by the common practice of insurers in using death certificates as evidence of age when it is to their advantage to do so?
2. What regulatory procedure does the author suggest as a way to eliminate the abuse practiced by some insurers in the matter of settling death claims? What does this illustrate about the practical nature of insurance regulation?
3. The author suggests that life insurance companies may not be paying out all the sums due beneficiaries under life insurance policies from other policies in force (such as through dividend options) but unknown to the beneficiary. How could this possible abuse be corrected?

# 36. GENERAL LIABILITY INSURANCE RATEMAKING *

Jeffrey T. Lange

Liability insurance is designed to protect an individual against the possibility that he will be held responsible in a court of law for injury to another's person, property, or other interests. The property owner is held responsible for accidents happening on his property if negligence can be established or legal liability exists by statute. Similarly, the contractor is held responsible for accidents that result from his operations, and the manufacturer for accidents arising from the use of his product, while the professional may even be held liable for the advice he gives. The insurance for these diverse forms of liability is provided by several lines of insurance which are generally grouped together under the title "Liability Other Than Automobile." or "General Liability Insurance." Manuals of rules and rates for general liability insurance are published by the National Bureau of Casualty Underwriters, by the Mutual Insurance Rating Bureau, and by several independent insurance companies. These rules and rates are also the basis of the liability rates appearing in the multi-peril manuals published by the Multi-Line Insurance Rating Bureau and the various state fire rating bureaus.

The rating techniques used by the general liability underwriter are in some ways similar to those used by fire underwriters despite their superficial antitheses. Both liability and fire insurance premiums are determined by a complex process in which the rates are influenced by the business of the insured occupying the premises and by risk characteristics that modify the hazard (e.g., the existence of elevators); however, the actuarial procedures used to establish the rates charged by the general liability underwriter are closely related to the other casualty lines rather than property insurance. The determination of the overall rate level change closely resembles the procedure used for automobile liability insurance, while the determination of class rates mixes techniques borrowed from both automobile and workmen's compensation ratemaking with some unique procedures. Unlike many other lines of insurance, there is no single general liability insurance rate filing in a given state. Individual rate filings are made for each subline of general liability insurance and for each coverage. The findings for individual sublines differ considerably from each other because the form of liability insured under each of them is quite different; therefore, some knowledge of the coverage provided by the various sublines is essential in understanding

---

* From *Proceedings, Casualty Actuarial Society* (May, 1966), pp. 26-60. Reprinted by permission.

the ratemaking procedures.[1] It should be noted that the ratemaking techniques discussed in this paper are those developed and used by the National Bureau of Casualty Underwriters. Similar procedures are used by the Mutual Insurance Rating Bureau in their findings.

## Lines of Insurance

Although each liability line corresponds to a particular type of liability hazard, there is some overlap between lines for a particular hazard. The basic hazard is generally considered to be the liability which arises out of the existence of the premises occupied by the insured and his operations. There are four ways of providing this coverage:

1. Owners', Landlords' and Tenants' (OL&T) covers the liability which arises out of the existence of the premises and *necessary and incidental* operations.
2. Manufacturers' and Contractors' (M&C) covers the liability which arises out of the existence of the premises and *all* operations.
3. Farmers' Comprehensive Personal Liability (FCPL) covers premises, farm operations, and personal liability of the insured.
4. Comprehensive Personal Liability (CPL) covers premises and personal liability but not business operations of the insured.

Each of the four is a basic coverage component, or part, which is separately rated and which may be purchased by the insured as a separate policy or as an integral part of a broader liability package. The typical commercial risk would need either the OL&T or the M&C coverage; in addition, CPL coverage might be added to the basic policy by endorsement to cover the personal liability of the owner of the business.

OL&T and M&C coverages do not include liability hazards which may be separately identified and rated; for example, an OL&T policy would not cover liability imposed by a workmen's compensation statute. Such hazards may be covered by separate policies and/or by other coverage components in the basic general liability policy. In the following list those hazards which may be covered in a general liability insurance policy are listed first (items 1-7) and are followed by hazards which are covered in other liability policies. (There are other liability hazards which are generally not covered by insurance, e.g., resulting from war, revolution, etc.) In a few cases, a part of the hazards mentioned below is covered in the basic policy (e.g., some automobile liability coverage is given in an OL&T policy). A discussion of the details of the insuring agreements and exclusions is beyond the scope of this paper, but the following list is specific enough to indicate what type of hazard is covered by each liability line:

---

[1] Magee, J. H., General Insurance (Richard D. Irwin, 1964). Seventh Edition, Chap. 15.

1. Liability arising out of the existence and use of elevators located on the premises of the insured (Elevator Liability Insurance).
2. Liability arising from the use of products sold or distributed by the insured or from operations of the insured after the insured has relinquished control over the operations (Product Liability Insurance).
3. Liability arising out of the operations of independent contractors employed by the insured (Owners' or Contractors' Protective Insurance).
4. Liability assumed by the insured under written agreement (Contractual Liability Insurance).
5. Liability resulting from the sale of alcoholic beverages (Liquor Law Liability).
6. Liability resulting from sprinkler leakage, etc. (Water Damage Liability).
7. Liability resulting from the rendering of (or failure to render) medical care or professional service (Professional Malpractice Liability).
8. Liability imposed by workmen's compensation statute (Workmen's Compensation Insurance).
9. Liability arising out of the ownership of an automobile (Automobile Liability Insurance).
10. Liability arising out of the ownership of aircraft (Aircraft Liability Insurance).
11. Liability resulting from the operation of an atomic reactor, the production of nuclear energy, etc. (Nuclear Energy Liability).

## Class Rating

The variation in hazard presented by the diverse risks seeking to purchase general liability insurance necessitates a wide range of rates. Schedule rating of the type used in fire insurance rating is unknown in the general liability field. Individual risk rating techniques similar to those which apply for workmen's compensation are used for general liability insurance. In addition, the experience rating plan applicable in most states provides credits and debits for certain general management characteristics such as cooperation with the insurance company. A majority of the liability risks do not develop premium and loss experience of sufficient volume to have any significant degree of credibility, and therefore fail to qualify for the application of rating plans. As a result, in most cases neither experience nor schedule rating techniques can be used to tailor the manual rate to the individual risk; therefore, general liability underwriters have relied upon the use of a large number of manual classifications in order to arrive at a premium for an individual risk which as closely as possible represents the hazard of that risk, and which needs little further modification for most risks. The rates for these numerous classes may be varied by state, or even by city, depending upon the nature of the coverage provided. For example, the class rates for Owners', Landlords' and Tenants' subline vary by rate territory, resulting in a total of over 30,000 individual manual rates.

The multiplicity of classifications coupled with the large number of sublines, each covering a specific type of liability insurance, results in a rating technique which, in end result, parallels fire schedule rating even though the techniques employed seem quite different. A typical fire rating schedule provides an extensive list of credits and debits which are used to modify the basic class rate for the risk; these credits and debits reflect various risk characteristics which have some bearing on the hazard. In rating an individual risk for general liability insurance, there is no one basic manual rate and no lengthy list of credits or debits. Instead there are a number of manual rates which apply to the risk; these rates reflect various liability hazards (line of insurance) as well as risk type and characteristics (class rates). For example, in rating the liability insurance of the owner of an individual building, the underwriter might first have to apply several different OL&T rates to provide the basic premises coverage. The section of the building used as a store by the owner would take a higher rate than that used for offices. A section of the building occupied by a tenant would be rated a still lower rate. Having applied the appropriate OL&T rates reflecting type of occupancy and location, the underwriter would then rate any other public liability hazard. For example, the owner would be charged separately for any elevators on the premises, and for the hazard resulting from products he sells. In each case, it might be necessary to use more than one class rate. The overall general liability premium reflects those risk characteristics which tend to increase or lessen the hazard, just as the overall fire premium does; however, for liability insurance this has been accomplished by a schedule of coverages and by the use of a number of class rates for each coverage rather than a schedule of credits and debits modifying a single class rate.

There is one more significant difference between the fire and liability approaches. Whereas the credits and debits used for fire insurance must of necessity be established on a judgment basis, the various class rates used in rating liability risks may be established statistically. To assess statistically the credits and debits of a fire rate schedule, it would be necessary to apportion each individual fire loss among those risk characteristics which contributed to the loss. Since many factors influence the loss, and as the loss is destructive, this is impossible. Liability losses, on the other hand, usually result from a specific accident at a single location. Such a loss can generally be assigned to a particular subline and class.

Setting rates for the individual classes within each of the sublines is in many respects comparable to attempting to determine statistically the appropriate credits and debits in a fire rating schedule. Since the latter is considered impossible, it should not be surprising that the former is somewhat abstruse.

## RATEMAKING

Each of the various general liability insurance sublines is considered independently for ratemaking purposes. The sublines are further subdivided by coverage: bodily injury, property damage, medical payments, and personal injury coverages are each rated independently. In addition, the basic limits experience is reviewed separately from excess limits. Manual rates are generally published for limits of $5,000 per person and $10,000 per accident for bodily injury coverage and $5,000 per accident for property damage coverage.[2] These rates are generally termed basic limits rates, and the charges for limits of liability above basic limits are referred to as excess, or increased limits, rates. The rate filings discussed in the following sections are filings of basic limits manual rates; therefore, premiums exclude any charges for excess limits coverages and losses are limited to basic limits (e.g., if a claimant were paid $15,000, only the first $5,000 would be included in the basic limits losses and the remaining $10,000 would be considered excess losses). The determination of excess limits charges is quite different from the determination of the basic limits rates, and a discussion of excess limits rate-making is beyond the scope of this paper.

The ratemaker is presented with the problem of setting basic limits manual rates for a particular coverage and a particular subline. With a limited volume of statistical data, he must revise several thousand individual rates. In most cases, there are so many classes that a number of years of experience would be necessary to obtain credible experience for individual classes even on a countrywide basis. As liability loss levels are sensitive not only to inflationary trends but also to changes in the legal climate, the ratemaker should rely only on the latest data in setting rates. Finally, in many cases he must develop rates that vary by state and even by city. The result is a two-fold dilemma: to assure credibility many years of statistics should be used, but to assure responsponsiveness only the latest data should be used; to assure credibility the statistics for broad geographic regions should be used, but to assure responsiveness to the local situation statistics should be analyzed by state and city.

This dilemma has been solved by a rather involved procedure. The latest experience of all classes on a combined basis is used to establish the overall rate change needed in a particular state (or countrywide). This rate change is distributed by rate territory (if any) using a longer experience period. The resulting overall rate changes are then used to develop class rates by means of a procedure which gives recognition to class experience both in the state and countrywide. The complex procedures used to establish class rates for the various sublines represent an attempt to give recognition to the experience of individual classes whose data has very low credibility. This is accomplished by grouping similar classes and analyzing the experience of each group of classes in the state

---

[2] For Professional Malpractice Liability Insurance basic limits are $5,000 per person and $15,000 in aggregate. For Product bodily injury liability, and for certain property damage liability sublines, aggregate limits apply in addition to the limit per accident.

and the experience of the individual classes countrywide. For a typical subline the individual class rate results from an analysis of the class experience on a countrywide basis, the experience of similar classes in the state during the past five years, the experience of all classes in the rating territory during the last five years, and the experience of all classes in the state during the last year or two. The exact method of accomplishing this varies by subline of insurance.

## Determination of Overall Rate Level

The first step in the development of manual rates for a subline of insurance is to determine the overall rate change. For the major sublines this is usually done on a statewide basis while for the minor sublines it is done on a regional or countrywide basis. While the ratemaking procedures are not identical for the various sublines, it is possible to make certain general statements which hold true for most sublines.

For most of its rate filings the National Bureau uses the experience of members, subscribers, and some other companies; however, some filings include the experience of the Mutual Insurance Rating Bureau. Experience is tabulated on a policy year basis and the loss ratio method is used in ratemaking. A comparison is made between basic limits incurred losses and the premiums at present manual rates, which are computed by multiplying the earned exposures for each class in each territory by the appropriate basic limits manual rate.

The reported losses include all allocated loss adjustment expense; for ratemaking purposes they are multiplied by 1.16 to reflect unallocated loss adjustment expense. This countrywide factor is obtained from the Insurance Expense Exhibit by taking the three year average of the ratios of unallocated loss adjustment expenses to the sum of losses and allocated loss adjustment expense.[3] The losses must be adjusted to the present cost level since they will be compared to premiums at present rates. This is accomplished in two steps: first, these losses must be adjusted for subsequent changes in the level of reserves and for incurred but not reported losses, i.e., for loss development; second, the losses must be adjusted to reflect changes in the level at which claims are being paid, i.e., for the trend in average paid claim costs.

The calculation of loss development factors is accomplished in the manner outlined by Stern in "Rate Making Procedures for Automobile Liability Insurance."[4] It should be noted that for certain general liability sublines (e.g., Professional Malpractice) the loss development factors are much more significant numerically than are those shown in the example in Stern's paper.

---

[3] Separate reporting of allocated and unallocated loss adjustment expenses are required in a supplement to the Insurance Expense Exhibit.

[4] Stern, P. K., "Ratemaking Procedures for Automobile Liability Insurance," *PCAS VOL. LII*, p. 162.

The calculation of average paid claim cost trend factors is carried out as outlined by Benbrook in "The Advantages of Calendar—Accident Year Experience and the need for Appropriate Trend and Projection Factors in the Determination of Automobile Liability Rates."[5] For those lines of insurance where the exposure basis is payroll, sales, or receipts, no trend factor has been used in the past because the exposure base itself rises during periods of inflation.

At least five years of premium and loss experience at present level are available for the determination of the overall rate level change; however, in order to achieve responsiveness it is customary to use a weighted average of the loss ratios for the latest two years with weights of 30% for the earlier year and 70% for the later year. This average loss ratio is adjusted by the factor reflecting the change in the level of average paid claim costs, and it is then credibility weighted with the expected loss ratio, i.e., the provision in the rates for losses and loss adjustment expenses. The resulting loss ratio is divided by the expected loss ratio to obtain the indicated rate change.

The expected loss and loss adjustment ratio is obtained as it is in all liability lines by substracting from unity the total service and overhead expense provisions in the manual rates. For some expense items the actual amount will vary by line, i.e., inspection costs for elevator liability insurance are much greater than in other general liability lines. Taxes may differ by state, while the 5% provision for underwriting profit and contingencies is constant for all liability insurance lines in most states. These expense provisions are grouped under the following headings (with typical percentages shown in parenthesis): total production cost (25%); administration (8.5%); inspection, exposure audit, and bureau (4.5%); taxes, licenses, and fees (3%); underwriting profit and contingencies (5%).

Credibility is based upon the number of claims in the last two years. The standard for 100% credibility is 683 claims which corresponds to 95% probability of being within 7.5% of the true value for a Poisson process (see L. H. Longley-Cook, "An Introduction to Credibility Theory").[6] Partial credibilities are obtained from a table based upon the formula

$$Z = \sqrt{(\text{number of claims}) \div 683}$$

The calculation of the overall rate change may be expressed algebraically as follows:

[5] Benbrook, P., "The Advantages of Calendar-Accident Year Experience and Need for Appropriate Trend and Projection Factors in the Development of Automobile Liability Rates," *PCAS VOL. XLV*, p. 20. The actual calculation of a trend factor is outlined in a discussion of Mr. Benbrook's paper by R. Lino, *PCAS Vol. XLVI*, p. 301, and in Stern, op. cit., p. 172.

[6] Longley-Cook, L. H., "An Introduction to Credibility Theory," *PCAS Vol. XLIX*, p. 200.

WLR = weighted average of the loss ratios for the two most recent years

ELR = expected loss ratio

T = trend factor

Z = credibility

$$\text{Rate change} = \frac{\text{WLR} \times \text{T} \times \text{Z}}{\text{ELR}} + (1.00 - \text{Z})$$

The numerical example in Exhibit 1 illustrates the determination of the overall rate change. The actual data was drawn from a recent OL&T filing in an average sized state. As is frequently the case in general liability insurance ratemaking, the proposed rate change is somewhat less than the indicated rate change. At the rating bureaus, the proposed change is generally selected by the underwriters after a review of the indicated rate change and the individual components of the rating formula.

## Classification Rates

Having established the overall rate change statewide, the next question is: How shall each class rate in each territory be modified in order to achieve the desired overall change—how should the rate change be "distributed"?

Most states are divided into rating territories for only one major subline—Owners', Landlords' and Tenants' Liability; for many other major general liability sublines only the two or three largest states are subdivided into rate territories and for some lines, several states are combined into one rate territory.

General liability sublines are subdivided into a number of risk classifications. The two major sublines—Owners' Landlords' and Tenants', and Manufacturers' and Contractors'—are subdivided into 264 and 192 classes respectively. Due to the number and diversity of these classes, it is impossible to use countrywide differentials to a single base class (as is done for private passenger automobile insurance). While some recognition must be given to the classification experience by state in setting the rates, the experience for individual classifications by state is too sparse to permit the use of a classification relativity procedure like that used in workmen's compensation insurance.

Although there are differences in the methods of analyzing class and territory experience, the essential features are the same. The term territory relativity (or classification relativity) is generally applied to this analysis because its aim is to establish how much the individual territory (or class) differs from the average. The experience of each territory

EXHIBIT 1

DETERMINATION OF OVERALL RATE CHANGE

| (1) Policy Year | (2) Premium at Present Manual Rates | (3) Basic Limits Incurred Losses Incl. all Loss Adj. | (4) Loss Development Factor | (5) Incurred Losses Including Development (3)×(4) | (6) Number of Claims | (7) Loss Ratio (5)÷(2) |
|---|---|---|---|---|---|---|
| 1959 | 473,553 | 239,430 | .98 | 234,641 | 468 | .495 |
| 1960 | 514,836 | 261,620 | .98 | 256,388 | 621 | .498 |
| 1961 | 541,217 | 286,624 | .98 | 280,892 | 501 | .519 |
| 1962 | 593,528 | 312,510 | .98 | 306,260 | 589 | .516 |
| 1963 | 662,678 | 366,816 | .99 | 363,148 | 598 | .548 |
| Total | 2,785,812 | 1,467,000 | | 1,441,329 | 2,777 | .517 |

( 8) Weighted loss and loss adjustment ratio at present rates (30% 1962 + 70% 1963) ................................................................. .538
( 9) Factor to adjust losses for average claim cost changes subsequent 33 months based on average paid claim cost data ................................. 1.061
(10) Product (8) × (9). .................................................. .571
(11) Expected loss and loss adjustment ratio ................................. .540
(12) Credibility based on policy years 1962-1963 number of claims ............ 1.000
(13) Indicated change [(10) ÷ (11)] × (12) + [1.00 − (12)] ...................... 1.057
(14) Proposed statewide rate level change ..................................... +5%

(or class) is used to the extent it is credible; the complement of credibility is applied to our "prior estimate" of the experience for that territory (or class). The average experience of all territories receives the remainder of the credibility in a territory relativity; the average for all similar classes or the countrywide experience for that class receives it in a class relativity. Algebracially, the index representing the relative experience of the $i$th territory (or class) may be represented as follows:

$$\text{Index} = FLR_i \div [(\sum_{i=1}^{n} P_i \times FLR_i) \div \sum_{i=1}^{n} P_i]$$

where  $P_i$ = the premium at present rates in the $i$th territory
  $FLR_i$ = The formula loss ratio for the $i$th territory
  $FLR_i$ = $Z_i \times LR_i + (1 - Z_i) \times SLR$
  $Z_i$ = credibility for the $i$th territory (based upon the number of claims during the past five years)
  $SLR$ = statewide average loss ratio
  $LR_i$ = loss ratio for the $i$th territory

In the following example, the five year loss ratios shown in column three were obtained by dividing the basic limits incurred losses (including all loss adjustment) by premium at present manual rates:

| Territory or Class (1) | Premium at Present Rates for the latest year (2) | 5 Year Loss Ratio (3) | Credibility (4) | Formula Loss Ratio (5) | Index (6) |
|---|---|---|---|---|---|
| 1 | $ 75,203 | .506 | .40 | .519 | .961 |
| 2 | 69,373 | .485 | .60 | .502 | .930 |
| — | — | — | — | — | — |
| — | — | — | — | — | — |
| — | — | — | — | — | — |
| Total or Average | 662,678 | .527 | 1.00 | .540 | 1.000 |

The indices developed in the last column are a measure of how much better or worse the individual loss ratio is than the average. These indices can be multiplied by the overall rate change to determine territory (or class) rate changes to be applied to the present rates. For some lines of insurance such indices are computed independently by territory (all classes combined) and by class group (all territories combined), and a composite index is used to develop class rates within each territory.

Although the experience of major classifications will have some credibility by state, the experience of most classes will have little or no credibility by state; therefore, for several sublines, classifications have been divided into groups in which they are related to base classifications by differentials. In the classification relativity, the experience of the class group is treated as a single class and an index is developed for the group as a whole. This index multiplied by the territory rate change is used to modify the group average rate which is divided by the average differential to obtain the base rate. Class rates are determined by multiplying the base rate by the class differentials. The differentials themselves are developed from countrywide statistical experience.

A different way of using countrywide data to overcome low credibility by class by state is the introduction of "national loss ratios" in the classification relativity within an individual state. The national loss ratio is simply the countrywide loss ratio for the class. In the classification relativity the complement of the class credibility is applied to the class national loss ratio (adjusted to the overall state rate level) instead of the experience of all classes in the state.

Other variations in the manner of obtaining class rates are possible. In fact, each of the major sublines uses a different procedure for establishing class rates. The manner of establishing class rates is the major difference between the ratemaking procedure for each of the sublines, as the method for establishing the overall rate change for each subline varies only in minor details. For every subline, the procedure has the same general pattern: the class experience is used to the extent it is credible, and the complement of credibility is applied to the "prior estimate of the class experience." The procedural variations may best be studied by reviewing the key exhibits from the rate filings for several sublines. Attention is first directed to the two major bodily injury insurance rate filings. Following a detailed discussion of these filings the distinguishing features of ratemaking for other sublines are discussed. It should be noted that the ratemaking techniques discussed are the standard ones employed in almost all states but that some states, notably New York, employ slightly different techniques.

## RATE FILINGS

### Owners', Landlords' and Tenants' Bodily Injury Liability Insurance

This is the largest of the general liability sublines and probably best illustrates general liability ratemaking. The basic rate filing includes approximately 130 rate classes, including classes with several different exposure bases: area, frontage, pupil day (schools), admissions (theatre), and miscellaneous bases.[7] Rates for this subline vary not only by class but also by rate territory (of which there are almost 150). An overall rate change is established in each state using the method set forth in the previous section: the weighted average of the basic limits loss ratios for the two most recent years is adjusted for the trend in average paid claim costs and then, after reflecting credibility, compared to the expected loss ratio.

The overall rate change is then distributed by rate territory using a relativity procedure like that described in the last section. The five year average basic limits loss ratio,[8] computed using premium at present rates for each rate territory, is first credibility weighted with the statewide five year average loss ratio. This formula loss ratio is then divided by the average formula loss ratio in the state to obtain a measure of how much better or worse each individual territory is than the statewide average. The statewide rate change is multiplied by these territorial indices to obtain the indicated rate change for each territory. This two-stage rating procedure makes possible the use of the latest two years of experience for development of the statewide rate change while using a longer experience period in each territory where the statistical data is sparser and hence less credible. Credibility weighting, as explained above, permits inclusion of the experience of territories too small to be rated independently. The numerical example in Exhibit 2 illustrates this procedure:

---

[7] Separate rate filings are made for certain minor OL&T classes which present unusual hazards (e.g., amusement parks).

[8] In large states only three years of data are used in setting rates by territory.

EXHIBIT 2

DETERMINATION OF PROPOSED RATE CHANGES BY TERRITORY

OL&T Bodily Injury Liability

| (1) | (2) | (3) | (4) | (5) | (6) | (7) |
|-----|-----|-----|-----|-----|-----|-----|
| | | | | | | Proposed |
| | Basic Limits | Loss & Loss | Credi- | Formula | | Territory |
| | Premium at | Adj. Ratio | bility | Loss & | Indices | Rate Change |
| Terri- | Present Rates | Pol. Yrs. | Pol. Yrs. | Loss Adj. | (5) − | Factor |
| tory | Pol. Yr. 1963 | 1959-1963 | 1959-1963 | Ratio | Tot. (5) | (6) × 1.050 |
| 01 | 382,054 | .474 | 1.00 | .474 | .894 | .839 |
| 02 | 108,201 | .575 | .70 | .561 | 1.058 | 1.111 |
| 03 | 172,423 | .634 | 1.00 | .634 | 1.196 | 1.256 |
| | 662,678 | .527 | | .530 | 1.000 | 1.050 |

Formula loss ratio = (3) (4) + [1.00 − (4)] [total (3)]

Having established the needed rate changes by territory, the rate-maker must now determine the appropriate adjustment for each class. Since individual class experience by territory and state (and even countrywide for some classes) is so thin as to be unreliable, individual classes are grouped, based upon inherent hazard, about certain large classes for ratemaking purposes. The major class in each group is called the base class and the rates for the other classes are related to the rate for the base class through the use of countrywide rate relationships or differentials. For example, the eleven school and church classifications are grouped together with the church class as the base classification. The differentials relating the rate for each individual class to the base class are developed from an analysis of countrywide statistical experience. A list of the classification groups is set forth below:

OL&T CLASSIFICATION GROUPS

| Group Number | Number of Classes | Major Types of Classes Included in Group |
|--------------|-------------------|------------------------------------------|
| 1 | 3 | Apartments and hotels |
| 2 | 4 | Offices and office buildings |
| 3 | 11 | Candy stores, salesrooms, etc. |
| 4 | 8 | Grocery stores, department stores |
| 5 | 1 | Supermarkets |
| 6 | 2 | Restaurants, bars |
| 7 | 28 | Clubs, pools |
| 8 | 22 | Miscellaneous |
| 9 | 6 | Hospitals, rest homes |
| 10 | 11 | Schools, churches |
| 11 | 21 | Theatres, halls |
| 12 | 15 | Storekeepers [9] |

---

[9] The term "storekeepers" refers to a liability insurance package; see the Owners' Landlords' and Tenants' Liability Insurance Manual, National Bureau of Casualty Underwriters, p. 211 ff.

Within each state, the experience of the 12 classification groups is analyzed on a statewide basis using a relativity procedure similar to that used in computing territorial rate changes. The five year average basic limits loss ratio at present rates is computed for each class group. The loss ratio for the group is credibility weighted with the loss ratio for all classes to obtain a formula loss ratio. The group's formula loss ratio is compared to the statewide average formula loss ratio for all classes to determine whether the group's experience has been better or worse than average. The effect of this class grouping procedure is to permit a selected group of classes to develop its own level of rates, as a group, within the framework of the state's overall experience indications. Individually, each class would have taken a ratio reflecting more closely the statewide change for all classes combined, because of its limited credibility, if this grouping procedure were not used. Exhibit 3 illustrates the method outlined above.

The group indices developed above show how much the rates for an individual class group should be changed relative to the average; the individual class differential for a class within a group reflects the proper relationship among classes; the territorial rate change combines the needed overall increase with indications of the individual territory. All that remains is to combine these elements of the class rate change.

The present average rate for the class group in each territory is computed by dividing the premium at present rates for the class group by the exposures. The proposed average rate for the group is equal to this

EXHIBIT 3

DEVELOPMENT OF GROUP INDICES

OL&T Bodily Injury LIiability

| (1) | (2) | (3) 1959-1963 Basic Limits Loss & Loss Adj. Ratio | (4) | (5) | (6) |
|---|---|---|---|---|---|
| Classification Group | 1963 Premium at Present Rates | | Credi- bility | Formula Loss Ratio | Group Index |
| 1 | 75,203 | .506 | .40 | .519 | .961 |
| 2 | 69,373 | .485 | .60 | .502 | .930 |
| 3 | 116,457 | .607 | .80 | .591 | 1.094 |
| 4 | 57,458 | .558 | .60 | .546 | 1.011 |
| 5 | 61,326 | .737 | .70 | .674 | 1.248 |
| 6 | 44,185 | .544 | .40 | .534 | .989 |
| 7 | 49,861 | .576 | .50 | .552 | 1.022 |
| 8 | 93,467 | .390 | .50 | .459 | .850 |
| 9 | 25,227 | .528 | .30 | .527 | .976 |
| 10 | 23,333 | .420 | .40 | .484 | .896 |
| 11 | 16,586 | .494 | .60 | .507 | .939 |
| 12 | 30,202 | .474 | .40 | .506 | .937 |
| Total | 662,678 | .527 | 1.00 | .540 | 1.000 |

present average rate times the territory rate change times the group index adjusted for an overall rate change produced by the group indices in the given rate territory. (The group indices are computed on a statewide basis; hence, although they are balanced on a statewide basis, they need not be balanced in any given territory.) By dividing the proposed average rate by the average differential, we obtain the base rate for the group. The base rate times the class differentials gives the proposed class rates.

CALCULATION OF RATES FOR GROUP 1 IN TERRITORY 01

OL&T BODILY INJURY LIABILITY

(1) Group 1 present average rate ................................. .400
(2) Index for Group 1 ............................................ .961
(3) Rate change for Territory 01 ................................ .940
(4) Adjustment for change produced by group index in rate territory [10] .998
(5) Group 1 proposed averate rate, (1) × (2) × (3) × (4) ......... .360
(6) Group 1 average differential .................................. 1.200
(7) Group 1 base rate, (5) ÷ (6) ................................. .300
(8) Class rates, (7) × (Class differential)
    a) Base class (differential 1.00) ............................. .300
    b) Other classes (differential  .50) ............................ .150
                     (differential 2.00) ........................... .600

## Questions

1. How does the author contrast commercial liability rate making with commercial fire insurance rate making?
2. The author states a dilemma in liability ratemaking: to assure credibility many years of statistics should be used, but to assure responsiveness only the latest data should be used; to assure credibility the statistics for broad geographic regions should be used, but to assure responsiveness to a local situation statistics should be analyzed by state and city. Show how this dilemma is resolved by reference to the illustrative example on page 000.
3. If a given class of liability insurance, such as churches, does not produce sufficient exposure to be "credible," how does the ratemaker handle this problem? Discuss.

---

[10] $[\sum_{i=1}^{n} (\text{Index}) (P_i)] \div \sum P_i$ where the summations are carried out by group within each territory.

# 37. RATES OF RETURN IN THE NONLIFE INSURANCE INDUSTRY *

Stephen W. Forbes †

## ABSTRACT

Risk-return relationships within the nonlife insurance industry during 1955-1967 are examined in light of the earnings performances of 82 randomly selected stock nonlife insurers. Seven annual measures of return are calculated for each insurer and evaluated using weighted and unweighted earnings bases and alternative temporal methologies. The study results suggest that returns on capital and surplus were inadequate during the period using either the Plotkin methodology or correlating mean temporal returns and corresponding standard deviations. Other results indicate (1) little significant relationship between insurer size and rate of return, (2) the measurement technique has an important bearing on the risk-return relationship recorded for the nonlife insurance industry, (3) the question of the most appropriate methodology to be used in evaluating industry risk-return relationships remains unresolved, and (4) what is true for aggregate industry behavior need not necessarily hold for the behavior of individual firms within the nonlife insurance industry.

There has been a great deal of controversy in recent years regarding the profitability of nonlife insurance companies. Insurers have argued that their earnings have not been commensurate with those of firms within other industries facing similar financial risks. Others have felt that nonlife insurance companies have achieved an adequate return through the years but that this result has failed to be disclosed to the public because of departures from generally accepted accounting principles.[1] The one recent study on the subject has been widely criticized for certain assumed weak conceptual foundations and statistical errors.[2]

---

* From *The Journal of Risk and Insurance* (September, 1971), pp. 409-422.

† Assistant Professor of Finance, University of Illinois.

[1] See for example Gilbert B. Friedman, "Why Automobile Insurance Rates Keep Going Up," *The Atlantic* (September, 1960), pp. 58-63 and replies in the January, 1970 issue, pp. 28-29.

[2] *Prices and Profits in the Property and Liability Insurance Industry,* Report to the American Insurance Association, Arthur D. Little, Inc., November, 1967. Two recent evaluations of the Little Report include a review by Alfred E. Hofflander and R. Hal Mason in the *Journal of Risk and Insurance,* XXXV (June, 1968), pp. 293-298 and J. D. Hammond and N. Shilling, "A Review Article: The Little Report on Prices and Profits in the Property and Liability Insurance Industry," *Journal of Risk and Insurance,* XXXVI (March, 1969), pp. 129-145. For a rejoinder to these reviews, see *Prices and Profits in the Property and Liability Insurance Industry,* statements of Dr. David M. Boodman and Dr. Irving H. Plotkin before the Subcommittee on Antitrust and Monopoly Legislation of the Committee on the Judiciary, United States Senate, November 25, 1969. For additional discussions of the pricing and profit issue, see Irving H. Plotkin, "Rates of Return in the Property and Liability Insurance Industry," *Journal of Risk and Insurance,* XXXVI (June, 1969), pp. 173-200 and "Comments on the Plotkin Paper" by John D. Long on Pages 201-216 of the same issue.

The purpose of this paper is to evaluate alternative measures of return for a sample of firms operating within the nonlife insurance industry during 1955-1967. This period has been selected for study because it has been characterized by the industry as one lacking relative profitability. The truth of this supposition depends in part upon the appropriateness of the measure of return used to evaluate insurance company earnings and its application.

## PROBLEMS IN MEASURING RETURN

The problem involved in measuring the financial return of a nonlife insurance company arise from insurance accounting procedures which differ markedly from those used by mercantile and manufacturing companies. Generally accepted accounting principles dictate that a firm attempt to match appropriate revenues with appropriate costs in determining its earnings or losses for a period. In mercantile and manufacturing accounting this objective is achieved through the use of uniform accounting procedures (e.g., consistent depreciation and amortization methods) and accrual accounting involving accurate determinations of unpaid liabilities on hand at the end of the period.

Manufacturing accounting remains a highly uncertain process because of such problems as the amortization of research and development costs, the treatment of goodwill in acquisitions, the reporting of earnings of foreign subsidiaries, the proper method of evaluating inventories, depreciation, intangible drilling and mining costs, plant start-up costs, and numerous other factors.

Nonlife insurance companies also face unique problems in matching revenues and costs. While revenues may be determined accurately by measuring the earned premium for a period, inaccurate unpaid loss and loss adjustment expense reserve estimates make an accurate determination of underwriting costs impossible, even for a large nonlife insurance company.[3] Such inaccuracies in loss and loss adjustment expense reserves are not a reflection on insurance accounting or on reserve estimation procedures but in the typical situation are the inevitable result of being forced to put a value on a loss before the amount can be determined with certainty.

Further complicating the problem, statutory insurance accounting procedures require the deduction of the acquisition expense in full in the year an insurance policy is issued rather than its amortization over the life of the contract. This usually results in an overstatement of the underwriting expenses incurred during a period.

---

[3] For empirical evidence, see Rafal J. Balcarek, "The Effects of Loss Reserve Margins on Calendar Year Results," *Proceedings of the Casualty Actuarial Society,* LIII, Part I, Nos. 99 and 100, pp. 1-16.

It is possible to adjust earnings for a failure to amortize the acquisition expense through the use of one of two relatively simple formulas.[4] However, an earnings adjustment for an inaccurate loss and loss adjustment expense reserve is ordinarily not made because the calculations are complex and the required information is not readily available.[5]

## Selecting a Measure of Return

A further problem arises in selecting an appropriate measure of return for a nonlife insurance company. There are several alternatives, none of which is entirely satisfactory. One involves the following formula:

(1) Total   Adjusted      Interest,   Realized   Federal   Unrealized   Tax Adjustment
    Return = Underwriting + Dividends± Capital   −Income ± Capital      ±for Unrealized
             Result        and Rents  Gain (Loss) Tax      Gain (Loss)  Capital Gain
                                                                        (Loss)

This measure is deficient to the extent that the adjusted underwriting result is not corrected for the influence of an inaccurate loss and loss adjustment expense reserve. The addition of the unrealized capital gain or subtraction of the unrealized capital loss from earnings is also artifical to the extent that an unrealized gain in one period may become a loss in the next and vice versa.[6] Finally, the tax adjustment, assuming the realization of the unrealized capital gain or loss, is somewhat arbitrary due to the nature of the taxation of nonlife insurance companies.[7]

This latter problem is corrected through the use of the following simplified measure of return which disregards the unrealized capital gain or loss during a period:

---

[4] One formula involves multiplying the earned premium by the sum of two ratios in order to derive an adjusted total incurred loss, loss adjustment expense, and underwriting expense. The first ratio divides incurred underwriting expenses by the net written premium in order to amortize the first year acquisition expenses. The second ratio divides the incurred loss and loss adjustment expenses by the earned premium in order to derive a pure loss ratio.

Under an alternative approach, statutory underwriting results are converted to adjusted results by adding to the statutory amount a percentage of the increase or subtracting a percentage of the decrease in the unearned premium reserve for the period. The percentage is derived from the proportion of the unearned premium assumed to represent prepaid expenses.

A completely accurate adjustment is only possible after all of the claims have been settled and thus the incurred losses and loss adjustment expenses are known with certainty.

[5] A misstatement in the loss and loss adjustment expense reserve may involve an inaccurate unpaid liability estimate for (1) claims incurred in prior periods, (2) claims incurred in present period, and/or (3) claims incurred but not yet reported. The cost of these claims is known only after they all have been closed. Given the influences of the statute of limitations and court docket waiting periods, the period for complete settlement usually ranges from six to nine years beyond the end of the accounting period.

For an outline of a procedure used to adjust the underwriting results for the influences of inaccurate loss and loss adjustment expense reserve involving the Schedule P, Part 5, of policy-accident year incurred loss developments in the Convention Annual Statement, see Rafal J. Balcarek, op. cit., pp. 2-5.

[6] Recognizing this, discounted net cash flow models estimating rates of return for alternative investments base their projections solely upon realized results.

[7] Mutual and stock nonlife insurance companies are taxed on capital gains in the same manner as other corporations. Thus, net, long-term capital gains are excluded from taxable

(2) Total        Adjusted              Interest,       Realized        Federal
    Return = Underwriting + Dividends, ± Capital      − Income
             Result               and Rents       Gain (Loss)    Tax

This formula has a disadvantage to the extent that it fails to give recognition to the role an unrealized capital gain or loss plays in earnings of a nonlife insurance company.

A third measure of return involves the following formula:

(3) Total        Statutory             Interest,       Realized        Federal,   Unrealized
    Return = Underwriting + Dividends, ± Capital      − Income  ± Capital
             Result               and Rents       Gain (Loss)    Tax          Gain (Loss)

This measure, used in the Arthur D. Little study, has been criticized because the statutory underwriting result fails to amortize the acquisition expense and the unrealized capital gain or loss is not adjusted to account for the federal income tax impact of its realization.[8]

All three measures of return are calculated and compared among the insurers in this study in order to determine if differences in valuation methods significantly affect the earnings reported by the nonlife insurance industry.

## Selecting an Earnings Base

The selection of an appropriate earnings base to enable a consistent comparison of returns among nonlife insurance companies also remains arbitrary because each base contains certain deficiencies. The alternative measures include; (1) admitted assets, (2) capital and surplus, (3) adjusted capital and surplus, and (4) the Arthur D. Little earnings base involving the sum of the loss and the loss adjustment expense reserve, the unearned premium reserve, and capital and surplus.

**Admitted Assets.** There are several problems in using admitted assets as an earnings base. Complete consistency would require that the assets be carried at either book or market value. In practice, nonlife insurance companies use a combination of valuation methods, carrying bonds which meet the prescribed regulatory requirements at amortized value, the remainder of securities at market, and real estate at book, capitalized, or appraised value.

---

income. A tax is computed on the balance and an amount equal to 25 percent of the net long-term capital gain is added to the tax as computed. This tax is payable if it is less than the tax computed in the regular manner including the net long-term capital gain.

A net capital loss of either class (short-term or long-term) is fully deductible against a net capital gain of the other class. If all capital losses exceed all capital gains, the net loss is not deductible in the current year but may be utilized in the five succeeding years as a short-term capital loss.

There are also special tax laws for nonlife insurance companies involving capital losses incurred to meet abnormal insurance losses. For a discussion of these see Richard L. Denney, Anthony P. Rua, and Robert J. Schoen, *Federal Taxation of Insurance Companies* (New York: The Ronald Press Co., 1966), pp. 10.8-10.10.

[8] See Hammond and Shilling, *op. cit.*, pp. 136-37.

Secondly, the admitted asset measure fails to recognize the value, if any, of nonadmitted assets.[9] While such a value will usually be minor when compared with the value of admitted assets, it should be included in an asset earnings base if complete consistency in comparing returns is to be maintained among nonlife insurance companies.

Finally, since the earnings or losses are generated throughout the year, they should be measured against the average assets available during the year rather than against the assets on hand at the end of the year. The use of an average asset base may not be entirely representative if there are wide fluctuations in asset levels during the year.

**Capital and Surplus.** The use of capital and surplus as an earnings base also carries deficiencies. As in the situation of admitted assets, this measure will be affected by differences in methods of valuing stocks, bonds, and real estate and the exclusion of any value arising from nonadmitted assets. This measure will also be understated by the amount of any overstatement in the loss and loss adjustment expense reserve and overstated by the amount of any understatement in this reserve. Capital and surplus also fails to recognize the value of any prepaid expenses which may exist in the unearned premium reserve.

As in the situation of admitted assets, an average capital and surplus base should be used since the earnings or losses are generated throughout the year. Such an average may not be entirely representative if the surplus fluctuates widely during the year.

**Adjusted Capital and Surplus.** When adjusting statutory underwriting results for the hidden equity in the unearned premium reserve, it has been argued by Plotkin and others (e.g., Standard and Poor's) that accounting consistency also calls for making an adjustment by adding the same percentage of the ending unearned premium reserve to the capital and surplus earnings base. Such an adjustment appears entirely reasonable and appropriate if consistent accounting principles are to be maintained.

**The Arthur D. Little Measure.** The earnings base used in the Arthur D. Little study involves the sum of the loss and loss adjustment expense reserve, the unearned premium reserve, and capital and surplus. It was intended to provide a measure to enable the comparison of the returns of nonlife insurance companies with the returns on the shareholder's equity and long term debt of manufacturing corporations. The sum of the loss and loss adjustment expense reserve and the unearned premium reserve was intended to be analogous to long term debt in this evaluation process.

---

[9] Nonadmitted assets include company's stock owned, loans on company's stock, deposits in suspended banks less estimated amount recoverable, agents' balances or uncollected premiums over three months due, bills receivable past due taken for premiums, excess of bills receivable not past due taken for risks over the unearned premiums thereon, equipment, furniture, and supplies, bills receivable not taken for premiums, and loans on personal security, endorsed or not.

As Hammond and Shilling have observed:

The reserves are a necessary by-product of the insurance transaction
. . . they bear interest; they do not cost it . . . comparability of the
return ratio over industries, therefore, disappears. Moreover, it is distorted in such a way as to make the return of the insurance industry
appear low; the denominator is expanded by the addition of costless
funds.[10]

Irving H. Plotkin has counterargued:

. . . insurance policies are examples of conditional promises to pay (debts)
and demand deposits are examples of unconditional promises to repay
persons who in essence provide debt capital. The capital they provide
contributes to the long-term, permanently investable funds in the operations of these financial intermediaries. From society's point of view, there
is an opportunity cost for the monies being channeled into the insurance
industry through the purchase of insurance policies, as there is an opportunity cost for the monies channeled into the banking and other non-
bank financial intermediaries. An evaluation of the overall efficiency
of capital employment requires viewing the total permanently invested
assets in any of the industries compared. It is for these reasons that
the two major reserve accounts are included as sources of permanently
invested funds in the insurance enterprise.[11]

It would appear that the Plotkin analysis is complicated by the fact
that insurance is a necessity and that reserve funds must be invested in
relatively liquid low yielding securities if the insurance mechanism is to
perform its function. The argument regarding the proper allocation of
investable funds on a yield-risk basis must be modified when applied to
the insurance industry. "The opportunity cost of the funds tied up in
one's own business is the interest (or profits corrected for differences in
risk) that could be earned on these funds in other ventures." [12] Yet the
policyholder funds flowing into the nonlife insurance industry arise from
a desire to reduce the uncertainties surrounding an investment yield, a
conceptually different framework.

Furthermore, in the absence of the insurance arrangement all resource allocation would suffer and society as a whole would be less well
off. It is clear from this that the rationale and motivations underlying
the insurance purchase decision are qualitatively different from other
investment decisions and that it is therefore inappropriate to compare
nonlife insurance contracts with other investment media within an opportunity cost framework.

In light of this reality, the return on shareholder's equity rather than
the Arthur D. Little measure of investable funds would appear to be the
more appropriate measure affecting the present and future capacity of
the nonlife insurance industry to absorb expanded underwriting needs.
Here the opportunity cost framework is clearly both appropriate and
applicable.

---

[10] Hammond and Shilling, *op. cit.*, p. 137.

[11] Irving H. Plotkin, *op. cit.*, p. 184.

[12] William W. Haynes, *Managerial Economics: Analysis and Cases* (Homewood,
Illinois: Richard D. Irwin, Inc., 1963), p. 31.

## Selecting a Measure of Risk

Either a spatial or temporal measure of risk may be calculated for a given set of rates of return.

**The Spatial Measure of Risk.** The spatial measure of risk is represented by the variance of the mean rate of return experienced during a given year by all of the firms under study. The Arthur D. Little study took averages of these annual mean returns and variances in order to derive a risk-return relationship for a particular industry.

Hammond and Shilling have observed that (1) firms could experience constant individual annual rates of return and demonstrate a high spatial measure of risk and (2) firms could experience widely fluctuating annual rates of return and demonstrate a zero spatial measure of risk.[13] They conclude from this analysis that an investor cannot equate industry risk with the spatial variation of returns. Rather, the investor should be concerned with the variability in the returns of a particular firm over time. They further observe that shifts in exogenous variables will not affect the spatial measure of risk "to the extent that all firms' rates of return change in response to these external factors by the same amount."[14]

Irving H. Plotkin has counterargued that Hammond and Shilling's statistical examples "portray situations never found in the real world" and that "if the insurance industry is compared with other industries on the basis of its return versus a measure of its temporal risk, it ranks even lower as an economic opportunity than it does when cross-sectional measures of risk are used."[15] Plotkin further contends that the spatial measure of risk minimizes the impact of realized and unrealized capital gains upon the industry risk measure.[16] While neither attacking nor defending the Plotkin methodology, it may be questioned whether these responses provide an adequate answer to the theoretical questions raised by Hammond and Schilling or whether a different issue is being discussed by Plotkin, namely, the relationship between methodology and result.

**The Temporal Measure of Risk.** The temporal measure of risk is represented by the variance of the mean annual rate of return. This measure is deficient to the extent that it fails to give recognition to the role of steadily growing or declining earnings in the investor's return. The greater the rate of growth in earnings. the greater the temporal risk although the investor would not view the problem this way. Similarly, if earnings are steadily declining, the temporal risk will tend to undervalue the negative effects of this trend.

---

[13] Hammond and Shilling, *op. cit.*, pp. 132-33.

[14] *Ibid.*, p. 134.

[15] Boodman and Plotkin, *op. cit.*, pp. 87-88.

[16] Irving H. Plotkin, *op. cit.*, p. 180.

While not refuting the value of the spatial measure of risk, the temporal standard deviation was found to be statistically significant in explaining differences in the average rates of return on capitalization for firms within selected industries during 1946-60 in a study by Cootner and Holland.[17]

Cootner and Holland attempted to give explicit recognition to positive or negative trends in earnings movements through the development of a measure of the asymmetry of the distribution of yearly earnings, the reasoning being that "other things equal, the more skewed the distribution of earnings on the low side, the higher the rate of return; the more more skewed on the high side, the lower the rate of return,"[18] As an additional measure of temporal risk, the standard deviation of year-to-year changes in the rates of return around their mean change was taken for each firm in their study. In both instances, the correlation results between these measures and the average rates of 1946-60 return among the firms within the selected industries were disappointing.[19]

In relation to the skewness measure, Cootner and Holland observed:

> Not only does it add very little to the correlation coefficient, but the sign of the coefficient is the opposite of what we would expect, and the coefficient is just barely statistically significant...it is not completely clear why we get these results. It may simply mean that there is no relation, but it may also be due in part to (the fact that) any relation that should be there is already covered in the first two variables (temporal measures of risk) ...or it may be a conceptual error—that is, the skewness we were really interested in is the probability of making losses or rates of return less than the interest rate or some other lower bound ... finally, it may be a spurious result due to the fact that companies with negative skewness had low rates of return in some years and these pulled down the average rate of return.[20]

An additional problem arises because the annual return may be affected by shifts in exogenous variables. Firms within an industry thus may demonstrate a high or low temporal measure of risk depending upon the period selected for study. In relation to this, Joyce and Vogel have observed:

> If variance is in fact the best measure of risk, the question remains: which variance? In the case of a stock portfolio the variance in the rate of return for an individual stock may be calculated from price information recorded over a shorter or longer period of time; moreover, observations from the same period of time when aggregated using different schemes produce different estimates of variance.[21]

---

[17] Paul H. Cootner and Daniel M. Holland, *Risk and Rate of Return,* Massachusetts Institute of Technology, DSR Project No. 9565, Revised Issue, February 1964.

[18] *Ibid.,* p. 73.

[19] *Ibid.,* pp. 86-87.

[20] *Ibid.*

[21] Jon M. Joyce and Robert C. Vogel, "The Uncertainty in Risk: Is Variance Unambiguous?" *The Journal of Finance,* XXV (March, 1970), p. 128.

Despite these limitations, the temporal risk represents an improvement over the spatial risk to the extent that it enables a direct evaluation of the earnings performances of individual firms within an industry. Beyond this application, its usefullness may be questioned.

When discussing methodology in measuring industry earnings behavior, it becomes clear that many mean and variance combination measurements are possible. The selection of the proper measure from these alternatives, for purposes of inter-industry comparison is not certain. Arguments can be made against using combinations of aggregate means and variances, in that these measures do not give proper weight to individual performance. A segment of an industry might be performing exceedingly well and this performance might be masked in the aggregate experience.

Displaying the results of individual firms on a grid makes impossible the comparison of industry-wide statistics but is more meaningful to the extent that the performances of individual economic units and resulting shareholder interests are measured.

Further complicating the analysis, the future does not mirror the past in symmetrical fashion and therefore projections cannot be made from historical statistics. The results of this study presented in light of aggregate and individual firm behavior thus may not be extended into generalizations regarding a particular firm or industry.

## CALCULATED RATES OF RETURN

Seven annual rates of return (denoted A, B, C, D, E, F and G, respectively) are calculated during 1955-1967 for each insurer in the study. Measures A and B involve the returns in formulas (1) and (2), above, divided by the average capital and surplus bases. The statutory underwriting results are converted to adjusted results under the assumption of a 30 percent hidden equity in the unearned premium reserve.[22] A tax adjustment for the unrealized capital gain or loss is made under the assumption of a 25 percent capital gains tax rate.

Measurers C and D involve procedures identical to those used for returns A and B except that the average capital and surplus bases are adjusted under the assumption of a 30 percent hidden equity in the unearned premium reserve.[23]

Rates of return E and F involve the returns in formulas (1) and (2), above, divided by the average admitted asset bases. The statutory results

---

[22] The statutory results are converted to adjusted results by adding to the former 30 percent of the net increase (or subtracting 30 percent of the net decrease) in the unearned premium reserve for the period.

[23] In order to derive the adjusted average capital and surplus base, 30 percent of the unearned premium reserve at the end of the period and 30 percent of the reserve at the beginning of the period are added to the sum of the ending and beginning capital and surplus bases before dividing by two.

are converted to adjusted results using the same prepaid expense and capital gains tax assumptions as those for rates of return A and B.

Rate of return G, the Arthur D. Little measure, involves the return in formula (3), above, divided by the sum of the loss and loss adjustment expense reserve, the unearned premium reserve, and capital and surplus at the end of the period.

## SELECTION OF INSURERS

Eighty-two stock insurers were randomly selected from the 1957 edition of *Best's Fire and Casualty Insurance Reports*. The population used in the selection process involved only those insurers with a complete time series of 1955-1967 earnings data; therefore, there is a bias in the sample against companies that failed during the period and also against new insurers.

## RESULTS OF THE STUDY

### Aggregate Results

The 1955-1967 mean annual spatial and temporal returns and standard deviations for the insurers are presented in Table 1. The bracketed sections of the Table involve mean returns weighted by the earnings bases of the respective insurers. For example, mean weighted return A of 16.59 percent for 1955 is derived by dividing the aggregate earnings reported by the insurers by the average of the aggregate capital and surplus bases on hand at the end of 1954 and 1955, respectively. This procedure, used in modified form in the Arthur D. Little study, gives greater weight to the earnings performances of the larger insurers.[24]

The unweighted mean returns, on the other hand, give each annual return equal weight regardless of insurer size. For example, the mean unweighted return A of 18.31 percent for 1955 involves dividing the total individual rates of return reported that year by the total number of insurers studied.

The purpose of comparing both weighted and unweighted returns is to study a question first raised by Hammond and Shilling, namely, the extent to which weighting affects the returns reported by the nonlife insurance industry.[25] As the mean 1955-1967 results at the bases of the columns in Table 1 indicate, the differences between the weighted and unweighted measures are minor for most of the returns, the greatest difference being 1.92 percent for return B (with the unweighted return being larger). This result is unexpected in light of the wide ranges of asset and surplus sizes studied in the sample.

---

[24] In a conversation and correspondence with Dr. Irving Plotkin, it was found that the Arthur D. Little methodology involved this weighting procedure using the investable funds bases; however, there was no averaging of bases.

[25] Hammond and Shilling, *op. cit.*, p. 143.

## TABLE 1

### RATES OF RETURN IN THE NONLIFE INSURANCE INDUSTRY: 1955-1967[a]

| Year | Rate of Return A[c] Mean Unweighted Annual Return (Percent)[b] | Rate of Return A[c] Mean Weighted Annual Return (Percent) | Rate of Return B[d] Mean Unweighted Annual Return (Percent) | Rate of Return B[d] Mean Weighted Annual Return (Percent) | Rate of Return C[e] Mean Unweighted Annual Return (Percent) | Rate of Return C[e] Mean Weighted Annual Return (Percent) | Rate of Return D[f] Mean Unweighted Annual Return (Percent) | Rate of Return D[f] Mean Weighted Annual Return (Percent) | Rate of Return E[g] Mean Unweighted Annual Return (Percent) | Rate of Return E[g] Mean Weighted Annual Return (Percent) | Rate of Return F[h] Mean Unweighted Annual Return (Percent) | Rate of Return F[h] Mean Weighted Annual Return (Percent) | Rate of Return G[i] Mean Unweighted Annual Return (Percent) | Rate of Return G[i] Mean Weighted Annual Return (Percent) |
|---|---|---|---|---|---|---|---|---|---|---|---|---|---|---|
| 1955 | 18.31 | (16.59) | 15.29 | (8.86) | 13.62 | (13.66) | 11.24 | (7.30) | 6.40 | (6.93) | 5.12 | (3.70) | 6.13 | (8.04) |
| 1956 | 7.38 | (8.31) | 7.70 | (6.85) | 5.84 | (6.89) | 6.11 | (5.68) | 2.48 | (3.51) | 2.64 | (2.89) | 1.73 | (2.83) |
| 1957 | 3.59 | (.21) | 5.86 | (6.10) | 3.01 | (.17) | 4.69 | (4.96) | 1.51 | (.08) | 2.21 | (2.42) | .34 | (-1.81) |
| 1958 | 18.94 | (25.49) | 11.03 | (9.41) | 14.78 | (20.74) | 8.62 | (7.66) | 6.87 | (10.12) | 3.71 | (3.74) | 7.43 | (10.83) |
| 1959 | 15.92 | (12.28) | 14.28 | (9.51) | 12.10 | (10.12) | 10.89 | (7.84) | 4.95 | (5.06) | 4.36 | (3.92) | 4.18 | (4.63) |
| 1960 | 12.59 | (10.70) | 11.91 | (11.05) | 9.66 | (8.74) | 9.17 | (9.03) | 4.18 | (4.20) | 3.97 | (4.34) | 3.90 | (3.12) |
| 1961 | 18.30 | (21.32) | 10.86 | (9.11) | 14.57 | (17.59) | 8.51 | (7.51) | 6.98 | (8.43) | 3.78 | (3.60) | 7.87 | (9.38) |
| 1962 | 3.30 | (2.40) | 7.29 | (9.52) | 2.45 | (1.99) | 5.76 | (7.88) | .92 | (.95) | 2.69 | (3.77) | .21 | (-.48) |
| 1963 | 14.15 | (17.00) | 10.50 | (9.41) | 11.26 | (14.01) | 8.20 | (7.76) | 5.56 | (6.53) | 3.87 | (3.62) | 5.25 | (6.71) |
| 1964 | 11.19 | (14.43) | 8.65 | (7.43) | 8.94 | (12.03) | 6.87 | (6.20) | 4.51 | (5.77) | 3.33 | (2.97) | 4.16 | (5.98) |
| 1965 | 10.68 | (11.02) | 9.71 | (8.35) | 8.16 | (9.25) | 7.54 | (7.01) | 3.59 | (4.48) | 3.35 | (3.39) | 2.93 | (4.28) |
| 1966 | 8.27 | (1.71) | 14.69 | (10.18) | 6.26 | (1.42) | 11.41 | (8.41) | 2.63 | (.65) | 5.29 | (3.87) | .65 | (-1.16) |
| 1967 | 17.21 | (18.89) | 13.08 | (10.06) | 13.53 | (15.48) | 10.18 | (8.25) | 6.01 | (6.94) | 4.41 | (3.70) | 5.99 | (7.24) |
| (A) Mean of Annual Spatial Mean Returns | 12.29 | (12.33) | 10.83 | (8.91) | 9.55 | (10.16) | 8.39 | (7.34) | 4.35 | (4.89) | 3.74 | (3.53) | 3.87 | (4.58) |
| (B) Standard Deviation of Annual Spatial Mean Returns About Mean of Annual Spatial Mean Returns | 5.25 | (7.45) | 2.86 | (1.34) | 4.06 | (6.09) | 2.07 | (1.09) | 1.94 | (2.92) | .88 | (.49) | 2.56 | (3.84) |
| Coefficient of Variation (B) ÷ (A) | .43 | (.60) | .26 | (.15) | .43 | (.60) | .25 | (.15) | .45 | (.60) | .24 | (.14) | .66 | (.84) |
| (C) Mean Insurer Temporal Standard Deviation[j] | 12.79 | | 10.71 | | 9.75 | | 7.65 | | 3.79 | | 4.65 | | 5.22 | |
| Coefficient of Variation (C) ÷ (A) | 1.04 | | .99 | | 1.02 | | .91 | | .87 | | 1.24 | | 1.35 | |

[a] Based upon 82 randomly selected insurers.

[b] Aggregate earnings reported by insurers divided by the average of the aggregate earnings bases at the end of this and the prior year.

[c] Rate of return on average capital and surplus including unrealized capital gains (losses) adjusted for federal income tax liability.

[d] Rate of return on average capital and surplus excluding unrealized capital gains (losses).

[e] Same as rate of return A except that 30 percent hidden equities in the respective beginning and ending unearned premium reserves are added to the respective capital and surplus bases before averaging.

[f] Same as rate of return B except for adjustment in footnote e.

[g] Rate of return on average admitted assets including unrealized capital gains (losses) adjusted for federal income tax liability.

[h] Rate of return on average admitted assets excluding unrealized capital gains (losses).

[i] The Arthur D. Little measure of return.

[j] Total 1955-1967 temporal standard deviations divided by total number of insurers studied.

A more important question is the difference in the risk-return relationship between the weighted and unweighted results. As the coefficients of variation in Table 1 indicate, the means of the weighted annual spatial mean returns do not have significantly larger temporal standard deviations than their unweighted counterparts.[26]

In another measure, a mean insurer standard deviation was calculated for each return by dividing the total of the individual insurer temporal 1955-1967 standard deviations by the number of insurers studied. As the resulting coefficients of variation in the last row of Table 1 indicate, the coefficients portrayed by the mean insurer measures are significantly larger than those involving the standard deviations of the means of the unweighted annual spatial mean returns.[27]

Both the weighted and unweighted values of the 1955-1967 mean annual returns at the bases of the columns do vary significantly between returns on capital and surplus A and B, returns on adjusted capital and surplus C and D, and returns on assets E and F. Thus the inclusion or exclusion of unrealized capital gains or losses in the measure of return does significantly affect the final result. The weighted measure of return G of 4.58 percent also closely approximates the results found in the Arthur D. Little Report.

Another comparison may be made between both the unweighted and weighted mean returns on capital and surplus A and C without and with adjusted earnings bases, respectively. As the results in Table 1 indicate, the adjustment of the earnings base for a 30 percent hidden equity in the unearned premium reserve does significantly lower than mean returns recorded for the insurers. This relationship also is maintained for returns on equity B and D which exclude unrealized capital gains or losses.

Table 2, taken from Statements of Dr. David M. Boodman and Dr. Irving H. Plotkin before the Subcommittee on Antitrust and Monopoly

---

[26] There has been some confusion regarding the specific methodology used in the Arthur D. Little study and its rationale. The best available discussion of this topic is provided by the mathematical supplement included in the reprint of Gordon R. Conrad and Irving H. Plotkin, "Risk/Return: U.S. Industry Pattern" in the March-April 1968 issue of the *Harvard Business Review*. In the supplement, Conrad and Plotkin argue that "neither industry temporal variance nor average company temporal variance possesses much independent explanatory power with respect to return once the interspatial variance is considered."

An industry temporal standard deviation is used to generate the first set of coefficients of variation in Table 1. This measure involves the standard deviation of the annual spatial mean returns. Squaring it would result in the measure of industry temporal variance used by Plotkin in the supplement.

It is interesting to observe that Conrad and Plotkin did not test the industry or average temporal variance in relation to return excluding the spatial measure. Alternative measures of temporal risk were tested by Cootner and Holland in relation to return and were found to be statistically significant (see Cootner and Holland, *op. cit.*, pp. 52-58).

[27] It can be demonstrated by mathematical proof that the mean of the unweighted annual mean spatial returns equals the total insurer mean temporal returns divided by the number of insurers. Therefore, the mean returns used in calculating the sets of unweighted coefficients of variation in Table 1 are the same.

TABLE 2
STANDARD AND POOR'S INDUSTRIALS RATES OF RETURN ON NET WORTH

| Year | Rate of Return | Number of Companies | Number of Industries |
|---|---|---|---|
| 1967 | 11.8% | 826 | 120 |
| 1966 | 13.2 | 826 | 120 |
| 1965 | 13.1 | 821 | 119 |
| 1964 | 12.3 | 818 | 119 |
| 1963 | 11.3 | 817 | 118 |
| 1962 | 10.8 | 814 | 118 |
| 1961 | 10.0 | 807 | 118 |
| 1960 | 10.4 | 799 | 118 |
| 1959 | 11.2 | 786 | 117 |
| 1958 | 10.0 | 768 | 116 |
| 1957 | 12.0 | 752 | 116 |
| 1956 | 12.8 | 734 | 116 |
| 1955 | 13.7 | 718 | 116 |
| Mean of Annual Spatial Mean Returns | 11.7 | | |
| Coefficient of Variation of Mean of Annual Spatial Mean Returns | .12 | | |

$$\text{Rate of Return} = \frac{\text{Aggregate Net Income After Taxes for all Firms}}{\text{Aggregate Net Worth for all Firms}}$$

Source: Standard and Poor's COMPUSTAT Annual Industrial Tape.

Legislation of the United States Senate, provide mean annual weighted returns for 1955-1967 for individual firms developed by Arthur D. Little from Standard and Poor's Compustat Annual Industrial Tape.[28] These returns measure aggregate net income after taxes against the aggregate net worth of all of the firms reporting data.

In comparing the weighted returns on equity C and D with the Table 2 measures, the resulting coefficients of variation involving the standard deviations of the annual spatial mean returns about the respective means of the annual spatial mean returns would indicate that the non-life insurance industry is underearning relative to industrial firms during the period of study. Plotkin would argue that this relationship portrays an unfavorable risk-return relationship for the nonlife insurance industry in comparison with the other industries. [29]

This conclusion requires the acceptance of the annual spatial mean return and its standard deviation about the overall mean as the relevant industry risk-return measure. The use of weighted spatial return measures which evaluate the firms within an industry collectively for purposes of risk-return comparison may be questioned in that this statistical approach to some extent masks individual firm behavior.

Conrad and Plotkin have rejected the application of individual firm temporal standard deviations in risk-return comparisons on the following theoretical grounds: (1) individual firm financial performance data is "muddy" and may be adjusted to mask a risk situation, (2) the individual firm may be too small and/or too unusual a unit to rely upon as a basis for measurement (e.g., its performance may be governed by such things

[28] See Boodman and Plotkin, *op. cit.*, pp. 42-59.
[29] *Ibid.*

as luck or managerial inertia), and (3) the financial performance reported by a firm may be insensitive to the cyclicality it is experiencing.[30]

## Regression Results

Whether one accepts or rejects the Conrad-Plotkin arguments in regard to industry risk and return measures, the individual insurer performances portrayed in Figure 1 correlating mean 1955-1967 returns on adjusted capital and surplus and corresponding standard deviations, suggest an unfavorable risk-return performance for the majority of insurers during the period.[31] The coefficient of determination of .397 for the Figure however indicates a significant correlation between the mean temporal returns and the corresponding standard deviations.[32] The reasons for the wide variations in the standard deviations portrayed in the Figure derive in part from the many negative annual rates of return recorded for the insurers in the study.

### FIGURE 1

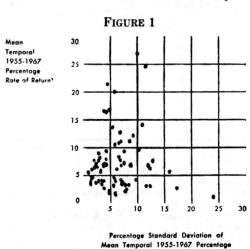

Mean
Temporal
1955-1967
Percentage
Rate of Return[a]

Percentage Standard Deviation of
Mean Temporal 1955-1967 Percentage
Rate of Return

[a] Rate of return equals adjusted underwriting results plus interest, dividends, and rent plus or minus realized capital gains or losses minus federal income taxes, divided by average capital and surplus. Adjustments to earnings and the earnings base assume a 30 percent hidden equity in the unearned premium reserve.

---

[30] For a full discussion of these issues, see the Conrad-Plotkin supplement cited in footnote 26.

[31] For reasons of economy of space, Transport Insurance Company and Texas General Indemnity Company with mean temporal 1955-1967 returns on adjusted average capital and surplus of 75 and 72 percent respectively and excluded from the Figure. These usually high returns derived primarily from underwriting profits.

[32] The coefficient of determination was calculated with the temporal standard deviation treated as the dependent variable. The Transport Insurance Company and Texas General Indemnity Company were included in the calculation of the coefficient. The test of significance involved a .05 level of significance.

## Distribution of Return Values

The distribution of the mean 1955-1967 rates of return on average adjusted capital and surplus for the insurer sample in Table 3 is highly skewed. Approximately 40 percent of the insurers reporting a positive mean return for the period earned less than five percent on capital and surplus whereas 76 percent of these firms earned less than 10 percent. If the six insurers earning negative rates of return are included in the sample distribution, these percentages become greater.

TABLE 3

DISTRIBUTION OF MEAN 1955-1967 RATE OF RETURN ON AVERAGE CAPITAL AND SURPLUS:  82 RANDOMLY SELECTED STOCK NONLIFE INSURERS [a]

| Percentage Rate of Return | | Percentage of Total Insurers Studied [b] |
|---|---|---|
| At Least | And Less Than | |
| 0% | 5% | 39.5% |
| 5 | 10 | 36.8 |
| 10 | 15 | 11.8 |
| 15 | 20 | 3.9 |
| 20 | 25 | 3.9 |
| 25 | 30 | 1.3 |
| .. | .. | |
| 70 | 75 | 1.3 |
| 75 | 80 | 1.3 |
| TOTAL | | 99.8% [c] |

[a] The annual return equals the total adjusted underwriting result plus interest, dividends, and rents plus or minus realized capital gains or losses minus federal income taxes divided by average adjusted capital and surplus.  The adjustment of the statutory underwriting result and the capital and surplus earnings base is made under the assumption of a 30 percent hidden equity in the unearned premium reserve.

[b] Percentage of total insurers reporting a positive mean 1955-1967 rate of return.  Six insurers in the sample reported negative mean rates of return on capital and surplus for the period ranging from .03 to 7.7 percent.

[c] Total does not equal 100 percent due to rounding.

In comparing the Figure 1 and Table 3 results with temporal performances involving other investment media, the relevant question becomes the following: "Could comparable average returns have been earned outside of the nonlife insurance industry during the period at lower risk?" While the appropriate methodology to be used in analyzing such a question may be debated, at the five percent level, a risk free investment in the form of a federally insured savings and loan account would have been available during the period. Risk free government securities would have produced comparable yields. Cootner and Holland concluded in their empirical investigation that "a return of 5.3 percent for a company which had no year-to-year earnings variability in an industry where all firms earned at the same rate seemed 'reasonable,' i.e., nonfoolish to us."[33] Yet the five percent returns in the insurer sample involve a high degree of risk.

## Insurer Size and Rate of Return

It has been suggested that the size distribution of firms should be given recognition in an analysis of risk-return relationships within the nonlife insurance industry.[34]

In order to examine the question of size and return, the insurers in the study are divided into four size categories based upon 1954 admitted assets.[35] The data in Table 4 reveal little significant difference in the mean temporal returns on adjusted capital and surplus reported among the categories. However, the coefficients of variation in the third column in the Table suggest a greater variability in the mean temporal returns among the insurers in the categories involving less than 50 million dollars in 1954 admitted assets than among the larger firms. This suggests a greater differential in average earnings performances among smaller nonlife insurance companies.

TABLE 4

MEAN TEMPORAL MEAN RATES OF RETURN FOR 1955-1967:
FOUR SIZE CATEGORIES OF NONLIFE INSURERS [a]

| Admitted Assets at end of 1954 (in millions of dollars) | | Mean Temporal Mean 1955-1967 Rate of Return [b] (Percent) (1) | Standard Deviation of Mean Temporal Mean 1955-1967 Rate of Return (Percent) (2) | Coefficient of Variation of Mean Temporal Mean 1955-1967 Rate of Return ( [2] ÷ [1] ) |
|---|---|---|---|---|
| At Least | And Less Than | | | |
| 50 | — | 6.4 | 3.6 | .6 |
| 10 | 50 | 7.4 | 5.8 | .8 |
| 1 | 10 | 10.5 | 16.3 | 1.6 |
| — | 1 | 6.5 | 7.4 | 1.2 |

[a] Adjusted underwriting result plus interest, dividends, and rent, plus or minus realized capital gains or losses minus federal income taxes divided by adjusted average capital and surplus for 82 randomly selected nonlife insurers under the assumption of a 30 percent hidden equity in the unearned premium reserve.

[b] Total mean temporal 1955-1967 rates of return for size category divided by total number of insurers in category.

Table 5 examines the more important question of the variability in annual earnings among nonlife insurance companies. As the results in the first column indicate, the mean coefficients of variation of the temporal returns on adjusted capital and surplus are significantly greater for insurers with less than 50 million dollars in 1954 admitted assets than for the larger firms. This result indicates a tendency for smaller insurers to exhibit less stability in annual earnings compared with larger insurers. The coefficients of variation in the third column in Table

---

[33] Cootner and Holland, op. cit., p. 84.

[34] See Hofflander and Mason, op. cit., p. 297.

[35] The respective size categories (in terms of 1954 admitted assets to the nearest million dollars) and corresponding numbers of insurers are the following: at least 50, 11; at least 10 and less than 50, 20; at least one and less than 10, 35; less than one, 16.

TABLE 5

COEFFICIENTS OF VARIATION OF MEAN TEMPORAL RATES OF RETURN FOR 1955-1967:
FOUR SIZE CATEGORIES OF NONLIFE INSURERS [a]

| Admitted Assets at End of 1954 (in millions of dollars) | | Mean Coefficient of Variation of 1955-1967 Rates of Return [b] (1) | Standard Deviation of Mean Coefficient of Variation (2) | Coefficient of Variation of Coefficients of Variation ( [2]÷[1] ) |
|---|---|---|---|---|
| At Least | And Less Than | | | |
| 50 | — | .5 | .4 | .8 |
| 10 | 50 | 1.1 | 1.0 | .9 |
| 1 | 10 | 1.8 | 3.3 | 1.8 |
| — | 1 | 1.2 | 1.0 | .8 |

[a] Adjusted underwriting result plus interest, dividends, and rent plus or minus realized capital gains or losses minus federal income taxes divided by average adjusted capital and surplus for 82 randomly selected nonlife insurers under the assumption of a 30 percent hidden equity in the unearned premium reserve.

[b] Coefficient of variation equals the temporal standard deviation of the 1955-1967 mean return divided by the mean return. The mean coefficient of variation equals the total coefficients of variation within each size category divided by the total number of insurers in the category.

5 also indicate relative stability in interfirm dispersions of temporal risk among the categories.

## SUMMARY

This paper has examined risk-return relationships within the non-life insurance industry during 1955-1967 in light of the earnings performances of 82 randomly selected nonlife insurers. The study results suggest that returns on capital and surplus were inadequate during the period, using the Plotkin methodology of measuring risk and return. If one rejects this methodology on theoretical grounds, this result still appears to be confirmed at the five percent rate of return level when correlating mean temporal returns and corresponding standard deviations.

Further support for the hypothesis that the industry was under-earning during the period is provided by the distribution of adjusted returns on capital and surplus recorded for the sample. Approximately 40 percent of the insurers reporting a mean positive return for 1955-1967 earned less than five percent on capital and surplus whereas 76 percent of these firms earned less than 10 percent.

Other study results indicate that (1) there is little significant relationship between insurer size and return; however, the smaller insurers record greater variability in earnings performances, (2) the measurement technique has an important bearing on the return value recorded for the nonlife insurance industry (e.g., the inclusion or exclusion of unrealized capital gains or losses in the measure of return, the adjustment or failure to adjust the earnings base for the prepaid expense in the unearned premium reserve), (3) significant differences in risk-return relationships result from the application of different methodologies, (4) the question of the "best" or most appropriate methodology to be used in evaluating risk-return behavior remains unresolved, and (5) what is true for aggregate industry behavior need not necessarily hold for the behavior of individual firms within the industry. In regard to the latter issue, the use of aggregate values to measure industry performance to some extent masks individual firm risk-return behavior which may vary widely.

## Questions

1. Describe the two following accounts in the nonlife insurance company financial reports: (a) loss and loss adjustment expense reserve and (b) unearned premium reserve. Would you describe these accounts as current liabilities or fixed liabilities of the company? Discuss.
2. What is the distinction between a spatial and a temporal measure? Why is it important in the measure of risk proposed by the author?
3. What implied definition of risk is used in measuring the risk involved in the rate of return studied in this article? How does the definition compare with the definition of risk in your textbook?

# CONTRIBUTING AUTHORS